THE HAMLYN DICTIONARY OF

HOUSE AND GARDEN
PLANTS

Autumn border showing a fine specimen of *Cortaderia selloana*

THE HAMLYN DICTIONARY OF
HOUSE AND GARDEN
PLANTS

ROB HERWIG

HAMLYN

The model gardens in Lunteren
Rob Herwig lives in a 100-year-old farmhouse in Lunteren, Holland, and started laying out his model gardens in its grounds in 1972. Using examples from these gardens, he offers the public advice and guidance on gardening, garden design and allied subjects. Nearly four acres of land are divided into ten smaller garden plots. There are also borders, small greenhouses, ponds, an organic kitchen garden, examples of paving, a rock garden, and various types of hedging and fencing on view.

A tour around these gardens is accompanied by a helpful taped commentary, and at the end of the tour the visitor is encouraged to put any questions he may have about plants, books, garden design, and so on.

Acknowledgments
Drawings: Anke van Vulpen, Amersfoort
Photographs: with a few exceptions are by the author

Translated from the Dutch by Arnold Pomerans

Jacket photography by the author

First published by Zomer & Keuning-Ede under the title *2850 Tuin & Kamerplanten*
© Copyright 1984 Zomer & Keuning Boeken B.V., Ede

This edition published in 1985 by
Hamlyn Publishing, a division of The Hamlyn Publishing Group Ltd.,
Bridge House, London Road, Twickenham, Middlesex, England

© Copyright 1985 English language edition Hamlyn Publishing,
a division of The Hamlyn Publishing Group Limited

ISBN 0 600 30636 4

Printed and bound by Graficromo s.a., Cordoba, Spain

Contents

Preface

People with a professional interest in gardening, no less than those who have made it their hobby, have a constant need for a book that will help them to identify as many plants as possible. Such books are not easy to find, oddly enough, and this lack has led to the writing of this volume, in which the most important house and garden plants are illustrated and described.

You may wonder what is meant by 'the most important', and that, of course, is a tricky question. Something that arouses enthusiasm in one person will leave another cold. The main criteria I have applied are availability, decorative effect, suitability for private homes and gardens, and personal taste. This last, in particular, stamps the book as an expression of my own view of indoor and outdoor gardening. That is only to be expected. All I can hope is that you do not disagree too strongly with my selection of 2,850 house, greenhouse, container and garden plants out of the tens of thousands of possible choices.

After much reflection, the publisher and I decided simply to divide the book into two parts: house plants and garden plants. We could, of course, have used a more complicated division, for instance herbaceous perennials, shrubs, conifers and so on, but without knowing to what group a particular plant belonged, the reader would have had difficulty in looking it up. Within these two groups, plants have been listed in the alphabetical order of their botanical names.

I am particularly pleased with the idea of putting the most important characteristics of each plant immediately beneath its picture. Each entry contains as much information as can be fitted into a few lines, and for that reason I have used symbols and concise indications.

Two extensive lists at the end of the book group together plants with the same demands and properties, which should help you when stocking a room or garden to choose the plants best adapted to widely different circumstances.

I have very much enjoyed working on the book, and I wish amateur gardeners and students every success with it. I could not have written it without the enthusiastic support of Ellen Lubbers-de-Beer, Hannelie Boks, Esther van Leeuwen and Trix Stortenbeek, each of whom contributed in her own way a great deal.

I should be very grateful for any comments from either expert or amateur gardeners, particularly concerning the choice, the naming and the description of the plants I have shown.

Lunteren, Spring 1984

Climatic Zones

The United States, a large country with many different climates, has long been divided into zones, each with a number, and garden books usually tell you in which zone a particular plant is completely hardy.

In Europe, it is not common practice to mention climatic zones in plant books, but since this book is intended for a wide readership, we have assigned a hardiness zone to most trees and shrubs. The lower the number of that zone, the hardier the plant. Thus 'Zone 5' indicates that the shrub in question is hardy down to and including that zone, (see map) and that it will tolerate a mean winter temperature of −20°C to −25°C (−40°F to −13°F), though it can, of course grow in zones with a higher figure.

There are two problems about this division. The first is that the mean minimum winter temperature is not the only factor determining the hardiness of a plant – wind, precipitation and other factors are also involved. Thus it can happen that a plant assigned to Zone 5 may not in fact be hardy below Zone 7. The second problem is the difficulty of dividing Europe into zones, taking account of the warming influence of the Gulf Stream in the west and the chilling effect of the great land mass of Central Asia which lies in the east.

Some gardening books assign most of Holland and Belgium to Zone 8, which is shown as stretching from almost as far south as Madrid to almost as far north as the coast of Norway. This would assume that a plant that is hardy in Bordeaux would also be hardy in Bergen. Moreover, Zone 8 is given a minimum winter temperature of between −6°C and −12°C (21°F to 11°F), and the standard plants quoted for the zone include *Choisya ternata*, *Olearia haasti*, *Pittosporum tobira* and *Viburnum tinus*. These species may indeed survive out of doors in Bordeaux, but not in Amsterdam and certainly not in Bergen.

We have prepared an alternative zone map which – and this must be said with emphasis – is based not on scientific data (such as isotherms) but on practical estimates.

Undoubtedly, this is not the ideal solution either, but we hope that our map may prove useful to the gardener. Needless to say, the author will be most grateful for any additional information and suggestions.

Hardiness and Wind Resistance

The British Isles fall into two zones, 8 and 9. Because plants come from all parts of the world, many are not hardy in our latitudes. They can, however, be grown in our gardens if given a little extra protection in bad weather. The symbol ⊘ in a plant description indicates that it is only common sense to give it this extra protection in the winter.

Herbaceous perennials are usually quite safe from frost because they die down to the ground before the winter comes. If the whole plant does

Climatic zones of Western Europe

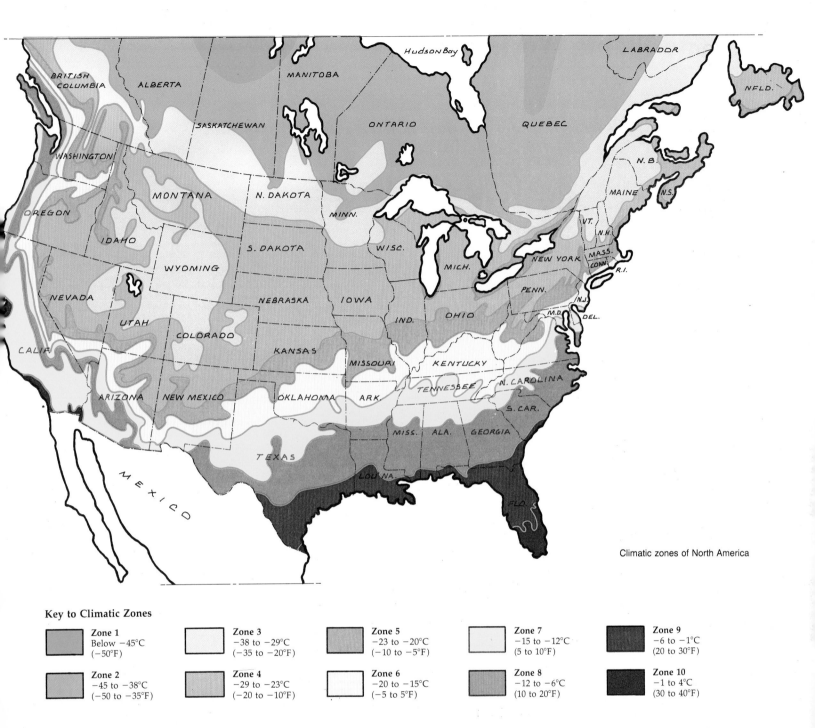

Climatic zones of North America

Key to Climatic Zones

	Zone 1 Below −45°C (−50°F)		Zone 3 −38 to −29°C (−35 to −20°F)		Zone 5 −23 to −20°C (−10 to −5°F)		Zone 7 −15 to −12°C (5 to 10°F)		Zone 9 −6 to −1°C (20 to 30°F)
	Zone 2 −45 to −38°C (−50 to −35°F)		Zone 4 −29 to −23°C (−20 to −10°F)		Zone 6 −20 to −15°C (−5 to 5°F)		Zone 8 −12 to −6°C (10 to 20°F)		Zone 10 −1 to 4°C (30 to 40°F)

Gardens can look attractive even in winter

die it is generally because the soil is too wet. Sensitive plants should therefore be grown on a well-drained site.

Matters are quite different with shrubs, which do not die down to the ground in the winter. Evergreen shrubs have an even harder time, because they lose a great deal of water by transpiration through their leaves. They are in danger of drying up rather than freezing up in the winter.

The symbol ⊕ indicates that the plant must be protected against the wind. This is done by siting it in, for instance, the middle of a mature, sheltered garden, behind a hedge, a timber fence, or so-called windbreak netting. Plants can be protected against the cold by covering with straw, leaves, bracken and the like. The larger a plant, of course, the more difficult it becomes to protect it.

How do Plants Work?

In this chapter is a brief description of how plants work, that is, how they grow and multiply, what organs they use and why, and what the various parts of a plant are called.

Sexual Reproduction

Most of the plants described are seed-bearing plants: they produce seeds which germinate and give rise to new plants. We shall also be dealing with spore-bearing plants (ferns), which differ from seed-bearing plants in several respects that need not concern the practical gardener.

A 'normal' – or rather, a complete – flower will be found to contain female and male organs of reproduction. The male organs are called stamens and produce pollen; the female organs are called pistils and contain the ovary. Both are usually protected by the floral leaves: the (usually) coloured corolla of petals and the (often) green calyx of sepals. The well-known story of the flowers and the bees which you were probably taught as a child is true in so far as bees may carry the pollen from the stamen to the pistil. From there it reaches the ovary through the stigma and the style, after which the seed can mature.

The same flower does not necessarily contain both types of sexual organ. These may be found in separate flowers of the same plant, which is then said to be bisexual and monoecious. If the two separate flowers are found on two separate plants, the latter are said to be dioecious. The amateur gardener should be on his guard whenever he hears the word 'dioecious', for if he fails to make sure that his garden contains both a female and a male specimen of such a plant, he may never see any fruit on the female plant, for the simple reason that no pollen can reach it. Sometimes a bee may, of course, oblige by carrying in some pollen from a neighbour's garden, but this is something that cannot always be counted on.

Pollination, that is the transfer of pollen to the stigma, is not wholly dependent on the help of insects. It may also be done by the wind, or water, or sometimes the pollen may simply fall on the female organ. Indoors, where there are few insects and wind is not a common phenomenon, it may be necessary to resort to artificial pollination, which is usually done with a feather or a soft brush.

Seed Development

When the seed has matured – and that can take a long time – it may produce a new plant which does not have to be identical with either or both of its parents, for various species can be crossed with one another and will then produce new strains. This may also happen spontaneously in nature. With specially bred garden varieties we can never count on producing seedlings that resemble their parents. Almost everyone knows that an apple pip will not produce a tree that bears the same apples as before, because modern apple trees are not grown from seed but have been grafted on to a 'wild' rootstock. Much the same is likely to happen with the seeds of F_1 (first-generation) hybrids. If a plant is capable of reproducing its own kind we say that it comes true.

If conditions are favourable, mature seeds may germinate. Most of them need warmth and moisture to do so. Sometimes they must first pass through a cool period, or even a hard frost. While some seeds will only germinate in the dark (that is, when covered with soil), others will germinate regardless of light conditions.

A seed can have one, two or more seed leaves

or cotyledons, and it is on this fact that an important division of the plant kingdom is based. We shall not go into the details here, but shall simply look at the germination of a seed with two leaves, for instance a bean. At the point where the two seed leaves are joined lies the plant embryo. It contains a rudimentary stem and root.

As the seed germinates, the root usually starts to grow first, forcing its way downwards to seek food in the soil. Next, the stem begins to grow and the cotyledons then emerge from the seed and turn green. They contain reserve food, sometimes very little, but sometimes a great deal, in which case the seedling can live on its own reserves for quite a long time. The stem makes use of that stored energy to lengthen further and to produce the first true leaves, whose shape is quite different from that of the cotyledons. As soon as the first leaves have appeared, the plant becomes self-supporting, as can be seen from the illustration.

Germination of a bean

What the Roots Do

The roots of a plant generally grow downward into the soil, into crevices in rocks or wind round trees. They give the plant support and absorb essential nutrients.

There are countless root systems; some adapted to dry soil, others to humid conditions, and some to marshy soil. All of them are built for maximum efficiency. Whether our plants are grown indoors or out, it is as well to find out what their natural conditions or original habitats are, so that we will not make the mistake of trying to grow an epiphytic orchid in clay or an edelweiss at the edge of a pond.

Plants absorb food through the tips of their roots, the root hairs. When house plants are repotted, the white root hairs are often found

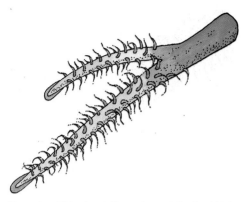
Tap root and lateral root. The root cap at the tip which is green in our illustration is usually white in nature, as are the food-absorbing root hairs

to be matted like felt around the edge of the soil ball. Food reaches the rest of the plant dissolved in the large quantities of water which the plant draws up and gives off again through transpiration. If the solution is too strong, however, the roots will refuse to absorb it and the plant will 'scorch'.

Different plants will not always absorb the same nutrients from the soil. This means that each plant chooses its own diet. In particular, the acidity, or pH, of the soil plays an important role in the absorption of nutrients. In practice, this means that we distinguish between lime-loving and lime-hating plants.

Plants as Chemical Factories

The nutrients absorbed by the roots are transported along vessels in the stems to the green parts of the plant, generally the leaves. Here they are assimilated, transformed into plant tissue. Assimilation is a fairly complicated process known as photosynthesis and involves the presence not only of nutrients from the soil, but also of carbon dioxide from the air, as well as sunlight (or possibly artificial light). In this process, chlorophyll plays the part of a catalyst. Water molecules which enter the plant through

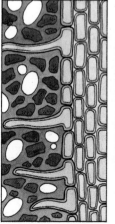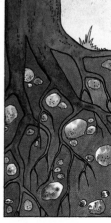
A greatly magnified section (left) of one of the roots shown on the right. The white blobs are air bubbles; the brown ones soil particles and the blue areas water in the soil. Together they make up the medium in which the root hairs (the protruding cells on the left) do their work

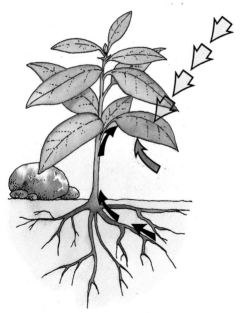
Under the influence of sunlight (yellow arrows), the leaves transform mineral substances in the soil (black arrows) and carbon dioxide in the air (blue arrow) into plant food. In the course of this process, the plant releases oxygen into the atmosphere

its roots are split into hydrogen and oxygen. The oxygen leaves the plant and the hydrogen is used to reduce the carbonic acid into a carbohydrate, from which fresh plant tissue is built up.

You may well think that all these processes involve small quantities of matter, but in fact a well-maintained lawn measuring 100 square metres (just over 1,000 square feet) produces enough oxygen in one season to fill the lungs of two people for a whole year. Moreover, the leaf of a single sunflower will pass 360,000 litres (about 80,000 gal) of air on a sunny day in order to fix about 25 g (1 oz) of carbon. Leaves continuously make carbohydrates in daylight; at night this process ceases and the carbohydrates are transported to other parts of the plant. In the morning, the leaf is 'empty' again.

Another chemical process used by plants is the assimilation of nitrogen and the consequent formation of proteins. Plants are the only living organisms capable of transforming elements directly into proteins. And they do so very economically.

Plant Organs

The leaf
The leaf is the plant's chief organ of food production. It is generally green and any parts lacking chlorophyll (green leaf pigment) play a subsidiary role in food assimilation. Leaves are covered with an upper skin or epidermis. On their lower surface, they have pores or stomata: leaves whose function it is to release a great deal of moisture (ferns, for example) have a very large number of pores, while desert plants such as cacti have very few. Pores usually close up in poor light and also when the air is very dry.

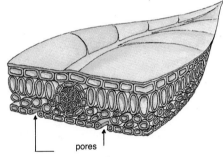

Magnified section illustrating the cellular structure of leaves

Leaves generally grow on stalks, on which they adopt characteristic positions and grow to a fixed size. This is a rather vague definition, and deliberately so, for leaves come in all sorts of strange shapes, sizes and colours. Their most common shapes are shown in the illustration on this page.

Seen from above the leaves are usually attached to the stem in a regular spiral. If the stem is very compact then the leaves will form a rosette. A common arrangement is for the leaves to be borne in pairs along the stem. They are then said to be opposite, and the next pair may sometimes be at right angles to the first (decussate arrangement). Less often, three or more leaves are distributed together at the same node, and are then said to be whorled.

If the leaf blade is divided as far as the midrib to give rise to several leaflets, it is known as a compound leaf.

Leaves are generally attached to a stalk or petiole. At the point where this joins the stem the leaf axils are found. These as a rule contain a bud that will eventually open. Underneath the leaf stalk there may be some tiny leaves, the so-called stipules. In the absence of a stalk, the leaf is said to be sessile. Different forms of leaf may be found on one and the same plant.

Leaves rarely live for more than one growing season, though some shrubs have evergreen leaves that persist for two or more years. Such

Some leaf shapes found in nature

leaves must not release too much moisture, for which reason they are usually very narrow (conifers) or leathery (*Rhododendron*). Some perennials, too, have evergreen leaves.

The stem
The stem is a plant organ that (generally) bears leaves. Higher plants carry buds on their stems and these eventually give rise to leaves. Thus when the leaf has not yet unfolded, it is called a bud; when it does unfold, the next bud will be found in the leaf axil.

Most stems end in a terminal bud which is often the most vigorous of all. When it is present the plant will grow mainly upwards, which explains, for example, the shape of trees. Stems may produce side shoots as well as leaves.

The stem carries a number of vessels, called vascular bundles, which ensure the transport of various nutrients. The stems (and leaves) of most herbaceous perennials (including bulbs and corms) die at the end of the growing season,

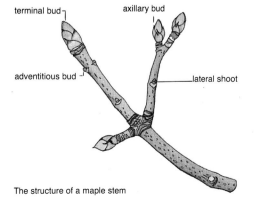

The structure of a maple stem

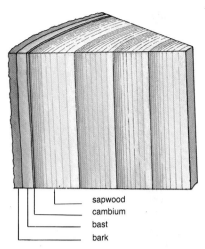

sapwood
cambium
bast
bark

and are replaced by new stems in the following year. Woody perennials behave differently: their stems lay down wood in the winter, a cork layer being formed on the outside. Such stems, which are called twigs or shoots in the first year, become branches in successive years, and grow thicker with each year.

The structure of a woody stem is shown in the illustration. The outermost layer is the bark and serves as protection. Below it lies a layer of bast which carries the sap downwards. Next comes an extremely thin layer – just one cell deep. It is called the cambium and is of the utmost importance for it lays down bast on the outside and wood on the inside. The next layer is therefore called wood, or more precisely sapwood, young wood formed in recent years. It carries the tubes conducting the sap, that is the water and nutrients, from the roots upwards to the leaves. Still further towards the centre lies the heartwood, sapwood that has died but which by its rigidity helps the tree or shrub to stand upright.

The root
Roots never bear leaves and invariably grow downwards. The size of root systems varies considerably from one plant to the next. The two main functions of roots are the absorption of food, and anchorage of the plant. Plants have the most varied types of roots, among which can be distinguished:

Normal roots These branch in the same way as stems, spreading more or less evenly through the soil. We distinguish between deep-rooted plants, in which the roots extend far down into the soil to seek water, and surface-rooting plants, which will only flourish on permanently moist soil.

Bulbs A bulb may be thought of as a stem carrying leaves known as scales. These scales store reserve food. The centre of the bulb consists of a bud that is extremely well protected against desiccation. Typical examples are a tulip, a hyacinth, and an onion.

Corms Corms are thickened stem bases usually covered with a papery skin. If a corm is cut through the middle the difference between it and a bulb becomes obvious: instead of scales, the corm is made up of a solid piece of tissue. Every year a new corm is formed on top of the old. A corm produces just one bud. Examples are the gladiolus and a crocus.

Tubers These are thickened fleshy roots or underground stems. They generally bear more than one bud and their shape is irregular. Examples are the potato, tuberous begonia, and dahlia.

Rhizomes These are thickened, horizontal, underground stems with adventitious roots beneath and stem-producing buds on top. A new stem appears above ground every growing season and the rhizome keeps spreading outwards. Older rhizomes stop producing buds and eventually die. Examples are the bearded iris, lily-of-the-valley, and ferns.

A root system of the type found in most herbaceous and in all woody plants

A bulb is composed of fleshy modified leaves or scales and bears roots underneath

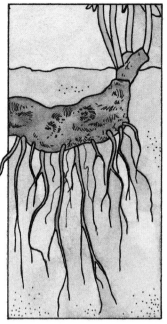

A rootstock or rhizome is a creeping and thickened underground stem

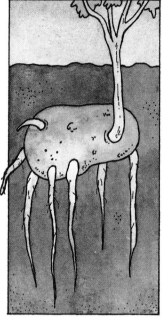

A tuber is an irregular fleshy root often bearing several buds from which stems may eventually emerge

The flower

The flower is considered to be a radically modified stem in which the leaves have been tightly pressed together. The receptacle is a fairly short part of the flower stalk on which the remaining parts of the flower are attached in whorls or spirals. The outer whorls may be of two kinds: a calyx of sepals surrounding a corolla of petals, the two differing in shape or colour. Petals and sepals together are known as the perianth and there may be no difference between them.

The perianth surrounds the plant's reproductive organs: the pistils and stamens. The stamens, too, are arranged in whorls or spirals and produce the pollen grains containing the

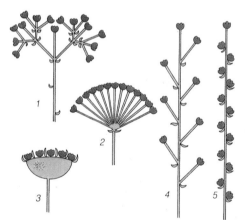

Types of inflorescence: 1. panicle 2. umbel 3. capitulum 4. raceme and 5. spike

male reproductive cells. The pistils contain the ovaries holding the female sex cells.

There is an immense difference in the structure of different flowers, and the systematic division and classification of the plant kingdom is based on these differences.

It is rare for a plant to bear just one flower; more often it will bear flowers in clusters or inflorescences. Depending on the way in which these clusters are arranged we speak of spikes, racemes, panicles or umbels. In the *Compositae*, the largest family of flowering plants, differently shaped flowers – a central mass of disk florets surrounded by ray florets – emerge from a common receptacle.

Male and female flowers contain either stamens or pistils. If both sets of reproductive organs are found on the same plant the plant is called monoecious; if they occur on different individual plants, such plants are said to be dioecious.

The corolla is usually coloured and drops off after the flowering period. Its petals may either be separate or fused into tubular shapes, funnels, bells, cups and so on.

In double flowers, the stamens have been modified into petals, a process the plant grower can encourage by selection and cross-breeding.

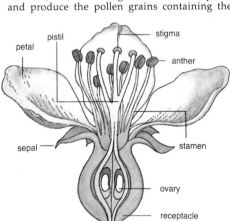

The structure of a bisexual flower

labels: petal, pistil, stigma, anther, sepal, stamen, ovary, receptacle

A combination of various types of inflorescence adds interest to a garden

The Naming of Plants

In this book, plants are listed in the alphabetical order of their Latin botanical names. There are several reasons for doing this. First, many plants have a number of different common names – thus *Dicentra spectabilis*, for instance, is known variously as Bleeding Heart, Lock and Keys, or Lyreflower. Moreover, it goes without saying that the popular names of flowers differ from country to country, and even from region to region, and since this book is being published abroad, an alphabetical list of local common names would have meant the rearrangement for each country of all the illustrations. We have therefore followed custom and kept to the Latin or scientific names.

But even here there is some confusion. If you consult different plant books you will find that not every author uses the same Latin names. Plant catalogues may use yet another set of names. It is enough to drive anyone mad: Latin names apparently have a tendency to alter.

The reason is the so-called priority rule introduced by the Swiss botanist A. de Landolle (1806–1893). This rule states that the oldest listed name is the correct one. Now it may have happened that, a few centuries ago, someone discovered, described and named a plant without drawing attention to this fact. Ten years later, somebody else comes upon the same plant, thinks he is the first to discover it, describes and names it in his turn. Naturally the name he chooses is different from the first, for he does not realise that the plant has already been identified. The second name becomes established and holds good for many decades. But one day, an archivist comes across the older description and, in accordance with the priority rule, the plant must now be renamed. The current name is placed behind it, as a synonym, and put between brackets. Some plants have as many as five such synonyms, and this can lead to a great deal of confusion. Thus Woodruff, always known as *Asperula odorata*, has suddenly become *Galium odoratum*, and the plant previously known as *Scindapsus* and renamed *Rhaphidophora*, must, according to the latest findings, be changed again to *Epipremnum*.

Nor is the priority rule the only reason for changing the names of plants. For closer scientific study may reveal that a given plant does not really belong the genus to which it has been assigned. In that case, scientists in various parts of the world may disagree, so that one and the same plant will have been given different scientific names in, say, Germany and the U.S.A.

Fortunately only a few plants change names every year, and many changes take a very long time to find wide acceptance. But sadly, not everyone is told about the latest changes in good time, or takes the trouble to implement them straightaway. As a result, confusion is compounded further. There are, however, some authoritative works in which the most recent names of all plants are listed. One of these is Zander's *Handwörterbuch der Pflanzennamen*. We have unreservedly followed the 11th edition of that work in this book, so that the names used here can be said to be fairly up to date. However, to facilitate the search for older names, as many synonyms as possible have been added in brackets.

The plant kingdom is divided into classes, sub-classes, orders, families, genera, species, sub-species and varieties. In this book, only the last five catagories are used, because classes, sub-classes and orders do not really concern the practical gardener.

In the first line of each plant description you will find the generic name, for example *Rosa*, followed by the specific name, such as *rubiginosa*. This agrees nicely with the way people are listed in telephone books – Smith, John. Now it can happen that the various species in the genus *Rosa* have been crossed and mixed up in so many ways that no one can really tell to what species a particular rose must be assigned. In that case we may employ a group name, such as Floribunda Rose, and list the plant under that.

Much the same system has been used for other plants as well, for instance *Gaillardia* hybrids or *Rhododendron* hybrids. Under the group name you will then find a number of cultivars (see below) of uncertain origin but with obviously shared characteristics.

If we still do not know from what species a particular cross has been derived then a new Latin name may be assigned to it. That name is always preceded by an ×-sign; *Rosa × borboniana*. Both parents can additionally be listed in brackets, *(R. chinensis × R. × damascena)*. The attentive reader will have realised that the second plant is itself a cross between two species of rose.

It happens occasionally that not two species, but two or more genera have been crossed, in which case the ×-sign must be placed in front of the generic name. This happens particularly in the case of orchids. Thus × *Odontocidium* is a cross between the genera *Odontoglossum* and *Oncidium*.

Varieties are sub-divisions of species that have arisen from natural causes. If there is space, we always add the abbreviation var., for instance, *Rosa gallica* var. *versicolor*. A shorter listing is *Rosa gallica versicolor*.

If a variety has not arisen from natural causes but through human intervention (crossing, selection, or radiation), then we refer to it as a cultivated variety, or 'cultivar'. In this book we also use the terms 'garden form' or 'strain' to refer to precisely the same product. The names of cultivars must always be written with a capital letter and placed between single inverted commas.

Occasionally we refer to sub-species (abbreviation: ssp.) or to forms (abbreviation: f.), the precise significance of which need not concern us here.

In the second line of each description, you will first find the most usual common name (if, indeed, there is one), followed by the family name. The latter may be useful to the gardener, because members of one and the same family of plants often (but by no means always!) demand the same kind of care.

The Plan of this Book

This book has been arranged on particularly simple lines. It begins with house and greenhouse plants, that is, plants that are not usually hardy in our climate. Container plants, those that stand outside in the summer in a tub or other container and which must be protected against the frost in winter, are also included in this section.

The second part of the book lists garden plants, most of them hardy, but some of them less so than others. We have refrained from grouping together such categories as shrubs, herbaceous perennials and conifers, but have instead listed all plants in alphabetical order. The advantage of this method is that if you know nothing about a plant but its name you will still be able to find it quickly.

A set of systematic tables of plants starts on page 345, beginning with house, greenhouse and container plants and continuing with garden plants.

The main criterion used in compiling the tables of house, greenhouse and container plants has been the amount of light they need:
Full sun
Full sun or semi-shade
Semi-shade
Semi-shade or shade
Shade

Subsidiary classifications are the temperature and amount of moisture needed, from high to low.

The main criteria used in compiling the tables of garden plants have been the amount of light and the moisture in the soil they need:
Full sun
Full sun and moist soil
Full sun and dry soil
Full sun and semi-shade
Full sun, semi-shade, moist soil
Full sun, semi-shade, dry soil
Full sun, semi-shade and shade
Semi-shade and moist soil
Semi-shade and dry soil
Semi-shade and shade
Shade

The tables are subdivided further according to whether the plants included in them are:
Annuals
Biennials
Herbaceous perennials
Bulbs
Tubers
Shrubs
Trees

The index of house, greenhouse and container plants begins on page 384, that of garden plants on page 387.

Cultivation of Indoor Plants

No plant grows naturally in a room or a greenhouse, and strictly speaking, therefore, there is no such thing as an indoor or house plant. All are outdoor plants that man has discovered somewhere in the world, cultivated, often crossed or improved, and now uses to adorn his living room, balcony, patio, office or greenhouse.

The chief characteristic of house plants, one that they nearly all have in common, is that they are not hardy. If they were, they could be grown outside in the garden without further ado. Beyond that, different house plants make different demands on their environment. In this book we have expressed these demands by means of symbols, so that the reader can tell at a glance how much light, heat, water, air and soil humidity a particular plant requires. These are their chief needs, and we shall now examine them in more detail.

Light

Light is a form of energy, which explains, for instance, why solar panels can be used to raise the temperature of our bath water. Light is also a form of wave motion with an extremely small wavelength – in the case of visible light, between 380 and 780 nanometres. Light comes in all the colours of the rainbow but we see it as white alone. Only when it falls on objects that absorb some of it do we see the objects in a certain colour, say blue. The sensitivity of the human eye is greatest in the spectral range that includes green and yellow. Plants, for their part, grow fastest in red light.

The amount of light which falls on a certain area is measured in lux, a unit based on the spectral sensitivity of the human eye, but also used to express the light requirements of plants. Here mistakes can easily be made, for instance when gauging the amount of light emitted by a neon tube. The human eye is not very sensitive to it so that it might be thought that the tube does not emit a great deal of light. But plants particularly like its red factor, and would, if they could, record a much greater amount of light value. Be that as it may, we shall pretend that there is only one level of sensitivity and measure everything in lux, otherwise things become too complicated.

Directly behind a window at noon on a sunny day in May or July, an illumination of 160,000 to 320,000 lux would be recorded. The minimum illumination a plant needs to survive in the middle of winter is 700 lux. These figures determine the range in which nearly all plants grow. The light reaching the earth is only a fraction of the light produced by the sun. On top of a mountain, for instance, you will notice a vast increase in light intensity. The atmosphere is cleaner up there and the path of the light less impeded by the countless dust and vapour particles present in the lower atmosphere.

Closer to the sun, the light quickly becomes unbearably intense. This is because the intensity of light increases at the square of the distance to its source. In other words, twice as far from the sun means a quarter the light.

If you look upon your window therefore as the 'sun', that is, the source of light, you will record a quarter the light at distance B, twice as far from the window as distance A. You can easily check these values with a photographic light meter. So if you grow plants indoors, the reason why they suddenly begin to droop as they are moved further away from the window is readily understood: they lack light. In practice, half a metre (yard) can make all the difference.

Three symbols are used in this book to indicate the amount of light each house plant needs:

○ Full sun. The plant tolerates unshaded sunlight for an unlimited number of hours each day. It can therefore be placed in or very close to a south-facing window.

◐ Semi-shade. The plant needs a great deal of light but must be protected from the strongest rays of the sun, that is from about 10.00 a.m. to 5.00 p.m. In a south-facing window, therefore, it should be shaded by blinds or thin net curtains. Alternatively, it can be placed in a window facing east from which the sun disappears at about ten in the morning, or a west-facing window which the sun does not reach until about five in the afternoon.

◑ Shade. The plant must not be exposed to direct sunlight, particularly during the summer. A north-facing window is ideal, or somewhere further away from any window in what is otherwise a light room. But be careful not to choose *too* dark a spot.

The number of daylight hours also has an effect on the growth of plants. In winter, the days draw in appreciably so that there is much less light in any one day. Moreover, the sky is usually more overcast than it is in summer. It follows that plants receiving more than enough light in the summer may suffer from lack of light in the winter. If possible they should then be placed a little closer to the window. It is also possible for a plant to receive so little light that it simply stops growing. It really then needs a resting period (see page 14).

The number of daylight hours may also influence the flowering period and the growth of plants. Two distinctions can be made:

Short-day plants These make flower buds when there are less than 12 daylight hours. Nurserymen make use of this characteristic by keeping plants artificially dark. In that way poinsettias, for instance, can be brought on early for the Christmas trade (normally they would only bloom after Christmas).

Long-day plants These flower when there are more than 12 daylight hours. Here, too, the nurseryman can make use of this characteristic by growing the plants concerned in artificial light during the winter. They will then come into flower much earlier in the spring.

The householder, too, can influence the growth and flowering of various house plants by keeping them darker or by giving them a little extra light. Thus if a poinsettia is removed to a darkened cupboard for a few hours each day at the end of August so that it does not receive more than 12 hours (or better still, 10 hours) of light per day, it will produce buds within a week or so and can then be put back in its normal position in the room.

Again, if you would like an African violet or a begonia to flower throughout the winter, put it beside a table lamp in the evenings.

It is common nowadays for people to try to grow plants in parts of the room where there really is too little light, especially during the winter. The answer may be artificial illumination. Unfortunately, the light from an ordinary electric light bulb is not of much help. Plants greatly prefer fluorescent tubes, high-pressure vapour lamps, or, best of all, one of the many wide-spectrum, gas-discharge, plant-growing lamps sold under various trade names. These lamps can be left on for up to 18 hours at a time, but can also be used to extend the number of daylight hours – they can be turned on in the morning before it is light outside and in the evening, after dark. Unfortunately, many people know very little about the amount of light emitted by plant lamps. Suspended one metre (yard) above a plant (and that is very low indeed!), a 32-watt fluorescent tube emits

520 lux, a 160-watt wide-spectrum lamp about 700 lux and a high-pressure mercury lamp gives 1,200 lux. Generally, however, the lamps are hung from the ceiling at a height of 2 to 3 m (6 to 10 ft) above the plant with the result that the light will bring some benefit to the top of the plants only.

To illuminate plants effectively in, say, an office, a whole battery of lamps may be needed. To run them is an expensive business and it may well prove cheaper simply to replace the plants now and then.

Plant-growing lamps are best turned on and off with the help of a time switch, for people tend to be forgetful and the rhythm of plants is easily disrupted.

Temperature

Most house plants do well thanks to the relatively high and even temperature of our homes. That does not mean, however, that they should have as much heat as possible. Indeed, different house plants demand different temperatures, and in particular different summer and winter temperatures.

In this book the temperature needs of house plants are indicated by various thermometer symbols: warm, moderately warm and cool. Our distinguishing criterion has been the minimum night temperature in temperate zones during the summer (generally reckoned to last from the end of May to the beginning of October). We decided against using the minimum day temperature because it can fluctuate considerably indoors: measurements have shown that in front of a glass window in the sun the temperature can quickly rise to 40°C (104°F) and more. No plant actually needs so high a temperature, though most house plants will tolerate it. On the other hand, a very cold night temperature can prove fatal to many tropical plants, which is why it is reliable guideline. In fact, we might simply have called it the minimum summer temperature, for if the thermometer does fall below, say, 10°C (50°F) at night, it will certainly not drop below that value during the day.

Many house plants like a cooler temperature in the winter than in the summer, and then pass through a resting period (see page 14).

We have used the following three temperature symbols:

⊕ Cultivate at a warm temperature. Minimum (night) temperature in summer 16 to 20°C (60 to 68°F).

⊕ Cultivate at a moderately warm temperature. Minimum (night) temperature in summer 10 to 16°C (50 to 60°F).

☺ Cultivate at a cool temperature. Minimum (night) temperature in summer 3 to 10°C (37 to 50°F).

In general, plants from tropical regions fall in the first category and plants from subtropical regions in the last. In the subtropics the temperature can, after all, be very cold in spring; indeed it may dip below freezing point. Plants in the last category can be placed outside from April to the middle of October in the south of the country and from the middle of May to the end of September in the north.

Fluctuations in temperature do not in general favour plants but may be tolerated provided they go together with fluctuations in the amount of light. This is logical, for when the sun shines it is usually warmer. Differences between day and night temperatures are another matter: they are common in natural habitats and for that very reason they are beneficial to indoor and container plants, and may

Davallia mariesii is one of many attractive ferns which make fine houseplants

even encourage their growth. The thermostat can therefore safely be turned down by 4 to 6°C (7 to 11°F) at bedtime. It must however be remembered that in winter the temperature near a single-glazed window can drop extremely quickly, so that much damage can be suffered by plants such as anthuriums.

In greenhouses, where the temperature is generally regulated by a thermostat, people often forget to provide different day and night temperatures. The thermostat may be set at 18°C (64°F) on an overcast winter's day and be left at that level for 24 hours. That is not very profitable, and certainly not for your pocket. A better idea is to install a time switch and to set the temperature at 19 to 20°C (66 to 68°F) during the day and at 16°C (60°F) at night. The extra thermostat and time switch will have paid for themselves within a year in an electrically heated greenhouse, and the plants will, moreover, have benefited greatly.

In places where plants are stored over the winter, such as conservatories or unheated greenhouses, the temperature must not be allowed to rise too high. The minimum temperature is usually 5°C (41°F) in cool greenhouses, but in the winter or spring sunshine, the temperature inside can easily reach 20 to 25°C (68 to 77°F) during the day. This is not desirable, since the plants will start growing much too quickly. The answer is ventilation.

Not only the length of the day, but the temperature, too, can influence bud development.

Many succulents will only produce buds if they have been kept at a low temperature for some time, and chrysanthemums will not come into bud unless the temperature is at least 16°C (60°F). Once the buds have been formed the temperature can of course be changed.

Water

Every plant needs water, but there are vast differences in the requirements of, say, a cactus and a fern, whose transpiration rates vary considerably. Transpiration ensures that the roots work like a pump, sending the nutrients dissolved in the water up to the green parts of the plant. The transpiration rate of plants is regulated by the pores, which are capable of opening and closing.

In every plant the water intake and the transpiration rate must be balanced. If a plant loses more water by transpiration than the roots can take up, the plant will begin to wilt.

Transpiration is most strongly influenced by the temperature of the plant's surroundings. Other factors are humidity and potential draughts. On a sunny day you may well have to give a plant in front of a south-facing window three times as much water as when the sky outside is overcast. Again, a plant you have just cut back severely will need much less water next day. Every rule stating that a particular plant needs a given amount of water daily is therefore

wrong in principle. You must look at it afresh each day, and then let your actions be dictated by the circumstances.

There are several ways of determining how much water a particular plant needs. The simplest is to feel the soil with your fingers. You can also determine how dry the soil is simply by looking at it, or you can tell by the weight of the plant and its pot: the less it weighs, the drier the soil. Moisture meters, which are pushed into the potting mixture, work very accurately and will tell you exactly how moist the soil is.

In this book we shall use three symbols to indicate how much water a plant needs during its growing season. If it has different demands in its resting period, these will be mentioned in the text. Moisture symbols used are:

◎◎ Moist. The soil must feel damp to the touch at all times but must not be saturated. Water should not be left to stand in the saucer. Plastic pots are most suitable for plants with these requirements.

◎ Moderately moist. The potting mix may be allowed to become quite dry between waterings, but not so much that the plant begins to droop. In particular, the pots must be well drained.

◎ Dry. Water only when it is warm; the plant will lose most of its water by transpiration. The soil must not be allowed to dry out completely, or it will not be able to absorb moisture easily at the next watering. Pots should contain a thick layer of crocks, pebbles or other drainage material.

In order to control the soil mixture, all house plants should be grown in plastic or clay pots with a drainage hole from which the excess water can run into a matching saucer. There are just a few plants that need water in the saucer at all times (this will be indicated in the text); under normal conditions the saucer should remain dry. Many of the photographs in this book show ornamental pots with a separate matching saucer. All other kinds of ornamental pots, plant cylinders or what have you, no matter how beautiful, are not really suitable because it is impossible to judge whether they are holding too much water. Millions of plants are killed every year by drowning.

Watering is best carried out using a reasonably sized can with a long spout. Allow cold water to reach room temperature first, or use tepid water. This is especially important in winter. Simply water the earth from the top; if there is not enough room, fill the saucer with water, wait for half an hour or so until the soil has absorbed all it needs and then throw the extra water away.

Some plants in the categories 'moist' and 'moderately moist' like an occasional plunge. This means that the pot should be completely submerged. The air expelled from the potting compost will be seen rising as bubbles. Later, when the pot is allowed to drain, fresh air will automatically be absorbed by the soil. Giving a plant a weekly plunge during the growing season will ensure that it always has moist soil which does not contain too many waste materials. In the growing season, plant food can can be added to the water used in the can or for plunging. Once a week is normally sufficient (see Feeding, page 15).

The quality of tap water is becoming an increasing cause of concern to gardeners in many parts of the country, for it contains more and more salts and poisonous substances in solution, with particularly dire consequences for plants. Very hard water contains calcium and magnesium which in moderation does not affect most plants too badly, although it is harmful to lime-hating plants. Tap water is therefore not always the best choice. Rainwater is better in many cases, but not if it is contaminated, as will be the case in most industrial areas.

The answer is to soften tap water, which can

be done with chemicals or with a filter. The filter must work on the ion-exchange principle but must not be the kind that has to be charged with kitchen salt and which replaces calcium and magnesium ions with sodium ions. Most plants have a particular dislike of the latter and will simply stop growing. It is better to use distilled water, which is not very expensive and can be obtained at any garage, where it is used for filling batteries. It is a good idea to use a mixture of distilled water and ordinary tap water (say, 50:50) for watering your plants. More sensitive plants, such as orchids, will need a mixture of 2 parts distilled water to 1 part tap water.

In the nature of things, the soil in the pot, particularly the uppermost layer, acts as a filter and can absorb harmful materials. In the course of time this top layer becomes saturated with matter toxic to plants and should be replaced. In other words, regular repotting may help to counteract the effects of impure water.

Humidity

The air around us contains a certain amount of water vapour. If it is fully saturated with water vapour so that it can absorb no more, we speak of relative (atmospheric) humidity of 100 per cent or 100. Conversely, if there is no water vapour at all in the atmosphere, the relative humidity is 0.

All that is quite straightforward. But, to complicate matters, there is a law of nature which states that warm air can absorb more water vapour than cold air.

Take just one example: a cubic metre (yard) of air at 5°C (41°F) cannot hold more than 6.8 g (¼ oz) of water. The relative humidity is then 100 per cent. If the temperature of the air is raised to 20°C (68°F), then it can hold 17.4 g (⅔ oz) of water, almost three times as much!

The lower the relative humidity, the greater the demands on the devices used by man, animals and plants to protect themselves from desiccation. Plants differ in their responses to a drop in humidity. Thus a cactus which thrives in the dry desert wind is obviously proof against such contingencies, but a fern from the rain forest will fare considerably worse.

In rooms and greenhouses, atmospheric humidity often plays tricks on us, particularly in winter when the central heating is turned up. The air is artificially warmed, but the amount of moisture in it remains the same, with the result that the relative humidity drops sharply. Air admitted from outside (for instance when doors or windows have to be opened), is often very moist, but it is also cold. In absolute terms it adds very little water to the inside: when it is heated to 20°C (68°F) – and that happens automatically – it will prove to be relatively drier than the air already inside. In winter, therefore, every draught tends to lower the relative humidity of the air inside. Plants that benefited in the summer, when the central heating was off, from breaths of warm, moist air from outside with a relative humidity of, say, 60 to 80 per cent, are now suddenly forced to cope with a relative humidity of 40 to 50 per cent, as a hygrometer will quickly show. Plants unable to adapt to a dry atmosphere will show signs of leaf scorch: the leaves will curl up, turn brown and finally drop off.

Because plants show marked differences in their need for moist air, we have divided them into three categories, with the following symbols:

◑ High relative humidity (above 60 per cent) is essential. In winter such plants are best kept under glass, as they are unlikely to survive the winter in a normal centrally heated room.

◑ Moderate relative humidity (50 to 60 per cent) is desirable. Indoors this degree of humidity can only be maintained in winter if special provisions are made.

An easy-to-read hygrometer

◑ Low relative humidity (less than 50 per cent) is sufficient. These plants can be kept in heated rooms during winter without special treatment (as least as far as the relative humidity is concerned).

Increases in the relative humidity in living rooms is something about which few people in countries with cold winters have given much thought. Plants are not alone in suffering from dry air – it can also afflict human beings with dry skins, chapped lips, dried-out mucous membranes that render them more susceptible to colds, and so on. Furniture shows signs of shrinking and splitting. Dry air also feels colder than moist air, so that a room with dry air encourages us to turn the heat up even higher and the air then becomes drier still, and so on.

There are various ways of increasing the relative humidity of the air. You can hang small containers of water on the central heating radiators, spray the plants with water, or group plants together on a shallow tray above water. All these methods are very good in theory but do not help greatly in practice. In a normal house at least 10 litres (18 pints) of water is evaporated in 24 hours when the heating is on high, and that cannot be made up using the above methods.

The best solution is to use an electric humidifier, a handsome container holding water kept constantly just below the boil. It will cut out before it runs dry, it makes no noise, it does not pollute the environment (as can happen with vaporisers) and its energy consumption is relatively low. The extra electricity used may be easily offset by turning the thermostat down a little. No one will notice the difference because moist air always feels a little warmer. In the circumstances, it is quite extraordinary that so few people use humidifiers.

Resting Periods

We have seen that plants need a given amount of light and a given temperature to grow and that they absorb water and food. If any of these factors is reduced, the plant will develop less rapidly, or may stop growing altogether. This is only to be expected, of course. In temperate zones most trees lose their leaves in winter and stop growing, and buds lie dormant until the weather grows warmer and the days become longer again.

Many house plants, too, may have a dormant period in their natural habitat. As far as the amount of light is concerned, our winters do indeed oblige in that respect. However, the temperature in a living room will not drop, since we ourselves like to keep nice and warm. For most plants this is an abnormal state of affairs – in nature a reduction in daylight almost invariably goes together with a fall in temperature. In a warm room, a plant is encouraged

to grow but because of the lack of light that growth will be abnormally thin and lanky. To begin with, the plant will not assimilate food properly, and so will suffer a shock to its system. In addition, many plants need a low temperature in order to form buds. In short, they need a rest, which in their case means less light and a lower temperature.

Now, where can such conditions be found in a normal home? It might be possible to find an unused, or at least cool, bedroom, and place all plants needing a rest close to the window – they all need what little daylight they can get in winter. The thermostat should be set very low, but not lower than 5°C (41°F). Since minimum resting temperatures differ, consult the plant descriptions.

A greenhouse is, of course, the ideal resting place. For resting purposes, a distinction may be made between a cool greenhouse with a minimum temperature of 5°C (41°F) and an intermediate greenhouse in which the temperature is never allowed to drop below 12°C (54°F).

In the past, succulents and cacti used to be kept in a conservatory, brick-built with high windows, which was kept frost-free in winter. This arrangement was not ideal because of the small amount of light admitted – most plants need as much light as possible in winter. The exceptions are deciduous plants, some of which (for instance fuchsias) respond to what appears rough treatment: they can be cut back very hard, and over winter protected by a deep mulch of straw, leafmould or peat. In the spring, when they are uncovered, the plants will not look very attractive, but they will still be alive and quickly shoot beautifully again.

In the spring, the temperature in the winter storage area – whether it is a greenhouse, a bedroom or a conservatory – must not be allowed to rise too quickly, for if that happens the plant will start to grow while there is not yet enough light. The answer is the use of shading and of short periods of ventilation until about the middle of April, by which time the amount of light will be sufficient.

While a plant is resting, it will still need a very small amount of water. Needs vary considerably, but are invariably more modest than

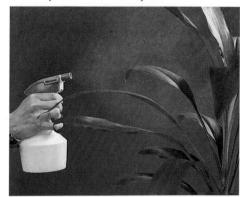
Spraying helps to raise the humidity slightly

An electric humidifier is more efficient

during the growing period. Most succulents (cacti included) can overwinter in completely dry soil provided the temperature is low enough, but plants with winter foliage need a little tepid water every now and then.

In this book resting periods have not been given special symbols, but are mentioned in the text, together with the appropriate temperature.

Feeding

Most house plants obtain their food from the potting compost, which, if it is good, should contain the correct combination of nutrients. However, in due course the nutrients will, of course, have become depleted. These shortages will have to be made good or else plant growth will stagnate.

The main plant nutrients are combinations of nitrogen, phosphates, potash and sometimes lime. Other elements needed in very small quantities, and which are therefore called trace elements, are iron, magnesium, zinc, molybdenum, copper, boron and chlorine.

There are two ways in which we can make up for food shortages in our plants: by feeding and repotting. The second alternative is often overlooked, but is an obvious solution and one that has additional advantages: it helps to remove the harmful salts that have been accumulating in the old potting compost. If we simply keep adding food, the concentration of toxic materials can become too great.

Plants can be fed with a variety of fertilisers, some of which are organic and some inorganic. Organic fertilisers are natural products (chicken manure, farmyard manure, blood meal and so on), and inorganic fertilisers come from the chemical factory. Both types can help you to obtain good results, and the choice is a matter of personal preference.

You can also choose between powders and liquids. Here, too, the results will be the same, so that you can use whatever suits you best.

Most plant fertilisers are compound, that is, they contain nitrogen, phosphate and potash (NPK). A good ratio for the average indoor plant is 6:4:6, although some plants do better with different proportions. Succulents for instance like a little less nitrogen and a little more potash, 4:7:9. Nor are these the only acceptable proportions.

Plants should only be fed when they are growing and the quantity of fertiliser must always be matched to their growth rate. It is only common sense that a small cactus should need considerably less food than a large, quick-growing ficus. In general, a weekly or fortnightly application of fertiliser during the growing season is all a plant needs. If it has just been repotted, you can safely wait for about four weeks before feeding it, as the potting compost contains a good supply of nutrients.

Some fertilisers release their nutrients very slowly and need only be added once or twice a season. In their case, it is almost impossible to overfeed, but that can easily happen with traditional fertilisers, especially of the inorganic type. If the prescribed dosage is exceeded, the plant may start to scorch, which you can tell from the fact that the leaves begin to curl, or turn yellow or brown. It is therefore always best to dilute fertilisers in plenty of water and never to apply a concentrated solution to a dry pot.

Feeding is mentioned under the plant descriptions only if the plant's needs vary from those described here.

Repotting

Nearly all the plants described in this book absorb food from the soil through their roots. Now 'soil' is not always identical with 'earth' since many indoor plants are epiphytes, that is, they grow on trees. Their roots draw up nutrients from all sorts of accumulations of humus found in tropical rain forests. It might be added,

Plant food either in powder form or in liquid form can be added directly to the watering can

for the sake of completeness, that some plants can live practically on air, for example bromeliads of the widespread *Tillandsia* genus.

Normally speaking, a potting compost – perhaps better described as a growing medium – must contain or be able to hold adequate amounts of water, food and air (to supply the plant roots with all the oxygen they need) and must also provide the roots with support. In addition, it must be of the right balance of acidity – many plants have a clear preference for a potting compost with a given pH. Provided these conditions are fulfilled, plants will put up with practically anything: they can grow in a medium of nothing but synthetic stone, or even in just a nutrient solution (see Hydroculture, page 19).

In the past, it was customary to prepare a special mix of various materials for each type of house plant, in an attempt to simulate its natural habitat. And that was, of course, an excellent idea and it has to be said that such mixes did most plants a great deal of good. However, for greater efficiency, people have increasingly gone over to the use of standard potting composts in which as many plants as possible can thrive, and the writer is happy to report that these mixes are not only the same in all countries but that they do equally well everywhere. Britain has its various John Innes Composts, Germany uses TKS and Holland the RHPA mix. We can safely take it that nowadays at least 80 per cent of all house plants will thrive in such mixes. They contain little actual soil and consist mainly of peat. Now, because these humus-rich mixtures are acid by nature, their acidity has to be reduced, with the help of lime, to a more generally acceptable pH of 5.5 to 6.5. Lime-hating plants (for instance azaleas and calceolarias) require special mixtures and for lime-loving plants a little extra lime can be added to the potting mix. Artificial composts are usually

enriched with artificial fertilisers, but there are some completely organic mixes available.

About 20 per cent of house plants – cacti, orchids, bromeliads – will refuse to grow in such standard mixes under any circumstances. It is sometimes possible to buy special mixes for these groups such as cactus mixture, or anthurium mixture, but in many cases the amateur indoor gardener will have to make up his own.

Three symbols have been used to indicate which potting compost is best for each plant:

⊛ The plant does well in standard potting mixture, such as John Innes and Levington composts in Britain and Black Magic Soilless planting medium and Swiss Farm's potting soils in the United States.

⊚ The plant prefers an acid medium – 2 parts standard potting compost, 1 part peat and some extra food, or a special acid potting compost.

⊙ The plant only does well in the special potting mixture described in the text.

The descriptions of some plants will sometimes contain two of these symbols together, which indicates that the plant will be quite happy with the standard potting mixture, but that it will probably do better still if you take the trouble to make up a special mixture. The composition of that mixture is described in the appropriate entry.

Standard John Innes potting composts are of three kinds. No. 1 is made up of:
7 parts medium loam
3 parts peat
2 parts washed river sand
To each bushel (0.036 kg) of potting mixture is added 21 g (¾ oz) of ground chalk and 110 g (4 oz) of fertiliser made up of
2 parts (by weight) of hoof and horn meal
2 parts (by weight) of calcium superphosphate
1 part (by weight) of potassium sulphate
John Innes Compost No. 2 contains double the quantity of fertiliser, and No. 3 three times as much.

Special potting composts for such lime-hating plants as azaleas and cyclamens can be brought. They usually contain a much larger proportion of peat, have added leafmould and, of course, no ground chalk.

Cactus compost usually contains less humus and is more porous than the normal mixture. And there are also a number of special proprietary composts for orchids and bromeliads.

Some manufacturers also market mixtures containing leafmould, stable manure, pinewood soil, and other ingredients, but on the whole most garden centres do not provide a very wide choice of potting composts.

As the reader may like to make up his own potting compose, we shall describe the most important of these, first listing the ingredients.

Leafmould Most gardeners prefer well broken-down beech leaves. The leaves are piled up, left for a few years and then sieved.

It is not difficult to prepare your own potting mix

15

The job of pruning is often best combined with repotting

Turf soil Turf grown on clay soil is preferred. The turves are put in a pile and allowed to rot.

Compost This can be made from garden and kitchen refuse. The disadvantage is that the compost is likely to contain the seeds of many weeds.

Farmyard manure Cow manure is most commonly used, although pig and chicken manure are alternatives. The manure must be at least one year old and well rotted. This point is reached when the manure no longer smells bad.

Peat dust Bought in bags. It must not contain too much salt.

Peat Well-rotted black peat, also bought in bags.

Sphagnum moss Also called peat moss, it was customarily used by florists as a support in flower arrangements. Artificial foam is now used, but many florists still keep a small supply of sphagnum.

Pinewood soil This is the rotted litter from the floor of a pine forest.

Clay or clayey loam This must be friable, since otherwise it is difficult to mix. Collect it yourself, for instance from a roadside verge. Clay from molehills is particularly suitable.

Sharp or river sand It must not contain too much lime, and is usually washed first to remove extraneous matter.

Perlite This is a variety of obsidian consisting of masses of pearly globules each a few millimetres in diameter. It is normally rich in lime, but the horticultural variety is neutral. It helps to aerate the soil. Usually obtainable from cactus growers.

Charcoal Widely obtainable because of its use in barbecues. It also helps to aerate the soil.

Ground chalk Used to increase the alkalinity or pH of the potting mixture. It is sold in packets at garden centres.

Blood, hoof and horn or bonemeal Ideal for people who do not want to use artificial fertilisers in their potting mixture. It contains nitrogen, phosphorous, potassium, calcium and trace elements in balanced proportions, and can also be used as a top dressing. Sold in bags.

Expanded clay granules Used in hydroculture to aerate the solution.

These are the main ingredients with which most mixes may be made up, except for those suitable for orchids which must also contain chopped fern roots, tree bark and fragments of tree fern. These items are difficult to obtain except from an orchid grower.

Now for a few potting mixtures you can make up yourself.

Potting mixture for normal plants, as a substitute for the standard mixture, symbol ⊕:
  4 parts finely sieved leafmould
  1 part sharp sand
  1 part well-rotted farmyard manure
  To each litre (quart) add 5 g (¼ oz) ground chalk and 5 g (¼ oz) dried blood, hoof and horn or bonemeal. Mix thoroughly and set aside for some time before use.

Potting mixture for acid-loving plants, symbol ⊞:
  3 parts pinewood soil
  2 parts peat
  1 part well-rotted farmyard manure
  To each litre (quart) add 2 g (a pinch) of ground chalk, and 2 g (a pinch) of powdered NPK fertiliser 12:10:18

Seed compost, also suitable for cuttings:
  2 parts medium loam
  1 part peat
  1 part washed sand
  To each litre (quart) add 2 g (a pinch) of ground chalk and 4 g (⅛ oz) superphosphate.

Cactus mixture, suitable for all succulents:
  1 part standard potting mixture
  1 part perlite (horticultural quality)

For other special mixes see the individual plant description.

These are the ingredients of various potting mixtures – now for something about potting itself. It is true to say that the roots of nearly all house plants have not been designed to be crammed unnaturally into a pot or a bowl. Anyone who has seen a philodendron growing among the trees in a tropical jungle and then thinks of the little plastic pot in his living room will readily appreciate this.

The best way of caring for house plants is to repot them regularly, as a rule once a year. Only very large, older plants should be repotted less

A ceramic combination pot

A mirror pot

Repotting. Notice how the roots have filled the soil ball

often. As already said, repotting not only helps to replenish the supply of nutrients but also helps to eliminate waste matter that has accumulated in the potting mixture.

How often you have to repot a plant depends on its vigour. A strongly growing plant bought in the spring when small may be repotted several times during the growing season, while a small succulent, which grows very slowly, can safely be left in a fairly small pot for a whole year. In all cases, the space available for the roots must be kept in proportion to the space occupied by the plant above the pot, or else the plant will not flourish.

You can tell whether it is time to repot by checking the extent of root growth in the soil ball. No harm is done at all to the plant by the removal of the soil ball from the pot, provided the roots are not disturbed. If a fair amount of soil is still visible, perhaps so much that the ball almost falls apart, you can safely put off repotting. If several roots can be seen, but also some soil, the plant may be allowed to grow on in the old pot a little longer. But if hardly any soil can be seen for the mass of roots, then the plant is potbound and it is high time that it is repotted.

Most plants grow best in an ordinary flower pot with a drainage hole. Such pots are made either of baked clay or of plastic. Plastic pots are increasingly popular, the old story that plants prefer clay pots having been proved a fallacy. The main difference between plastic and clay pots is their respective rate of evaporation: a clay pot, which is very porous, loses a great deal of moisture, and the plant in it must therefore be watered much more frequently. Some of the water is taken up by the plant, and some by the pot. A plastic container, on the other hand, does not allow water to pass through it, so that all the moisture is available for the plant.

The potting mixture contains nutrients and these dissolve in the water you add, much like the salts and other material present in tap water. Some of these salts finish up in the wall of the clay pot, often to be seen as an unsightly white sediment.

Deep-rooting plants such as palms like extra-deep pots. Surface-rooting plants such as azaleas, on the other hand, are best grown in a shallow pot. Because pots can be bought in all shapes and sizes, these requirements are easily satisfied.

To repot a plant, one must, of course, first remove the soil ball from the old pot. With smooth, plastic pots this generally causes few problems, but the ball often refuses to budge from clay pots. If this should happen, hold the plant upside-down and tap the pot against the edge of the table. This will usually release the ball, but if it does not then there is no alternative but to smash the old pot with a hammer. The crocks will come in handy for drainage purposes.

Often the roots grow out of the drainage hole in the bottom of the pot. Try to leave them

Moving a *Ficus benjamina* to a large container

undamaged, for cutting them off will severely hamper the absorption of food. The same is true of all the root hairs which form a felty white layer round the soil ball, particularly with plants grown in clay pots. Some books advise you to trim this layer off, but that is a sure way of doing irreparable damage to the plant. The cutting of roots is always a mistake, unless, of course, part of the root system is rotten. The unhealthy parts must then be removed with a sharp knife, and the wounds treated with charcoal powder.

From time to time, it is a good idea to try and remove the old potting compost that clings to the roots. The top layer will usually drop off by itself, and that is all to the good, because it is usually the most contaminated. Even inside the ball there is often a great deal of loose soil, and this can sometimes be removed by a gentle kneading of the soil ball. If this is unsuccessful, it does not matter greatly and it may safely be left in place.

The new pot must be one or two sizes larger than the old, so that the entire soil ball can be surrounded by fresh potting compost.

Start with the drainage layer, usually consisting of crocks, which serve to prevent the roots from blocking the drainage hole. Often one large crock alone will do, its convex side uppermost, although plants that need particularly thorough drainage must have a deeper layer. In the case or orchids, half the pot is often filled with crocks.

A thin layer of potting compost should then be laid on top of the drainage layer and the plant placed in the pot. Make sure that it is neither too high nor too low in the pot. Fill in around the soil ball with potting compost and firm down well. Then add another 2.5 cm (1 in) or so of compost on top of the ball and again firm it down leaving a distance of about 2.5 cm (1 in) to the top of the pot, which is the watering space. If you fill the pot right to the top with soil, you will make watering extremely dif-

It is important to allow space for watering

ficult – the water will simply run off the surface and over the edge of the pot.

After repotting, keep the plant out of the full sun (if that is where it is normally kept) for a few weeks while the roots recover their strength, and new roots form.

Repotting is usually carried out when a plant has temporarily stopped growing, for instance at the end of the winter. However, in principle it is possible to repot plants throughout the year, provided that the soil ball is left intact.

During repotting, many plants can also be divided, amongst them orchids, in which case only the younger parts should be used.

Propagation

Many house plants are quite easy to propagate, and home propagation is not only a simple way of obtaining more plants but it is also a pleasant hobby. In our descriptions of indoor plants, the letter P indicates the method of propagation: by division, cuttings, seed, layering or grafting.

An electrically heated propagator

Each of these methods is described separately, but first here are a few general tips.

For seed to germinate, but also for stems to root, warmth, moisture and air are essential. Not much food is needed at the beginning; tender roots are quickly satisfied – after all, you don't feed a two-week old baby on entrecôte steak.

Seed or propagating compost can usually be bought ready-made, but you can also make it yourself by mixing standard potting compost and peat in equal parts. Succulents prefer to make roots in 100 per cent sharp sand. Roots can also be formed in sphagnum moss, in perlite and even in water, though roots grown in water alone have a different structure from normal roots and the plant has to adapt when transferred to pots containing compost. That is why it is a mistake to place a cutting in a jar of water and let it grow roots if it is later to be potted up. The method may work but it is unnecessarily cumbrous.

There are special small germination or rooting pots, of which those made of peat are particularly useful because they do not have to be broken or discarded: they can be planted intact and the roots will simply grow through the walls.

To restrict transpiration, which is advisable with small cuttings, you can cover the pots with glass, plastic or other materials that admit light. Indoor propagation boxes are becoming increasingly popular.

Extra warmth is almost invariably a good way of giving cuttings and seedlings a start. The small pots, bowls or propagators can be placed on or near central-heating radiators, though care must be taken that the temperature of the soil does not rise above 35°C (95°F), 20°C (68°F) being quite enough in most cases. Remember that the higher the temperature, the greater the transpiration, and make sure that the potting compost is never allowed to dry out.

Sowing

You can collect your own indoor plant seeds. The advantage of propagation from seed is that seeds may be sent easily all over the world. Not every seed retains its germination power so that it is advisable to sow seeds as soon as possible. Very hard-coated seeds should first be soaked, but generally seeds will germinate as soon as they are placed in a warm and moist environment.

Before seed is sown in a small pot or bowl, the compost should be firmed down, and the surface made level. The seeds can then be scattered. Make sure that fine seeds do not fall too close together – a typical beginner's mistake – or there will not be enough room when they start to grow. The seeds should then be covered with a thin layer of sharp sand, which is best applied through a tea strainer. Seeds that take a very long time to germinate can also be covered with very fine gravel, or coarser sand. Algae does not grow so quickly on sand or small stones as on damp compost, and a covering of algae will seal off the compost and prevent oxygen from reaching the seeds. Cactus seeds will sometimes take six months to germinate and in their case the prevention of algal growth is of especial importance.

Another way of preventing algal growth is to cover the seedtray with a newspaper or something similar so that no light can enter. The tray will then have to be checked daily for seedlings, for these will need light immediately they come up.

Trays, small pots and bowls with freshly sown seed must be provided with drainage holes, and preferably with a thin drainage layer, in which case they can be watered from below by placing the pot or bowl in a basin of water. Saturation of the compost is complete as soon as the surface darkens with moisture. As a rule no more water will be needed until the seeds have germinated.

Seed pots or bowls are usually covered with glass or polythene to reduce transpiration. When the seedlings come out, they should remain covered for a while, but after a few days a little air can be carefully admitted to reduce the humidity. This process is called hardening off and is of great importance.

Seedlings first send up seed leaves or cotyledons, followed later by true leaves. As soon as the latter have appeared it is time to prick the seedlings out to give them more space, preferably by placing each in a pot of its own. Pricking out must be done very carefully lest the tender roots or other parts be damaged. Put your hand under the compost and push the entire plant upwards until it can be removed quite easily. Often, a taped pair of tweezers or a small wooden plant label with a wedge-shaped notch can be used as an aid. In its new home, the seedling can safely be planted a little more deeply, so that it stands up. Do not forget to give it a little water.

A plastic bag placed over plant and pot provides an ideal micro-climate

It is only sensible to keep plants that have just been pricked out protected under glass or polythene for another few days. Under no circumstances should they be placed in the sun. Only when you are sure that they are growing should you harden them off again.

After a few weeks many plants must be pricked out once more, or rather repotted. At this stage, a standard potting compost or any other suitable mixture can be used.

Division

All plants that send up more than one stem can be divided. Knock the plant out of its pot and try to divide the soil ball into two or more pieces with your hands. Each piece must have at least one stem and one root, otherwise the plant cannot grow. Tubers with more than one bud can also be divided. If it cannot be done by hand, then a sharp knife may be used. It does not matter too much if some of the roots are severed, but try to cut as few as possible. Wounds on fleshy roots and tubers should be treated with charcoal powder and allowed to dry out a little before the tubers are replanted.

If many of the roots are damaged during division it is best to keep the affected plant under glass or polythene for a while so as to reduce transpiration.

Cuttings

It is possible with many plants simply to cut off a part without roots and allow that section to make its own roots. This remarkable process is known as 'taking a cutting'. It is made possible by the fact that many plants are able to produce roots as well as shoots from certain growing points.

Just like a germinating seed, a cutting is encouraged to make roots by warmth and moisture. More so, however, than with seeds, it is important not to let the cutting dry out, since, lacking roots, it is unable to absorb water from the soil, and unlike a seed protected by a seed case, it has a high rate of transpiration. Hence it is best to grow nearly all cuttings under glass or polythene.

Cuttings are of the following kinds:

Softwood cuttings: shoot or tip cuttings These are young shoot tips that have not yet turned woody. They should have a few leaves and should be cut off cleanly just below a bud. The bottom leaves are carefully removed and the lowermost part of the shoot should be inserted in the rooting medium. Roots will develop from buds in the lower leaf axils.

Eye cuttings Similar to the last, except that a stem section having just one leaf should be chosen. The eye in the leaf axil will produce both roots and a new shoot. The leaf and petiole (if there is one) are left on the stem, but to reduce transpiration large leaves, for instance those of *Ficus*, should be rolled up. A rubber band will keep them in place.

The stem is cut approximately 1 cm (⅓ in) below the bud. It should thus be possible to obtain quite a few cuttings from a single stem, and the tip may also be used as a rule. The

Inserting cuttings in sharp sand

Air-layering

stem, the eye and a small part of the leaf stalk are then inserted in the rooting medium, and the leaf is allowed to protrude.

Leaf cuttings Leaves, too, with or without stalks, are capable of forming roots. The leaves of such plants as evergreen begonias, in particular, can safely be cut into sections measuring 1 square cm (six to the square inch). If the sections are laid flat on the rooting medium and pegged down, roots and shoots will be formed.

With other plants, the African violet for instance, a complete leaf, together with a section of the stalk, must be placed vertically in the rooting medium. The elongated leaves of *Streptocarpus* (Cape Primrose), on the other hand, may be divided horizontally through the central vein and both halves inserted upright in the rooting medium. In due course, a number of plantlets will develop along the line of the central vein.

Root and stem cuttings Sections of the root or of the stem can be cut off and placed in the rooting medium. In time, eyes will be formed to produce shoots and roots.

Nearly all cuttings grow better if the rooting medium is heated, generally to 20°C (68°F) but sometimes as high as 35°C (95°F). Transpiration should be limited lest the cuttings dry out. Sometimes it helps to treat the cut with a hormone rooting powder. All cuttings will respond well in an electrically heated propagator, something that will give pleasure for many years.

Cuttings from succulent plants should be allowed to dry for a while before being placed in the rooting medium, or they may rot. The drying period may last from one to fourteen days, depending on the plant.

The optimum temperature for taking cuttings of most house plants mentioned in this book that lend themselves to this method of propagation is indicated in the text.

Air-layering

Layering is a method of propagation in which the stem of a living plant is cut in such a way that it remains attached to the parent. It is a rather clumsy method, in fact, used for the most part by those who are not happy about taking cuttings. It is useful for overgrown plants, for instance a *Ficus* or a *Monstera* threatening to go through the ceiling. In such cases, air-layering will produce roots halfway up the long stem, which can then be severed below the roots and the top section can then be potted up separately. (It is not generally realised that the lower part will continue to grow, making an even more attractively branched plant.)

The way to do it is to make an oblique cut one-third of the way through the stem directly below an eye, keeping the wound open by inserting a piece of matchstick. The whole section is wrapped in moist sphagnum moss, which is then covered with polythene film and

bound to the stem above and below the moss. A weekly check should be made to make sure the sphagnum moss is still damp. The pot should be watered less than usual so that the plant is kept slightly hungry. This will stimulate root formation inside the sphagnum wrap.

It may take months, but eventually roots will begin to grow in the moss. When they have reached a reasonable size, the stem can be severed just below the roots and the upper part of the plant potted up separately. Cover it temporarily with a polythene bag to limit transpiration, since the roots are not yet capable of taking up a great deal of moisture.

Grafting

In this method of propagation, living portions of two related plants are joined together. The portion to be increased is called the scion, and the portion to which it is joined (an established root system) is called the stock, or rootstock.

In the case of indoor and hothouse plants, grafting is largely confined to cacti. The reason is that in temperate zones many cacti do not grow well with their own root systems, since they receive too little light. The best stock is a species that assimilates nutrients readily and has assimilation products to spare, so that the excess food can be transferred to the scion. The latter rewards this act of generosity with strong and healthy growth. The stock must not be too short, generally about 8 cm (3 in), since otherwise its green surface area will be too small. The popular red and yellow globular cacti (*Gymnocalycium* species) must invariably be grafted because they lack chlorophyll and cannot therefore form any assimilation products. Many green cacti, too, must be grafted, usually because they are too weak to survive alone outside their normal habitat.

A vigorous rootstock for grafting cacti is provided by *Eriocereus jusbertii* and *Trichocereus spachianus*. Both can be grown from seed or cuttings. When they are between six and eighteen months old, the stock should be cut off smoothly at a height of about 8 cm (3 in) and the crown slightly rounded off.

The scion is cut off smoothly too, so that no roots are left on it. The cut surface of the scion can safely be slightly smaller than that of the stock. Both parts are then held together with a rubber band. After a few weeks stock and scion will have united and the rubber band can be removed.

As well as cacti, standard azaleas may be propagated by grafting. Grafting is otherwise rarely used for the propagation of house plants.

Pelargonium and *Fuchsia* standards are not propagated by grafting but by the removal of side shoots. The main shoot is staked and the growing tip pinched out when it has reached the required height.

Grafting cacti

Hydroculture and Watering Systems

Plants do not necessarily have to grow in soil, but may also thrive in nutrient solutions, as Justus von Liebig discovered in the nineteenth century. This method of plant cultivation is called hydroculture.

A plant does not produce the same roots in water as it does in soil – the two types of root have distinct structures, and although it is true that either type can develop into the other, the process takes several months. This explains why growers offering plants grown by hydroculture describe them as especially suited to growing in hydropots. It is, of course, possible to root your own cuttings in water, in which case you can do without the services of the nurseryman.

In hydroculture, only part of the root system grows under water. Because the roots are unable to absorb oxygen in the water, the plant usually produces other roots that grow in the damp atmosphere just above the surface of the water.

The most common hydroculture system today comprises a large pot filled with porous clay aggregates and water up to a third or half of its depth. The level is regularly checked with a gauge. The clay granules give the roots all the support they need.

Nutrient tablets or solutions, available from good gardening shops, are dissolved in the water. There are also long-acting nutrient cartridges that work on the ion-exchange principle: nutrients from the cartridge enter the water and waste products from the water are returned to the cartridge. Such cartridges last for up to six months. Special pellets are also available.

In the absence of an ion-exchange system, it is advisable to pump the nutrient solution out once a year and to replace it. With ion-exchange systems it is possible, in theory at least, to continue indefinitely, but the water does, of course, collect dust and other extraneous matter, so that it is best to use a fresh solution even here, if only occasionally. The hydropot must be topped up in any case to offset transpiration by the plant.

There is also a patent watering system which resembles hydroculture but is based on an altogether different principle, and which comes in several versions, in all of which the plants are rooted in soil. Water containers are placed below the pots or tray, and the water is drawn up into the pot soil by means of a strip of absorbent material. The absorption rate must be so calculated that the soil is never too moist or too dry. The plant itself then chooses how much moisture is required and the indoor gardener need do no more than keep the reservoir topped up. The water level must, of course, be easy to check.

Since nutrients can be dissolved in the water, a plant should be able to be kept for years with such a watering system.

Hydroculture calls for specially grown plants, which are therefore more expensive than ordinary plants. On the other hand, they can usually be supplied with enough water to be left unattended for much longer periods. Again, not all house plants do equally well with hydroculture. It is, of course, an unnatural method, however remarkable some of its results, but it is of especial value in office buildings or public areas where plants may be left untended for lengthy periods.

Watering systems are unsuitable for plants that do not like to grow in very moist soil, although this drawback can be offset by leaving the reservoir empty for a week or so every now and then. It is true to say that watering miscalculations are nowadays easily avoided in either method. The choice is yours.

Pests and Diseases

House plants are subject to all sorts of complaints of which attacks by pests are the most

Aphids can be a nuisance even indoors

common. They may also be badly affected by mould, viruses and bacteria. How can these plagues be avoided?

We are responsible for removing plants from their natural environment in order to brighten up our surroundings. The plants themselves did not ask us to do so and if we do not ensure the best conditions for them it is evident that their powers of resistance will suffer and they will sicken.

The secret of keeping plants healthy, therefore, is prevention. For that reason it is very important to follow the directions, in both symbols and words, given in this book. If you allow, say, a *Stephanotis* to spend the entire winter in too warm a room, you may take it for granted that it will be covered with scale insects the next summer. Moreover, the plant has been deprived of its resting period, and that is asking for trouble.

If you take proper care, a plant should not succumb to pests or diseases. But none of us is perfect and it may well happen one day that you come upon one of your house plants covered with some nasty infestation. What do you do? Often, the best solution is to repot it, in other words to move it to a better environment. After repotting, it is best to cut it back, and the new shoots will probably then be free of trouble.

If the plant continues to be plagued with pests or diseases then you have no alternative but to throw it away or to spray with pesticides. Here you have the choice between proprietary brands, many of which are highly toxic, and home-made mixtures.

Let us start with the latter. A solution of 20 g (¾ oz) green soap and 10 g (¼ oz) methylated spirits in 1 litre (1¾ pints) of water is a good remedy against aphids, and also helps against other pests, particularly when applied on several days in succession.

Pure methylated spirits can be dabbed straight on to scale insects and leaf-hoppers, and should also be applied repeatedly. An infusion of pipe tobacco contains nicotine and is effective against all sorts of pests. It can be sprayed on the plant and also over the soil to deal with any parasites that may be concealed. It must be remembered however, that nicotine is very toxic.

Of the proprietary mixtures those containing pyrethrum are the least harmful, because pyrethrum is of plant origin (though there are also synthetic pyrethrins). The effects, however, are not long-lasting. Small pyrethrum 'spikes' are available which when inserted into the soil in the pot release their poisonous substances gradually and these are then absorbed by the roots and spread to the entire plant.

If none of these methods proves adequate, you may have to resort to 'heavier' chemicals.

Woolly aphids on a *Grevillea robusta* plant

An infestation of scale insects on a *Pseuderanthemum atropurpureum*

This should be done out of doors on a still day and the pesticides kept well out of reach of pets and children.

Plants bought from a shop will as a rule have been pumped full of extremely poisonous pesticides and inhibitors by the nurseryman. If you want a plant that is completely biologically pure, the best guarantee you can have is to grow it yourself from seed or from a cutting rather than buying it.

Cultivation of Garden Plants

In addition to house, greenhouse and container plants, this book lists and describes some 1,700 garden plants in alphabetical order. We have decided against combining them into such groups as herbaceous perennials, shrubs and bulbs because in many cases that would make them harder to look up. Moreover, it is not always certain to which of these groups a particular plant belongs, and there are many alternative forms. If preferred, plants can always be found under the group headings in the tables and indexes at the end of the book.

With garden plants we have used symbols to indicate their preferred garden sites, their features and special uses. There are 25 symbols in all, and we shall start with a brief explanation.

Light

Full sun is not the place for all plants. In nature, but also in man-made landscapes, there is a great deal of shade cast by trees, houses and so on, and many plants have become adapted to these conditions and will simply no longer grow in full sunlight.

We have accordingly divided plants into three categories: those that thrive in full sun, and those preferring semi-shade or shade. The associated symbols are:

○ Full sun. Any outside spot which is in the sun (if it is out!) with no obstruction for at least 7 hours a day in May, June, July and August. Don't make the mistake of concluding from the fact that a particular plant happens to be standing in the sun that it necessarily enjoys full sun all the time. Check that the situation remains the same for at least 7 hours.

◑ Semi-shade. Any outside spot which is in the sun for at least 3 to 5 hours, or for longer but with the light filtered slightly through trees.

◐ Shade. Any spot with less than 3 hours of full sun a day, or a spot shaded more heavily by trees. (If a plant is in full sun for 2 hours a day and in the shade for the rest of the time, it will fall in this category).

It is very important to remember these distinctions, since if they are ignored many plants will become stunted or diseased. People are generally too optimistic, that is, they often choose too dark a site for their plants. They also choose sunny sites for their shade-loving plants, in which case their mistake very quickly becomes obvious as the leaves begin to droop. Many plants are, however, less fussy about the amount of sunlight they need, and we have given these more than one light symbol.

In general, plants flower more profusely the more light they receive. If you want a large number of flowers you must choose the sunniest possible spot.

Soil Moisture

The absence of a soil-moisture symbol in the description indicates that the plant likes normally moist garden soil. What is meant by that? It means soil that is neither sopping wet nor bone dry. In other words, the water table must not be too high, particularly where large shrubs or trees with deep roots are concerned. The ideal water table in a fairly humus-rich soil is about 2 m (6 ft) below the surface. During dry spells in summer the soil must usually be watered to restore an adequate moisture level.

There are also plants that prefer a slightly drier or moister habitat than the normal. These plants have been given the following two symbols:

⊖ The plant requires a fairly dry, usually chalky soil. The soil should never be wet, particularly in winter.

⊗ The plant requires a very wet soil at all times, usually acid.

Hardiness of Plants

Garden plants can be damaged by various external factors, chief among them frost and wind (see also under hardiness and wind resistance, page 6). The following symbols have been used to indicate their response:

⊗ The plant is sensitive to frost, and in severe winters should be covered with earth, peat, straw, bracken or other protective material. The cover should be removed as soon as the thaw sets in.

⊝ The plant is resistant to strong winds and is therefore suitable for growing in coastal areas. It may or may not be frost-resistant.

⊛ The plant is vulnerable to strong winds and should always be placed in a sheltered site.

Groups of Plants

Garden plants can be classified in various ways. It is usual to distinguish between annuals, biennials, herbaceous perennials, bulbs, tubers, shrubs and trees. In this book we shall indicate to what group a plant belongs with the following symbols:

⊙ Annual. Flowers the year it is sown and then dies.

⊙ Biennial. This is sown late in the season, overwinters, flowers the second year, and then dies.

○ Herbaceous perennial. The parts of the plant above ground usually die down each winter, while the roots generally remain alive. The following spring new shoots appear.

⊘ Bulbs. Plants with underground storage organs consisting of fleshy scales which grow out of a short piece of tissue. The plant usually dies down to the ground after the vegetative period, the underground bulb staying alive. Not all bulbs are hardy; some have to be lifted and stored in the autumn.

⊛ Tubers. Plants with thickened underground stems (rhizomes) or roots (see page 9). Not all are hardy, and they must therefore be lifted and stored in autumn.

⊛ Shrubs. Plants that develop several woody stems. They can be either deciduous or evergreen.

⊛ Trees. Shrubs that develop just one woody stem or trunk. This group includes artificially grown trees, that is, trees grown by various grafting methods.

Features of Plants

The most important features of garden plants are indicated by the following symbols:

Ⓨ Flowering plant. The main attraction of this plant is its beautiful flower(s).

⊚ Foliage plant. The leaves of this plant are particularly handsome and of special decorative value.

⊛ Evergreen plant. The leaves of this plant stay green in the winter (or partly green in very severe winters). Evergreens can be found among herbaceous perennials as well as among

shrubs and trees, which also includes conifers.

⊛ A plant with particularly striking fruits or berries.

◎ Poisonous plant. Some or all parts of this plant are more or less poisonous, sometimes when touched, but usually only when eaten. Care should therefore be taken, though there is no need for anxiety.

Special Uses of Plants

The following symbols are used for plants with important special uses:

⊕ Specimen plant. This plant is particularly suitable for growing on its own in a solitary position.

⊗ Rock plant. This plant is especially suited for use in rock gardens or crevices in paving. Rock plants usually require a particularly well-drained site in the winter; too much moisture causes rotting.

⊞ Hedging plant. This plant can be used to form a loose or dense hedge.

⊖ Ground-cover plant. This plant will, in a few seasons, cover the surface of the soil so closely that it is almost impossible for weeds to grow.

⊗ Good for cutting. The plant can be specially grown to produce flowers for cutting. Other parts of the plant, such as branches or fruit, may also be used for cutting.

Flowering Period

As a rule the first entry after the symbols indicates the flowering period of the plant, if it does indeed flower. Ferns, for instance, do not, and the text will say so.

The flowering period listed is always an approximation. It may differ from one part of the country to another, though as the season advances, the differences generally even out. The fact that the flowering period is listed does not necessarily mean that the flowers are especially attractive – quite the contrary may sometimes be the case.

Colour

By colour we always refer to the colour of the flowers, unless otherwise stated. The colour names have been based largely, but not entirely, on the R.H.S. Colour Chart, published by the Royal Horticultural Society in 1966.

For example, the colour between yellow and orange is given as yellow-orange. If a flower has two distinct colours, one yellow, the other orange, this is indicated by being described as yellow/orange.

In general, only the colour of the plant in the illustration is given. If the plant comes in a number of colours, not all of which can be listed, then this may be indicated as var. or mixed colours.

Height

After the colour comes the height, always indicated by the letter H. Low values are given in centimetres (cm) and inches (in), higher values in metres (m) and feet (ft). Generally the minimum and maximum heights are given, but particularly with trees we sometimes give only, say, 20 m (65 ft), which indicates the maximum eventual height. Since the tree may grow for a

A red and purple corner in the gardens of Ladham House, Goudhurst, Kent

century before reaching that height, it is not necessarily unsuitable for smaller gardens. Where no height is given, that is because it is irrelevant, for instance in the case of an aquatic plant that floats on the surface of the water.

Width

The letter W indicates the maximum spread, particularly of shrubs, over which people often tend to make mistakes. Thus a blue Atlas cedar will often be seen planted a mere 2 m (6 ft) or so from the front of a house, a little too close when it is realised that the eventual width of the tree may be more than 10 m (33 ft)!

Planting Distance

In the case of herbaceous perennials, annuals and biennials, bulbs and tubers, we have indicated the planting distance (distance apart = A) rather than the width of the plant. They both come to the same thing, of course, since half the spread is equal to half the planting distance. Knowledge of the precise planting distance is, however, very useful in the designing and planting of borders and other garden areas.

Depth

With a number of plants, such as bulbs and tubers, the planting depth is of great importance. It is indicated by the letter D and is the measurement from the top of the bulb or tuber to the surface of the soil. Well-developed bulbs should be planted at a slightly greater depth and small bulbs of the same species at a slightly lesser depth.

D is also used to indicate the water depth of aquatic plants or those growing on river banks.

Soil

It is very important to grow garden plants in the soil appropriate to them. Demands can differ considerably, an important distinction being made, for instance, between lime- (or chalk-) loving and lime-hating plants. In general, acid soils are moist soils whereas chalky soils are porous and more or less dry. But there are exceptions. Sandy soil is generally acid, but chalky on sandy coasts. Clay soil generally contains a great deal of chalk, but can also be acid. Peat soils are always acid, and so is valley soil. Loamy soils contain chalk.

In order to make gardening as simple as possible we use the concept of so-called normal garden soil. By that we mean soil with an average acidity, neither very acid nor very alkaline, that is with a pH of between 5 and 6. In addition, it is fairly rich in humus and all the necessary nutrients. Drainage must be adequate, and during dry weather the soil must be watered. It is the kind of soil you would get if you were to follow the advice of a professional soil-analysis expert.

For plants that need special soil, it is always possible to dig a hole and to fill it with the kind of soil that is suitable.

The letter S indicates these soil requirements. 'Not critical' means that the plant in question is not fussy about the soil it grows in. 'Poor soil' means soil that must be poor in nutrients. 'Normal soil' has been described above. 'Fertile' or 'rich' means that the soil must be given a top dressing at least once a year.

'Lime-rich' or 'chalky' is a matter of pH. Once you have determined the pH of the soil (which can be done with a soil-testing kit) you can calculate how much lime must be added to increase the pH. A soil is said to be rich in lime if it has a pH of about 7. A light soil needs about 30 kg (66 lb) of calcium carbonate per 100 m² (1,100 sq ft) if the pH is to be increased by one point. On somewhat heavier soil it is better to use 15 to 20 kg (33 to 44 lb) of agricultural lime per 100 m² (1,100 sq ft). If the pH has to be increased by more than one point, then it is best to do so by stages over two or three years. But these are exceptional cases.

'Loamy soil' speaks for itself. It is far easier to start with such soil than to have to import it at great expense.

'Acid, moist soil' can be produced by mixing a great deal of peat into the soil. Lime should never be added to such soils.

Propagation

Like house plants, many garden plants are easily propagated. There are two main methods:
  generative or sexual propagation;
  vegetative or asexual propagation.
The first comprises propagation by seed or by spores. The second covers all forms of propagation by which a part or organ of the plant is removed and encouraged to lead an independent existence.

In the descriptions, the letter P indicates which of the following methods of propagation are the most suitable.

Sowing

In principle every plant can be grown from seed (or from spores) but whether it will be identical to its parent is another matter. Moreover, many garden plants do not produce seed in our latitudes. That is the main reason why alternative methods of propagation are suggested.

Few if any grafted plants breed true from seed. Thus you will not obtain a James Grieve apple tree from the pip from a James Grieve apple. Only wild apples can be grown from seed; garden varieties originally produced by chance cross-pollination can only be maintained by vegetative propagation, that is by grafting (see page 23).

The first generation of crosses between two individuals, the so-called F₁ hybrids, will also not breed true from seed – the two parental lines must always be crossed anew to produce the seed of further F₁ hybrids.

Many garden plants, produced by selection and crossing, have double flowers, that is, many of their stamens have been transformed into petals. If no stamens are left, then the plant cannot, of course, propagate itself by sexual means: it has become sterile. And there are many other reasons, too, why it is not possible for some plants to be propagated from seed. Luckily, there are large numbers of plants with which it can be done.

In principle garden plants are sown and pricked out in the same way as house plants (see page 17). With garden plants, however, you are likely to want to sow more seed than would fit into a small pot. Seed may have to be sown under glass; if warmth is required, the text will say so, otherwise no heat should be applied. Heated frames or greenhouses are usually built of wood or aluminium and glass, and the temperature of the soil in them is raised to 20 to 30°C (68 to 86°F) with the help of natural gas or paraffin heaters or electric cables. A cold frame or unheated greenhouse can only be used for raising seed when the weather is milder, say from the beginning of April onwards.

After hardening off, the plants can be planted

Sowing seeds in drills filled with sowing compost

outside (generally not before the middle of May). The required planting distances are listed.

The sowing of plants outside should not be started before mid April. If the plants are sensitive to frost, delay until the end of April and frost should no longer be a threat by the time the seedling appears.

Plants can be sown outside in three ways: in drills (narrow furrows or grooves), on little mounds or by scattering. Unfortunately garden soil is full of weeds which will germinate at the same time as the seeds you have been sowing. The difference between garden plants and weeds is very difficult to tell at the beginning, certainly for beginners, and if the weeds are not removed in time they may choke the good plants. However, if you sow your seeds in drills or on little mounds then the difference will be much more obvious, since weeds do not come up spaced out at regular intervals.

Because plants are almost always sown far too close together, the seedlings have to be thinned out. This can be done by pulling the unwanted seedlings up, pinching them out or snipping them off. The letter A in the plant description indicates how far apart the remaining seedlings should be. Thinning out is often done in several stages, but it is very important to do it in time, or the seedlings will touch each other and their growth will be retarded.

When planting outside it is a good idea to apply some sowing compost first, in drills or in mounds. The layer of compost should be about 5 to 7 cm (2 to 2¾ in) thick. Germination will be encouraged because sowing compost holds moisture more efficiently than ordinary garden soil and there will be many fewer weeds since a good sowing compost contains no weed seeds.

Biennials should be sown from the end of May onwards, generally straight outdoors in a shady site. The seedlings should be pricked out and in September planted out with their soil ball to the site where they are to flower next year. In the winter give them more protection against frost, although most species are fairly hardy.

Division

We now come to the various methods of asexual reproduction, and of these division is certainly the easiest.

Herbaceous perennials that grow in clumps and have several growth buds can, in principle, be divided. This must generally be done when the plant is dormant, that is in spring or late autumn. However, some plants, for instance irises, are best divided and transplanted in the summer.

When dividing a plant, the clump should be lifted and the excess soil shaken off. You will then see a tangle of roots with the growing

points on top (these are most obvious in the spring when they have begun to sprout). In many plants the centre of the clump may be quite old, with few or weakly developed growth buds. If that is the case, choose the outer parts of the clump for replanting. The clump can sometimes be separated by hand, but more often a sharp knife or spade is needed. In principle, you can cut the clump into as many pieces as you want, provided only that each part has at least one growth bud and one small root. Generally, however, fairly large sections are taken. These are then replanted and watered, and nature will do the rest.

Tubers are usually divided under glass (see page 18), and once they have started to grow they are hardened off and planted outside. Bulbs often produce tiny offset bulblets at the bottom. These bulbets can be pulled off and moved to a separate seed bed. After a few years they will be large enough to produce flowers of their own.

Layering and stooling

As could be seen with indoor plants (page 18), air-layering is a method of allowing cuttings to grow on the mother plant, so to speak. In the case of garden plants two related methods of layering are used, layering and stooling.

Layering is almost entirely confined to those shrubs that cannot be propagated from cuttings, which would be a very much simpler method of increase. The shrub in question should also have pliable branches, for the idea is to bend one or more shoots downwards so that they can be partly buried in the soil, and kept in place by a wooden or wire peg. A slit is first made in the part of the shoot to be in contact with the soil, if possible at the level of a bud, and kept open with a small stone or wedge. A hollow is made in the ground and filled with rooting compost, and the tip of the shoot buried in it and left until it produces roots. Layering is usually done in the autumn. The rooted shoots can be separated from the mother plant in the following year. The layering technique can also be used with herbaceous perennials, for instance carnations. The method is identical.

Stooling is a method used with small shrubs that produce easily rooting shoots. The whole plant is cut back and covered with humus-rich soil (for instance potting compost mixed with peat), so that only the tips of the shoots show. After some time these shoots will form roots and when these are large enough, the shoots can be cut off and planted out separately.

Cuttings

This is a reliable and common technique for increasing both herbaceous perennials and shrubs. Various methods are used. Herbaceous perennials are usually treated in the way described for house plants on page 18, using rooting compost, sometimes rooting powder, and in many cases adding extra warmth to speed up root formation. Transpiration must again be restricted by covering the plant with glass or polythene, and the cuttings must be kept out of the sun.

Some herbaceous perennials are propagated from root cuttings, for instance plants of the family *Papaveraceae*: root sections are placed in seed boxes filled with rooting compost and overwintered.

Shrubs, including conifers, can be increased by two sorts of cuttings, summer or semi-hard cuttings and winter or hardwood cuttings.

We shall begin with the second method because it is the simpler.

In early autumn take 10- to 20-cm (4- to 8-in) long cuttings which should have a heel – a small strip of the bark – and be from shoots of the current season's growth. They must be overwintered, protected both from the frost and from drying out. They are usually inserted in sharp sand, but some growers also protect their winter cuttings by wrapping them in polythene and refrigerating them at 1°C (34°F).

During the winter, the cuttings will form a callus and in the spring they will start to root, often as early as April. If not, the cuttings should be potted up and given some bottom heat.

The pots must again be covered with glass or polythene to reduce transpiration. Roots should now appear fairly quickly followed by buds and leaves. Harden the cuttings off and plant them outside, either in their flowering site or in a nursery bed.

Summer cuttings are taken in June, July or August, again of shoots of the same year's growth. Any shoot tips about 5 to 15 cm (2 to 6 in) long can be used. Cut them just beneath a bud, as you would with house plants (see page 18). The bottom leaves should be cut off, the top leaves left on, and a heel is usually left on the cutting. It is then dipped into rooting powder and inserted in a potting mix. The mix should be given some bottom heat and transpiration slowed down. Growers often take cuttings that dry out quickly, for instance those of rhododendrons and conifers, and use mist propagation which ensures that nearly every cutting will root.

The roots are formed in this case before winter, which means that the cuttings should be potted up separately and protected from frost during the winter. In the spring they can be planted out in a nursery bed.

Summer and winter cuttings are susceptible to attack by moulds, which is not surprising when you consider that they have to be kept moist and warm for a long time. It is therefore advisable to add some fungicide to the mister or watering can.

Grafting

One method of propagating trees and shrubs is to graft a portion of the variety to be increased (the scion) on to a chosen rootstock. Many garden plants are propagated by grafting, among them apples, pears and roses. The rootstock is usually grown from seed and the scion is a shoot.

There are various types of grafting. In splice grafting, which is used when stock and scion are of equal diameter, the two are sliced through diagonally, fitted neatly together, bound with raffia and sealed with a grafting wax. The stock must have a few leaves to allow the plant to photosynthesise. When the graft has taken, all growth from the stock is cut off. The stock will probably make new shoots again later, either from the stem or from the roots. These should

be removed at once so that all the plant's energy goes into the scion.

Crown grafting is used when the scion is thinner than the stock. The scion is prepared by making diagonal cuts at one end and it is then pushed under the bark of the stock which has been slit to admit it. Again, the two cut surfaces must be bound together and sealed with grafting wax.

Budding is the simplest method of grafting, and is used particularly to increase ornamental shrubs such as roses. The work is done in the summer, when the roses are in flower. The stock (usually a dog rose) should have been planted and pruned to the requisite height in the previous autumn. Now take a shoot of the current season's growth of the chosen variety, remove the growing tips, all leaves (but not the leaf stalks) and all thorns and then use a very sharp knife to cut out one of the scion buds in such a way as to retain some bark and the leaf stalk beneath. The scion is now inserted into a T-shaped opening in the bark of the stock and the two are bound firmly together with raffia. If the leaf stalk drops off naturally within a week, the graft has taken. Quite often a shoot will have grown from the bud before the onset of winter.

Before frost sets in, the small stems should be earthed up loosely. In March the rootstock is cut down to within 1 cm (½ in) above the bud. The rose may be left in a nursery bed for another year before it is ready for delivery. Here, too, 'wild' shoots or suckers will often come up from the old rootstock and these should be removed at once.

Pests and Diseases

Garden plants suffer from much the same pests and diseases as house plants (see page 19). The best protection we can give them is to choose a good site and to bear their special requirements in mind.

Insecticides and pesticides are a fiercely debated subject. Commercial growers are unlikely to dispense with what they euphemistically call 'plant-protection methods'. The amateur gardener, too, with a large variety of exotic plants in his garden, will want to do something to protect them. But he always has the choice of a harmless and biological, or a poisonous and chemical remedy. Now any pesticide or insecticide will, of course, include some poisonous material, since otherwise it would not work. But there is a vast difference

between spraying with pyrethrum and spraying with parathion.

Nowadays more and more pesticides are being manufactured to destroy the specific agent attacking a plant, and that agent only. Thus they will leave harmless insects alone, insects, that is, which may often be of use to the gardener. There is one pesticide, for instance, containing a virus that kills caterpillars only. Unfortunately, it kills all caterpillars, and one dead caterpillar means one less butterfly. Other pesticides kill aphids only but not ladybirds, which, as you know, are voracious aphid eaters. In short, we may be moving in the right direction but we still have a long way to go.

Harmless remedies which you can prepare yourself include spirits of soap: dissolve 20 g (¾ oz) soft soap and 10 g (¼ oz) methylated spirits in 1 litre (1¾ pints) of water against aphids; nettle essence: steep stinging nettles in water for a few days and add 1 per cent soft soap against various insects; equisetum tea: boil 300 g (11 oz) dried equisetum leaves in 1 litre (1¾ pints) of water for 30 minutes, cool and filter, then mix 5 cc of liquid with 1 litre (1¾ pints) of water and spray against mildew; and rhubarb soap: chop 1 kg (2¼ lb) rhubarb leaves and boil for 30 minutes in 2 litres (3½ pints) of water, filter and add 25 g (1 oz) of soft soap as a spray against aphids. Any book on gardening without poisons will tell you more about the subject.

It is very important to try to establish a biological balance in your garden. Many harmful organisms are eaten and thus kept in check by other, less harmful, organisms. The more natural protection you afford your plants, the greater the chance that the natural balance will be preserved.

Our gardens are usually full of plants grown for years and for the sake of their beautiful large flowers. We tend to overlook their less obvious qualities, for instance their resistance to disease. In the past that was certainly the case with roses, and anyone starting to grow old-fashioned roses (very popular because of that lovely fragrance and charm) will find that though they have been planted in the best position and manured well, it is very likely that they will suffer from mildew. There is little that can be done about that apart from spraying with one of the several very effective fungicides.

We could mention many more examples, but nowadays garden plants have been bred not only for their beauty but also for their resistance, with the result that most of them are healthy enough.

Key to Symbols

The symbols used throughout the book are intended as a quick, at-a-glance guide to the type of plant and its cultivation requirements. Other outstanding features are also represented by a symbol – for instance, attractive berries or suitability as ground cover for planting under shrubs. For easy reference, the list of symbols is reproduced with its key on the back flap, which has been enlarged so that it can be used as a book marker. However, if the cover should become worn or lost, the list is also repeated here.

Abbreviations used in text

H – maximum height
W – maximum spread
A – planting distance
D – planting depth
S – soil
P – method of propagation

Symbols

Garden plants

 Needs direct sunlight (at least 7 hours a day in the summer)

 Needs semi-shade (only 3–5 hours of direct sunlight in the summer)

 Can grow in the shade (less than 3 hours of full sunlight in the summer)

 Needs well-drained alkaline soil

 Needs moist, acid soil

 Protect from frost in severe winters

 Wind resistant

 Protect from strong winds

 Annual

 Biennial

 Hardy perennial

 Bulb

 Corm, tuber or rhizome

 Shrub

 Tree

 Particularly attractive flowers

 Particularly attractive foliage

 Evergreen

 Bears attractive fruit or berries

Wholly or partly poisonous plant

 Useful as a specimen plant

 Useful in rock and paved gardens

 Good hedging plant

 Good ground cover

 Good as cut flowers

House plants

 Needs direct sunlight whenever possible

 Needs light, but protect from direct sunlight between 10am and 5pm

 Needs relatively small amount of light

 Needs warmth. Minimum night temperature in the summer 16–20°C (60–68°F)

 Needs less warmth. Minimum night temperature in the summer 10–16°C (50–60°F)

 Needs little warmth. Minimum night temperature in the summer 3–10°C (37–50°F)

 Keep moist at all times. Soil must not be allowed to dry out

 Keep fairly moist. Soil should be allowed to dry out between waterings

 Keep fairly dry. Water moderately, but only when there is adequate warmth

 High relative humidity (above 60%)

 Moderate relative humidity (50–60%)

 Low relative humidity (below 50%)

 Standard potting mix, pH 5.5–6.5

 Acid potting mix, pH 4.5–5.5

 Needs special potting mix (see text)

House, Greenhouse and Container Plants

Stephanotis floribunda

Abutilon

**Abutilon hybrid 'Feuerglocke'
fam. Malvaceae**
○ ◑ ⬡ ⬡ ∞ ⬡ ⬡
Easily grown house plant, combining
vigorous growth with attractive appearance.
Regular repotting prevents infestation by
aphids and red spider mites.

**Abutilon hybrid 'Golden Fleece'
fam. Malvaceae**
○ ◑ ⬡ ⬡ ∞ ⬡ ⬡
Hybrid between *A. darwinii* and *A. striatum*.
Flowers from May to October. Put outside in
summer. Minimum winter temp. 12–15°C (54–
59°F). P seed.

**Abutilon megapotamicum 'Variegatum'
fam. Malvaceae**
○ ◑ ⬡ ⬡ ∞ ⬡ ⬡
Can be grown as a small tree if side shoots
are removed until required height is reached
Then pinch out. P cuttings.

**Abutilon striatum 'Thompsonii'
fam. Malvaceae**
○ ◑ ◑ ⬡ ⬡ ∞ ⬡ ⬡
As with all other variegated abutilons, the
mottled leaves are due to a virus. Flowers from
August to November. P cuttings.

**Acacia armata (A. paradoxa)
fam. Leguminosae**
○ ⬡ ∞ ⬡ ⬡
Likes a cool and well-lit position in winter. If
necessary cut back after flowering. Put out in
sheltered spot in summer. P seed, or cuttings
in April or in July–August.

**Acalypha hispida (A. sanderi)
Red-hot Cat's Tail / fam. Euphorbiaceae**
◑ ⬡ ⬡ ∞ ⬡ ⬡
For best effect, pinch out occasionally and pot
in a mixture of leafmould, well-rotted
farmyard manure, sharp sand and fine clay or
loam. P cuttings at 20°C (68°F).

**Acalypha wilkesiana 'Musaica'
fam. Euphorbiaceae**
◑ ⬡ ⬡ ⬡ ∞ ⬡ ⬡ ⬡ ⬡
A. wilkesiana varieties have more attractive
leaves but far less striking flower spikes than
A. hispida. Minimum winter temperature 16°C
(60°F). Needs extra feeding in summer.

**Achimenes erecta (A. coccinea, A. rosea)
fam. Gesneriaceae**
◑ ⬡ ∞ ⬡ ⬡
In winter store rootstock in dry sand or peat
at 10–15°C (50–59°F). In spring pot at D 1–2 cm
(½–¾ in) and cover with glass. P division, seed
or cuttings.

**Achimenes hybrid 'India'
fam. Gesneriaceae**
◑ ⬡ ⬡ ∞ ⬡ ⬡
Another most attractive hybrid. S equal parts
peat, leafmould and sharp sand with a little
farmyard manure. P cuttings, division.

Achimenes hybrid 'Johanna Michelsen'
fam. *Gesneriaceae*
Ⓘ Ⓓ ∞ Ⓢ 🗊
Profusely flowering hybrid, its large blooms
set off strikingly by the dark green leaves. To
avoid leaf burn, choose a well-lit spot but
avoid direct sun.

Achimenes hybrid 'Little Beauty'
fam. *Gesneriaceae*
Ⓘ Ⓓ ∞ Ⓢ 🗊
A hybrid that does credit to its name. It is
easily satisfied and produces small, carmine-
pink flowers in great profusion.

Achimenes hybrid 'Paul Arnold'
fam. *Gesneriaceae*
Ⓘ Ⓓ ∞ Ⓢ 🗊
A hybrid with large flowers. When buds
appear, spray liberally to raise the humidity.
Direct spraying on open flowers causes
spotting.

Acorus gramineus 'Aureovariegatus'
Sweet Flag / fam. *Araceae*
Ⓘ Ⓠ ∞ Ⓢ 🗊
A grassy plant. 'Argenteostriatus' has white-
striped leaves. The green species tolerates
more shade. Add a little clay to the potting
compost.

Adiantum fulvum
Maidenhair Fern / fam. *Adiantaceae*
Ⓘ Ⓓ ∞ Ⓢ 🗊
Pot this graceful fern in special fern mixture,
or mix two parts potting compost with one
part peat and one part sand. P seed or
division.

Adiantum raddianum (*A. cuneatum*)
Delta Maidenhair / fam. *Adiantaceae*
Ⓘ Ⓓ ∞ Ⓢ 🗊
Will grow up to 50 cm (20 in). There are many
cultivars. Young leaves stand erect but
eventually arch over. Treat the same as
A. fulvum.

Adiantum raddianum 'Goldelse'
Delta Maidenhair / fam. *Adiantaceae*
Ⓘ Ⓓ ∞ Ⓢ 🗊
Attractive, bright yellow and green leaves,
reddish at juvenile stage. P division.
'Brilliantelse' grows more vigorously.
P spores and division.

Adiantum tenerum 'Scutum'
Maidenhair Fern / fam. *Adiantaceae*
Ⓘ Ⓓ ∞ Ⓢ 🗊
Less bushy and with more delicate leaves
than *A. raddianum.* 'Scutum' has green,
'Scutum roseum' pink juvenile leaves. Treat
like *A. fulvum.*

Adromischus trigynus
fam. *Crassulaceae*
Ⓞ Ⓠ ⊙ Ⓢ 🗊
Compact habit. Erect, flat, greyish-green
leaves with brown spots on either side.
S cactus mixture. P break off leaves and root
them in a sandy mixture.

Aechmea

Aechmea fasciata (Billbergia fasciata)
fam. Bromeliaceae

Bromeliads flower just once, but offsets at base of old plant can be potted up and grown on, preferably under glass. S bromeliad compost, or sphagnum, leafmould, fern roots and farmyard manure.

Aechmea fulgens
fam. Bromeliaceae

Like most aechmeas, an epiphyte from tropical and subtropical Central and South America. The variety *discolor* has purple leaves which are woolly grey underneath.

Aechmea recurvata var. benrathii
fam. Bromeliaceae

An unusual aechmea with small rosettes. Leaves spotted silver on both sides. Treat like *A. fasciata.*

Aechmea weilbachii
fam. Bromeliaceae

Produces leaves up to 60 cm (24 in) long, serrated except for the tips. 'Leodiensis' has copper-green leaves, wine red at the base. Treat like *A. fasciata.*

Aeonium arboreum
fam. Crassulaceae

A striking, branching shrub with bright green or brown compact rosettes. Older leaves drop off, leaving scars on the stem. Yellow flowers. S cactus mixture. P cuttings.

Aeonium tabuliforme
Saucer Plant / **fam. Crassulaceae**

Forms sessile rosettes. Densely branched inflorescences are produced from the growing point. Yellow flowers. Plant dies after flowering. S cactus mixture. P cuttings.

Aerangis rhodosticta
fam. Orchidaceae

The waxy blooms of this winter-flowering plant are most fragrant in the evening. Water less frequently when resting. Minimum temperature 15°C (59°F). S sphagnum and osmunda. P cuttings.

Aeschynanthus lobbianus (Trichosporum lobbianus) / **fam. Gesneriaceae**

A plant with arching stems and leaves in whorls of two or three. Pot in a loose mixture of leafmould, sphagnum, loam and sand. P seed and cuttings.

Aeschynanthus marmoratus (Trichosporum marmoratus) / **fam. Gesneriaceae**

Most attractive hanging plant with waxy, marbled foliage. Always apply and spray with lukewarm softened water. Treat like *A. lobbianus.*

Aeschynanthus radicans (Trichosporum javanicum)/fam. Gesneriaceae

Nicknamed 'Lipstick Vine' because its brown sepals resemble lipstick cases from which the scarlet flowers emerge slowly. Treat like *A. lobbianus*.

Aeschynanthus speciosus (Trichosporum speciosum)/fam. Gesneriaceae

The stems of this vigorous plant from Java can attain a height of more than 50 cm (20 in) and carry large, erect flowers. Treat like *A. lobbianus*.

Agave albicans 'Albopicta'
fam. *Agavaceae*

This plant, which is suitable for containers, has fleshy, stiff, greyish blue leaves with a lighter central stripe. The plant dies after flowering. S cactus mixture.

Agave americana
Century Plant/fam. Agavaceae

The leaves of this plant may reach 175 cm (5¾ ft) long by 20 cm (8 in). Flower spikes, up to 11 m (36 ft) tall, bear yellow-green flowers. Keep cool and dry in winter. S cactus mixture. P cuttings.

Agave americana 'Marginata'
fam. *Agavaceae*

Like all agaves, this attractive plant does not flower before the age of 10 to 30 years. After flowering, the rosette dies. Makes a good container plant. P offsets.

Agave americana 'Stricta'
fam. *Agavaceae*

This plant can grow very tall. Leafy flower spikes up to 6 m (20 ft) long appear from the rosettes of older plants. P offsets.

Agave ferdinandi-regis
fam. *Agavaceae*

This small agave with spreading leaves likes full sunlight. Water generously in summer whenever the soil feels dry. Minimum winter temperature 3–8°C (37–46°F). S cactus mixture.

Agave parrasana
fam. *Agavaceae*

This agave from the Sierra de Parras has grey-blue leaves up to 30 cm (1 ft) long with a 2.5-cm (1-in) terminal spine. For minimum winter temperature, see *A. americana*. S cactus mixture. P cuttings.

Agave schidigera
fam. *Agavaceae*

This decorative plant has a rosette of elongated dark green leaves. Needs a great deal of fresh air in summer. Minimum winter temperature 3–8°C (37–46°F). S cactus mixture. P cuttings.

29

Agave stricta
fam. *Agavaceae*
Bears dense rosettes of narrow green leaves up to 35 cm (14 in) long with a 2.5-cm (1-in) terminal spine. Flower spike up to 2 m (6 ft) long. Does not die after flowering, and eventually produces numerous heads.

Aglaonema commutatum
fam. *Araceae*
Strong foliage plant, sometimes with attractive berries. Pot in March to April in mixture of sphagnum, peat, sand and standard potting compost. P seed, cuttings, division.

***Aglaonema commutatum* 'Pseudobracteatum'**
fam. *Araceae*
The variegated forms demand more light than the green, but too much light may encourage red spider mites. Treat like *A. commutatum.*

Aglaonema costatum
fam. *Araceae*
Dense foliage plant up to 30 cm (1 ft) in height. Treat like *A. commutatum.* While plant is growing, add lime-free nutrient solution every two weeks.

***Aglaonema modestum* 'Variegatum'**
fam. *Araceae*
This cultivar from Puerto Rico must be sprayed with lukewarm soft water. P cuttings, division. Treat like *A. commutatum.*

Aglaonema nitidum* f. *curtisii
fam. *Araceae*
Like other aglaonemas this plant has shallow roots and therefore needs wide, shallow pots. Take care: roots break off very easily. Treat like *A. commutatum.*

***Aglaonema treubii* 'Silver King'**
fam. *Araceae*
In *A.* 'Silver King' as well as in *A.* 'Silver Queen', large parts of the leaf are silver-grey. *A.* 'Silver King' has blotchy leaves. Treat like *A. commutatum.*

***Aglaonema treubii* 'Silver Queen'**
fam. *Araceae*
A. 'Silver Queen' has green leaf stalks. Do not spray directly on the leaves or they will become spotted. Treat like *A. commutatum.*

Allamanda cathartica
fam. *Apocynaceae*
Glorious climber for the heated greenhouse. Rest in winter at minimum temp. of 18°C (64°F). Then pot in equal parts clay, farmyard manure, leafmould and a little sharp sand. P cuttings.

Page 62. Michelia Figo
Page 123. Cantua Buxifolia
124. Euphorbia Characias
128 Yucca Whipplei

Alloplectus capitatus
fam. *Gesneriaceae*
Ⓘ🕐🈂🈁🔲
Unusual plant with racemes of red and yellow
flowers. If plant looks poorly, rest it at a
minimum temperature of 18°C (64°F). P seed
and cuttings at about 28°C (82°F).

Alocasia lowii
fam. *Araceae*
Ⓘ🕐🈂🈁🔲
Rest variegated species at minimum winter
temperature of 18°C (64°F), then pot in a
mixture of leafmould, peat, sphagnum moss
and charcoal. P seed, runners, division.

Aloe arborescens
Tree Aloe / fam. *Liliaceae*
◯🕐◉🌓🔲
Leaf sap has a soothing effect on burns. Small,
orange-red flowers borne in loose clusters
laterally between the leaves. S sandy.
P cuttings.

Aloe barbadensis (A. vera; A. vulgaris)
fam. *Liliaceae*
◯🕐◉🌓🔲
Leaves up to 60 cm (2 ft) long. Flower spikes
up to 90 cm (3 ft) high with 2-cm (¾-in) yellow
or red flowers. S 2 parts potting compost, 1
part sharp sand or perlite. P cuttings.

Aloe ferox (A. supralaevis)
fam. *Liliaceae*
◯🕐◉🌓🔲
Bears long racemes of red flowers. Margins
and surfaces of leaves covered with spines.
Likes to be outside in the summer. S sandy.
P offsets.

Aloe mitriformis
fam. *Liliaceae*
◯🕐◉🌓🔲
Leaves up to 15 cm (6 in) long. Dense clusters
of red flowers in summer. Older plants bear
dense groups of prickly rosettes. S cactus
mixture. P leaf cuttings.

Aloe plicatilis
fam. *Liliaceae*
◯🕐◉🌓🔲
The stems of this plant often fork out. Every
branch ends in a fan of narrow, flat and rigid
leaves arranged in two ranks. The red flowers
are borne in racemes.

Aloe spinosissima
fam. *Liliaceae*
◯🕐◉🌓🔲
Stemless at first but forms stems later. Up to
1 m (3 ft) in height. Leaves up to 30 cm (1 ft)
long. Non-branching flower stalks up to 60 cm
(2 ft) long carry orange-red flowers in clusters.
S sandy. P offsets.

Aloe striata (A. albo-cincta)
fam. *Liliaceae*
◯🕐◉🌓🔲
Has fleshy greyish-blue leaves, their margins
set off with white or red lines. Can grow very
large. Branching flower stalk with clusters of
red flowers. S cactus mixture. P cuttings.

Aloe

Aloe variegata
Partridge Breast / fam. *Liliaceae*
○ ◔ ◑ ◒ ⊡
Rosettes of fleshy, dark green leaves marked with bands of white and arranged in three ranks. Readily bears racemes of tubular red flowers. Keep cool in winter. P offsets.

Alpinia sanderae
fam. *Zingiberaceae*
◑ ⊞ ⊗ ◒ ⊡
Not very well-known member of the ginger family. Pot in rich mixture of loam, well-rotted farmyard manure and peat. P division of creeping rhizomes.

Amaryllis belladonna 'Carina'
Belladonna Lily / fam. *Amaryllidaceae*
○ ⊞ ⊗ ◒ ⊡
Bulbous plant with stout flower stems carrying six to twelve flowers each in the autumn. Overwinter in a sunny, frost-free greenhouse. Put outside in the summer. P seed.

Ampelopsis brevipedunculata maximo-wiczii 'Elegans' / fam. *Vitaceae*
◑ ◐ ⊗ ◒ ⊡
Creeper that loses all or some of its leaves in the autumn. Rest at 5°C (41°F). Repot in the spring. P cuttings in the summer at 15–18°C (59–64°F).

Ananas comosus 'Aureovariegatus'
Pineapple / fam. *Bromeliaceae*
○ ⊞ ⊗ ◒ ◓ ⊡
Pineapples may be kept indoors all year. P offsets in March / April or from leaf rosettes on top of fruit. Dry for 24 hours then pot up.

Anastatica hierochuntica
Rose of Jericho / fam. *Cruciferae*
○ ⊞ ⊗ ◒ ⊡
Annual. The rosette turns brown when dry but unfolds and turns green in water. P sow in March under heat.

Anthurium andreanum
Painter's Pallette / fam. *Araceae*
◑ ⊞ ⊗ ◒ ⊡
Likes a bright and warm spot in winter. Repot every two to three years in special anthurium compost. P division, stem cuttings, rooted side shoots or seed.

Anthurium crystallinum
fam. *Araceae*
◑ ⊞ ⊗ ◒ ⊡
Anthuriums grown for their foliage need more shade than those grown for their flowers. They do best in a heated greenhouse. Treat like *A. andreanum*.

Anthurium magnificum
fam. *Araceae*
◑ ⊞ ⊗ ◒ ⊡
Its trailing velvety leaves make this a very striking plant. Like all other anthuriums, it is very sensitive to salts. Use soft water and lime-free nutrients.

Anthurium scherzeranum
Flamingo Flower / fam. *Araceae*
Ⓘ Ⓓ ∞ Ⓖ Ⓣ
The strongest of all anthuriums. For profuse
flowers keep dryer than usual for two months
in the winter and at a minimum temperature
of 15°C (59°F). See also under *A. andreanum*.

Aphelandra aurantiaca var. *roezlii*
fam. *Acanthaceae*
Ⓘ Ⓓ ∞ Ⓒ Ⓖ Ⓣ
Does best in a warm greenhouse. In the
house, keep the soil moist with soft water. Do
not allow the soil ball to dry out. After
flowering, rest at 10–14°C (50–57°F). P stem or
eye cuttings.

Aphelandra maculata (Stenandrium lindenii)
fam. *Acanthaceae*
Ⓘ Ⓓ ∞ Ⓒ Ⓣ
A trailing plant for the heated greenhouse.
Does well in a mixture of peat, well-rotted
farmyard manure and pinewood soil.
P division and tip cuttings; root under glass.

Aphelandra squarrosa
Zebra Plant / fam. *Acanthaceae*
Ⓘ Ⓓ ∞ Ⓒ Ⓖ Ⓣ
The best known aphelandra, it comes in a
large number of races and varieties, most with
finer marking than the species. Treat like
A. maculata.

Aphelandra squarrosa hybrid
fam. *Acanthaceae*
Ⓘ Ⓓ ∞ Ⓒ Ⓖ Ⓣ
Aphelandras do not usually branch unless
they are pinched out, in which case, however,
they bear smaller flowers. Treat like
A. maculata.

**Aporocactus flagelliformis (Cereus flagelli-
formis)** / Rat's Tail Cactus / fam. *Cactaceae*
Ⓞ Ⓓ ∞ Ⓖ Ⓣ
Long, thin stems about 1 cm (½ in) thick with
pink flowers up to 10 cm (4 in) long which
appear as early as March. Overwinter in a
cool and light place. S cactus compost. P seed
or cuttings.

Arachis hypogea
Peanut / fam. *Leguminosae*
Ⓞ Ⓓ ∞ Ⓖ Ⓣ
Annual. Very sensitive to excess moisture and
subject to attack by whitefly. Water with
discretion. P seed; germinate fresh peanuts at
20°C (68°F).

Araucaria heterophylla 'Gracilis'
Norfolk Island Pine / fam. *Araucariaceae*
Ⓘ Ⓐ ∞ Ⓖ Ⓣ
May be put out in summer. Keep in a light
spot and protect against frost in winter. Repot
every two to three years in acid potting
compost. P shoot tips.

Ardisia crenata (A. crispa)
fam. *Myrsinaceae*
Ⓘ Ⓓ ∞ Ⓖ Ⓣ
This attractive plant also comes in the
variegated form 'Albomarginata'. Spraying
during flowering time impedes pollination.
P cuttings or seed.

Areca lutescens
fam. *Palmae*

Elegant feather palm which is slow to develop. Use tall, narrow pots with a mixture of clay, leafmould, well-rotted farmyard manure and sharp sand. P seed.

Arequipa paucicostata
fam. *Cactaceae*

At first globular but later cylindrical cactus with only a few ribs. Carmine flowers covered with hair. S cactus compost. P offsets.

Arisaema candidissimum
fam. *Araceae*

Heel in outside in October and bring back indoors in the spring. Mix extra peat and leafmould with the potting compost to prevent drying out. P offsets in March–April.

Arpophyllum giganteum
fam. *Orchidaceae*

This epiphyte flowers in March–April and prefers a greenhouse or conservatory. Pot in special orchid mixture. P division or seed.

Asparagus asparagoides (A. medeoloides)
Smilax / **fam. *Liliaceae***

Attractive hanging plant with fragrant greeny-white flowers. Rest in winter at 8–10°C (46–50°F) giving slightly less water. Feed and plunge in water during growing period. P division or seed.

Asparagus densiflorus 'Meyeri'
Plume Asparagus / **fam. *Liliaceae***

'Meyeri' has a much more attractive shape than *A. d.* 'Sprengeri'. *A. densiflorus* strains overwinter well indoors provided they are fed and watered sparingly.

Asparagus densiflorus 'Myriocladus'
Asparagus Fern / **fam. *Liliaceae***

Attractive and easily grown indoor plant. Treat like *A. densiflorus* 'Meyeri'. Cut back slightly when the (pseudo) leaves are yellow.

Asparagus densiflorus 'Sprengeri'
Asparagus Fern / **fam. *Liliaceae***

One of the strongest indoor plants. Responds well if extra clay is added to the potting compost. Small bright pink flowers are followed by red berries yielding excellent black seed.

Asparagus falcatus
fam. *Liliaceae*

A very strong plant that can attain a height of 1 m (3 ft). Bears spines and is therefore not very suitable for the windowsill. Treat like *A. densiflorus* 'Meyeri'.

Asparagus setaceus (A. plumosus)
Asparagus Fern/fam. *Liliaceae*
Ⓘ ⬤ ⬤ ⬤ ⬤ ⬤ ⬤
Fully grown specimens become climbers with
white flowers and violet berries. Sensitive to
dry air. Add leafmould and peat to potting
mixture. Minimum winter temp. 12–15°C
(54–59°F).

Aspidistra elatior
fam. *Liliaceae*
Ⓘ ⬤ ⬤ ⬤ ⬤ ⬤ ⬤
A vigorous plant that will tolerate draughts
and will survive winter temperatures of 7–
10°C (45–50°F). P division; must be done very
gently.

***Aspidistra elatior* 'Variegata'**
fam. *Liliaceae*
Ⓘ ⬤ ⬤ ⬤ ⬤
Requires slightly more light and warmth than
the species. Excessive water in pot causes root
rot. Transplant large specimens every three
years.

Asplenium bulbiferum
Spleenwort/fam. *Aspleniaceae*
Ⓘ ⬤ ⬤ ⬤ ⬤
This fern will grow to a height of 1 m (3 ft). P
(rooted) plantlets on the fronds or spores in
March, July or August. Repot in clay, sharp
sand and leafmould in proportions 1:1:2.

Asplenium daucifolium (A. viviparum)
fam. *Aspleniaceae*
Ⓘ ⬤ ⬤ ⬤ ⬤
Somewhat stiffer and more erect in habit than
A. bulbiferum. Minimum winter temperature
12°C (54°F). Treat like *A. bulbiferum*.

Asplenium nidus
Bird's Nest Fern/fam. *Aspleniaceae*
Ⓘ ⬤ ⬤ ⬤ ⬤ ⬤
An epiphyte that likes a mixture of well-rotted
leafmould, well-rotted farmyard manure and
coarse peat. Minimum winter temperature
16°C (60°F). P spores.

Astrophytum capricorne senile
Goat's Horn Cactus/fam. *Cactaceae*
○ ⬤ ⬤ ⬤ ⬤ ⬤
A cactus with curved spines resembling
horns. The eight ribs are densely covered
with woolly tufts. The silky flowers, 7 cm
(2¾ in) across, are yellow with a red centre.
S cactus compost. P seed.

Astrophytum myriostigma
Bishop's Cap/fam. *Cactaceae*
○ ⬤ ⬤ ⬤ ⬤ ⬤
Spineless pentagonal plant, spherical to
cylindrical, covered in grey flakes. Height to
15 cm (6 in). Yellow flowers. Overwinter in a
light, cool place at 5–10°C (41–50°F). S cactus
compost. P seed.

Astrophytum ornatum
fam. *Cactaceae*
○ ⬤ ⬤ ⬤ ⬤ ⬤
Globular to cylindrical cactus. The eight ribs
are covered with bands of silvery tufts.
Flowers canary yellow. This species grows
very slowly. S cactus mixture. P seed.

35

Austrocephalocereus

Austrocephalocereus dybowskii
fam. Cactaceae
◯ ⊞ ⊗ ⊙ ⊞
Completely covered with silky white hairs.
Long central spines up to 3 cm (1 in). White
flowers, 4 cm (1½ in) long. Will not flower
unless overwintered in a cool, dry
environment. S cactus mixture. P seed.

Barkeria lindleyanum
fam. Orchidaceae
◖ ⊞ ⊗ ⊙ ⊞
Fairly rare, winter-flowering orchid for the
warm greenhouse. Repot every two years in
a mixture of osmunda, sphagnum moss and
some clay granules. P division.

Beaucarnea recurvata (Nolina recurvata)
fam. Agavaceae
◯ ⊞ ⊗ ⊙ ⊞
This container plant may be kept outside from
May to October. Minimum winter
temperature 5°C (41°F). Pot in equal parts
loam, leafmould and sand. P seed or cuttings.

Begonia acutifolia (B. acuminata)
fam. Begoniaceae
◖ ⊞ ⊗ ⊙ ⊞
Overwinter at about 15°C (59°F). Pot up in
spring in equal parts potting compost and
peat mixed with a little sand and well-rotted
farmyard manure. P side shoot, tip and leaf
cuttings, seed.

Begonia boweri
fam. Begoniaceae
◖ ⊞ ⊗ ⊙ ⊞
Produces small white flowers in winter.
'Nigramarga' has black veins. Best kept at 15–
18°C (59–64°F). Cultivation and propagation
as for B. acutifolia.

Begonia chlorosticta
fam. Begoniaceae
◖ ⊞ ⊗ ⊙ ⊞
Summer-flowering begonia with slightly
fragrant little flowers. Leaf markings are likely
to disappear if light is inadequate. Treat like
B. acutifolia. P seed, side shoot and tip
cuttings.

Begonia conchifolia
fam. Begoniaceae
◖ ⊞ ⊗ ⊙ ⊞
Profusely flowering species. Spraying
begonia flowers and leaves directly will
encourage mildew and grey mould. Treat like
B. acutifolia.

Begonia corallina
fam. Begoniaceae
◖ ⊞ ⊗ ⊙ ⊞
Vigorous grower, up to 2 m (6 ft) high. Cut
out old steams every two to three years.
'Lucerna' is the best known of the various
strains. Treat and propagate like B. acutifolia.

Begonia decora
fam. Begoniaceae
◖ ⊞ ⊗ ⊙ ⊞
A small species with very hairy leaves.
Flowers in the summer. Treat like B. acutifolia.
P seed, cuttings.

Begonia elatior hybrid, 'Rieger' type
fam. Begoniaceae
Rieger begonias are less susceptible to mildew and bud blast than other *B. elatior* varieties. Will flower longest in a cool spot, 16°C (60°F). P cuttings.

Begonia × erythrophylla
fam. Begoniaceae
This pink-flowered plant is the result of a cross between *B. manicata* and *B. hydrocotylifolia*. Remarkable for its creeping rhizomes. P see *B. acutifolia*.

Begonia foliosa
fam. Begoniaceae
As the plant ages its originally upright stems begin to arch over. Inconspicuous white little flowers sometimes appear in the leaf axils. Treat like *B. acutifolia*.

Begonia heracleifolia
fam. Begoniaceae
Long petioles carry pink or white flowers. The leaves of 'Punctata' are less deeply cut. Treat like *B. acutifolia*.

Begonia hispida var. cucullifera
fam. Begoniaceae
Produces clusters of white flowers and has large leaves. Adventitious buds along the main veins give rise to young plants. Treat like *B. acutifolia*.

Begonia hydrocotylifolia
fam. Begoniaceae
Produces masses of little pink flowers in the summer. Overwinter at 15–18°C (59–64°F). Water rhizomatous begonias sparingly. Treat like *B. acutifolia*.

Begonia imperialis
fam. Begoniaceae
A very attractive, compact begonia. 'Smaragdina' has emerald green leaves. Treat like *B. acutifolia*.

Begonia limmingheana
fam. Begoniaceae
This glorious begonia makes an excellent hanging plant thanks to its pliant stems. Grows to a height of 80 cm (32 in). Treat like *B. acutifolia*.

Begonia lorraine hybrid
fam. Begoniaceae
This plant produces mostly pink or white flowers in the winter. Grown from crossing *B. socotrana* with *B. dregei*. P leaf cuttings; in the summer also from stem cuttings.

Begonia

Begonia maculata 'Picta'
fam. Begoniaceae
◐ ⊞ ∞ ⊖ ⊞
This species (syn. *B. argyrostigma*) has small white spots on its leaves. Remove old stems every two to three years. Treat like *B. acutifolia*.

Begonia manicata 'Aureomaculata'
fam. Begoniaceae
◐ ⊞ ∞ ⊖ ⊞
This species bears green leaves and small pink flowers in the winter. 'Crispa' has a crinkled leaf edge. Treat like *B. acutifolia*.

Begonia masoniana 'Iron Cross'
fam. Begoniaceae
◐ ⊞ ∞ ⊖ ⊞
Bears attractive leaves as well as clusters of greenish-white flowers. Keep at 15–18°C (59–64°F) and do not feed. Water moderately. P leaf cuttings.

Begonia metallica
fam. Begoniaceae
◐ ◐ ⊞ ∞ ⊖ ⊞
Vigorous grower, up to 1 m (3 ft) in height. Cut out old stems from time to time to prevent straggling. Treat like *B. acutifolia*.

Begonia rex hybrid
fam. Begoniaceae
◐ ◐ ⊞ ∞ ⊖ ⊞
Grown for its red, black, silver and green foliage. Flowers mostly pink. Keep at 15–18°C (59–64°F). P leaf cuttings.

Begonia semperflorens hybrid
fam. Begoniaceae
◐ ◐ ⊞ ∞ ⊖ ⊞
The species and its hybrids with green or dark red leaves and pink or red flowers are also used as bedding plants. P seed; double-flowered varieties from cuttings.

Begonia serratipetala
fam. Begoniaceae
◐ ◐ ⊞ ∞ ⊖ ⊞
Shrub-like plant with pink flowers. Cut out old stems from time to time. Overwinter at 15–18°C (59–64°F). P leaf cuttings. Treat like *B. acutifolia*.

Begonia socotrana
fam. Begoniaceae
◐ ◐ ⊞ ∞ ⊖ ⊞
A winter-flowering plant often used for crossing. Keep at 18–20°C (64–68°F) when in flower. Minimum summer temperature 15°C (59°F). P leaf and stem cuttings.

Beloperone guttata
Shrimp Plant / fam. Acanthaceae
○ ◐ ◐ ⊞ ∞ ⊖ ⊞
Protect from midday sun in the summer. Overwinter at 12–15°C (53–59°F). Cut back in the spring to maintain bushy appearance. P seed or cuttings at 20°C (68°F).

**Bertolonia maculata
fam. *Melastomataceae***

Sow new specimens every year, as young
plants are by far the most attractive. Minimum
winter temperature 18°C (64°F). S pinewood
soil mixed with peat fibre. P seed, cuttings.

**Bertolonia marmorata
fam. *Melastomataceae***

Small plant with bright violet flowers.
'Bruxellensis' has silver leaves with small
green spots. Minimum winter temperature
18°C (64°F). S pinewood soil mixed with peat.
P cuttings and seed.

**Billbergia nutans
Queen's Tears / fam. *Bromeliaceae***

This bromeliad may be put outside in
summer. Water from below as well as from
above. In winter, water from above only.
Minimum temperature 16°C (60°F). P division.

**Blechnum gibbum
fam. *Blechnaceae***

Graceful fern that can grown to 1 m (3 ft).
Summer air temperature 20–35°C (68–95°F),
winter 13–25°C (55–77°F). Water freely in
March–June, sparingly for the rest of the year.
P division or spores.

**Blechnum occidentale
fam. *Blechnaceae***

Very leafy fern with a creeping rootstock. Do
not spray the leaves. Treat like *B. gibbum*.

**Borzicactus samaipatanus
fam. *Cactaceae***

Cactus with branching stems, often prostrate.
8 to 12 ribs with white spines. Red flowers,
often present in young plants. Overwinter at
about 10°C (50°F). S cactus mixture. P seed.

**Bougainvillea 'Harrisii'
fam. *Nyctaginaceae***

Striking, bushy plant with white flowers
surrounded by violet bracts. Treat like
B. spectabilis 'Alexandra'.

**Bougainvillea spectabilis 'Alexandra'
fam. *Nyctaginaceae***

Prune after flowering. A cool winter rest at
8–10°C (46–50°F) encourages bud formation.
Add fertiliser every week in summer.
P cuttings in spring at soil temperature of 30–
35°C (86–95°F).

**Bouvardia hybrid 'Mary'
fam. *Rubinaceae***

It is important to overwinter at a cool 5–10°C
(41–50°F). May go outside in summer.
S standard compost plus a little peat and well-
rotted manure. P stem or root cuttings.

Bowiea

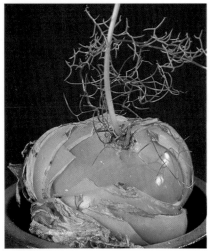

Bowiea volubilis
fam. *Liliaceae*
Ⓘ Ⓖ Ⓜ Ⓣ
Rare bulbous plant useful as a climber or for a hanging basket. Possibly add a little extra loam to the potting compost. Resting period: dry at 6–10°C (43–50°F). P offsets.

Brassavola nodosa
fam. *Orchidaceae*
Ⓘ Ⓖ Ⓜ Ⓣ
Pot in a mixture of 2 parts osmunda fibre and 1 part sphagnum or tie to clumps of dried bracken. Minimum winter day temperature 16–18°C (60–64°F) and 13–16°C (55–60°F) at night. P division and seed.

Brassavola perrinii
fam. *Orchidaceae*
Ⓘ Ⓖ Ⓜ Ⓣ
This summer-flowering orchid must be given special orchid food from March to September Water sparingly in winter. Treat like *B. nodosa*.

Brassia maculata (B. guttata)
fam. *Orchidaceae*
Ⓘ Ⓖ Ⓜ Ⓢ Ⓣ
Graceful epiphyte which can easily be grown indoors. Winter day temperature 17–20°C (62–68°F) and 13–17°C (55–62°F) at night. Pot in osmunda fibre and sphagnum moss. P seed and division.

× Brassolaeliacattleya 'Heron Gyll'
fam. *Orchidaceae*
Ⓘ Ⓖ Ⓜ Ⓢ Ⓣ
A cross between various species of orchids. Pot in a mixture of osmunda fibre and sphagnum moss. Minimum winter temperature 13°C (55°F). P seed and division.

Breynia disticha 'Rosea Pictum' (B. nivosa)
fam. *Euphorbiaceae*
Ⓘ Ⓖ Ⓜ Ⓢ Ⓣ Ⓔ
This species from the South Pacific has green stems and white-spotted green leaves. Minimum winter temperature 16°C (60°F). P division or cuttings.

Brosimum alicastrum
fam. *Moraceae*
Ⓘ Ⓘ Ⓖ Ⓜ Ⓢ Ⓣ
A plant needing little special care. Do not allow the root ball to dry out. Can remain all year in a warm room. P shoot tip cuttings, under glass.

Browallia speciosa (B. major)
fam. *Solanaceae*
Ⓘ Ⓖ Ⓜ Ⓢ Ⓣ Ⓔ
Sub-shrub up to 50 cm (20 in) in height with a very long flowering season. Can remain indoors all year. S loamy, humus-rich. P seed, cuttings.

Brunfelsia pauciflora var. calycina
fam. *Solanaceae*
Ⓘ Ⓖ Ⓜ Ⓢ Ⓣ
A resting period from November to January at 10–12°C (50–53°F) will encourage bud production. Second resting period after flowering in May–June. P shoot tip cuttings under glass at 30°C (86°F).

40

Bulbophyllum becquartii
fam. *Orchidaceae*
Ⓘ ⊕ ⊛ ⊗ ⊙
Rare orchid which flowers in late summer and autumn. Minimum winter temperature 18°C (64°F). Pot in a shallow basket filled with osmunda fibre. P seed, division.

Caladium bicolor 'Candidum'
fam. *Araceae*
Ⓘ ⊕ ⊛ ⊗ ⊙
The foliage of this plant dies in the autumn. Overwinter in dry soil at a minimum of 18°C (64°F). Pot in a mixture of leafmould, peat and well-rotted manure. P division, seed.

Caladium bicolor 'Crimson Glow'
fam. *Araceae*
Ⓘ ⊕ ⊛ ⊗ ⊙
Do not spray the leaves of *Caladium* hybrids. The arum-lily shaped flowers are borne on a spadix and have bracts. Treat like *C. b.* 'Candidum'.

Calanthe masuca (Bletia masuca)
fam. *Orchidaceae*
Ⓘ ⊕ ⊛ ⊗ ⊙
Evergreen species flowering in summer–autumn. Overwinter at about 10°C (50°F). S mixture of osmunda fibre, tree fern, loam and well-rotted manure. Feed frequently. P seed.

Calanthe vestita 'William Murray'
fam. *Orchidaceae*
Ⓘ ⊕ ⊛ ⊗ ⊙
Deciduous plant. Remove from pot at the beginning of the year and keep dry at 13°C (55°F). Pot in sphagnum moss, leafmould, sand and fibrous peat. P division, seed.

Calathea crocata
fam. *Marantaceae*
Ⓘ ⊕ ⊛ ⊗ ⊙
The only species in which the flowers are the main attraction. Calatheas have a triangular receptacle. Treat like *C. lancifolia*.

Calathea lancifolia (C. insignis)
Rattlesnake Plant / fam. *Marantaceae*
Ⓘ ⊕ ⊛ ⊗ ⊙
Best kept in a heated greenhouse or conservatory. Minimum winter temperature 13–16°C (55–60°F). Must be repotted each year in potting compost with added peat, sand and loam. P division.

Calathea lietzei (Maranta lietzei)
fam. *Marantaceae*
Ⓘ ⊕ ⊛ ⊗ ⊙
One of the few calatheas to produce upright shoots and runners. The oblong leaf is up to 16 cm (6½ in) long. Treat like *C. lancifolia*.

Calathea makoyana (Maranta makoyana)
Peacock Plant / fam. *Marantaceae*
Ⓘ ⊕ ⊛ ⊗ ⊙
A popular house plant up to 60 cm (2 ft) in height, with strikingly marked leaves up to 20 cm (8 in) in length. Treat like *C. lancifolia*.

41

Calathea

Calathea ornata 'Sanderiana'
fam. Marantaceae
ⓘ ⊕ ⊛ ⊕ 🔲
C. ornata can reach a height of more than 1 m
(3 ft). It has very long leaf stems and broader
leaves than the species. Treat like C. lancifolia.

Calathea zebrina
Zebra Plant / **fam. Marantaceae**
ⓘ ⊕ ⊛ ⊕ 🔲
Plant up to 60 cm (2 ft) in height with velvety
leaves. C. z. binotii is smaller in all its parts;
the light green leaves have darker stripes.
Treat like C. lancifolia.

Calceolaria hybrid (C. × herbeohybrida)
Slipper Plant / **fam. Scrophulariaceae**
ⓘ ☺ ⊕ ⊖ 🔲
Annual which dies after flowering. Needs a
draught-free spot at 10–12°C (50–53°F) and
acid potting compost. P cuttings, seed.

Calliandra tweedyi
fam. Leguminosae
ⓘ ⊕ ⊛ ⊖ 🔲 🔲
Decorative shrub which can be placed in a
sunny spot in autumn and winter. Minimum
winter temperature 15°C (59°F). Cut back
slightly in the spring. P cuttings.

Callisia elegans (Setcreasea striata)
fam. Commelinaceae
ⓘ ⊕ ⊛ ⊖ 🔲
Attractive creeping and hanging plant with
small white flowers. Minimum winter
temperature 10°C (50°F). Feed weekly in spring
and summer. P shoot tip cuttings at 20°C (68°F)
in sand / peat or in water.

Callistemon citrinus (C. lanceolatus)
Bottle Brush / **fam. Myrtaceae**
○ ⊕ ⊛ ⊖ 🔲
A container plant from Australia. Overwinter
at 6–8°C (43–46°F), put out in the summer. Cut
back after flowering. Pot in pinewood soil.
P cuttings at 18–20°C (64–68°F) under glass.

Calocephalus brownii (Leucophyta brownii)
fam. Compositae
○ ⊕ ⊛ ⊖ 🔲
Small shrub from Australia up to 30 cm (1 ft)
tall with clusters of tubular yellow flowers.
May be put out in summer. Mininum winter
temperature 5°C (41°F). P cuttings at
moderately warm temperature.

Camellia japonica
Common Camellia / **fam. Theaceae**
ⓘ ☺ ⊛ ⊖ 🔲
There are many beautiful camellia hybrids, all
of which hate sudden change. If the pot is
turned, buds will drop off. P shoot tip
cuttings in January or August at 18–22°C (64–
71°F).

Camellia sinensis (Thea sinensis)
Tea Bush / **fam. Theaceae**
ⓘ ☺ ⊛ ⊖ 🔲
Evergreen shrub with small white scented
flowers. Keep in a light, cool place indoors,
and use as a container plant outside in the
summer. The leaf is used for tea.

***Campanula fragilis* 'Carol Forster'**
Bellflower / fam. *Campanulaceae*
○ ◔ ⊗ ◑ ▣
Not well known but an attractive Bellflower.
Watering depends on the situation, but the
root ball must not be allowed to dry out.
Overwinter at 6–8°C (43–46°F). P seed.

***Campanula isophylla* 'Alba'**
Star of Bethlehem / fam. *Campanulaceae*
○ ◐ ◔ ⊗ ◑ ▣
This attractive hanging plant is easy to grow.
Can be put out in the summer. Minimum
winter temperature 6–8°C (43–46°F). P seed or
shoot tip cuttings at maximum 15°C (59°F).

***Campanula isophylla* 'Mayi'**
Star of Bethlehem / fam. *Campanulaceae*
○ ◐ ◔ ⊗ ◑ ▣
'Mayi' has slightly larger flowers than 'Alba'.
Both flower throughout the summer. A good
potting mixture can be made of loam,
leafmould and well-rotted farmyard manure.
Treat like *C. i.* 'Alba'.

***Canna indica* hybrid 'Lucifer'**
fam. *Cannaceae*
○ ◐ ⊕ ⊗ ◑ ▣
One of the many beautiful hybrids that flower
indoors as well as out in summer. The
rhizomes should be overwintered in
moderately moist peat at 15°C (59°F).
P division, seed.

Capsicum annuum
Red Pepper / fam. *Solanaceae*
○ ⊕ ⊗ ◑ ▣
Many varieties with fruit of striking colour
are grown as annuals. P sow in about March
at 15–18°C (59–64°F). Grow at 15°C (59°F). May
be put out in the summer.

***Carex brunnea* 'Variegata' (C. elegantis-
sima)** / Sedge / fam. *Cyperaceae*
◐ ⊕ ⊗ ◑ ▣
Variegated grasslike plant, as easily grown as
the green species. Overwinter at 8–16°C (46–
60°F). P division. Seed will yield green plants
only.

***Carissa spectabilis (Toxicophlaea spec-
tabilis)*** / fam. *Apocynaceae*
○ ⊕ ⊗ ◑ ▣
Fairly large, poisonous plant producing
fragrant flowers from February to April.
Overwinter at 12–15°C (53–59°F). P seed and
cuttings. Take care with children and
domestic pets!

Caryota mitis (C. sobolifera)
Fishtail Palm / fam. *Palmae*
◐ ⊕ ⊗ ◑ ⊚
An attractive palm from South East Asia.
Makes a great many roots. Pot in a mixture of
loam, leafmould and sand. Overwinter at 16°C
(60°F). P division.

Catasetum callosum (Myanthus callosus)
fam. *Orchidaceae*
◐ ⊕ ⊕ ⊗ ◑ ⊚
Easily grown orchid. Needs a lot of light,
warmth and moisture while growing. Keep
fairly dry during resting period. S osmunda
fibre. Never place in too large a pot.

43

Catasetum trulla
fam. Orchidaceae
○ ◑ ⊕ ⊛ ⊝ ⊡
An easily grown autumn bloomer.
Overwinter at 12–15°C (53–59°F). Repot
regularly in osmunda fibre or tie to pieces of
tree fern. P seed, division.

Catharanthus roseus 'Ocellatus' (Vinca
rosea)/fam. *Apocynaceae*
○ ⊕ ⊛ ⊝
The species has rose-red, 'Alba' has white,
flowers. Mostly grown as an annual. To take
cuttings, overwinter at 12–18°C (53–64°F).
P seed or cuttings.

Cattleya bowringiana
fam. Orchidaceae
◑ ⊕ ⊛ ⊝ ⊡
Suitable for intermediate greenhouse or
windowsill. Minimum winter temperature
12°C (53°F); 15°C (59°F) while growing.
S 2 parts osmunda fibre to 1 part sphagnum
moss. P division.

Cattleya forbesii (C. vestalis)
fam. Orchidaceae
◑ ⊕ ⊛ ⊝ ⊡
Summer-flowering orchid from Brazil with
fragrant flowers that last well. Treat like *C.
bowringiana*. For good flowers, provide plenty
of light. P division.

Cattleya labiata (C. l. var. autumnalis)
fam. Orchidaceae
◑ ⊕ ⊛ ⊝ ⊡
Autumn flowering. 'Candida' has white
flowers. Minimum winter temperature 12°C
(53°F). Pot in 2 parts osmunda fibre to 1 part
sphagnum moss. P division.

Cattleya mossiae
fam. Orchidaceae
◑ ⊕ ⊛ ⊝ ⊡
Resembles *C. labiata* but is less robust, and
fairly variable. Flowering period: late spring
and summer. Treat like *C. bowringiana*.
P division.

Cattleya skinneri
fam. Orchidaceae
◑ ⊕ ⊛ ⊝ ⊡
This orchid flowers in the spring. Flowering
must be followed by a resting period during
which the temperature may drop by 2 to 3°C
(3 to 5°F). Treat like *C. labiata*.

Cephalocereus senilis (Cephalophorus
senilis)/Old Man Cactus/fam. *Cactaceae*
○ ⚇ ⊛ ⊙ ⊝ ⊡
Columnar cactus which produces pink
flowers in later life. The flowers open at night.
Resting period in winter at 15°C (59°F). Root
collar sensitive to moisture. S special cactus
mixture. P seed.

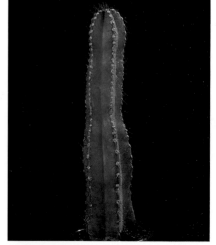

Cereus peruvianus
fam. Cactaceae
○ ⊛ ⊙ ⊝ ⊡
Easily grown house plant. Height in native
habitat up to 12 m (40 ft). Flowers on old parts
of the plant; light pink. Overwinter in a fairly
dry environment. P seed or cuttings.

Cereus peruvianus 'Monstrosus'
fam. *Cactaceae*
Grows slowly and has a distorted growing point to which it owes its peculiar shape. The large white flowers open at night. P cuttings left to dry before insertion, or seed.

Ceropegia barkleyi
Hearts Entangled / fam. *Asclepiadaceae*
Arching stems without cormlets. Green, oval leaves. Long tubular flowers terminating in five flaps. S cactus mixture. P seed or cuttings.

Ceropegia sandersonii
Hearts Entangled / fam. *Asclepiadaceae*
Entangled stems with heart-shaped leaves and yellow–green flowers, funnel shaped at the tip. Reminiscent of parachutes. S cactus mixture. P pot up stem with cormlet.

Ceropegia woodii ssp. woodii
Rosary Vine / fam. *Asclepiadaceae*
Popular hanging plant. Stems with kidney-shaped leaves on short leaf stalks grow many metres (yards) long. Pink flowers with dark brown lobes. Cormlets root readily. S cactus mixture.

Chamaecereus silvestrii
fam. *Cactaceae*
Offsets produce groups of stems, each the length of a finger. Funnel-shaped, scarlet flowers. S cactus mixture. P seed or offsets dried out and allowed to root in a sandy mixture.

Chamaedorea elegans (Neanthe bella, Collinia elegans) / fam. *Palmae*
Palm up to 1 m (3 ft) in height. 'Bella' is smaller in all parts. Resting period from October to February at 5–12°C (41–53°F). S mixture of leafmould, well-rotted manure and sand. P sow at 25°C (77°F).

Chamaerops humilis
fam. *Palmae*
Fan palm up to 7 m (23 ft) in height, but rarely taller than 1 m (3 ft) when grown as a container plant. Protect against frost in winter. Pot up in loam, leafmould and sand. P seed.

Chlorophytum comosum 'Variegatum' (C. sternbergianum) / Spider Plant / Liliaceae
Extremely strong house plant. Variegated types need good light and warmth. Mininum temperature 7°C (44°F). Loamy mixture. P seed, division or from plantlets.

Chrysanthemum indicum hybrid
fam. *Compositae*
Short-day plants that can be made to flower all the year round by adjustment of artificial light. Best grown as an annual but can be overwintered at 4–6°C (39–43°F). P cuttings.

Chysis aurea
fam. Orchidaceae

This epiphyte flowers in May–June and makes a good indoor plant. Minimum winter day temperature 16–18°C (60–64°F), 13–16°C (55–60°F) at night. S 2 parts osmunda fibre to 1 part sphagnum moss. P seed.

Cissus antarctica
fam. Vitaceae

Attractive climber best overwintered at 8°C (46°F). If kept in the house, it must be sprayed freely. Potting mixture may contain a little extra chalk. P seed.

Cissus discolor
fam. Vitaceae

A heated greenhouse plant which should be overwintered at 15°C (59°F). Grows vigorously. Potting mixture based on leafmould or standard mix. No extra chalk. P cuttings.

Cissus rhombifolia (Rhoicissus rhomboidea)
fam. Vitaceae

Extremely strong house plant with inconspicuous flowers followed by small berries. Overwinter at a minimum of 8°C (46°F). Pot in a loamy humus mixture or standard potting compost. P cuttings.

Cissus rhombifolia 'Ellen Danica'
fam. Vitaceae

A very vigorous variety with triple leaves (like the species) but more deeply cut and hence more decorative. Treat like *C. rhombifolia.*

Cissus striata
fam. Vitaceae

Attractive hanging plant – the perfect cissus for smaller houses. Minimum winter temperature 8°C (46°F). Pot in a mixture of loam and humus or in ordinary potting compost. P cuttings.

Citrus limon (C. limonum, C. medica var. limon)/Lemon Tree/fam. Rutaceae

A container plant with white flowers followed by lemons which ripen in about a year. Overwinter at 4–6°C (39–43°F). Pot in rich mixture of loam and humus. P cuttings.

Citrus microcarpa (C. mitis)
Calamondin Orange/fam. Rutaceae

Small clusters of three or four fragrant white flowers each. Flowers and fruits profusely from an early age. Fruits up to 4 cm (1½ in) long. Treat like *C. limon.*

Cleistocactus strausii (Cereus strausii)
fam. Cactaceae

Columnar cactus with no fewer than 25 ribs. Areoles densely covered with white spines. Carmine tubular flowers up to 7.5 cm (3 in) long appear on older plants. P seed.

Clerodendrum speciosissimum (C. fallax)
fam. **Verbenaceae**
◑ ⊞ ∞ ◐ ⊡
Rest in winter at 10–12°c (50–53°F). Cut back in late February and pot up in equal parts leafmould, well-rotted farmyard manure and loam. P cuttings, seed or root fragments.

Clerodendrum thomsoniae
Glory Bower / fam. **Verbenaceae**
◑ ⊞ ∞ ◐ ⊡
Vigorous climber with the protruding stamens so typical of *Clerodendrum* species. This is the only species that will also grow indoors. Treat like *C. speciosissimum*.

Cleyera japonica 'Tricolor' Eurya
ochnacea) / fam. Theaceae
◑ ⊞ ⊙ ∞ ◐ ⊡
Slow grower. 'Tricolor' leaves are at first touched with pink. Winter temperature 10–12°c (50–53°F), summer 8–18°c (46–64°F). P shoot tip cuttings in the spring at 18–20°c (64–68°F).

Clivia miniata
fam. **Amaryllidaceae**
◑ ◑ ⊞ ∞ ◐ ⊡
Pot immediately after flowering in a very fertile mixture of loam and humus. Rest in October at 8–10°c (46–50°F), keeping the soil fairly dry. P seed or offshoots.

Clivia miniata 'Citrina'
fam. **Amaryllidaceae**
◑ ⊞ ⊙ ∞ ◐ ⊡
When the flower stem has grown to 15 cm (6 in) after the resting period, apply a little more heat and water. This applies to all clivias. Treat like *C. miniata*.

Coccoloba uvifera
fam. **Polygonaceae**
◑ ⊞ ∞ ◐ ◐ ⊡
Its leathery leaves help to protect this plant from a dry indoor atmosphere. Pot in a loamy and fertile mixture. Overwinter at 12°c (53°F). P seed, layering and shoot tip cuttings.

Cocculus laurifolius
fam. **Menispermaceae**
○ ◑ ⊞ ∞ ◐ ⊡
Suitable as a container plant. Puts out inconspicuous axillary inflorescences. Rest from October–May at 4–10°c (39–50°F). P seed, stem and root cuttings.

Cocos nucifera
Coconut Palm / fam. **Palmae**
◑ ⊞ ∞ ∞ ◐ ⊡
Water less from October and sparingly in winter when this palm should be kept at 16°c (60°F). Germinate coconuts at 20–25°c (68–77°F). Germination takes half a year. P seed.

Codiaeum variegatum var. pictum (C.
pictum) / Croton / fam. Euphorbiaceae
◑ ⊞ ⊞ ∞ ∞ ◐ ⊡
Magnificent foliage plants with a host of varieties differing in shape and leaf colour. Moist air is important. For cultivation see the next entry.

***Codiaeum variegatum* var. *pictum* (flowers)**
Croton / fam. *Euphorbiaceae*
◐ ⊞ ⊞ ⊗ ⊖ ⊖ ⊡
Keep the temperature as even as possible and
never less than 18–20°C (64–68°F). Pot in
leafmould, well-rotted manure and clay-based
loam in the proportions 2:2:1. P cuttings,
seed, layering.

Codonanthe crassifolia
fam. *Gesneriaceae*
◐ ⊞ ⊗ ⊖ ⊖ ⊡
Hanging plant resistant to dry indoor
atmospheres. Minimum temperature 16°C
(60°F). Pot in a humus-rich mixture with a
good deal of pine forest soil. P cuttings, and
more easily from seed.

Coelia bella (Bifrenaria bella)
fam. *Orchidaceae*
◐ ⊞ ⊗ ⊖ ⊡
A striking orchid for the heated greenhouse.
Minimum winter temperature 16–18°C (60–
64°F). Do not repot unless absolutely
unavoidable; use osmunda fibre or finely
chopped tree fern. P seed.

Coelogyne flaccida
fam. *Orchidaceae*
◐ ⊞ ⊗ ⊖ ⊡
Orchid for the intermediate greenhouse: rest
in winter at minimum temperature of 16°C
(60°F). Do not repot frequently. S equal parts
osmunda fibre and sphagnum. P seed and
division.

Coffea arabica
Coffee Plant / fam. *Rubiaceae*
◐ ⊞ ⊗ ⊗ ⊖ ⊡
A plant up to 2 m (6 ft) high with fragrant
white flowers. Keep at 16–20°C (60–68°F) from
October to March. Pot in loam, leafmould,
compost and sand. P seed.

***Coleus blumei* hybrid**
Flame Nettle / fam. *Labiatae*
○ ◐ ⊞ ⊞ ⊗ ⊞ ▣
Easily grown house plant provided it has
sufficient light and water. Potting mixture,
water and food must not contain too much
lime. Winter temperature 12–15°C (53–59°F).
P seed or cuttings.

***Coleus blumei* hybrid 'Pagoda'**
Flame Nettle / fam. *Labiatae*
○ ◐ ⊞ ⊞ ⊗ ⊖ ▣
The leaves of flame nettles often come in the
most fantastic combinations of colours. P very
easy from shoot tip or eye cuttings and from
seed. Treat like C. 'Sabre Pastel'.

***Coleus blumei* hybrid 'Sabre Pastel'**
Flame Nettle / fam. *Labiatae*
○ ◐ ⊞ ⊞ ⊗ ⊖ ▣
Overwinter these plants for the sole purpose
of taking cuttings in spring. The white-and-
blue flower clusters are best pinched out to
maintain a bushy habit.

Colletia cruciata
fam. *Rhamnaceae*
○ ⊞ ⊕ ⊘ ⊖ ⊡
Vigorous, prickly container plant with
fragrant small flowers. Overwinter in a cold
greenhouse at 4–6°C (39–43°F). Pot in compost
mixed with loamy soil rich in humus.
P cuttings, seed.

Columnea × banksii
fam. Gesneriaceae
◐ ⊞ ∞ ◔ ▣
Successful cross between *C. oerstedtiana* and
C. schiediana. Winter temperature 10–15°C
(50–59°F). S friable mixture rich in humus.
P cuttings at 20°C (68°F).

Columnea gloriosa
fam. Gesneriaceae
◐ ⊞ ∞ ◔ ▣
These epiphytes must be kept at 18–22°C (64–
71°F), but down to 14–16°C (57–60°F) when
resting. S forest soil with sphagnum,
osmunda fibre, charcoal and well-rotted
manure. P cuttings.

Columnea gloriosa 'Purpurea'
fam. Gesneriaceae
◐ ⊞ ∞ ◔ ▣
Attractive and unusual hanging plant. Grow
on tree ferns or in an orchid basket. More
suitable for the greenhouse than for indoor
cultivation. Treat like *C. gloriosa*.

Columnea hirta
fam. Gesneriaceae
◐ ⊞ ∞ ◔ ▣
Attractive trailing or hanging epiphyte with
stems that make roots at the nodes. Dry
resting period encourages flowering. Treat
like *C. gloriosa*.

Columnea microphylla
fam. Gesneriaceae
◐ ⊞ ∞ ◔ ▣
Epiphyte with stems up to 1 m (3 ft) long.
'Stavanger' is larger in all parts and demands
a winter temperature of 18°C (64°F). Treat like
C. gloriosa.

Comparettia speciosa
fam. Orchidaceae
◐ ⊞ ∞ ◔ ▣
Summer-flowering epiphyte from Ecuador.
Pseudobulbs bear one leaf. Winter
temperature 18°C (64°F). Does well on tree
bark or in an orchid basket. P seed.

Conophytum corculum
fam. Aizoaceae
○ ⊞ ◉ ◔ ▣
Leaves are fused into a spherical body with a
split in the centre from which the small yellow
flowers emerge. Flowering August–
September. Resting period December–July.
P seed.

Conophytum cornatum
fam. Aizoaceae
○ ⊞ ◉ ◔ ◔ ▣
The leaves are fused into a spherical body –
the corpusculum – with a split in the centre
from which the orange flowers emerge.
Flowering period August–September. P seed
and cuttings.

Conophytum wettsteinii
fam. Aizoaceae
○ ⊞ ◉ ◔ ▣
Corpuscula flat on top and fairly large. Red
flowers up to 3 cm (1 in) high. Repot every
three years in cactus mixture or sandy,
humus-rich soil with loam. P seed, cuttings.

49

Coprosma

Coprosma baueri 'Marginata'
fam. *Rubiaceae*

This species has green leaves and greenish flowers followed by orange–yellow berries. Give it a rest period in winter at 5–10°C (41–50°F). Do not repot older plants every year. P cuttings.

Cordyline indivisa
fam. *Agavaceae*

The unbranched stems can reach a height of 1.5 m (5 ft) when grown in a pot. The leaves are leathery and come to a long point. Winter temperature 4–7°C (39–45°F). Treat like *C. terminalis*.

Cordyline terminalis
fam. *Agavaceae*

The leaves of this cordyline easily develop brown spots when the air humidity is low. Winter temperature 10–13°C (50–55°F). S pinewood soil. P shoot tip cuttings.

Cordyline terminalis 'Mme André'
fam. *Agavaceae*

This plant comes in a number of varieties with gloriously coloured leaves. 'Firebrand' has purple leaves with a brighter vein. Treat like *C. terminalis*.

Cordyline terminalis 'Tricolor'
fam. *Agavaceae*

Much happier indoors than the species. Plants that become unsightly below can be layered. Treat like *C. terminalis*.

Corynocarpus laevigatus
fam. *Corynocarpaceae*

Overwinter this container plant at 3–14°C (37–57°F). Pot in a mixture of proprietary potting compost, loam and well-rotted farmyard manure. Prune in the spring. P cuttings at 18–20°C (64–68°F).

Coryphantha cornifera
fam. *Cactaceae*

Globular grey-green cactus that eventually becomes cylindrical. Has large cushions bearing attractive spines. Striking yellow flowers with red stamens. Keep cool in winter. P seed.

Coryphantha hesterii
fam. *Cactaceae*

Grows into an oblong cactus with offsets. It has a woolly white head and purple flowers. Can tolerate winter temperature down to 0°C (32°F) provided it is kept absolutely dry. S cactus mixture.

Costus igneus
fam. *Zingiberaceae*

Fairly rare greenhouse plant which must be rested in winter at a minimum 12°C (53°F). Cut back in spring. S proprietary potting compost with extra loam. P division, eye and stem cuttings.

50

Cotyledon orbiculata
fam. *Crassulaceae*
○ ⊕ ⊚ ⊖ ⊡
Branching succulent with grey-white
bloomed leaves and yellow, tubular flowers.
Do not touch the leaves or you will damage
their bloom. P cuttings.

Cotyledon undulata
Silver Ruffles / **fam.** *Crassulaceae*
○ ⊕ ⊚ ⊖ ⊡
Small shrub with densely bloomed, fleshy
leaves with a wavy edge. Do not touch the
leaves. Keep cool and dry in winter. S cactus
mixture.

Crassula arborescens (Cotyledon arbor-
escens) / **fam.** *Crassulaceae*
○ ⊕ ⊚ ⊖ ⊡
Can grow into a 3-m (10-ft) high shrub. The
thick, fleshy leaves have red edges and dark
speckles on top. S cactus mixture. P leaf or
shoot tip cuttings.

Crassula conjuncta
fam. *Crassulaceae*
○ ⊕ ⊚ ⊖ ⊡
The fleshy leaves of this plant are ranged
round the stem. In the summer, place in a
protected spot outside. S cactus mixture. P
up shoots in sand and peat.

Crassula falcata (Rochea falcata)
fam. *Crassulaceae*
○ ⊕ ⊚ ⊖ ⊡
Sickle-shaped leaves in two rows pointing
alternately to left and right. The wide heads
of red flowers are shaped like paint brushes.
Very attractive if not allowed to grow too tall.

Crassula lycopodioides
fam. *Crassulaceae*
○ ⊕ ⊚ ⊖ ⊡
A succulent particularly suited to indoor life.
The erect stems are covered with scaly leaves
fitting together like roof tiles. Inconspicuous
white flowers.

Crassula portulacea
fam. *Crassulaceae*
○ ⊕ ⊚ ⊖ ⊡
Indestructible house plant with a very thick
stem. Leaves opposite. The white flowers
appear in the winter. S cactus mixture. P leaf
or side shoot cuttings.

Crassula rupestris
fam. *Crassulaceae*
○ ⊕ ⊚ ⊖ ⊡
Erect stems with pairs of triangular leaves.
The yellowish flowers are born in umbels.
Overwinter at 6–10°C (43–50°F). S cactus
mixture. P seed or cuttings.

Crassula tetragona
fam. *Crassulaceae*
○ ⊕ ⊚ ⊖ ⊡
With its decussate spherical and pointed
leaves this plant looks like a series of small
trees. Keep cool and well lit in winter.
Excessive humidity encourages mildew.

51

***Crossandra infundibuliformis* 'Mona Wallhed'** / fam. *Acanthaceae*

⟐ ⊛ ⊕ ∞ ⊝ ⊟ ⊡

This Swedish variety is more compact and grows more vigorously than the species. Minimum winter temperature 13°C (55°F). Pot in light, humus-rich, slightly acid soil. P softwood cuttings.

Cryptanthus beuckeri fam. *Bromeliaceae*

⟐ ⊛ ⊕ ∞ ⊝ ⊝ ⊟ ⊡

Variegated species should be overwintered at 20–22°C (68–71°F); the rest at 18°C (64°F). S standard potting compost with a little sphagnum, leafmould and sand. P young rosettes.

Cryptanthus bivittatus fam. *Bromeliaceae*

⟐ ⊛ ⊕ ∞ ⊝ ⊝ ⊟ ⊡

Like other *Cryptanthus* species, this bromeliad has a small root system. Will grow well in flat pots or bowls, or on tree ferns as an epiphyte. Treat like *C. beuckeri*.

Cryptanthus fosteranus fam. *Bromeliaceae*

⟐ ⊛ ⊕ ∞ ⊝ ⊟ ⊡

The plant dies down after flowering, but by then new rosettes have usually been formed, separating soon afterwards. Treat like *C. beuckeri*.

***Crypanthus zonatus* 'Zebrinus'** fam. *Bromeliaceae*

⟐ ⊛ ⊕ ∞ ⊝ ⊝ ⊟ ⊡

Grown largely for its leaf markings. The leaves are beset with fine spines and are white and woolly underneath. Treat like *C. beuckeri*.

Ctenanthe lubbersiana (Phrynium lubbersianum) / fam. *Marantaceae*

⟐ ⊛ ⊕ ∞ ⊝ ⊟

One of the most attractive and hardy species, 60–80 cm (24–32 in) high. Minimum winter temperature 16°C (60°F). S coarse leafmould and peat with a little sand and farmyard manure. P offshoots.

***Ctenanthe oppenheimiana* 'Variegata'** fam. *Marantaceae*

⟐ ⊛ ⊕ ∞ ⊝ ⊡

To obtain the best leaf markings, place this plant in a well-lit spot, just out of the direct sun. Treat like *C. lubbersiana*.

Ctenanthe rubra fam. *Marantaceae*

⟐ ⊛ ⊕ ∞ ⊝ ⊡

Green foliage plant which is more tolerant of shade than other ctenanthes. Does well in a greenhouse, conservatory or mixed container. Treat like *C. lubbersiana*.

Cuphea ignea (C. platycentra) Cigar Plant / fam. *Lythraceae*

⟐ ⟐ ⊕ ⊛ ∞ ⊝ ⊟

The cigar-shaped flowers are out from April–November. Then cut back and keep at 7°C (44°F). May be put outside in the summer. P cuttings in spring or autumn; seed.

Cyanotis kewensis (Erythrotis beddomei)
Teddy Bear Vine / fam. *Commelinaceae*
○ 🌢 ⊗ ⊗ 😊 🔲
Small creeper, conspicuously covered in
brown hair on all parts above the ground.
Violet flowers. Can also be grown as a
hanging plant. Minimum winter temperature
14°C (57°F). P seed or cuttings.

Cycas revoluta
Sago Palm / fam. *Cycadaceae*
◑ 🌢 ⊗ 😊 😊 🔲
Ancient, very elegant plant. Overwinter at 12–
15°C (53–59°F). Repot every two to three years
in equal parts of clay-based loam and
leafmould. P sow at 25–30°C (77–86°F).

Cyclamen persicum hybrid
fam. *Primulaceae*
◑ 🌢 ⊗ 😊 🔲
The tuberous *C. persicum* comes in a great
many varieties, differing in colour, shape and
size of flowers. The variety depicted here has
fringed petals. For cultivation see next entry.

Cyclamen persicum 'Vuurbak'
fam. *Primulaceae*
◑ 🌢 ⊗ 😊 🔲
Variety with entire petals. Keep flowering
plants at 10–16°C (50–60°F). Overwinter the
tuber inside the pot at 10–12°C (50–53°F). Pot
in loamy, fertile soil. P seed.

Cyclamen persicum 'Wellensiek'
fam. *Primulaceae*
◑ 🌢 ⊗ 😊 🔲
Beautiful, small-flowered variety produced by
crossing large-flowered varieties with the
botanical species. Keep moist or plunge the
pot in tepid water. Treat like *C. p.* 'Vuurbak'.

Cycnoches chlorochilum
fam. *Orchidaceae*
◑ 🌢 ⊗ 😊 😊 🔲
Graceful orchid which can flower twice a year.
Minimum winter temperature 14°C (57°F).
S osmunda fibre and sphagnum moss in a
proportion of 2:1 with a little fibrous peat
and charcoal. P seed.

Cymbidium hybrid 'Norma Talmadge'
fam. *Orchidaceae*
◑ 🌢 ⊗ 😊 🔲
Overwinter at 13–16°C (55–60°F) during the
day and at 7–12°C (45–53°F) at night. Repot
every three years in osmunda fibre,
sphagnum moss, pine bark and beech leaves,
in proportions 3:2:2:1. P seed.

Cymbidium 'Zuma Beach'
fam. *Orchidaceae*
◑ 🌢 ⊗ 😊 🔲
One of many *Cymbidium* cultivars with pastel-
coloured flowers that keep in water for weeks.
The one depicted here has small flowers. Treat
like previous entry.

Cyperus alternifolius
Umbrella Plant / fam. *Cyperaceae*
◑ 🌢 ⊗ 😊 🔲
Attractive ornamental grass with conspicuous
inflorescences. 'Variegata' has multi-coloured
leaves. Treat like *C. argenteostriatus*, but keep
constantly moist. P cuttings, seed, division.

53

Cyperus argenteostriatus (C. laxus)
fam. Cyperaceae
Very strong plant that demands moist soil but
should not be constantly soaked like C.
alternifolius. Overwinter at 12°C (53°F).
S loamy. P division and seed.

Cyperus diffusus
Umbrella Plant / fam. **Cyperaceae**
Small plant that must be overwintered at 17°C
(62°F). Flowers readily. Repot in normal
potting compost in the spring. Do not keep
this species in excessively moist soil.
P division, seed.

Cyperus haspan
fam. Cyperaceae
A smaller version of C. *papyrus*, 50 cm (20 in)
tall. Flowers in the summer. Do not leave too
much water in the saucer. P clay-based loam,
leafmould, farmyard manure.

Cyperus papyrus
Egyptian Paper Rush / fam. **Cyperaceae**
Plant 2–3 m (6–10 ft) in height. Thrives if it is
stood in a tray of water. Overwinter at 17°C
(62°F) and provide sufficient light. S fertile
soil. P division and seed.

Cyrtanthus parviflorus
fam. Amaryllidaceae
Attractive small bulbous plant that can be put
out in a sheltered spot in the summer.
Possibly add a little extra loam to the potting
compost. Minimum winter temperature 5°C
(41°F). P seed.

Cyrtomium falcatum (Aspidium falcatum;
Polystichum falcatum) / Holly Fern / fam.
Aspidiaceae
Vigorous plant; give it a rest at 7–10°C (44–
50°F) from October to March. Pot in a mixture
of leafmould and well-rotted farmyard
manure. P division, spores.

Cytisus × racemosus
Genista / fam. **Leguminosae**
'Everestianus' has darker yellow flowers.
Keep at 12–18°C (53–64°F) when in flower. Put
outside in summer. Overwinter at 4–8°C (39–
46°F). P semi-hardwood cuttings in spring or
summer at 17°C (62°F).

Darlingtonia californica
fam. Sarraceniaceae
Carnivorous plant for the greenhouse. Repot
every other July in peat and sphagnum moss
mixed with charcoal and sharp sand.
Overwinter at 5°C (41°F). P cuttings, seed.

Dasylirion serratifolium (D. laxiflorum,
Yucca serratifolium) / fam. **Agavaceae**
Container plant; spinous leaves. Overwinter
at 0–5°C (32–41°F). Repot in clay-based loam,
leafmould, well-rotted manure and sand in
porportions 2:2:1:1, not necessarily every
year. P seed.

Datura candida 'Plena'
fam. *Solanaceae*
○ 🐛 ⊗ ⊗ 🌱 🗓
Very striking though rather poisonous house
and container plant. Overwinter at 7°C (44°F).
Add extra loam, well-rotted farmyard manure
and sand to the potting compost. P cuttings.

Datura hybrid
fam. *Solanaceae*
○ 🐛 ⊗ ⊗ 🌱 🗓
These plants do best when they are planted
out in a cold greenhouse. Spinous fruits. Treat
like *D. candida* 'Plena'.

Datura suaveolens
fam. *Solanaceae*
○ 🐛 ⊗ ⊗ 🌱 🗓
This shrub can reach a height of 5 m (16 ft).
Flowers have a strong, sweet fragrance.
'Plena' has white double flowers. Treat like
D. candida 'Plena'.

Davallia mariesii (D. bullata var. mariesii)
Rabbit's Foot Fern / fam. *Davalliaceae*
🌓 🐛 🌓 ⊗ 🌱 🗓
A fern with delicate fronds and conspicuous
hairy rhizomes. Minimum winter temperature
15°C (59°F). S leafmould, sphagnum moss,
farmyard manure and a little loam. P spores,
division.

Dendrobium ciliatum
fam. *Orchidaceae*
🌓 🐛 ⊗ 🌓 🌱 🗓
Graceful autumn-flowering species for the
warm greenhouse. Minimum temperature 18–
20°C (64–68°F). Pot in fairly small containers
of pure osmunda fibre or orchid mixture.

Dendrobium phalaenopsis hybrid
fam. *Orchidaceae*
🌓 🐛 ⊗ 🌱 🗓
Tropical plants for the warm and intermediate
greenhouse. No definite resting period. These
plants demand a great deal of light.
S osmunda fibre. P division.

**Dendrobium phalaenopsis var.
schroederianum** / fam. *Orchidaceae*
🌓 🐛 ⊗ 🌓 🌱 🗓
Autumn-flowering orchid for the warm
greenhouse. Minimum winter temperature
16°C (60°F). Pot in fern or beech root mixed
2:1 with sphagnum moss. P division after
flowering.

Dichorisandra reginae (Tradescantia reginae)
fam. *Commelinaceae*
🌓 🐛 ⊗ 🌓 🗓
Slow grower bearing lavender flowers.
Mininum winter temperature 15°C (59°F). Pot
in equal parts peat, leafmould and loam with
a little sand. P seed, division, cuttings.

Didymochlaena truncatula (D. lunulata)
fam. *Aspidiaceae*
🌓 🐛 ⊗ 🌓 🗓
These ferns need a rest from October to
February at 12–14°C (53–57°F). Then cut back
and repot in standard potting compost mixed
with leafmould. P division and spores.

55

Dieffenbachia

Dieffenbachia amoena 'Tropic Snow'
fam. _Araceae_
◑ ⊞ ⊗ ⊝ ⊡
Large foliage plant with lily-like flowers.
Overwinter at 15–18°C (59–64°F). Repot in the
spring in leafmould, clay-based loam and
farmyard manure, 3:1:1. P shoot tip and stem
cuttings.

Dieffenbachia × bausei
fam. _Araceae_
◑ ⊞ ⊗ ⊝ ⊡
Like all dieffenbachias, this plant is
poisonous in all parts, and can cause skin
irritation and mucous catarrh. Grow like
D. amoena 'Tropic Snow'.

Dieffenbachia bowmannii 'Arvida'
(D. reginae)/fam. _Araceae_
◑ ⊞ ⊗ ⊝ ⊡
The largest of all dieffenbachias. If the plant
grows too large, air-layer it. Healthy plants
will bush out if they are cut back to 10–15 cm
(4–6 in). Treat like _D. amoena_ 'Tropic Snow'.

Dieffenbachia maculata (D. picta)
fam. _Araceae_
◑ ⊞ ⊞ ⊗ ⊝ ⊡
This species has a great many cultivars,
including particularly 'Jenmannii' with white
bands between the lateral veins. Treat like
D. amoena 'Tropic Snow'.

Dionaea muscipula
Venus Flytrap/fam. _Droseraceae_
○ ◑ ⊞ ⊗ ⊝ ⊡
Carnivorous plant needing a great deal of
light. Has to be overwintered at 3–10°C (37–
50°F). S mixture of peat, heathland soil and
sphagnum moss. P division, leaf cuttings,
seed.

Dipladenia atropurpurea
fam. _Apocynaceae_
◑ ⊞ ⊗ ⊝ ⊡
Seldom flowers until late in life. Overwinter
at 13°C (55°F); in March keep at 16°C (60°F),
then increase gradually. S leafmould,
farmyard manure, clay-based loam and peat,
at 2:2:1:1. P cuttings.

Dipladenia boliviensis
fam. _Apocynaceae_
◑ ⊞ ⊗ ⊝ ⊡
A less common climber producing fragrant
white flowers with a yellow centre. These
appear in the spring, summer or autumn.
Treat like _D. atropurpurea_.

Dipladenia sanderi 'Rosea'
Pink Allamanda/fam. _Apocynaceae_
◑ ⊞ ⊗ ⊝ ⊡
This is the best-known commercially
obtainable variety, stronger than the species
and with larger flowers. Dipladenias flower
on the twining stems. Treat like _D.
atropurpurea_.

**Dipteracanthus devosianus (Ruellia
devosiana)/fam. _Acanthaceae_**
◑ ⊞ ⊗ ⊝ ⊟
Small ground-cover plants with striking
foliage and white and lilac small flowers. Keep
warm throughout the year. If these plants
become unsightly, replace with young
specimens. P cuttings or seed.

***Dipteracanthus makoyanus (Ruellia
makoyana)*/fam. *Acanthaceae***
🌓 🌗 ∞ ⊖ ⊡
Very suitable for double-glazed picture
windows, terraria and bottle gardens. Do not
spray the leaves directly. Treat like
D. devosianus.

***Dizygotheca elegantissima (Aralia
elegantissima)*/fam. *Araliaceae***
🌓 🌗 ∞ ⊖ ⊡
The older this plant grows, the broader its
leaves become. The leaf shape alters because
the length does not increase in proportion.
Treat like *D. veitchii.*

***Dizygotheca veitchii (Aralia veitchii)*
fam. *Araliaceae***
🌓 🌗 ∞ ⊖ 🌑 ⊡
Rest from October to February at a minimum
temperature of 15°c (59°F). Pot in standard
potting compost or pinewood soil. P seed, or
grafting on *Meryta denhamii.*

***Dizygotheca veitchii* 'Castor'
fam. *Araliaceae***
🌓 🌗 ∞ ⊖ 🌑 ⊡
This is much smaller than the species and of
very compact habit. The lowermost leaves will
drop off if the air is too dry. Treat like
D. veitchii.

***Dizygotheca veitchii* 'Gracillima'
fam. *Araliaceae***
🌓 🌗 ∞ ⊖ 🌑 ⊡
This variety looks like an immature copy of
D. elegantissima. Very suitable as a specimen
plant. Treat like *D. veitchii.*

**× *Doritaenopsis* 'Jason Beard' × *manni*
fam. *Orchidaceae***
🌓 🌗 ∞ ⊖ ⊡
A cross between *Doritis* and *Phalaenopsis.*
Minimum winter temperature 16–18°c (60–
64°F). Pot in a mixture of osmunda fibre and
sphagnum moss. P division.

***Doritis pulcherrima*
fam. *Orchidaceae***
🌓 🌗 ∞ ⊖ ⊡
An orchid for the warm greenhouse.
Overwinter at minimum temperature of 16–
18°c (60–64°F). Pot in a mixture of osmunda
fibre and sphagnum moss or tie to tree bark.
P seed.

***Doryopteris palmata*
fam. *Sinopteridaceae***
🌓 🌗 ∞ ⊖ ⊡
This fern has both fertile and sterile fronds. It
produces plantlets on its leaves. Overwinter
at 12°c (53°F). Mix some extra peat and forest
soil into the potting compost. P spores.

***Dracaena deremensis* 'Warneckii'
Dragon Tree/fam. *Agavaceae***
🌓 🌗 ∞ ⊖ 🌑 ⊡
This cultivar can reach 5 m (16 ft) and tolerates
more shade than the species. Minimum
winter temperature 13°c (55°F). S leafmould,
manure and peat at 2:1:1, or normal potting
compost. P seed or cuttings.

Dracaena

Dracaena draco
Dragon Tree / fam. *Agavaceae*
A vigorous species with a tree-like stem and leaves in rosettes. Overwinter at a minimum temperature of 7°C (44°F), otherwise treat like *D. deremensis*.

***Dracaena fragrans* 'Massangeana'**
Corn Palm / fam. *Agavaceae*
One of several varieties. Makes a good Ti Tree. 'Lindenii' has leaves with creamy longitudinal stripes and yellow-green margins. Treat like *D. deremensis*.

***Dracaena fragrans* 'Victoria'**
fam. *Agavaceae*
One of the most attractive of all the cultivars of this species. In later life it bears flowers with a delightful fragrance. Treat like *D. deremensis*.

Dracaena marginata
Madagascar Dragon Tree / fam. *Agavaceae*
A very strong plant tolerant of some shade. 'Tricolor' has leaves with green, cream and red stripes. Treat like *D. deremensis*.

***Dracaena reflexa* 'Song of India'**
Dragon Tree / fam. *Agavaceae*
This plant branches very readily and is easily turned into a many-stemmed specimen. Overwinter at a minimum temperature of 10°C (50°F). Treat like *D. deremensis*.

Dracaena sanderiana
Ribbon Plant / fam. *Agavaceae*
A smaller species but one that is very strong. There are a number of attractive cultivars including a completely green type. Minimum winter temperature 10°C (50°F). Treat like *D. deremensis*.

Dracaena surculosa (D. godseffiana)
Dragon Tree / fam. *Agavaceae*
The habit differs from that of most dracaenas. Bears early, greeny-yellow, fragrant flowers, followed by red berries. Winter temperature 10°C (50°F). Treat like *D. deremensis*.

Duchesnea indica
Indian Strawberry / fam. *Rosaceae*
Attractive hanging and balcony plant or good ground cover. Can overwinter in the garden under a cover of straw. Keep indoors at 10–12°C (50–54°F). P seed or runners.

Echeveria agavoides
fam. *Crassulaceae*
An agave-like echeveria. Produces dense rosettes of leaves with attractive reddish-brown pointed tips. Reddish-yellow flowers on long stems in May–June.

Echeveria agavoides 'Cristata'
fam. _Crassulaceae_
○ ⊕ ⊗ ⊙ ⊖ ▣
Comb-shaped cultivar whose leaves turn an
attractive red in a sunny situation. S cactus
mixture. P offsets or leaf cuttings.

Echeveria elegans (E. perelegans)
Mexican Snowball / fam. _Crassulaceae_
○ ⊕ ⊗ ⊙ ⊖ ▣
Up to 15-cm (6-in) wide rosettes with a white,
waxy protective layer. Do not spray the leaves
or pour water into the rosettes. Reddish
yellow flowers. P offsets.

Echeveria gibbiflora var. carnunculata
fam. _Crassulaceae_
○ ⊕ ⊗ ⊙ ⊖ ▣
Large rosettes of fleshy grey-green leaves
with wart-like outgrowths on the upper
surface causing the leaf edges to curl. Red
flowers. Keep cool in winter.

Echeveria gigantea
fam. _Crassulaceae_
○ ⊕ ⊗ ⊙ ⊖ ▣
Large, fleshy, purplish leaves. P tip cuttings.
Older stems will quite often produce new
shoots that can be removed, dried and used
as cuttings.

Echeveria harmsii
fam. _Crassulaceae_
○ ⊕ ⊗ ⊙ ⊖ ▣
Branching stems with up to 7-cm (2¾-in) wide
rosettes. Narrow leaves up to 4 cm (1½ in) long.
Elongated flower stems bearing one to three
bell-shaped red flowers with a yellow centre.
S cactus mixture.

Echeveria leucotricha
fam. _Crassulaceae_
○ ⊕ ⊗ ⊙ ⊖ ▣
Loose rosettes of lanceolate leaves covered in
white wool and up to 8 cm (3 in) long.
Vermilion flowers. Woolly species must be
watered carefully and never sprayed.

Echeveria pulvinata 'Ruby'
fam. _Crassulaceae_
○ ⊕ ⊗ ⊙ ⊖ ▣
Loose rosettes to 15 cm (6 in) across with
leaves smaller than those of the species;
margins turn reddish in sunny positions.
Lateral inflorescences with red flowers.
S cactus mixture. P cuttings.

Echeveria secunda 'Pumila'
fam. _Crassulaceae_
○ ⊕ ⊗ ⊙ ⊖ ▣
Glaucous rosettes up to 15 cm (6 in) across.
The leaves come to a sharp point with a
brown tip. Inflorescence with up to 20 red
and yellow flowers. Flowering period May–
April.

Echeveria setosa
fam. _Crassulaceae_
○ ⊕ ⊗ ⊙ ⊖ ▣
Dense short-stemmed rosettes of green leaves
densely covered in white hair. Red flowers
with yellow tips. Flowering period April–
July. P seed.

Echinocactus

Echinocactus grusonii
Golden Barrel Cactus / **fam.** ***Cactaceae***
○ ⊞ ∞ ⊕ ⊙
Globular plant with a diameter of up to nearly 1 m (3 ft) and 20 to 37 prominent ribs; woolly crown. Older plants may bear yellow flowers. Slow grower. P seed.

Echinocereus scopulorum
fam. ***Cactaceae***
○ ⊞ ∞ ⊕ ⊙
Columnar cactus densely covered with spines. Large, light purple flowers with green stigmas. Winter rest needed to encourage bud formation in spring. S cactus mixture. P seed.

Echinofossulocactus zacatecasensis
(Stenocactus zacatecasensis) / **fam.** ***Cactaceae***
○ ⊞ ∞ ⊕ ⊙
Globular cactus with several densely packed, sharp, wavy ribs and three brownish central spines of which the middle one is flat. S cactus mixture. P seed.

Echinopsis intricatissima
fam. ***Cactaceae***
○ ◑ ⊞ ⊕ ⊙
Globular, later columnar, freely branching cactus. Large white, fragrant flowers that open wide in sunny weather. S cactus mixture. P seed or cuttings.

Elettaria cardamomun (Amomum cardamomum) / **Cardamom** / **fam.** ***Zingiberaceae***
◑ ⊞ ∞ ⊕ ⊙
Vigorous house plant. The white flowers have a blue and white striped lip and a yellow margin. Keep at 14–16°c (57–60°F) in winter. P seed or shoot tip cuttings.

Elisena longipetala
fam. ***Amaryllidaceae***
○ ⊞ ∞ ⊕ ⊙
This bulbous plant must be kept at 15°c (59°F) from October on. Pot in March in proportions of loam, leafmould, sand and farmyard manure 2:2:1:1. P offsets, which will flower within a few years.

Encyclia vitellina
fam. ***Orchidaceae***
◑ ⊞ ∞ ⊕ ⊙
Autumn-flowering plant from Central America. Minimum temperature 18°c (64°F). S osmunda fibre, sphagnum moss and beech leaves in proportions 4:2:1. P seed and division.

Epidendrum ciliare
fam. ***Orchidaceae***
◑ ⊞ ⊙ ⊕ ⊙
Fragrant winter-flowering orchid which needs a lot of light. Winter at 10°c (50°F). Grow on tree ferns or in baskets filled with osmunda fibre, sphagnum moss and beech leaves, 4:2:1. P seed, division.

Epidendrum cochleatum
fam. ***Orchidaceae***
◑ ⊞ ⊙ ⊕ ⊙
Fragrant winter-flowering orchid. Minimum winter temperature 12°c (53°F). Spray and keep moist with soft water only. Treat like *E. ciliare.*

Epidendrum fragrans
fam. Orchidaceae
Ⓘ ⓖ ⊙ ⊚ ⓣ
Bears very fragrant flowers in the spring.
Suitable for indoor cultivation. Maintain a
winter temperature of 12°C (53°F). Treat like
E. ciliare.

Epidendrum radiatum
fam. Orchidaceae
Ⓘ ⓖ ⊙ ⊚ ⓣ
Attractive epiphyte which flowers between
the beginning of May and the end of July.
Rest in winter at a minimum temperature of
12°C (53°F). Treat like E. ciliare.

Epiphyllum hybrid 'Anton Gunther'
Leaf Cactus/**fam. Cactaceae**
Ⓘ ⓖ ⊚ ⊝ ⓣ
Erect stems, sometimes flat and sometimes
triangular. Large red flower. Rest in winter at
8–10°C (46–50°F), then do not turn plant once
buds appear. S cactus mixture. P cuttings.

Epipremnum aureum (Rhaphidophora aurea,
Scindapsus aureus)/**fam. Araceae**
Ⓘ Ⓜ ⊕ ⊚ ⊝ ⊙ ⊞ ⓣ
Easily grown climbing or hanging plant.
Minimum winter temperature 15°C (59°F).
S pinewood soil, lumps of fibrous peat and a
little farmyard manure. P shoot tip and eye
cuttings, layering.

Epipremnum aureum 'Marble Queen'
(Rhaphidophora aurea)/**fam. Araceae**
Ⓘ ⓖ ⊕ ⊚ ⊝ ⊞ ⓣ
This cultivar is more tolerant of shade and
grows faster than the species. Winter at 15°C
(59°F). S pinewood soil with fibrous peat and
farmyard manure. P cuttings will root easily.

Episcia cupreata
fam. Gesneriaceae
Ⓘ Ⓜ ⊕ ⊚ ⊝ ⊙
A rewarding house plant in the summer. Best
to winter it in the greenhouse at a minimum
16°C (60°F). S pinewood soil with well-rotted
farmyard manure. P runners, leaf and stem
cuttings.

Episcia cupreata 'Silver Queen'
fam. Gesneriaceae
Ⓘ Ⓜ ⊕ ⊚ ⊝ ⓣ
One of several cultivars which also include
'Emerald Queen', 'Ajacou', 'Frosty' and
'Metallica', all differing from the species in
leaf colour and leaf size. Treat like E. cupreata.

Episcia dianthiflora
fam. Gesneriaceae
Ⓘ Ⓜ ⊕ ⊚ ⊝ ⓣ
Trailing plant with very conspicuous white
flowers, sometimes hidden beneath the
leaves. Treat like E. cupreata.

Episcia lilacina (E. chontalensis)
fam. Gesneriaceae
Ⓘ Ⓜ ⊕ ⊚ ⊝ ⊙
Fast-growing plant which makes excellent
ground cover but is very sensitive to cold. It
is therefore best grown in a container.
Flowers from September to December. Treat
like E. cupreata.

61

Erica gracilis
Heather / fam. *Ericaceae*
Ⓘ Ⓐ Ⓧ Ⓖ Ⓣ
Will flower outside or in a cool room from
September to December. Do not overwinter.
S pinewood soil. P cuttings in the summer or
in January–March at 16°C (60°F).

Erica × willmorei (E. × willmoreana)
Heather / fam. *Ericaceae*
Ⓘ Ⓐ Ⓧ Ⓖ Ⓣ
Spring-flowering heather. Cut back after
flowering. Put outside in the summer and
overwinter at 6–8°C (43–46°F). Repot in
pinewood soil with a little peat and sand.
P cuttings.

Eriocactus leninghausii
fam. *Cactaceae*
Ⓞ Ⓐ Ⓧ Ⓖ Ⓣ
At first broadly globular but later branching
to produce golden-yellow cylinders covered
with spines. Woolly white sloping caps;
yellow flowers. S special cactus mixture.
P seed.

Eriocactus magnifucus var. nigrispinus
fam. *Cactaceae*
Ⓞ Ⓐ Ⓧ Ⓖ Ⓣ
Globular cactus. The ribs bear areoles with
white or yellow spines. Grafting encourages
flowering. Winter temperature about 10°C
(50°F). S special cactus mixture. P seed.

Erythrina crista-galli
Coral Tree / fam. *Leguminosae*
Ⓞ Ⓐ Ⓧ Ⓖ Ⓣ
Strong container plant which should be
overwintered at 5°C (41°F). Cut back to 15 cm
(6 in) from the base in the spring. S potting
compost with extra loam and sand. P seed,
division, cuttings.

Espostoa lanata (Pilocereus lanatus)
fam. *Cactaceae*
Ⓞ Ⓐ Ⓧ Ⓖ Ⓣ
A cactus wrapped in fine hairs. Cultivated
specimens will grow to a height of about 1 m
(3 ft) without branching. Keep above 15°C
(59°F) in winter. Can be grafted. S special
cactus mixture. P seed.

Eucalyptus cinerea (E. cephalophora)
fam. *Myrtaceae*
Ⓞ Ⓐ Ⓧ Ⓖ Ⓖ Ⓣ
The illustration shows the foliage in its
youthful form. Later the leaves grow more
elongated. A container plant which should be
overwintered at 5°C (41°F). S loamy mixture.
P seed.

Eucharis grandiflora (E. amazonica)
fam. *Amaryllidaceae*
Ⓘ Ⓐ Ⓧ Ⓖ Ⓣ
Fragrant bulbous plant that can flower three
times a year in a warm greenhouse. Rest for
one month at about 15°C (59°F) after flowering.
S fertile and humus-rich. P offsets.

Eucomis bicolor
fam. *Liliaceae*
Ⓞ Ⓐ Ⓧ Ⓖ Ⓢ
This summer-flowering plant must be potted
up in February and grown on at 8–10°C (46–
50°F). Put outside in late May. Overwinter in
a frost-free and dry spot. P seed, offsets.

Eugenia paniculata
fam. *Myrtaceae*
Produces white flowers in the spring followed by rose-red fruits. Var. *australis* is smaller. Winter temperature 5°C (41°F). S humus-rich, loamy and fertile. P cuttings.

Eulophia porphyroglossa
fam. *Orchidaceae*
Marsh orchid for the warm greenhouse or flower window. Minimum winter temperature 18°C (64°F). Pot in sphagnum moss, peat and osmunda fibre. P seed.

***Euonymus japonicus* 'Albomarginatus'**
fam. *Celastraceae*
This plant comes in many kinds, all with different leaf markings. The variegated types demand more light. Overwinter at 4–6°C (39–43°F) and put outside after April. P tip cuttings.

Euphorbia cap st. mariensis
fam. *Euphorbiaceae*
Hairy stems with crenated leaves at their tips. Insignificant flowers, unusual rather than attractive. Overwinter at 10–15°C (50–59°F). S special cactus mixture. P seed and cuttings.

Euphorbia fulgens
Scarlet Plume / fam. *Euphorbiaceae*
Shrub up to 125 cm (4 ft) in height. Lanceolate green leaves. Bright orange or white little flowers borne on the stem in winter. Good for cutting. S special cactus mixture. P seed.

Euphorbia grandicornis
fam. *Euphorbiaceae*
A 1 to 2-m (3- to 6-ft) high branching shrub with wide 3-ribbed lateral stems of annual segments. Up to 7-cm (2¾-in) long paired, tough spines. S special cactus mixture.
P cuttings or seed.

Euphorbia heteracantha
fam. *Euphorbiaceae*
Rectangular densely branched plant. Like all other euphorbias, it has a white milky sap that can be very poisonous and cause various irritations. Cover wounds with ash.
P cuttings.

Euphorbia horrida
fam. *Euphorbiaceae*
This plant forms groups of pillars up to 1.5 m (5 ft) in height from the base. New growths have small leaves. P cuttings.

Euphorbia lophogona (E. fournieri)
fam. *Euphorbiaceae*
Pentagonal, often branching stems. Inflorescences grow in the axils of the stiff, leathery leaves. This plant is self-fertile and seeds itself. S special cactus mixture.

Euphorbia

Euphorbia meloformis
fam. *Euphorbiaceae*
Spherical, low-growing plant with eight to
ten ribs. Embedded growing point. Bears no
leaves. Lignified inflorescences with yellow-
green flowers. P very simple from seed.

Euphorbia milii
Crown of Thorns / fam. *Euphorbiaceae*
Woody, round, slightly fluted stems covered
in spines. Infloresences have a sticky stem.
Once the leaves have been shed, do not water
for one month. No winter rest needed.

Euphorbia pseudocactus
fam. *Euphorbiaceae*
Three to five-edged, articulated, up to 5-cm
(2-in) wide stems with yellow-green
markings between the ribs. Yellow flowers
are borne on the upper part of the plant.
Winter rest at 10°c (50°F). P seed.

Euphorbia pugniformis
fam. *Euphorbiaceae*
The inflorescences are borne on the main stem
and lateral branches. P plunge cuttings into
water to prevent 'bleeding' – otherwise the
sap will seal off the cut surface and impede
rooting.

Euphorbia pulcherrima
Poinsettia / fam. *Euphorbiaceae*
A plant with large red, white or salmon-pink
bracts. Place in a dry and dark spot once the
leaves drop off. Cut back in spring. P tip
cuttings.

Euphorbia tirucalli
fam. *Euphorbiaceae*
Round branches with pencil-shaped green
sideshoots bearing small leaves that drop off
in the autumn. Can grow to a very large size.
S special cactus mixture. P seed.

Euphorbia trigona
fam. *Euphorbiaceae*
Erect stems with three- to four-sided
branches. Deciduous; oval leaves. Needs little
water in the winter. S special cactus mixture.
P seed or cuttings, dried and potted in sand.

Euterpe edulis
Assai Palm / fam. *Palmae*
Graceful palm that can reach a height of 30 m
(100 ft) in nature. Overwinter at 14–18°c (57–
64°F). Pot in proprietary potting compost with
extra loam. P seed.

Exacum affine
Persian Violet / fam. *Gentianaceae*
Biennial grown as an annual. Flowers from
July to October, then discard. S proprietary
potting compost with extra peat and sand.
P sow in February–March at 18°c (64°F).

× _Fatshedera lizei_
fam. _Araliaceae_
◐ ⊕ ☺ ⊗ ▣
Evergreen plant up to 5 m (16 ft) in height.
May be put out in summer; overwinter at 9°C
(48°F). Repot in a mixture of pinewood soil
and farmyard manure. P cuttings or seed.

× _Fatshedera lizei_ 'Variegata'
fam. _Araliaceae_
◐ ⊕ ☺ ⊗ ⊝ ▣
Grows more slowly than the species and
needs a little more warmth and light. Pinch
out to obtain bushier plants. Treat like × _F.
lizei_. P cuttings.

Fatsia japonica (Aralia japonica)
Japanese Aralia / fam. _Araliaceae_
◐ ☺ ⊗ ⊝ ▣
Strong plant with panicles of greenish-white
flowers and black berries. Can overwinter
outside in sheltered spots if well covered.
S standard potting mixture. P cuttings, seed,
air-layering.

Fatsia japonica 'Albomarginata'
Japanese Aralia / fam. _Araliaceae_
◐ ☺ ⊗ ⊝ ▣
The variegated forms demand more light and
warmth and grow more slowly than the
species. Treat like _F. japonica_. P cuttings or
air-layering.

Faucaria tigrina
Tiger's Jaws / fam. _Aizoaceae_
○ ⊕ ⊗ ◐ ⊝ ⊝ ▣
Broad greyish-green leaves covered with
white dots. Leaf margins have sharply
toothed 'jaws'. Ray-shaped yellow flowers.
Rest in winter at 5°C (41°F). P seed or cuttings.

**_Ferocactus acanthodes (Echinocactus
acanthodes)_ / fam. _Cactaceae_**
○ ⊕ ☺ ◐ ⊝ ⊝ ▣
A cactus densely covered with red spines.
Central spine up to 12 cm (4½ in) long.
Reddish-yellow flowers. To form buds, rest in
winter at 5°C (41°F). S special cactus mixture.
P seed, cuttings.

**_Ferocactus latispinus (Echinocactus
corniger)_ / Fish Hook Cactus / fam. _Cactaceae_**
○ ⊕ ☺ ◐ ⊝ ⊝ ▣
Flat, spherical body with about 20 ribs. Red,
hooked central spines. Red flowers appear
vary rarely. Rest from October–March.
S special cactus mixture. P seed.

Ferocactus recurvus
fam. _Cactaceae_
○ ⊕ ☺ ◐ ⊝ ▣
Bright green globular plant with about 13
ribs. Areoles beset with eight yellowish
spines. The central spine is flat, red and hook
shaped. The carmine flowers appear very
rarely.

Ficus altissima
fam. _Moraceae_
◐ ⊕ ⊗ ⊝ ▣
Most _Ficus_ species make strong plants which
can be overwintered in a normally heated
room. Water occasionally. S standard potting
compost. P cuttings.

Ficus

Ficus aspera 'Parcellii' (F. parcellii)
fam. Moraceae

This plant will quickly bear small figs. Overwinter at a minimum temperature of 18°C (64°F). Demands a great deal of light. S loam and leafmould at 3:1, and a little sand and peat. P cuttings.

Ficus australis
fam. Moraceae

A very strong ficus which can be grown at a somewhat lower temperature than most. Minimum winter temperature 10°C (50°F). Do not be afraid to cut back if this plant grows too tall. P cuttings and seed.

Ficus benghalensis (F. indica)
fam. Moraceae

Grows into a very robust plant. 'Krishnae' is a most attractive form with ivory-coloured veins. Cultivate and propagate like *F. altissima*.

Ficus benjamina (F. nitida)
Weeping Fig / fam. Moraceae

Very popular plant with a graceful appearance. In nature grows as a strangler and produces a great many aerial roots. Treat like *F. altissima*.

Ficus benjamina 'Rijssenhout'
Weeping Fig / fam. Moraceae

One of many cultivars now sold in garden shops. Another popular cultivar is *F. b.* 'Exotica'. Treat like *F. altissima*.

Ficus benjamina 'Variegata'
Variegated Weeping Fig / fam. Moraceae

This cultivar needs more light, warmth and greater humidity than the species and grows more slowly. Treat like *F. altissima*. P cuttings

Ficus cyathistipula
fam. Moracea

One of the few species to produce 3- to 4-cm (1- to 1½-in) wide thick, round pseudo-fruits at an early age. Treat like *F. altissima*. P seed and cuttings.

Ficus deltoidea (F. diversifolia)
Mistletoe Fig / fam. Moraceae

Lives as an epiphyte on various trees. Produces pea-sized pseudo-fruits at an early age. Slow grower, reaching a height of up to 80 cm (32 in). Treat like *F. altissima*. P seed, cuttings.

Ficus elastica 'Belgaplant'
Rubber Plant / fam. Moraceae

A relatively new variety with very beautifully marked leaves. Needs a great deal of light to retain its fine markings. Treat like *F. altissima* P cuttings, air-layering.

Ficus elastica 'Decora'
Rubber Plant / fam. *Moraceae*
Ⓘ ⊞ ∞ ⊜ 🗑
Formerly used for rubber tapping; now only grown as a house plant in various decorative shapes. Treat like *F. altissima*. P seed, cuttings, air-layering.

Ficus elastica 'Schryveriana'
Rubber Plant / fam. *Moraceae*
Ⓘ ⊞ ∞ ⊜ 🗑
This plant is one of a large number of cultivars of *F. elastica*. Variegated forms need more light and warmth. Treat like *F. altissima*. P cuttings, air-layering.

Ficus lyrata (F. pandurata)
Fiddle Leaf Fig / fam. *Moraceae*
Ⓘ ⊞ ∞ ⊜ ⊜ 🗑
Tall, sparingly branched plant. Ensure there is enough air humidity, otherwise treat like *F. altissima*. P seed, cuttings, air-layering.

Ficus pumila (F. repens)
Creeping Fig / fam. *Moraceae*
Ⓘ ⊞ ∞ ∞ ⊜ 🗑 ⊡
Climbing, creeping or hanging plant. Can overwinter at anything from 5–18°C (41–64°F) but is much more demanding over air humidity: spray frequently. P cuttings, seed.

Ficus rubiginosa 'Variegata'
fam. *Moraceae*
Ⓘ ⊞ ∞ ∞ ⊜ 🗑
The species is a shrub with branching stems that root where they touch the ground. Minimum winter temperature 10°C (50°F); the variegated type needs more warmth. S humus-rich loam. P cuttings.

Ficus sagittata 'Variegata' (F. radicans 'Variegata') / fam. Moraceae
Ⓘ ⊞ ∞ ⊜ 🗑 ⊡
This ficus makes attractive ground cover and can also be grown as a climbing or hanging plant. When repotting, cut back a little to keep it in good shape. Treat like *F. altissima*. P cuttings.

Ficus schlechteri
fam. *Moraceae*
Ⓘ ⊞ ∞ ⊜ 🗑
A tree from New Caledonia, where it bears yellow figs. A rewarding plant that can stand a great deal of shade. Treat like *F. altissima*. P seed, cuttings.

Ficus triangularis
fam. *Moraceae*
Ⓘ ⊞ ∞ ⊜ 🗑
A tree with striking leaves producing small 'figs' at an early age. Tolerant of shade. Treat like *F. altissima*. P seed, cuttings.

Fittonia verschaffeltii
fam. *Acanthaceae*
Ⓘ ⊞ ∞ ∞ ⊜ ⊡
A glorious foliage plant with inconspicuous flowers, suitable for a warm greenhouse. Minimum winter temperature 13°C (55°F). S potting compost, peat and a little clay. P cuttings, runners.

67

Fittonia

Fittonia verschaffeltii 'Argyroneura'
fam. *Acanthaceae*

Like other fittonias, this is best grown at 20°C (68°F). The minimum winter temperature is slightly higher than for the others, at 16°C (60°F). Otherwise treat like *V. verschaffeltii*.

Fittonia verschaffeltii 'Pearcei'
fam. *Acanthaceae*

If grown in pots indoors, this plant will produce smaller leaves than it does in a greenhouse border. Treat like *F. verschaffeltii*.

Fuchsia hybrid 'Alice Hofman'
fam. *Onagraceae*

A popular plant; one of hundreds of cultivars. This particular type is of dwarflike habit. P cuttings; from seed only to produce new varieties. Treat like *F.* 'Bernadette'.

Fuchsia hybrid 'Bernadette'
fam. *Onagraceae*

Put out in a sheltered spot in summer and feed weekly; keep at 5°C (41°F) in winter or mulch roots with bracken. S leafmould, loam, farmyard manure and a little dried blood. P cuttings.

Fuchsia hybrid 'Cover Girl'
fam. *Onagraceae*

Double-flowered fuchsia that should be pinched out for attractive and bushy plants. Never place in full sun. Treat like *F.* 'Bernadette'.

Fuchsia hybrid 'Dollarprinzessin'
fam. *Onagraceae*

One of the best-known double fuchsias. Cuttings root easily in water or in a mixture of peat and sand, at 15–20°C (59–68°F). Treat like *F.* 'Bernadette'.

Fuchsia hybrid 'El Camino'
fam. *Onagraceae*

Attractive double fuchsia suitable for growing as a small standard. To that end, take cuttings in September. Treat like *F.* 'Bernadette'.

Fuchsia hybrid 'Gartenmeister Bonstedt'
fam. *Onagraceae*

One of the Triphylla hybrids produced from crosses of *F. triphylla* first used by the German grower, Bonstedt. Treat like *F.* 'Bernadette'.

Fuchsia hybrid 'La Campanella'
fam. *Onagraceae*

Attractive hanging fuchsia. Once the slips have taken they should not be pinched out because they will be expected to make long shoots. Treat like *F.* 'Bernadette'.

Fuchsia hybrid 'Mme Cornelissen'
fam. Onagraceae
This hybrid is often grown as a standard: the stem is allowed to reach the required height and then pinched out except for the top six pairs of leaves. Treat like *F.* 'Bernadette'.

Fuchsia hybrid 'Pink Galore'
fam. Onagraceae
One of the most attractive double, arching fuchsias. Pinch out as little as possible. Treat like *F.* 'Bernadette'.

Fuchsia hybrid 'Pink Temptation'
fam. Onagraceae
Single fuchsia that can be made to flower later than usual by protracted stopping. Treat like *F.* 'Bernadette'.

Fuchsia hybrid 'White Prixii'
fam. Onagraceae
Very attractive variety in beautiful colours and with graceful flowers. Can be grown as a standard. Treat like *F.* 'Bernadette'.

Gardenia jasminoides (G. florida, G. radicans) / Cape Jasmine / fam. Rubiaceae
May be put out in the summer. Overwinter at 5–10°C (41–50°F). Repot older plants every three years in leafmould, loam and sand. P tip cuttings or possibly from seed.

Gasteria caespitosa
fam. Liliaceae
Clump-forming plant. Leaves slightly rounded, up to 14 cm (5½ in) long with light spots. Graceful reddish flowers on long stems. S special cactus mixture. P offsets.

Gasteria maculata
fam. Liliaceae
Tongue-shaped leaves up to 20 cm (8 in) in length, dark green with white spots and with horny spines. Red flowers. To encourage flowering, rest at 10°C (50°F). P leaf cuttings.

Gasteria verrucosa
Warty Aloe / fam. Liliaceae
Long, pointed leaves, concave on top and rounded underneath with white pearly tubercles. Long inflorescences bearing red flowers with green tips. S special cactus mixture. P leaf cuttings.

Gerbera hybrid 'Orange Queen'
fam. Compositae
Single-flowered cultivar particularly suitable for cutting: flowers will keep in water for a long time. Older plants flower less profusely than young. Treat like *G. jamesonii*.

Gerbera jamesonii
fam. *Compositae*

Flowers most profusely when planted out in a border in equal parts of clay-based loam, leafmould and farmyard manure. Minimum winter temperature 12°C (53°F). P seed, cuttings, divison.

Glecoma hederacea 'Variegata' (Nepeta hederacea)/fam. *Labiatae*

Vigorous trailing or hanging plant with fragrant leaves and small blue flowers. Overwinter at 6–10°C (43–50°F). Will root spontaneously if nodes touch the ground. P cuttings.

Gloriosa rothschildiana
Glory Lily / fam. *Liliaceae*

Overwinter the tuber in its pot at 10–12°C (50–53°F). Repot in the spring in loam, leafmould and sand and keep at 20°C (68°F). P seed, offsets.

Glottiphyllum nelii
fam. *Aizoaceae*

Fleshy leaves in two rows. Short-stemmed yellow flowers blooming from September to January. Growing period from April to July. Keep cool in winter. S special cactus mixture. P seed.

Graptopetalum amethystinum (Pachyphytum amethystinum)/fam. *Crassulaceae*

Procumbent stems with heavily bloomed, amethyst leaf rosettes at the top. Red flowers. Rest in winter at 5–10°C (41–50°F). S cactus mixture. P shoot tip or leaf cuttings but also from seed.

Grevillea robusta
Silk Oak / fam. *Proteaceae*

Graceful plant for a cool room. Rest in winter at 6–10°C (43–50°F). S leafmould, loam and a little farmyard manure. Propagation from seed is easier than from cuttings.

Guzmania dissitiflora
fam. *Bromeliaceae*

Very suitable for the warm greenhouse or flower window. Minimum winter temperature 16–18°C (60–64°F). Pot in osmunda fibre, sphagnum moss, beech leafmould and a little sand. P seed, offshoots.

Guzmania lindenii
fam. *Bromeliaceae*

Stemless plant with a large rosette. The leaves are up to 70 cm (28 in) long and have attractive markings. Treat and propagate like *G. dissitiflora*.

Guzmania lingulata (G. cardinalis)
fam. *Bromeliaceae*

Forms up to 80 cm (32 in) wide and 30 cm (1 ft) high rosettes that need space. 'Splendens' has leaves more strongly marked with red. Treat like *G. dissitiflora*.

Guzmania minor 'Orange'
fam. Bromeliaceae
A cultivar with mostly red-tinged leaves and red bracts. *G. m.* 'Orange Variegata' has leaves with a yellowish longitudinal stripe. Treat like *G. dissitiflora*.

Guzmania zahnii
fam. Bromeliaceae
Foliage covered with red lines in the spring. The use of growth regulators make it possible to market flowering guzmanias throughout the year. Treat like *G. dissitiflora*.

Gymnocalycium bicolor (Echinocactus bicolor)/**fam. Cactaceae**
Flat-capped globular plant that makes no offsets. Funnel-shaped pink and white flowers carried at the top of the stem. Flower tube scaly outside. Needs a rest period for flower formation.

Gymnocalcyum mihanovichii (Echinocactus mihanovichii)/**fam. Cactaceae**
From left to right: 'Rosea', 'Black Cap', and 'Optima Rubra'. The caps have no chlorophyll and can only live if grafted. When grafting, cut off stock and scion and squeeze together.

Gymnocalycium pileomayensis (Weingartia pileomayensis)/**fam. Cactaceae**
Bluish-green spherical cactus with a profusion of yellow flowers. Will do very well outside in the summer. Resting period from October to March. S special cactus mixture. P seed.

Gymnocalycium quehlianum (Echinocactus quehlianus)/**fam. Cactaceae**
Eight to thirteen knobbly ribs and groups of five curved spines. Flattened spherical shape. Often turns brown in the sun. White flowers up to 7 cm (2¾ in) long. S special cactus mixture. P seed or cuttings.

Gynura aurantiaca
fam. Compositae
Hanging or upright plant, very popular because of its unusual colours. Minimum winter temperature 12–15°C (53–59°F). Pot in leafmould, loam and farmyard manure. P cuttings root very easily.

Haageocereus chosicensis
fam. Cactaceae
Cylindrical cactus with 16 or more ribs and reddish-brown spines. White flowers open at night. Rest in winter at 5–10°C (41–50°F). S special cactus mixture. P seed or cuttings.

Habenaria rhodocheila (H. pusilla)
fam. Orchidaceae
Sensitive autumn-flowering orchid which needs a lot of water and fertiliser when growing. Rest at a minimum 18°C (64°F) keeping it fairly dry. S loam, farmyard manure, osmunda fibre. P division.

71

Habranthus robustus (Zephyranthes robusta)
fam. *Amaryllidaceae*

◯ ⊕ ∞ ◔ ◷ ▭

Bulbous plant which can be put out in
summer and should be overwintered in an
unheated greenhouse at 5°C (41°F). Flowers in
the summer. P offsets, seed or division.

Haemanthus albiflos
fam. *Amaryllidaceae*

◑ ◐ ⊕ ∞ ◷ ▭

Beautiful but unfortunately rare plant.
Overwinter at 12–15°C (53–59°F). Do not allow
leaves to die off completely. S equal parts
clay-based loam, leafmould and farmyard
manure. P division, seed.

Haemanthus multiflorus
fam. *Amaryllidaceae*

◯ ⊕ ∞ ◷ ▭

Water so sparingly in the autumn that the
foliage dies. Overwinter the bulb at 12°C
(53°F). Repot in the spring in equal parts clay-
based loam, leafmould and farmyard manure.
P offsets, seed.

Hamatocactus setispinus
fam. *Cactaceae*

◯ ⊕ ◔ ◷ ▭

Globular, later cylindrical plant with 12–15
ribs and hook-shaped central spines. Large
yellow flowers with a red throat. Keep dry
and at about 5°C (41°F) in winter. P seed.

Harpephyllum caffrum
fam. *Anacardiaceae*

◯ ◐ ◔ ∞ ◷ ▣ ▭

Container plant which should be put out in a
sheltered place during the summer and kept
at 5°C (41°F) in winter. S loamy. P seed.

Hatiora cylindrica
Coral Cactus / **fam.** *Cactaceae*

◐ ⊕ ∞ ◷ ▭

Strongly branching cactus with red-spotted,
round joints. Flowers red and orange. May
safely be put out in the summer. A cool, dry
resting period is needed to encourage
flowering. P from joints.

Haworthia attenuata
fam. *Liliaceae*

◐ ⊕ ◔ ◯ ◷ ▭

Small, spreading, rosette-forming plant with
elongated and pointed leaves covered with
small white tubercles. White flowers. S cactus
mixture. P dry off and pot up young rosettes.

Haworthia fasciata
fam. *Liliaceae*

◐ ⊕ ◔ ◯ ◷ ▭

Rosette with slightly incurving leaves,
smooth on top and covered with small white
'pearls' underneath. White, bell-shaped
flowers in loose clusters on long stems.
P cuttings.

Haworthia reinwardtii
fam. *Liliaceae*

◐ ⊕ ◔ ◯ ◷ ▭

Species with a pyramidal habit. The short
green leaves are densely covered by white
tubercles. Flowers in September. Stop
watering from October. Leaves tend to turn
red in excessive sunlight.

Hebe andersonii hybrid
fam. *Scrophulariaceae*
An autumn-flowering cross between *H. speciosa* and *H. salicifolia*. Keep at 5°C (41°F) in the winter. S pinewood soil mixed with a little peat and manure. P tip cuttings at 20–25°C (68–77°F).

Hebe andersonii hybrid 'Variegata'
fam. *Scrophulariaceae*
Other cultivars are 'Albertine' with violet pink, 'Imperial Blue' with violet blue, and 'Snowflake' with white flowers. Treat and propagate like *H. andersonii* hybrid.

Hebe speciosa
fam. *Scrophulariaceae*
Good autumn-flowering species which must be kept in a cool place if it is not to shed its leaves and flowers too quickly. Treat like *H. andersonii* hybrid.

Hechtia stenopetala
fam. *Bromeliaceae*
Striking foliage plant. Overwinter at 10–15°C (50–59°F). Pot in a mixture of osmunda fibre, sphagnum moss, beech leafmould and sand. P seed, rooted shoots.

Hedera helix 'Erecta'
Ivy / fam. *Araliaceae*
One of the many attractive cultivars in which *H. helix* is so rich. Keep at 0–10°C (32–50°F) in winter. In summer, too, tend carefully: it is not really ideal for indoors. P shoot tip cuttings.

Hedera helix 'Garland'
Ivy / fam. *Araliaceae*
Non-climbing variety. Needs soft water and must be given extra food during the growing period. Maximum winter temperature during the day about 15°C (59°F). Treat like *H. helix* 'Erecta'.

Hedera helix 'Goldheart' ('Jubilee')
Ivy / fam. *Araliaceae*
Ivy with relatively small leaves. 'Pittsburgh' has small but entirely bright green leaves. 'Shamrock' is green with crinkly leaf margins. Treat like *H. h.* 'Erecta'.

Hedera helix 'Harald'
Ivy / fam. *Araliaceae*
This variegated ivy has fairly large leaves in various shades of green and white. P shoot tip cuttings. Treat like *H. h.* 'Erecta'.

Hedera helix spp. canariensis 'Variegata'
(Hedera canariensis) / Ivy / fam. *Araliaceae*
Formerly known as 'Gloire de Marengo'. Winter temperature 10–18°C (50–64°F). A true indoor climber, tolerating more warmth than other ivies. Do not place in too dark a position. P cuttings.

Heliconia

Heliconia illustris 'Aureostriata'
fam. *Musaceae*

◯ ◑ ⊞ ⊗ ⊖ ▣ 𝄇

Minimum winter temperature 20°C (68°F) in
the daytime; 16°C (60°F) at night. Pot up in
leafmould or pinewood soil with farmyard
manure and sand. P division; then keep in a
heated greenhouse.

Helleborus niger
Christmas Rose / fam. *Ranunculaceae*

◑ ⊞ ⊗ ⊜ ⊖ 𝄇

Forced plants will flower indoors at about
Christmas time. After flowering plant out,
filling the planting hole with turfy loam.
P seed and division.

Hemigraphis alternata (H. colorata)
fam. *Acanthaceae*

◑ ⊞ ⊗ ⊖ 𝄇

Unusually coloured plant for the heated
greenhouse. Keep all year at about 20°C (68°F)
during the day and 15°C (59°F) at night.
S equal parts loam, leafmould and lumps of
peat. P cuttings.

Heterocentron elegans
fam. *Melastomataceae*

◑ ⊞ ⊗ ⊜ ▣ 𝄇

Hanging plant or ground cover. Minimum
winter temperature 10°C (50°F). Possibly mix
potting compost with extra sphagnum moss
and peat. P shoot tip cuttings.

Hibbertia scandens (H. volubilis)
fam. *Dilleniaceae*

◑ ⊞ ⊗ ⊖ 𝄇

This plant has winding twigs and flowers
with an unpleasant smell. Minimum winter
temperature 7°C (45°F). Mix a little clay soil
with the potting compost. P cuttings, seed.

Hibiscus rosa-sinensis (double pink)
Chinese Rose / fam. *Malvaceae*

◯ ⊞ ⊗ ⊖ ▣ 𝄇

Cultivated forms are less hardy than the
original species. Keep this cultivar at an even
temperature and even humidity. Treat like *H.
rosa-sinensis* 'Holiday'.

Hibiscus rosa-sinensis 'Cooperi'
Chinese Rose / fam. *Malvaceae*

◯ ⊞ ⊗ ⊖ ▣ 𝄇

This and 'Albovariegata' are the only
variegated strains. Flowers are smaller than
those of the green-leaved varieties. Treat like
H. rosa-sinensis 'Holiday'.

Hibiscus rosa-sinensis 'Holiday'
Chinese Rose / fam. *Malvaceae*

◯ ⊞ ⊗ ⊖ ▣ 𝄇

Needs a winter rest at 10–15°C (50–59°F).
Prune in the spring and repot in equal parts
loam, leafmould and farmyard manure or in
standard potting compost. P cuttings.

Hippeastrum hybrid
fam. *Amaryllidaceae*

◯ ⊞ ⊞ ⊗ ⊖ ▣

For early flowers, keep dry from August.
From September, 4–5 weeks at 17°C (63°F),
then 4 weeks at 23°C (73°F). Pot up at bottom
heat of 20°C (68°F). S and P as *H.* 'Fire Dance'.

Hippeastrum hybrid 'Belinda'
fam. *Amaryllidaceae*
○ ⊕ ⊕ ⊗ ⊝ ⊟
Pot the bulbs in mid-winter, allowing their
necks to protrude above the soil. Place in a
warm spot and water sparingly. When the
flower stem is 20 cm (8 in) long, place the plant
in a well-lit window.

Hippeastrum hybrid 'Fire Dance'
fam. *Amaryllidaceae*
○ ⊕ ⊕ ⊗ ⊝ ⊟
May be put in summer. Cut down on watering
in early September, allowing the foliage to
die. Keep at 16°C (60°F) until flowering is to
be forced – see *H.* 'Belinda'. P seed, offsets.

Hippeastrum hybrid 'Picotee'
fam. *Amaryllidaceae*
○ ⊕ ⊕ ⊗ ⊝ ⊟
Picotee varieties have striking flowers with
edges in contrasting colours. Add a top
dressing when the leaves are growing.
Otherwise treat like *H.* 'Fire Dance'.

Homalocladium platycladum (Mueh-
lenbeckia platyclados) / fam. *Polygonaceae*
○ ⊕ ⊗ ⊝ ⊟ ⊡
Easily grown house plant which may be put
out in the summer. Winter temperature 8–16°C
(46–60°F). Best to add a little loam to the potting
compost. P cuttings and seed.

Howeia belmoreana (Kentia belmoreana)
Kentia Palm / fam. *Palmae*
◑ ⊕ ⊗ ⊝ ⊟
Less hardy than the next species. Needs
adequate light and a fairly constant
temperature. Further treatment like *H.*
fosteriana. P seed.

Howeia fosteriana (Kentia fosteriana)
Kentia Palm / fam. *Palmae*
◑ ⊕ ⊗ ⊝ ⊟
Graceful palm requiring a winter temperature
of 14–18°C (57–64°F). Plant in a deep pot of
leafmould, farmyard manure and sand. P fresh
seed in March.

Hoya bella
Miniature Wax Plant / fam. *Asclepiadaceae*
◑ ⊕ ⊗ ⊝ ⊟
Flowers best when grafted on to Wax Plant.
Winter temperature 18°C (64°F). S loam,
leafmould, farmyard manure and sand in
proportions 2:2:1:1, with a little extra
sphagnum moss. P grafting on *H. carnosa.*

Hoya carnosa (Asclepias carnosa)
Wax Plant / fam. *Asclepiadaceae*
○ ◑ ⊕ ⊗ ⊝ ⊟ ⊡
Has larger, more upright flowers than *H. bella.*
Keep dry and cool from October at 10–14°C
(50–57°F). S see last entry. P shoot tip or eye
cuttings at 20–25°C (68–77°F).

Hoya carnosa 'Exotica' (H. marmorata)
Wax Plant / fam. *Asclepiadaceae*
◑ ⊕ ⊗ ⊝ ⊟
A mutant of *H. carnosa.* Treat in the same way
but make sure that this is not placed in the full
sun. P tip or eye cuttings at 20–25°C (68–77°F).

75

Hoya multiflora
Wax Flower / fam. *Asclepiadaceae*
Climbing plant from Malaysia with prominent flowers. Not really suitable for growing outside a heated greenhouse or flower window. Treat like *H. bella*. P cuttings.

Huernia brevirostris
fam. *Asclepiadaceae*
Sinuous serrated stems. Star-shaped flowers with attractive markings, but with an unpleasant smell. P cuttings or seed.

Hyacinthus orientalis hybrid 'Blue Jacket'
Hyacinth / fam. *Liliaceae*
Heel in at 12°C (53°F) in the autumn or place in a dark cupboard. When you can feel the flower bud, bring the bulb into the light. S equal parts compost and sand, or grow in water. P offsets.

Hydrangea macrophylla ssp. **m. f. otaksa**
(pink) / Hortensia / fam. *Saxifragaceae*
Sheds its leaves in the autumn. Overwinter at 4–6°C (39–43°F). Return to 18°C (64°F) in February. Repot in pinewood soil after summer pruning. P shoot tip cuttings.

Hydrangea macrophylla ssp. **m. f. otaksa**
(blue) / Hortensia / fam. *Saxifragaceae*
The white or pink sepals are turned blue by ammonia fertiliser. Hydrangeas like a top dressing. No lime. Treat like last entry.

Hymenocallis narcissiflora (Pancratium
narcissiflorum) / fam. *Amaryllidaceae*
Bulbous plant with fragrant flowers. Dies down in the autumn. Dry resting period at minimum temperature of 15°C (59°F). Mix proprietary potting compost with extra clay. P offsets.

Hymenocallis speciosa (Pancratium
speciosum) / fam. *Amaryllidaceae*
The leaves of this bulb do not die in the winter. Rest at 15°C (59°F) making sure to keep the plant dry. Treat like *H. narcissiflora*.

Hypocyrta glabra
fam. *Gesneriaceae*
A resting period at 10–14°C (50–57°F) from December to February is needed for bud formation. S leafmould, sphagnum moss, charcoal. P seed, shoot tip cuttings, division.

Hypoestes phyllostachya (H. sanguinolenta)
Polka-dot Plant / fam. *Acanthaceae*
Eminently suited to a heated greenhouse; will not flourish indoors unless tended very carefully. No resting period is needed. Cut back in the spring. P seed, shoot tip cuttings.

Illicium verum
fam. *Illiciaceae*
○ ◑ 🌢 ⊛ 🌢 🗑
Container plant with fragrant flowers.
Overwinter at 5°C (41°F). May be put out in
the summer. Pot in pinewood soil and well-
rotted farmyard manure. P seed, shoot tip
cuttings.

Impatiens balsamina (Balsamina hortensis)
Balsam / fam. *Balsaminaceae*
○ 🌢 ⊛ 🌢 🗑
A rewarding annual which needs a great deal
of water in the summer. Overwinter indoors
and take cuttings in the spring. P seed and
shoot tip cuttings at 18–20°C (64–68°F).

Impatiens hybrid 'Confetti'
Buzy Lizzie / fam. *Balsaminaceae*
○ ◑ 🌢 ⊛ 🌢 🗑
There is a constant stream of new Busy Lizzies
of which the compact forms make particularly
suitable house plants. Treat like *I. balsamina*.

Impatiens walleriana (I. holstii, I. sultanii)
Busy Lizzie / fam. *Balsaminaceae*
○ ◑ 🌢 ⊛ 🌢 🗑
Herbaceous perennial; flowers in numerous
shades. 'Petersiana' is reddish in all parts.
Treat like *I. balsamina*.

Iresine herbstii (Achyranthes
verschaffeltii) / fam. *Amaranthaceae*
○ 🌢 ⊛ 🌢 🗑
Small foliage plant which may be put outside
in May. Minimum winter temperature 15°C
(59°F). P shoot tip cuttings in the spring; will
root in water. Nip out growing tips every so
often.

Iresine herbstii 'Acuminata'
fam. *Amaranthaceae*
○ 🌢 ⊛ 🌢 🗑
More decorative than the species thanks to its
pointed leaves. Another cultivar,
'Brilliantissima', has chestnut-coloured leaves
with bright red veins. Treat like *I. herbstii*.

Iresine herbstii 'Aureoreticulata'
fam. *Amaranthaceae*
○ 🌢 ⊛ 🌢 🗑
This plant will produce its finest leaves if it is
placed in the full sun. Treat like *I. herbstii*.
Plant several young plants in one pot.

Ixora hybrid
fam. *Rubiaceae*
◑ 🌢 ⊛ 🌢 🗑
Creamy to orange-red flowers. Cut back after
flowering and overwinter in a warm
greenhouse at a minimum 18°C (64°F).
S pinewood soil with manure. P shoot tip
cuttings at about 28°C (82°F).

Jacaranda mimosifolia (J. ovalifolia)
fam. *Bignoniaceae*
◑ 🌢 ⊛ 🌢 🗑
Grow young plants under heat; minimum
winter temperature during the first four years
not below 12°C (53°F). Older plants excellent
for containers; winter minimum 5°C (41°F).
P seed.

77

Jacobinia carnea (Justicia carnea, Cyrtanthera magnifica)/fam. Acanthaceae

Flowers in late summer, then cut back and rest at 12–15°C (53–59°F). Repot regularly in loam, leafmould and farmyard manure. P shoot tip cuttings under glass.

Jacobinia pauciflora (Libonia floribunda, Sericographis pauciflora)/fam. Acanthaeae

May be put out all summer. Move to an unheated greenhouse to flower in December–February. S loam, leafmould and a little farmyard manure. P shoot tip cuttings in January–February.

Jasminum officinale 'Grandiflorum'
Jasmine/fam. Oleaceae

A winter resting period at 2–8°C (35–46°F) is essential for good flowering. Repot early in the year in loam, beech leafmould and a little farmyard manure and sand. P cuttings, layering.

Jatropha pandurifolia
fam. Euphorbiaceae

Evergreen shrub up to 1 m (3 ft) in height. Not very well known but easy to tend. Do not overfeed. S normal potting compost with a little clay added. P seed.

Jatropha podagrica
fam. Euphorbiaceae

Unusual but easily tended plant. May be left in the house all the year round. Repot in clay-based loam and leafmould, but not every year. Do not feed. P seed.

Kalanchoe blossfeldiana 'Kuiper's Orange'
Flaming Katy/fam. Crassulaceae

A cultivar with orange flowers; other hybrids come with yellow and lilac flowers. If this plant gets too much sun its leaves will turn red. Minimum winter temperature 15°C (59°F).

Kalanchoe blossfeldiana hybrid 'Solferino Purper'/Flaming Katy/fam. Crassulaceae

Easily cultivated plant but it needs a good deal of fresh air. Lilac flowers. S potting compost with a little extra loam. P seed or rooting of side shoots.

Kalanchoe daigremontiana (Bryophyllum daigremontianum)/fam. Crassulaceae

Upright plant with long triangular leaves marked with purple spots underneath. The leaf margins are adorned with buds bearing easily rooted plantlets.

Kalanchoe farinacea
fam. Crassulaceae

Fleshy, greyish-green, oval leaves. Clusters of orange, bell-shaped flowers in spring. S cactus mixture. P remove one of the small fleshy leaves and allow to dry for a few days before rooting.

Kalanchoe hybrid 'Wendy'
fam. Crassulaceae
○ ◖ ⊞ ⊗ ⊖ ▣
Small, decorative variety with cymes of usually three red lantern-shaped flowers, often more than 2 cm (¾ in) in length. Sessile leaves. P cuttings.

Kalanchoe laxiflora 'Fedschenko' (Bryophyllum crenatum; K. crenata) / fam. Crassulaceae
○ ⊞ ⊗ ⊖ ▣
Erect plant with small leaves covered in a bluish bloom and with milled edges. Overwinter dry at 5°C (41°F). Plant will turn straggly at higher temperatures.

Kalanchoe manginii
fam. Crassulaceae
○ ◖ ⊞ ⊗ ⊖ ▣
Lanceolate or spatular leaves. Red, pendent flowers, buds appearing when the day is shorter than 12 hours. Flowering period is in spring. P special cactus mixture.

Kalanchoe tomentosa
Panda Plant / fam. Crassulaceae
○ ◖ ⊗ ⊙ ⊖ ▣
One of the most beautiful species. The matted leaves have brown and milled tips and their arrangement on the stem is decussate. Do not water in cool weather. S special cactus mixture.

Kalanchoe tubiflora (Bryophyllum tubiflorum) / fam. Crassulaceae
○ ⊞ ⊗ ⊖ ▣
Small plant with thin, cylinder-shaped leaves. Plantlets formed exclusively at the leaf tips. P pot up the young plantlets.

Kohleria amabilis (Tydaea amabilis, Isoloma amabilis) / fam. Gesneriaceae
◖ ⊞ ⊗ ⊖ ▣
Small greenhouse plant which must be overwintered at 10–12°C (50–53°F). Pot up every spring in a mixture of leafmould, farmyard manure and sand. P seed, shoot tip cuttings, division of rhizomes.

Kohleria bogotensis (Isoloma bogotensis, Tydaea picta) / fam. Gesneriaceae
◖ ⊞ ⊗ ⊖ ▣
The scaly rhizome of this kohleria is occasionally offered for sale. Leaves must not be allowed to die off completely in the winter. Treat like K. amabilis.

Kohleria eriantha (Isoloma erianthum)
fam. Gesneriaceae
◖ ⊞ ⊗ ⊖ ▣
Flowering period August–September. This species comes in several richly flowering cultivars chiefly found in the greenhouses of amateurs specialising in them. Treat like K. amabilis.

Lachenalia aloides hybrid (Phormium aloides) / fam. Liliaceae
○ ◖ ⊖ ⊗ ⊖ ▣ ▣
Pot the bulbs in September in loamy soil and keep at 9–14°C (48–57°F). Blooms in February–March and then sheds its leaves. Keep dry from May onwards. P offsets.

79

Lachenalia bulbifera (L. pendula)
fam. *Liliaceae*
○ ❀ ☻ ∞ ☺ ▣
An attractive bulbous plant which likes to be put out in the summer. Keep in an unheated greenhouse or cool room during the winter. Flowers from January to March. Treat like *L. aloides* hybrid.

× ***Laeliocattleya 'Hugo de Groot'***
fam. *Orchidaceae*
◑ ❀ ☻ ∞ ☺ ▣
A cross between *Cattleya* and *Laelia*. Rest this large-flowered orchid at 15°C (59°F). S equal parts sphagnum moss and osmunda fibre. P division in the spring.

Lagerstroemia indica
fam. *Lythraceae*
○ ❀ ☻ ∞ ☺ ▣
Deciduous container plant with very beautifully shaped flowers. Overwinter at 2–5°C (35–41°F). Cut back, especially older plants, in March–April. S loamy. P seed and cuttings.

Lampranthus blandus
fam. *Aizoaceae*
○ ❀ ☻ ☺ ▣
Plant with procumbent stems carrying small fleshy leaves, round and flattened on top. Large purple flowers in profusion. S cactus mixture. P shoot tip cuttings will root easily.

Lapeirousia laxa (Gladiolus laxus, Anomatheca cruenta) / fam. *Iridaceae*
○ ❀ ☻ ∞ ☺ ▣
Pot the tubers in September and keep at about 12°C (53°F). Water less after flowering in spring, allowing the foliage to die off. Keep the tubers dry. P seed, offsets.

Laurus nobilis
Sweet Bay / fam. *Lauraceae*
○ ❀ ☻ ∞ ☺ ▣
Container plant. Overwinter at no less than 2°C (35°F). Prevent premature budding in the spring. S potting compost with a little extra loam. P shoot tip cuttings in September. Protect from frost.

Leptocladodia elongata (Mammillaria elongata) / fam. *Cactaceae*
○ ❀ ☻ ☻ ☺ ▣
Freely clustering cactus with cylindrical joints. Flowers yellow or white with a central red stripe. Keep cool and dry in the winter. P seed or cuttings.

Leptospermum scoparium
fam. *Myrtaceae*
○ ❀ ☻ ∞ ☺ ▣
A rather variable species with fragrant leaves. Keep this container plant at 5–12°C (41–53°F) in winter. Put out in summer. S loam, sand, leafmould and manure. P shoot tip cuttings, seed.

Leuchtenbergia principis
fam. *Cactaceae*
○ ❀ ☻ ☻ ☺ ▣
Cactus with an elongated tap root. The blunt tubercles are topped with straw-yellow, paper-like spines. Yellow flowers are borne on young tubercles. P seed.

Lycaste

Liriope muscari 'Variegatus' (Ophiopogon muscari 'Variegatus')/fam. Liliaceae

The flowers are followed by black berries. Winter temperature 5–15°C (41–59°F). Keep indoors in the summer. The green-leaved species is more tolerant of shade. P division, seed.

Liriope spicata (Ophiopogon spicatus) fam. Liliaceae

Beautiful and easily cultivated plant. Treat like L. muscari. A little extra clay can be mixed with the potting ground but this is not essential.

Lithops bromfieldii
Living Stones / fam. Aizoaceae

Two flat, semicircular leaves with red markings serve this plant as a water reservoir. The yellow daisy-like flowers appear in slits between the leaves in September.

Lithops ruschiorum
Living Stones / fam. Aizoaceae

The two very thick leaves of this plant are fused together except for a small groove. Keep dry and cool in winter. A new corpusculum is formed under the old, shrivelled skin in May.

Littonia modesta
fam. Liliaceae

Pot up in March in loam, leafmould and farmyard manure. Place in a warm spot but move to a cooler position when leaves have come out. Keep dry in winter at 12°C (53°F). P seed, root cuttings.

Lobivia famatimensis (L. pectinifera) fam. Cactaceae

Cylindrical, reddish-brown cactus with 20 ribs and short spines. Yellow bell-shaped flowers with a green throat. Winter rest essential for flowering. S cactus mixture. P seed or cuttings.

Lobivia hertrichiana
fam. Cactaceae

Bright green plant with six to eleven ribs. Begins to produce large, scarlet blooms when still very young. Overwinter dry at 5–8°C (41–46°F). Needs a great deal of fresh air. Propagate like L. famatimensis.

Lobivia nealeana
fam. Cactaceae

Low cylindrical cactus with 14 ribs, short, needle-shaped spines and large, bright red flowers. Easy to grow and free flowering, provided it has a winter rest. P as L. famatimensis.

Lycaste cruenta
fam. Orchidaceae

Spring-flowering orchid, suitable indoors or for the cool greenhouse. Minimum winter temperature 5°C (41°F). Pot in osmunda fibre, sphagnum moss, leafmould, loam and argex granules. P division.

81

Lycaste lasioglossa (Maxillaria lasioglossa)/fam. Orchidaceae

Spring-flowering plant for the intermediate greenhouse or for the house. Minimum winter temperature 12°C (53°F). Ensure a good supply of fresh air. Cultivate like *L. cruenta*.

Lycaste virginalis (L. skinneri) fam. Orchidaceae

This winter-flowering orchid is the best-known species of *Lycaste*. In contrast to the other species it reacts badly to temperature fluctuations. Treat like *L. cruenta*.

Macroplectrum sesquipedale (Angraecum sesquipedale)/fam. Orchidaceae

Winter-flowering orchid for the heated greenhouse. Minimum winter temperature 16°C (60°F). S osmunda fibre or beech root and sphagnum moss. P seed (a job for specialists!).

Malvastrum capense fam. Malvaceae

An old-fashioned plant, now rarely seen. Put out in the summer; winter temperature 8–10°C (46–50°F). You might add a little loam to the potting mixture. P tip cuttings and seed.

Malvaviscus arboreus fam. Malvaceae

An attractive winter-flowering plant with flowers in a striking colour. Winter temperature 10–15°C (50–59°F). Add a little extra loam to the potting mixture. P cuttings or seed.

Mammillaria albicans fam. Cactaceae

Originally spherical but later cylindrical, freely clustering cactus with woolly axils. Relatively large pink flowers. Keep dry at 6–12°C (43–53°F) in winter. P seed or cuttings.

Mammillaria bachmannii fam. Cactaceae

Dark green semi-spherical cactus with a slightly sunken cap. Woolly zones between the axils; black central thorns; pink flowers. S special cactus mixture. P seed.

Mammillaria bellacantha fam. Cactaceae

Globular, dark green cactus with white radial and reddish-brown central spines. Woolly axils; pink flowers. S cactus mixture. P seed at soil temperature of 25°C (77°F).

Mammillaria elongata var. echinaria fam. Cactaceae

Resembles *Leptocladodia elongata* but has pale yellow spines. The central spines are 1 cm (½ in) long. Bears white or cream flowers just beneath the top. S cactus mixture.

Mammillaria parkinsonii
fam. *Cactaceae*
○ ⊕ ⊗ ⊙ ⊤
Often develops new growing points to form large clumps. Yellow flowers, up to 2 cm (¾ in) across. P seed.

Mammillaria pennispinosa
fam. *Cactaceae*
○ ⊕ ⊗ ⊙ ⊤
Light marginal spines and red, hooked central spines, all feathery. White flowers with a pink central stripe. The photograph shows a specimen bearing fruits.

Mammillaria plumosa
fam. *Cactaceae*
○ ⊕ ⊙ ⊙ ⊤
Very popular cactus with white, softly feathered spines resembling fluffs of down. Grafting ensures that plants are vigorous. P cuttings or seed.

Mammillaria prolifera var. *texana*
fam. *Cactaceae*
○ ⊕ ⊗ ⊙ ⊙ ⊤
Easily grown, clustering variety with brown spines and yellowish flowers. Very decorative red fruits. S cactus mixture. P offsets root readily.

Mammillaria rhodantha
fam. *Cactaceae*
○ ⊕ ⊕ ⊗ ⊙ ⊤
Globular, later cylindrical cactus that often divides to form large clumps. Conical tubercles; white woolly areoles. Magenta-red flowers. P seed.

Mammillaria sheldonii
fam. *Cactaceae*
○ ⊕ ⊙ ⊙ ⊤
Large-flowered mammillaria which is sometimes difficult to cultivate, and is therefore best grafted. Large pink, white-edged flowers. P offsets, seed.

Mammillaria spinosissima
fam. *Cactaceae*
○ ⊕ ⊗ ⊙ ⊙ ⊤
Cylindrical cactus with woolly caps and axils. The areoles have 20–30 radial and 7–10 central spines. Rest in winter at 5–10°c (41–50°F).

Mammillaria vagaspina
fam. *Cactaceae*
○ ⊕ ⊙ ⊙ ⊤
Globular grey-green cactus with a short stem and woolly growing point. Grey-brown central spines up to 6 cm (2¼ in) long. Creamy white flowers. Overwinter in a cool spot. S cactus mixture. P seed.

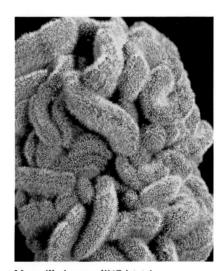

Mammillaria vaupelii 'Cristata'
fam. *Cactaceae*
○ ⊕ ⊙ ⊙ ⊤
Really a misshapen variety of the spherical *M. vaupelii*. The crests will sometimes emerge spontaneously from seed.

Mammillaria

Mammillaria winteriae
fam. Cactaceae
○ ⊕ ⊙ ⊚ ⊖ Ⓣ
Globular, bluish-green cactus with square tubercles and woolly axils. Radial spines up to 3 cm (1 in) long. Creamy flowers up to 3 cm (1 in) across with a yellow central stripe. S cactus mixture. P seed.

Mammillaria zeilmanniana
fam. Cactaceae
○ ⊕ ⊗ ⊙ ⊖ Ⓣ
A cluster-type cactus densely covered in spines. Central spines hook-shaped. Flowers readily with beautiful, bell-shaped reddish-violet or less frequently white flowers. P seed or cuttings.

Manettia inflata
fam. Rubiaceae
◐ ⊕ ⊗ ⊙ ⊖ Ⓣ
This climbing plant flowers from spring to autumn, preferably in an intermediate greenhouse. Winter temperature 12–25°C (53–59°F). Add a little extra loam to the potting compost. P seed or cuttings.

Maranta bicolor (Calathea bicolor)
fam. Marantaceae
◐ ⊕ ⊗ ⊚ Ⓣ
Glorious small foliage plant for the heated greenhouse. Minimum winter temperature 14°C (57°F). Pot in pinewood soil mixed with well-rotted farmyard manure. Will do well in a border. P division.

Maranta leuconeura
fam. Marantaceae
◐ ⊕ ⊗ ⊚ Ⓣ
This species is not offered for sale very often because the cultivars are less demanding and have more spectacular leaves. Treat like *M. bicolor*.

Maranta leuconeura 'Erythroneura'
fam. Marantaceae
◐ ⊕ ⊗ ⊚ Ⓣ
One of several cultivars fairly well suited to indoor cultivation. Water and spray with tepid soft water. Cultivate like *M. bicolor*.

Maranta leuconeura 'Fascinator'
fam. Marantaceae
◐ ⊕ ⊗ ⊚ Ⓣ
Magnificent foliage plant that can be kept indoors with a little special care. Excellent in a mixed plant container. Treat like *M. bicolor*.

Maranta leuconeura 'Kerchoveana'
Prayer Plant / fam. Marantaceae
◐ ⊕ ⊗ ⊚ Ⓣ
The easiest maranta to grow as a house plant. Like all others it carries insignificant white or pink flowers in a raceme. Treat like *M. bicolor*.

Masdevallia 'Doris'
fam. Orchidaceae
◐ ◑ ⊙ ⊗ ⊚ Ⓣ
Autumn-flowering orchid for a cool, shady spot. Minimum temperature 10°C (50°F). Does not have a proper resting period. Pot in sphagnum moss and osmunda fibre. P division.

Medinilla magnifica
fam. *Melastomataceae*
Ⓘ 🌡 ⊚ ⊜ 🔟
Unusual plant, best in a heated greenhouse.
Minimum winter temperature 15°C (59°F).
S loam, leafmould, well-rotted manure and
sand, at 2:2:1:1. P shoot tip cuttings at soil
temperature 30–35°C (86–95°F).

Melocactus bahiensis
Turk's Cap / fam. *Cactaceae*
○ 🌡 ⊙ ⊜ 🔟
Mature specimens may develop a cephalium,
a woolly reddish swelling at the top from
which the flowers appear and later make fruit.
P seed.

Melocactus maxonii
Melon Cactus / fam. *Cactaceae*
○ 🌡 ⊙ ⊜ 🔟
Cactus with 12 prominent ribs with covered
reddish spines. Produces a cephalium when
mature. Minimum winter temperature 10°C
(50°F). S special cactus mixture. P seed or
possibly grafts of young plants.

Microcoelum weddellianum (Cocos weddel-
liana) / Dwarf Coconut Palm / fam. *Palmae*
Ⓘ 🌡 🌡 ⊚ ⊜ 🔟
A palm for the heated greenhouse. It can be
kept indoors provided it receives extra
attention. Minimum temperature 18°C (64°F) all
the year. S pinewood soil with a little farmyard
manure. P seed.

Microlepia platyphylla (Davallia
lonchitidea) / fam. *Dennstaedtiaceae*
Ⓘ 🌡 🌡 ⊚ ⊜ 🔟
Fern with mellow green leaves for the heated
greenhouse. Overwinter at 15–17°C (59–62°F).
Pot in the spring in leafmould, farmyard
manure and sand, in porportions 3:2:1.
P division, spores.

Microlepia speluncae
fam. *Dennstaedtiaceae*
Ⓘ 🌡 🌡 ⊚ ⊜ 🔟
'Cristata' has fronds that are broadened at the
tip. Feed every two weeks during the growing
period. Treat like *M. platyphylla.*

Mikania ternata (M. apiifolia)
fam. *Compositae*
○ Ⓘ 🌡 ⊚ ⊜ 🔟
Small hanging or creeping plant with foliage
in an unusual colour. Rest at 12–15°C (53–59°F).
Pot in leafmould and loam mixed with
farmyard manure and sand. P division,
cuttings, seed.

Miltonia hybrid
fam. *Orchidaceae*
Ⓘ 🌡 🌡 ⊚ ⊜ 🔟
The flowers of this orchid are reminiscent of
pansies though they are much showier. Treat
like *M. paterson* × 'Limelight'. P division.

Miltonia paterson × 'Limelight'
fam. *Orchidaceae*
Ⓘ 🌡 🌡 ⊚ ⊜ 🔟
Keep as cool as possible from May on. At the
end of October raise temperature to 6–10°C
(43–50°F). After flowering, pot in sphagnum
moss and osmunda fibre with expanded clay
granules. P division.

85

Miltonia spectabilis* var. *bicolor
fam. *Orchidaceae*

Has solitary flowers like the species. The pseudobulbs bear two tongue-shaped leaves. Flowers appear in August. Cultivate and propagate like *Miltonia paterson* × 'Limelight'.

Miltoniopsis vexillaria (Odontoglossum vexillarium)* / fam. *Orchidaceae

This orchid flowers in May when it should be moved to brighter position at 10°C (50°F). Feed lightly every two weeks in the growing period. Pot in special orchid mixture. P division and seed.

Mimosa pudica
Humble Plant / fam. *Leguminosae*

At 18°C (64°F) or more the leaflets fold together when touched. Grow annually from seed. S leafmould, loam, farmyard manure and sand. P seed with soil temperature 20–25°C (68–77°F).

Monstera deliciosa (Philodendron pertusum)
Swiss Cheese Plant / fam. *Araceae*

Only older leaves have the characteristic perforations. Very vigorous plant. Minimum winter temperature 12°C (53°F). S standard potting compost. P seed, cuttings, air-layering.

***Monstera deliciosa* 'Variegata'**
Swiss Cheese Plant / fam. *Araceae*

Demands more light than the species if the leaf markings are to be brought out to full effect. 'Borsigiata' has green leaves but is smaller in all parts than the species. Treat like *M. deliciosa*.

Monstera obliqua* var. *expilata (M. o.* 'Leicht-linii') / Swiss Cheese Plant / fam. *Araceae

All the leaves of this plant have perforations. Not very vigorous grower and hence not so popular. Treat like *M. deliciosa*. P division, seed.

Murraya paniculata (M. exotica)
fam. *Rutaceae*

Unusual plant with deliciously fragrant flowers. Winter temperature 12–15°C (53–59°F). Pot in equal parts pinewood soil, farmyard manure and sand. P shoot tip cuttings and seed at 30°C (86°F).

Musa* × *paradisiaca (M.* × *sapientum)
Banana / fam. *Musaceae*

Very large plant which needs extra light on dark winter days. Keep at a minimum temperature of 12°C (53°F). Pot in equal parts loam, leafmould and farmyard manure. P suckers.

Myrtillocactus geometrizans
fam. *Cactaceae*

Cylindrical cactus covered with a light blue bloom. Six regular ribs with few spines. Several fragrant white flowers can emerge from one and the same areole. The fruits resemble bilberries.

Myrtus communis
Myrtle / fam. **Myrtaceae**
○ 🌱 ∞ 🌿 🕐
Old-fashioned container plant with fragrant leaves and flowers. Winter temperature 4–12°C (59–53°F). S pinewood soil with farmyard manure. P shoot tip cuttings, seed.

Narcissus 'Carlton'
Narcissus / fam. **Amaryllidaceae**
🌓 🌱 ∞ 🌿 🕐
Pot bulbs in October in equal parts proprietary potting compost and sand, and bury pots outside. Bring indoors towards the end of January and stand in a cool place.

Narcissus 'Grand Soleil d'Or'
Narcissus / fam. **Amaryllidaceae**
🌓 🌱 ∞ 🌿 🕐
This and 'Paperwhite' are the only cultivars which do not need a plunging period in darkness. Plant in bowls containing gravel or a mixture of potting compost and sand between September and February.

Nautilocalyx lynchii (Alloplectus lynchii)
fam. **Gesneriaceae**
🌓 🌱 ∞ 🌿 🕐
The creamy flowers with light red throat are borne in clusters. Winter temperature 16–18°C (60–64°F). Pot in leafmould or small chunks of peat with manure and sand. P tip cuttings or seed.

Nematanthus strigillosus (Hypocyrta strigillosa) / fam. **Gesneriaceae**
🌓 🌱 ∞ 🌿 🕐
Winter temperature of 10–14°C (50–57°F) encourages good bud formation. May be put out in summer. Pot in leafmould with sphagnum moss and charcoal. P seed, shoot tip cuttings, division.

Nematanthus strigillosus 'Variegatus'
fam. **Gesneriaceae**
🌓 🌱 ∞ 🌿 🕐
This attractive variegated cultivar is not often offered for sale. Excellent for growing in hanging baskets. Cultivate like N. strigillosus.

Neoporteria paucicostata
fam. **Cactaceae**
○ 🌱 ⊙ 🌿 🕐
Bluish-green globular cactus with off-white areoles. Sturdy spines, black at first, later rather lighter in colour. Rose-white flowers. Winter rest starts September. Flowers as early as February.

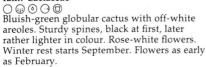

Neoporteria senilis (N. gerocephala)
fam. **Cactaceae**
○ 🌱 ⊙ 🌿 🕐
The spines of this cactus are irregularly curved and intertwined across the entire body. Red flowers. Grafting is recommended. P seed.

Neoporteria wagenknechtii
fam. **Cactaceae**
○ 🌱 ⊙ 🌿 🕐
Globular, later cylindrical, cactus with long, hard, greyish-brown spines and purple flowers. Grafting encourages growth and flowering. S cactus mixture. P seed.

Neoregelia carolinae (Aregelia c., Nidularium meyendorffii)/fam. Bromeliaceae

Must be grown in a warm greenhouse. Minimum winter temperature, 15–18°C (59–64°F). Foliage at flowering time an attractive colour. S leafmould, sphagnum moss and manure. P offsets, seed.

Neoregelia carolinae 'Stricata' fam. Bromeliaceae

Shops generally offer specimens already flowering. These are, in fact, in the process of dying, so there is no problem about cultivation. Otherwise treat like *N. carolinae.* P offsets.

Neoregelia carolinae 'Tricolor' fam. Bromeliaceae

Flowering specimens will retain their appeal longer if kept cool at about 12°C (53°F). The flowering rosette dies after about six months. Cultivate like *N. carolinae.* P offsets.

Neoregelia concentrica (Aregelia c., Nidularium acanthocrater)/fam. Bromeliaceae

Small blue flowers are borne deep in the 'vase' of the rosette of this plant. A number of attractive cultivars are grown. Treat like *N. carolinae.* P seed, offsets.

Nepenthes hybrid Pitcher Plant/fam. Nepenthaceae

Carnivorous epiphyte for the warm greenhouse. Minimum winter temperature 18°C (64°F). Pot in a hanging basket in osmunda fibre, leafmould, sphagnum moss and manure. P leaf cuttings.

Nephrolepis cordifolia 'Plumosa' Sword Fern/fam. Oleandraceae

Graceful fern for the greenhouse. Can be kept indoors for a year if it is tended very carefully. Winter temperature 14–18°C (57–64°F). S leafmould, farmyard manure and sand. P stolons.

Nephrolepis exaltata 'Maassii' Sword Fern/fam. Oleandraceae

Unlike *N. cordifolia,* this fern has no tubers. Over the years, a great many cultivars have appeared. Cultivate like *N. c.* 'Plumosa'.

Nephrolepis exaltata 'Rooseveltii' Sword Fern/fam. Oleandraceae

Sword Ferns often do well in bathrooms where there is plenty of shade and moisture. Feed lightly during the growing period. Treat like *N. cordifolia* 'Plumosa'.

Nephrolepsis exaltata 'Teddy Junior' Sword Fern/fam. Oleandraceae

This, like other Sword Fern cultivars, can only be propagated from stolons. The natural species can also be grown from spores. Treat like *N. cordifolia* 'Plumosa'.

Nerium oleander (double, pink)
Oleander / fam. ***Apocynaceae***
○ ⬚ ⊛ ⬚ ⬚
Attractive container plant with a great need
for fresh air. Winter temperature 5–10°C (41–
50°F). S loam, leafmould, farmyard manure
and blood meal, in a plastic container. P seed,
cuttings.

Nerium oleander (white)
Oleander / fam. ***Apocynaceae***
○ ⬚ ⊛ ⬚ ⬚
This container plant should be put outside
early in the spring – a touch of night frost
does less damage than premature growth.
Treat like last entry.

Nertera granadensis (N. depressa)
Bead Plant / fam. ***Rubiaceae***
○ ⬚ ⊛ ⬚ ⬚
Try to keep the temperature below 13°C (55°F)
at all times. Minimum winter temperature 5–
10°C (41–50°F). Pot in loam, leafmould and
well-rotted farmyard manure. P seed and
division.

***Nopalxochia phyllanthoides* 'Grandiflorum'**
fam. ***Cactaceae***
◐ ⬚ ⊛ ○ ⬚ ⬚
Large fleshy leaves bearing very large, 10-cm
(4-in) long, red flowers. Do not turn this plant
once buds appear. S cactus mixture. P leaf
cuttings.

Notocactus horstii (Malacocarpus horstii)
fam. ***Cactaceae***
○ ◐ ⊞ ⊛ ⬚ ⬚
Cylindrical cactus topped with white wool.
Older plants have curving ribs. Yellow
flowers. S cactus mixture. P graft weaker
specimens; otherwise grow from seed.

Notocactus leninghausii (Eriocactus
leninghausii)* / fam. *Cactaceae
○ ◐ ⊞ ⊛ ⬚ ⬚
Branching cylindrical cactus with
approximately 30 ribs. Elongated, densely
packed golden-yellow spines. Older
specimens bear large, glossy, yellow flowers
on one side of the stem.

***Notocactus mammulosus* 'Masollerensis'**
fam. ***Cactaceae***
○ ◐ ⊞ ⊛ ⬚ ⬚
Green cactus, slightly cylindrical in shape,
with 18–20 ribs. The top is covered with
white wool. Sulphur-yellow flowers, reddish
on the outside and with red stigmas. S cactus
mixture. P seed.

Notocacus ottonis (Malacocarpus ottonis)
fam. ***Cactaceae***
○ ◐ ⬚ ⊛ ⬚ ⬚
Bright green cactus with 10–13 ribs, yellow
radial spines, reddish-brown central spines.
Flowers readily, producing brilliant white
flowers, woolly brown outside. These stay open
for well over four days.

Notocactus purpureus (Malacocarpus
purpureus)* / fam. *Cactaceae
○ ◐ ⊞ ⊛ ⬚ ⬚
Globular, later somewhat cylindrical species.
Top woolly and slightly sunken. Flowers,
purple to salmon coloured, appear at the top.
Overwinter at 10°C (50°F). P sow at 25°C (77°F).

Obregonia denegrii
fam. *Cactaceae*

◯ ⊕ ⊗ ⊝ ⊡

The stem of this cactus is covered with leaf-like tubercles set with tiny spines. The woolly top carries small white flowers. Not suitable for indoor cultivation. S cactus mixture.

Ochna serrulata (O. multiflora)
fam. *Ochnaceae*

◯ ⊕ ⊗ ⊝ ⊡

The fruits of this uncommon plant are black. Flowers in March–April. Minimum winter temperature 10–15°C (50–59°F). S potting mixture with a little extra loam. P seed, cuttings.

× Odontioda 'Lilly Menuet'
fam. *Orchidaceae*

◐ ⊕ ⊗ ⊝ ⊡

One of many beautiful crosses between *Cochlioda* and *Odontoglossum*. Winter temperature 15°C (59°F). Pot in sphagnum moss and osmunda fibre. P division.

× Odontocidium 'Anneliese Rothenberger'
fam. *Orchidaceae*

◐ ⊕ ⊗ ⊝ ⊡

A cross between *Odontoglossum* and *Oncidium*. Minimum winter temperature 15°C (59°F). Pot in basic mixture of sphagnum moss and osmunda fibre. P division.

× Odontocidium 'Tiger Hambuhren'
fam. *Orchidaceae*

◐ ⊕ ⊗ ⊝ ⊡

Spring-flowering cross between *Odontoglossum* and *Oncidium*. Feed lightly during the growing period. Treat like *O*. 'Anneliese Rothenberger'.

Odontoglossum bictoniense
fam. *Orchidaceae*

◐ ⊕ ⊖ ⊗ ⊝ ⊡

Autumn-flowering orchid for indoor cultivation. Keep dry for one month after flowering. Winter temperature about 10°C (50°F). Pot in mixture of sphagnum moss and osmunda. P seed, division.

Odontoglossum grande
fam. *Orchidaceae*

◐ ⊕ ⊖ ⊗ ⊝ ⊡

The strongest and best-known species for cultivation as a house plant. Several cultivars are available. Feed lightly during the growing period. Treat like *O. bictoniense*.

Odontoglossum pulchellum
fam. *Orchidaceae*

◐ ⊕ ⊖ ⊗ ⊝ ⊡

Flowering period February–April. The attractive white flowers have a delightful fragrance. Always water with tepid, lime-free water, preferably rainwater. Treat like *O. bictoniense*.

× Odontonia 'Boussole Blanche'
fam. *Orchidaceae*

◐ ⊕ ⊗ ⊝ ⊡

A cross between *Miltonia* and *Odontoglossum*. Pot in a mixture of osmunda fibre and sphagnum moss. P division.

Olea europea
Olive / fam. *Oleaceae*
〇 🐛 🕸 🜃 📖
Container plant which prefers a winter
temperature of 5–10°C (41–50°F). Feed every
two weeks in the growing period. S potting
compost with a little extra loam. P seed,
softwood tip cuttings.

Oncidium flexuosum
fam. *Orchidaceae*
◑ 🐛 🕸 🜃 📖
Usually flowers between September and
December. Rest in winter at 12–16°C (53–60°F).
Pot in a mixture of 2 parts osmunda fibre to 1
part sphagnum moss. P division, seed.

Oncidium incurvum (O. albo-violaceum)
fam. *Orchidaceae*
◑ 🐛 🕸 🜃 📖
Autumn-flowering orchid from Mexico. Rest
during the winter at 10–12°C (50–53°F). Pot in
sphagnum moss and osmunda fibre in
proportions of 1:2. P division, seed.

Oncidium krameranum
fam. *Orchidaceae*
◑ ◑ 🐛 🕸 🜃 📖
Will flower for years in succession from the
same stem, which should therefore not be cut.
Winter temperature 15–18°C (59–64°F). Pot in
osmunda fibre and sphagnum moss at 2:1.
P division, seed.

Oncidium sphacelatum
fam. *Orchidaceae*
◑ 🐛 🕸 🜃 📖
An orchid from Central America. Flowering
period April–June. Rest and keep fairly dry
at 15–18°C (59–64°F). S osmunda fibre and
sphagnum moss in proportions of 2:1.
P division, seed.

Ophiopogon jaburan 'Vittatus'
fam. *Liliaceae*
〇 ◑ 🐛 🕸 🜃 📖
The evergreen species will tolerate less light
than this variety. Overwinter at minimum
temperature of 5°C (41°F). Feed every two
weeks during the growing period. P seed,
runners, division.

Oplismenus hirtellus (Panicum hirtellum)
fam. *Gramineae*
◑ 🐛 🕸 🜃 📖
Attractive hanging plant or ground cover.
Overwinter at 10–16°C (50–60°F). 'Variegatus'
is a splendid strain with variegated leaves.
P rooted runners or tip cuttings.

**Opuntia clavarioides (Austrocylindropuntia
clavarioides)** / fam. *Cactaceae*
〇 🐛 🕸 🜃 📖
Brownish joints, often in the shape of a hand,
sometimes fan shaped. Must be grafted on to
a vigorous *Opuntia*. Yellow-brown flowers,
rarely seen in cultivation.

Opuntia clavarioides var. cristata 'Minima'
fam. *Cactaceae*
〇 🐛 🐛 🕸 🜃 📖
Crested variety with elongated, almost
spherical joints. This variety, too, has to be
grafted. S cactus mixture. P graft offsets on to
a vigorous *Opuntia*.

Opuntia

Opuntia ficus-indica
Indian Fig Cactus / fam. *Cactaceae*
〇⊕⊕⊕◎⊖⊛⊜⊡
Oblong discs up to 50 cm (20 in) long. Thin, nearly spineless pads of a yellowish colour and orange-red flowers. Suitable as a stock for grafting. S cactus mixture. P rooting of discs.

Opuntia microdasys 'Albispina'
Bunny Ear / fam. *Cactaceae*
〇⊕⊕⊛◎⊖⊡
Small, flat, nearly circular discs, their areoles covered with bundles of white tufts. Yellow flowers. S standard potting compost.
P cuttings (joints).

Opuntia microdasys var. *undulata*
fam. *Cactaceae*
〇⊕⊕⊛◎⊖⊛⊜⊡
Flattened joints fairly densely covered with golden-yellow tufts. On the slightest contact, the short spines will enter the skin and are awkward to remove.

Opuntia rufida
Cinnamon Cactus / fam. *Cactaceae*
〇⊛⊛⊛◎⊖⊜
Circular joints up to 15 cm (6 in) long, greyish green with thick reddish-brown tufts. Yellow or orange flowers, rarely seen on cultivated plants. P cuttings of joints; seeds soaked in water.

Opuntia scheeri
fam. *Cactaceae*
〇⊕⊕⊛◎⊖⊛⊜⊡
Large, flat, bluish-green oval joints up to 30 cm (1 ft) long. Areoles covered with brownish tufts. Bright yellow flowers. Keep cool in winter but not completely dry.
P cuttings.

Opuntia tunicata (Cylindropuntia tunicata)
fam. *Cactaceae*
〇⊕⊛⊛◎⊖⊡
The round joints are densely covered with near-white long spines which readily drop off. These are tipped by barbs which stick in the skin on contact.

Opuntia vulgaris (O. monacantha)
fam. *Cactaceae*
〇⊕⊕⊛◎⊖⊛⊜⊡
Bright green oval joints with small leaves on new growth. Usually one spine to each areole. S potting compost or cactus mixture.
P oblique disc cuttings.

Oreocereus celsianus
fam. *Cactaceae*
〇⊛⊛⊛⊖⊡
Cylindrical cactus covered in wool, with 10–20 ribs, tough yellow spines and rose-red flowers. Needs high daytime warmth but must be cool at night, down to 0°c (32°F).
S cactus mixture. P seed.

Oreopanax capitatus (O. nymphaeifolius)
fam. *Araliaceae*
〇⊕⊛⊛⊖⊜
Fast-growing plant reminiscent of ivy, even including its inflorescences. Overwinter at 10–15°c (50–59°F). P root tip cuttings under glass at 30–35°c (86–95°F).

Pachystachys

Oxalis deppei (O. esculenta)
Lucky Clover / **fam.** *Oxalidaceae*
This hardy four-leaved clover is usually sold
at about Christmas time, when it can be kept
for a time in a cool room. P loamy soil.
P offsets, division.

Oxalis purpurea (O. variabilis)
fam. *Oxalidaceae*
This clover is suitable for indoor cultivation.
Flowers in an attractive colour appear in
October–December. Overwinter at 10°C (50°F).
S light, loamy soil. P division, offsets.

Oxalis vulcanicola
fam. *Oxalidaceae*
This clover prefers a border in the
greenhouse, where it can serve as ground
cover or as a hanging plant. Treat like *O.
purpurea*. P division, offsets.

Pachycereus pringlei
fam. *Cactaceae*
Cylindrical cactus which can reach a height
of 11 m (36 ft). The funnel-shaped flowers
appear on older plants. Overwinter at a cool
temperature; water sparingly or the plant may
grow straggly.

Pachyphytum funifera
fam. *Crassulaceae*
Easily grown succulent with thick, oval leaves
which do not form a proper rosette. Red
flowers. Water carefully. Keep cool and dry in
the winter. P leaf cuttings.

Pachyphytum marneriana
fam. *Crassulaceae*
Fleshy small leaves with a blue bloom in a
loose rosette. Red flowers. Overwinter dry at
5°C (41°F). S cactus mixture. P rooted leaves or
tip cuttings.

Pachypodium lamerei
fam. *Apocynaceae*
Resembles a cactus. Cylindrical body crowned
with lanceolate leaves. When the foliage dies,
it is time to stop watering. Minimum winter
temperature 13°C (55°F). P imported seed.

Pachypodium lamerei var. cristata
fam. *Apocynaceae*
Crested form of *P. lamerei*. Hairless spines.
New leaves may appear on the top after
winter, in which case resume watering but be
very sparing. S mixture of leafmould and clay-
based loam.

Pachystachys lutea
fam. *Acanthaceae*
The chief attraction of these plants is their
yellow bracts. Overwinter at 14–18°C (57–
64°F). Feed every two weeks during the
growing season. P cuttings.

93

Pachyveria

×*Pachyveria clavifolium*
fam. *Crassulaceae*
○ ⊕ ⊛ ○ ◔ ⊡
Blue-green leaves with reddish margins form
an extended rosette widest above the centre.
Flowers white outside, red inside. P leaf or
tip cuttings.

×*Pachyveria* 'Glauca'
fam. *Crassulaceae*
○ ⊕ ⊛ ○ ◔ ⊡
Cross between *Echeveria* and *Pachyphytum*.
Rosette with 6-cm (2¼-in) long spatular, fleshy
leaves. Overwinter cool and dry. Red flowers.
S cactus mixture. P leaf and tip cuttings.

Pandanus veitchii
Screw Pine / fam. *Pandanaceae*
◑ ⊕ ⊛ ⊜ ◔ ⊡
Keep out of reach of people passing, as the
spines are exceedingly sharp. Minimum
water temperature 18°C (64°F). S potting
compost, loam and beech leafmould. P offsets.

Paphiopedilum fairieanum
Slipper Orchid / fam. *Orchidaceae*
◑ ⊕ ⊛ ⊜ ◔ ⊡
An orchid for the cold to intermediate
greenhouse flowering summer and early
autumn. Minimum winter temperature 14°C
(57°F). Repot February in sphagnum with 5
per cent osmunda fibre. P division.

Paphiopedilum hybrid 'F. M. Ogilvie'
Slipper Orchid / fam. *Orchidaceae*
◑ ⊕ ⊛ ⊜ ◔ ⊡
A cultivar liked for its cut flowers. Minimum
winter temperature 14°C (57°F). Dress with
lime-free fertiliser during the growing period.
S sphagnum moss with 5 per cent osmunda
fibre. P division.

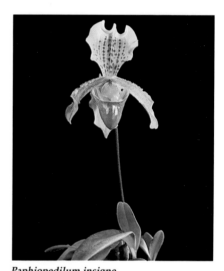

Paphiopedilum insigne
Slipper Orchid / fam. *Orchidaceae*
◑ ◔ ⊛ ⊜ ◔ ⊡
This species comes in many varieties.
Flowering period autumn to spring.
Minimum winter temperature 10°C (50°F).
Repot in February in sphagnum moss with 5
per cent osmunda. P division.

Paphiopedilum sukhakulii
Slipper Orchid / fam. *Orchidaceae*
◑ ⊕ ⊛ ⊜ ◔ ⊡
Suitable for a heated greenhouse or room.
Maintain a winter temperature of 18°C (64°F).
Repot in June in sphagnum moss with 5 per
cent osmunda fibre. Flowers in autumn.
P division.

Paphiopedilum venustum
Slipper Orchid / fam. *Orchidaceae*
◑ ⊕ ◔ ⊛ ⊜ ⊡
Species with variegated leaves which needs
to be kept cool. Winter temperature about
14°C (57°F). Flowers in late autumn to winter.
S sphagnum moss with 5 per cent osmunda.
P division.

Parodia aureispina
fam. *Cactaceae*
○ ⊕ ⊛ ○ ◔ ⊡
Small cactus with hooked spines. Very woolly
tufts appear near the growing point from
which several yellow flowers may emerge at
once. S cactus mixture.

Parodia chlorocarpa
fam. *Cactaceae*
○ ⊕ ○ ◯ ▣
Small cactus with large yellow flowers, several of which generally open together. P seed. Seedlings develop very slowly, so that grafting may be preferable.

Parodia commutans
fam. *Cactaceae*
○ ⊕ ○ ◯ ▣
Globular cactus which later becomes elongated. Woolly top. Central spines 2–5 cm (¾–2 in) long and browny-yellow. Yellow flowers. Keep dry and at 5–10°C (41–50°F) in winter. S cactus mixture. P seed.

Parodia gracilis
fam. *Cactaceae*
○ ⊕ ○ ◯ ▣
Originally spherical but later an ovoid cactus. White woolly top bearing yellow flowers. Winter temperature 8–12°C (46–53°F). Keep fairly dry in winter. S cactus mixture. P seed.

Parodia minima
fam. *Cactaceae*
○ ⊕ ○ ◯ ▣
Small cactus which does well when grafted on a rootstock. In that case the plant will flower earlier than it otherwise would. Water the rootstock sparingly in the winter.

Parthenocissus henryana (Vitis henryana)
Chinese Virginia Creeper / fam. *Vitaceae*
○ ◑ ⊕ ○ ∞ ◯ ▣ ▣
Self-attaching climber with tiny green flowers in branched cymes. Minimum winter temperature 2–10°C (35–50°F). Repot in loamy mixture in spring. P half-ripe shoot tip cuttings in summer.

Passiflora alata
Passion Flower / fam. *Passifloraceae*
○ ◑ ⊕ ∞ ◯ ◯ ▣
Likes the border of a cool or intermediate greenhouse. Minimum winter temperature 5–10°C (41–50°F). P layering, seed or half-ripened tip cuttings.

Passiflora caerulea
Passion Flower / fam. *Passifloraceae*
○ ♨ ∞ ◯ ▣
The best Passion Flower for indoor cultivation – it can even be overwintered in a sheltered spot outdoors. Indoor temperature 5–10°C (41–50°F). P see *P. alata*.

Passiflora violacea
Passion Flower / fam. *Passifloraceae*
○ ◑ ⊕ ∞ ◯ ▣
This graceful climber prefers to be in a greenhouse but can be brought indoors from time to time. Winter temperature 5–10°C (41–50°F). P layering, seed or half-ripened tip cuttings.

Pavonia multiflora (P. wiotii)
fam. *Malvaceae*
◑ ⊕ ⊕ ∞ ◯ ▣
The most striking features of this plant are the red sepals. Keep at 12–15°C (53–59°F) in the winter. S leafmould, pinewood soil and farmyard manure. P tip cuttings at 30–35°C (86–95°F).

Pedilanthus

Pedilanthus tithymaloides 'Variegata'
fam. Euphorbiaceae

The species has bright green leaves and
flowers with bright red bracts. Winter
temperature 15–18°c (59–64°F). P shoot tip
cuttings in spring; let the sap coagulate, then
root at 25°c (77°F).

Pelargonium × citrosum 'Variegatum' (P.
crispum) / Lemon-scented Geranium / fam.
Geraniaceae

The leaves smell of lemon. To obtain flowers,
overwinter at 10–12°c (50–53°F). Cut back
slightly in the spring. P cuttings in August.

Pelargonium grandiflorum hybrid 'Marechal
Foch' / French Geranium / fam. Geraniaceae

Sensitive to cold and hence cultivated
indoors. Winter temperature 8–10°c (46–50°F).
Provide sufficient moisture on hot days.
P cuttings in mid-August.

Pelargonium graveolens 'Variegatum'
Rose-scented Geranium / fam. Geraniaceae

Extremely vigorous indoor plant with rose-
scented leaves. The variegated form demands
more light than the green species. Winter
temperature 10–12°c (50–53°F). P cuttings in
August.

Pelargoniaum peltatum 'l'Elegante'
Ivy-leaved Geranium / fam. Geraniaceae

Trailing plant for the balcony that can be put
outside in the middle of May. Will tolerate
winter temperatures down to freezing point.
P very easily from cuttings, preferably in mid-
August.

Pelargonium tetragonum
fam. Geraniaceae

Succulent species with long stems and several
hairy, nearly circular leaves. Overwinter dry
at 10°c (50°F). S cactus mixture. P rooted
cuttings or seed.

Pelargonium zonale hybrid (P. × hortorum)
fam. Geraniaceae

Nearly hardy geranium which can be
overwintered at about 5°c (41°F). Can be put
outside from the middle of May. Feed during
growing period. P cuttings in mid-August.

Pelargonium zonale hybrid 'Dawn'
fam. Geraniaceae

The leaves of *P. zonale* hybrids smell of herbs
when bruised. One and two-year-old
specimens are the most attractive. Treat like
P. zonale hybrid.

Pelargonium zonale hybrid 'Friesdorf'
fam. Geraniaceae

Dwarf variety with fairly small flowers and
deeply cut leaves. Treat like *P. zonale* hybrid.

Pelargonium zonale hybrid 'Lady Cullum'
fam. *Geraniaceae*
○ ◐ ⊗ ⊖ ▣
Striking variegated geranium which must not
be fed too much if the leaf markings are to
remain at their best. Treat like *P. zonale*
hybrid.

Pellaea falcata
fam. *Sinopteridaceae*
◐ ⊕ ⊗ ⊖ ▣
These ferns can be kept in the house all year,
but prefer a winter rest at 12–15°C (53–59°F).
S beech leafmould, peat and farmyard
manure. Does not mind a little chalk.
P division, spores.

Pellaea rotundifolia
fam. *Sinopteridaceae*
◐ ⊕ ⊗ ⊖ ▣
The best-known representative of this genus.
Feed every two weeks in the summer. Treat
like *P. falcata*. P division, spores.

Pellionia pulchra (Elatostema pulchrum)
fam. *Urticaceae*
◐ ⊕ ⊗ ⊖ ▣
Variegated ground-cover plant for the
greenhouse or container. Minimum winter
temperature 12°C (53°F). S leafmould, peat and
farmyard manure; no chalk. P shoot tip
cuttings.

**Pellionia repens (Elatostema repans, P.
daveauana)**/fam. *Urticaceae*
◐ ⊕ ⊗ ⊖ ▣
Adequate light is essential if the attractive
leaf markings are to be preserved. In summer,
feed lightly once every two weeks. Otherwise
treat like *P. pulchra*.

Pentas lanceolata (P. carnea)
fam. *Rubiaceae*
◐ ⊕ ⊗ ⊖ ▣
A plant for the intermediate greenhouse
which can temporarily be kept indoors.
Winter temperature about 12°C (53°F).
S humus-rich loam. P seed, cuttings. Pinch
out the stem tips repeatedly.

**Peperomia argyreia (P. arifolia var.
argyreia)**/fam. *Piperaceae*
◐ ⊕ ⊕ ⊙ ⊖ ▣
The green, lanceolate leaves have half-moon
shaped silver markings and long red stalks.
S see *P. glabella*. P leaf cuttings.

Peperomia blanda
fam. *Piperaceae*
◐ ⊕ ⊕ ⊙ ⊖ ▣
A plant with brownish-red, upright stems.
Leaves in groups of three or four. S see *P.
glabella*. P root the tip cuttings in sandy soil
during the spring.

Peperomia caperata
fam. *Piperaceae*
◐ ⊕ ⊕ ⊙ ⊖ ▣
The ovoid leaves are very waxy and
corrugated between the ribs. P cuttings of leaf
with a short bit of the leafstalk. S see *P.
glabella*.

97

Peperomia

Peperomia clusiifolia (P. obtusifolia var. clusiifolia) / fam. Piperaceae

Large leathery leaves without stalks. The slightly down-curving leaf margins are red. Thin white flower spikes. P leaf cuttings. S see *P. glabella*.

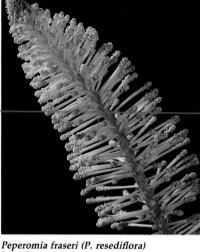

Peperomia fraseri (P. resediflora) fam. Piperaceae

Erect, fleshy branches with heart-shaped, dark green leaves arranged in rosette form along the stem. Shown here is the flower spike with fragrant small white flowers.

Peperomia glabella 'Variegata' fam. Piperaceae

Hanging plant with heart-shaped leaves full of yellow, green and white spots. Very vigorous grower. S mixture of well-rotted leafmould, farmyard manure, peat fibre and sharp sand.

Peperomia griseo-argentea (P. hederifolia) fam. Piperaceae

Long red-striped leaf stalks bearing near-circular green leaves with dark ribs. Pot in well-drained, broad and shallow bowls.

Peperomia metallica fam. Piperaceae

Unbranched upright stems with lanceolate leaves on red leafstalks. The leaves have a green central stripe. S see *P. glabella*. P shoot tip cuttings.

Peperomia obtusifolia (P. magnoliifolia) Desert Privet / fam. Piperaceae

Stiff, shiny, fleshy leaves on short stalks with yellow and green markings. This species needs a great deal of light to retain the beautiful markings. P leaf cuttings.

Peperomia puteolata fam. Piperaceae

Hanging plant with lanceolate, leathery leaves, dark green with five yellow and shiny grooves on the surface. A well-drained pot is essential.

Peperomia rotundifolia (P. nummulariifolia) fam. Piperaceae

Hanging plant with very thin, creeping stems. Small round leaves. If possible give rainwater at room temperature. S see *P. glabella*. P shoot tip cuttings rooted in warm sand at 16°C (60°F).

Peperomia serpens (P. scandens) fam. Piperaceae

Creeping stems with small oval, waxy, bright green leaves. Poor drainage, cold water or excessively moist soil may cause foot rot.

**Pereskia godseffiana (Peireskia godsef-
fiana)/Leaf Cactus/fam. Cactaceae**
○ ⊞ ∞ ⊙ ▣
Stems bearing red and apricot-yellow leaves
with green spots. The stems are covered with
spines. When the leaves have fallen reduce
watering. P shoot tip cuttings.

**Perilepta dyeriana (Strobilanthes
dyerianus)/fam. Acanthaceae**
◐ ⊞ ∞ ⊙ ▣ ⊙
Attractive foliage plant for the greenhouse.
Small violet flowers. Overwinter at 14–18°C
(57–64°F). P shoot tip cuttings. Take regular
cuttings as young plants have attractive
leaves.

**Persea americana (P. gratissima)
Avocado/fam. Lauraceae**
○ ◐ ⊞ ∞ ⊙ ⊙
Vigorous indoor plant easily grown from a
stone. Winter temperature 10–12°C (50–53°F).
S leafmould, loam and farmyard manure.
P seed. Feed in summer.

**Phalaenopsis amabilis var.
fam. Orchidaceae**
◐ ⊞ ∞ ⊙ ⊙
This plant comes in many varieties. Flowers
in October–January. One dry month at 12°C
(53°F) encourages flowering. S osmunda fibre
with a little sphagnum moss. P seed.

**Phalaenopsis amboinensis
fam. Orchidaceae**
◐ ⊞ ∞ ⊙ ⊙
Flowers in December–January. Feed with
orchid fertiliser in the summer. Otherwise
treat like *P. amabilis*. Can also be grown in
expanded clay and peat granules, or on tree
ferns.

**Phalaenopsis fasciata
fam. Orchidaceae**
◐ ⊞ ∞ ⊙ ⊙
Flowers in late summer and autumn. Likes
tepid rainwater – spraying with cold water
causes leaf spots. Treat like *P. amabilis*.

**Phalaenopsis hybrid
fam. Orchidaceae**
◐ ⊞ ∞ ⊙ ⊙
Of the numerous *Phalaenopsis* hybrids in
cultivation, many are grown specially for their
long-lasting cut flowers. Keep in the shade
from March onwards. Treat like *P. amabilis*.

**Phalaenopsis hybrid (pink)
fam. Orchidaceae**
◐ ⊞ ∞ ⊙ ⊙
A glorious *Phalaenopsis* hybrid with long-
lasting flowers. Make sure the pot is well
drained at all times. Repot in May, once every
two years. Otherwise treat like *P. amabilis*.

**Philodendron domesticum (P. hastatum)
fam. Araceae**
◐ ◐ ⊞ ∞ ⊙ ⊙ ⊙
Philodendrons are eminently suitable for
hydroculture. They can remain indoors
during the winter. Minimum temperature
14°C (57°F). S pinewood soil and farmyard
manure. P see *P. elegans*.

99

Philodendron

Philodendron elegans
fam. Araceae
🔘🔘🔘🔘🔘🔘🔘🔘
Climber with deeply divided leaves. P shoot
tip cuttings, eye cuttings, stem cuttings with
aerial roots, seed and air-layering. Cuttings
must be rooted at 25–30°C (77–86°F).

Philodendron erubescens hybrid
fam. Araceae
🔘🔘🔘🔘🔘🔘🔘🔘
Striking red sheaths round young foliage.
Popular cultivars include 'Red and Emerald
Green' and 'Bourgogne'. Treat like *P.
domesticum*. P see *P. elegans*.

**Philodendron laciniatum (P. amazonicum, P.
pedatum) / fam. Araceae**
🔘🔘🔘🔘🔘🔘🔘🔘
The leafstalks of this species can grow to a
length of 50 cm (20 in). Use only tepid water
for spraying and watering. Treat like *P.
domesticum*.

Philodendron longilaminatum
fam. Araceae
🔘🔘🔘🔘🔘🔘🔘🔘
Vigorous house plants. Leaves have a
conspicuous central rib. Treat like *P.
domesticum*. P see *P. elegans*.

**Philodendron melanochrysum 'Andreanum'
(P. andreanum) / fam. Araceae**
🔘🔘🔘🔘🔘🔘🔘🔘
'Andreanum' is the adult, 'Melanochrysum'
the juvenile form with small arrow-shaped
leaves. Treat like *P. domesticum*. P see *P.
elegans*.

Philodendron micans
fam. Araceae
🔘🔘🔘🔘🔘🔘🔘🔘
Small climbing or hanging plant. The leaves
have a purple underside. Treat like *P.
domesticum*. P root tip or eye cuttings under
glass.

Philodendron panduriforme
fam. Araceae
🔘🔘🔘🔘🔘🔘🔘🔘
Vigorous plant with 25–35-cm (10–14-in) long
leafstalks and violin-shaped leaves. Sponge
the leaves regularly. Treat like *P. domesticum*.
P see *P. elegans*.

Philodendron radiatum (P. dubium)
fam. Araceae
🔘🔘🔘🔘🔘🔘🔘🔘
A strong plant with large leaves. The foliage
of the juvenile form is smaller and less deeply
divided. Treat like *P. domesticum*. P see *P.
elegans*.

Philodendron sagittifolium 'Ilsemannii'
fam. Araceae
🔘🔘🔘🔘🔘🔘🔘
Magnificent climber with 40-cm (16-in) long
leaves covered with green, rose-red and cream
spots. Grows very slowly. Treat like *P.
domesticum*. P see *P. elegans*.

Philodendron scandens (P. cordatum, P. cuspidatum)/fam. Araceae
One of the best known philodendrons. Does well in a hanging basket but also makes a good climber. Treat like *P. domesticum*.
P shoot tip or eye cuttings.

Philodendron selloum
fam. Araceae
Up to 1.5 m (5 ft) tall, a non-climbing species of *Philodendron*. The stout leaves have many translucent spots. Treat like *P. domesticum*.
P see *P. elegans*.

Philodendron sodiroi (P. laucheanum)
fam. Araceae
Climbing plant with blue-green foliage shot with silver. Red veins on the undersurface of the leaves. Treat like *P. domesticum*. P see *P. elegans*.

Philodendron squamiferum
fam. Araceae
A graceful climber with very hairy leafstalks. Leaf and leafstalk up to 30 cm (1 ft) long. Treat like *P. domesticum*. P see *P. elegans*.

Phlebodium aureum (Polypodium aureum)
fam. Polypodiaceae
Ferns with blue-green leaves than stand up well to dry air indoors. Minimum winter temperature 16°c (60°F). S leafmould, farmyard manure and sand. P division, spores.

Phlebodium aureum 'Mandaianum'
fam. Polypodiaceae
This cultivar has wavy, irregularly curled and divided leaves. Feed every two weeks during the growing season. Treat like *P. aureum*.

Phoenix canariensis
Canary Date Palm/fam. Palmae
Container plant which should spend the summer outside. Minimum winter temperature 4°c (39°F). Use deep, narrow pots with a mixture of loam, leafmould, manure and sand. P seed.

Phoenix roebelenii
Pygmy Date Palm/fam. Palmae
Demands a minimum temperature of 16°c (60°F) throughout the year. Give tepid, soft water. S fill narrow, tall pots with a loamy mixture. P seed, division.

Phyllanthus angustifolius
fam. Euphorbiaceae
The flowers are borne on the margins of the phylloclades (flattened stems functioning as leaves). Overwinter at 16°c (60°F).
S leafmould, sand and farmyard manure.
P seed and cuttings.

101

***Phyllitis scolopendrium (Scolopendrium
vulgare)***/Hart's Tongue Fern/fam.
Aspleniaceae

Hardy garden plant also attractive in cool
positions indoors. Winter temperature 2–6°C
(35–43°F). Feed in summer. P spores, division,
root cuttings.

Phyllitis scolopendrium 'Undulatum'
Hart's Tongue Fern/fam. ***Aspleniaceae***

Cultivar with very curly leaf edges. Treat like
P. scolopendrium. Apply lime-free water only.
P division and root cuttings.

Pilea cadierei
Aluminium Plant/fam. ***Urticaceae***

A well-lit position is needed to maintain the
attractive leaf colour. Winter temperature 12–
15°C (53–59°F). S leafmould, well-rotted turf,
manure and sand in proportions 2:1:1:1.
P cuttings.

Pilea involucrata (P. pubescens)
Friendship Plant/fam. ***Urticaceae***

Do not spray the leaves of this plant as that
may cause black spots. Treat like *P. cadierei*.
P shoot tip cuttings in May in warm medium.

***Pilea microphylla (P. muscosa, P. calli-
trichoides)***/Artillery Plant/fam. ***Urticaceae***

This species with extremely small leaves may
be put out in the middle of May in a
somewhat shady, sheltered spot. Treat like *P.
cadierei*. P cuttings.

Pilea spruceana 'Norfolk'
fam. ***Urticaceae***

Foliage plant very suitable as ground cover in
large plant containers. Treat like *P. cadierei*.
P cuttings in a warm propagating case.

Pilea spruceana 'Silver Tree'
fam. ***Urticaceae***

The older pileas are, the less attractive they
look, so it is advisable to take frequent
cuttings. Treat like *P. cadierei*.

Pinus 'Silver Crest'
Pine/fam. ***Pinaceae***

Conifers are becoming increasingly popular
as indoor plants. Winter temperature 0–5°C
(32–41°F). Pot in standard potting compost
mixed with sand. P seed, cuttings.

Piper crocatum
Pepper/fam. ***Piperaceae***

Can be grown as a climber or as a hanging
plant. Minimum winter temperature 12°C
(53°F). The best growing medium is
leafmould, farmyard manure and sand.
P shoot tip and eye cuttings.

Piper nigrum
Pepper / fam. *Piperaceae*
◐ ◑ ⊕ ⊗ ▣ ▣
This is the strongest of the peppers. The
flowers are followed by clusters of green fruits
that later turn red and finally black. Treat like
P. crocatum. P shoot tip and eye cuttings.

Pisonia umbellifera 'Variegata'
(Heimerliodendron umbellifera 'Variegata')
fam. *Nyctaginaceae*
◐ ⊕ ⊗ ⊙ ▣ ▣
Heated greenhouse, or indoors with extra
care. Minimum winter temperature 16–18°C
(60–64°F). S leafmould, loam, manure. P shoot
tip and eye cuttings.

Pittosporum eugenioides
fam. *Pittosporaceae*
○ ◐ ◑ ⊙ ⊗ ▣ ▣
Clusters of fragrant cream flowers in summer.
'Variegatum' has decorative leaves. Winter
temperature 5–10°C (41–50°F). Put out in June.
S clay and leafmould, 2:1. P shoot tip
cuttings, seed.

Pittosporum tobira
fam. *Pittosporaceae*
○ ◐ ◑ ⊙ ⊗ ▣ ▣
Fragrant flowers in the spring. Will do best
in a bright but shaded position. Treat like *P.
eugenioides*. P seed, shoot tip cuttings in
August.

Pittosporum tobira 'Variegatum'
fam. *Pittosporaceae*
○ ◐ ◑ ⊙ ⊗ ▣ ▣
Attractive container plant with fragrant
flowers from March to May. Treat like *P.
eugenioides*. Feed every two weeks during the
growing season. P seed, shoot tip cuttings.

Pittosporum undulatum
fam. *Pittosporaceae*
○ ◐ ◑ ⊙ ⊗ ▣ ▣
The fragrant cream-coloured flowers come out
in May–June. Treat like *P. eugenioides*. P half
ripe shoot tip cuttings in August under glass,
or fresh seed.

Platycerium bifurcatum (P. alcicorne)
Stag's Horn Fern / fam. *Polypodiaceae*
◐ ◑ ⊕ ⊙ ⊗ ▣ ▣
Grow this hanging plant in a wicker basket
filled with pinewood soil, osmunda fibre and
farmyard manure. Winter temperature 10–
15°C (50–59°F). P plantlets and spores.

Platycerium grande
Stag's Horn Fern / fam. *Polypodiaceae*
◐ ◑ ⊕ ⊙ ⊗ ▣ ▣
The sterile leaves of this plant are nest
shaped; the fertile leaves antler shaped, and
pendulous. Treat like *P. bifurcatum*. P sow
spores under glass at 25°C (77°F).

Plectranthus coleoides 'Marginatus'
fam. *Labiatae*
◐ ◑ ⊕ ⊙ ⊗ ⊗ ▣ ▣
Only one variety of this species is in
cultivation. Overwinter at about 15°C (59°F).
Feed in the summer. P tip cuttings root very
easily both in the soil and also in water.

103

Plectranthus fruticosus
fam. *Labiatae*

○ ◐ ⊕ ⊕ ⊗ ⊚ ▣

Small semi-shrub with fragrant leaves, easily grown indoors. Minimum winter temperature 12°C (53°F). Grow annually from cuttings; these will root quickly in the soil and also in water.

Plumbago auriculata (P. capensis)
Cape Leadwort / **fam. *Plumbaginaceae***

◐ ◐ ⊗ ⊚ ▣

Put outside in the summer for flowering until the autumn. 'Alba' has white flowers. Minimum winter temperature 7°C (45°F). S equal parts of loam, leafmould and farmyard manure. P cuttings.

Plumbago indica
fam. *Plumbaginaceae*

A plant for the intermediate greenhouse. Minimum winter temperature 13°C (55°F). Repot in spring in equal parts leafmould, loam and farmyard manure and cut back hard. P seed, stem cuttings.

Podocarpus macrophyllus (P. chinensis)
fam. *Podocarpaceae*

○ ◐ ⊕ ⊚ ⊚ ▣

A conifer which can be put out in summer and returned to the cold greenhouse in winter. Repot in a mixture of loam, leafmould, peat and manure. P shoot tip cuttings rooted under glass.

Polyscias balfouriana* 'Pennockii' (*Aralia balfouriana* 'Pennockii') / fam. *Araliaceae

◐ ⊕ ⊕ ⊗ ⊚ ⊚ ▣

'Pennockii' has larger leaves than the species. Winter temperature about 15°C (59°F). Pot in pinewood soil with farmyard manure. P tip cuttings rooted at 25–30°C (77–86°F) under glass.

Polyscias fruticosa (Panax fruticosus, Aralia fruticosa) / fam. *Araliaceae

◐ ◐ ⊕ ⊕ ⊗ ⊚ ⊚ ▣

Slightly more tolerant of shade than the variegated forms. Treat like *P. balfourinana*. Best potted in loam, leafmould, farmyard manure and sand. P shoot tip cuttings.

Polyscias guilfoylei (Aralia guilfoylei, Nothopanax guilfoylei) / fam. *Araliaceae

◐ ⊕ ⊕ ⊗ ⊚ ⊚ ▣

Attractive variegated foliage plant. 'Victoriae' has deeply and irregularly divided small leaves. Treat like *P. balfouriana*. P shoot tip cuttings.

Polystichum tsus-simense
Tsus-sima Holly Fern / **fam. *Aspidiaceae***

◐ ⊕ ⊕ ⊗ ⊚ ⊚ ▣

The best-known species. Does well in mixed plant containers. Minimum winter temperature 10°C (50°F). Repot in leafmould with farmyard manure and sand. P division, spores.

***Primula malacoides* 'Pink Panther'**
Fairy Primrose / **fam. *Primulaceae***

◐ ◐ ⊕ ⊗ ⊚ ⊚ ▣

One of many attractive varieties. Difficult to bring into flower a second time. Put out in the summer; keep at about 8°C (46°F) in winter. P seed.

Primula obconica
Poison Primrose / fam. *Primulaceae*
This plant sometimes causes skin rashes.
Overwinter at minimum temperature of 5°C
(41°F). Can sometimes be made to flower
twice. P seed.

Primula praenitens (P. sinensis)
Chinese Primrose / fam. *Primulaceae*
Varieties with cut and fringed petals belong
to the Fimbriata group. After a cool period at
a minimum temperature of 5°C (41°F), this
species may bloom again. P germinate seed
at 16°C (60°F).

Primula vulgaris (P. acaulis)
Primrose / fam. *Primulaceae*
Often sold as a house plant when it is in fact
a garden plant. After flowering, plant out in a
cool, moist spot of the garden. P seed.

Pseuderanthemum atropurpureum
'Tricolor' / fam. *Acanthaceae*
Flowering plant for the small container.
Maintain a minimum winter temperature of
16°C (60°F). S leafmould, farmyard manure
and sand. P shoot tip cuttings.

Pseuderanthemum sinuatum (Eranthemum cooperi) / fam. *Acanthaceae*
Older plants are often less attractive, so it is
best to propagate new plants regularly from
cuttings. Treat like *P. atropurpureum*
'Tricolor'. P shoot tip cuttings.

Pseudomammillaria camptotricha (Dolichothele camptotricha) / fam. *Cactaceae*
A cluster-formed cactus with entangled
yellow, spinous hairs and prominent
tubercles. Fragrant white flowers. Keep dry
and cool in winter. S cactus mixture. P offsets.

Pteris cretica 'Albolineata'
Variegated Table Fern / fam. *Pteridaceae*
This fern has many cultivars. The variegated
forms need a winter temperature of 16–18°C
(60–64°F). S beech leafmould, farmyard
manure and sand. P division, spores.

Pteris cretica 'Alexandrae'
Table Fern / fam. *Pteridaceae*
Feed weekly during the growing period at
half the usual concentration. S see *Pteris
cretica* 'Albolineata'. P division, spores.

Pteris cretica 'Major'
Table Fern / fam. *Pteridaceae*
Green-leaved Table Ferns are more tolerant of
shade than the variegated forms. Winter
temperature may drop to 12°C (53°F).
S leafmould with farmyard manure and sand.
P division and spores.

105

Pteris cretica 'Parkeri'
Table Fern / fam. *Pteridaceae*
Ⓘ 🖐 🕸 ⊗ 🌢 🖥 🕘
The broad fronds of this cultivar feel rough to the touch. Treat like *P. c.* 'Major'. Feed lightly during the growing period. P division and spores.

Pteris ensiformis 'Victoriae' (*P. crenata* 'Victoriae') / Silver Lace Fern / fam. *Pteridaceae*
Ⓘ 🖐 🕸 ⊗ 🌢 🖥 🕘
This cultivar sometimes turns into *P. e.* 'Evergemiensis' and vice versa. Treat like *P. c.* 'Albolineata'. P spores; division in the spring when repotting.

Pteris quadriaurita
Table Fern / fam. *Pteridaceae*
Ⓘ 🖐 🕸 ⊗ 🌢 🖥 🕘
A graceful fern with straw-coloured leafstalks. Treat like *P. c.* 'Major'. Always supply and spray with soft water. P division, spores.

Punica granatum 'Nana'
Dwarf Pomegranate / fam. *Punicaceae*
○ 🖐 🕸 🌢 🕘
Container plant that needs a minimum winter temperature of 5°C (41°F). Put out in a sunny spot in the summer. Repot in a loamy mixture in the spring. P seed, cuttings.

Pyrrhocactus reconditus (*Neochilenia recondita*) / fam. *Cactaceae*
○ 🕸 ⊙ 🌢 🕘
Grey-green globular cactus with slightly sunken areoles and grey spines. Pale pink flowers. Keep dry and at 5°C (41°F) in the winter. S cactus mixture. P seed at 25°C (77°F).

Pyrrhocactus scoparius
fam. *Cactaceae*
○ 🕸 ⊙ 🌢 🕘
Spherical cactus with tough, black to grey spines. Cream-coloured flowers. Grafted specimens look better and make better flowers. P seed, but only with great difficulty.

Rebutia aureiflora (*Mediolobivia aureiflora*)
fam. *Cactaceae*
○ 🕸 ⊙ 🌢 🕘
Flattened globular cactus with 15–20 soft, yellow or red bristle-shaped spines. S cactus mixture. P cuttings or seed: seed germinates readily.

Rebutia deminuta (*Aylostera deminuta*)
fam. *Cactaceae*
○ 🕸 ⊙ 🌢 🕘
A cluster-type globular cactus with eight to ten bristly, yellow-white spines. Red to orange-red flowers. S cactus mixture. P plant offsets in sandy soil.

Rebutia gracilis
fam. *Cactaceae*
○ 🕸 ⊙ 🌢 🕘
Cluster-forming spherical cactus with orange-red flowers. When the buds appear in the spring, spray carefully at first and then go on to watering sparingly. P see *R. deminuta*.

Rebutia minuscula* var. *grandiflora
fam. *Cactaceae*

○ 🕸 🐛 🌢 🗓

A flattened spherical green cactus with 20–30 bristly spines to each tubercle. Red flowers appear in the spring right round the lower part of the globe.

Rebutia senilis
fam. *Cactaceae*

○ 🕸 🐛 🌢 🗓

A flattened globular cactus densely covered with white spines. Bright red flowers. Cultivars have yellow, lilac or orange flowers. Overwinter dry at 5°C (41°F). S cactus mixture.

Rechsteineria cardinalis (Gesneria cardinalis)
Cardinal Flower / fam. *Gesneriaceae*

◑ 🕸 🐛 🌢 🗓

Keep the tubers at 12°C (53°F). Pot up in spring in peat, leafmould and farmyard manure, the eyes just above the surface, under glass at 20–25°C (68–77°F). P seed, division, cuttings.

Rechsteineria leucotricha
Cardinal Flower / fam. *Gesneriaceae*

◑ 🕸 🐛 🐜 🌢 🗓

Really a greenhouse plant but it can be temporarily brought indoors while it is in flower. Treat like *R. cardinalis*. P leaf and softwood cuttings, seed, division of tubers.

Rehmannia elata
fam. *Gesneriaceae*

◑ 🕸 ◔ 🐜 🌢 🖤

Generally grown as a biennial. Very attractive plant as long as it is kept in a cool spot. Winter temperature 8–10°C (46–50°F). P seed, softwood cuttings.

Rhipsalidopsis gaertneri (Schlumbergera
gaertneri)* / Easter Cactus / fam. *Cactaceae

◑ 🕸 🐛 🐜 🌢 🗓

Strongly branching cactus with arching stems and flat joints. Terminal scarlet flowers in groups of one to three appear in April.
P remove joints, dry and insert in peat-based compost.

Rhipsalidopsis rosea (Rhipsalis rosea)
fam. *Cactaceae*

◑ 🕸 🐛 🐜 🌢 🗓

Small upright joints with fragrant pink flowers. Rest in winter at 10–15°C (50–59°F) and keep almost dry to ensure good flowers. S anthurium mixture.

Rhodochiton atrosanguineum (R. volubilis,
***Lophospermum atrosanguineum)* / fam.**
Scrophulariaceae

○ ◑ 🕸 🐛 🌢 🗓

A most graceful climber, usually cultivated as an annual. S humus-rich soil with leafmould, peat and a little farmyard manure and loam. P seed.

Rhododendron obtusum
Japanese Azalea / fam. *Ericaceae*

◑ 🕸 ◔ 🐛 🌢 🖤

This small shrub can also be used as a garden plant. Dead-head regularly, flower stalks included. Further treatment like *R. simsii*. P cuttings, grafting.

Rhododendron

Rhododendron simsii (Azalea indica)
Indian Azalea / fam. *Ericaceae*
Ⓘ ⊕ ⊙ ⊗ ⊖ ⊟
Keep at a maximum 15°C (59°F) when in
flower and then at 6–10°C (43–50°F). Put
outside in a sheltered spot in summer.
S pinewood soil with farmyard manure.
P shoot tip cuttings, grafting.

Rhododendron simsii (Azalea indica)
Indian Azalea / fam. *Ericaceae*
Ⓘ ⊕ ⊙ ⊗ ⊖ ⊟
This plant also has a great many cultivars, one
of which is shown here. All flower at different
periods; can also be grown as standards.
Cultivate like previous entry. P cuttings,
grafting.

**Rhoeo spathacea 'Vittata' / Moses in the
Cradle / fam. *Commelinaceae***
Ⓘ ⊕ ⊗ ⊖ ⊟
The species has evenly dark green leaves with
a purple underside. Minimum winter
temperature 15°C (59°F). Repot every spring.
P shoot tip cuttings and seed.

Rhoicissus capensis (Cissus capensis)
fam. *Vitaceae*
Ⓘ Ⓘ ⊕ ⊗ ⊖ ⊟
Vigorous climber that likes to be kept cool in
the winter. Minimum temperature 7°C (44°F).
P eye cuttings with the leaf rolled up or tip
cuttings, three cuttings to a pot.

Rivinia humilis (R. laevis)
fam. *Phytolaccaceae*
Ⓘ ⊕ ⊕ ⊗ ⊖ ⊟
Climber with attractive berries which only
ripen if the flowers are not sprayed. Older
plants are less attractive, so take regular
cuttings or grow from seed.

Rochea coccinea (Crassula coccinea)
Crassula / fam. *Crassulaceae*
Ⓘ ⊕ ⊙ ⊙ ⊖ ⊟
Stiff, upright, branching little shrub with
leaves in rows along the stem. Tubular red
flowers in terminal clusters. S cactus mixture.
P cut off tops and insert in compost.

Rodriguezia secunda
fam. *Orchidaceae*
Ⓘ ⊕ ⊕ ⊗ ⊖ ⊟
An orchid for the warm greenhouse;
minimum temperature 18°C (64°F). Grow on
tree ferns or in a mixture of sphagnum moss
and osmunda fibre. P seed.

Saintpaulia ionantha
African Violet / fam. *Gesneriaceae*
Ⓘ ⊕ ⊗ ⊖ ⊖ ⊟
Profusely flowering small plant; keeps
making blooms in bright light. Needs a
minimum rest of one month at 16°C (60°F).
S pinewood soil with farmyard manure. P leaf
cuttings, division.

Saintpaulia ionantha
African Violet / fam. *Gesneriaceae*
Ⓘ ⊕ ⊗ ⊖ ⊖ ⊟
African violets have numerous cultivars with
single and double flowers in all sorts of
colours. Treat like last entry.

108

Sandersonia aurantiaca
fam. *Liliaceae*
○ ⊞ ⊗ ⊖ ⊡
A plant for the intermediate greenhouse but can be kept temporarily in the house. Keep tubers dry at 10–12°C (50 to 53°F). Pot up in spring in peat, loam and beech leafmould. P division.

Sansevieria trifasciata (S. guineensis)
Snake Plant / fam. *Agavaceae*
○ ⊞ ◐ ⊖ ⊡
Indestructible indoor plant. Minimum temperature 14°C (57°F). Feed with fertilisers low in nitrogen. P division; leaf cuttings left to dry.

Sansevieria trifasciata 'Golden Hahnii'
Snake Plant / fam. *Agavaceae*
○ ⊞ ◐ ⊖ ⊡
Though Snake Plants will grow in shady positions, the leaf markings of the variegated forms in particular will be less spectacular. Cultivate like *S. trifasciata*. P division.

Sansevieria trifasciata 'Laurentii'
Snake Plant / fam. *Agavaceae*
○ ⊞ ◐ ⊖ ⊡
One of the most popular Snake Plants. Treat like *S. trifasciata*. P division. Be careful not to overwater or to let the temperature drop too low.

Sauromatum venosum (S. guttatum, Arum guttatum) / fam. *Araceae*
◑ ◓ ⊗ ⊖ ⊡
Tuberous plant good for drying. The typical aroid inflorescences have an unpleasant smell. Put out in the garden after flowering. Overwinter at 0–5°C (32–41°F). P offsets.

Saxifraga cotyledon (S. pyramidalis)
fam. *Saxifragaceae*
○ ◓ ◐ ⊖ ⊡
Hardy plant. Rosettes do not flower for two to four years. Flowers are plume-like sprays of small white blooms. After flowering put the plant back outside.

Saxifragra stolonifera (S. sarmentosa)
Mother of Thousands / *Saxifragaceae*
◑ ⊞ ⊗ ⊖ ⊡
Small plant with thin runners bearing young plantlets. Keep at 5–10°C (41–50°F) in winter and water very sparingly. P seed, division, runners.

Saxifraga stolonifera 'Tricolor'
fam. *Saxifragaceae*
◑ ⊞ ⊗ ⊖ ⊡
Demands much light and a minimum winter temperature of 16°C (60°F). Otherwise treat like *S. stolonifera*. Grow young plantlets under glass.

Schefflera actinophylla (Brassaia actinophylla) / fam. *Araliaceae*
◑ ⊞ ⊗ ⊖ ⊡
Makes a good container plant and will also thrive in a cool spot indoors. Retains its leaves at a minimum temperature of 12°C (53°F). P sow at 20–25°C (68–77°F) under glass.

Schefflera

***Schefflera digitata (S. cunninghamii,
Aralia schefflera)*/ fam. *Araliaceae***

A less vigorous grower than *S. actinophylla*.
Put outside in a sheltered spot in summer.
Treat like *S. actinophylla*. P seed.

***Schefflera octophyllum*
fam. *Araliaceae***

Has a more modest form than *S. actinophylla*.
Needs to be fed just once a month in summer.
Treat like *S. actinophylla*. P seed.

***Schefflera venulosa (Heptapleurum
venulosum)*/ fam. *Araliaceae***

Young scheffleras grow particularly fast and
may have to be repotted twice during their
first year. Treat like *S. actinophylla*. P seed.

***Schizanthus pinnatus* 'Dwarf Bouquet'
fam. *Solanaceae***

An annual which, when sown in August, will
add much colour to the greenhouse from
February to April. Repot seedlings
frequently and keep cool until buds appear.

***Schlumbergera* hybrid (*Zygocactus truncatus*)
Christmas Cactus / fam. *Cactaceae***

After flowering, rest for 6–10 weeks. Put
outside in late May. Rest inside in September
until buds appear. S cactus mixture.
P cuttings of joints beneath areoles; also
grafting.

***Scindapsus pictus* 'Argyreus'
fam. *Araceae***

Attractive hanging or climbing plant for the
warm greenhouse. Keep at 12–18°C (53–64°F)
in winter. S turf, beech leafmould, sphagnum
moss and farmyard manure. P eye and stem
cuttings.

***Scirpus cernuus*
fam. *Cyperaceae***

Grassy plant that can be kept indoors all the
year round, preferably at 16–20°C (60–68°F).
P divide at least once a year or try seed.

***Sedum griseum*
fam. *Crassulaceae***

Compact little shrub with erect stems bearing
green, cylindrical leaves and white flowers.
Overwinter cool and dry. S cactus mixture.
P tip cuttings.

***Sedum morganianum*
Burro's Tail / fam. *Crassulaceae***

Spectacular hanging plant with stems
resembling tails. The cylindrical leaves
overlap like roof tiles. Pink flowers. P rooting
of leaves.

Sedum pachyphyllum
Jelly Bean Plant / **fam.** *Crassulaceae*
◯ ⊕ ⊙ ⊖ ⊡
The erect, small stems carry about 4-cm
(1½-in) long club-shaped, blue-green leaves
with reddish tips. Yellow flowers. S cactus
mixture. P stem and leaf cuttings.

Sedum rubrotinctum
Jelly Bean Plant / **fam.** *Crassulaceae*
◯ ⊕ ⊙ ⊖ ⊡
Thin, erect little stems with cylindrical, bright
green leaves that snap off easily and have
club-shaped, reddish-brown tips. In sunny
positions the whole plant turns red. Yellow
flowers.

Sedum sieboldii 'Variegatum'
fam. *Crassulaceae*
◯ ⊕ ⊙ ⊖ ⊡
Flexible stems with blue-green, white-edged
leaves, always in groups of three. Pink flowers
in October. Keep cool and dry in winter.
S cactus mixture. P stem or leaf cuttings.

Sedum stahlii
fam. *Crassulaceae*
◯ ⊕ ⊙ ⊖ ⊡
Thin, protruding stems with 1–1.5-cm (½–⅝-
in) long, cylindrical, green to browny leaves,
their colour depending on the sun. Otherwise
they look like coffee beans. Yellow flowers.

Sedum suaveolens
fam. *Crassulaceae*
◯ ⊕ ⊙ ⊖ ⊡
Rosette of fleshy, bluish leaves. Overwinter
at about 5°C (41°F) and keep almost completely
dry – the leaves are full of reserve moisture.
S cactus mixture. P leaf cuttings.

Seemannia latifolia
fam. *Gesneriaceae*
◑ ⊕ ⊗ ⊜ ⊡
Unusual plant flowering in the summer
and / or autumn. Overwinter at minimum
temperature of 16°C (60°F). S leafmould with a
little farmyard manure and sand. P seed,
cuttings.

Selaginella apoda
fam. *Selaginellaceae*
◑ ⊕ ⊗ ⊜ ⊡
This moss grows to a height of 30 cm (1 ft).
Cultivate at 15°C (59°F) and higher
temperatures, preferably under glass. Add
some extra sphagnum moss and peat to the
potting mixture. P division.

Selaginella kraussiana
fam. *Selaginellaceae*
◑ ⊕ ⊗ ⊜ ⊡
This moss thrives in a humid atmosphere.
Minimum temperature 15°C (59°F). S standard
potting mix with added peat and sphagnum
moss. P division; watch out for slugs.

Selaginella lepidophylla
fam. *Selaginellaceae*
◑ ⊕ ⊗ ⊜ ⊡
During dry spells the feathery side shoots curl
up; when moistened they spread out again.
Reminiscent of Rose of Jericho. Treat like *S.
kraussiana*.

111

Selaginella martensii
Creeping Moss/fam. *Selaginellaceae*
The originally upright but later procumbent stems are covered with aerial roots. 'Watsoniana' has silvery-white tips. Treat like *S. kraussiana*.

Senecio citriformis
fam. *Compositae*
Short procumbent stems with lemon-shaped leaves up to 20 cm (8 in) long, covered with bluish bloom and bearing translucent small lines. White flowers on long stems. S cactus mixture. P cuttings.

Senecio cruentus (Cineraria hybrid)
fam. *Compositae*
This plant is best discarded once it has flowered. Grow from seed: sow in July–August and overwinter at 5°C (41°F) in a cold greenhouse. Flowers in the spring.

Senecio herreanus (Kleinia gomphophylla)
fam. *Compositae*
Is often confused with *S. rowleyanus*, but has pointed short leaves. Overwinter in a cool and dry atmosphere. S cactus mixture. P rooted cuttings.

Senecio macroglossus 'Variegatus'
Variegated Wax Vine/fam. *Compositae*
Hanging plant with small ivy-like, variegated leaves. Overwinter in a cool and dry atmosphere. S cactus mixture. P dried tip cuttings inserted in rooting mix.

Senecio rowleyanus
String-of-Beads/fam. *Compositae*
Hanging plant with stems covered in small leaves resembling peas. White-and-purple flowers. Overwinter cool and dry. S cactus mixture. P rooted cuttings.

Senecio serpens (Kleinia repens)
fam. *Compositae*
Procumbent, branching shoots with rounded, bloomed leaves. Small white flowers. Overwinter cool and dry. S cactus mix. P rooted tip or leaf cuttings.

Serissa foetida 'Variegata'
fam. *Rubiaceae*
Unusual plant, best overwintered in a greenhouse at 5–10°C (41–50°F). Cut back in the spring and repot in a loamy, humus-rich mixture. P cuttings.

Setcreasea purpurea
fam. *Commelinaceae*
Small purple flowers. Plentiful light will ensure the best leaf colour. Keep at 10–15°C (50–59°F) in the winter. Feed lightly in summer. P tip cuttings.

Siderasis fuscata (Tradescantia fuscata)
fam. _Commelinaceae_

Plant with a conspicuous cover of hair and attractively set-off flowers. Minimum winter temperature 16°C (60°F). P division; possibly also from cuttings or seed.

Sinningia speciosa (Gloxinia speciosa)
Gloxinia / fam. _Gesneriaceae_

Gloxinias come in various colours and even in two-coloured forms. Store tubers at 15°C (59°F) and pot up in February in leafmould, peat and farmyard manure. P basal shoots, cuttings, seed.

Smithiantha cinnabarina (Naegelia
cinnabarina) / fam. _Gesneriaceae_

Overwinter rhizomes dry at minimum temperature of 12°C (53°F). Pot in leafmould, peat and farmyard manure. Start into growth at 20–25°C (68–77°F). P leaf cuttings, division of rhizomes.

Smithiantha hybrid
Temple Bells / fam. _Gesneriaceae_

Cross between _S. multiflora_ and _S. zebrina_. Garden shops offer the hybrids for sale more often than they do the species. Treat like _S. cinnabarina_.

Solanum pseudocapsicum (Capsicum capsi-
castrum / Winter Cherry / fam. _Solanaceae_

The orange or red berries of this plant are a familiar sight at Christmas. Overwinter at 10°C (50°F). Put outside in the summer. P seed or tip cuttings.

Soleirolia soleirolii (Helxine soleirolii)
fam. _Urticaceae_

Excellent ground-cover or hanging plant for the kitchen or bathroom. Overwinter at minimum temperature of 10°C (50°F). P division. Also silvery and golden-green leaved varieties.

Sonerila margaritacea
fam. _Melastomataceae_

A plant for the warm greenhouse that can temporarily live indoors in summer. Overwinter at minimum of 16°C (60°F). S pinewood soil with farmyard manure. P tip cuttings at 20–25°C (68–77°F).

Sparmannia africana
African Hemp / fam. _Tiliaceae_

Flowering period January–April. Put outside in late May, choosing a sheltered spot. Bring back inside in September and keep at a minimum 5°C (41°F). P stem cuttings.

Spathiphyllum wallisii
fam. _Araceae_

Warm greenhouse plant that with extra care can also be kept indoors. Minimum winter temperature 16°C (60°F). Feed every two weeks in summer. P division, seed.

113

Sprekelia formosissima (Amaryllis formosissima)/Jacobean Lily/fam. **Amaryllidaceae**

Pot the bulb in winter or spring and treat like an amaryllis. When the leaves have died, the bulb must be stored at 15°C (59°F). P seed and offsets.

Stapelia variegata
Carrion Flower/fam. **Asclepiadaceae**

Rectangular stems, grey-green but reddening in the sun. Foetid flowers 5–8 cm (2–3 in) across, yellow and reddish-brown. S cactus mixture. P break off stems, dry and use as cuttings.

Stenocarpus sinuatus
fam. **Proteaceae**

A fairly uncommon plant for a container. Winter temperature 4–10°C (39–50°F). Feed in the summer. P sow in January at 20°C (68°F) or stem cuttings in August.

Stephanotis floribunda
Madagascar Jasmine/fam. **Asclepiadaceae**

The fragrant flowers normally come out in the summer. Overwinter at 12–14°C (53–57°F). S loam, leafmould, farmyard manure and sand. P seed or eye cuttings.

Steriphoma paradoxum
fam. **Caprifoliaceae**

Very attractive plant for the warm greenhouse. Minimum winter temperature 18°C (64°F). Add a little extra loam to the potting compost. P seed or cuttings.

Strelitzia reginae
Bird of Paradise/fam. **Musaceae**

Container plant for the intermediate greenhouse, or a warm room for a time. Overwinter at 8–14°C (46–57°F). Flowers December–January. S loam, leafmould and farmyard manure. P division, seed.

Streptocarpus caulescens
Cape Primrose/fam. **Gesneriaceae**

If tended carefully, Cape Primulas will flower profusely from May to October. Rest in winter at 12°C (53°F). P seed and leaf cuttings. A most beautiful species.

Streptocarpus hybrid (pink)
Cape Primrose/fam. **Gesneriaceae**

Dead-head flowers as soon as possible and occasionally remove some of the older leaves at flowering time. For further treatment see *S. caulescens*. P leaf cuttings.

Streptocarpus hybrid 'Laura Nimf'
Cape Primrose/fam. **Gesneriaceae**

Varieties differ in leaf shape and in the colour and size of their flowers. Feed every two weeks in the growing season. Treat like *S. caulescens*. P leaf cuttings.

Streptocarpus polyanthus
Cape Primrose / fam. *Gesneriaceae*
One of the strange *Streptocarpus* species that
have only one large leaf in nature. Treat like
S. caulescens. P leaf cuttings and seed.

Stromanthe amabilis
fam. *Marantaceae*
Most unusual plant for the heated
greenhouse. Can go indoors temporarily in
summer. Winter temperature 18–22°C (64–
71°F). Mix Styromull into standard potting
compost. P division.

Syngonium podophyllum
fam. *Araceae*
All syngoniums will occasionally produce
aroid flowers. Tie up the climbing varieties.
Minimum winter temperature 15°C (59°F).
S pinewood soil. P tip or eye cuttings,
layering.

Syngonium podophyllum 'Albolineatum'
fam. *Araceae*
Variegated types demand more light than the
green-leaved ones. Treat like *S. podophyllum*.
Feed every two weeks during the growing
season.

Syngonium podophyllum 'Greengold'
fam. *Araceae*
Variegated kind with large leaves. Cultivate
and propagate like *S. podophyllum*. An
alternative growing medium is fibrous peat,
leafmould and farmyard manure.

Syngonium vellozianum 'Albolineatum'
fam. *Araceae*
One of the syngoniums that should really be
trained on a moss stick. Lead the aerial roots
down to the ground. Treat like *S.
podophyllum*.

Testudinaria elephantipes (Dioscorea
elephantipes) / Elephant's Foot / fam.
Dioscoreaceae
Unusual climbing or hanging plant for a
heated greenhouse. Yellow-green flowers.
Resting period at 12°C (53°F). S rich in humus
and chalky. P (imported) seed.

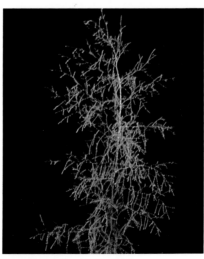

Tetraclinis articulata (Callitris
quadrivalvis) / fam. *Cupressaceae*
This little cypress is best grown in a
container. Put out in a sheltered spot during
the summer. Minimum winter temperature
5°C (41°F). S clay, leafmould and farmyard
manure. P seed.

Tetrastigma voinierianum (Vitis
voinieriana) / fam. *Vitaceae*
Thrives in a greenhouse and sometimes
indoors as well. Temperature between 12 and
18°C (54–64°F). Minimum winter temperature
10°C (50°F). Feed during the growing season.
P eye cuttings at 25°C (77°F).

Thunbergia

Thunbergia alata
Black-Eyed Susan / fam. *Acanthaceae*
○ ⊕ ∞ ⊖ ⊟
Usually grown as an annual but can be
overwintered at 5–10°C (41–50°F). Cut back in
the spring. Feed in the summer. P germinate
seed at 20°C (68°F).

Tillandsia flabellata
fam. *Bromeliaceae*
◑ ⊕ ∞ ⊖ ⊟
Each rosette flowers just once. P pot up young
offshoots with a piece of root attached in
beech leafmould, osmunda fibre and
Styromull. Overwinter in a heated
greenhouse at 18–20°C (64–68°F).

Tillandsia ionantha
fam. *Bromeliaceae*
○ ⊕ ⊙ ⊖ ⊟
A very variable species with many cultivars.
Can be put outside in summer. Minimum
winter temperature 12°C (53°F). S attach to a
twig adding sphagnum moss and osmunda
fibre.

Tillandsia leiboldiana
fam. *Bromeliaceae*
◑ ⊕ ∞ ⊖ ⊟
Up to 60 cm (2 ft) tall, this is a plant with most
striking inflorescences. Treat like *T. flabella*.
Give, and spray with, softened water.
P offshoots.

Tillandsia lindenii (T. lindeniana)
fam. *Bromeliaceae*
◑ ⊕ ∞ ⊖ ⊟
One of the best known tillandsias. The
inflorescence consists of deep blue and white-
throated flowers set off strikingly from coral-
pink bracts. Treat and propagate like
T. flabellata.

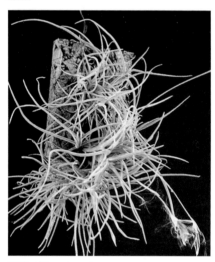

Tillandsia recurvata
fam. *Bromeliaceae*
◑ ⊕ ⊙ ⊖ ⊟
Unusual epiphyte that needs much light and
fresh air. Minimum winter temperature 12°C
(53°F). Tie to a piece of tree fern or to a
bromeliad tree. P offsets.

Tillandsia tricholepis (T. polytrichioides)
fam. *Bromeliaceae*
◑ ⊕ ⊙ ⊖ ⊟
A fairly rare tillandsia highly reminiscent of a
moss until it produces its spectacular
inflorescences. Typical greenhouse plant.
P see *T. recurvata*.

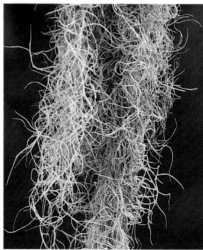

Tillandsia usneoides
Spanish Moss / fam. *Bromeliaceae*
◑ ⊕ ⊙ ⊖ ⊟
Rootless epiphyte which can form a very long
'beard'. Must be attached to a bromeliad tree.
Inconspicuous yellow-green flowers. Treat
and propagate like *T. recurvata*.

Tillandsia xerographica
fam. *Bromeliaceae*
◑ ⊕ ⊙ ⊖ ⊟
Not very well known, this species has scaly
grey leaves. Cultivate and propagate like *T.
recurvata*. Occasionally syringe with special
leaf fertiliser in the growing season.

Tolmiea menziesii
Pick-a-Back Plant / fam. *Saxifragaceae*
◑ ⊕ ⊗ ⊖ ▣
Produces green to brown flowers in May–
June. Very easily cultivated. May go outside
in the summer. Minimum winter temperature
5°C (41°F). P division; also from leaves bearing
plantlets.

Torenia fournieri
fam. *Scrophulariaceae*
◑ ⊕ ⊗ ⊖ ▣
Sow these annuals in February at 18°C (64°F)
under glass. They will flower throughout the
summer, even in a sheltered spot outside.
'Alba' has white flowers with violet spots.

Tradescentia albiflora 'Albovittata'
Wandering Jew / fam. *Commelinaceae*
◑ ⊕ ⊗ ⊖ ▣
Stem-rooting plant easily propagated from
cuttings. Minimum winter temperature 10°C
(50°F). Feed in the summer. Prune regularly.

Tradescantia blossfeldiana 'Variegata'
fam. *Commelinaceae*
◑ ⊕ ⊗ ⊖ ▣
Attractive hanging plant with beautifully
striped leaves. A well-lit position helps to
bring out the markings. Cultivate and
propagate like *T. albiflora* 'Albovittata'.

Trevesia burckii (T. sanderi)
fam. *Araliaceae*
◑ ⊕ ⊗ ⊖ ▣
Young foliage is covered with greyish-white
scales and more deeply divided than the
adult. Cultivate and propagate like *T. palmata*.

Trevesia palmata
fam. *Araliaceae*
◑ ⊕ ⊗ ⊖ ⊖ ▣
A plant with striking leaves and insignificant
flowers. Winter temperature 14–16°C (57–
60°F). May be put outside in a sheltered spot
during the summer. P seed, stem cuttings,
layering.

Trichocereus pasacana
fam. *Cactaceae*
○ ⊕ ⊗ ⊖ ▣ ▦
Globular cactus which can grow to a very
large size. Very long spines. Overwinter at
about 5°C (41°F) and keep dry. S cactus
mixture. P seed or cuttings.

Trichocereus spachianus
fam. *Cactaceae*
○ ⊕ ⊗ ⊖ ▣ ▦
Cylindrical cactus with 10–15 ribs and yellow-
brown spines. White flowers. Often used as
rootstock for grafting difficult or sensitive
species. S cactus mixture. P seed or cuttings
at 20°C (68°F).

Tritonia crocata hybrid
fam. *Iridaceae*
○ ⊕ ⊗ ⊖ ▣ ▦
Corm for the cool greenhouse. Flowering
period May–June. Thereafter, water less until
the leaves die. Keep dry and at 5°C (41°F) in
winter. S potting compost with extra clay.
P offsets.

117

Tulipa

Tulipa 'Brilliant Star'
Tulip / fam. _Liliaceae_
◐ ⊕ ☺ ∞ ⊖ ⬛
Place the bulbs in pots with equal parts sand and potting compost in mid-October. Bring indoors in February at a maximum of 15°C (59°F). When the buds begin to colour, temperature may be raised.

Tulipa (early single) 'Prince Carnaval'
Tulip / fam. _Liliaceae_
◐ ⊕ ☺ ∞ ⊖ ⬛
Treat like _T._ 'Brilliant Star'. Stored tulips may be brought indoors as soon as their noses are 7 cm (2¾ in) long and the flower buds can be felt.

Tulipa (Darwin) 'Rose Copeland'
Tulip / fam. _Liliaceae_
◐ ⊕ ☺ ∞ ⊖ ⬛
Treat like _T._ 'Brilliant Star'. The bulbs can be forced indoors in an absolutely dark room at 9°C (48°F). Keep the soil slightly moist.

Vallota speciosa (Crinum speciosum, Amaryllis purpurea) / fam. _Amaryllidaceae_
○ ⊕ ∞ ⊖ ⬛
Pot the bulbs in March–April. Flowers in the summer. Rest in winter at 5–10°C (41–50°F). Feed weekly during the growing period. P seed, offsets.

Vanda coerulea
fam. _Orchidaceae_
◐ ⊕ ∞ ⊖ ⬛
Grow on bark or on pieces of tree fern or in wicker baskets filled with sphagnum moss, osmunda fibre, coarse peat and expanded clay granules. Do not rest. P side shoots, seed.

Vanda roeblingiana
fam. _Orchidaceae_
◐ ⊕ ∞ ⊖ ⬛
Orchid for the intermediate greenhouse. Cultivate and propagate like _V. coerulea._ Ensure adequate light and fresh air. Give tepid, completely soft water.

Veltheimia capensis (V. glauca)
Forest Lily / fam. _Liliaceae_
○ ◐ ☺ ∞ ⊖ ⬛
Pot bulbs in autumn in leafmould, clayey loam and manure. Keep at 20°C (68°F) until leaves come out, then at a maximum 12°C (53°F). Rest in summer after winter flowering. P offsets, seed.

Vriesea carinata
fam. _Bromeliaceae_
◐ ⊕ ∞ ⊖ ⬛
Grow at 18–20°C (64–68°F) in a mixture of beech leafmould, sphagnum moss, coarse peat and farmyard manure. Minimum temperature throughout the year 18°C (64°F). P rooted offshoots, seed.

Vriesea hieroglyphica
King of Bromeliads / fam. _Bromeliaceae_
◐ ⊕ ∞ ⊖ ⬛
Leaves with striking markings. This species flowers rarely, and is more difficult to grow than species with green or grey leaves. Treat like _V. carinata._

Vriesea × poelmannii
fam. Bromeliaceae
Cross between *V. gloriosa* and *V. vangeertii.*
Treat like *V. carinata.* P young offshoots.
Plants grown from seed will not bear flowers
for years.

Vriesea psittacina
fam. Bromeliaceae
The rosette of this plant dies after flowering.
Grow new plants from offshoots – seed takes
a long time. Cultivate and propagate like *V.
carinata.*

Vriesea rodigasiana
fam. Bromeliaceae
Small rosette in comparison with the long
inflorescence. Cultivate and propagate like
V. carinata. During the growing period, soft
water may be poured into the funnel.

**Vriesea splendens 'Major' (V. longebract-
eata)** / Flaming Sword / **fam. Bromeliaceae**
The best known species. Cultivars have large
inflorescences. Cultivate and propagate like
V. carinata. Will also grow on tree ferns or
bark.

Vriesea viminalis 'Rex'
fam. Bromeliaceae
If young plants refuse to come into flower,
apply some acetylene (the gas given off by
ripe apples) to the funnel. Treat like *V.
carinata.*

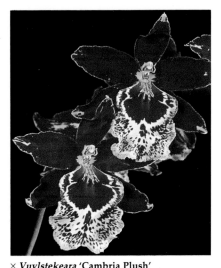

× Vuylstekeara 'Cambria Plush'
fam. Orchidaceae
Cross between *Cochlioda, Miltonia* and
Odontoglossum. Winter temperature 8–12°c
(46–53°F). S osmunda fibre, sphagnum moss
and expanded clay granules. P division. A
sturdy species.

Washingtonia filifera (Pritchardia filifera)
fam. Palmae
Undivided young foliage. Good container
plant. Minimum winter temperature 5°c
(41°F). Put outside in a sheltered spot in
summer. S loam, leafmould and manure.
P sow at 25–30°c (77–86°F).

× Wilsonara hybrid
fam. Orchidaceae
Cross between *Cochlioda, Odontoglossum* and
Oncidium. Winter temperature 8–12°c (46–
53°F). S osmunda fibre, sphagnum moss and
a few expanded clay granules. P division.

Xanthosoma nigrum (X. violaceum)
fam. Araceae
Vigorous, fast-growing plant for the heated
greenhouse. Minimum winter temperature
15°c (59°F). S leafmould, pinewood soil, coarse
peat and farmyard manure. Feed generously.
P division.

119

***Yucca aloifolia* 'Marginata'**
Spanish Bayonet / fam. *Agavaceae*
○ 🌸 ⊕ ∞ 🌗 🔲
Sharp-pointed yucca with a decorative stem.
This species also includes green-leaved types.
Container plant. Overwinter at minimum 5°C
(41°F). S humus-rich loam. P stem cuttings.

Yucca elephantipes (Y. guatemalensis)
Spineless Yucca / fam. *Agavaceae*
○ 🌸 ⊕ ∞ 🌗 🔲
Stem grossly thickened at the base. If you
repot this plant annually you do not need to
feed it. Treat like *Y. aloifolia* 'Marginata'.

Zamia pumila
fam. *Cycadaceae*
🌓 🌸 ☺ ∞ 🌗 ⊡ 🔲
Unusual house or greenhouse plant with an
underground stem. Pot in humus-rich loam.
Overwinter at 12–16°C (53–60°F). P seed.

Zantedeschia aethiopica (Calla aethiopica)
Arum Lily / fam. *Araceae*
○ 🌓 🌸 ∞ 🌗 🔲
Produces fragrant flowers in the spring or
early summer. Follow with one month's rest.
Can be put out in the garden during the
summer. Second rest in winter at 10°C (50°F).
S loamy. P division.

***Zantedeschia aethiopica* 'Green Goddess'**
Arum Lily / fam. *Araceae*
○ 🌓 🌸 ∞ 🌗 🔲
This cultivar with most striking inflorescence
does best in a greenhouse. Treat like *Z.
aethiopica*. The leaves drop off during the dry
overwintering period.

Zebrina pendula (Tradescentia zebrina)
fam. *Commelinaceae*
🌓 🌸 🌸 ∞ 🌗 🔲
Attractive hanging plant with white to rose-
red small flowers. Good light ensures best leaf
markings. Minimum winter temperature 12°C
(53°F). P cuttings.

***Zebrina pendula* 'Quadricolor'**
fam. *Commelinaceae*
🌓 🌸 🌸 ∞ 🌗 🔲
Needs even more light than the species. Feed
very lightly in the summer; otherwise
cultivate and propagate like *Z. pendula*. Prune
regularly.

Zebrina purpusii
fam. *Commelinaceae*
🌓 🌸 🌸 ∞ 🌗 🔲
Larger plant than *Z. pendula*. 'Minor' has less
red in its leaves and is less robust. Repot and
cut back every year. Otherwise treat and
propagate like *Z. pendula*.

Zephyranthes candida
fam. *Amaryllidaceae*
○ 🌸 🌙 ∞ 🌗 🔲
This bulb flowers between July and October.
Put out in a sheltered spot during the
summer. Minimum winter temperature 5°C
(41°F); keep very slightly moist. P division,
seed, offsets.

Garden Plants

Photographed at Great Dixter, Northiam, East Sussex, England.

Abies balsamea* f. *hudsonia
Balsam Fir / Fam. *Pinaceae*
H 1 m (3 ft) W 1.25 m (4 ft). Zone 3. S slightly acid. P seed, cuttings. A spreading bush with densely packed, glossy leaves having two white bands on the underside.

Abies grandis
Giant Fir / fam. *Pinaceae*
H 30 m (100 ft). W 6 m (20 ft). Zone 6. S not too poor. P seed. Attractive pyramidal tree. Leaves laid flat. Cones upright. Not suitable for gardens.

Abies koreana
Korean Fir / fam. *Pinaceae*
May. Female flowers red, green, male reddish brown, yellow. H 15 m (50 ft). W 5 m (16 ft). Zone 5. S normal. P seed. Profusely flowering small tree with particularly attractive cones.

Abies lasiocarpa* var. *arizonica
Silver Fir / fam. *Pinaceae*
May. Female flowers purple, male violet blue. H 2 m (6 ft). W 6 m (20 ft). Zone 5. P seed. Slim shape. Branches covered in short hair. Fine blue leaves; purple cones.

***Abies pinsapo* 'Glauca'**
Spanish Fir / fam. *Pinaceae*
H 2 m (6 ft). W 7 m (23 ft). Zone 6. S slightly acid. P cuttings. Pyramidal tree with radially spreading leaves covered in a blue bloom. Cylindrical cones.

Acacia dealbata (A. decurrens* var. *dealbata)* / Mimosa / fam. *Leguminosae
January–April. Yellow. H 2 m (6 ft). W 5 m (16 ft). Zone 9. S normal garden soil. P seed. Tree with fern-like, grey-green leaves and fragrant flowers borne in long panicles.

Acaena anserinifolia (A. sanguisorbae)
New Zealand Burr / fam. *Rosaceae*
June–August. Purple. H 15 cm (6 in). A 30 cm (12 in). S chalky. P division, seed. Ground-cover plant with hairy grey-blue leaves and reddish-purple burrs.

Acaena buchananii
New Zealand Burr / fam. *Rosaceae*
June–August. Brown. H 5 cm (2 in). A 30 cm (12 in). S chalky. P division, seed. Well-known ground-cover plant with blue-green leaves and amber-brown burrs.

Acaena novae-zealandiae
New Zealand Burr / fam. *Rosaceae*
June–August. Red. H 10 cm (4 in). A 30 cm (12 in). S chalky. P division, seed. Hardy ground-cover plant with purple-red burrs and dark green leaves.

Acantholimon olivieri (A. venustum)
fam. *Plumbaginaceae*
○ ⊜ ⊘ ⊛ ⊗ ⊗
July–August. Pink. H 20 cm (8 in). A 20 cm
(8 in). S normal garden soil. P seed, cuttings.
Hardy plant with blue-green leaves and
profuse flowers in loose spikes.

Acanthus mollis
Bear's Breeches / fam. *Acanthaceae*
○ ⓘ ○ ⊘ ⊛ ⊘ ⊕ ⊗
June–August. White / purple. H 1 m (3 ft).
A 1 m (3 ft). S chalky. P root cuttings, division,
seed. Hardy. White-lipped petals with purple
veins. Long, loose flower spikes.

Acer capillipes
Maple / fam. *Aceraceae*
○ ⓘ ⓘ ⊛ ⊘ ⊛ ⊕
May. Greeny white. H 6 m (20 ft). W 3 m (10 ft).
Zone 5. S humusy. P seed, layering. Small tree
with striped trunk and branches, and leaves
that change colour. Juvenile leaves are red.

Acer cappadocicum (A. laetum)
Maple / fam. *Aceraceae*
○ ⓘ ⓘ ⊛ ⊘ ⊛ ⊕
May–June. Yellow. H 2 m (6 ft). W 8 m (26 ft).
Zone 5–6. S humus-rich. P grafting, seed.
Tree with winged seeds and golden-yellow
leaves that change colour.

Acer griseum
Maple / fam. *Aceraceae*
○ ⓘ ⓘ ⊛ ⊘ ⊛ ⊕
May. Yellow. H 12 m (40 ft). W 5 m (16 ft). Zone
5. S humus-rich. P seed. Small tree with
flaking buff-coloured bark and leaves that
turn red and scarlet in the autumn.

***Acer japonicum* 'Aconitifolium'**
Japanese Maple / fam. *Aceraceae*
○ ⓘ ⓘ ⊛ ⊘ ⊛ ⊘ ⊕
May. Red. H 5 m (16 ft). W 3 m (10 ft). Zone 5.
S humus-rich. P grafting, layering. Shrub or
small tree with deeply divided light green
leaves that change colour.

***Acer japonicum* 'Aureum'**
Japanese Maple / fam. *Aceraceae*
○ ⓘ ⊛ ⊘ ⓦ ⊛ ⊘ ⊕
May. Red. H 5 m (16 ft). W 3 m (10 ft). Zone 5.
S humus-rich. P grafting, layering. Fairly
dense, slow-growing shrub with yellow-
green leaves that change colour.

Acer negundo* spp. *californicum
Box Elder / fam. *Aceraceae*
○ ⓘ ⊛ ⊘ ⓦ ⊛ ⊘ ⊛ ⊛
April. Yellow-green. H 15 m (50 ft). W 10 m
(33 ft). Zone 2. S humus-rich. P grafting,
layering. Shrub or tree with glaucous
branches and leaves, and large winged seeds.

***Acer palmatum* 'Atropurpureum'**
Japanese Maple / fam. *Aceraceae*
○ ⓘ ⓘ ⊗ ⊛ ⊘ ⓦ ⊘ ⊕
June. Red. H 6 m (20 ft). W 3 m (10 ft). Zone 5.
S humus-rich and chalky. P layering, grafting.
Shrub or small tree with dark red, deeply
divided leaves and winged seeds.

Acer

Acer palmatum 'Corallinum'
Japanese Maple / fam. *Aceraceae*
○ ◐ ⊛ ⊕ ⊛ ⓦ ⊘
June. Red. H 3 m (10 ft). W 2 m (6 ft). Zone 5.
S humus-rich and chalky. P layering, grafting.
Shrub with coral-red bark and deeply
divided, light green leaves that change colour.

Acer palmatum 'Dissectum' (summer)
Japanese Maple / fam. *Aceraceae*
◐ ⊛ ⊕ ⊛ ⓦ ⊕
June. Red. H 3 m (10 ft). W 3 m (10 ft). Zone 5.
S humus-rich, acid. P cuttings, grafting.
Compact habit. Branches often twisted.
Suitable for gardens and small parks.

Acer palmatum 'Dissectum' (autumn)
Japanese Maple / fam. *Aceraceae*
◐ ⊛ ⊕ ⊛ ⓦ ⊘ ⊕
June. Red. H 3 m (10 ft). W 3 m (10 ft). Zone 5.
S humus-rich, acid. P cuttings, grafting. The
light green leaves turn a glorious russet in
autumn.

Acer palmatum 'Ornatum'
Japanese Maple / fam. *Aceraceae*
◐ ⊛ ⊕ ⓦ ⊘
June. Red. H 4 m (13 ft). W 4 m (13 ft). Zone 5.
S humus-rich, chalky. P cuttings, grafting.
Shrubby small tree with finely divided russet
leaves that change colour in autumn.

Acer palmatum 'Roseomarginatum'
Japanese Maple / fam. *Aceraceae*
○ ◐ ⊛ ⊕ ⓦ ⊘
June. Red. H 6 m (20 ft). W 3 m (10 ft). Zone 5.
S humus-rich, chalky. P grafting, cuttings.
Upright shrub with deeply divided leaves
having pink margins.

Acer palmatum var. *heptalobum*
Japanese Maple / fam. *Aceraceae*
○ ◐ ⊛ ⓦ ⓥ ⊘ ⊕
June. Red. H 4.5 m (15 ft). W 2.5 m (8 ft). Zone
5. S humus-rich, chalky. P cuttings, seed.
Shrubby tree with large, lobate, light green
leaves that change colour in autumn.

Acer pennsylvanicum (A. striatum)
Snake Bark Maple / fam. *Aceraceae*
○ ◐ ⊛ ⊛ ⓦ ⊘
May. Yellow. H 8 m (26 ft). W 6 m (20 ft).
S humus-rich. P cuttings, seed. Small tree
with white-striped bark and leaves that
change colour. Suitable for medium-sized
gardens.

Acer platanoides
Norway Maple / fam. *Aceraceae*
○ ◐ ⊛ ⊘
April–May. Greeny yellow. H 20 m (65 ft).
W 10 m (33 ft). Zone 3. S humus-rich. P seed.
Robust tree with a broad crown and bright
green leaves that change colour. For parks and
streets.

Acer platanoides 'Drummondii'
Norway Maple / fam. *Aceraceae*
○ ◐ ◐ ⊛ ⊘ ⊕
April–May. Yellow. H 15 m (50 ft). W 10 m
(33 ft). Zone 3. S humus-rich. P budding.
Moderately tall tree with white-edged, bright
green leaves. For medium-sized gardens.

Acer platanoides 'Globosum'
Norway Maple / fam. *Aceraceae*
◯ ◑ ✳ ⊕ ⊕
April–May. Yellow. H 5 m (16 ft). W 10 m
(33 ft). Zone 3. S humus-rich. P grafting. Tree
with a flat-topped, spherical shape and dark
green leaves. For parks, squares and streets.

Acer platanoides 'Goldsworth Purple'
Norway Maple / fam. *Aceraceae*
◯ ◑ ✳ ⊕
April–May. Yellow. H 20 m (65 ft).
W 10 m (33 ft). Zone 3. S humus-rich.
P grafting, cutting. Tree with dull, deep
purple-brown leaves that do not change
colour in autumn.

Acer pseudoplatanus 'Atropurpureum'
Sycamore / fam. *Aceraceae*
◯ ◑ ✳ ⊕ ⊕
May. Yellow green. H 15 m (50 ft). W 12 m
(40 ft). Zone 5. S humus-rich. P grafting,
cuttings. Tree with a broad conical crown.
Vigorous grower with attractive bronze
leaves.

Acer pseudoplatanus 'Brilliantissimum'
Sycamore / fam. *Aceraceae*
◑ ✳ ⊕
May. Yellow green. H 7 m (23 ft). W 5 m (16 ft).
Zone 5. S humus-rich. P grafting, cuttings.
Small tree with a dense, pyramidal crown and
yellowish leaves speckled with pink.

Acer pseudoplatanus 'Costorphinense'
Sycamore / fam. *Aceraceae*
◯ ◑ ✳ ⊕
May. Yellow green. H 30 m (100 ft). W 10 m
(33 ft). Zone 5. S humus-rich. P grafting,
cuttings. Tree with a broad pyramidal crown
and leaves changing from bright yellow to
mat green.

Acer pseudoplatanus 'Luteo-virescens'
Sycamore / fam. *Aceraceae*
◯ ◑ ✳ ⊕
May. Greeny yellow. H 20–30 m (65–100 ft).
W 10 m (33 ft). Zone 5. P budding. Magnificent
tree for parks and avenues. Five-lobed leaves
with fairly large yellow spots.

Acer pseudoplatanus 'Prinz Handjery'
Sycamore / fam. *Aceraceae*
◯ ◑ ✳ ⊕
May. Yellow-green. H 3 m (10 ft). W 3 m (10 ft).
Zone 5. S humus-rich. P grafting, cutting.
Resembles *A. pseudoplatanus*
'Brilliantissimum' except that the leaves have
a light purple undersurface.

Acer rubrum 'Scanlon'
Red Maple / fam. *Aceraceae*
◯ ◑ ⊕ ✳ ⊕
March–April. Red. H 15 m (50 ft). W 10 m
(33 ft). Zone 3. S humus-rich. P cuttings,
grafting. A fairly slow-growing tree with a
dense conical crown and most attractive
leaves.

Acer saccharinum (A. dasycarpum)
Silver Maple / fam. *Aceraceae*
◯ ◑ ⊕ ✳ ⊕
April. Green. H 30 m (100 ft). W 15 m (50 ft).
Zone 3. S lime-free. P seed. Robust tree with
a broad, loose crown and brittle branches.
Suitable for parks. Foliage changes colour.

125

Acer tegmentosum
Maple / fam. *Aceraceae*
○ ◐ ✿ ⊛
May. Yellow. H 9 m (30 ft). W 4 m (13 ft). Zone
5. S humus-rich. P seed. Small tree with bare
light green juvenile branches which later
develop lighter stripes.

Achillea 'Coronation Gold'
Yarrow / fam. *Compositae*
○ ◐ ◑ ◎ ⊗ ⊗
June–September. Yellow. H 75–100 cm (30–
36 in). A 40 cm (16 in). S normal garden soil.
P division. Probably a cross between *A.
clypeolata* and *A. filipendulina*. Flowers
profusely.

Achillea filipendulina
Yarrow / fam. *Compositae*
○ ◐ ◑ ◎ ⊗ ⊗
July–August. Yellow. H 120 cm (4 ft). A 50 cm
(20 in). S normal garden soil. P division, seed.
Very good and strong plant for the border.
Flowers good for drying.

Achillea millefolium
Yarrow / fam. *Compositae*
○ ◐ ◑ ◎ ⊗ ⊗
June–July (October). Red. H 50–75 cm (20–
30 in). A 30 cm (1 ft). S normal garden soil.
P division, seed. Suitable for wild gardens.
Can be dried for winter decoration.

Achillea taygetea
Yarrow / fam. *Compositae*
○ ◐ ◑ ◎ ⊗ ⊗
July–September. Yellow. H 40 cm (16 in).
A 20 cm (8 in). S normal garden soil.
P division, seed. Flowers prufusely. Erect
stems. Divide frequently. Grown chiefly for
its creamy colour.

**Achnatherum calamagrostis (Agrostis
calamagrostis) / fam. *Gramineae***
○ ⊖ ⌃ ◎ ⊗ ⊗
June–July. Yellow-white. H 60–100 cm (2–
3 ft). A 20 cm (8 in). S porous, chalky. P seed,
division. Attractive grass with flat leaves and
7–15-cm (2¾–6-in) long panicles. Suitable for
drying.

Acidanthera bicolor var. murielae
fam. *Iridaceae*
○ ⊖ ✣ ⊕ ◎ ⊗
August–September. White. H 30–40 cm (12–
16 in). A 15 cm (6 in). D 5 cm (2 in). S normal
garden soil. P offsets. Fragrant flowers.
Overwinter bulbs at 12–18°C (53–64°F). Plant
out in April.

Aconitum × arendsii
Monkshood / fam. *Ranunculaceae*
◐ ◑ ◎ ⊗ ⊗
September–October. Blue. H 100–130 cm (3–
4 ft). A 60 cm (2 ft). S normal garden soil.
P division, seed. Loose racemes. Picturesque
appearance. For clearings in woods.

Aconitum carmichaelii (A. fischeri)
Monkshood / fam. *Ranunculaceae*
◐ ◑ ◎ ⊗ ⊗
August–October. Violet. H 50–100 cm (20–
36 in). A 35 cm (14 in). S humus-rich. P seed,
division. Attractive, low-growing plant with
sturdy, upright, almost bare stems.

Aconitum fischeri
Monkshood / fam. *Ranunculaceae*
◖◯🌣🌢⊗
August–October. Purple. H 40–70 cm (16–28 in). A 30 cm (1 ft). S normal garden soil. P seed, division. Attractive upright plant; palmate, three-lobed leaves; big flowers in loose racemes.

Aconitum henryi
Monkshood / fam. *Ranunculaceae*
◖◯🌣🌢⊗
July–August. Violet blue. H 130–160 cm (4–5 ft). A 60 cm (2 ft). S normal garden soil. P seed, division. Loose racemes. Most suitable for a border. Colour more pronounced in shady positions.

Aconitum lamarckii (A. pyrenaicum)
Monkshood / fam. *Ranunculaceae*
◖◯🌣🌢⊗
June–August. Yellow. H 1 m (3 ft). A 60 cm (2 ft). S normal garden soil. P division, seed. Sturdy stems. Moderately moist position such as the edge of woods and clearings.

Aconitum napellus ssp. *pyramidale*
Monkshood / fam. *Ranunculaceae*
◖◯🌣🌢⊗
June–August. Deep blue. H 150 cm (5 ft). A 60 cm (2 ft). S normal garden soil. P division, seed. Palmate leaves. Cool position. Flowers best on fertile, slightly moist soil.

Actaea pachypoda (A. alba)
Baneberry / fam. *Ranunculaceae*
◖◖▦◯🌼🌣⊗
May–June. White. H 40–50 cm (16–20 in). A 20 cm (8 in). S fertile, humus-rich. P seed, division. Grows in woods. Decorative foliage; red, thickened fruit stalks and white berries.

Actaea rubra
Red Baneberry / fam. *Ranunculaceae*
◖◖▦◯🌼🌣
May–June. Red fruits. H 40 cm (16 in). A 20 cm (8 in). S fertile. P division, seed. Poisonous berries. Trilobate to doubly trilobate, crenate leaves. Tends to grow wild.

Actinidia chinensis
Chinese Gooseberry / fam. *Actinidiaceae*
◯◖▦🌣🌢🍂🌼
May–June. Cream-white. H 8 m (26 ft). W 2 m (6 ft). Zone 5–6. S humus-rich. P seed, cuttings. Vigorous climber. Young twigs covered with russet hairs. Edible fruits.

Actinidia kolomikta
Kolomikta Vine / fam. *Actinidiaceae*
◯◖◿▦🌣🌢🍂🌼
May. White. H 2 m (6 ft). W 3 m (10 ft). Zone 4. S humus-rich. P seed, cuttings. Fairly slow-growing climber with fragrant unisexual flowers. Yellowish fruits.

Adiantum pedatum
Maidenhair Fern / fam. *Adiantaceae*
◖◖◖◯🌣⊗
No flowers. H 25–50 cm (10–20 in). A 20 cm (8 in). S humus-rich. P division, spores. Attractive, hardy fern. Must not lack water during the growing period.

Adonis aestivalis
fam. *Ranunculaceae*
○ ⊖ ☉ ☽ ❀ ⊘ ⊗
Sow in autumn. Thin out to 10 cm (4 in). H 30–
50 cm (12–20 in). Red-black. S not critical. An
old-fashioned annual with finely cut leaves
and bowl-shaped flowers.

Adonis vernalis
fam. *Ranunculaceae*
○ ⊖ ☿ ❀ ⊘ ⊗
April–May. Yellow. H 15–30 cm (6–12 in).
A 20 cm (8 in). S chalky. P division, seed. Rock
plant needing full sun to produce flowers in
profusion. Attractive foliage.

***Aegopodium podagraria* 'Variegatum'**
Ground Elder / fam. *Umbelliferae*
◗ ○ ✿ ⊘
June–September. White. H 20–40 cm (8–
16 in). A 20 cm (8 in). S normal garden soil.
P division. Attractive variegated cultivar.
Spreads like a weed. Plant as ground cover
under shrubs.

Aesculus* × *carnea
Red Horse Chestnut / fam. *Hippocastanaceae*
○ ◗ ❀ ✿ ☿ ⊘ ☉ ⊕
May. Rose pink. H 15 m (50 ft). W 12 m (40 ft).
Zone 3. S humus-rich. P seed or grafting. Tree
with few conkers, suitable for the medium-
sized garden.

***Aesculus hippocastanum* / Common Horse**
Chestnut / fam. *Hippocastanaceae*
○ ◗ ❀ ☿ ✿ ☉ ⊕
May. White. H 30 m (100 ft). W 15 m (50 ft).
Zone 3. S humus-rich. P seed. Tall tree with a
very broad crown, large leaves and prickly
fruits.

***Aesculus hippocastanum* 'Memmingeri'**
Horse Chestnut / fam. *Hippocastanaceae*
○ ◗ ❀ ☿ ✿ ☉ ⊕
May. White. H 30 m (100 ft). W 15 m (50 ft).
Zone 3. S humus-rich. P grafting. A tall tree
with light green or greyish leaves and prickly
fruits.

Aesculus pavia (A. rubra)
Red Buckeye / fam. *Hippocastanaceae*
○ ◗ ❀ ☿ ✿ ☉ ⊕
June. Red. H 15 m (50 ft). W 12 m (40 ft). Zone
5. S humus-rich. P seed. A smaller Horse
Chestnut with five-lobed leaves and flowers
in long panicles.

***Aethionema* hybrid 'Warley Ruber'**
fam. *Cruciferae*
○ ⊖ ⊘ ○ ☿ ⊗
April–May. Purple. H 10–25 cm (4–10 in). A
20 cm (8 in). S normal garden soil. P division,
cuttings. Shrub-like rockplant. Profuse
flowers. Spreading. Strongly resembles *Iberis*.

Agapanthus praecox* ssp. *orientalis
fam. *Liliaceae*
○ ⊘ ○ ☿ ⊗
July–August. Violet. H 30–70 cm (12–28 in).
A 30 cm (1 ft). S potting compost. P division,
seed. Suitable for containers. Protect against
frost with deep layers of bracken or
weathered ashes.

Agastache foeniculum
fam. *Labiatae*
○ ◑ ○ ☯
June–August. Purple. H 70 cm (28 in). A 25 cm
(10 in). S normal garden soil. P division, seed.
Not very well known but a particularly fine
and easily managed border plant. Flowers
profusely.

Ageratum 'Dondo'
fam. *Compositae*
○ ◑ ○ ☯
Sow in February–March under glass at 16–
18°C (60–64°F). Plant out 15–30 cm (6–12 in)
apart. H 15 cm (6 in). Violet blue. S normal
garden soil. Deadhead regularly and remove
second-growth leafstalks.

Ageratum houstonianum (A. mexicanum)
fam. *Compositae*
○ ◑ ○ ☯
Sow in Feburary–March in heated
greenhouse. Harden off. Plant out 15–30 cm
(6–12 in) apart. H 30–60 cm (1–2 ft). Violet-
blue, purple, white. S normal soil. Profusely
flowering. P also from cuttings.

Agrostemma githago
Corn Cockle / fam. *Caryophyllaceae*
○ ○ ☯ ☢ ⊗
Sow in April in flowering site. Thin out to
30 cm (1 ft) apart. H 80 cm (32 in). Purple. S not
critical. Good for cutting; occasionally found
in fields and by roadsides. Seeds poisonous.

Ailanthus altissima (A. glandulosa)
fam. *Simaroubaceae*
○ ◑ ❋ ☯ ❀
July. Orange. H 20 m (65 ft). W 15 m (50 ft).
Zone 4. S not critical. P seed, suckers. Robust
tree with thick branches and twigs, large
flower clusters and winged seeds.

Ajuga reptans
Bugle / fam. *Labiatae*
◑ ◑ ○ ☯
May–June. Blue. H 20 cm (8 in). A 20 cm (8 in).
S humus-rich soil. P division. Hardy, well-
known ground-cover plant tending to spread
by runners.

Ajuga reptans 'Rubra'
Bugle / fam. *Labiatae*
◑ ○ ☯ ☢ ⊖
May–June. Blue. H 30 cm (1 ft). A 30–45 cm
(12–18 in). S normal garden soil. P root
cuttings. Showy brown-red leaves, bronze in
winter. Hardy.

Akebia quinata
fam. *Lardizabalaceae*
○ ◑ ◑ ☯ ❀
April–May. Purple. H 10 m (33 ft). W 5 m
(16 ft). Zone 4. S humus-rich. P layering,
cuttings. Fast-growing, twining shrub;
fragrant flowers; violet, glaucous fruits.

Alcea rosea (Althaea rosea)
Hollyhock / fam. *Malvaceae*
○ ◒ ⊕ ○ ☯ ☢ ⊗
Sow in May in flowering position. Thin out
to 70 cm (28 in) apart. H 3 m (10 ft). Red.
S fertile. Single-flowered hollyhock suitable
for cottage gardens. Susceptible to rust.

129

Alcea

Alcea rosea (Althaea rosea)
Hollyhock / fam. *Malvaceae*
◯ ⊜ ⊛ ☉ ⊙ · ☯ ⊕ ⊗
For description and propagation see last
entry. Double-flowered hollyhock; outer
petals larger than innermost. *Alcea* has
medicinal properties.

Alcea rosea 'Chater's Double Choice'
Hollyhock / fam. *Malvaceae*
◯ ⊜ ⊛ ☉ ⊙ ☯ ⊕ ⊗
For description and propagation see previous
entry. Decorative plant, densely crowded
flower. Remove side shoots at the foot of the
plant and treat as cuttings.

Alcea rosea 'Silver Puffs'
Hollyhock / fam. *Malvaceae*
◯ ⊛ ☉ ⊙ ☯ ⊕ ⊗
Sow in February in heated greenhouse, April
in flowering site. Thin to 40 cm (16 in) apart.
H 150 cm (5 ft). Violet-pink. S fertile. A
popular annual, good for the back of the
border.

Alchemilla mollis (A. acutiloba)
Lady's Mantle / fam. *Rosaceae*
◯ ⊖ ◑ ◐ ☯ ⊛ ⊗
June–August. Yellow. H 30–40 cm (12–16 in).
A 20 cm (8 in). S normal garden soil.
P division, seed. Excellent border plant. Cut
back stems hard after flowering. Leaves catch
raindrops.

Alisma plantago-aquatica
Water Plantain / fam. *Alismataceae*
◯ ◑ ⊗ ◐ ☯ ⊗
June–October. White. H 40–80 cm (16–32 in).
A 30 cm (1 ft). S clay. P division, seed. Suitable
for marshy land or ponds 20 cm (8 in) deep.
Seeds itself readily. Good for drying.

Allium cernuum
fam. *Liliaceae*
◯ ⊖ ⊚ ◐ ☯
May–July. Purple. H 60 cm (2 ft). A 20 cm
(8 in). D 5–10 cm (2–4 in). S normal garden
soil. P seed, splitting of bulbs. Beautiful, fairly
rare decorative species with masses of flowers
in a fine colour.

Allium christophii (A. albopilosum)
fam. *Liliaceae*
◯ ⊖ ⊚ ◐ ☯ ⊗
June–July. Purplish-mauve. H 60 cm (2 ft).
A 20–30 cm (8–12 in). D 7–10 cm (3–4 in).
S normal. P seed, split bulbs. A fine species
from Turkestan. Flowers in 20–25-cm (8–10-
in) globular heads.

Allium flavum
fam. *Liliaceae*
◯ ⊖ ⊚ ◐ ☯
July–August. Yellow. H 30 cm (1 ft). A 10–
15 cm (4–6 in). D 5 cm (2 in). S normal garden
soil. P seed, splitting of bulbs. Makes good
border plant. The bulbs need not be lifted for
many years.

Allium giganteum
fam. *Liliaceae*
◯ ⊖ ⊛ ⊚ ◐ ☯ ⊕ ⊗
June–July. Deep lilac. H 175 cm (5¾ ft). A 20 cm
(8 in). D 10 cm (4 in). S normal garden soil.
P seed, split bulbs. Fine for cutting, though
only for large arrangements. Also good for
drying.

130

Allium karataviense
fam. *Liliaceae*
○ ⊖ ⊛ ⓨ ⊗
April–May. Pale pink. H 30 cm (1 ft). A 10–
15 cm (4–6 in). D 5 cm (2 in). S normal. P seed,
split bulbs. Unusual species. The broad leaves
have a metallic sheen. Short-stemmed flower
heads.

Allium moly
fam. *Liliaceae*
◑ ⊖ ⊛ ⓨ ⊗
May–June. Yellow. H 25 cm (10 in). A 5–10 cm
(2–4 in). D 3–5 cm (1–2 in). S humus-rich,
moist. P seed. Best-known garden onion with
golden-yellow flower heads. Suitable for
naturalisation.

Allium oreophilum (A. ostrowskianum)
fam. *Liliaceae*
○ ⊖ ⊛ ⓨ ⊗
June. Rose coloured. H 15 cm (6 in). A 5–10 cm
(2–4 in). D 5 cm (2 in). S normal graden soil.
P seed, bulb splitting. Only two to three
lanceolate leaves. Best in rock gardens.

Allium sphaerocephalon
fam. *Liliaceae*
○ ⊖ ⊛ ⓨ ⊗
July–August. Reddish brown. H 30–60 cm (1–
2 ft). A 5–15 cm (2–6 in). D 5 cm (2 in).
S normal garden soil. P seed, bulb splitting.
Colour and profusion make this onion
suitable for borders.

Allium ursinum
Ramsons / fam. *Liliaceae*
◑ ⊖ ⊛ ⓨ ⊗
May. White. H 15–40 cm (6–16 in). A 5 cm
(2 in). D 5 cm (2 in). S humus-rich, moist soil.
P seed. The best-known species. Grows wild
in moist woods.

Alnus glutinosa
Grey Alder / fam. *Betulaceae*
○ ◑ ⊖ ⊛ ✳ ⓨ ⊛ ▥ ⊗
February–March. H 25 m (80 ft). W 10 m (33 ft).
Zone 3. S fertile. P seed. Tree with an
irregular crown and attractive, long catkins.
Good as a wind break.

Alnus glutinosa
Grey Alder / fam. *Betulaceae*
○ ◑ ⊛ ➔ ✳ ⓨ ⊛ ▥ ⊗
For description and propagation see last
entry. Native to Europe and Siberia. Leaves
obovate, doubly serrated. Beautiful long
catkins in the winter.

Alnus incana 'Aurea'
Golden Alder / fam. *Betulaceae*
○ ◑ ⊖ ⊛ ✳ ⓨ ⊛ ⊗
February–March. Orange. H 6 m (20 ft).
W 4 m (13 ft). Zone 2. S not critical. P cuttings
or layering. Tree with yellow-green leaves
and yellowish branches and catkins. Suitable
for smaller gardens.

Alonsoa warscewiczii (A. grandiflora)
Mask Flower / fam. *Scrophulariaceae*
○ ○ ⓨ
Sow in March in warm, or in April–May in
cool, greenhouse. Plant out at A 20 cm (8 in).
H 30–90 cm (1–3 ft). Orange red. S humus-
rich. Bushy semi-shrub of narrowly
pyramidal habit.

131

Alstroemeria

Alstroemeria aurantiaca 'Lutea'
Peruvian Lily / fam. *Amaryllidaceae*
○ ⊘ ⊙ ⊗
June–August. Yellow-orange. H 60–120 cm
(2–4 ft). A 70 cm (28 in). S normal garden soil.
P division. This attractive border plant with
tuberous roots bears 10 to 30 flowers.

Alstroemeria aurantiaca 'Orange King'
Peruvian Lily / fam. *Amaryllidaceae*
○ ⊙ ⊗
June–August. H 60–120 cm (2–4 ft). A 70 cm
(28 in). S normal garden soil. P division, seed.
Not quite hardy. Will not prosper if the
ground is moist for long periods.

Alternanthera bettzickiana
fam. *Amaranthaceae*
○ ⊙ ⊛ ⊗
H 20 cm (8 in). S humus-rich. P cuttings in
January at 20–22°c (68–71°F). Plant out at
A 20–30 cm (8–12 in). Graceful, upright, bushy
little plant with attractively coloured leaves.

Alyssum montanum ssp. *montanum*
fam. *Cruciferae*
○ ⊖ ⊙ ⊛ ⊗
June–July. Yellow. H 10–20 cm (4–8 in).
A 15 cm (6 in). S chalky. P seed, cuttings
(July–September). Cut the plants back slightly
after flowering or they will become straggly.

Alyssum saxatile
Gold Dust / fam. *Cruciferae*
○ ⊖ ⊙ ⊛ ⊗
April–May. Yellow. H 15–30 cm (6–12 in).
A 20 cm (8 in). S chalky. P seed, cuttings
(July–September). Hardy semi-shrub, its
leaves densely covered with grey hairs.

Alyssum saxatile 'Dudley Neville'
Gold Dust / fam. *Cruciferae*
○ ⊖ ⊙ ⊛ ⊗
April–May. Creamy yellow. H 15–30 cm (6–
12 in). A 20 cm (8 in). S chalky. P cuttings (July
to September). Double flowers. Suitable for
rock gardens, steep banks and edging.

Amaranthus caudatus
Love-Lies-Bleeding / fam. *Amaranthaceae*
○ ⊙ ⊛ ⊗
Sow in March in heated greenhouse or in May
in flowering position. Thin out to A 45 cm
(18 in). H 1 m (3 ft). Red. S fertile. Most
popular species for a border. Stems turn red
in autumn.

Amaranthus tricolor 'Splendens'
Joseph's Coat / fam. *Amaranthaceae*
○ ⊙ ⊛ ⊗
Sow in April in heated greenhouse. Plant out
at A 30–45 cm (12–18 in). H 1 m (3 ft). Red.
S fertile, chalky. Strong-growing plant with
scarlet leaves overlaid with dark green,
bronze and yellow.

Amberboa moschata 'Imperialis'
fam. *Compositae*
○ ⊛ ⊙ ⊛ ⊗
Sow in February in heated greenhouse. Plant
out at A 25 cm (10 in). H 80 cm (32 in). White,
reddish violet. S normal soil. Good for
cutting. The toothed and fragrant flowers
have a silky sheen.

132

Amelanchier canadensis (A. oblongifolia)
Shadbush/fam. *Rosaceae*
○ ◐ 🌱 ✳ 🌱 🪴 ❀
April. White. H 8 m (26 ft). W 4 m (13 ft). Zone
4. S normal garden soil, chalky. P seed,
cuttings. Large shrub with oblong leaves and
erect racemes.

Amelanchier florida (A. alnifolia)
June Berry/fam. *Rosaceae*
○ ◐ ❀ 🌱 ✳ 🌱 🪴 ❀
May. White. H 4 m (13 ft). W 3 m (10 ft). Zone
2. S normal but chalky. P seed, cuttings.
Shrub or small tree with small flowers and
edible blue-black berries.

Amelanchier lamarckii (A. canadensis)
Shadbush/fam. *Rosaceae*
○ ◐ 🌱 ✳ 🌱 🪴 ❀
April–May. White. H 10 m (33 ft). W 4 m
(13 ft). Zone 4. S not critical. P seed, cuttings.
Slender shrub with leaves which turn a
beautiful colour. Bears edible fruits.

Ammobium alatum 'Grandiflorum'
Winged Everlasting/fam. *Compositae*
○ ◐ 🌱 ❀
Sow in April under glass. Plant out at A 25 cm
(10 in). H 50 cm (20 in). White/yellow. S not
critical. Plant covered in white hair. Winged
stems, good for drying.

Amorpha fruticosa
fam. *Leguminosae*
○ ❀ 🌱 ❀
June–August. Purple. H 5 m (16 ft). W 4 m
(13 ft). Zone 4. S not critical. P seed, cuttings.
Fairly broad shrub. Flowers in clusters, with
conspicuous yellow stamens. Variable
species.

Ampelopsis brevipedunculata (summer)
fam. *Vitaceae*
○ ◐ 🌱 🪴 ❀
June–July. Green. H 12 m (40 ft). W 5 m (16 ft).
Zone 4. S humus-rich. P seed, cuttings,
layering. Very vigorous climber with flowers
in dense clusters and fruits that change
colour.

Ampelopsis megalophylla (autumn)
fam. *Vitaceae*
○ ◐ 🌱 🪴 ❀
For description and P see last entry. A self-
clinging shrub with thick, bare twigs. Large
winter buds. Oval leaves, round fruits.

Anagallis arvensis
Scarlet Pimpernel/fam. *Primulaceae*
○ ⊙ 🌱 ❀
Sow in March under glass or in May in
flowering position. Thin out to A 15 cm (6 in).
H 5 cm (2 in). Red, blue. S normal soil. Low-
spreading or prostrate little plant for the
border or rock garden.

Anagallis arvensis ssp. coerulae
Scarlet Pimpernel/fam. *Primulaceae*
○ ⊙ 🌱 ❀
Sow in March under glass or in May in
flowering position. Thin out to A 15 cm (6 in).
H 5 cm (2 in). S normal garden soil. More
rarely found growing wild than *A. arvensis*,
but much cultivated.

133

Anaphalis

Anaphalis margaritacea (Gnaphalium m.)
Pearl Everlasting / fam. *Compositae*
○ ◐ ⊜ ⊖ ⊙ ⊗ ⊛ ⊗
June–September. White. H 50–75 cm (20–
30 in). A 30 cm (1 ft). S normal soil (sandy).
P division, seed. Strong-growing,
proliferating plant. Does best in a warm
position. Good for drying.

Anaphalis triplinervis 'Schwefellicht'
fam. *Compositae*
○ ◐ ⊜ ⊙ ⊙ ⊗ ⊛
July–September. H 25–50 cm (10–20 in).
A 20 cm (8 in). S normal garden soil.
P division. Does not spread. Good for drying.
Fragrant flowers. Suitable for a border.

Anchusa azurea (A. italica) 'Loddon
Royalist' / Bugloss / fam. *Boraginaceae*
○ ⊙ ⌃ ⊙ ⊙
June–July / September. Blue. H 90 cm (3 ft).
A 90 cm (3 ft). S chalky. P basal cuttings. Long
flowering period and attractive flowers. Often
grown as an annual in colder areas.

Anchusa capensis 'Blue Bird'
Bugloss / fam. *Boraginaceae*
○ ○ ⊙ ⊗
Sow in April under glass or in May in
flowering position. Thin out to A 15–25 cm
(6–10 in). H 45 cm (18 in). Blue. S normal
garden soil. A striking plant with forget-me-
not-like flowers throughout the summer.

Andromeda polifolia
Bog Rosemary / fam. *Ericaceae*
○ ◐ ⊜ ⊙ ⊛ ⊛ ⊙ ⊗
May–August. Pink. H 10–30 cm (4–12 in).
W 40 cm (16 in). Zone 2. S humus-rich, acid.
P seed, cuttings, division. Foliage used for
tanning and as black dye. Contains poisonous
substances.

Androsace sarmentosa
Rock Jasmine / fam. *Primulaceae*
○ ◐ ⊜ ⊙ ⊙ ⊗
June–July. Deep pink. H 12 cm (5 in). A 10–
20 cm (4–8 in). S normal garden soil.
P division, seed, cuttings. For the rock
garden. Protect against too much rain in
winter.

Anemone apennina
Windflower / fam. *Ranunculaceae*
○ ◐ ⊛ ⊙ ⊙ ⊗
April–May. Various colours. H 15–20 cm (6–
8 in). A 15 cm (6 in). D 5 cm (2 in). S humus-
rich, acid. P seed, division. Good for edge of
woods. Dies down after flowering. Tubers
keep. Very hardy.

Anemone blanda / Mountain Windflower of
Greece / fam. *Ranunculaceae*
○ ◐ ⊛ ⊙ ⊙ ⊗
March–April. Various colours. H 15 cm (6 in).
A 5 cm (2 in). D 5 cm (2 in). S normal garden
soil. P division of rhizomes after top growth
has died down.

Anemone coronaria 'Sylphide'
Poppy Anemone / fam. *Ranunculaceae*
○ ⌃ ⊛ ⊙ ⊙ ⊗
April–May. Mauve. H 25–35 cm (10–14 in).
A 5 cm (2 in). D 5 cm (2 in). S normal garden
soil. P root cuttings. Very variable in size,
colour and number of flowers.

Anemone × fulgens 'Annulata Grandiflora'
Windflower / fam. *Ranunculaceae*
◯ ◐ ◭ ⊛ ☻ ⊚ ⊗ ⊛
March–May. Red. H 30 cm (1 ft). A 10–15 cm
(4–6 in). D 5 cm (2 in). S normal garden soil.
P root cuttings. A hairy perennial with finely
cut leaves. Plant in the autumn.

Anemone hupehensis var. japonica
Windflower / fam. *Ranunculaceae*
◯ ◐ ◑ ☻ ⊚ ⊗
August–September. Pink. H 50–75 cm (20–
30 in). A 30 cm (1 ft). S fertile soil. P division.
Windflowers may send up new plants from
small root remains after replanting.

**Anemone japonica 'Elegans' / Japanese
Anemone / fam. *Ranunculaceae*
◯ ◐ ◭ ◑ ☻ ⊚ ⊗
August–October. White. H 50–100 cm (20–
36 in). A 70 cm (28 in). S fertile. P division.
Fine autumn-flowering plant. Replant only in
spring. Very long flowering period.

Anemone nemorosa
Wood Anemone / fam. *Ranunculaceae*
◐ ◑ ◭ ☻ ⊚
March–May. White; pink outside. H 15–25 cm
(6–10 in). A 20 cm (8 in). S humus-rich.
P division, seed. Common in woods except
on acid soil.

**Anemone ranunculoides 'Plena' / Yellow
Wood Anemone / fam. *Ranunculaceae*
◐ ◑ ◭ ☻ ⊚
April–May. Yellow. H 15–25 cm (6–10 in).
A 20 cm (8 in). S humus-rich. P division, seed.
Attractive plant with a strong resemblance to
A. nemorosa. Rarely seen in garden shops.

Anemone sylvestris 'Macrantha'
Windflower / fam. *Ranunculaceae*
◯ ◐ ◑ ☻ ⊚
April–May and sometimes August–
November. White. H 20–40 cm (8–16 in).
A 30 cm (1 ft). S chalky. P seed, division.
Flowers have silky hairs underneath. Fruits
silvery and woolly.

Anemone tomentosa 'Albadura'
Windflower / fam. *Ranunculaceae*
◯ ◐ ◭ ◑ ☻ ⊚ ⊗
August–September. Pink. H 30–50 cm (12–
20 in). A 40 cm (16 in). S fertile garden soil.
P division. Woolly plant. Good in borders.
Cover in severe winters.

Anemone tomentosa 'Robustissima'
Windflower / fam. *Ranunculaceae*
◯ ◐ ◭ ◑ ☻ ⊚ ⊗
August–September. Deep pink. H 30–50 cm
(12–20 in). A 40 cm (16 in). S fertile garden
soil. P division. Good in borders.
'Robustissima' is the best and hardiest garden
variety.

Anethum graveolens var. hortorum
Dill / fam. *Umbelliferae*
◯ ⊙ ☻ ⊛ ⊗
Sow in April–June and thin out to A 30 cm
(1 ft). H 1 m (3 ft). Yellow. S fertile soil.
Herbaceous plant whose leaves and seeds are
used in the kitchen and for medicinal
purposes.

135

Antennaria

Antennaria dioica 'Rubra'
fam. Compositae
○ ◐ ⊛ ⊘ ⊛ ⊗
May–June. Red. H 8–20 cm (3–8 in). A 10 cm
(4 in). S normal garden soil. P division. Strong
plant tolerant of a great deal of sunlight. Good
for rock gardens.

Anthemis cupaniana
Chamomile / **fam. Compositae**
○ ⊝ ○ ⊛ ⊗
July–August. White. H 60 cm (2 ft). A 30 cm
(1 ft). S dry (gravelly). P cuttings, division.
Attractive plant for rock gardens and walls.
Renew every two years for profuse flowers.

Anthemis tinctoria
Ox-eye Chamomile / **fam. Compositae**
○ ⊝ ○ ⊛ ⊗
June / July–August. Yellow. H 30–80 cm (12–
32 in). A 50 cm (20 in). S dry (gravelly).
P cuttings, division. Flowers fairly large and
on tall stems. Will grow straggly if overfed.

Anthericum liliago
St Bernard's Lily / **fam. Liliaceae**
○ ○ ⊛ ⊛ ⊗
May–June. White. H 40–80 cm (16–32 in).
A 40 cm (16 in). S light soil. P division, seed.
Small, numerous and fragrant flowers. It takes
several years for these plants to thicken out.

Antirrhinum majus 'Butterfly Little Darling'
Snapdragon / **fam. Scrophulariaceae**
○ ◐ ⊙ ⊛ ⊗
Sow in February–March in warm, or in April
in cool, greenhouse. Plant out at A 12 cm
(5 in). H 45 cm (18 in). S good garden soil.
Mixed colours. Belongs to the Penstemon
group.

Antirrhinum majus 'Madame Butterfly'
Snapdragon / **fam. Scrophulariaceae**
○ ◐ ⊙ ⊛ ⊗
P see last entry. H 35 cm (14 in). Orange-red.
S good garden soil. Very attractive double-
flowered form of the Penstemon type with
small, open flowers.

Antirrhinum majus 'Panorama'
Snapdragon / **fam. Scrophulariaceae**
○ ◐ ⊙ ⊛ ⊗
P see A. 'Butterfly Little Darling'. H 80 cm
(32 in). Red / yellow. S good garden soil.
Belongs to the Maximum group of tall
snapdragons. Particularly suitable for cutting.

Apocynum adrosaemifolium
fam. Apocynaceae
◐ ⊝ ○ ⊛ ⊗
July–September. Red. H 30 cm (1 ft). A 20 cm
(8 in). S sandy garden soil. P division,
cuttings. Unusual, shrub-like plant. Aromatic.
The flowers catch flies.

Aponogeton distachyus
Water Hawthorn / **fam. Aponogetonaceae**
○ ◐ ⊛ ⊛ ⊛ ⊗
June–October. White. H 10 cm (4 in). A 80 cm
(32 in). S clayey. P division, seed. Aquatic
plant that often flowers twice. Will not
survive the winter if the ground freezes.

Aquilegia flabellata
Columbine / fam. *Ranunculaceae*
May–June. Red/white. H 15–20 cm (6–8 in).
A 20 cm (8 in). S normal garden soil.
P division, seed. Early-flowering rock plant.
Likes a cool, slightly moist position (no
midday sun).

Aquilegia hybrid
Columbine / fam. *Ranunculaceae*
May–June. Various colours. H 120 cm (4 ft).
A 60 cm (2 ft). S normal garden soil. Graceful
plant with unusually shaped flowers having
fused petals.

Aquilegia vulgaris
Columbine / fam. *Ranunculaceae*
May–June. Purple. H 40–80 cm (16–32 in).
A 30 cm (1 ft). S normal garden soil.
P division, seed. Grows wild throughout
almost the whole of Europe. Large, nodding
flowers.

Arabis aubrietioides
fam. *Cruciferae*
April–May. Purple-violet. H 15–25 cm (6–
10 in). A 20 cm (8 in). S porous. P division,
seed, cuttings. Forms mats. Will often die in
moist positions during the winter. Rewarding
plant.

Arabis caucasica (A. albida)
Rock Cress / fam. *Cruciferae*
March–April. White. H 10–30 cm (4–12 in).
A 20 cm (8 in). S normal garden soil.
P division, seed, cuttings. Mat-forming plant
with upright stems and grey-green leaves.

Arabis ferdinandi-coburgi 'Variegata'
fam. *Cruciferae*
April–June. White. H 10–25 cm (4–10 in).
A 20 cm (8 in). S well drained. P division,
cuttings. Very striking rock and ground-cover
plant with white-edged leaves.

Aralia elata (Dimorphanthus elatus)
Angelica Tree / fam. *Araliaceae*
August–September. White. H 5 m (16 ft).
W 3 m (10 ft). Zone 3. S humus-rich. P root
cuttings. Tree-like shrub with spiny stems,
big leaves and large flowers in long panicles.

Aralia elata 'Variegata'
Angelica Tree / fam. *Araliaceae*
August–September. White. H 2 m (6 ft). W 2 m
(6 ft). Zone 3. S humus-rich. P root cuttings.
Tree-like, picturesque shrub with white-
edged leaves and spiny branches.

Araucaria araucana (A. imbricata) / Chile
Pine, Monkey Puzzle / fam. *Araucariaceae*
Striking, pyramidal conifer with snake-
shaped branches, triangular leathery leaves
and cones after about 30 years. H 20 m (65 ft).
W 10 m (33 ft). S humus-rich. P seed, cuttings.
Zone 6.

137

Arbutus menziesii
Strawberry Tree / fam. *Ericaceae*
○ ◐ ⍟ ⊘ ◎ ⍟ ◐
May. White. H 20 m (65 ft). W 5 m (16 ft). Zone
7. S fertile. P seed. Tree with a thick trunk,
smooth cinnamon-coloured bark and dark
green leaves.

Arctotis hybrid
African Daisy / fam. *Compositae*
○ ⊙ ⍟ ⊗
Sow in March in heated greenhouse or in
April in flowering site. Thin out to A 30 cm
(1 ft). H 60 cm (2 ft). Various colours. S not
critical. Good for a border and bedding.
Flowers keep in water.

Arenaria balearica
Sandwort / fam. *Caryophyllaceae*
◐ ◍ ∧ ○ ⍟ ◎ ◎ ⊖
April–August. White. H 5 cm (2 in).
A 20 cm (8 in). S well drained, sandy.
P division, cuttings. Mat-forming plant with
numerous star-shaped little flowers.

Argemone mexicana
Prickly Poppy / fam. *Papaveraceae*
○ ⊙ ⍟
Sow in March–April in heated greenhouse.
Plant out at A 30–40 cm (12–16 in). H 60–80 cm
(24–32 in). Yellow/orange. S humus-rich.
Graceful plant resembling a poppy. From
tropical America.

Aristolochia macrophylla (A. durior)
Dutchman's Pipe / fam. *Aristolochiaceae*
○ ◍ ◎ ◎ ⍟
June–August. Mid-green. H 10 m (33 ft).
W 1 m (3 ft). Zone 4. S normal garden soil.
P seed, layering. Climbing plant with
enormously large leaves and small flowers
resembling pipe bowls.

Armeria maritima
Thrift / fam. *Plumbaginaceae*
○ ○ ⍟ ◎ ◎ ◎ ⊖
May–June. Purple. H 15 cm (6 in). A 15 cm
(6 in). S normal garden soil. P division.
Attractive edging plant that forms a grass-like
mat. Must be dead-headed.

***Armeria maritima* 'Rosea'**
Thrift / fam. *Plumbaginaceae*
○ ○ ⍟ ◎ ◎ ◎ ⊖
May–June. Pink. H 15 cm (6 in). A 15 cm (6 in).
S normal garden soil. P division. Dense,
bright green, spherical heads. Liked for its
restful colour.

Aronia melanocarpa (Sorbus melanocarpa)
fam. *Rosaceae*
○ ◐ ◍ ◎ ⍟
May–June. White. H 1 m (3 ft). W 1 m (3 ft).
Zone 4. S not critical. P seed or cuttings.
Shrub with suckers, browny-red autumn
foliage and shiny black fruits.

Aronia prunifolia (A. floribunda)
fam. *Rosaceae*
○ ◐ ◎ ◎ ⍟
May–June. White. H 4 m (13 ft). W 2 m (6 ft).
Zone 4. S not critical. P seed or cuttings.
Shrub with red autumn foliage and dark red,
early fruits.

Arrhenatherum elatius ssp. **bulbosum** 'Variegatum' / fam. **Gramineae**
○ ◑ ⊖ ◯ ⊘ ⊗
June–July. White. H25–50 cm (10–20 in).
A30 cm (1 ft). S normal garden soil.
P division. Low-growing ornamental grass.
Erect stems with bulbous swellings at the base.

Artemisia lactiflora
White Mugwort / fam. **Compositae**
○ ◑ ⊖ ◯ ⊙ ⊘
September–October. White. H130–160 cm (4–5 ft). A60–80 cm (24–32 in). S normal garden soil. P division. Robust plant for the autumn border. Small, cream-coloured, fragrant flowers.

Artemisia ludoviciana
White Sage / fam. **Compositae**
○ ◑ ⊖ ◯ ⊘ ⊗
July–August. White. H75–100 cm (30–36 in).
A40–50 cm (16–20 in). S normal garden soil.
P division. Spreads rapidly. Creeping, shrubby plant with woolly grey foliage.

Artemesia schmidtiana
fam. **Compositae**
○ ◑ ⊖ △ ◯ ⊘ ⊗
August. White. H30–60 cm (1–2 ft). A30 cm (1 ft). S normal garden soil. P division. Very attractive, compact plant which is often lost during severe winters.

Artemisia 'Silver Queen'
fam. **Compositae**
○ ◑ ⊖ ◯ ⊘ ⊗
June–August. White. H75–100 cm (30–36 in).
A50 cm (20 in). S normal garden soil.
P division. Silver-grey variety of unknown origin. Suitable for a white border.

Arum conophalloides subvar. **virescens**
fam. **Araceae**
◑ ◐ ≈ △ ⊘ ⊛
April–May. Red. H30 cm (1 ft). A20 cm (8 in).
S fertile. P division, seed. Rhizomatous plant with unusual inflorescences and large, ornamental leaves.

Arum italicum 'Pictum'
fam. **Araceae**
◑ ◐ ≈ △ ⊘ ⊛
April–May. Red. H30 cm (1 ft). A20 cm (8 in).
S fertile. P division. Shiny, white-ribbed leaves in the autumn. Grows near south coast in Britain.

Aruncus aerthusifolius
Goat's Beard / fam. **Rosaceae**
○ ◑ ◐ ◯ ⊙ ⊕
June–July. White. H1–2 m (3–6 ft). A1 m (3 ft).
S normal garden soil. P division, seed.
Vigorous ornamental plant. Not attractive after flowering. Rarely seen.

Aruncus dioicus (A. sylvestris)
Goat's Beard / fam. **Rosaceae**
◑ ◐ ◯ ⊙ ⊘ ⊕
June–July. White. H2 m (6 ft). A1 m (3 ft).
S normal garden soil. P division, seed.
Ornamental specimen plant for growing on lawns or near water. Feathery leaves.

139

Arundinaria pumila (Sasa pumila)
Dwarf Bamboo / fam. *Gramineae*
Ⓘ ⊗ Ⓞ ⊗ ⊗
H 60 cm (2 ft). W 40 cm (16 in). Zone 5.
S humus-rich. P division, root cuttings.
Creeping shrub. Very invasive. May turn
yellow in the winter.

Arundo donax
fam. *Gramineae*
◯ ⌃ Ⓞ ⊗
Rarely flowers. H 1.75–3 m (5¾–10 ft). S fertile
soil. P division. Attractive, strong-growing,
ornamental grass with thick, woody rhizomes
and sturdy, erect woody stems.

Asperula orientalis (A. azurea)
fam. *Rubiaceae*
◯ Ⓘ ⊙ Ⓨ
Sow in∙April in flowering position and thin
out to A 45 cm (18 in). H 25 cm (10 in). Blue.
S humus-rich. Attractive, strongly fragrant
annual with leaves arranged in whorls.

Asperula tinctoria (Galium triandrum)
fam. *Rubiaceae*
◯ Ⓘ Ⓞ Ⓨ
June–July. White. H 50 cm (20 in). A 30 cm
(1 ft). S chalky. P division, seed. Richly
flowering plant. Bushy habit. Moist but well-
drained soil.

Asphodeline lutea
fam. *Liliaceae*
◯ ⊖ ⌃ Ⓞ Ⓨ ⊗
May–June. Yellow. H 60–80 cm (24–32 in).
A 40 cm (16 in). S sandy, chalky. P division,
seed. An attractive plant which adds variety
to the border.

Aster alpinus
fam. *Compositae*
◯ ◯ Ⓨ ⊗ ⊖
May–June. Purple-blue. H 15–25 cm (6–10 in).
A 25 cm (10 in). S normal garden soil. Very
attractive rock plant. Hairy leaves and flower
stalks. Place at the front of the border.

Aster amellus 'Rudolf Goethe'
fam. *Compositae*
◯ Ⓞ Ⓨ ⊗
July–September. Deep lavender. H 60–70 cm
(24–28 in). A 15 cm (6 in). S good garden soil.
P division, cuttings. Very attractive border
plant. Not large enough to need tying.

Aster divaricatus (A. corymbosus)
fam. *Compositae*
◯ Ⓘ Ⓞ Ⓨ ⊗
September–October. White. H 60 cm (2 ft).
A 30 cm (1 ft). S normal garden soil.
P division, seed. Thrives in fairly shady
positions. Tolerant of sandy soil.

Aster dumosus 'Alice Haslam'
fam. *Compositae*
◯ Ⓞ Ⓨ ⊗
September–November. Purple. H 25 cm
(10 in). A 30 cm (1 ft). S good garden soil.
P division, cuttings. Good border plant. The
erect stems branch strongly at the top and
have no hairs.

Aster

Aster dumosus 'Little Boy Blue'
fam. *Compositae*
○ ○ Ⓨ ⊗
September–November. Violet. H 40 cm
(16 in). A 30 cm (1 ft). S good garden soil.
P division, cuttings. Broad, bushy plant
covered in flowers. Fast growing.

Aster ericoides 'Delight'
fam. *Compositae*
○ ○ Ⓨ
September–October. White. H 60–100 cm (2–
3 ft). A 40 cm (16 in). S normal garden soil.
P division, seed. Attractive border plant with
branching stems. Flowers profusely. Small
flower heads.

Aster farreri 'Berggarten'
fam. *Compositae*
○ ○ Ⓨ ⊗
May–June. Pale purple. H 50 cm (20 in).
A 50 cm (20 in). S normal garden soil.
P division. Popular spring-flowering aster.
Strong plant with a profusion of flowers.
Grows in any soil.

Aster × frikartii
fam. *Compositae*
○ ○ Ⓨ ⊗
August–September. Violet-purple. H 60–
70 cm (24–28 in). A 60 cm (2 ft). S normal
garden soil. P division. Cross between *A.
amellus* and *A. thomsonii*, with larger flowers
than the first.

Aster himalaicus
fam. *Compositae*
○ ◐ ⊖ ○ Ⓨ ⊗
May–June. Purple. H 15–30 cm (6–12 in).
A 20 cm (8 in). S normal garden soil.
P division. Attractive rock plant entirely
covered with hair. Thrives in slight shade.

Aster linosyris (Linosyris vulgaris)
Goldilocks / fam. *Compositae*
○ ○ Ⓨ ⊗
July–October. Yellow. H 40–60 cm (16–24 in).
A 30 cm (1 ft). S good garden soil. P division,
cuttings. Attractive plant with upright stems,
lanceolate leaves and tubular flowers.

Aster novae-angliae 'Dr Eckener'
Michaelmas Daisy / fam. *Compositae*
○ ○ Ⓨ ⊗
August–October. Purple. H 130–160 cm (4–
5 ft). A 60–80 cm (24–32 in). S normal garden
soil. P division. Hairy stems. May get mildew
in bad weather. Attractive autumn-flowering
aster.

Aster novae-angliae 'Roter Stern'
Michaelmas Daisy / fam. *Compositae*
○ ○ Ⓨ ⊗
September–October. Purple. H 135 cm (1½ ft).
A 50 cm (20 in). S good garden soil. P division,
cuttings. Attractive border plant with robust,
upright and hairy stems branching at the top.

Aster novae-angliae 'Rudelsberg'
Michaelmas Daisy / fam. *Compositae*
○ ○ Ⓨ ⊗
September–October. Purple-violet. H 120 cm
(4 ft). A 50 cm (20 in). S good garden soil.
P division, cuttings. Michaelmas Daisy leaves
tend to turn black with time. Best to replant.

141

Aster

Aster novi-belgii 'Dauerblau'
Michaelmas Daisy / fam. *Compositae*
○ ◐ ⓨ ⊗
September–October. Violet. H 100–125 cm (3–4 ft). A 60 cm (2 ft). S normal garden soil. P division. Very good, profusely flowering border plant. *Novi-belgii* stems have no hairs.

Aster novi-belgii 'Eventide'
Michaelmas Daisy / fam. *Compositae*
○ ◐ ⓨ ⊗
September–October. Violet. H 1 m (3 ft). A 50 cm (20 in). S good garden soil. P division, cuttings. Very good border plant, tall and erect and with hairless stems.

Aster sedifolius (A. acris)
fam. *Compositae*
○ ◐ ⓨ ⊗
August–September. Lavender-blue. H 60–100 cm (2–3 ft). A 40 cm (16 in). S good garden soil. P division, cuttings. Low-growing, bushy plant with dense foliage and clusters of small flowers.

Aster shortii
fam. *Compositae*
○ ◐ ⓨ ⊗
September–October. Pale purple. H 75–100 cm (30–36 in). A 60 cm (2 ft). S normal garden soil. P division. Border plant with a profusion of small flowers. Not very sturdy – needs tying.

Aster tongolensis 'Wartburgstern'
fam. *Compositae*
○ ◐ ⓨ ⊗
May–June. Purple. H 30–40 cm (12–16 in). A 30 cm (1 ft). S normal garden soil. P division. Early flowering. Excellent as an edging plant or front of the border in larger groups.

Astilbe chinensis var. pumila
fam. *Saxifragaceae*
○ ◐ ◑ ○ ⓨ ⊖
August–September. Rose-purple. H 30 cm (1 ft). A 30 cm (1 ft). S not critical. P division. The only *Astilbe* tolerant of dry conditions. Creeping habit. Flowers in short panicles.

Astilbe hybrid 'Emden'
fam. *Saxifragaceae*
◑ ⊛ ○ ⓨ ⊗
June–August. Red. H 50–75 cm (20–30 in). A 30 cm (1 ft). S normal garden soil. P division. The waving spikes of this plant can often be seen along the water's edge.

Astilbe hybrid 'Fanal'
fam. *Saxifragaceae*
○ ◑ ⊛ ○ ⓨ ⊗
June–August. Dark garnet red. H 50–75 cm (20–30 in). A 30 cm (1 ft). S normal garden soil. Excellent for the border. Flowers profusely. Definitely needs a moist position.

Astilbe hybrid 'Möwe'
fam. *Saxifragaceae*
○ ◑ ⊛ ⊗ ○ ⓨ ⊖
June–July. Pink. H 50–60 cm (20–24 in). A 30 cm (1 ft). S normal garden soil. P division. Glossy leaves. Dense panicles. Very good ground cover. Needs a lot of moisture.

Astilbe hybrid 'Peach Blossom'
fam. *Saxifragaceae*
◐ ◑ ⊗ ◯ ⊗ ⊗
June–July. Peach. H 50–60 cm (20–24 in).
A 30 cm (1 ft). S normal garden soil.
P division, seed. Can be placed in full sun
provided the soil is moist.

Astilbe hybrid 'Vesuvius'
fam. *Saxifragaceae*
◯ ◐ ⊗ ◯ ⊗ ⊗
June–August. Red. H 50–75 cm (20–30 in).
A 30 cm (1 ft). S normal garden soil.
P division. Does best in moist positions, on
all good garden soils.

Astilboides tabularis (Rodgersia tabularis)
fam. *Saxifragaceae*
◐ ⊗ ◯ ⊗ ⊗ ⊗
June–July. White. H 75–125 cm (30–48 in). 50–
60 cm (20–24 in). S normal garden soil.
P division, seed. Resembles *Rodgersia*. Needs
very moist soil (near water).

Astrantia carniolica
Masterwort / fam. *Umbelliferae*
◐ ◯ ⊗ ⊗
June–August. White. H 50–75 cm (20–30 in).
A 30 cm (1 ft). S heavy soil. P division, seed.
Modest but attractive border plant. Protect
from midday sun.

Astrantia carniolica 'Rubra'
Masterwort / fam. *Umbelliferae*
◐ ◯ ⊗ ⊗
June–August. Red. H 50–75 cm (20–30 in).
A 30 cm (1 ft). S heavy soil. P division, seed.
Border plant, not very well known but of an
attractive colour.

Astrantia major
Masterwort / fam. *Umbelliferae*
◐ ◯ ⊗ ⊗
June–July. White / purple-pink. H 30–60 cm
(1–2 ft). A 30 cm (1 ft). S normal garden soil.
P division, seed. Valuable border plant,
originally from mountain meadows. The best-
known species.

Athyrium filix-femina (Polypodium filix-
femina) / Lady Fern / fam. *Athyriaceae*
◐ ◑ ⊗ ◯ ⊗
No flowers. H 60–100 cm (2–3 ft). A 50 cm
(20 in). S humus-rich. P division, spores. Very
attractive native fern with bipinnate fronds.

Aubrieta hybrid (A. × cultorum)
fam. *Cruciferae*
◯ ⊖ ⊗ ⊗ ⊗
April–May. Various shades. H 5–10 cm (2–
4 in). A 10 cm (4 in). S chalky. P division,
cuttings. Well-known cushion-forming,
spring-flowering plant for rock gardens, dry
stone walls and crevices.

Aubrieta libanotica
fam. *Cruciferae*
◯ ⊖ ⊗ ⊗ ⊗
April–May. Violet-purple. H 5–10 cm (2–4 in).
A 10 cm (4 in). S chalky. P division, seed,
cuttings. Flowers profusely. Will grow more
vigorously on humus-rich ground but will die
in the winter.

143

***Aucuba japonica* 'Variegata'**
Spotted Laurel / fam. ***Cornaceae***
March–April. White. H 3 m (10 ft). W 1.5 m
(5 ft). Zone 7. S fertile. P cuttings. Evergreen,
dioecious shrub with spotted leaves and red
fruits.

Azolla filiculoides
Fairy Moss / fam. ***Azollaceae***
May. Red. P stem segments. Drifting aquatic
plant. Spread quickly, especially in warm
weather. Turns reddish brown after frosts.

Basella alba (B. rubra)
Indian Spinach / fam. ***Basellaceae***
Sow in March in a heated greenhouse. Plant
out at A 15 cm (6 in). H 10–20 cm (4–8 in). Red-
purple. S humus-rich. Creeping ground-cover
plant with fleshy, undivided leaves. For the
garden and greenhouse.

***Begonia semperflorens* hybrids**
fam. *Begoniaceae*
Sow Semperflorens begonias in a heated
greenhouse in the winter. Adequate humus
is essential for good flower production. Shield
against midday sun.

***Begonia semperflorens* 'Organdy'**
fam. *Begoniaceae*
Sow in January–February in a heated
greenhouse. Plant out at A 20 cm (8 in).
H 20 cm (8 in). S humus-rich, acid. Single-
flowered dwarf variety in red, reddish purple
and white.

Begonia × tuberhybrida
Tuberous Begonia / fam. ***Begoniaceae***
For propagation see last entry. Do not bury
seed but press down lightly. Moist
atmosphere. Prick out seedlings. Harden off
in cold greenhouse in May.

Begonia × tuberhybrida
Tuberous Begonia / fam. ***Begoniaceae***
See last entry. Cut the plants back hard after
flowering, remove soil from the tubers, dry
and overwinter at 5–6°C (41–43°F) in dry peat
dust.

Begonia × tuberhybrida
Tuberous Begonia / fam. ***Begoniaceae***
See previous entry. A member of the
Fimbriata group with striking flowers
resembling carnations. Each petal is most
delicately fringed.

Begonia × tuberhybrida
Tuberous Begonia / fam. ***Begoniaceae***
See previous entries. A member of the
Marginata group with flowers in strikingly
beautiful shapes and contrasting petal edges.
Flowers profusely. Useful in all parts of the
garden.

Begonia × *tuberhybrida*
Tuberous Begonia / fam. *Begoniaceae*
Ⓜ Ⓐ Ⓨ
See previous entries. A member of the
Maxima group with numerous, smaller
double flowers. Do not plant out before late
May to avoid danger of frost.

Begonia × *tuberhybrida* (small-flowered)
Tuberous Begonia / fam. *Begoniaceae*
Ⓜ Ⓐ Ⓨ
May–September. Various colours. H 15–25 cm
(6–10 in). A 20 cm (8 in). D 5 cm (2 in).
S humus-rich. P cuttings, division. Single or
semi-double flowers, small but numerous.
Ideal for bedding.

Begonia × *tuberhybrida* 'Bertinii'
Tuberous Begonia / fam. *Begoniaceae*
Ⓜ Ⓐ Ⓨ
May–September. Various colours. H 15–25 cm
(6–10 in). A 20 cm (8 in). D 5 cm (2 in).
S humus-rich. P seed, cuttings, division.
Small nodding flowers in profusion. For
balconies or containers.

Bellis perennis 'Hortensis'
Meadow Daisy / fam. *Compositae*
○ Ⓜ ⌃ ⊙ Ⓨ
Sow in July–August under glass. Plant out at
A 20 cm (8 in). H 15 cm (6 in). White / red.
S fertile soil. Hardy perennial often grown as
a biennial. Flowers from March to October.

Berberis 'Barbarossa'
Barberry / fam. *Berberidaceae*
○ ⌃ Ⓜ Ⓨ ⊛ ⊛ ⊗
June. Yellow. H 90–150 cm (3–5 ft). W 2 m
(6 ft). Zone 5. S not critical. P cuttings,
layering. Semi-hardy shrub with erect to
arching stems. Fruit round to oblong.

Berberis 'Bunch o' Grapes'
Barberry / fam. *Berberidaceae*
○ ⌃ Ⓜ Ⓨ ⊛ ⊛ ⊗
For description and P see last entry. Compact
shrub. Berries in grape-like clusters. Habit
erect to arching.

Berberis candidula
Barberry / fam. *Berberidaceae*
○ Ⓜ ⌃ Ⓜ Ⓨ ⊛ ⊛ ⊛ ⊗
May. Yellow. H 50 cm (20 in). W 150 cm (5 ft).
Zone 5. S not critical. P seed, cuttings,
layering. Attractive, dense shrub with black
berries. For edging and slopes.

Berberis × *carminea* 'Buccaneer'
Barberry / fam. *Berberidaceae*
○ Ⓜ Ⓨ ⊛
May–June. Yellow. H 1 m (3 ft). W 1 m (3 ft). Zone 5.
S not critical. P seed, cuttings, layering.
Robust shrub with small leaves, red fruits and
triple spines.

Berberis gagnepainii var. *lanceifolia*
Barberry / fam. *Berberidaceae*
○ Ⓜ Ⓜ Ⓜ Ⓨ ⊛ ⊛ ⊗
May–June. Yellow. H 2 m (6 ft). W 1.5 m (5 ft).
Zone 5. S not critical. P seed, cuttings,
layering. Robust shrub with broad, erect
clusters of flowers, deep green leaves and
black fruits.

145

Berberis giraldii
Barberry / fam. *Berberidaceae*
June. Yellow. H 2 m (6 ft). W 3 m (10 ft). Zone 5. S not critical. P seed, cuttings, layering. Broad shrub with dark green leaves and single spines.

Berberis* × *hydridogagnepainii
Barberry / fam. *Berberidaceae*
May–June. Yellow. H 1.5 m (5 ft). W 1 m (3 ft). Zone 5. S not critical. P seed, cuttings, layering. Shrub with an attractive, compact habit. Dark green glossy leaves and blue fruits.

***Berberis* × *media* 'Parkjuweel'**
Barberry / fam. *Berberidaceae*
May–June. Yellow. H 1 m (3 ft). W 2 m (6 ft). Zone 5. S not critical. P cuttings, layering. Compact shrub with fairly large, glossy, dark green leaves. Rarely flowers.

Berberis sieboldii
Barberry / fam. *Berberidaceae*
May. Yellow. H 1 m (3 ft). W 2 m (6 ft). Zone 5. S not critical. P seed, cuttings, layering. Shrub with dark red, bare and rectangular branches and glossy red fruits.

Berberis* × *stenophylla
Barberry / fam. *Berberidaceae*
May. Golden yellow. H 2 m (6 ft). W 3 m (10 ft). Zone 5. S not critical. P cuttings, layering. Very attractive shrub with gracefully arching branches and inflorescences. Black fruits.

Berberis thunbergii
Barberry / fam. *Berberidaceae*
May. Yellow. H 1.5 m (5 ft). W 2 m (6 ft). Zone 4. S not critical. P seed, cuttings, layering. Densely branching shrub with magnificent glossy scarlet berries. Autumn colouring.

Berberis vulgaris
Barberry / fam. *Berberidaceae*
May. Yellow. H 2 m (6 ft). W 2 m (6 ft). Zone 3. S not critical. P seed, cuttings, layering. Dense shrub with elongated clusters of profuse flowers and ovoid red berries.

Berberis wilsoniae
Barberry / fam. *Berberidaceae*
May–June. Yellow. H 1 m (3 ft). W 2 m (6 ft). Zone 5. S not critical. P seed, cuttings, layering. Very densely branching shrub with narrow leaves that change colour. Salmon-pink berries.

***Berberis wilsoniae* 'Orangeade'**
Barberry / fam. *Berberidaceae*
June. Yellow. H 1 m (3 ft). W 1 m (3 ft). Zone 5. S not critical. P cuttings, layering. Semi-prostrate shrub with red autumn foliage. Flowers in clusters. Fairly resistant to frost.

Bergenia hybrid 'Morgenröte'
fam. *Saxifragaceae*
Ⓜ️ⓋⓄⒶⓉⓀⒶ⊖
April–May. Purple. H 30–50 cm (12–20 in).
A 30–40 cm (12–16 in). S normal garden soil.
P division. Plant with large decorative leaves
and heavy flower clusters. Good for the edge
of ponds.

Bergenia hybrid 'Silberlicht'
fam. *Saxifragaceae*
Ⓜ️ⓋⓄⒶⓉⓀⒶ⊖
April–May. White changing to pink. H 30–
50 cm (12–20 in). A 40 cm (16 in). S normal
garden soil. P division. Grows everywhere
but prefers moist soil and semi-shade. Plant
in groups.

Bergenia × schmidtii
fam. *Saxifragaceae*
Ⓜ️ⓋⓄⒶⓉⓀⒶ⊖
March–May. Light purple. H 30–50 cm (12–
20 in). A 40 cm (16 in). S normal garden soil.
P division. Leaves ciliate and wedge-shaped
at the base. Flowers profusely. Sensitive to
late frost.

Betula albosinensis septentrionalis
Birch / fam. *Betulaceae*
ⓄⓋⓀⓀⓀⒶ
April–May. Yellow-green. H 25 m (80 ft).
W 10 m (33 ft). Zone 5. S not critical. P seed.
Tree with catkins and peeling orange to
orange-brown bark.

Betula costata
Birch / fam. *Betulaceae*
ⓄⓋⓀⓀⓀⒶ
April–May. Yellow-green. H 15 m (50 ft).
W 6 m (20 ft). Zone 5. S not critical. P seed.
Attractive parkland tree with a creamy yellow
trunk and erect catkins.

**Betula jacquemontii (B. utilis var. jacque-
montii)** / Birch / fam. *Betulaceae*
ⓄⓋⓀⓀⓀⓀⒶ
April–May. Yellow-green. H 12 m (40 ft).
W 8 m (26 ft). Zone 5. S not critical. P seed.
Low-branching tree with peeling white bark
and elliptical leaves.

Betula nigra
Black Birch / fam. *Betulaceae*
ⓄⓋⓀⓀⒶ
April. Greeny yellow. H 20 m (65 ft). W 10 m
(33 ft). Zone 4. S not critical, acid. P seed.
Fairly tall tree of graceful habit. Silvery bark,
reddish brown when peeling.

Betula papyrifera (B. papyraceae)
Paper or Canoe Birch / fam. *Betulaceae*
ⓄⓋⓀⓀⒶ
April–May. Yellow-green. H 25 m (80 ft).
W 12 m (40 ft). Zone 2. S not critical. P seed.
Tall tree with peeling white bark over a
brownish-red trunk.

Betula pendula (B. alba, B. verrucosa)
Silver Birch / fam. *Betulaceae*
ⓄⓋⓀⓀⒶ
April–May. Yellow-green. H 20 m (65 ft).
W 10 m (33 ft). Zone 2. S not critical. P seed.
Tree with gracefully drooping, warty
branches. Peeling white bark.

147

Betula

***Betula pendula* 'Dalecarlica'**
Silver Birch / fam. ***Betulaceae***
○ ❀ ❁ ❃ ❄ ⊕
April–May. Yellow-green. H 20 m (65 ft).
W 6 m (20 ft). Zone 2. S not critical. P seed.
Tall, elegant tree with fairly large, deeply cut
leaves and blunt terminal buds.

***Betula pendula* 'Youngii'**
Young's Weeping Birch / fam. ***Betulaceae***
○ ⊖ ❁ ❃ ❄ ⊕
April–May. Yellow-green. H 4 m (13 ft).
W 6 m (20 ft). Zone 2. S not critical. P seed.
Dome-shaped tree with long and thin
weeping branches.

Betula pubescens (B. alba)
Silver Birch / fam. ***Betulaceae***
○ ❀ ❁ ❃ ❄ ⊕
April–May. Yellow-green. H 20 m (65 ft).
W 10 m (33 ft). Zone 3. S not critical. P seed.
Tall tree with slightly arching branches
covered with down and peeling white bark.

Borago officinalis
Borage / fam. ***Boraginaceae***
○ ◑ ⊙ ❂ ⊗ ⊗
Sow in April in flowering position and thin
out to A 30 cm (1 ft). H 60 cm (2 ft). Blue. S not
critical. Culinary and medicinal herb with
hairy stems and star-shaped flowers that have
to be tied.

Brachycome iberidifolia
Swan River Daisy / fam. ***Compositae***
○ ⊙ ❂
Sow in April under glass or in May in the
open. Thin out to A 20 cm (8 in). H 45 cm
(18 in). White, lilac, purple-blue. S fertile.
Strongly branching border plant with fragrant
flowers.

***Brassica oleracea* 'Plumosa'**
fam. ***Cruciferae***
○ ◑ ⊙ ❁
Sow in March under glass or in May in the
open. Thin out to A 45 cm (18 in). H 25 cm
(10 in). Yellow-white. S fertile. Ornamental
cabbage with attractively shaped and
coloured leaves.

Briza maxima (B. rubra)
Pearl Grass / fam. ***Gramineae***
○ ◑ ⊙ ❂ ⊗ ⊗
Sow in March–April and thin out to A 15–
25 cm (6–10 in). H 50 cm (20 in). Brown.
S normal garden soil. Grass with loose
panicles of pendent spikelets on very thin
stems. Good for drying.

Bromus macrostachys
Brome Grass / fam. ***Gramineae***
○ ◑ ⊙ ❂ ⊗
Sow in April and thin out to A 25 cm (10 in).
H 60 cm (2 ft). Brown. S not critical.
Ornamental grass with compact spikelets.
Especially suitable for dried bouquets.

Broussonetia papyrifera
Paper Mulberry / fam. ***Moraceae***
○ ◑ ◐ ⊙ ❂ ❃
May. Off-white. H 4 m (13 ft). W 4 m (13 ft).
Zone 6. S not critical. P semi-hardwood
cuttings. Dioecious shrub or small tree with
large leaves and orange-red fruits.

Browallia americana (B. demissa, B. elata)
fam. *Solanaceae*
◍ ⌣ ⊙ ⊗
Sow in Feburary in heated greenhouse or in
August in cold frame. Thin and plant out at
A 20 cm (8 in). H 60 cm (2 ft). Blue, white.
S normal garden soil. Easily grown plant with
hairy stem and calyx.

Bruckenthalia spiculifolia
fam. *Ericaceae*
◯ ◍ ⍟ ⊗ ⍟
June–July. Reddish purple. H 15 cm (6 in).
W 30 cm (1 ft). Zone 5. S humus-rich. P seed,
cuttings. Evergreen heather with needle-
shaped leaves and flowers in dense spikes.

**Brunnera macrophylla (Anchusa
myosotidiflora)** fam. *Boraginaceae*
◍ ⊗ ◯ ⊗ ⍟ ⍟
April–June. Blue. H 30–40 cm (12–16 in).
A 30 cm (1 ft). S humus-rich. P division, seed.
Sprays of forget-me-not-like flowers. Suitable
for the front of the border.

Buddleia alternifolia
fam. *Buddleiaceae*
◯ ⊖ ⍟ ⍟ ⍟ ⊗
June. Violet. H 4 m (13 ft). W 5 m (16 ft). Zone
5. Fertile soil. P cuttings, seed. Shrub with
long, thin, drooping branches and fragrant
clusters of flowers.

Buddleia davidii (B. variabilis)
Butterfly Bush / fam. *Buddleiaceae*
◯ ⍟ ⍟ ⊗
September–October. White. H 3 m (10 ft).
W 3 m (10 ft). Zone 5. S fertile soil. P cuttings,
seed. Shrub with long, slightly overhanging
branches, large leaves and fragrant flowers.

Buddleia davidii 'Fascination'
Butterfly Bush / fam. *Buddleiaceae*
◯ ⍟ ⍟ ⊗
July–August. Purple-violet. H 3 m (10 ft).
W 3 m (10 ft). Zone 5. S fertile soil. P cuttings.
Strong-growing little shrub with fragrant
flowers in very long plume-shaped clusters.

Buddleia davidii 'Nanho Purple'
Butterfly Bush / fam. *Buddleiaceae*
◯ ⍟ ⍟ ⊗
August-September. Reddish purple. H 1 m
(3 ft). W 3 m (10 ft). Zone 5. S fertile soil.
P cuttings. A new hybrid from Boskoop in
Holland with long and spreading flower
clusters.

Buddleia davidii var. nanhoensis
Butterfly Bush / fam. *Buddleiaceae*
◯ ⍟ ⍟ ⊗
August–September. Purple. H 1.5 m (5 ft).
W 2 m (6 ft). Zone 5. S fertile soil. P cuttings.
Compact shrub with small leaves and thin,
wide-spreading branches. Late flowerer.

**Buglossoides purpurocaeruleum (Lithosper-
mum purpurocaeruleum)** / fam. *Boraginaceae*
⍟ ⊗ ⊖
May–June. Blue. H 20–40 cm (8–16 in).
A 20 cm (8 in). S chalky. P seed, cuttings,
division. Attractive plant with erect flowering
shoots. Flowers purple-red at first.

149

Bulbocodium vernum (Colchicum vernum)
Spring Meadow Saffron/fam. *Liliaceae*
○ ⊗ ⊛ ⊙ ⊛
February–March. Purple. H 20 cm (8 in).
A 10 cm (4 in). D 10 cm (4 in). S humus-rich.
P seed, offsets. Small, poisonous little corms.
Good for naturalising in grass. Fairly rare.

Buphthalmum salicifolium
Yellow Oxeye/fam. *Compositae*
○ ○ ⊛ ⊗
June–August. Yellow. H 20–60 cm (8–24 in).
A 30 cm (1 ft). S normal garden soil.
P division, seed. Strong border plant which
does not blow over easily and flowers for a
long period. Must be dead-headed.

Butomus umbellatus
Flowering Rush/fam. *Butomaceae*
○ ⊗ ○ ⊛
May–September. Red. H 80–120 cm (32–
48 in). A 40 cm (16 in). S any type. P division.
Grows wild on banks but also suitable for
garden pools. Water depth to 50 cm (20 in).

Buxus sempervirens 'Argenteovariegata'
Box/fam. *Buxaceae*
○ ⊕ ⊕ ⊛ ⊛ ⊛ ⊕ ⊛
April–May. Yellow. H 2 m (6 ft). W 1 m (3 ft).
Zone 5. S not critical. P cuttings. Upright
shrub with oval to elliptical, white-edged
leaves. Needs more light than green varieties.

Buxus sempervirens 'Aureovariegata'
Box/fam. *Buxaceae*
○ ⊕ ⊕ ⊛ ⊛ ⊛ ⊕ ⊛
April–May. Yellow. H 2 m (6 ft). W 1 m (3 ft).
Zone 5. S not critical. P cuttings. Erect shrub
with oval to elliptical, yellow-green
variegated leaves.

Buxus sempervirens 'Suffruticosa'
Box/fam. *Buxaceae*
○ ⊕ ⊕ ⊛ ⊛ ⊛ ⊕ ⊛
April–May. Yellow. Zone 5. S not critical.
P cuttings, layering. Low shrub with small
leaves. Excellent for topiary work.

Cajophora lateritia (Loasa lateritia)
fam. *Loasaceae*
○ ○ ⊛
July–October. Yellow-orange. H 3 m (10 ft).
A 80 cm (32 in). S normal garden soil. P seed.
Striking climber densely covered with
stinging hairs. Feathery leaves on long stalks.

Calamagrostis × acutiflora 'Karl Foerster'
fam. *Gramineae*
○ ⊕ ⊕ ○ ⊛ ⊛ ⊗
June–July. Yellow-orange. H 150 cm (5 ft).
A 50 cm (20 in). S not critical. P division. Tall
grass with long erect spikelets and broad
reed-like leaves which come out early in the
year.

Calceolaria integrifolia (C. rugosa)
fam. *Scrophulariaceae*
○ ⊕ ⊙ ⊛
Sow in March under glass or in April in the
open. Thin out to A 15 cm (6 in). H 60 cm (2 ft).
Yellow. S normal garden soil. Particularly
suitable for balcony containers.

Calceolaria tripartita (C. scabiosifolia)
fam. *Scrophulariaceae*
◯ ◑ ⊙ ⊗
Sow in January–March in heated greenhouse.
Plant out at A 20 cm (8 in). H 40–70 cm (16–
28 in). Yellow. Normal garden soil. Most
attractive of all calceolarias. Easily cultivated
in a cool environment.

Calendula officinalis
Pot Marigold / fam. *Compositae*
◯ ◑ ⊙ ⊗ ⊗
Sow in March. Thin out to A 30–40 cm (12–
16 in). H 60 cm (2 ft). Yellow-orange. S not
critical. The original species has single
flowers. Makes curved seeds with barbed
hooks.

Calendula officinalis 'Golden King'
Pot Marigold / fam. *Compositae*
◯ ◑ ⊙ ⊗ ⊗
Sow in March. Thin out to A 30–40 cm (12–
16 in). H 60 cm (2 ft). Yellow-orange. S not
critical. Attractive cultivar with large double
flowers. Suitable for the border or for cutting.

Calendula officinalis 'Plena'
Pot Marigold / fam. *Compositae*
◯ ◑ ⊙ ⊗ ⊗
Sow in March. Thin out to A 30–40 cm (12–
16 in). H 60 cm (2 ft). Yellow-orange. S not
critical. Shrubby, erect plant with solitary,
double, characteristically scented flowers.

Calendula officinalis 'Radio'
Pot Marigold / fam. *Compositae*
◯ ◑ ⊙ ⊗ ⊗
Sow in March. Thin out to A 30–40 cm (12–
16 in). H 60 cm (2 ft). Orange. S not critical.
Easily cultivated plant with oddly quilled and
curled petals.

Calla palustris
fam. *Araceae*
◯ ◑ ⊗ ◯ ⊗ ⊗ ⊙ ⊖
May–June. White. H 20–40 cm (8–16 in).
A 30 cm (1 ft). S marshy. P seed, division.
Aquatic or marsh plant with creeping
rhizomes and attractive but poisonous red
berries.

Callicarpa bodinieri var. giraldii
fam. *Verbenaceae*
◑ ⊼ ⊗ ⊗ ⊗ ⊗
July–August. Violet. H 2 m (6 ft). W 2 m (6 ft).
Zone 5–6. S good garden soil. P cuttings.
Erect shrub with dull green leaves that change
colour, and small purple fruits.

Callicarpa dichotoma (C. purpurea)
fam. *Verbenaceae*
◑ ⊗ ⊗ ⊗
August. Pink. H 1.5 m (5 ft). W 2 m (6 ft).
S good garden soil. P cuttings. Small shrub,
very hardy, with small violet-purple fruits
and flowers in racemes.

Callistephus chinensis 'Azure Blue'
China Aster / fam. *Compositae*
◯ ◯ ⊙ ⊗ ⊗
Sow in March in a heated greenhouse or in
May in the open. Plant out at A 30 cm (1 ft).
H 60 cm (2 ft). Various colours. S fertile. Large
double flowers; oval, coarse-toothed leaves.
Useful for bouquets.

151

Callistephus

Callistephus chinensis 'Deep Blue'
China Aster/fam. *Compositae*
○ ⊙ ⓨ ⊗
Sow in March in a heated greenhouse or in
May in the open. Thin/plant out at A 15–
20 cm (6–8 in). H 30 cm (1 ft). Violet blue, red,
white. S fertile soil. Dwarf variety. Good
bedding plant.

**Callistephus chinensis 'Hellblaue
Prinzessin'/China Aster/fam. *Compositae***
○ ⊙ ⓨ ⊗
Sow in March in a heated greenhouse or in
May in the open. Thin/plant out at A 30 cm
(1 ft). H 75 cm (30 in). Various colours.
S fertile. Giant strain. Guard against wilt by
plant rotation.

**Callistephus chinensis 'Pinocchio's Mittel-
blau'/China Aster/fam. *Compositae***
○ ⊙ ⓨ ⊗
Sow in March in a heated greenhouse or in
May in the open. Thin/plant out at A 15–
20 cm (6–8 in). H 45 cm (18 in). Various
colours. S fertile soil. Small flowers on long
stems.

Calluna vulgaris 'Darkness'
Heather, Ling/fam. *Ericaceae*
○ ◑ ⓜ ⓨ ⊛ ⊝ ⊗
August–September. Purple-red. H 35 cm
(14 in). W 40 cm (16 in). Zone 4. S humus-rich.
P cuttings, layering. Very attractive recent
introduction with flowers in dense and erect
terminal spikes.

Calluna vulgaris 'Elsie Purnell'
Heather, Ling/fam. *Ericaceae*
○ ◑ ⓜ ⓨ ⊛ ⊝ ⊗
September–October. Pink. H 60 cm (2 ft).
W 70 cm (28 in). Zone 4. S humus-rich.
P cuttings, layering. Strongly branching
shrub with double flowers in graceful, erect
racemes.

Calluna vulgaris 'Golden Rivulet'
Heather, Ling/fam. *Ericaceae*
○ ◑ ⓜ ⓨ ⊛ ⊝ ⊗
August–September. Pale purple. H 20 cm
(8 in). W 40 cm (16 in). Zone 4. S humus-rich.
P cuttings, layering. Small shrub of compact
habit. Has yellow-bronze leaves that change
colour.

Calluna vulgaris 'Gold Haze'
Heather, Ling/fam. *Ericaceae*
○ ◑ ⓜ ⓨ ⊛ ⊝ ⊗
August–September. White. H 25 cm (10 in).
W 40 cm (16 in). Zone 4. S humus-rich.
P cuttings, layering. Small shrub with long
branches. Of erect habit with golden-yellow
leaves.

Calluna vulgaris 'H. E. Beale'
Heather, Ling/fam. *Ericaceae*
○ ◑ ⓜ ⓨ ⊛ ⊝ ⊗
September–October. Purple-pink. H 60 cm
(2 ft). W 70 cm (28 in). Zone 4. S humus-rich.
P cuttings, layering. Small shrub of compact,
erect habit. Double flowers with a silvery
sheen.

Calluna vulgaris 'Marleen'
Heather, Ling/fam. *Ericaceae*
○ ◑ ⓜ ⓨ ⊛ ⊝ ⊗
September–November. Purple-red. H 30 cm
(1 ft). W 40 cm (16 in). Zone 4. S humus-rich.
P cuttings, layering. Spreading to upright
little shrub. The white flowers have a purple
point.

Calluna vulgaris 'Multicolor'
Heather, Ling / fam. *Ericaceae*
○ ◑ ⚙ ✿ ⊛ ⊖ ⊗
August–September. Purple. H 20 cm (8 in).
W 40 cm (16 in). Zone 4. S humus-rich.
P cuttings, layering. Small shrub of very
compact habit with yellow-bronze leaves that
change colour.

Calluna vulgaris 'Peter Sparkes'
Heather, Ling / fam. *Ericaceae*
○ ◑ ⚙ ✿ ⊛ ⊖ ⊗
September–October. Purplish pink. H 60 cm
(2 ft). W 40 cm (16 in). Zone 4. S humus-rich.
P cuttings, layering. Attractive cultivar of
compact and spreading habit with double
flowers.

Calluna vulgaris 'Radnor'
Heather, Ling / fam. *Ericaceae*
○ ◑ ⚙ ✿ ⊛ ⊖ ⊗
August–September. Pink. H 30 cm (1 ft).
W 40 cm (16 in). Zone 4. S humus-rich.
P cuttings, layering. New cultivar of erect
habit. Double flowers.

Calocedrus decurrens (Libocedrus decur-rens) / Incense Cedar / fam. *Cupressaceae*
○ ✳ ⚙ ⊛ ⊕
Tall pyramidal, ascendant tree with flattened
fan-like leaves and smooth, oval cones. H 30 m
(100 ft). W 5 m (16 ft). S fertile garden soil.
P seed. Zone 5.

Caltha palustris
Marsh Marigold / fam. *Ranunculaceae*
○ ◑ ⊗ ⊖ ⚙ ✿ ⊚
April–June. Yellow, H 25–50 cm (10–20 in).
A 30 cm (1 ft). S humus-rich, acid. P division,
seed. Attractive bright green leaves. Stout
stems. For moist or marshy ground by ponds.

Caltha palustris 'Plena' ('Multiplex')
Marsh Marigold / fam. *Ranunculaceae*
○ ◑ ⊗ ⊖ ⚙ ✿ ⊚
April–June. Yellow. H 25–50 cm (10–20 in).
A 30 cm (1 ft). S humus-rich, acid. P division.
Double flowers. Very attractive at the edge of
pools or ponds.

Calycanthus floridus
Carolina Allspice / fam. *Calycanthaceae*
○ ◑ ⚙ ⚙ ✿ ⊚ ⊛ ⊚
May–June. Reddish brown. H 3 m (10 ft).
W 2 m (6 ft). Zone 4. S not critical. P seed,
cuttings, layering. Shrub with large oval
leaves and fragrant flowers, leaves, roots and
branches.

Calycanthus occidentalis
Carolina Allspice / fam. *Calycanthaceae*
○ ◑ ⚙ ✿ ⊛ ⊚
June–August. Reddish brown. H 3 m (10 ft).
W 2 m (6 ft). Zone 4. S not critical. P seed,
cuttings, layering. Shrub with fragrant,
quickly fading and not very abundant
flowers.

Camassia cusickii
Quamash / fam. *Liliaceae*
○ ◑ ⊗ ⊙ ⚙ ⊚
May–June. Light blue. H 1 m (3 ft). A 10–20 cm
(4–8 in). D 7–10 cm (2¾–4 in). S normal garden
soil. P offsets. Plant in October, preferably in
groups. Light blue-green leaves, 5 cm (2 in) in
width.

153

Camellia

Camellia japonica
Common Camellia / fam. ***Theaceae***
○ ◑ ⊘ ⊕ ⊛ ♈ ⊛ ⊗

Janurary–April. Varied. H 4 m (13 ft). W 4 m
(13 ft). Zone 7. S fertile, acid. P seed, cuttings,
layering. Shrub with glossy green leaves and
single, semi-double or double flowers in
various colours.

***Camellia japonica* 'Beatrice Burns'**
Camellia / fam. ***Theaceae***
○ ◑ ⊘ ⊕ ⊛ ♈ ⊛ ⊗

January–April. Red. H 4 m (13 ft). W 4 m
(13 ft). Zone 7. S fertile, acid. P cuttings,
layering. A hardy variety for sheltered
positions developed in Boskoop, Holland.

Campanula carpatica
Bellflower / fam. ***Campanulaceae***
○ ◑ ○ ♈ ⊗

June–September. Violet. H 15–45 cm (6–
18 in). A 30 cm (1 ft). S normal garden soil.
P division, seed. Solitary flowers on thin
stems. Long flowering period. For the front
of a border.

Campanula cochleariifolia (C. pusilla)
Bellflower / fam. ***Campanulaceae***
◑ ◑ ⊖ ♈ ⊗

June–July. Violet-blue. H 10–15 cm (4–6 in).
A 30 cm (1 ft). S normal garden soil. P seed,
division. Fine rock-garden plant. Makes a
carpet of small leaves and graceful bell-
shaped flowers.

Campanula glomerata
Bellflower / fam. ***Campanulaceae***
○ ◑ ○ ♈ ⊗

June–August. Purple. H 25–60 cm (10–24 in).
A 40 cm (16 in). S humus-rich, chalky.
P division, seed. Flowers erect in dense
globular heads. Hardy plant for the border.

Campanula lactiflora
Great Bellflower / fam. ***Campanulaceae***
○ ◑ ○ ♈ ⊗

June–August. Lavender-blue. H 80–150 cm
(32–60 in). A 50 cm (20 in). S normal garden
soil. P division, seed. Stout flower stems
which need no support. Attractive plant for a
border.

***Campanula lactiflora* 'Loddon Anna'**
Bellflower / fam. ***Campanulaceae***
○ ◑ ○ ♈ ⊗

June–August. Mushroom-pink. H 1 m (3 ft).
A 50 cm (20 in). S normal garden soil.
P division. Cultivar with soft-coloured
flowers. Especially suitable for a border.

***Campanula lactiflora* 'Pouffe'**
Bellflower / fam. ***Campanulaceae***
○ ◑ ○ ♈

June–August. Violet. H 30 cm (1 ft). A 30 cm
(1 ft). S normal garden soil. P division. Low-
growing variety. Very attractive border plant.
Should be planted in fairly large groups.

***Campanula lactiflora* 'Pritchard'**
Bellflower / fam. ***Campanulaceae***
○ ◑ ○ ♈ ⊗

June–August. Violet. H 60 cm (2 ft). A 50 cm
(20 in). S normal garden soil. P division. Stout
flower stems which need no support. The
best-known garden variety.

Campanula latifolia 'Alba'
Bellflower / fam. *Campanulaceae*
◯ ◖ ◫ ◖ ◯ ⊗ ⊗
July–August. White. H 50–150 cm (20–60 in).
A 50 cm (20 in). S normal garden soil.
P division. Large and elongated bell-shaped
flowers. Sturdy stems. Will flower even in the
shade.

Campanula latifolia 'Macrantha'
Bellflower / fam. *Campanulaceae*
◯ ◖ ◯ ◯ ⊗ ⊗
July–August. Violet-purple. H 1 m (3 ft).
A 50 cm (20 in). S normal garden soil.
P division. Magnificent and particularly
strong garden variety.

Campanula medium
Canterbury Bell / fam. *Campanulaceae*
◖ ◯ ⌢ ⊙ ⊗ ⊗
Sow in June under glass. Plant out in August
at A 30 cm (1 ft). H 1 m (3 ft). Various colours.
S fertile garden soil. Robust plant with large
bell-shaped flowers in clusters.

Campanula persicifolia / Peach-leaved
Bellflower / fam. *Campanulaceae*
◯ ◖ ◯ ◯ ⊗ ⊗
June–August. Violet. H 40–100 cm (16–36 in).
A 50 cm (20 in). S humus-rich garden soil.
P division, seed. Flowers in loose clusters,
rigid stems. Excellent for the border. 'Alba'
has white flowers.

Campanula portenschlagiana 'Birch Hybrid'
Bellflower / fam. *Campanulaceae*
◯ ◖ ◯ ◯ ⊗ ⊗
June–August. Pale bluish-mauve. H 10 cm
(4 in). A 10 cm (4 in). S normal garden soil.
P division, cuttings. Creeping plant, excellent
for rock gardens and dry walls.

Campanula poscharskyana
Bellflower / fam. *Campanulaceae*
◯ ⌢ ◯ ◯ ⊗ ⊗
June–August. Violet. H 10–20 cm (4–8 in).
A 20 cm (8 in). S normal garden soil.
P division, seed. Strong-growing, attractive
plant for rock and wall gardens. Procumbent
stems. Flowers profusely.

Campunala pyramidalis
Chimney Bellflower / fam. *Campanulaceae*
◖ ◯ ⌢ ⊗ ⊗
Sow in June under glass. Plant out in August
at A 30 cm (1 ft). H 150 cm (5 ft). Violet-blue,
white. S humus-rich. Profusely flowering
ornamental plant. Flowers keep well in water.

Campsis radicans (Bignonia radicans)
Trumpet Creeper / fam. *Bignoniaceae*
◯ ⌢ ⇗ ⋓ ⊗
July–September. Orange, yellow. H 10 m
(33 ft). W 5 m (16 ft). Zone 5. S fertile. P seed,
cuttings, layering. Climbing shrub, self-
clinging. Light green pinnate leaves; trumpet-
shaped flowers.

Canarina canariensis
fam. *Campanulaceae*
◯ ⌢ ◯ ◯ ⊗ ⊗
November–March. Orange. H 1–2 m (3–6 ft).
A 50 cm (20 in). S prepacked compost. P seed,
division. Zone 10. Really a greenhouse
climber, resting in summer. Minimum 12–
15°C (53–59°F) during growing period.

155

Canna

Canna indica* hybrid *(C. × generalis)
fam. *Cannaceae*
○ ⊕ ⊗ ⊕ ⊕

June–September. Various colours. H 50–150 (20–60 in). A 40–50 cm (16–20 in). D 5 cm (2 in). S fertile garden soil. P division. Lift rhizones in late September. Plant out again in May.

Cardamine pratensis
Cuckoo Flower / **fam.** *Cruciferae*
○ ◖ ⊗ ○ ⊕

March–May. Lilac. H 30–40 (12–16 in). A 20 cm (8 in). S normal garden soil. P division, seed. Charming, profusely flowering native plant. Suitable for the edge of pools and ditches.

Cardiocrinum giganteum (Lilium giganteum)
Giant Lily / **fam.** *Liliaceae*
○ ⌃ ◔ ⊕

July–August. White. H 3–4 m (10–13 ft). A 80 cm (32 in). D half-buried. S humus-rich. P offsets. Unusual plant rarely cultivated. Has fragrant lily-like flowers.

Carex pendula (C. maxima)
Sedge / **fam.** *Cyperaceae*
○ ◖ ⧄ ⊗ ⊕ ⊕ ⊕

June–July. Green. H 60–150 cm (2–5 ft). A 60 cm (2 ft). S normal garden soil. P division, seed. Arching stems. Cut back hard after frost damage. Plant in small groups.

Carex plantaginea
Sedge / **fam.** *Cyperaceae*
○ ◖ ⊗ ⊕ ⊗

May–June. Greeny-white. H 30 cm (1 ft). A 20 cm (8 in). S normal garden soil. P seed, division. Grass-like plant with overhanging green leaves and triangular stems.

Carlina acaulis
fam. *Compositae*
○ ⊖ ○ ⊕ ⊗ ⊗

July–September. White. H 10–15 cm (4–6 in). A 50 cm (20 in). S normal garden soil. P seed. Very attractive thistle for the rock garden. Small leaves with spinuous teeth.

Carpinus betulus
Common Hornbeam / **fam.** *Betulaceae*
○ ◖ ⊛ ⊗ ⊞

June. Yellow-green. H 20 m (65 ft). W 12 m (40 ft). Zone 5. S not critical. P seed. This tree makes an excellent and easily pruned hedge.

Carpinus betulus
Common Hornbeam / **fam.** *Betulaceae*
○ ◖ ⊛ ⊗ ⊕ ⊞

June. Yellow-green. H 20 m (65 ft). W 12 m (40 ft). Zone 5. S not critical. P seed. Fairly tall tree or robust shrub. Flowers in catkins; winged nutlets.

Caryopteris × clandonensis
fam. *Verbenaceae*
○ ⌃ ⊗ ⊕

September. Blue. H 125 cm (4 ft). W 125 cm (4 ft). Zone 5. S not critical. P cuttings. Low shrub with narrow greyish-green leaves, fragrant branches. Flowers on one-year-old wood.

***Castanea sativa* 'Glabra'**
Sweet Chestnut / fam. *Fagaceae*
○ ◐ ❀ ⊕ ⊕
May. Greeny-yellow. H 20 (65 ft). W 10 cm
(33 ft). Zone 5. S not critical. P seed. Robust
tree with large, coarse, dark green, glossy
leaves and edible nuts.

Catalpa bignonioides
Indian Bean Tree / fam. *Bignoniaceae*
○ ◑ ❀ ⓨ ⊛ ⊕ ⊕
June–July. White. H 10 m (33 ft). W 4 m (13 ft).
Zone 4. S normal garden soil. P cuttings. Tree
or tall shrub with an umbrella-shaped crown.
Long, thin, pendulous seed pods shaped like
beans.

***Catalpa* × *erubescens (C. bignonioides* ×
C. ovata)** / **Bean Tree** / fam. *Bignoniaceae*
○ ❀ ⓨ ⊛ ⊕ ⊕
June–July. White. H 10 (33 ft). W 5 m (16 ft).
Zone 5. S normal garden soil. P cuttings.
Leaves slightly lobate; flowers borne in
clusters.

***Catalpa* × *erubescens* (seed pods)**
Bean Tree / fam. *Bignoniaceae*
○ ❀ ⓨ ⊛ ⊛ ⊕
For description and P see last entry. Hardy
tree. Vigorous grower with a rounded shape.
Attractive leaves and very long thin and
pendent seed pods.

Catalpa ovata (C. kaempferi)
Bean Tree / fam. *Bignoniaceae*
○ ❀ ⓨ ⊛ ⊛ ⊕
July. White. H 10 m (33 ft). W 10 m (33 ft). Zone
4. S normal garden soil. P cuttings, seed.
Sturdy tree with a broad crown, lobed leaves
and clusters of small flowers.

Catananche caerulea
Cupid's Dart / fam. *Compositae*
○ ⊖ ◎ ⓥ ⊗
July–August. Purple-blue. H 40–80 cm (16–
32 in). A 40 cm (16 in). S normal garden soil.
P division, seed. Resembles the cornflower.
Native plant, suitable for rock gardens. Good
for cutting.

***Ceanothus* hybrid 'Gloire de Versailles'**
Californian Lilac / fam. *Rhamnaceae*
○ ⌂ ⊕ ⓦ ⓨ
August–September. Soft powder blue. H 1 m
(3 ft). W 1.5 m (5 ft). Zone 5. S fertile.
P cuttings, division, layering. Strong-growing
shrub with a profusion of flowers in large
panicles. One of the hardiest varieties.

***Cedrus atlantica* 'Glauca'**
Blue Atlas Cedar / fam. *Pinaceae*
○ ❀ ⊛ ⓨ ⊛ ⊕
Fairly quick-growing conifer with grey-blue
leaves and barrel-shaped cones. Very hardy.
H 30 m (100 ft). W 10 m (33 ft). S normal garden
soil. P grafting. Zone 5–6.

Cedrus deodara
Deodar / fam. *Pinaceae*
○ ❀ ⊛ ⓨ ⊛ ⊕
More sensitive to frost than *C. a.* 'Glauca'.
Trees less than 40 years old rarely have cones.
Blue-green, long needles. H 20 m (65 ft). W 8 m
(26 ft). S normal garden soil. P seed. Zone 6.

***Cedrus deodara* 'Aurea'**
Deodar / fam. *Pinaceae*
○ ❋ ❀ ❀ ⊛ ⊕
Same pyramidal habit as the species but
grows more slowly. Needles lose some of their
golden-yellow colour in autumn and winter.
H 10 m (33 ft). W 6 m (20 ft). P cuttings,
grafting. Zone 7.

Cedrus libani (C. libanotica)
Cedar of Lebanon / fam. *Pinaceae*
○ ❋ ❀ ❀ ⊛ ⊕
Very slow-growing tree with a flat crown and
reddish-brown aromatic wood. H 25–40 m
(80–135 ft). W 12 m (40 ft). Zone 6. S normal.
P seed, grafting.

Celastrus orbiculatus (C. articulatus)
Staff Vine / fam. *Celastraceae*
○ ◑ ❀ ❀ ❀ ⊛
June. Yellow-green. H 10 m (33 ft). W 5 m
(16 ft). Zone 4. S not critical. P seed, cuttings,
layering. Vigorous climber with variably
shaped oval leaves and decorative orange
fruits.

Celastrus scandens
Staff Vine / fam. *Celastraceae*
○ ◑ ❀ ❀ ❀ ⊛
June. Yellow-green. H 7 m (23 ft). W 3 m (10 ft).
Zone 2. S not critical. P layering, cutting,
seed. Dioecious climbing shrub. The
attractive leaves change colour. Dehiscent
fruits.

Celosia argentea var. cristata (C. cristata)
Cockscomb / fam. *Amaranthaceae*
○ ☉ ❦
Sow in February–March in heated
greenhouse. Plant out at A 20 cm (8 in).
H 30 cm (1 ft). Red. S fertile, fairly heavy.
Compact plant with large heads of crested
flowers. Needs light and warmth.

Centaurea cyanus
Cornflower / fam. *Compositae*
○ ☉ ❦ ⊗
Sow in May and thin out to A 25–40 cm (10–
16 in). H 1 m (3 ft). Blue, white, red, purple.
S not critical. Good for cutting. Grows as a
weed in cornfields. Soft stems; attractive
flowers.

***Centaurea cyanus* 'Blue Diadem'**
Cornflower / fam. *Compositae*
○ ☉ ❦ ⊗
Sow in May and thin out to A 25–40 cm (10–
16 in). H 1 m (3 ft). Blue. S not critical. A new,
tall garden variety with extra large flowers.
Attractive in borders.

Centaurea macrocephala
Cornflower / fam. *Compositae*
○ ⊜ ❦ ⊗
July–August. Yellow. H 40–90 cm (16–36 in).
A 50 cm (20 in). S chalky. P division, seed.
Fleshy and leafy stems bear spherical flower
heads up to 9 cm (3½ in) in diameter. Looks
like a thistle.

***Centaurea montana* 'Alba'**
Cornflower / fam. *Compositae*
○ ◑ ❦ ⊗
May–August. White. H 30–50 cm (12–20 in).
A 20–30 cm (8–12 in). S normal garden soil.
P division, cuttings. Cut back stems hard after
flowering, for a second show in the autumn.

Centranthus macrosiphon
Valerian / fam. *Valerianaceae*
○ ⊖ ⊙ ⊚
Sow in March under glass or in April outside.
Plant or thin out to A 30 cm (1 ft). H 40 cm
(16 in). Rosy carmine. S not critical.
Oustanding border plant blending well with
grey and purple.

Centranthus ruber
Red Valerian / fam. *Valerianaceae*
○ ○ ⊚ ⊗
May–July. Deep pink. H 80 cm (32 in). A 50 cm
(20 in). S chalky. P division, seed. Hard to
combine with other colours in the border.
Seeds itself.

Centranthus ruber 'Roseus'
Red Valerian / fam. *Valerianaceae*
○ ○ ⊚ ⊗
May–July. Pink. H 80 cm (32 in). A 50 cm
(20 in). S chalky. P division. Very long
flowering period. Will grow between stones.
Striking colour.

Cephalaria gigantea (C. tatarica)
fam. *Dipsacaseae*
○ ◑ ⓦ ⊚ ⊗
July–August. Yellow. H 130–160 cm (4–5 ft).
A 80 cm (32 in). S normal garden soil.
P division, seed. Large, ornamental plant.
Flowers resemble *Scabiosa*. Stems erect,
sometimes arching.

Cephalotaxus harringtonia 'Fastigiata'
fam. *Cephalotaxaceae*
○ ◑ ⓦ ⊛ ⊛ ⊛ ⊚
Columnar habit and very long dark green,
radially arranged needles. Grows very slowly
at first. H 5 m (16 ft). W 2 m (6 ft). P seed,
cuttings. Zone 5.

Cerastium biebersteinii (C. repens)
Snow-in-Summer / fam. *Caryophyllaceae*
○ ⊖ ○ ⓦ ⊚ ⊖
May–June. White. H 30 cm (1 ft). A 20 cm
(8 in). S normal garden soil. P division.
Woolly, silver-grey leaves. Invasive. Suitable
for rock gardens and containers.

Ceratostigma plumbaginoides
fam. *Plumbaginaceae*
○ ◑ ⓦ ⊚ ⊚ ⊖
September–October. Blue. H 30 cm (1 ft).
W 50 cm (20 in). Zone 8. S not critical.
P cuttings, division. Semi-shrub with leaves
that change colour. Prostrate or slightly raised
stems.

Ceratostigma willmottianum
fam. *Plumbaginaceae*
○ ◑ ⓦ ⊚
September–October. Blue. H 1 m (3 ft). W 2 m
(6 ft). Zone 8. S not critical. P cuttings,
division. Semi-shrub with a protracted
flowering period in late summer. Suitable for
small gardens.

Cercidiphyllum japonicum (autumn)
fam. *Cercidiphyllaceae*
○ ◑ ⊚ ⊛ ⓦ ⊕
April–May. Red. H 10 m (33 ft). W 8 m (26 ft).
Zone 4. S not critical. P seed. Dioecious shrub
with attractively branched stems and lovely
autumn colours.

159

Cercidiphyllum

Cercidiphyllum japonicum (summer)
fam. *Cercidiphyllaceae*
○ ◑ ⊗ ❋ ⊛ ⊕ ⚘
April–May. Red. H 10 m (33 ft). W 8 m (26 ft).
Zone 4. S not critical. P seed. Fine foliage
shrub. Leaves red when unfolding. Foliage
assumes beautiful autumn tints.
Inconspicuous flowers.

Cercis siliquastrum
Judas Tree / fam. *Leguminosae*
○ ⊘ ❋ ⊙ ⓨ ⊛ ⚘
April–May. Rose-purple. H 7 m (23 ft). W 5 m
(16 ft). Zone 6. S fertile, chalky. P seed. Small
tree or tall shrub with flat green seeds.
Flowers on naked stems.

Cestrum 'Newellii' *(Habrothamnus newellii)*
fam. *Solanaceae*
○ ◑ ⊘ ⓨ ⊛ ⚘
May–September. Red. H 3 m (10 ft). W 2.5 m
(8 ft). Zone 10. S fertile, chalky. P cuttings.
Shrub grown from crosses between unknown
parents; resembles C. *purpureum*.

Cestrum purpureum (C. elegans)
fam. *Solanaceae*
○ ◑ ⊙ ⊛ ⓨ ⊛ ⚘
April–September. Purple-red. H 3 m (10 ft).
W 1.5 m (5 ft). Zone 10. S fertile, chalky.
P cuttings. Graceful climbing shrub with
lanceolate, dark green, downy leaves.

Chaenomeles japonica (Cydonia japonica)
Maule's Quince / fam. *Rosaceae*
○ ◑ ⊗ ⚘ ⓨ ⊛ ⊙
March–April. Red. H 2.5 m (8 ft). W 3 m (10 ft).
Zone 4. S humus-rich. P seed, cuttings,
layering. Wide-spreading dwarf shrub with
fine spines and yellow-green fragrant fruits.

Chaenomeles speciosa 'Simonii'
Japonica / fam. *Rosaceae*
○ ◑ ⊗ ⚘ ⓨ ⊛ ⊙ ⊖
March–April. Red. H 50 cm (20 in). W 1.25 m
(4 ft). Zone 4. S humus-rich. P cuttings,
layering. Dwarf shrub with spreading
branches. Bears spines and semi-double or
single flowers.

Chaenomeles × superba (fruits)
Ornamental Quince / fam. *Rosaceae*
○ ◑ ⊗ ⚘ ⓨ ⊛ ⊙
March–April. Red. H 2 m (6 ft). W 4 m (13 ft).
Zone 4. S humus-rich garden soil. P layering,
cuttings. Fruits edible but not tasty unless
used for jam or jelly.

Chaenomeles × superba 'Crimson and Gold'
Ornamental Quince / fam. *Rosaceae*
○ ◑ ⊗ ⚘ ⓨ ⊛ ⊙ ⊖
March–April. Crimson. H 1 m (3 ft). W 2 m
(6 ft). Zone 4. S humus-rich. P cuttings,
layering. Wide-spreading shrub; dense
foliage, single flowers and yellow fruits with
red cheeks.

**Chamaecyparis lawsoniana (Cupressus
lawsoniana)** / Lawson Cypress / fam.
Cuppressaceae
○ ◑ ❋ ⊛ ⊙ ⊕ ⊖ ▥
Narrow conical tree with tiny blue-green
leaves smelling of parsley when crushed.
H 35 m (115 ft). W 10 m (33 ft). S humus-rich.
P seed, cuttings, layering. Zone 5.

***Chamaecyparis lawsonia* 'Albovariegata'**
Lawson Cypress / fam. *Cupressaceae*
○ ◑ ✳ ⊘ ⊛ ⊛ ⊚ ⊕
Compact round shrub, tolerant of frost in
unsheltered positions but more decorative
with adequate protection. H 7 m (23 ft). W 4 m
(13 ft). S humus-rich. P cuttings. Zone 6.

***Chamaecyparis lawsoniana* 'Alumii'**
Lawson Cypress / fam. *Cupressaceae*
○ ◑ ✳ ⊘ ⊛ ⊛ ⊚ ⊕
Strong-growing conifer, narrowly conical.
Dull blue-grey form. Very popular. H 20 m
(65 ft). W 8 m (26 ft). S humus-rich. P cuttings.
Zone 5.

***Chamaecyparis lawsoniana* 'Blue Nantais'**
Lawson Cypress / fam. *Cupressaceae*
○ ◑ ✳ ⊘ ⊛ ⊛ ⊚ ⊕
Broadly conical shrub with fine leaves, blue-
green on the upper surface and bluish white
underneath. H 10 m (33 ft). W 4 m (13 ft).
S humus-rich. P cuttings. Zone 6.

***Chamaecyparis lawsoniana* 'Dow's Gem'**
Lawson Cypress / fam. *Cupressaceae*
○ ◑ ✳ ⊘ ⊛ ⊛ ⊚
Attractive, compact conifer with gracefully
arching branch tips and thuja-like foliage.
H 3 m (10 ft). W 3 m (10 ft). S humus-rich.
P cuttings. Zone 6.

***Chamaecyparis lawsoniana* 'Ellwoodii'**
Lawson Cypress / fam. *Cupressaceae*
○ ◑ ✳ ⊘ ⊛ ⊛ ⊚ ⊕
Well-known conifer with a columnar habit
and fine needle-shaped young leaves. Blue-
green scales. Also grown in containers. H 6 m
(20 ft). W 2 m (6 ft). S humus-rich. P cuttings.
Zone 5.

***Chamaecyparis lawsoniana* 'Ellwood's White'**
Lawson Cypress / fam. *Cupressaceae*
○ ◑ ✳ ⊘ ⊛ ⊛ ⊚ ⊕
Cultivar of *C. l.* 'Ellwoodii'. Attractive light
yellow new growth. Grows very slowly. H 8 m
(26 ft). W 2 m (6 ft). S humus-rich. P cuttings.
Zone 6.

***Chamaecyparis lawsoniana* 'Erecta Aurea'**
Lawson Cypress / fam. *Cupressaceae*
○ ◑ ⋓ ⊘ ⊛ ⊛ ⊚
Slow-growing conical conifer with scaly
leaves and numerous globular cones after a
few years. H 4 m (13 ft). W 2 m (6 ft). S humus-
rich. P cuttings. Zone 6.

***Chamaecyparis lawsoniana* 'Filiformis
Compacta'** / Lawson Cypress / fam.
Cupressaceae
○ ◑ ⋓ ⊘ ⊛ ⊚
Slow-growing conifer often confused with
C. pisifera 'Filifera Nana'. H 2 m (6 ft). W 1.5 m
(5 ft). S humus-rich. P cuttings. Zone 5.

***Chamaecyparis lawsoniana* 'Fletcheri'**
Lawson Cypress / fam. *Cupressaceae*
○ ◑ ✳ ⊘ ⊛ ⊛ ⊚ ⊕
Usually multi-columnar with blue-green
leaves, very feathery in the juvenile stage.
H 12 m (40 ft). W 4 m (13 ft). S humus-rich.
P cuttings. Zone 5.

Chamaecyparis

***Chamaecyparis lawsoniana* 'Gimbornii'**
Lawson Cypress / fam. *Cupressaceae*
○ ⦾ ⦿ ⊛ ⦿ ⊙
Compact and slow-growing conifer with
purple leaf tips. Should not be pruned.
H 80 cm (32 in). W 80 cm (32 in). S humus-rich.
P cuttings. Zone 5.

***Chamaecyparis lawsoniana* 'Intertexta'**
Lawson Cypress / fam. *Cupressaceae*
○ ⦾ ⦿ ⊛ ⦿ ⊙
A tree that needs space. Open, erect habit.
Gracefully arching branches. Not suitable for
smaller gardens. H 20 m (65 ft). W 10 m (33 ft).
S humus-rich. P cuttings. Zone 5.

***Chamaecyparis lawsoniana* 'Lanei'**
Lawson Cypress / fam. *Cupressaceae*
○ ❋ ⦿ ⦾ ⊛ ⦿ ⊙ ⊕
One of the most beautiful golden-yellow
varieties. Upright, slim habit with spreading
branches. Needles are yellow underneath.
H 6 m (20 ft). W 3 m (10 ft). S humus-rich.
P cuttings. Zone 5–6.

***Chamaecyparis lawsoniana* 'Lutea'**
Lawson Cypress / fam. *Cupressaceae*
○ ❋ ⦿ ⦾ ⊛ ⦿ ⊙ ⊕
A tree which will grow in most surroundings.
Narrow columnar habit with slightly arching
branches and yellow-green foliage. H 10 m
(33 ft). W 3 m (10 ft). S humus-rich. P cuttings.
Zone 5.

***Chamaecyparis lawsoniana* 'Minima Aurea'**
Lawson Cypress / fam. *Cupressaceae*
○ ⦾ ⦿ ⊛ ⦿ ⊙ ⊕
Slow-growing conifer of very compact habit.
Bright yellow scales. Best colour in winter.
H 1.5 m (5 ft). W 1.5 m (5 ft). S humus-rich.
P cuttings. Zone 5.

***Chamaecyparis lawsoniana* 'Minima Glauca'**
Lawson Cypress / fam. *Cupressaceae*
○ ⦙⦙ ⦾ ⦿ ⊛ ⦿ ⊙ ⊕
Slow-growing shrub of compact globular
habit with blue-grey scales. H 1.5 m (5 ft).
W 1.5 m (5 ft). S humus-rich. P cuttings.
Zone 5.

***Chamaecyparis lawsoniana* 'Nana'**
Lawson Cypress / fam. *Cupressaceae*
○ ⦙⦙ ⦾ ⦿ ⊛ ⦿ ⊙ ⊕
Broadly conical shrub with a thick trunk and
horizontally spreading branches. Difficult to
distinguish from 'Minima Glauca'. H 1.25 m
(4 ft). W 1 m (3 ft). Zone 5.

***Chamaecyparis lawsoniana* 'Nidiformis'**
Lawson Cypress / fam. *Cupressaceae*
○ ⦙⦙ ⦾ ⦿ ⊛ ⦿ ⊙ ⊕
Ornamental plant resembling a large, blue-
green bird's nest. Attractive habit. Suitable
dimensions for a small garden. H 1.5 m (5 ft).
W 2 m (6 ft). S humus-rich. P cuttings. Zone 5.

***Chamaecyparis lawsoniana* 'Nyewoods'**
Lawson Cypress / fam. *Cupressaceae*
○ ⦙⦙ ❋ ⦾ ⦿ ⊛ ⦿ ⊙ ⊕
Slow-growing, broadly columnar shrub with
a broad, wavy crown and fine needle-shaped,
blue-grey juvenile foliage. H 10 m (33 ft).
W 4 m (13 ft). S humus-rich. P cuttings.
Zone 6.

***Chamaecyparis lawsoniana* 'Pendula'**
Lawson Cypress / fam. *Cupressaceae*
○ ❀ ✿ ⊕ ⊛ ◎ ⊕
Conical, fairly open habit, arching branches,
dark green foliage and purple male flowers.
H 20 m (65 ft). W 10 m (33 ft). S humus-rich.
P cuttings. Zone 5.

***Chamaecyparis lawsoniana* 'Pygmaea
Argentea'** / Lawson Cypress / fam.
Cupressaceae
◐ ❂ ◑ ✿ ⊛ ◎ ⊕
Attractive, slow-growing conifer. Protect
against leaf-tip burn from full sun or frost.
H 1 m (3 ft). W 1 m (3 ft). S humus-rich.
P cuttings. Zone 6.

***Chamaecyparis lawsoniana* 'Triomf van Bos-
koop'** / Lawson Cypress / fam. *Cupressaceae*
○ ◐ ◑ ❀ ⊛ ◎ ⊕ ⊕
Columnar tree. The silvery leaves have a blue
bloom. Pruning is essential for dense foliage.
H 15–18 m (50–60 ft). W 4 m (13 ft). Zone 5.
S humus-rich. P cuttings, layering.

***Chamaecyparis lawsoniana* 'Winston
Churchill'** / Lawson Cypress / fam.
Cupressaceae
○ ❀ ✿ ⊛ ◎ ⊕
One of the best golden Lawsons, with full
colour all the year. Relatively slow-growing.
H 8 m (26 ft). W 3 m (10 ft). S humus-rich.
P cuttings. Zone 5–6.

***Chamaecyparis nootkatensis* 'Pendula'**
Nootka Cypress / fam. *Cupressaceae*
○ ◑ ❀ ✿ ⊛ ◎ ⊕
Weeping form with horizontal, upward-
sweeping branches, gracefully drooping
branchlets and coarse green scales. H 10 m
(33 ft). W 5 m (16 ft). S humus-rich. P cuttings.
Zone 4.

***Chamaecyparis obtusa* (*Retinispora obtusa*)**
Hinoki Cypress / fam. *Cupressaceae*
○ ◐ ◑ ✿ ⊛ ⊛ ◎ ⊕
Attractive slow-growing, conical tree, pruned
here in the Japanese manner. Green leaves,
silvery markings on the underside. H 8 m
(26 ft). W 6 m (20 ft). S humus-rich. P seed,
cuttings.

***Chamaecyparis obtusa* 'Nana Gracilis'**
Hinoki Cypress / fam. *Cupressaceae*
○ ◑ ✿ ⊛ ◎ ◎ ⊕
One of the most decorative semi-dwarf
conifers with fan-shaped branches and of
compact conical habit. H 2.5 m (8 ft). W 1 m
(3 ft). S humus-rich. P cuttings. Zone 5.

***Chamaecyparis obtusa* 'Pygmaea'**
Hinoki Cypress / fam. *Cupressaceae*
○ ◐ ⌂ ◑ ✿ ⊛ ⊛
Low, spreading shrub of broadly globular
habit. The stiff fan-shaped branches bear
horizontal needles. H 75 cm (30 in). W 1.5 m
(5 ft). S humus-rich. P cuttings. Zone 5.

***Chamaecyparis obutsa* 'Tetragona Aurea'**
Hinoki Cypress / fam. *Cupressaceae*
○ ◐ ◑ ◑ ✿ ⊛ ⊛ ◎ ⊕
Attractive, irregularly growing golden
conifer. Prune lightly for shape and
compactness. H 4 m (13 ft). W 3 m (10 ft).
S humus-rich. P cuttings. Zone 5.

Chamaecyparis

***Chamaecyparis pisifera* 'Boulevard'**
Sawara Cypress / fam. *Cupressaceae*
Attractive shape. Broadly conical, compact
habit. Striking grey-blue needle-shaped
foliage (juvenile form). H 4 m (13 ft). W 3 m
(10 ft). S humus-rich. P cuttings. Zone 5.

***Chamaecyparis pisifera* 'Compacta'**
Sawara Cypress / fam. *Cupressaceae*
Delightful small and compact bun-shaped
bush. The green adult foliage turns browny
green in the winter. H 50 cm (20 in). W 75 cm
(30 in). S humus-rich. P cuttings. Zone 5.

***Chamaecyparis pisifera* 'Filifera Aurea'**
Sawara Cypress / fam. *Cupressaceae*
Bright golden cultivar grown as a round bush
or small tree. Slightly globular habit. Thread-
like foliage. H 5 m (16 ft). W 3 m (10 ft).
S humus-rich. P cuttings. Zone 5.

***Chamaecyparis pisifera* 'Filifera Nana'**
Sawara Cypress / fam. Cupressaceae
Very compact globular bush with grey-green
foliage hanging in long threads. H 50 cm
(20 in). W 1 m (3 ft). S humus-rich. P cuttings.
Zone 5.

***Chamaecyparis pisifera* 'Nana'**
Sawara Cypress / fam. *Cupressaceae*
One of the most compact of all conifers which
ultimately grows into a dome-shaped bush.
H 60 cm (2 ft). W 1.5 m (5 ft). S humus-rich.
P cuttings. Zone 5.

***Chamaecyparis pisifera* 'Plumosa Aurea
Nana' / Sawara Cypress / fam. *Cupressaceae***
Compact habit. Slow growing. Retains its
golden colour throughout the winter.
Resinous aroma. H 1.5 m (5 ft). W 1 m (3 ft).
S humus-rich. P cuttings. Zone 5.

***Chamaecyparis pisifera* 'Plumosa Minima'**
Sawara Cypress / fam. *Cupressaceae*
Irregularly growing, globular bush of compact
habit. Feathery foliage, slightly prickly but
soft looking. H 1 m (3 ft). W 1.5 m (5 ft).
S humus-rich. P cuttings. Zone 5.

***Chamaecyparis pisifera* 'Pygmaea'**
Sawara Cypress / fam. *Cupressaceae*
Slow-growing shrub of compact conical habit,
densely covered in very fine juvenile foliage.
H 2 m (6 ft). W 2 m (6 ft). S humus-rich.
P cuttings. Zone 5.

***Chamaecyparis pisifera* 'Squarrosa
Pygmaea' / Sawara Cypress / fam.
*Cupressaceae***
Dense circular dwarf shrub with a flat top and
occasionally protruding branches. Attractive
juvenile foliage. H 80 cm (32 in). W 1 m (3 ft).
S humus-rich. P cuttings. Zone 5.

Chamaecyparis thyoides 'Ericoides'
fam. *Cupressaceae*
Upright bronze-green conifer which retains
its juvenile foliage permanently. Though
foliage turns reddish-purple in autumn it is
not a *Thuja*. H 2 m (6 ft). W 1 m (3 ft). S humus-
rich. P cuttings. Zone 5.

Chamaedaphne calyculata var. nana
fam. *Ericaceae*
April–May. White. H 30 cm (1 ft). W 50 cm
(20 in). S humus-rich. P seed, cuttings. Dwarf
shrub with horizontal branches and small
leaves. Dense habit. For the heather garden.

Chamaemelum nobile (Anthemis nobilis)
Sweet Chamomile / fam. *Compositae*
July–October. White. H 30 cm (1 ft). A 20 cm
(8 in). S normal garden soil. P division, seed.
Strongly resembles the Common Chamomile
(which has hollow receptacles).

Chamomilla recutita (Matricaria recutita)
Wild Chamomile / fam. *Compositae*
Sow in March under glass or in May in the
open. Plant / thin out to A 15 cm (6 in).
H 40 cm (16 in). White / yellow. S normal
garden soil. The dried flowers have medicinal
applications.

Cheiranthus cheiri (Erysimum cheiri)
Wallflower / fam. *Cruciferae*
Sow in May under glass. Plant out at A 25–
30 cm (10–12 in), first in a seed bed. H 40 cm
(16 in). Various colours. S chalky, fertile.
Fragrant plant for the border or for bedding.

Chelone obliqua
Turtlehead / fam. *Scrophulariaceae*
July–September. Deep rose. H 60 cm (2 ft).
A 50 cm (20 in). S humus-rich. P division,
seed. Fairly rare hardy perennial, better in
natural groups than in the border. Good for
cutting.

**Chiastophyllum oppositifolium (Cotyledon
oppositifolia)** / Lamb's Tail / *Crassulaceae*
June–July. Yellow. H 10–25 cm (4–10 in).
A 20 cm (8 in). S normal garden soil.
P division, seed. Flowers in profusion. Likes
crevices between rocks. Moderately moist.

Chionanthus virginicus
fam. *Oleaceae*
June. White. H 2–3 m (6–10 ft). W 2–3 m (6–
10 ft). Zone 4. S loamy. P seed, grafting,
layering. Broad, erect shrub with fragrant
flower plumes and dark blue, oval fruits.

Chionodoxa gigantea
Glory of the Snow / fam. *Liliaceae*
March–April. Blue. H 20 cm (8 in). A 5–7 cm
(2–2¾ in). D 5 cm (2 in). S normal garden soil.
P offsets. Unlike *C. luciliae*, this species has
three to four flowers to each flower spike.

165

Chionodoxa

Chionodoxa luciliae
Glory of the Snow / fam. *Liliaceae*
○ ◐ ◍ ⊕ ⊙
March–April. Blue. H 12–15 cm (4½–6 in). A 5–
7 cm (2–2¾ in). D 5 cm (2 in). S normal garden
soil. P offsets. These bulbs with star-shaped
little flowers should be planted close in large
groups.

***Chrysanthemum arcticum* (*Dendranthema
arcticum*) / fam. *Compositae***
○ ○ ⊕
September–October. Light yellow. H 30–
40 cm (12–16 in). A 25–30 cm (10–12 in).
S normal garden soil. P division, cuttings.
Creeping habit. Flowers profusely in autumn.
Branching stems with many leaves.

***Chrysanthemum coccineum* 'Brenda'
fam. *Compositae***
○ ○ ◍ ⊕ ⊙
June–July. Red. H 1 m (3 ft). A 50 cm (20 in).
S normal garden soil. P division, seed.
Flowers profusely. Lift every three years,
divide and replant. Good border plant.

***Chionodoxa luciliae* 'Pink Giant'**
Glory of the Snow / fam. *Liliaceae*
○ ◐ ◍ ⊕ ⊙
March–April. Pink. H 12–15 cm (4½–6 in). A 5–
7 cm (2–2¾ in). D 5 cm (2 in). S normal garden
soil. P offsets. Very good for the front row of
the border.

***Chrysanthemum carinatum* (*C. tricolor*)**
fam. *Compositae*
○ ○ ⊙ ⊕ ⊗
Sow in February in heated greenhouse or in
April in the open. Thin / plant out at A 25 cm
(10 in). H 60 cm (2 ft). Various colours.
S normal garden soil. Summer flowering.
Good for cutting.

Chrysanthemum corymbosum
fam. *Compositae*
○ ○ ⊕ ⊗
June–August. White. H 120 cm (4 ft). A 60 cm
(2 ft). S normal garden soil. P division, seed.
Outstanding edging plant with hedges. Cut
back to the ground.

Choisya ternata
Mexican Orange / fam. *Rutaceae*
○ ◐ ◍ ⊕ ⊙ ⊛ ♣
May–June. White. H 1 m (3 ft). W 1 m (3 ft).
Zone 7. S fertile soil. P cuttings. Shrub with
dense foliage. Leaves leathery and aromatic;
fragrant flowers.

***Chrysanthemum carinatum* 'Merry'**
fam. *Compositae*
○ ○ ⊕ ⊗
Sow in February in heated greenhouse or in
April in the open. Thin / plant out at A 25 cm
(10 in). H 60 cm (2 ft). S normal garden soil.
Recommended cultivar. Single flowers of
various colours.

***Chrysanthemum* 'Balcombe Perfection'**
fam. *Compositae*
○ ∧ ◍ ⊕ ⊗
August–November. Orange. H 120 cm (4 ft).
A 30 cm (1 ft). S humus-rich. P cuttings,
division. Incurved petals forming a loose
globe. Very decorative.

Chrysanthemum 'Blanche Poiteviene'
fam. Compositae
○ ⊘ ◐ Ⓣ ⊗
August–November. White. H 120 cm (4 ft).
A 30 cm (1 ft). S humus-rich. P cuttings,
division. Loosely arranged and irregularly
incurving petals.

Chrysanthemum 'Fairweather'
fam. Compositae
○ ⊘ ◐ Ⓣ ⊗
August–November. Purple-red. H 120 cm
(4 ft). A 30 cm (1 ft). S humus-rich. P cuttings,
division. Incurved flowers: the densely
packed and sturdy florets form a complete
sphere.

Chrysanthemum 'Golden Chance'
fam. Compositae
○ ⊘ ◐ Ⓣ ⊗
August–November. Yellow. H 60 cm (2 ft).
A 30 cm (1 ft). S humus-rich. P cuttings,
division. Cut stems after flowering. New
growths appear close to the stem.

Chrysanthemum 'Jimmy Mottram'
fam. Compositae
○ ⊘ ◐ Ⓣ ⊗
August–November. Orange-red. H 60 cm
(2 ft). A 30 cm (1 ft). S humus-rich. P cuttings,
division. Reflexed type: florets fall outwards
and slightly downwards.

Chrysanthemum 'Maiko'
fam. Compositae
○ ⊘ ◐ Ⓣ ⊗
August–November. Purple. H 1 m (3 ft).
A 30 cm (1 ft). S humus-rich. P cuttings,
division. Lift and overwinter in a light and
frost-free position, preferably on the
greenhouse floor.

Chrysanthemum 'Perfection'
fam. Compositae
○ ⊘ ◐ Ⓣ ⊗
August–November. Reddish-purple. H 80 cm
(32 in). A 30 cm (1 ft). S humus-rich.
P cuttings, division. Force stools in the spring
at about 18°C (64°F). Take cuttings of 5–7 cm
(2–2¾ in).

Chrysanthemum 'Red Breast'
fam. Compositae
○ ⊘ ◐ Ⓣ ⊗
August–November. Red. H 60 cm (2 ft).
A 30 cm (1 ft). P cuttings, division. Plant out
when the danger of night frosts is over. Stop
young plants after two weeks.

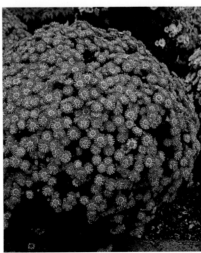

Chrysanthemum 'Ringdove'
fam. Compositae
○ ⊘ ◐ Ⓣ ⊗
August–November. Reddish-purple. H 60 cm
(2 ft). A 30 cm (1 ft). S humus-rich. P cuttings,
division. Frequent stopping and disbudding
helps to produce more flowers.

Chrysanthemum 'Rytop'
fam. Compositae
○ ⊘ ◐ Ⓣ ⊗
August–November. Rose-purple. H 80 cm
(32 in). A 30 cm (1 ft). S humus-rich.
P cuttings, division. Large-flowered florists'
chrysanthemum. Remove lateral stems for
long flowers.

Chrysanthemum

***Chrysanthemum* 'Ugetsu'**
fam. *Compositae*
○ ⊙ ◐ ⊕ ⊗
August–November. White. H 120 cm (4 ft).
A 30 cm (1 ft). S humus-rich. P cuttings,
division. Protect against bad weather – plastic
bags will help to ensure good colour.

Chrysanthemum frutescens
fam. *Compositae*
○ ⊙ ⊕
Sow in February–March in heated
greenhouse. Plant out at A 30 cm (1 ft).
H 45 cm (18 in). White / yellow. S normal.
Semi-shrub, generally grown for bedding.
Single and double flowers.

Chrysanthemum leucanthemum
(*Leucanthemum vulgare*) / Ox-eye Daisy
fam. *Compositae*
○ ◐ ⊕ ⊗
June–September. White / yellow. H 40–60 cm
(16–24 in). A 30 cm (1 ft). S not critical. P seed.
Hardy perennial. Native plant that is easily
naturalised in flower meadows.

***Chrysanthemum maximum* hybrid**
'Marvellous' / Shasta Daisy / fam. *Compositae*
○ ◐ ⊕ ⊗
July–August. White / yellow. H 40–70 cm (16–
28 in). A 30–40 cm (12–16 in). S normal soil.
P division. Large, white, summer-flowering
daisy. Dislikes moist soil. Not very long-
lived.

Chrysanthemum millefoliatum* (*Tanacetum
millefolium*) / fam. *Compositae
○ ⊜ ◐ ⊕ ⊛ ⊗
July–September. Yellow. H 10–50 cm (4–
20 in). A 30 cm (1 ft). S normal garden soil.
P division, seed. Demands a dry and warm
position. Rarely available commercially.

Chrysanthemum paludosum
fam. *Compositae*
○ ⊙ ⊕
Sow in February in heated greenhouse or
April in the open. Thin / plant out at A 25 cm
(10 in). H 25 cm (10 in). White / yellow.
S normal soil. Dead-head. Flowers May–
August, depending when sown.

***Chrysanthemum parthenium* 'Ball's White'**
Feverfew / fam. *Compositae*
○ ⊙ ⊕
Sow in February in heated greenhouse or
April in the open. Thin / plant out at A 20 cm
(8 in). H 40–80 cm (16–32 in). White / yellow.
S normal garden soil. Bushy plant with
chamomile smell. Good for borders.

***Chrysanthemum parthenium* 'Snowball'**
Feverfew / fam. *Compositae*
○ ⊙ ⊕
Sow in February in heated greenhouse or
April in the open. Thin / plant out at A 20 cm
(8 in). H 20–70 cm (8–28 in). White / yellow.
S normal garden soil. Long-lasting pompon-
like flowers.

***Chrysanthemum rubellum* 'Clara Curtis'**
fam. *Compositae*
○ ⊙ ◐ ⊕ ⊗
September–October. Clear pink. H 80–100 cm
(32–36 in). A 50 cm (20 in). S humus-rich.
P division. Stems branch near the top. Good
border plant. Cut down stems immediately
after flowering.

168

***Chyrsanthemum segetum* 'Eastern Star'**
Corn Marigold / fam. *Compositae*
○ ⊙ ⊗ ⊛
Sow in February in heated greenhouse or
April in the open. Thin / plant out at A 25 cm
(10 in). H 30–60 cm (1–2 ft). Yellow / brown.
S normal garden soil. Single flowers in July–
September.

***Chrysanthemum segetum* 'Eldorado'**
Corn Marigold / fam. *Compositae*
○ ⊙ ⊗ ⊛
Sow in February in heated greenhouse or in
April in the open. Thin / plant out at A 25 cm
(10 in). H 30–60 cm (1–2 ft). Yellow / brown.
S normal garden soil. Excellent cultivar for
borders; flowers profusely.

Chrysanthemum serotinum (C. uliginosum)
Moon Daisy / fam. *Compositae*
○ ○ ⊗ ⊛
September–October. White / yellow. H 1 m
(3 ft). A 50 cm (20 in). S normal soil.
P division, seed. Flowers 3–5 cm (1–2 in)
across. Usually quite rigid. For the back row
of the border.

Chrysogonum virginianum
fam. *Compositae*
○ ⊜ ⊗ ⊛ ⊛
May–July. Yellow. H 20–40 cm (8–16 in).
A 20 cm (8 in). S normal soil. P division, seed.
Long flowering period (until September).
Suitable for border or rock garden. Not
widely known.

Chusquea culeou
fam. *Gramineae*
◐ ⊘ ⊛ ⊛ ⊛
Insignificant flowers. H 3 m (10 ft). W 2 m
(6 ft). Zone 6. S fertile. P division. A bamboo
with herbaceous, bare, black, solid stems.
Rarely seen.

Cimicifuga dahurica
Bugbane / fam. *Ranunculaceae*
○ ◐ ⊗ ○ ⊛
August–October. White. H 2 m (6 ft). A 50 cm
(20 in). S fertile, acid. P seed, division. The
most attractive autumn-flowering species for
the border. Slender, wand-like flower spikes.

Cimicifuga ramosa
Bugbane / fam. *Ranunculaceae*
○ ◐ ⊗ ○ ⊛ ⊛
September. White. H 100–150 cm (3–5 ft).
A 50 cm (20 in). S fertile, acid. P seed,
division. Attractive plant for the border, with
dark green leaves and seed cases which make
good dried bouquets.

***Cimicifuga simplex (C. racemosa* var.
simplex) / Black Snake-Root / fam.
*Ranunculaceae***
○ ◐ ⊗ ○ ⊛
September–October. White. H 80–125 cm (32–
48 in). A 30–35 cm (12–14 in). Good garden
plant, with solitary, slightly arching flower
spikes and bipinnate leaves.

***Cirsium rivulare* 'Atropurpureum'**
fam. *Compositae*
○ ○ ⊗ ⊛ ⊛
June–July. Deep crimson-purple. H 140 cm
(4½ ft). A 70 cm (28 in). S sandy, porous.
P division, seed. One to five flower heads.
Ornamental plant. Leaves in large tufts.

Cladanthus arabicus (Anthemis arabica)
fam. *Compositae*
◯ ⊜ ⊛ ⊗ ⊗
Sow in April under glass. Plant out at A 20–30 cm (8–12 in). H 40–70 cm (16–28 in). Yellow. S not critical. Undemanding, free-flowering, highly fragrant plant. Sends out a host of lateral shoots.

Cladastris lutea (Virgilia lutea)
fam. *Leguminosae*
◯ ⊛ ⊛ ⊗ ⊕
May–June. White-pink. H 10 m (33 ft). W 8 m (26 ft). Zone 3. S chalky. P seed. Multi-stemmed tree with smooth bark, fragrant flowers and yellow wood.

***Clarkia unguiculata* 'Ruby King'**
fam. *Onagraceae*
◯ ◯ ⊛ ⊗
Sow in April and thin out to A 20 cm (8 in). H 60 cm (2 ft). Various colours. S normal garden soil. Graceful summer-flowering plant making few demands. Brief flowering period.

***Clematis alpina* 'Willy'**
fam. *Ranunculaceae*
◯ ◑ ⊜ ⊛ ⊛ ⊛ ⊗ ⊗
May–July. Rose-purple. H 3 m (10 ft). W 1 m (3 ft). Zone 5. S humus-rich, fertile. P cuttings, layering. Attractive early-flowering plant with decorative fruits. Prune in early August.

***Clematis* hybrid 'Ernest Markham'**
fam. *Ranunculaceae*
◯ ◑ ⊛ ⊛ ⊗ ⊗
July–September. Glowing red. H 4 m (13 ft). W 1 m (3 ft). Zone 4. S humus-rich and fertile. P cuttings. Climber with a profusion of large flowers. Viticella type. Needs pruning.

***Clematis* hybrid 'Fairy Queen'**
fam. *Ranunculaceae*
◯ ◑ ⊛ ⊛ ⊗ ⊗
June–August. Soft pink. H 3 m (10 ft). W 1 m (3 ft). Zone 5. S humus-rich, fertile. P cuttings. Large-flowered climber of the Lanigunosa type. Needs pruning.

***Clematis* hybrid 'Hagley Hybrid'**
fam. *Ranunculaceae*
◯ ◑ ⊛ ⊛ ⊗ ⊗
June–September. Deep satin-pink. H 2 m (6 ft). W 1 m (3 ft). Zone 5. S humus-rich, fertile. P cuttings. Free-flowering, large-bloomed hybrid of the Jackmanii type. Prune in February.

***Clematis* hybrid 'Jackmanii Superba'**
fam. *Ranunculaceae*
◯ ◑ ⊛ ⊛ ⊗ ⊗
July–August. Violet-blue. H 10 m (33 ft). W 1 m (3 ft). Zone 5. S humus-rich, fertile. P cuttings. Deciduous, large-bloomed hybrid. Flowers in profusion. The strongest variety.

***Clematis* hybrid 'Mrs Cholmondeley'**
fam. *Ranunculaceae*
◯ ◑ ⊛ ⊛ ⊗ ⊗
May–August. Pale blue. H 3 m (10 ft). W 1 m (3 ft). Zone 5. S humus-rich, fertile. P cuttings. Climber. Large-flowered hybrid of the Lanigunosa type. Flowers profusely. Needs pruning.

Clematis hybrid 'Nelly Moser'
fam. Ranunculaceae
○ ◑ ⊕ ⊗ ⊗ ⊗
May–June. Pale mauve/pink. H 4 m (13 ft).
W 2 m (6 ft). Zone 5. S humus-rich, fertile.
P cuttings. Large-flowered climber of the
Lanigunosa type. Prune after flowering.

Clematis hybrid 'The President'
fam. Ranunculaceae
○ ◑ ⊕ ⊗ ⊗ ⊗
June–July. Blue-purple. H 4 m (13 ft). W 2 m
(6 ft). Zone 5. S humus-rich, fertile. P cuttings.
Climber with flowers 15 cm (6 in) across.
Large-flowered hybrid of the Lanigunosa
type.

Clematis hybrid 'Ville de Lyon'
fam. Ranunculaceae
○ ◑ ⊕ ⊗ ⊗ ⊗
May–September. Red. H 4 m (13 ft). W 1 m
(3 ft). Zone 5. S humus-rich, fertile. P cuttings.
Large-flowered climber of the Viticella type.
Flowers profusely. Needs pruning.

Clematis hybrid 'Vyvyan Pennell'
fam. Ranunculaceae
○ ◑ ⊕ ⊗ ⊗ ⊗
May–June. Violet-purple. H 4 m (13 ft). W 2 m
(6 ft). Zone 5. S humus-rich, fertile. P cuttings.
Large-flowered climber of the Patens type.
Double flowers. Needs pruning.

Clematis integrifolia
fam. Ranunculaceae
○ ◑ ⊘ ○ ⊕ ⊗ ⊗
June–August. Violet. H 80–150 cm (32–60 in).
A 30 cm (1 ft). S humus-rich. P division,
cuttings. Slender plant with a profusion of
flowers. Base of main stem and roots must be
protected from the sun.

Clematis integrifolia 'Hendersonii'
fam. Ranunculaceae
○ ◑ ⊘ ○ ⊕ ⊗ ⊗
June–August. Violet. H 25–50 cm (10–20 in).
A 30 cm (1 ft). S humus-rich. P division,
cuttings. Attractive smaller variety that needs
less support.

Clematis × jackmanii (C. lanuginosa × C.
viticella)/fam. Ranunculaceae
○ ◑ ⊕ ⊗ ⊗ ⊗
July–October. Violet-blue. H 4 m (13 ft). W 2 m
(6 ft). Zone 5. S humus-rich, fertile. P cuttings.
Sturdy climber usually with three-leaf leaflets
and 10-cm (4-in) wide flowers.

Clematis macropetala
fam. Ranunculaceae
○ ◑ ⊕ ⊗ ⊗
May–June. Violet-blue. H 3 m (10 ft). W 1 m
(3 ft). Zone 5. S humus-rich, fertile. P seed,
layering. Slender climber with bell-shaped
flowers. Bushy habit.

Clematis macropetala 'Maidwell Hall'
fam. Ranunculaceae
○ ◑ ⊕ ⊗ ⊗
May–June. Blue. H 3 m (10 ft). W 1 m (3 ft).
Zone 5. S humus-rich, fertile. P cuttings.
Slender climber with a bushy appearance,
and bell-shaped flowers.

Clematis

Clematis macropetala 'Markhamii'
fam. *Ranunculaceae*
○◑◉◍ⓨ◉
May–June. Rose pink. H 3 m (10 ft). W 1 m
(3 ft). Zone 5. S humus-rich, fertile. P cuttings.
Slender climber of bushy habit and bell-
shaped flowers.

Clematis montana 'Rubens'
fam. *Ranunculaceae*
○◑◉ⓨ◉
May–June. Pale pink. H 10 m (33 ft). W 5 m
(16 ft). Zone 5. S humus-rich, fertile.
P cuttings. Vigorous climber with dark green
leaves and profuse flowers. Very robust.

Clematis montana 'Tetrarose'
fam. *Ranunculaceae*
○◑◉ⓨ◉
May–June. Lilac-pink. H 10 m (33 ft). W 5 m
(16 ft). Zone 5. S humus-rich, fertile.
P cuttings. Vigorous climber with dark green
leaves. Flowers in profusion. Very robust.

Clematis tangutica
fam. *Ranunculaceae*
○◑◉◍ⓨ◉◉⊗
August–October. Yellow. H 6 m (20 ft).
W 2.5 m (8 ft). Zone 5. S humus-rich, fertile.
P seed, division. Slender, vigorous climber
with grey-green leaves, bell-shaped flowers
and decorative seed pods.

Clematis vitalba (fruits)
Traveller's Joy / fam. *Ranunculaceae*
○◑◉◍◉ⓨ◉◉
July–September. White. H 15 m (50 ft). W 2 m
(6 ft). S humus-rich, fertile. P seed, layering.
Often found twining on tall trees. Bears
fragrant flowers in large plumes.

Clematis viticella 'Minuet'
fam. *Ranunculaceae*
○◑⊖◉◍ⓨ◉
August–September. Purple-red. H 3 m (10 ft).
W 1 m (3 ft). Zone 6. S humus-rich, fertile.
P cuttings. Climbing shrub with composite
leaves; stems covered in reddish-brown hairs.

Cleome spinosa 'Kirschkönigin'
Spider Flower / fam. *Capparaceae*
○☉ⓨ⊕
Sow in March in heated greenhouse. Plant
out at A 30–40 cm (12–16 in). H 125 cm (5 ft).
Purple-red. S fertile, humus-rich. Fragrant
plant flowering profusely in spider-like
heads.

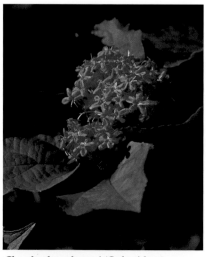

Clerodendrum bungei (C. foetidum)
fam. *Verbenaceae*
○◑△◍ⓨ◉◉
August–September. Red. H 2.5 m (8 ft). 2.5 m
(8 ft). Zone 6. S fertile garden soil. P division,
cuttings. Shrub with long, slender stems and
fragrant flowers. Leaves smell unpleasant.

Clerodendrum trichotomum (flowers)
fam. *Verbenaceae*
○◍ⓨ◉
August–September. White. H 8 m (26 ft).
W 6 m (20 ft). Zone 5. S fertile garden soil.
P cuttings. Shrub of bushy habit or small tree
with a round crown. Leaves have an
unpleasant smell.

Clethra alnifolia
Sweet Pepper Bush / fam. *Clethraceae*
○ ◍ ◍ ✿ ✐
July–September. White. H 2 m (6 ft). W 1 m
(3 ft). Zone 3. S humus-rich. P seed, cuttings,
layering. Shrub with bright yellow foliage in
autumn. Fruit remains on the tree all winter.

Clethra barbinervis
fam. *Clethraceae*
○ ◍ ◍ ✿
July–September. White. H 4 m (13 ft). W 2 m
(6 ft). Zone 5. S humus-rich. P seed, cuttings,
layering. Tall shrub with reddish-brown,
wide-spreading branches and fragrant
flowers in long racemes.

Cobaea scandens
Cup and Saucer Vine / fam. *Polemoniaceae*
○ ☉ ✿
Sow in March in a heated greenhouse. Plant
out at A 60 cm (2 ft) in May. Violet-blue. H 3 m
(10 ft). S not critical. Fast-growing, tendril
climber, self-supporting. Needs much
warmth.

Colchicum autumnale
Meadow Saffron / fam. *Liliaceae*
○ ◍ △ ✿ ✿
September–October. Lilac to white. H 20 cm
(8 in). A 20 cm (8 in). D 10 cm (4 in). S fertile
soil. P offsets. Native to moist meadows in
Europe. Leaves come out in the spring.

Colchicum bowlesianum
Autumn Crocus / fam. *Liliaceae*
○ ◍ △ ✿ ✿
September–October. Purple-red. H 10–20 cm
(4–8 in). A 15–20 cm (6–8 in). D 10 cm (4 in).
S fertile soil. P offsets. Species named after
E. A. Bowles, a specialist grower of autumn
crocuses.

Colchicum byzantinum
Autumn Crocus / fam. *Liliaceae*
○ ◍ △ ✿ ✿
September–October. Lilac-pink. H 15–20 cm
(6–8 in). A 15–20 cm (6–8 in). D 10 cm (4 in).
S fertile soil. P offsets. Flowers profusely
indoors without water or soil. Put outside
after flowering.

Colchicum speciosum
Autumn Crocus / fam. *Liliaceae*
○ ◍ △ ✿ ✿
Description and propagation as for last entry.
Elongated bulb. Unusually large flowers in
vivid shades of mauve. Very good edging
plant, particularly in a shrub border.

Collinsia heterophylla (C. bicolor)
fam. *Scrophulariaceae*
○ ◍ ☉ ✿
Sow March–April and thin out to A 15 cm
(6 in). H 30 (1 ft). Violet / white. S normal
garden soil. Slender, often slightly woolly
plant with short-lived but very showy
flowers.

Colutea arborescens
Bladder Senna / fam. *Leguminosae*
○ ◍ ◍ ◍ ✿ ✐ ✿
June–August. Yellow. H 3 m (10 ft). W 3 m
(10 ft). Zone 5. S not critical. P seed, cuttings.
Shrub of bushy, open habit, bearing light
green pinnately divided leaves and inflated
pods.

173

Convallaria

Convallaria majalis
Lily of the Valley / fam. *Liliaceae*
May. White. H 15–25 cm (6–10 in). A 20 cm
(8 in). S humus-rich (slightly acid). P division,
seed. Profusely flowering and thick stemmed.
Especially useful under trees and shrubs.

Convolvulus tricolor
fam. *Convolvulaceae*
Sow in April–May, thin out to A 15–25 cm (6–
10 in). H 20–40 cm (8–16 in). Various colours.
S not critical. Hairy and shrubby with erect
to creeping stems and striking flowers.

**Corbularia bulbocodium (Narcissus
bulbocodium)** / Hoop-petticoat Daffodil
fam. *Amaryllidaceae*
March–April. Yellow. H 10 cm (4 in). A 4 cm
(1½ in). D 2 cm (¾ in). S fertile. P offsets. This
bulb has small flowers but holds its own with
invasive plants.

Coreopsis basalis 'Goldkrone'
Tickweed / fam. *Compositae*
Sow in April and thin out to 25 cm (10 in).
H 50 cm (20 in). Yellow / purple-red. S normal
garden soil. Undemanding, long-flowering
summer flower. A cultivar with larger than
usual flowers.

Coreopsis grandiflora 'Sunburst'
Tickweed / fam. *Compositae*
July–August. Yellow. H 60–100 cm (2–3 ft).
A 40–50 cm (16–20 in). S normal garden soil.
P division. Suitable for a border; generally
hardy. Large flowers. Excellent for cutting.

Coreopsis lanceolata 'Babygold'
Tickweed / fam. *Compositae*
June–August. Yellow. H 50–60 cm (20–24 in).
A 30 cm (1 ft). S normal garden soil.
P division. Flowers profusely; excellent for
cutting. Cut back hard after flowering. For the
border.

Coreopsis tinctoria 'Tetra Mistigry'
Tickweed / fam. *Compositae*
Sow in April. Thin out to A 25 cm (10 in).
H 1 m (3 ft). Yellow / crimson-brown.
S normal garden soil. Bushy plant covered in
a mass of flowers. Will not keep very long in
water.

Coreopsis tripteris
Tickweed / fam. *Compositae*
June–August. Yellow. H 50–75 cm (20–30 in).
A 50 cm (20 in). S normal garden soil.
P division, seed. Erect stems with few leaves.
Good for cutting and excellent in borders.

Coreopsis verticillata
Tickweed / fam. *Compositae*
June–September. Yellow. H 50–75 cm (20–
30 in). A 50 cm (20 in). S normal garden soil.
P division, seed. Star-shaped flowers, finely
divided leaves. Appealling even after long
flowering period.

Coreopsis verticillata 'Grandiflora'
Tickweed / fam. *Compositae*
○ ◐ ⓨ ⊗
June–September. Yellow. H 50–75 cm (20–30 in). A 50 cm (20 in). S normal garden soil. P division. Flowers profusely. Will keep better and longer if regularly divided.

Coriaria japonica
fam. *Coriaraceae*
○ ⌃ ⓦ ⓨ ⊛ ◐
May. Green. H 1 m (3 ft). W 1 m (3 ft). Zone 5–6. S fertile soil. P seed, cuttings. Low-growing shrub. Petals become red and fleshy and later turn violet-black.

Cornus alba (C. tatarica)
Dogwood, Cornel / fam. *Cornaceae*
○ ◐ ⓦ ⊛ ◐
May–June. White. H 3 m (10 ft). W 3 m (10 ft). S humus-rich. P layering, cuttings. Tall shrub with red wood in the winter and ovate leaves, grey underneath.

Cornus alba 'Elegantissima'
Dogwood, Cornel / fam. *Cornaceae*
○ ◐ ⓦ ⊛ ◐
May–June. White. H 3 m (10 ft). W 3 m (10 ft). Zone 2. S humus-rich. P cuttings, layering. Robust, erect shrub with red branches in winter and white-edged leaves.

Cornus amomum
Dogwood, Cornel / fam. *Cornaceae*
○ ⊗ ⓦ ⓨ ⊛ ◐
May–June. Yellow-white. H 4 m (13 ft). W 2 m (6 ft). Zone 5. S humus-rich. P cuttings, division. Moderately tall, more or less compact shrub with bright blue or blue-black fruits.

Cornus canadensis
Dogwood, Cornel / fam. *Cornaceae*
◐ ○ ⓨ ⊛ ⊝
June. White. H 10–20 cm (4–8 in). A 15 cm (6 in). S normal or slightly acid garden soil. P division, seed. Graceful flowers. Edible red fruits top the whorls of leaves.

Cornus controversa 'Variegata'
Dogwood, Cornel / fam. *Cornaceae*
○ ◐ ⓦ ⓨ ⊛ ◐ ⊕
June–July. White. H 5 m (16 ft). W 3 m (10 ft). Zone 5. S humus-rich. P cuttings. Tree-like shrub. Branches form horizontal layers. Pendent, glaucous twigs.

Cornus florida 'Rubra'
Dogwood, Cornel / fam. *Cornaceae*
○ ◐ ⓦ ⓨ ⊛ ⊗ ⊕
May. Purple-red. H 6 m (20 ft). W 4 m (13 ft). Zone 4. S humus-rich. P seed, layering, cuttings. Bushy shrub or small tree; leaves change colour in autumn. Flowers surrounded by bracts.

Cornus kousa
Dogwood, Cornel / fam. *Cornaceae*
○ ◐ ⓦ ⓨ ⊛ ⊗ ⊕
June. White. H 6 m (20 ft). W 3.5 m (11 ft). Zone 5. S humus-rich. P seed, cuttings. Vigorous and tall shrub with dark green foliage. Flowers surrounded by bracts.

175

Cornus mas
Cornelian Cherry / fam. ***Cornaceae***
○ ◐ ◍ ◐ ◐ ◐ ◐ ◍ ⊗
February–April. Yellow. H 7 m (23 ft). W 4 m (13 ft). Zone 4. S humus-rich. P seed. Shrub or small tree with edible red berries in autumn – sometimes plentiful and sometimes absent.

Cornus mas
Cornelian Cherry / fam. ***Cornaceae***
○ ◐ ◍ ◐ ◐ ◐ ◐ ◍ ⊗
February–April. Yellow. H 7 m (23 ft). W 4 m (13 ft). Zone 4. S humus-rich. P seed. Shrub or small tree with firm, upright branches and thin twigs. Small flowers in rounded clusters.

***Cornus nuttallii* 'Ascona'**
Dogwood, Cornel / fam. ***Cornaceae***
○ ◐ ◍ ◐ ◐ ⊘ ⊕
May. White. H 6 m (20 ft). W 4 m (13 ft). Zone 6. S humus-rich. P cuttings, and layering. Tall shrub or small tree; beautiful autumn colouring. Flowers surrounded by bracts.

***Cornus sericea* 'Flaviramea'**
Dogwood, Cornel / fam. ***Cornaceae***
○ ◐ ◍ ◈ ◍ ◈
May–June. White. H 2.5 m (8 ft). W 3 m (10 ft). Zone 2. S humus-rich. P cuttings. Stooling shrub with yellow-green twigs in winter and bright green leaves.

Coronilla emerus* ssp. *emeroides
fam. ***Leguminosae***
○ ◐ ◍ ◐
May–June. Yellow. H 1 m (3 ft). W 1 m (3 ft). Zone 5. S fertile soil. P cuttings. Small shrub with green, overhanging twigs. Suitable for underplanting larger trees and shrubs.

Coronilla valentina* ssp. *glauca
fam. ***Leguminosae***
○ ◐ ⊖ ◍ ◐ ⊛
April–July. Yellow. H 1 m (3 ft). W 1 m (3 ft). Zone 7. S not critical. P cuttings. Small shrub with fragrant flower clusters. Effective between rocks or on sunny dry walls.

Cortaderia selloana (Gynerium argenteum)
Pampas Grass / fam. ***Gramineae***
○ ◁ ◈ ◉ ◐ ⊘ ⊕ ⊗
September-October. White. H 2–3 m (6–10 ft). A 1 m (3 ft). S fertile. P division, seed. Splendid silvery flowering plumes. Dioecious plant; male specimens are the more attractive.

Corydalis lutea
Yellow Corydalis / fam. ***Papaveraceae***
◐ ◐ ◍ ◐ ◐ ◈
June–September. Yellow. H 30 cm (1 ft). A 20 cm (8 in). S normal. P division, seed. Graceful but not very conspicuous plant. Invasive. Best when naturalised.

Corydalis solida
Purple Corydalis / fam. ***Papaveraceae***
◐ ◐ ◐ ◐ ◐
March–April. Purple. H 15–25 cm (6–10 in). A 20 cm (8 in). S normal. P division, seed. Very suitable for naturalising in open woodland where it seeds itself.

Corylopsis pauciflora
fam. *Hamamelidaceae*
○ ◑ ⊕ ⊛ ⊗
March–April. Yellow. H 1 m (3 ft). W 2 m (6 ft).
Zone 5. S humus-rich, preferably lime free.
P cuttings, layering. Graceful shrub with
early, fragrant flowers and leaves that change
colour.

Corylus avellana 'Contorta'
Corkscrew Hazel / fam. *Betulaceae*
○ ◑ ⊕ ⊛ ⊗
February–March. Yellow. H 3 m (10 ft). W 4 m
(13 ft). Zone 3. S normal soil. P cuttings,
layering. Ornamental shrub with twisted
branches, twigs and leaves and graceful,
pendent catkins.

Corylus avellana 'Pendula'
Hazel / fam. *Betulaceae*
○ ◑ ⊕ ⊛ ⊗
February–March. Yellow. H 5 m (16 ft). W 4 m
(13 ft). Zone 3. S normal garden soil.
P cuttings, layering. Weeping shrub with firm
green leaves, edible nuts and pendulous
catkins.

Cosmos bipinnatus 'Gloria'
fam. *Compositae*
○ ⊙ ⊛ ⊗
Sow in March under glass. Plant out at A 50–
60 cm (20–24 in). H 120 cm (4 ft). Purple-red.
S normal garden soil. Elegant, bushy plant of
the 'Sensation' type with finely cut leaves.

Cosmos bipannatus 'Purity'
fam. *Compositae*
○ ⊙ ⊛ ⊗
Sow in March under glass. Plant out at A 50–
60 cm (20–24 in). H 120 cm (4 ft). Pink.
S normal soil. 'Sensation' type with profuse
flowers. Vigorous; suitable for the back of the
border.

Cotinus coggygria (Rhus cotinus)
Smoke Tree / fam. *Anacardiaceae*
○ ◑ ⊛ ⊛ ⊗ ⊙ ⊕
For description and P see next entry. Freely
branching, upright shrub with ovate or
obovate leaves, colouring in autumn. Broken
twigs have an unpleasant smell. Side shoots
contain yellow dye.

Cotinus coggygria (flowers)
Smoke Tree / fam. *Anacardiaceae*
○ ◑ ⊛ ⊛ ⊗ ⊙ ⊕
June–July. Green. H 3 m (10 ft). W 2 m (6 ft).
Zone 5. S normal soil. P cuttings, layering.
Compact shrub with expanding hairy
inflorescences and leaves which colour well
in autumn.

Cotinus coggyria 'Royal Purple'
Smoke Tree / fam. *Anacardiaceae*
○ ◑ ⊛ ⊛ ⊗ ⊙ ⊕
June–July. Green. H 2 m (6 ft). W 2 m (6 ft).
Zone 5. S normal soil. P cuttings, layering. A
particularly fine cultivar with extra-large
plum-purple foliage. Grows vigorously.

Cotinus obovatus
Smoke Tree / fam. *Anacardiaceae*
○ ◑ ⊛ ⊛ ⊗ ⊙ ⊕
June–July. Green. H 6 m (20 ft). W 3 m (10 ft).
Zone 5. S normal soil. P cuttings, layering.
Tree-like shrub with red branches, foliage
colouring in autumn and expanding
inflorescences.

177

Cotoneaster

Cotoneaster dammeri (C. humifusus)
fam. *Rosaceae*
○ ◑ ⊞ ⊞ ⊛ ⊚ ⊛ ⊛ ⊝
May. White. H 20 cm (8 in). W 2 m (6 ft). Zone
5. S not critical. P seed, layering, cuttings.
Creeping shrub with dull green leaves and
gracefully arching branches. For low walls.

Cotoneaster dielsianus (C. applanatus)
fam. *Rosaceae*
○ ◑ ⊞ ⊛ ⊛
June. White. H 2 m (6 ft). W 4 m (13 ft). Zone 5.
S not critical. P seed, cuttings, layering. Bushy
and spreading ornamental shrub with
overhanging branches and dark green foliage.

Cotoneaster divaricatus
fam. *Rosaceae*
○ ◑ ⊛ ⊛
June. Pink. H 2 m (6 ft). W 3 m (10 ft). Zone 5.
S not critical. P seed, cuttings, layering. Shrub
with slender, arching stems and glossy dark
green foliage.

Cotoneaster horizontalis
fam. *Rosaceae*
○ ◑ ⊞ ⊛ ⊛
May–June. White. H 1 m (3 ft). W 2 m (6 ft).
Zone 4. S not critical. P seed, cuttings,
layering. Densely spreading shrub; branches
arranged in herringbone style. Suitable for
slopes and walls.

Cotoneaster racemiflorus
fam. *Rosaceae*
○ ◑ ⊞ ⊛ ⊛
May–June. White. H 2.5 m (8 ft). W 3.5 m
(11 ft). Zone 4. S not critical. P seed, cuttings,
layering. Tall and broad shrub with branches
covered in grey hairs. Early fruits.

Cotoneaster roseus
fam. *Rosaceae*
○ ◑ ⊛ ⊛ ⊛ ⊕ ⊗
June. White. H 3 m (10 ft). W 5 m (16 ft). Zone
5. S not critical. P seed, cuttings, layering.
Erect habit. Slender, arching branches.
Widely cultivated.

Cotoneaster salicifolius
fam. *Rosaceae*
○ ◑ ⊛ ⊛ ⊛ ⊛
June–July. White. H 4.5 m (15 ft). W 4.5 m
(15 ft) Zone 6. S not critical. P seed, cuttings,
layering. Shrub with hairy branches and
narrow, glossy green, willow-like leaves.
Suitable as ground cover.

Cotoneaster simonsii
fam. *Rosaceae*
○ ◑ ⊝ ⊛ ⊛ ⊛ ⊛
June–July. White. H 3 m (10 ft). W 2 m (6 ft).
Zone 5. S not critical. P seed, cuttings,
layering. A shrub of erect habit, with hairy
branches and glossy green leaves.

Cotoneaster × watereri 'Brandkjaer'
fam. *Rosaceae*
○ ◑ ⊛ ⊛ ⊕
June. White. H 4.5 m (15 ft). W 4.5 m (15 ft).
Zone 4. S not critical. P seed, cuttings,
layering. Shrub of erect habit with large
leaves. The big red berries often last well into
the winter.

Cotoneaster × watereri 'Pendula'
fam. Rosaceae
○ ◑ 🌢 △ ○ 🐝 ⊕
June. White. H 4.5 m (15 ft). W 4.5 m (15 ft).
Zone 5. S not critical. P seed, cuttings,
layering. Weeping habit with prostrate to
very pendulous branches and slightly
wrinkled leaves.

Cotula squalida (Leptinella squalida)
fam. Compositae
○ ◑ 🌢 △ ○ 🌢 🐝 ⊖
July–August. Green. H 5 cm (2 in). A 10 cm
(4 in). S not critical. P division. Very vigorous,
clustering plant with woolly leaves. Good for
crevices in paving.

Crambe cordifolia
Seakale / fam. Cruciferae
○ ◑ 🌢 🌢 🐝 🐝 🐝 ⊖
June–July. White. H 130–160 cm (4–5 ft). A 1 m
(3 ft). S normal or chalky soil. P division, seed.
Robust plant with thick roots that need a great
deal of space. Large, heart-shaped leaves.

× Crataegomespilus dardarii
fam. Rosaceae
○ ◑ 🌢 🌸 🐝 🐝 🐝
May. White. H 6 m (20 ft). W 4 m (13 ft). Zone
5. S not critical. P grafting. Tree with hairy,
pendulous, thorny branches, and small, entire
leaves.

Crataegus × grignonensis
Ornamental Thorn / fam. Rosaceae
○ ◑ 🌸 🐝 🐝
May–June. White. H 3.5 m (11 ft). W 4 m (13 ft).
Zone 5. S not critical. P grafting. Slow-
growing tree with a dense crown and
thornless green branches. Suitable for parks.

Crataegus laevigata 'Mutabilis'
Hawthorn / fam. Rosaceae
○ ◑ 🌸 🐝 🐝
June. White, double. H 4 m (13 ft). W 4 m
(13 ft). Zone 4. S not critical. P grafting. Tree
with a relatively dense crown, dark green
leaves and pink flower buds.

Crataegus laevigata 'Paul's Scarlet'
Hawthorn / fam. Rosaceae
○ ◑ 🌸 🐝 🐝 ⊕
May. Red. H 7 m (23 ft). W 4 m (13 ft). Zone 4.
S not critical. P grafting. Small tree with a
broad crown, or tall shrub. Double flowers. A
very beautiful hawthorn.

Crateaegus × lavallei
Ornamental Thorn / fam. Rosaceae
○ ◑ 🌢 🌸 🐝 🐝 ⊕
June. White. H 5 m (16 ft). W 4 m (13 ft). Zone
4. S not critical. P grafting. Compact tree with
reddish-brown branches, long thorns and
glossy, leathery leaves.

Crataegus monogyna 'Pendula'
Common Hawthorn / fam. Rosaceae
○ ◑ 🌢 🌸 🐝 🐝 ⊕
May–June. White. H 8 m (26 ft). W 6 m (20 ft).
Zone 4. S not critical. P grafting. Tree or shrub
with pendulous branches and twigs, long
upright thorns. Makes a good rootstock.

Crataegus nitida
Ornamental Thorn / fam. *Rosaceae*
◯ ◑ ✹ ✹ ✹
May. White. H 7 m (23 ft). W 4 m (13 ft). Zone
4. S not critical. P seed. Tall shrub with a
round crown, foliage changing colour in the
autumn, few thorns. Fruits last well.

Crataegus × prunifolia
Ornamental Thorn / fam. *Rosaceae*
◯ ◑ ✹ ✹ ✹ ✹
May–June. White. H 4 m (13 ft). W 3 m (10 ft).
Zone 4. S not critical. P grafting. Shrub or
small tree with olive-coloured branches,
flowers in downy clusters, thorns.

Crataegus pubescens f. stipulaceae
Ornamental Thorn / fam. *Rosaceae*
◯ ◑ ✹ ✹
April–May. H 4 m (13 ft). W 3 m (10 ft). Zone
5. S not critical. P grafting. Shrubby tree with
few thorns. Bears edible yellow fruits.

Crataegus punctata
Ornamental Thorn / fam. *Rosaceae*
◯ ◑ ✹ ✹ ✹
June. White. H 6 m (20 ft). W 4 m (13 ft). Zone
4. S not critical. P seed. Small tree, usually
with very thorny branches and spotted woolly
fruits.

Crataegus succulenta (C. macracantha)
Ornamental Thorn / fam. *Rosaceae*
◯ ◑ ✹ ✹ ✹
May. Pink. H 5 m (16 ft). W 4 m (13 ft). S not
critical. P seed. Small tree with reddish-
brown branches, numerous strong thorns and
flowers in umbels.

Crepis pyrenaica
Hawk's Beard / fam. *Compositae*
◯ ◑ ◯ ✹ ✹ ✹
June–July. Yellow. H 30–60 cm (1–2 ft).
A 30 cm (1 ft). S humus-rich, acid. P division,
seed. Attractive, fairly unknown but
profusely flowering rock plant.

**Crinum × powellii (C. bulbispermum ×
C. moorei)** / fam. *Amaryllidaceae*
◯ ◯ ✹ ✹ ✹
July–August. Red, white. H 120 cm (4 ft).
A 30–45 cm (12–18 in). D 15 cm (6 in). S fertile.
P seed, offsets. Has a round bulb with a short
neck and flower stems with slightly pendent
flowers.

**Crocosmia × crocosmiiflora (Montbretia
crocosmiiflora)** / Garden Montbretia / fam.
Iridaceae
◯ ◑ ✹ ✹ ✹ ✹ ✹
July–September. Orange. H 60–100 cm (2–
3 ft). A 5–7 cm (2–2¾ in). D 7 cm (2¾ in). S fertile
soil. P offsets. Long, sword-shaped leaves.
The flowers keep well in water.

Crocus biflorus
Scotch Crocus / fam. *Iridaceae*
◯ ◑ ✹ ✹ ✹
February–March. Purple-blue. H 10 cm (4 in).
A 7 cm (2¾ in). D 7–10 cm (2¾–4 in). S normal.
P seed, offsets. Spring-flowering crocus with
very narrow leaves. One to three flowers to
each smooth corm.

Crocus chrysanthus 'Blue Bird'
fam. *Iridaceae*
○ ◑ Ⓐ Ⓥ Ⓢ
February–March. White/blue. H 5–10 cm (2–4 in). A 2–5 cm (¾–2 in). D 5 cm (2 in). S normal garden soil. P offsets. The best-known botanical crocus. Very attractive in groups on the lawn.

Crocus chrysanthus 'Cream Beauty'
Crocus/**fam.** *Iridaceae*
○ ◑ Ⓐ Ⓥ Ⓢ
February–March. Creamy yellow. H 5–10 cm (2–4 in). A 2–5 cm (¾–2 in). D 5 cm (2 in). S normal garden soil. P offsets. Mowing the lawn too early exhausts the corm and prevents further flowering.

Crocus flavus (C. aureus)
Yellow Crocus/**fam.** *Iridaceae*
○ ◑ Ⓐ Ⓥ Ⓢ
March–April. Yellow. H 5–10 cm (2–4 in). A 2–5 cm (¾–2 in). D 5 cm (2 in). S normal garden soil. P offsets. A crocus with a large, flat corm. Most cultivars are derived from this species.

Crocus hybrids
fam. *Iridaceae*
○ ◑ Ⓐ Ⓥ Ⓢ
March–April. Various colours. H 5–10 cm (2–4 in). A 2–5 cm (¾–2 in). D 5 cm (2 in). S normal garden soil. P offsets. The corms will flower for many years without having to be lifted. Do not apply fresh manure.

Crocus kotschyanus (C. zonatus)
fam. *Iridaceae*
○ ◑ Ⓐ Ⓥ Ⓢ
September–October. Lilac-blue. H 5–10 cm (2–4 in). A 5 cm (2 in). D 5 cm (2 in). S normal garden soil. P offsets. Autumn-flowering crocus with a flat corm.

Crocus longiflorus (C. odorus)
fam. *Iridaceae*
○ ◑ Ⓐ Ⓥ Ⓢ
October–November. Deep lilac. H 10 cm (4 in). A 7 cm (2¾ in). D 10 cm (4 in). S humus-rich. P seed, offsets. Autumn-flowering crocus with very fragrant flowers, often striped on the outside.

Crocus speciosus
fam. *Iridaceae*
○ ◑ Ⓐ Ⓥ Ⓢ
September–October. Lilac-blue. H 15 cm (6 in). A 7 cm (2¾ in). D 10 cm (4 in). S humus-rich. P seed, offsets. Attractive autumn-flowering crocus. Plant before September. Leaves appear in the spring.

Crocus tommasinianus
fam. *Iridaceae*
○ ◑ Ⓐ Ⓥ Ⓢ
February–March. Pale mauve. H 5–10 cm (2–4 in). A 2–5 cm (¾–2 in). D 5 cm (2 in). S normal garden soil. P offsets. Goes particularly well with eranthus, galanthus, leucojums and scillas.

Crocus versicolor
fam. *Iridaceae*
○ ◑ Ⓐ Ⓥ Ⓢ
March–April. White. H 10 cm (4 in). A 7 cm (2¾ in). D 5–10 cm (2–4 in). S humus-rich. P seed, offsets. Sturdy spring-flowering species with one to four fragrant flowers and usually six leaves.

Cryptomeria japonica
Japanese Cedar / fam. *Taxodiaceae*
○ ◑ ⊕ ⊕ ⊛ ⊕
Pyramidal to columnar tree. The reddish bark peels off in long strips. Sickle-shaped needles. H 25 m (80 ft). W 5 m (16 ft). S humus-rich. P seed. Zone 5.

Cryptomeria japonica 'Cristata'
Japanese Cedar / fam. *Taxodiaceae*
○ ◑ ⊕ ⊕ ⊛ ⊕
Attractive conifer with pointed needles against the stem. Twig tops look like cock's combs. Globular cones. H 3 m (10 ft). W 2 m (6 ft). S humus-rich. P cuttings. Zone 5.

Cryptomeria japonica 'Elegans Nana'
Japanese Cedar / fam. *Taxodiaceae*
○ ◑ ⊕ ⊕ ⊛ ⊕
Compact, slow-growing conifer with densely packed branches and needles, bronze coloured in the winter. H 2 m (6 ft). W 2 m (6 ft). S humus-rich. P cuttings. Zone 6.

Cryptomeria japonica 'Globosa Nana'
Japanese Cedar / fam. *Taxodiaceae*
○ ◑ ⊛ ⊕ ⊛ ⊕
Broad shrub with a rounded crown and pendulous, densely packed needles. No visible stem. H 3 m (10 ft). W 4 m (13 ft). S humus-rich. P cuttings. Zone 6.

Cryptomeria japonica 'Pygmaea'
Japanese Cedar / fam. *Taxodiaceae*
○ ◑ ⊛ ⊕ ⊕ ⊛ ⊛ ⊘ ⊗
Slow-growing shrub of dense, compact and irregular habit. Slender twigs with short leaves. H 2 m (6 ft). W 2 m (6 ft). S humus-rich. P cuttings. Zone 6.

Cucurbita pepo var. *ovifera*
Ornamental Gourd / fam. *Cucurbitaceae*
○ ◑ ◐ ⊙ ⊗ ⊕ ⊕
Sow in April in heated greenhouse or in May in the open. Thin / plant out at A 2 m (6 ft). H 60 cm (2 ft). Orange-yellow. S humus-rich, fertile. Bitter-tasting, hard, oddly shaped fruits.

Cunninghamia lanceolata (C. sinensis)
fam. *Taxodiaceae*
○ ⊛ ⊕ ⊛ ⊛
Tree with peeling bark and rounded cones with up to 4-cm (1½-in) long oval and pointed seed scales. H 10–15 m (33–50 ft). W 6 m (20 ft). S humus-rich. P seed. Zone 7.

Cunninghamia lanceolata (C. sinensis)
fam. *Taxodiaceae*
○ ⊛ ⊕ ⊛ ⊛
Large, graceful tree with sharp needles 3–7 cm (1–2¾ in) long, 5–7 mm (¼ in) wide, with two blue-and-white stripes underneath. H 10–15 m (33–50 ft). W 6 m (20 ft). S humus-rich. P seed. Zone 7.

Cuphea ignea (C. platycentra)
Cigar Flower / fam. *Lythraceae*
○ ◑ ◐ ⊙ ⊗
Sow in March in a heated greenhouse or in May in the open. Thin / plant out at A 20 cm (8 in). H 30 cm (1 ft). Red / black. S normal soil. Bushy plant with tubular flowers borne singly.

× *Cupressocyparis leylandii* (hedge)
Leyland Cypress / fam. *Cupressaceae*
○ ◑ ❀ ⊘ ⊛ ⊕
Very vigorous garden hedge that needs space.
Cut back lateral shoots to encourage height.
H 20 m (65 ft). W 3 m (10 ft). S not critical.
P cuttings. Zone 5–6.

**× *Cupressocyparis leylandii* 'Castlewellan
Gold' / fam. *Cupressaceae***
○ ◑ ⊘ ❀ ⊛ ⊕
Very fast-growing conifer with columnar,
light green scales. Easily pruned. H 20 m
(65 ft). W 6 m (20 ft). S not critical. P cuttings.
Zone 5–6.

**× *Cupressocyparis leylandii* 'Haggerston
Grey' / fam. *Cupressaceae***
○ ◑ ❀ ⊘ ⊛ ⊕
Graceful, conical or columnar tree of more or
less open habit. Greyish-green foliage; very
fast growing. H 20 m (65 ft). W 6 m (20 ft).
S not critical. P cuttings. Zone 5–6.

Cupressus arizonica
Arizona Cypress / fam. *Cupressaceae*
○ ❀ ⊘ ⊛ ⊕
Broadly columnar tree with pointed, bluish-
green scales. Rare and graceful species. H 20 m
(65 ft). W 6 m (20 ft). S not critical. P seed,
cuttings. Zone 7.

Cyananthus microphyllus
fam. *Campanulaceae*
◑ ⊙ ○ ⊛
July–August. Blue. H 10–20 cm (4–8 in).
A 20 cm (8 in). S fertile. P division, seed,
cuttings. Attractive rock plant. Cover with
bracken in the winter. Moderately moist
position.

***Cyclamen coum* ssp. *hiemale* (C. hiemale)**
fam. *Primulaceae*
◑ ⊙ ○ ⊛
March–April. Purple-red. H 10 cm (4 in).
A 15 cm (6 in). D 2–4 cm (¾–1½ in). S humus-
rich. P seed. Hardy type. The small corms
have roots underneath only. Very variable.

Cyclamen hederifolium (C. neapolitanum)
fam. *Primulaceae*
◑ ⊙ ⊛
August–October. Pink. H 15 cm (6 in). A 7–
10 cm (2¾–4 in). D 2–5 cm (¾–2 in). S humus-
rich. P offsets. The leaves are marbled grey
like ivy leaves and look most decorative in
winter.

Cydonia oblonga (C. vulgaris)
Quince / fam. *Rosaceae*
○ ◑ ⊙ ⊛
May–June. White. H 8 m (26 ft). W 8 m (26 ft).
Zone 4. S normal garden soil. P seed, cuttings.
Ornamental tree with spineless branches and
edible fruits which can be used for preserves.

Cynara cardunculus
Cardoon / fam. *Compositae*
○ ⊙ ⊛ ⊕
August–October. Purple. H 150 cm (5 ft).
A 80 cm (32 in). S humus-rich. P seed. Related
to the artichoke though grown not for food,
but for its decorative appeal.

183

Cynoglossum

Cynoglossum amabile
Hound's Tongue / fam. ***Boraginaceae***
◐ ○ ◑ ⊙ ⊗
Sow in March in a heated greenhouse or in
April in the open. Thin / plant out at A 20 cm
(8 in). H 40–60 cm (16–24 in). Blue, white, red.
S fertile, chalky. Ideal for borders. Flowers
profusely.

Cypella herbertii
fam. ***Iridaceae***
○ ⊛ ⊗
June–August. Various colours. H 60–90 cm (2–
3 ft). A 10 cm (4 in). D 5 cm (2 in). S humus-
rich. P offsets. Bulbs are not hardy and should
be lifted in October and stored at 5°C (41°F).

Cypripedium calceolus
Lady's Slipper / fam. ***Orchidaceae***
◐ ◯ ⊙ ⊗
May–June. Maroon / yellow. H 25–40 cm (10–
16 in). A 20 cm (8 in). S chalky. P seed,
division. One of the most attractive plants
still growing in the wild. Protected species.

Cypripedium reginae (C. spectabile)
Lady's Slipper / fam. ***Orchidaceae***
◐ ◓ △ ⊙ ⊗
May–June. White / red. H 30–60 cm (1–2 ft).
A 30 cm (1 ft). S humus-rich. P seed, division.
Most attractive species with hairy lanceolate
to ovate leaves and large spikes bearing one
to two flowers each.

Cytisus ardoinii
Broom / fam. ***Leguminosae***
○ ⊝ △ ⊛ ⊗ ⊙ ⊠
April–May. Yellow. H 20 cm (8 in). W 1 m
(3 ft). Zone 7. S normal garden soil. P seed.
Trailing plant with hairy and striped
branches.

***Cytisus × dallimorei* 'Andreanus Splendens'**
Broom / fam. ***Leguminosae***
○ ⊛ ⊗ ⊙
May. Yellow / red. H 2.5 m (8 ft). W 2 m (6 ft).
Zone 6. S normal garden soil. P cuttings,
grafting. Shrub with sessile, trifoliate leaves
and brown, slightly hairy calyxes.

Cytisus decumbens (Sarothamnus
decumbens) / **Broom** / fam. ***Leguminosae***
○ ⊝ ⊛ ⊙ △ ⊠ ⊗
May–June. Yellow. H 1 m (3 ft). W 2 m (6 ft).
Zone 5. S normal garden soil. P seed.
Creeping shrub with simple leaves, branches
covered with few hairs and flowers in
profusion.

Cytisus × kewensis (C. ardoinii × C.
multiflorus) / **Broom** / fam. ***Leguminosae***
○ ⊛ ⊗ ⊙
May. Yellow. H 60 cm (2 ft). W 175 cm (5½ ft).
Zone 6. S normal garden soil. P seed. Fairly
low-growing shrub of creeping to prostrate
habit. Trifoliate leaves.

Cytisus nigricans (Lembotropis nigricans)
Broom / fam. ***Leguminosae***
○ ⊛ ⊗ ⊙
June–July. Yellow. H 1.5 m (5 ft). W 2 m (6 ft).
Zone 5. S normal garden soil. P seed. Erect,
bushy plant with trifoliate leaves, greyish
brown twigs and flowers in slender, erect
racemes.

184

Cytisus × praecox (C. multiflorus × C. purgans)/Broom/fam. Leguminosae
○ ⓦ ⓥ ⓢ ⓢ
April–May. Creamy-white. H 2 m (6 ft). W 2 m (6 ft). Zone 5. S normal garden soil. P cuttings. Erect, bushy shrub with arching twigs, fragrant flowers and grey-green leaves.

Cytisus × praecox 'Zeelandia' Broom/fam. Leguminosae
○ ⓦ ⓥ ⓢ ⓢ
April–May. Purple-red. H 1.8 m (6 ft). W 1.8 m (6 ft). Zone 5. S normal garden soil. P cuttings. Attractive, bushy and dense shrub with arching branches and fragrant flowers.

Cytisus purpureus (Chamaecytisus purpureus)/Broom/fam. Leguminosae
○ ⓐ ⓦ ⓥ ⓢ ⓢ
June–July. Pink. H 60 cm (2 ft). W 150 cm (5 ft). Zone 5. S normal garden soil. P seed. Broad, more or less prostrate shrub for the border and shrubbery.

Cytisus scorparius (Sarothamnus scoparius) Common Broom/fam. Leguminosae
○ ⓦ ⓥ ⓢ
May–June. Yellow. H 2 m (6 ft). W 2 m (6 ft). Zone 5. S normal garden soil. P seed. Shrub with erect to arching branches, elongated seed pods and a profusion of flowers.

Cytisus scoparius 'Luna' Common Broom/fam. Leguminosae
○ ⓦ ⓥ ⓢ
May–June. Yellow. H 2 m (6 ft). W 2 m (6 ft). Zone 5. S normal garden soil. P cuttings. Broad, erect and vigorous shrub with large flowers and angular green branches.

Daboecia cantabrica 'Atropurpurea' St Dabeoc's Heath/fam. Ericaceae
○ ⓘ ⓐ ⓦ ⓥ ⓐ
June–September. Purple-pink. H 40 cm (16 in). W 1 m (3 ft). Zone 5–6. S humus-rich. P cuttings, layering. Small sub-shrub with prostrate to erect branches and urn-shaped flowers in long racemes.

Dactylorhiza foliosa (Orchis foliosa) fam. Orchidaceae
○ ⓘ ⓘ ⓐ ⓐ ⓥ ⓢ
April–June. Purple-red. H 50–80 cm (20–32 in). A 40 cm (16 in). S chalky or acid. P seed, division. Will thrive on boggy as well as on clay soil. Not very hardy.

Dactylorhiza maculata (Orchis maculata) fam. Orchidaceae
○ ⓢ ⓐ ⓐ ⓥ ⓢ
June–July. Pale lilac. H 20–50 cm (8–20 in). A 30 cm (1 ft). S acid, humus-rich. P seed, division. Very variable species with spotted leaves. Does not tolerate chalk or artificial fertilisers.

Dahlia (anemone-flowered) fam. Compositae
○ ⓐ ⓥ ⓢ
August–October. Various colours. H 30–60 cm (2–3 ft). A 30 cm (1 ft). D 10 cm (4 in). S fertile soil. P cuttings, division. A ring of florets surrounds a dense group of short tubular florets.

185

Dahlia

Dahlia (cactus) 'Madeleine St Germain'
fam. _Compositae_

○ ⊕ ⊛ ⊕ ⊗

August–October. Purple-red. H 150 cm (5 ft).
A 50 cm (20 in). D 10–15 cm (4–6 in). S fertile
garden soil. P cuttings, division. Large double
blooms with rolled back and pointed ray
florets.

Dahlia (cactus) 'Television'
fam. _Compositae_

○ ⊕ ⊛ ⊕ ⊗

For description and P see previous entry.
Excellent for the rear of the border or for a
cut-flower bed. Very rewarding.

Dahlia (decorative) 'Emile Zola'
fam. _Compositae_

○ ⊕ ⊛ ⊕ ⊗

For description and P see previous entries.
Orange-red. Fully double blooms consisting
of ray florets only. These are broad, flat,
slightly twisted and bluntly pointed.

Dahlia (decorative) 'Frendy'
fam. _Compositae_

○ ⊕ ⊛ ⊕ ⊗

Description and P as first entry on this page.
Colour red/yellow. Tubers should be placed
in shallow boxes with moist peat in late
March and kept indoors until the middle of
May.

Dahlia (collerette)
fam. _Compositae_

○ ⊕ ⊛ ⊕ ⊗

August–October. Orange-red to yellow.
H 125 cm (4 ft). A 50 cm (20 in). D 10–15 cm (4–
6 in). S fertile soil. P cuttings, division. Flat
ray florets with inner ring of smaller florets
and central disc.

Dahlia (dwarf) 'Excellent Dwarf'
fam. _Compositae_

○ ⊕ ⊛ ⊕ ⊗

July–October. Orange-red. H 30–50 cm (12–
20 in). A 30 cm (1 ft). D 10–15 cm (4–6 in).
S fertile garden soil. P cuttings, division.
Good bedding and border plant. Must be
dead-headed. Cut flowers keep well.

Dahlia (orchid-flowered) 'Rote Giraffe'
fam. _Compositae_

○ ⊕ ⊛ ⊕ ⊗

August–October. Red. H 80 cm (32 in).
A 50 cm (20 in). D 10–15 cm (4–6 in). S fertile
garden soil. P cuttings, division. Small
flowers of an interesting shape. They keep
well in water.

Dahlia (paeony-flowered) 'Dandy'
fam. _Compositae_

○ ⊕ ⊛ ⊕ ⊗

For description and P see previous entry. For
extra large flowers, remove all but three
strong stems and leave only the terminal
flower buds.

Dahlia (pompon) 'Charles Dickens'
fam. _Compositae_

○ ⊕ ⊛ ⊕ ⊗

August–October. Purple-red. H 90 cm (3 ft).
A 40 cm (16 in). D 10 cm (4 in). S fertile garden
soil. P cuttings, division. Double blooms. Ray
florets rolled back or quilled.

Dahlia (pompon) 'Kinky'
fam. *Compositae*
○ ⊕ ⊛ ⊗ ⊗
P and description as previous entries. Purple-pink. Lift tubers immediately after first frost and then allow to dry with their foliage.

Dahlia (pompon) 'Kitty Hawk'
fam. *Compositae*
For description and P see previous entries. Purple. Overwinter tubers in cool but frost-free store, usually in boxes of dry peat.

Dahlia (pompon) 'Liane'
fam. *Compositae*
○ ⊕ ⊛ ⊗ ⊗
For description and P see previous entries. Red. Cultivation of dahlias is not difficult provided the plants are adequately fed.

Dahlia (semi-cactus) 'Hatsekatourian'
fam. *Compositae*
○ ⊕ ⊛ ⊗ ⊗
August–October. Yellow. H 50 cm (20 in). A 150 cm (5 ft). D 10–15 cm (4–6 in). S fertile garden soil. P cuttings, division. Ray florets broad at the base and quilled for half their length or less.

Dahlia (semi-cactus) 'Show'
fam. *Compositae*
○ ⊕ ⊛ ⊗ ⊗
For description and P see previous entry. Red/yellow. Flowers should only be cut when the disc has opened; dahlias cut too early fade fairly quickly.

Dahlia (single-flowered) 'Emilio Dahlio'
fam. *Compositae*
○ ⊕ ⊛ ⊗ ⊗
July–October. Purple. H 50 cm (20 in). A 30 cm (1 ft). D 10–15 cm (4–6 in). S fertile garden soil. P cuttings, division. Flower consists of a single ring of florets and a central, open disc.

Dahlia (single-flowered) 'Schneekönigin'
fam. *Compositae*
○ ⊕ ⊛ ⊗ ⊗
For description and P see last entry. White. Flowers relatively small but borne in large number, usually with a yellow centre. For borders and containers.

Dahlia (top mix) 'Top Mix Rose'
fam. *Compositae*
○ ⊕ ⊛ ⊗ ⊗ ⊗
July–October. Red. H 25 cm (10 in). A 20 cm (8 in). D 10–15 cm (4–6 in). S normal garden soil. P cuttings, division. Smallest of all dahlias but richly flowering. For border, bedding or containers.

Danae racemosa (Ruscus racemosus)
fam. *Liliaceae*
◑ ⦸ ⊗ ⌂ ⊕ ⊛ ⊗ ⊗
June–July. Yellow-green. H 1 m (3 ft). W 1.5 m (5 ft). Zone 6. S not critical. P seed, division. Sub-shrub with glossy, bright green, leaf-like stems. Resembles bamboo.

Daphne

Daphne × burkwoodii 'Somerset'
fam. *Thymelaeaceae*
○ ◑ ⚘ ⊛
May–June. White, pink. H 50 cm (20 in).
W 1 m (3 ft). Zone 5. S humus-rich. P seed,
cuttings. Erect, bushy shrub, branches hairy.
Aromatic flowers in dense terminal clusters.

Daphne cneorum
Garland Flower / fam. *Thymelaeaceae*
○ ◑ ⚘ ⊘ ⚘ ⊛
May–June. Pink. H 30 cm (1 ft). W 150 cm (5 ft).
Zone 4. S humus-rich. P seed, cuttings.
Creeping shrub with dark green elongated
leaves and fragrant flowers in dense terminal
clusters.

Daphne mezereum
Mezereon / fam. *Thymelaeaceae*
○ ◑ ⚘ ⚘ ⚘ ⊛
March–April. Purple-pink to violet-red. H 1 m
(3 ft). W 75 cm (30 in). Zone 4. S humus-rich.
P seed, cuttings. Erect shrub with large,
fragrant flowers in dense clusters. For the
small garden.

Davidia involucrata / Pocket Handkerchief
Tree / fam. *Davidiaceae*
○ ◑ ⚘ ⊛ ⚘ ⊕
May–June. White. H 15 m (50 ft). W 5 m (16 ft).
Zone 6. S normal garden soil. P seed, cuttings,
layering. Broad, erect shrub or tree. Flowers
obscured by bracts. Gives off an unpleasant
odour.

Decaisnea fargesii
fam. *Lardizabalaceae*
○ ◑ ⚘ ⊘ ⚘ ⊕
May–June. Yellow-green. H 2.5 m (8 ft). W 2 m
(6 ft). Zone 5. S well drained. P seed, cuttings.
Broad shrub with thick and erect stems, twigs
with a blue bloom and blue fruits.

Delosperma pruinosum (Mesembryanthe-
mum echinatum) / fam. *Aizoaceae*
○ ⊖ ⊙ ⚘ ⊛
Sow in March in heated greenhouse or in May
in the open. Thin / plant out at A 30 cm (1 ft).
H 50 cm (20 in). Purple-red. S not critical.
Dwarf trailing shrub. Also grown as a house
plant.

Delphinium ajacis 'Blue Bell'
Rocket Larkspur / fam. *Ranunculaceae*
○ ⊙ ⚘ ⚘ ⊗
Sow in March–April and thin out to A 15–
25 cm (6–10 in). H 1 m (3 ft). Violet-blue.
S normal garden soil. Profusely flowering,
bushy plant with very finely cut leaves.

Delphinium ajacis 'Brilliant Rose'
Rocket Larkspur / fam. *Ranunculaceae*
○ ⊙ ⚘ ⚘ ⊗
Sow in March–April. Thin out to A 15–25 cm
(6–10 in). H 1 m (3 ft). Rose-purple. S normal
garden soil. Particularly attractive cut flowers.
Can only be transplanted with difficulty.

Delphinium ajacis 'Giant Imperial'
Rocket Larkspur / fam. *Ranunculaceae*
○ ⊙ ⚘ ⚘ ⊗
Sow in March or September. Thin out to A 15–
25 cm (6–10 in). H 120 cm (4 ft). Various
colours. S fertile. Strongly branching stems.
Double flowers. Also for the greenhouse.

Delphinium hybrid 'Finsteraarhorn'
Larkspur / fam. *Ranunculaceae*
○ ⊕ ○ ⊙ ⊙ ⊗
July (September–October). Violet-purple.
H 170 cm (5½ ft). A 60 cm (2 ft). S very fertile.
P division, cuttings. Attractive German
strain. Disease resistant and hardy. Divide in
early spring.

Delphinium hybrid 'Gletscherwasser'
Larkspur / fam. *Ranunculaceae*
○ ⊕ ○ ⊙ ⊙ ⊗
June–July (September–October). Blue. H
180 cm (6 ft). A 60 cm (2 ft). S very fertile.
P division, cuttings. Cultivar from Germany,
disease resistant and hardy. Strong stems.

Delphinium hybrid 'Ouverture'
Larkspur / fam. *Ranunculaceae*
○ ⊕ ○ ⊙ ⊙ ⊗
June–July (September–October). Violet-
purple. H 160 cm (5¼ ft). A 60 cm (2 ft). S very
fertile. P division, cuttings. Early-flowering
hardy plant with stout stems; unusual
colouring.

Delphinium hybrid 'Sommerwind'
Larkspur / fam. *Ranunculaceae*
○ ⊕ ○ ⊙ ⊙ ⊗
June–July (September–October). Violet blue.
H 160 cm (5¼ ft). A 60 cm (2 ft). S very fertile.
P division, cuttings. Brilliantly coloured
flowers in stately spires. Needs a stout
support.

Delphinium hybrid 'Volkerfrieden'
Larkspur / fam. *Ranunculaceae*
○ ⊕ ○ ⊙ ⊙ ⊗
June–September. Blue. H 1 m (3 ft). 60 cm
(2 ft). S very fertile. P division, cuttings. Plant
of the Belladonna type with flowers in smaller
spikes. Very long flowering period.

Delphinium Pacific hybrid 'Galahad'
Larkspur / fam. *Ranunculaceae*
○ ⊕ ○ ⊙ ⊙ ⊗
July–August (September–October). White.
H 160–180 cm (5¼–6 ft). A 60 cm (2 ft). S very
fertile. P division, seed. Flowers profusely.
Stems need support. Mildew resistant. Good
for cutting.

Delphinium Pacific hybrid 'Oberon'
fam. *Ranunculaceae*
○ ⊕ ○ ⊙ ⊙ ⊗
July–August (September–October). Blue.
H 160–180 cm (5–6 ft). A 60 cm (2 ft). S very
fertile. P division, seed. Stems need support.
Resistant to mildew.

Delphinium Pacific hybrid 'Summer Skies'
fam. *Ranunculaceae*
○ ⊕ ○ ⊙ ⊙ ⊗
July–August (September–October). Violet.
H 160–180 cm (5–6 ft). A 60 cm (2 ft). S very
fertile. P division, seeds. Stems need support.
Resistant to mildew.

Delphinium × *ruysii* 'Pink Sensation'
Larkspur / fam. *Ranunculaceae*
○ ⊕ ○ ⊙ ⊙ ⊗
June–July (October). Pink. H 80 cm (32 in).
A 40 cm (16 in). S very fertile soil. P division,
seed. A cross between *D. nudicaule* and
D. × cultorum. Demands a great deal of
attention.

189

Deutzia

Deutzia × hybrida 'Mont Rosa'
fam. *Saxifragaceae*
○ ◐ ⊕ ⊛ ⊗
June. Pink. H 2 m (6 ft). W 2.5 m (8 ft). Zone 5.
S fertile. P cuttings. Bushy shrub of stiffly
erect habit with flowers in large round
clusters.

Deutzia × lemoinei (D. gracilis × D. parvi-flora)/fam. *Saxifragaceae*
○ ◐ ⊕ ⊛ ⊗
June. White. H 1 m (3 ft). W 1 m (3 ft). Zone 4.
S fertile. P cuttings. Small shrub with almost
perfectly globular flower clusters in
profusion. For the front of a shrub border.

Deutzia × lemoinei 'Boule de Neige'
fam. *Saxifragaceae*
○ ◐ ⊕ ⊛ ⊗
June. White. H 1 m (3 ft). W 1 m (3 ft). Zone 4.
S fertile. P cuttings. Bushy, upright shrub
with a profusion of large flowers in very
dense clusters.

Deutzia × magnifica (D. scabra × D. vilmori-nae)/fam. *Saxifragaceae*
○ ◐ ⊕ ⊛ ⊗
June. White. H 2.5 m (8 ft). W 2.5 m (8 ft). Zone
5. S fertile. P cuttings. Robust, upright shrub
with double flowers in broad panicles, large
leaves and peeling bark.

Deutzia × maliflora 'Boule Rose'
fam. *Saxifragaceae*
○ ◐ ⊕ ⊛ ⊗
May–June. White. H 1 m (3 ft). W 1 m (3 ft).
Zone 5. S fertile. P cuttings. Rounded shape.
Large numbers of flowers with pink edges.

Deutzia × rosea 'Campanulata'
fam. *Saxifragaceae*
○ ◐ ⊕ ⊛ ⊗
June–July. White. H 1 m (3 ft). W 1 m (3 ft).
Zone 5. S fertile. P cuttings. Low, compact
shrub with arching branches, bell-shaped
flowers and purple calyxes.

Deutzia scabra 'Macropetala'
fam. *Saxifragaceae*
○ ◐ ⊕ ⊛ ⊗
June–July. White. H 3 m (10 ft). W 2 m (6 ft).
Zone 5. S fertile. Stout shrub with erect stems.
Peeling brown bark. Large flowers.

Deutzia sieboldiana
fam. *Saxifragaceae*
○ ◐ ⊕ ⊛ ⊗
June. White. H 1 m (3 ft). W 1 m (3 ft). Zone 5.
S fertile. P cuttings. Graceful shrub with
peeling brown bark and hairy flower stems.

Deutzia taiwanensis
fam. *Saxifragaceae*
○ ◐ ⊕ ⊛ ⊗
June. White. H 1.5 m (5 ft). W 2 m (6 ft). Zone
5. S fertile. P cuttings. Shrub with elliptical,
finely toothed leaves and flowers in slender
racemes.

Deutzia vilmorinae
fam. *Saxifragaceae*
◯ ◍ ⬦ 🌢 ⊘ 🍂 ⊘
June. White. H 1.5 m (5 ft). W 1.5 m (5 ft). Zone
5. S fertile. P cuttings. Fast-growing shrub
with erect, arching stems and shiny brown
bark.

Dianthus × allwoodii
Pink / fam. *Caryophyllaceae*
◯ ⊖ ⬦ ◎ ◯ 🌢 ⊗
June–July (September–October). Pink. H 20–
35 cm (8–14 in). A 30 cm (1 ft). S well drained,
chalky. P cuttings taken in the summer. A
group of free-flowering, usually double pinks.

Dianthus barbatus 'Wee Willie'
Sweet William / fam. *Caryophyllaceae*
◯ ⊙ 🌢 ⊗
Sow in June and thin out to A 20 cm (8 in) in
September. H 15 cm (6 in). Red / white.
S good garden soil. Attractive biennial
bedding plant. Very compact habit. Also good
for cutting.

Dianthus 'Brilliancy'
Pink / fam. *Caryophyllaceae*
◯ ⊙ 🌢 ⊗
Sow in April in the open or in March under
glass. Thin / plant out at A 15 cm (6 in).
H 25 cm (10 in). Purple-red. S fertile soil. Well-
known free-flowering strain of uncertain
origin. Needs dead-heading.

Dianthus caryophyllus 'Juliet'
Carnation / fam. *Caryophyllaceae*
◯ ⊙ 🌢 ⊗
Sow in February–March in a heated
greenhouse. Plant out at A 20 cm (8 in).
H 25 cm (10 in). Red. S fertile soil. Double-
flowered carnation. In bad weather, bring
into flower under glass.

Dianthus chinensis 'Heddewigii'
Indian Pink / fam. *Caryophyllaceae*
◯ ⊙ 🌢
Sow in April in the open or in March under
glass. Thin / plant out at A 15 cm (6 in).
H 25 cm (10 in). Mixed red and white. S good
garden soil. Attractively marked single
flowers with no fragrance.

Dianthus deltoides hybrid
Maiden Pink / fam. *Caryophyllaceae*
◯ ⊖ ◎ 🌢 ⊗ ⊗ ⊖
June–September. Red. H 15–30 cm (6–12 in).
A 20 cm (8 in). S sandy, slightly acid. P seed,
division. The colour differs from that of the
species and the flowers are larger.

Dianthus gratianopolitanus (D. caesius)
Cheddar Pink / fam. *Caryophyllaceae*
◯ ⊖ ◎ 🌢 ⊗ ⊗ ⊖
May–July. Red. H 10–15 cm (4–6 in). A 10 cm
(4 in). S chalky. P division, cuttings. Fragrant
flowers borne singly or in pairs. Blue-green
foliage. Mat-forming, free-flowering plant.

Dianthus petraeus (D. spiculifolius)
Pink / fam. *Caryophyllaceae*
◯ ⊖ ◎ 🌢 ⊗ ⊗ ⊖
June–August. White. H 10–25 cm (4–10 in).
A 15 cm (6 in). S chalky. P division, seed.
Forms a flat, large, grey-green mat. Very
tolerant of drought.

191

Dianthus

Dianthus plumarius hybrids
Pink / fam. *Caryophyllaceae*
○ ⊖ ◐ 🌸 ⊗
May–June. Pink. H 10–25 cm (4–10 in).
A 15 cm (6 in). S chalky. P division, cuttings.
Very fragrant flowers. Blue-green foliage. Mat
forming. For beds and borders.

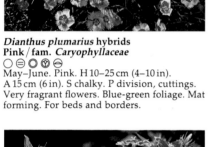

Dianthus 'Telstar'
Garden Pink / fam. *Caryophyllaceae*
○ ⊙ 🌸 ⊗
Sow in April in the open or in March under
glass. Thin / plant out at A 15 cm (6 in).
H 25 cm (10 in). White / purple-red. S fertile
soil. Recent addition; resembles *D. chinensis*.

Dictamnus albus (D. fraxinella)
Burning Bush / fam. *Rutaceae*
○ ⊙ 🌸 ⊗
June–July. Purple-red. H 60–100 cm (24–
36 in). A 80 cm (32 in). S chalky. P division,
seed. Decorative, very fragrant plant,
containing volatile oils. Grows slowly. Good
for dried flower bouquets.

Dianthus 'Queen of Hearts'
Garden Pink / fam. *Caryophyllaceae*
○ ⊙ 🌸 ⊗
Sow in April in the open or in March under
glass. Thin / plant out at A 15 cm (6 in).
H 25 cm (10 in). Red. S fertile soil. First F₁
hybrid. Uniform growth; weather-resistant.
Very variable.

Dicentra formosa
fam. *Papaveraceae*
◑ ◐ 🌸 ◉ ◔ ⊗
June–October. Red. H 20–40 cm (8–16 in).
A 40 cm (16 in). S normal garden soil. P seed,
division. Very valuable in borders thanks to
its unusually long flowering period. Robust
plant.

Didiscus caeruleus (Trachymene caerulea)
Blue Lace Flower / fam. *Umbelliferae*
○ ⊙ 🌸 ⊗
Sow in March under glass. Plant out at
A 25 cm (10 in). H 45 cm (18 in). Violet-blue.
S good garden soil. Bushy plant; deeply
divided, pale green leaves. Young stems and
foliage are sticky.

Dianthus seguieri ssp. *seguieri (D.*
sylvaticus) / fam. *Caryophyllaceae*
○ ◑ ◐ 🌸 ⊗
June–August. Purple-pink. H 30 cm (1 ft).
A 20 cm (8 in). S normal garden soil.
P division, seed. Needs little attention but is
quickly smothered by more invasive plants.

Dicentra spectabilis
Bleeding Heart / fam. *Papaveraceae*
◑ ◐ ○ 🌸 ⊗
April–June. Red / white. H 1 m (3 ft). A 80 cm
(32 in). S normal garden soil. P seed, division.
Graceful arching racemes. Blue-green foliage
which goes well with spring bulbs.

Dierama pendulum
Wand Flower / fam. *Iridaceae*
○ ⌃ 🌸 ○ ⊗
June–September. Violet. H 60 cm (2 ft).
A 40 cm (16 in). S normal garden soil, chalky.
P division, seed. Pendent flowers on arching
stems. Demands a sheltered and warm
position.

192

Digitalis ciliata
Foxglove / fam. *Scrophulariaceae*
◑ ☉ ⓨ ⊛
Sow in May–June. Space out seedlings at
A 15 cm (6 in), then move to flowering
position at A 30 cm (1 ft). H 1 m (3 ft). Purple-
red / yellow. S normal garden soil. Flowers in
loose spikes.

Digitalis grandiflora (D. ambigua)
Foxglove / fam. *Scrophulariaceae*
◑ ◐ ☉ ⓨ ⊛
Sow in May. Space out seedlings at A 15 cm
(6 in), then move to flowering position at
A 30 cm (1 ft). H 1 m (3 ft). Yellow / brown.
S normal garden soil. Lanceolate, toothed,
hairy leaves.

Digitalis nervosa
Foxglove / fam. *Scrophulariaceae*
○ ◑ ⓧ ∧ ⓨ ⊛
June–July. Yellow. H 120–180 cm (4–6 ft).
A 60 cm (2 ft). S humus-rich, not too dry.
P seed. Fairly rare, hardy species, appreciated
for its soft yellow flowers.

Digitalis purpurea
Foxglove / fam. *Scrophulariaceae*
◑ ☉ ⓨ ⓨ ⊛
Sow in June outside. Space out the seedlings
at A 15 cm (6 in), then move to flowering
position at A 60 cm (2 ft). H 1.5 m (5 ft). Purple-
red / white. S normal garden soil. The most
common species.

Digitalis purpurea 'Gloxiniaeflora'
Foxglove / fam. *Scrophulariaceae*
◑ ☉ ⓨ ⓨ ⊛
For cultivation see last entry. Various colours.
S normal garden soil. Improved and more
vigorous strain with large flowers in
impressive spikes.

Dimorphotheca pluvialis (D. annua)
Cape Marigold / fam. *Compositae*
○ ☉ ⓨ
Sow in March in heated greenhouse or in May
outside. Thin / plant out at 20 cm (8 in).
H 40 cm (16 in). White / violet / orange. S not
critical. Flowers close up when rainy weather
is expected.

Dimorphotheca sinuata (D. aurantiaca)
Star of the Veldt / fam. *Compositae*
○ ☉ ⓨ ⊛
Sow in March in heated greenhouse or in May
outside. Thin / plant out at A 20 cm (8 in).
H 30 cm (1 ft). Orange / brown. S not critical.
Yellow to orange hybrids look good in the
front row of a border.

Dipelta ventricosa
fam. *Caprifoliaceae*
○ ◑ ≋ ⚘ ⓨ ⊛
June–July. Rose-lilac. H 2 m (6 ft). W 2 m (6 ft).
Zone 5. S fertile. P cuttings. Shrub with
slightly toothed leaves, downy twigs and
heart-shaped bracts round its fruits.

Dipsacus sativus (D. fullonum)
Teasel / fam. *Dipsaceae*
○ ∧ ⓨ ⓨ ⊛
Sow in June and thin out to A 50 cm (20 in).
H 2 m (6 ft). Purple. S chalky and well drained.
Decorative plant, formerly used in weaving,
now only for bouquets of dried flowers.

Dipteronia sinensis
fam. *Aceraceae*
◯ ◐ ⬡ ❀ ⊗ ✤
June. Green. H 15 m (50 ft). W 8 m (26 ft). Zone
5–6. S good garden soil. P cuttings, layering.
Tree or tall shrub with large pinnate leaves
and erect inflorescences.

Dodecatheon jeffreyi
Shooting Star / fam. *Primulaceae*
◐ ◯ ⊙ ⊝ ⊗ ⊛
May–June. Purple. H 15–60 cm (6–24 in).
A 30 cm (1 ft). S humus-rich. P seed, division.
Needs a great deal of moisture in the spring.
Quickly smothered by invasive plants.

Dodecatheon meadia (D. pauciflorum)
Shooting Star / fam. *Primulaceae*
◐ ◯ ⊙ ⊝ ⊗ ⊛
May–June. Red. H 15–50 cm (6–20 in). A 30 cm
(1 ft). S well drained, acid. P seed, division.
Goes well with primulas in paved areas. Best
in semi-shade. Needs a great deal of moisture
in spring.

Doronicum orientale (D. caucasicum)
Leopard's Bane / fam. *Compositae*
◑ ◐ ⬡ ◯ ⊙ ⊗ ⊘ ⊗
April–late May. Yellow. H 30–50 cm (12–
20 in). A 40 cm (16 in). S normal garden soil.
P division, seed. Unattractive after flowering
– best left to fade behind later-flowering
plants.

Doronicum pardalianches
Great Leopard's Bane / fam. *Compositae*
◑ ◐ ⬡ ◯ ⊙ ⊗ ⊘ ⊗
June–July. Yellow. H 80–100 cm (32–36 in).
A 60–80 cm (24–32 in). S normal garden soil.
P division, seed. Very invasive, best suited
for large or wild gardens. Drought resistant.

Doronicum plantagineum 'Excelsum'
Leopard's Bane / fam. *Compositae*
◑ ◐ ⬡ ◯ ⊙ ⊗ ⊘ ⊗
April–June. Yellow. H 80 cm (32 in). A 40 cm
(16 in). S normal garden soil. P division, seed.
Good for cutting. Cut flowers curl up at first
and should be left in water for 24 hours.

Drosanthemum pulchellum
fam. *Aizoaceae*
◯ ⊜ ⊙ ⊗ ⊗
May–September. Red-purple. H 5–10 cm (2–
4 in). A 25 cm (10 in). S fairly dry, chalky.
P division, cuttings. Ground-cover plant from
the Mediterranean. Overwinter indoors; plant
out in spring.

Dryas octopetala
fam. *Rosaceae*
◯ ⊜ ◯ ⊙ ⊗ ⊛ ⊘ ⊝
July–September. White. H 15 cm (6 in).
A 15 cm (6 in). S humus-rich. P division, seed.
Creeping habit with prostrate stems that
quickly turn woody. Will creep across stones.

Dryopteris filix-mas
Male Fern / fam. *Aspidiaceae*
◑ ◐ ⬡ ⊜ ⊘ ◯ ⊙ ⊗
No flowers. H 120 cm (4 ft). A 60–80 cm (24–
32 in). S normal garden soil. P seed or
division. Short, scaly leafstalks. Almost
bippinnate fronds. Not the most beautiful of
ferns.

Eccremocarpus scaber
Chilean Glory Flower / fam. *Bignoniaceae*
○ ⊙ Ⓜ ⊛
Sow in February–March in heated frame.
Plant out at A 60 cm (2 ft). H 5 m (16 ft).
Orange-red, red, yellow. S humus-rich.
Attractive, free-flowering climber for a
sheltered south or south-west wall.

Echinacea purpurea (Rudbeckia purpurea)
Purple Cone Flower / fam. *Compositae*
○ ⊖ Ⓜ ⊥ ⊛
August–October. Purple-crimson. H 60–
100 cm (2–3 ft). A 60–80 m (24–32 in). S normal
garden soil. P division, seed. Upright stems
which eventually arch over. For the border.

Echinops bannaticus
Globe Thistle / fam. *Compositae*
○ ⊖ Ⓜ Ⓜ ⊛
July–August. Violet. H 100–110 cm (3–3½ ft).
A 60–90 cm (2–3 ft). S chalky. P division, seed.
Ornamental specimen plant frequented by
bees. Suitable for dried flower arrangements.

Echinops bannaticus 'Blue Globe'
Globe Thistle / fam. *Compositae*
○ ⊖ Ⓜ Ⓜ ⊥ ⊛
July–September. Violet-mauve. H 110 cm
(3½ ft). A 60–70 cm (24–28 in). S chalky.
P division, root cuttings. Fleshy and sturdy
stems covered with grey wool. Flowers
profusely. Very dark hue.

Echium platagineum (E. lycopsis)
Viper's Bugloss / fam. *Boraginaceae*
○ ⊙ Ⓜ
Sow in March in a heated greenhouse or in
May outside. Thin / plant out at A 45 cm
(18 in). H 90 cm (3 ft). Blue. S normal soil.
Bushy plant with oblong leaves and long,
branching inflorescences.

Echium plantagineum hybrid
Viper's Bugloss / fam. *Boraginaceae*
○ ⊙ Ⓜ
Sow in March in a heated greenhouse or in
May outside. Thin / plant out at A 20 cm (8 in).
H 40 cm (16 in). Violet-blue. S normal garden
soil. Pink to blue hybrids suitable for a
border.

Eichhornia crassipes
Water Hyacinth / fam. *Pontederiaceae*
○ ⊛ ⊛ Ⓜ Ⓜ
All summer. Violet. H 5–10 cm (2–4 in).
A 30 cm (1 ft). S not needed as this plant floats.
P seed, division. Aquatic plant that must be
stored in a frost-free greenhouse during the
winter.

Elaeagnus angustifolia
Oleaster / fam. *Elaeagnaceae*
○ ◑ ⏚ ⊛ ⊘ ⊛
June. Yellow. H 7 m (23 ft). W 5 m (16 ft). Zone
2. S not critical. P seed, cuttings, layering. Tall
shrub with spinous branches and scaly yellow
fruits.

Elaeagnus × ebbingei
fam. *Elaeagnaceae*
○ ◑ ⊖ ⏚ ⊛
May–June. White. H 3 m (10 ft). W 2 m (6 ft).
Zone 5. S not critical. P seed, cuttings,
layering. Broad shrub with erect stems and
fragrant flowers. Leaves silvery white
underneath.

195

Elaeagnus multiflora (E. edulis)
fam. *Elaeagnaceae*
◯ ◑ ⊜ ⊕ ⊛ ⊛
April–May. Pale yellow. H 2 m (6 ft). W 3 m
(10 ft). Zone 4. S not critical. P seed, cuttings,
layering. Very broad, fairly tall shrub with
dark brown to black branches and edible
fruits.

Elaeagnus pungens 'Maculata'
fam. *Elaeagnaceae*
◯ ◑ ⊜ ⊕ ⊛ ⊛
October–November. White. H 4 m (13 ft).
W 4 m (13 ft). Zone 5. S not critical. P seed,
cuttings, layering. Vigorous shrub with scaly
and often spinous brown branches and leaves
splashed with gold.

Elaeagnus umbellata (E. crispa)
fam. *Elaeagnaceae*
◯ ◑ ⊜ ⊜ ⊕ ⊛ ⊛
May–June. White. H 4 m (13 ft). W 4 m (13 ft).
Zone 3. S not critical. P seed, cuttings,
layering. Broad, vigorous shrub with yellow-
brown, mostly spinous branches and small
fruits.

Elymus arenarius
Lyme Grass / fam. *Gramineae*
◯ ◑ ⊜ ⊜ ⊛ ⊗
Rarely flowers. H 100–150 cm (3–5 ft). A 80 cm
(32 in). S normal garden soil. P division. Sand
dunes on coast. Leaves have a strong bluish
bloom.

Empetrum nigrum
Crowberry / fam. *Empetraceae*
◯ ◑ ⊛ ⊛ ⊗ ⊝
May. Red-purple. H 25 cm (10 in). W 40 cm
(16 in). Zone 3. S humus-rich. P seed,
cuttings, division. Prostrate stems, incurled
leaf edges and black berries.

Enkianthus campanulatus (flowers)
fam. *Ericaceae*
◯ ◑ ⊕ ⊕ ⊛ ⊙ ⊗ ⊗
May. Pink. H 3 m (10 ft). W 2 m (6 ft). Zone 4.
S humus-rich, acid. P seed, cuttings, layering.
A broad shrub of upright habit, with urn-
shaped flowers. Good autumn colour.

Enkianthus perulatus
fam. *Ericaceae*
◯ ◑ ⊕ ⊙ ⊗
May. White. H 2 m (6 ft). W 1.25 m (5 ft). Zone
5. S humus-rich. P seed, cuttings, layering.
Slow-growing, compact shrub with foliage
colouring in autumn and urn-shaped flowers.

***Epilobium angustifolium (Chamaenerion
angustifolium) / Rose Bay / fam. Onagraceae***
◯ ◯ ⊙
June–August. Rose-pink. H 150 cm (5 ft).
A 50 cm (20 in). S humus-rich. P seed,
division. Very attractive native plant with
numerous stolons.

Epimedium × cantabrigense
Barrenwort / fam. *Berberidaceae*
◑ ◑ ◯ ⊙ ⊗ ⊝
April–May. Orange-red. H 25–40 cm (10–
16 in). A 20 cm (8 in). S humus-rich. P seed,
division, root cuttings. Generally attractive
throughout the year. Spreads very quickly.

196

Epimedium perralderanum 'Fronleiten'
Barrenwort / fam. *Berberidaceae*

April–May. Yellow. H 35 cm (14 in). A 20 cm (8 in). S humus-rich. P division, root cuttings. Attractive cultivar that remains green well into the winter. Glossy foliage.

Epimedium pinnatum var. elegans
Barrenwort / fam. *Berberidaceae*

April–May. White. H 35 cm (14 in). A 20 cm (8 in). S humus-rich. P division, seed, root cuttings. White flowers, yellow inside, on leafless stalks. Stays green for a long time.

Epimedium × rubrum (E. coccineum)
Barrenwort / fam. *Berberidaceae*

April–May. Yellow / crimson. H 35 cm (14 in). A 20 cm (8 in). S humus-rich. P division, seed, root cuttings. Cross between *E. alpinum* and *E. grandiflorum*. Young foliage tinged purple-red. Large flowers.

Epimedium × versicolor
Barrenwort / fam. *Berberidaceae*

April–May. Pale yellow. H 35 cm (14 in). A 20 cm (8 in). S humus-rich. P division, seed, root cuttings. Cross between *S. grandiflorum* and *E. pinnatum. E. v.* 'Cupreum' is particularly attractive.

Epimedium × warleyense
fam. *Berberidaceae*

April–May. Orange-red. H 30 cm (1 ft). A 20 cm (8 in). S humus-rich. P division, seed, root cuttings. Cross between *E. alpinum* and *E. pinnatum colchicum*. Vigorous and compact plant.

Eranthis hyemalis
Winter Aconite / fam. *Ranunculaceae*

February–March. Yellow. H 10–15 cm (4–6 in). A 8 cm (3 in). D 2–5 cm (¾–2 in). S normal. P seed. Bare stems. Plant the fairly small spherical tubers early, preferably in September.

Eremurus elwesii
Foxtail Lily / fam. *Liliaceae*

May–June. Pink. H 2 m (6 ft). A 60–80 cm (24–32 in). S normal. P division, seed, root cuttings. Up to 1-m (3-ft) long light green leaves. Very conspicuous plant, dormant after flowering.

Eremurus himalaicus
Foxtail Lily / fam. *Liliaceae*

June. White. H 100–120 cm (3–4 ft). A 60–90 cm (2–3 ft). D 10 cm (4 in). S fertile. P seed, division. Attractive plant with long, leafless flower stems and radical leaves.

Eremurus robustus
Foxtail Lily / fam. *Liliaceae*

June–July. Pink. H 175–300 cm (5¾–10 ft). A 125 cm (4 ft). D 10 cm (4 in). S fertile. P seed, division. Splendid and vigorous plant with very large spikes of flowers that gradually turn white.

197

Eremurus

Eremurus 'Shelford Hybrids'
Foxtail Lily / fam. *Liliaceae*
⬭ ⬭ ⬭ ⬭ ⬭ ⬭
⬭ ⬭ ⬭ ⬭ ⬭
June–July. Pink. H 150–225 cm (5–7 ft). A 60–
90 cm (2–3 ft). D 10 cm (4 in). S fertile. P seed,
division. Attractive light green, lanceolate
leaves and flowers in 60–90-cm (2–3-ft) long
spikes.

Erica arborea var. *alpina*
Tree Heath / fam. *Ericaceae*
⬭ ⬭ ⬭ ⬭ ⬭ ⬭ ⬭
May–June. White. H 1.5 m (5 ft). W 1.5 m (5 ft).
Zone 7. S humus-rich. P seed, cuttings,
layering. Erect habit. Fresh green leaves,
fragrant flowers in long racemes.

Erica ciliaris 'Globosa'
Dorset Heath / fam. *Ericaceae*
⬭ ⬭ ⬭ ⬭ ⬭ ⬭ ⬭ ⬭
July–October. Rose-purple. H 35 cm (14 in).
W 50 cm (20 in). Zone 5. S humus-rich, acid.
P cuttings, layering. Hardiest variety with
greyish-green leaves and numerous flowers.

Erica cinerea 'Cevennes'
Bell Heather / fam. *Ericaceae*
⬭ ⬭ ⬭ ⬭ ⬭ ⬭ ⬭ ⬭
August–October. Pale lavender. H 25 cm
(10 in). W 30 cm (1 ft). Zone 5. S humus-rich,
acid. P cuttings, layering. Very compact habit,
bronze-coloured, golden-yellow leaves. Few
flowers.

Erica cinerea 'Golden Drop'
Bell Heather / fam. *Ericaceae*
⬭ ⬭ ⬭ ⬭ ⬭ ⬭ ⬭ ⬭
July–August. Red-purple. H 25 cm (10 in).
W 30 cm (1 ft). Zone 5. S humus-rich, acid.
P cuttings, layering. Very compact habit,
copper-red leaves, few flowers.

Eirca cinerea 'Pallas'
Bell Heather / fam. *Ericaceae*
⬭ ⬭ ⬭ ⬭ ⬭ ⬭ ⬭ ⬭
June–September. Purple. H 35 cm (14 in).
W 40 cm (16 in). Zone 5. S humus-rich.
P cuttings, layering. Very hardy, old cultivar.
Spreading, with a host of flowers.

Erica cinerea 'Pink Ice'
Bell Heather / fam. *Ericaceae*
⬭ ⬭ ⬭ ⬭ ⬭ ⬭ ⬭ ⬭
June–September. Rose-purple. H 20 cm (8 in).
W 35 cm (14 in). S humus-rich, acid.
P cuttings, layering. A particularly attractive
compact shrub with dark green leaves.

Erica × darleyensis 'Darley Dale'
fam. *Ericaceae*
⬭ ⬭ ⬭ ⬭ ⬭ ⬭ ⬭ ⬭
December–May. Rose-purple. H 40 cm (16 in).
W 1 m (3 ft). Zone 6. S chalky. P cuttings,
layering. Small shrub of spreading, erect and
fairly compact habit and with large flowers.

Erica erigena (*E. mediterranea*)
fam. *Ericaceae*
⬭ ⬭ ⬭ ⬭ ⬭ ⬭
March–May. Red. H 1.5 (5 ft). W 1.25 m (4 ft).
Zone 7. S not critical. P seed, cuttings,
layering. Erect, bushy shrub with pendent
flowers on woody, brittle stems.

Erica herbacea (E. carnea) 'Heathwood'
Winter Heath / fam. *Ericaceae*
○ ◑ ⚊ ⊛ ⊗ ⊗ ⊘ ⊗
December–April. Rose-purple. H 25 cm
(10 in). W 60 cm (2 ft). Zone 5. S not critical.
P cuttings, layering. Creeping, compact shrub
with dark green leaves and yellowish buds.

Erica herbacea (E. carnea) 'Myretoun Ruby'
Winter Heath / fam. *Ericaceae*
○ ◑ ⚊ ⊛ ⊗ ⊗ ⊘ ⊗
December–April. Red-purple. H 30 cm (1 ft).
W 50 cm (20 in). Zone 5. S not critical.
P cuttings, layering. Creeping, compact little
shrub with dark green leaves and brown
stems.

Erica tetralix 'Helma'
Cross-leaved Heath / fam. *Ericaceae*
○ ◑ ⚊ ⊛ ⊗ ⊗ ⊖ ⊗
July–September. Rose-purple. H 40 cm (16 in).
W 40 cm (16 in). S humus-rich. P cuttings,
layering. Erect habit. Flowers point in all
directions. Hairy leaves.

Erica tetralix 'Ken Underwood'
Cross-leaved Heath / fam. *Ericaceae*
○ ◑ ⚊ ⊛ ⊗ ⊗ ⊖ ⊗
June–September. Red-purple. H 30 cm (1 ft).
W 30 cm (1 ft). S humus-rich. P cuttings,
layering. Strikingly attractive cultivar with
grey-green leaves and numerous flowers.

Erica vagans 'George Underwood'
Cornish Heath / fam. *Ericaceae*
○ ◑ ⚊ ⊛ ⊗ ⊗ ⊖ ⊗
August–September. Rose-purple. H 25 cm
(10 in). W 40 cm (16 in). Zone 5. S not critical.
P cuttings, layering. New, vigorous cultivar
with flowers in long racemes. Fairly hardy.

Erica vagans 'Mrs D. F. Maxwell'
Cornish Heath / fam. *Ericaceae*
○ ◑ ⚊ ⊛ ⊗ ⊗ ⊖ ⊗
August–October. Deep cherry pink. H 35 cm
(14 in). W 65 cm (26 in). Zone 5. S not critical.
P cuttings, layering. Fairly dense and compact
habit. Flowers in long racemes.

Erica vagans 'St Keverne'
Cornish Heath / fam. *Ericaceae*
○ ◑ ⚊ ⊛ ⊗ ⊗ ⊖ ⊗
August–September. Rose-pink. H 35 cm
(14 in). W 40 cm (16 in). Zone 5. S not critical.
P cuttings, layering. Attractive and popular
cultivar with a fairly compact habit.

Erica × watsonii 'Truro'
fam. *Ericaceae*
○ ◑ ⚊ ⊛ ⊗ ⊗
July–October. Red-purple. H 15 cm (6 in).
W 25 cm (10 in). Zone 6. S humus-rich.
P cuttings, layering. Spreading shrub with
erect stems. Young growths yellowish to
bronze-red.

Erigeron hybrid 'Darkest of All'
Fleabane / fam. *Compositae*
○ ○ ⚊ ⊗
June–July. Purple. H 60 cm (2 ft). A 30 cm (1 ft).
S normal garden soil. P division. Flower
heads contain 100 to 160 ray florets. Yellow
centres.

Erigeron

Erigeron hybrid 'Foerster's Liebling'
Fleabane / fam. *Compositae*
○ ⊗ Ⓨ ⊗
June–July. Violet. H 60 cm (2 ft). A 30 cm (1 ft).
S normal garden soil. P division. A profusion
of semi-double flowers with a strong
resemblance to asters. For the border.

Erigeron hybrid 'Quakeress'
Fleabane / fam. *Compositae*
○ ⊗ Ⓨ ⊗
June–July. Light mauve-pink. H 70 cm (28 in).
A 30 cm (1 ft). S normal garden soil.
P division. Rejuvenate every three to five
years by division.

Erigeron hybrid 'Sommerabend'
Fleabane / fam. *Compositae*
⊗ Ⓨ ⊗
June–July. White. H 60 cm (2 ft). A 30 cm (1 ft).
S normal garden soil. P division. If cut back
after flowering, this hybrid will give a second
show of flowers.

Erigeron hybrid 'Strahlenmeer'
Fleabane / fam. *Compositae*
○ ⊗ Ⓨ ⊗
June–July. Violet. H 70 cm (28 in). A 30 cm
(1 ft). S normal garden soil. P division,
cuttings. Semi-double flowers. Oval to
lanceolate leaves.

Erigeron speciosus var. *macranthus*
Fleabane / fam. *Compositae*
○ ⊗ Ⓨ ⊗
June. Violet. H 40 cm (16 in). A 30 cm (1 ft).
S normal garden soil. P division, seed. A cross
between *E. speciosus* and *E. speciosus
macranthus*.

Eriogonum umbellatum
fam. *Polygonaceae*
○ ⊖ ⊜ ⌂ ⊕ Ⓜ Ⓨ ⊗
June–September. Yellow. H 20–30 cm (8–
12 in). W 30 cm (1 ft). Zone 6–7. S chalky.
P seed, division. Attractive semi-shrub for a
sunny and sheltered position.

Eriophorum latifolium
Cotton-grass / fam. *Cyperaceae*
April–May. White. H 50 cm (20 in). A 20–
30 cm (8–12 in). S moist, acid. P division,
seed. Marsh plant for the edge of ponds and
crevices in paving near water.

Eriophyllum lanatum
fam. *Compositae*
○ ⊗ Ⓨ ⊘ ⊗
June–August. Yellow. H 25 cm (10 in). A 15 cm
(6 in). S not critical. P division, seed, cuttings.
Rock plant with a woolly appearance and a
mass of flowers. Dislikes too much water; best
on slopes.

Eryngium alpinum
Sea Holly / fam. *Umbelliferae*
○ ⊜ ⊙ ⌂ Ⓨ ⊙ ⊘ ⊗
July–August. Violet. H 60–80 cm (24–32 in).
A 60 cm (2 ft). S chalky. P division, seed. Basal
leaves entire, heart-shaped and toothed. Stem
leaves finely divided.

Eryngium amethystinum
Sea Holly / fam. *Umbelliferae*
○ ⊜ ⦵ ⦵ ⦵ ⦵ ⦵
July–August. Violet. H 80 cm (32 in). A 60 cm
(2 ft). S chalky. P division, seed. Ornamental
plant for larger groups in the border. Very
good for drying.

Eryngium planum
Sea Holly / fam. *Umbelliferae*
○ ⊜ ⦵ ⦵ ⦵ ⦵
June–August. Violet. H 1 m (3 ft). A 60 cm
(2 ft). S chalky. P seed, root cuttings.
Attractive and graceful plant with a host of
flowers and oval- to heart-shaped leaves. A
sturdy species.

Erysimum × allionii 'Orange Queen'
Siberian Wallflower / fam. *Cruciferae*
○ ⦵ ⦵ ⦵
Sow in May under glass or in July outside.
Thin / plant out at A 25 cm (10 in). H 45 cm
(18 in). Orange. S chalky, well drained. Bushy
garden hybrid with fragrant flowers, of
unknown origin.

Erysimum decumbens
fam. *Cruciferae*
○ ⊜ ⦵ ⦵ ⦵ ⦵ ⦵
April–June. Yellow. H 25 cm (10 in). A 20 cm
(8 in). S dry, chalky. P division, seed. Very
good for rock gardens. Flowers in profusion.

Erysimum perovskianum
fam. *Cruciferae*
○ ⦵ ⦵
Sow in March–April and thin out to A 20 cm
(8 in). H 50 cm (20 in). Orange. S chalky, well
drained. Suitable for the front of a border.
Fragrant flowers in crowded heads.

Erythronium dens-canis
Dog Tooth Violet / fam. *Liliaceae*
⦵ ⦵ ⦵ ⦵ ⦵
April–May. Pink. H 10–20 cm (4–8 in).
A 15 cm (6 in). D 5 cm (2 in). S humus-rich.
P seed, offsets. Small plant with oblong,
whitish corms resembling dogs' teeth.
Spotted leaves.

Erythronium tuolumnense 'Pagoda'
fam. *Liliaceae*
⦵ ⦵ ⦵ ⦵
April. Yellow. H 25 cm (10 in). A 5 cm (2 in).
D 2–5 cm (¾–2 in). S humus-rich garden soil.
P offsets. Foliage mottled and bronze
coloured. Attractive and robust flowers, three
to four to the stem.

Escallonia hybrid 'Donard Seedling'
fam. *Saxifragaceae*
○ ⦵ ⦵ ⦵ ⦵
July–August. Pink. H 2 m (6 ft). W 1.5 m (5 ft).
Zone 5. S fertile, humus-rich. P cuttings.
Erect, fairly bushy and very vigorous shrub.
Long arching branches. Glossy and fleshy
leaves.

Escallonia × langleyensis
fam. *Saxifragaceae*
○ ⦵ ⦵ ⦵
July–August. White. H 2.5 m (8 ft). W 2 m
(6 ft). Zone 5. S fertile, humus-rich. P cuttings.
Vigorous shrub with long arching branches
and oval leaves.

201

Escallonia virgata
fam. *Saxifragaceae*
○ ⊙ ⊛ ⊛ ⊛
July–August. White. H 2 m (6 ft). W 2 m (6 ft).
Zone 6. S fertile, humus-rich. P cuttings, seed.
Shrub with branches that eventually arch;
very small leaves. The hardiest of all the
species.

Eschscholzia caespitosa 'Sundew'
California Poppy / fam. *Papaveraceae*
○ ⊙ ⊛ ⊛ ⊛
Sow in March–April or September–October
and thin out to A 25 cm (10 in). H 40 cm (16 in).
Yellow. S not critical. Striking cultivar with
thread-like leaves and blue-green seed pods.

Eschscholzia californica 'Mission Bells'
California Poppy / fam. *Papaveraceae*
○ ⊙ ⊙ ⊛ ⊛ ⊛
Sow in March–April or in September–
October and thin out to A 25 cm (10 in). H 30–
60 cm (1–2 ft). Various colours. S not critical.
Popular species. The petals close up in dull
weather.

Eucalyptus gunnii
Cider Gum / fam. *Myrtaceae*
○ ◑ ⊛ ⊛ ⊛ ⊛ ⊛
October–December. White. H 8 m (26 ft).
W 3 m (10 ft). Zone 8. S not critical. P seed.
Tree with blue-white branches, blue-green
juvenile leaves and long, green and pendent
adult leaves.

Eucalyptus niphophila
Alpine Snow Gum / fam. *Myrtaceae*
○ ⊛ ⊛ ⊛ ⊛
June–July. Green. H 7 m (23 ft). W 3 m (10 ft).
Zone 6–8. S not critical. P seed. The hardiest
of the *Eucalyptus* species, but slow growing
for the first few years.

Eucalyptus urnigera var. **glauca**
Urn-fruited Gum / fam. *Myrtaceae*
○ ◑ ⊛ ⊛ ⊛ ⊛
February–April. White. H 10 m (33 ft). W 3 m
(10 ft). Zone 8. S not critical. P seed. Tree with
arching juvenile branches, blue-green
juvenile leaves and glaucous or dark green
adult leaves.

Eucryphia × nymanensis
fam. *Eucryphiaceae*
○ ◑ ⊛ ⊛ ⊛ ⊛ ⊛
August–October. White. H 6 m (20 ft). W 3 m
(10 ft). Zone 6–7. S fertile, humus-rich.
P cuttings. Attractive late-flowering tree.
Generally hardy in the south but needs a
sheltered position.

Euonymus alatus
Winged Spindle Tree / fam. *Celastraceae*
○ ◑ ◐ ⊛ ⊛ ⊛
May–June. Greeny yellow. H 2 m (6 ft). W 2 m
(6 ft). S normal garden soil. P seed, cuttings.
Fairly dense shrub. Leaves turn crimson to
rose-scarlet in the autumn.

Euonymus europaeus 'Red Cascade'
Common Spindle Tree / fam. *Celastraceae*
○ ◑ ◐ ⊛ ⊛ ⊛ ⊛
May. White. H 3 m (10 ft). W 3 m (10 ft).
S normal garden soil. Fairly tall shrub with
numerous rose-red fruits (capsules) on
arching branches.

***Euonymus fortunei* 'Emerald Gaiety'**
Spindle Tree / fam. *Celastraceae*
May–June. White. H 2 m (6 ft). W 2 m (6 ft). Zone 5. S normal garden soil. P cuttings. Erect and bushy habit. Fairly large, silver-edged leaves. Suitable for containers.

***Euonymus fortunei* 'Silver Queen'**
Spindle Tree / fam. *Celastraceae*
May–June. White. H 2 m (6 ft). W 2 m (6 ft). Zone 5. S normal garden soil. P cuttings. Slow-growing shrub with broad, white-edged leaves. Not a climber.

Euonymus hamiltonianus* var. *hians
Spindle Tree / fam. *Celastraceae*
May. Creamy white. H 3 m (10 ft). W 3 m (10 ft). Zone 5. S normal garden soil. P cuttings, seed. Vigorous, erect shrub with obovate to narrowly elliptical leaves.

***Euonymus japonicus* 'Aureomarginatus'**
Spindle Tree / fam. *Celastraceae*
June–July. Green-white. H 3 m (10 ft). W 3 m (10 ft). Zone 5. S normal garden soil. P cuttings. Shrub with green, slightly angular branches and yellow-edged leaves.

Euonymus sachalinensis (E. planipes)
Spindle Tree / fam. *Celastraceae*
May. Red. H 3 m (10 ft). W 2.5 m (8 ft). Zone 5. S normal garden soil. P cuttings, seed. Vigorous, upright shrub with green branches, long purple-red terminal buds, and large leaves.

***Eupatorium purpureum* 'Glutball'**
Joe Pye Weed / fam. *Compositae*
September–October. Purple. H 2 m (6 ft). A 1 m (3 ft). S normal garden soil. P division. Excellent autumn-flowering plant for the back of a border.

Euphorbia characias* ssp. *wulfenii
Spurge / fam. *Euphorbiaceae*
May–June. Yellow. H about 90 cm (3 ft). A 40 cm (16 in). S normal garden soil. P division, seed. Of Mediterranean origin and therefore not particularly hardy.

***Euphorbia griffithii* 'Fireglow'**
Himalayan Spurge / fam. *Euphorbiaceae*
May–June. Orange. H 50 cm (20 in). A 20–30 cm (8–12 in). S normal garden soil. P seed, division. Of Tibetan origin and hence very hardy.

Euphorbia marginata (E. variegata)* / Snow on the Mountain / fam. *Euphorbiaceae
Sow in March in a heated greenhouse or in April–May outside. Thin / plant out at A 25 cm (10 in). H 90 cm (3 ft). White. S normal garden soil. Bushy habit. Put cut stems in hot water to prevent loss of sap.

Euphorbia

Euphorbia myrsinites
Spurge / fam. *Euphorbiaceae*
○⊖⊜⊘⊘⊘⊗
April–June. Yellow. H 10–20 cm (4–8 in).
A 20 cm (8 in). S humus-rich. P seed, cuttings.
Favourite for rock gardens. Prostrate stems
and fleshy, blue-green leaves.

Euphorbia polychroma (E. epithymoides)
Spurge / fam. *Euphorbiaceae*
○⊖⊙○⊘⊗
May–June. Yellow. H 30–40 cm (12–16 in).
A 30 cm (1 ft). S normal garden soil.
P division, seed. Very attractive plant for
growing between crevices in dry stone walls.
From Eastern Europe.

Exochorda giraldii var. wilsonii
fam. *Rosaceae*
○⊙⊕⊕⊗⊗⊕
April–May. White. H 3 m (10 ft). W 3 m (10 ft).
Zone 5. S humus-rich, chalky. P seed,
cuttings, grafting. Erect, broad shrub with
pink young twigs, ribs and leaf stalks.

Exochorda racemosa (E. grandiflora)
fam. *Rosaceae*
○⊘⊕⊗⊗⊕
May. White. H 3 m (10 ft). W 3 m (10 ft). Zone
4. S humus-rich, chalky. P seed, cuttings,
grafting. Tall, branching shrub with elegantly
down-curving branches and racemes of large
flowers.

Fagus sylvatica
Common Beech / fam. *Fagaceae*
○⊕⊛⊘⊗⊕⊞
April–May. Green. H 40 m (135 ft). W 20 m
(65 ft). Zone 4. S not critical. P seed. Tall tree
with a smooth grey trunk and a broad crown.
Edible fruits. Fresh green foliage which
makes a handsome hedge.

Fagus sylvatica 'Asplenifolia'
Fernleaf Beech / fam. *Fagaceae*
○⊕⊛⊘⊗⊕
April–May. Green. H 25 m (80 ft). W 12 m
(40 ft). Zone 4. S not critical. P grafting.
Graceful tree with deeply divided leaves and
edible fruits. Slow growing.

Fagus sylvatica 'Atropunicea'
Copper Beech / fam. *Fagaceae*
○⊕⊛⊘⊗⊕⊞
April–May. Green. H 40 m (135 ft). W 20 m
(65 ft). Zone 4. S not critical. P grafting, seed.
Robust tree with a broad crown, fairly large,
dark russet leaves and edible fruits.

Fagus sylvatica 'Fastigiata'
Dawyck Beech / fam. *Fagaceae*
○⊕⊛⊘⊗⊕
April–May. Green. H 20 m (65 ft). W 5 m
(16 ft). Zone 4. S not critical. P grafting. Tree
of columnar to broadly pyramidal habit.
Leaves like those of the species.

Fagus sylvatica 'Zlatia'
Hungarian Beech / fam. *Fagaceae*
○⊕⊛⊘⊗⊕
April–May. Green. H 40 m (135 ft). W 20 m
(65 ft). Zone 4. S not critical. P grafting. Large
tree with golden-yellow leaves in the spring
followed by yellow-green edible fruits.

Fallopia aubertii (Polygonum aubertii)
fam. *Polygonaceae*
◯ ⬤ ⬤ ⬤
July–October. White. H 12 m (40 ft). W 3 m
(10 ft). Zone 4. S not critical. P cuttings. Very
vigorous climbing shrub with a profusion of
small flowers in large, loose spikes.

Felicia bergerana (Aster bergeranus)
fam. *Compositae*
◯ ⨀ ⬤
Sow in March–April in a heated greenhouse.
Plant out at A 10 cm (4 in). H 15 cm (6 in).
Blue / yellow. S normal garden soil. Erect
plant covered with hair. For balconies, pots
and bedding.

Festuca cinerea (F. glauca)
Blue Fescue / fam. *Gramineae*
◯ ⬤ ⊖ ⬤ ⬤ ⬤ ⊖
August–September. White. H 20–40 cm (8–
16 in). A 30 cm (1 ft). S poor soil. P seed,
division. The blue-grey leaves are very thin.
For use in rock gardens and with paving.
Goes well with roses.

Festuca ovina 'Silberreiher'
Sheep's Fescue / fam. *Gramineae*
◯ ⬤ ⊖ ◯ ⬤ ⬤ ⊖
July–August. White. H 25 cm (10 in). A 30 cm
(1 ft). S poor soil. P division. Graceful, tuft-
forming grass that can be used as part ground
cover. Drought resistant.

Festuca scoparia (F. crinum-ursi)
fam. *Gramineae*
◯ ⬤ ◯ ⬤ ⬤ ⊖ ⊖
May–June. Creamy white. H 10–15 cm (4–
6 in). A 25 cm (10 in). S not critical. P seed,
division. Attractive grass forming bright
green compact clusters. Fine wire-shaped
blades.

Ficus carica
Fig / fam. *Moraceae*
◯ ⬤ ⬤ ⬤
May. Yellow-green. H 9 m (30 ft). W 5 m (16 ft).
Zone 6. S fertile. P cuttings, layering. Grown
as bush trees in South and West Britain or
fan-trained on south-facing walls further
north.

Filipendula rubra 'Venusta'
Queen of the Prairie / fam. *Rosaceae*
⬤ ⬤ ⬤ ⬤ ⬤ ⬤
June–July. Red. H 100–150 cm (3–5 ft). A 60–
80 cm (24–32 in). S well manured. P division.
Decorative plant with attractive, finely
divided leaves and deep pink flowers in
August. Plant near water.

Filipendula ulmaria 'Plena'
Meadow Sweet / fam. *Rosaceae*
⬤ ⬤ ◯ ⬤
June–September. White. H 60–125 cm (2–4 ft).
A 45 cm (18 in). S well manured. P division.
Attractive cultivar with fragrant double
flowers and pinnate, coarsely toothed leaves.

Foeniculum vulgare
Fennel / fam. *Umbelliferae*
◯ ◯ ⬤ ⬤ ⬤
August. Yellow. H 150 cm (5 ft). A 60–80 cm
(24–32 in). S sandy soil. P division, seed.
Herb, sometimes grown as a garden plant.
Replace from time to time.

205

Forsythia

Forsythia × intermedia
Common Forsythia / fam. *Oleaceae*
○ ◑ ⊞ ⊛ ⊗ ⊗
April–May. Yellow. H 2 m (6 ft). W 2 m (6 ft).
Zone 4. S not critical. P cuttings, layering.
Shrub with stiff and upright branches.
Flowers on naked wood. Dark green foliage.

Fortunella margarita (Citrus margarita)
Kumquat / fam. *Rutaceae*
○ ◑ ⊞ ⊛ ⊛
April–June. White. H 1.5 m (5 ft). W 1 m (3 ft).
Zone 8–9. S not critical. P seed, cuttings.
Small shrub without spines. Stout branches,
fragrant flowers and edible fruits.

Fothergilla major (F. alnifolia var. major)
fam. *Hamamelidaceae*
○ ◑ ⊜ ⊛ ⊛ ⊛ ⊗ ⊕
May. White. H 2 m (6 ft). W 3 m (10 ft). Zone 5.
S humus-rich. P layering, cuttings. Shrub of
erect and fairly broad habit with fragrant,
creamy-white flowers in long spikes.

Fothergilla major (F. alnifolia var. major)
fam. *Hamamelidaceae*
○ ◑ ⊜ ⊛ ⊛ ⊛ ⊗ ⊕
May. White. H 2 m (6 ft). W 3 m (10 ft). Zone 5.
S humus-rich. P layering, cuttings. Shrub of
erect and fairly broad habit with very
variable, large leaves which change colour in
autumn.

Fraxinus excelsior
Common Ash / fam. *Oleaceae*
○ ⊛ ⊛ ⊛ ⊛ ⊕
April–May. Yellow-green. H 40 m (135 ft).
W 10 m (33 ft). Zone 4. S normal garden soil.
P seed. Tall tree with a broad crown. Branches
and twigs densely covered with black buds.
Good autumn colour.

Fraxinus excelsior 'Aurea'
Common Ash / fam. *Oleaceae*
○ ⊛ ⊛ ⊛ ⊛ ⊕
April–May. Yellow-green. H 15 m (50 ft).
W 8 m (26 ft). S normal garden soil. P grafting.
Slow-growing tree with a broad crown,
yellow bark and golden-yellow young shoots.

Fraxinus excelsior 'Jaspidea
Golden Ash / fam. *Oleaceae*
○ ⊛ ⊛ ⊛ ⊛ ⊕
April–May. Yellow-green. H 20 m (65 ft).
W 10 m (33 ft). S normal garden soil.
P grafting. Tree with a broad, pyramidal
crown. Leaves turn yellow in autumn;
bronze-yellow branches in winter.

Fraxinus ornus
Manna Ash / fam. *Oleaceae*
○ ⊖ ⊛ ⊛ ⊛ ⊛ ⊕
May–June. White. H 10 m (33 ft). W 6–8 m (20–
26 ft). Zone 5. S humus-rich, loamy. P seed.
Bushy small tree with grey-green twigs.
Winged fruits. Suitable for smaller gardens.

Freesia hybrid 'Rijnveld's Golden Yellow'
fam. *Iridaceae*
○ ⊗ ⊗ ⊗
August–September. Yellow. H 25–30 cm (10–
12 in). A 5–7 cm (2–2¾ in). D 5 cm (2 in).
S normal garden soil. P offsets. Lift in
October; overwinter at 20°C (68°F). Store at
30°C (86°F) for 3 months before planting out.

Fritillaria imperialis
Crown Imperial / fam. *Liliaceae*
◯ ⊘ ⬡ ⓨ ⊙ ⎍
April–May. Orange. H 1 m (3 ft). A 20–35 cm
(8–14 in). D 15 cm (6 in). S normal garden soil.
P offsets. Flowers have an unpleasant smell.
Plant in September–November. Poisonous to
mice.

Fritillaria imperialis 'Lutea'
Crown Imperial / fam. *Liliaceae*
◯ ⊘ ⬡ ⓨ ⊙ ⎍
April–May. Lemon yellow. H 1 m (3 ft). A 20–
35 cm (8–14 in). D 15 cm (6 in). S normal
garden soil. P offsets. Leave undisturbed for
several years in sunny borders.

Fritillaria meleagris
Snake's Head Fritillary / fam. *Liliaceae*
◯ ◑ ◒ ⬡ ⊘ ⓨ ⓨ
April–May. Various colours. H 20–40 cm (8–
16 in). A 10 cm (4 in). D 7 cm (2¾ in). S fertile,
moist. P offsets. Especially suitable for
naturalisation. Most attractive near ponds.

Fritillaria persica 'Adiyaman'
Fritillary / fam. *Liliaceae*
◯ ⊘ ⬡ ⓨ ⊙
May. Dark purple. H 75 cm (30 in). A 15–20 cm
(6–8 in). D 10 cm (4 in). S normal garden soil.
P offsets. This relatively rare species makes
an exceptionally fine addition to a border.

Fuchsia magellanica 'Gracilis'
fam. *Onagraceae*
◯ ◑ ⊘ ⓦ ⓨ ⊗
May–September. Red. H 1 m (3 ft). W 1 m
(3 ft). Zone 5–6. S humus-rich and fertile.
P cuttings. Small shrub with gracefully
arching stems and very slender, pendent
flowers.

Fuchsia magellanica 'Riccartonii'
fam. *Onagraceae*
◯ ◑ ⊘ ⓦ ⓨ ⊗
May–September. Red / violet. H 2 m (6 ft).
W 1 m (3 ft). Zone 5–6. S humus-rich and
fertile. P cuttings. Robust and taller than
'Gracilis', with arching stems, larger and less
slender flowers.

Gaillardia pulchella var. *picta*
Blanket Flower / fam. *Compositae*
◯ ✻ ⊙ ⓨ ⊗
Sow in March in heated greenhouse or in
April outside. Thin / plant out at A 30 cm
(1 ft). H 45 cm (18 in). Various colours.
S normal garden soil. Best planted in groups.
Needs a lot of sunlight.

Gaillardia pulchella var. *picta* 'Lollipop'
Blanket Flower / fam. *Compositae*
◯ ◯ ⊙ ⓨ ⊗
Sow in March in a heated greenhouse or in
April outside. Thin / plant out at A 30 cm
(1 ft). H 45 cm (18 in). Various colours.
S normal garden soil. Recently more in
demand. Double flowers in profusion.

Gaillardia pulchella var. *picta* 'Lorentziana'
Blanket Flower / fam. *Compositae*
◯ ◯ ⊙ ⓨ ⊗
Sow in March in a heated greenhouse or in
April outside. Thin / plant out at A 30 cm
(1 ft). H 50 cm (20 in). S normal soil.
Magnificent cultivar with bicoloured double
flowers.

207

Galanthus nivalis
Common Snowdrop / fam. ***Amaryllidaceae***
Ⓘ Ⓘ Ⓞ Ⓥ Ⓐ ⊘
February–March. White. H 10–20 cm (4–8 in).
A 5–7 cm (2–2¾ in). D 2–5 cm (¾–2 in).
S humus-rich. P offsets. Bulbous plant
suitable for grassy areas, rock or wild gardens.

Galega × ***hartlandii* 'Duchess of Bedford'**
Goat's Rue / fam. ***Leguminosae***
Ⓞ Ⓞ Ⓞ Ⓥ ⊘
July–August. White / violet. H 150 cm (5 ft).
A 60–80 cm (24–32 in). S normal garden soil.
P seed, division. Flowers have sturdy, very
straight stems. Resembles a lupin. Good
border plant.

***Galeobdolon luteum* 'Herman's Pride'**
Yellow Archangel / fam. ***Labiatae***
Ⓘ Ⓘ Ⓞ Ⓥ Ⓐ Ⓐ ⊖
June–July. Yellow. H 30 cm (1 ft). A 40 cm
(16 in). S not critical. P division. New cultivar
with attractive foliage.

***Galeobdolon luteum* 'Variegatum'** *(Lamium*
galeobdolon **'Variegatum'**) / **Yellow**
Archangel / fam. ***Labiatae***
Ⓘ Ⓘ Ⓞ Ⓞ Ⓐ ⊖
May–June. Yellow. H 15–30 cm (6–12 in).
A 30–60 cm (1–2 ft). S humus-rich. P division,
cuttings. Very invasive plant. The oval leaves
are flecked with silver.

Galium odoratum (Asperula odorata)
Sweet Woodruff / fam. ***Rubiaceae***
Ⓘ Ⓘ ⊘ Ⓞ Ⓥ ⊝ ⊘
May–June. White. H 10–25 cm (4–10 in).
A 20 cm (8 in). S loamy forest soil. P division,
seed. Small woodland plant with a delightful
fragrance. Used in Germany for making May
wine.

Galtonia candicans (Hyacinthus candicans)
Giant Summer Hyacinth / fam. ***Liliaceae***
Ⓞ Ⓘ Ⓐ Ⓥ
July–September. White. H 100–125 cm (3–
4 ft). A 12–35 cm (4½–14 in). D 10–15 cm (4–
6 in). S normal garden soil. P offsets. Not
hardy. Lift the bulbs in the autumn and
overwinter at 5°C (41°F).

Gaultheria procumbens
Creeping Wintergreen / fam. ***Ericaceae***
Ⓘ Ⓘ Ⓘ Ⓐ Ⓐ Ⓥ ⊖
July–August. White / rose-purple. H 15 cm
(6 in). W 20 cm (8 in). Zone 3. S humus-rich.
P seed, cuttings. Dwarf shrub with bare stems
and dark purple leaves in winter. Flowers
borne singly.

***Gazania* hybrid 'Ministar'**
fam. ***Compositae***
Ⓞ ⊜ ⊙ Ⓥ ⊘
Sow in January–February in a heated
greenhouse. Plant out at A 30 cm (1 ft).
H 25 cm (10 in). Various colours. S fertile.
Low-growing plant with daisy-like flowers
which close up at night.

***Gazania* hybrid 'Ministar Yellow'**
fam. ***Compositae***
Ⓞ ⊜ ⊙ Ⓥ ⊘
Sow in January–February in a heated
greenhouse. Plant out at A 30 cm (1 ft).
H 25 cm (10 in). Yellow. S fertile. Vigorous,
free-flowering hybrid. Flowers look best at
close quarters.

Genista aetnensis
Mt Etna Broom / fam. *Leguminosae*
○ ⑨ ⑨ ⑨
July. Yellow. H 4 m (13 ft). W 2 m (6 ft). Zone
6. S normal garden soil, lime free. P seed. Tall
shrub with rush-like branches. Sheds its
leaves very quickly. Flowers in profusion.

Genista lydia
Broom / fam. *Leguminosae*
○ ⊗ ⑨ ⑨ ⑨
May–June. Yellow. H 60 cm (2 ft). W 2 m (6 ft).
Zone 7. S normal garden soil, lime free.
P seed. Wide-spreading shrub with arching
shoot tips and masses of flowers.

Gentiana cruciata
Gentian / fam. *Gentianaceae*
○ ① ⊗ ⊗ ○ ⑨
June–July / August. Blue. H 30 cm (1 ft).
A 20 cm (8 in). S humus-rich. P division, seed.
Densely packed, decussate leaves. Masses of
not particularly attractive flowers.

Gentiana septemfida
Summer Gentian / fam. *Gentianaceae*
○ ⊗ ⊗ ○ ⑨ ⊗ ⊖
August–September. Violet-blue. H 20–30 cm
(8–12 in). A 20 cm (8 in). S loamy. P division,
seed. Fairly upright, easily cultivated plant
with oval leaves and flowers with brown
spots.

Gentiana sino-ornata
Gentian / fam. *Gentianaceae*
○ ① ⊗ ⊗ ⑨ ⊗ ⊖
September–October. Blue H 15–20 cm (6–
8 in). A 15 cm (6 in). S loamy. P division, seed.
Creeping plant from West Tibet and China
with a profusion of flowers. Easily cultivated.

Gentiana verna
Spring Gentian / fam. *Gentianaceae*
○ ① ⊗ ⊗ ○ ⑨ ⊗
April–May. Blue. H 10 cm (4 in). A 10 cm (4 in).
S loamy. P division, seed. Native to Europe,
including Great Britain; often in small groups.
Not easy to cultivate. Protected plant.

Geranium cinereum 'Ballerina'
Cranesbill / fam. *Geraniaceae*
○ ① ① ○ ⑨ ⊗
June–July. Crimson / magenta. H 15 cm (6 in).
A 20 cm (8 in). S humus-rich. Under
favourable circumstance this cultivar will
keep flowering into September.

Geranium dalmaticum
Cranesbill / fam. *Geraniaceae*
○ ① ① ⊗ ○ ⑨ ⊗ ⊗ ⊖
June–August. Rose-purple. H 10 cm (4 in).
A 10 cm (4 in). S humus-rich. P division, seed.
Spreads quickly by means of runners,
especially between paving. Foliage turns red
in the autumn.

Geranium endressii
Cranesbill / fam. *Geraniaceae*
○ ① ① ○ ⑨ ⊗
June–August. Violet. H 25–30 cm (10–12 in).
A 20 cm (8 in). S humus-rich. P division, seed.
Free-flowering species with prostrate to erect,
slightly hairy stems.

Geranium

***Geranium × magnificum (G. platypetalum
hort.)***/Cranesbill/fam. *Geraniaceae*
Ⓞ Ⓘ Ⓥ Ⓨ Ⓦ Ⓧ
June–July. Violet-purple. H 35–70 cm (14–
28 in). A 50 cm (20 in). S humus-rich.
P division, seed. Leaves assume an attractive
bright colour in autumn. Not drought
resistant.

***Geranium meeboldii* 'Johnson's Blue'**
Cranesbill/fam. *Geraniaceae*
Ⓞ Ⓘ Ⓥ Ⓨ Ⓧ
June–July. Violet-blue. H 50 cm (20 in).
A 30 cm (1 ft). S humus-rich. P division.
Stems, leaves and flower stalks covered with
glandular hairs. Leaves are shed early.

Geranium palmatum (G. anemonifolium)
Cranesbill/fam. *Geraniaceae*
Ⓞ Ⓘ Ⓐ Ⓥ Ⓨ Ⓦ Ⓐ Ⓧ Ⓧ
July–September. Rose-purple. H 60–80 cm
(24–32 in). A 80 cm (32 in). S humus-rich,
chalky. P division, seed. Evergreen from the
Canary Islands and Madeira. Needs warmth.

Geraneum phaeum
Cranesbill/fam. *Geraniaceae*
Ⓞ Ⓘ Ⓘ Ⓥ Ⓧ
June–July. Purple. H 50 cm (20 in). A 30 cm
(1 ft). S humus-rich. P division, seed. From
South-east Europe. Suitable for the edge of
woods.

Geranium psilostemon (G. armenum)
Cranesbill/fam. *Geraniaceae*
Ⓞ Ⓘ Ⓘ Ⓥ Ⓧ
June–July. Vivid magenta. H 90 cm (3 ft).
A 50 cm (20 in). S humus-rich. P division,
seed. A spreading plant with erect stems.
Inconspicuous after flowering.

Geranium sanguineum* var. *prostratum
Bloody Cranesbill/fam. *Geraniaceae*
Ⓞ Ⓘ Ⓘ Ⓥ Ⓧ
June–July. Pink. H 15–25 cm (6–10 in). A 20 cm
(8 in). S humus-rich. P division, seed.
Creeping plant of British origin with graceful,
disease-resistant leaves. Fast growing.

Geranium sanguineum* var. *sanguineum
Bloody Cranesbill/fam. *Geraniaceae*
Ⓞ Ⓘ Ⓘ Ⓥ Ⓧ
May–September. Crimson-magenta. H 15–
25 cm (6–10 in). A 20 cm (8 in). S humus-rich.
P division, seed. Flowers in abundance. Good
in the first few rows of a border. Fast growing.
From Europe.

***Geranium sylvaticum* 'Mayflower'**
Wood Cranesbill/fam. *Geraniaceae*
Ⓘ Ⓞ Ⓥ Ⓧ
June–July. Purple-violet. H 60 cm (2 ft). A 30–
40 cm (12–16 in). S humus-rich. P division.
Flowers abundantly. For cool and shadowy
places, including slopes. From Europe.

Geranium tuberosum
Cranesbill/fam. *Geraniaceae*
Ⓞ Ⓞ Ⓥ Ⓧ
April–May. Purple. H 20–30 cm (8–12 in).
A 30 cm (1 ft). S humus-rich. P division, seed.
From the Mediterranean coast. Tuberous
rootstock.

Geum chiloense 'Mrs Bradshaw'
Avens / fam. *Rosaceae*
◯ ◑ ✿ ⊛ ⊗
May–August. Scarlet. H 40–60 cm (16–24 in).
A 30–40 cm (12–16 in). S normal garden soil.
P division. Attractive, long-flowering hybrid.
Long lived.

Geum hybrid 'Prinses Juliana'
Avens / fam. *Rosaceae*
◯ ◑ ✿ ⊛ ⊗
May–July. Orange. H 40–60 cm (16–24 in).
A 30–40 cm (12–16 in). S normal garden soil.
P division. Semi-double flowers. Densely
packed, dark green leaves.

Gillenia trifoliata
fam. *Rosaceae*
◯ ◑ ✿ ⊛ ⊗
June–August. White / red. H 60–70 cm (24–
28 in). A 50 cm (20 in). S normal. P seed,
division. White petals and red sepals. Of
North American origin. For borders.

Ginkgo biloba (Salisburia adiantifolia)
Maidenhair Tree / fam. *Ginkgoaceae*
◯ ❀ ✳ ⊛ ✿ ⊕
Dioecious tree of variable habit. Produces
creamy, rancid-smelling fruits following
warm summers. H 20 m (65 ft). W 8 m (26 ft).
S good garden soil. P seed, cuttings. Zone 4.

Gladiolus (Butterfly) 'A. Capella'
fam. *Iridaceae*
◯ ◑ ❀ ⊛ ⊕ ⊗
July–September. Yellow / red. H 80–120 cm
(32–48 in). A 10 cm (4 in). D 6–8 cm (2¼–3 in).
S fertile, chalky. P offsets. Very good for
cutting and very popular.

Gladiolus (Butterfly) 'Bambino'
fam. *Iridaceae*
◯ ◑ ❀ ⊛ ⊕ ⊗
For description see last entry. Reddish purple.
Sword-shaped leaves and flowers in
magnificent colours on long spikes.

Gladiolus (Butterfly) 'Norma'
fam. *Iridaceae*
◯ ◑ ❀ ⊛ ⊕ ⊗
For description see *Gladiolus* 'A. Capella'.
Orange / yellow. Not hardy. Lift in the
autumn and store in a dry and frost-free place.

Gladiolus (Butterfly) 'Prelude'
fam. *Iridaceae*
◯ ◑ ❀ ⊛ ⊕ ⊗
For description see *Gladiolus* 'A. Capella'.
White / red. Plant corms in well-dug and
well-fertilised, not too dry soil, from April to
May.

Gladiolus (Butterfly) 'Turandot'
fam. *Iridaceae*
◯ ◑ ❀ ⊛ ⊕ ⊗
For description see *Gladiolus* 'A. Capella'.
Yellow. Butterfly gladioli are low-growing
types with relatively small flowers, large
corms and stout stems.

Gladiolus

Gladiolus byzantinus
fam. *Iridaceae*
○ ◑ ⊛ ⊛ ⊛ ⊗
June–July. Wine-red. H 1 m (3 ft). A 10–15 cm
(4–6 in). D 10 cm (4 in). S chalky. P offsets.
Sturdy spikes with a host of densely packed
flowers.

Gladiolus hybrid 'Clio'
fam. *Iridaceae*
○ ◑ ⊛ ⊛ ⊛ ⊗
For description see *Gladiolus* hybrid (below).
Reddish purple / white. After planting in
frost-free weather, cover the corms with straw
or leaves.

Gladiolus hybrid 'Franz Liszt'
fam. *Iridaceae*
○ ◑ ⊛ ⊛ ⊛ ⊗
For description see *Gladiolus* hybrid (below).
Red / yellow. Tie taller specimens to very thin
sticks and plant in a sheltered position.

Gladiolus hybrid (G. × colvillei)
fam. *Iridaceae*
○ ◑ ⊛ ⊛ ⊛ ⊗
July. Red / white. H 100–150 cm (3–5 ft).
A 10 cm (4 in). D 6–8 cm (2¼–3 in). S fertile,
chalky. P offsets. Very early-flowering kinds
should be planted from the middle of
November to the middle of December.

Gladiolus hybrid 'Herman van der Mark'
fam. *Iridaceae*
○ ◑ ⊛ ⊛ ⊛ ⊗
For description see *Gladiolus* hybrid (above).
Red. Gladioli are propagated from cormlets
found at the base of the corm.

Gladiolus hybrid 'Melodie'
fam. *Iridaceae*
○ ◑ ⊛ ⊛ ⊛ ⊗
July–August. Various colours. H 100–150 cm
(3–5 ft). A 15–20 cm (6–8 in). D 10–15 cm (4–
6 in). S chalky. P offsets. Not hardy. Plant
early-flowering strains in November–
December and cover well.

Gladiolus hybrid 'Oscar'
fam. *Iridaceae*
○ ◑ ⊛ ⊛ ⊛ ⊗
For description see *Gladiolus* hybrid (above).
Red. Cormlets about the size of a pea appear
when the old corms are lifted in autumn.

Gladiolus hybrid 'Papilio'
fam. *Iridaceae*
○ ◑ ⊛ ⊛ ⊛ ⊗
For description see *Gladiolus* hybrid (above).
Violet / white / yellow. Store corms separately
in dry sand in a frost-proof place during the
winter. Plant out in the spring.

Gladiolus hybrid 'Sweepstake'
fam. *Iridaceae*
○ ◑ ⊛ ⊛ ⊛ ⊗
For description see *Gladiolus* hybrid. Orange-
red / yellow. Corms flower after two years,
though sometimes after only one year. Results
better after two years.

Gleditsia aquatica
Honey Locust / **fam.** *Leguminosae*
○ ⊖ ⏁ ✳ ⊘ ⊛ ⊥
June–July. Green. H 15 m (50 ft). W 5 m (16 ft).
Zone 4. S good garden soil. P seed. Slow-
growing tree with long branching spines.

Gleditsia japonica (G. horrida)
Honey Locust / **fam.** *Leguminosae*
○ ⊖ ⏁ ✳ ⊘ ⊛ ⊥
June–July. Green. H 20 m (65 ft). W 7 m (23 ft).
Zone 4. S good garden soil. P seed. Tree with
many 5–8-cm (2–3-in) long spines on stems
and branches. Sickle-shaped seed pods.

Gleditsia macrantha
Honey Locust / **fam.** *Leguminosae*
○ ⊖ ⏁ ✳ ⊛ ⊥
June–July. Green. H 15 m (50 ft). W 5 m (16 ft).
Zone 4. S good garden soil. P seed. Tree with
thick, glabrous branches, grey bark and large
spines on the trunk.

***Gleditsia triacanthos* 'Sunburst'**
Honey Locust / **fam.** *Leguminosae*
○ ⊖ ⏁ ✳ ⊘ ⊛ ⊥
June–July. Green. H 8 m (26 ft). W 5 m (16 ft).
Zone 4. S good garden soil. P grafting,
cuttings. Moderately tall tree with yellow
leaves that turn yellow-green in the autumn.
No spines.

***Glyceria maxima* 'Variegata'**
Reed Sweet Grass / **fam.** *Gramineae*
○ ◧ ◑ ⊘ ⊛
July–August. H 40–150 cm (16–60 in). A 60–
80 cm (24–32 in). S moist garden soil.
P division. Very invasive. Yellow in the
autumn. Suitable for banks.

***Godetia* hybrid**
fam. *Onagraceae*
○ ⊙ ⊛ ⊗
Sow in April and thin out to A 30–40 cm (12–
16 in). H 75 cm (30 in). Various colours.
S fertile soil. Tall, single and large-flowered
godetia. Flower buds must be peeled back.

***Godetia* hybrid (Azalea-flowered)**
fam. *Onagraceae*
○ ⊙ ⊛ ⊗
Sow in April and thin out to A 15–20 cm (6–
8 in). H 30 cm (1 ft). Various colours. S fertile
garden soil. Very popular variety.

Gomphrena globosa
Globe Amaranth / **fam.** *Amaranthaceae*
○ ⊙ ⊛ ⊗
Sow in March–April under glass. Thin / plant
out at A 20 cm (8 in). H 30 cm (1 ft). Various
colours. S humus-rich. Bushy plant with erect
stems, hairy leaves and flowers which can be
dried.

Gunnera manicata
fam. *Haloragaceae*
○ ◧ ⊜ ⊙ ⏁ ⊘ ⊛ ⊥
July–August. Brown. H 2–3 m (6–10 ft). A 5–
6 m (16–20 ft). S humus-rich. P division.
Brown cone-shaped panicles up to 1 m (3 ft)
high. Sensitive to frost. Needs careful
handling.

213

Gunnera

Gunnera tinctoria (G. chilensis)
fam. *Haloragaceae*
○ ◐ ⊗ ⊙ ① ⊘ ⊕
July–August. Brown-red. H 2–3 m (6–10 ft).
A 5–6 m (16–20 ft). S humus-rich. P division.
Resembles rhubarb. Needs a great deal of
moisture during the growing season.

Gymnocladus dioicus (G. canadensis)
Kentucky Coffee Tree / fam. *Leguminosae*
○ ✳ ⊘ ⊛ ②
May–June. Green-white. H 20 m (65 ft).
W 15 m (50 ft). Zone 4. S very fertile. P seed,
root cuttings. Loosely branching tree, rough
bark on mature stems. Slow growing.
Elongated brown pods.

Gypsophila elegans 'Alba'
Baby's Breath / fam. *Caryophyllaceae*
○ ⊜ ⊙ ⓨ ⊗
Sow in March–April and thin out to A 30 cm
(1 ft). H 60 cm (2 ft). White. S normal garden
soil, chalky. Easily grown variety. Very
attractive filler for a border.

Gypsophila hybrid 'Rosenschleier'
Baby's Breath / fam. *Caryophyllaceae*
○ ⊜ ⊝ ⓨ ⊗ ⊗
June–August. White-purple. H 30 cm (1 ft).
A 20 cm (8 in). S chalky. P division. Flowers
profusely for a long time. Drought resistant,
for example suitable for rock garden. Will
bush out.

Gypsophila paniculata
Baby's Breath / fam. *Caryophyllaceae*
○ ⊜ ⊖ ⊙ ⓨ ⊗
July–August. White-violet. H 1 m (3 ft). A 60–
80 cm (24–32 in). S chalky. P division, seed.
Needs a warm position. Flowers suitable for
drying.

Gypsophila repens 'Rosea'
Baby's Breath / fam. *Caryophyllaceae*
○ ⊜ ⊖ ⊙ ⓨ ⊗
May–June. Rose-purple. H 10 cm (4 in).
A 10 cm (4 in). S chalky. P division. Attractive
creeping plant for the rock garden. Older
plants are difficult to move.

Hakonechloa macra 'Aureola'
fam. *Gramineae*
◐ ⊗ ≈ ○ ⊘
Greeny yellow. H 25–50 cm (10–20 in). A 40 cm
(8 in). S normal garden soil. P division, seed.
Ornamental spreading grass from Japan.
Needs a moist and cool position. Not hardy.

Halesia carolina var. monticola
Snowdrop Tree / fam. *Styracaceae*
○ ◐ ⓦ ✳ ⓨ ⊛
April. White. H 6 m (20 ft). W 7.5 m (25 ft).
Zone 5. S normal garden soil, lime free.
P seed, layering. Tree-like shrub with wide-
spreading branches and pendent bell-shaped
flowers.

Hamamelis × intermedia 'Jelena'
Witch Hazel / fam. *Hamamelidaceae*
○ ◐ ⊕ ⓦ ⊘ ⊕ ⊗
January–February. Orange. H 3 m (10 ft).
W 3 m (10 ft). Zone 5. S humus-rich.
P grafting. Stout shrub with ascending
branches and very large flowers in profusion.

Hamamelis mollis (spring)
Chinese Witch Hazel / fam. *Hamamelidaceae*
Ⓘ ⊕ Ⓨ Ⓜ ⊛
January–March. Yellow. H 4 m (13 ft). W 4 m
(13 ft). Zone 5. S humus-rich. P cuttings, seed,
layering. Clusters of spicy-scented flowers
appear early before the leaves.

Hamamelis mollis (autumn)
Chinese Witch Hazel / fam. *Hamamelidaceae*
Ⓘ ⊕ Ⓨ Ⓜ ⊛
January–March. Yellow. H 4 m (13 ft). W 4 m
(13 ft). Zone 5. S humus-rich. P cuttings, seed,
layering. Large shrub with ascending
branches and broadly obovate woolly leaves,
turning yellow in the autumn.

Hamamelis virginiana / Common
Witch Hazel / fam. *Hamamelidaceae*
Ⓘ ⊕ Ⓜ ⊕ ⊕
September–October. Yellow. H 4 m (13 ft).
W 3.5 m (11 ft). Zone 4. S humus-rich.
P cuttings, seed, layering. Tall shrub of broad
habit. The green leaves turn yellow in
autumn. Small flowers.

Hebe × *andersonii* (*Veronica* × *andersonii*)
fam. *Scrophulariaceae*
◯ Ⓜ Ⓨ ⊛
August–October. Violet. H 1 m (3 ft). W 1 m
(3 ft). Zone 7. S fertile soil. P cuttings. Shrub
with wavy, oblong-lanceolate leaves and
flowers in long clusters.

Hebe armstrongii
fam. *Scrophulariaceae*
◯ ⌃ Ⓜ Ⓜ ⊛ ⊗
May–June. White. H 60 cm (2 ft). W 90 cm
(3 ft). Zone 5. S fertile. P cuttings. A bushy
conifer-like shrub with small scaly leaves that
change colour in the autumn.

Hebe 'Autumn Blue'
fam. *Scrophulariaceae*
◯ ⌃ ⊕ Ⓜ Ⓨ ⊛
September–October. Violet-blue. H 40 cm
(16 in). W 50 cm (20 in). Zone 7. S fertile.
P cuttings. One of many hybrids which are
hardy in South and West England.

Hebe salicifolia
fam. *Scrophulariaceae*
◯ Ⓜ Ⓨ ⊛
June–July. White-violet. H 3 m (10 ft). W 3 m
(10 ft). Zone 7. S fertile soil. P cuttings. Small
shrub with glabrous green branches, pointed
lanceolate leaves and flowers in long racemes.

Hebe traversii (Veronica traversii)
fam. *Scrophulariaceae*
◯ Ⓜ ⊛
June–August. White. H 2 m (6 ft). W 2 m (6 ft).
Zone 7. S fertile soil. P cuttings. Bushy habit.
Downy juvenile leaves. Flowers borne in long
racemes.

Hedera colchica 'Dentatovariegata'
Persian Ivy / fam. *Araliaceae*
◯ Ⓘ ⊳ ⌃ Ⓜ ⊕ ◯
September. Greeny yellow. H 9 m (30 ft).
W 1 m (3 ft). Zone 5. S not critical. P cuttings.
Vigorous climbing shrub with large, leathery,
glossy, white-edged leaves.

215

Hedera

Hedera helix
Common Ivy / fam. *Araliaceae*
◯ ⬤ ⬤ ⬤ ⬤ ⬤ ⬤ ⬤ ⊖
September–October. Greeny yellow. H 20 m
(65 ft). W 6 m (20 ft). Zone 5. S not critical. Tall
self-attaching climber with glossy dark green
leaves and black or yellow berries.

Hedera helix 'Arborescens'
Common Ivy / fam. *Araliaceae*
⬤ ⬤ ⬤ ⬤ ⬤ ⬤ ⬤ ⬤ ⊖
September–October. Greeny yellow. H 30 m
(100 ft). W 5 m (16 ft). Zone 5. S not critical.
P cuttings. Non-climbing ivy of bushy habit
and smaller leaves than the species.

Hedera helix 'Ovata'
Common Ivy / fam. *Araliaceae*
⬤ ⬤ ⬤ ⬤ ⬤ ⬤ ⬤ ⊖
September–October. Greeny yellow. H 20 m
(65 ft). W 6 m (20 ft). Zone 5. S not critical.
P cuttings. Attractive, green, lobate leaves.
A pleasing cultivar.

Hedera helix 'Sagittaefolia'
Common Ivy / fam. *Araliaceae*
⬤ ⬤ ⬤ ⬤ ⬤ ⬤
September–October. Greeny yellow. H 5 m
(16 ft). W 1 m (3 ft). Zone 5. S not critical.
P cuttings. Self-attaching climber with arrow-
shaped, five-lobed leaves. Not as vigorous as
the species.

Hedera helix 'Spectabilis Aurea'
Common Ivy / fam. *Araliaceae*
⬤ ⬤ ⬤ ⬤ ⬤ ⬤ ⬤
June–July. Green. H 10 m (33 ft). W 3 m (10 ft).
Zone 5–6. S moist. P cuttings. Unusual
climber with golden-yellow juvenile foliage.
Does not like too much shade.

Hedysarum multijugum
fam. *Leguminosae*
◯ ⬤ ⊖ ⬤ ⬤
June–September. Rose-purple. H 1 m (3 ft).
W 1 m (3 ft). Zone 4. S not critical. P cuttings,
layering. Ornamental shrub with zigzagging
branchlets and flowers in long racemes.

Helenium hybrid 'Altgoldriese'
Sneezeweed / fam. *Compositae*
◯ ⬤ ⬤ ⬤ ⊗
July–September. Red. H 2 m (6 ft). A 60 cm
(2 ft). S fertile. P division. Strong and tall
variety in an attractive shade of red. Not very
common. Suitable for larger borders.

Helenium hybrid 'Chipperfield Orange'
Sneezeweed / fam. *Compositae*
◯ ⬤ ⬤ ⬤ ⊗
July–September. Orange-yellow. H 2 m (6 ft).
A 60 cm (2 ft). S fertile. P division. Old-
fashioned, very tall variety in a striking
yellow hue. Robust border plant.

Helenium hybrid 'Julisonne'
Sneezeweed / fam. *Compositae*
◯ ⬤ ⬤ ⬤ ⊗
July–September. Yellow. H 1 m (3 ft). A 40 cm
(16 in). S fertile. P division. Compact variety
in a clear, soft yellow shade with matching
centre. Suitable for a smaller garden.

***Helenium* hybrid 'Superbum Rubrum'**
Sneezeweed / fam. *Compositae*
○ ○ ⊗ ⊗ ⊗
July–September. Orange. H 2 m (6 ft). A 60 cm
(2 ft). S fertile. P division. Stout plant which
shoots readily, suitable for borders and for
planting between shrubs.

***Helenium* hybrid 'Symbol'**
Sneezeweed / fam. *Compositae*
○ ○ ⊗ ⊗ ⊗
July–September. Yellow. H 150 cm (5 ft).
A 50 cm (20 in). S fertile. P division. Fine
yellow flowers with a brown centre. Excellent
and sturdy border plant.

***Helianthemum* hybrid 'Cerise Queen'**
Rock Rose / fam. *Cistaceae*
○ ⊜ ⊘ ⊕ ⊗ ⊛ ⊗
June–July. Red. H 15–25 cm (6–10 in). A 20 cm
(8 in). S dry, chalky. P cuttings. Grey-green
elliptical leaves. Flowers in abundance which
re-open in sunny weather.

***Helianthemum* hybrid 'Fire Dragon'**
Rock Rose / fam. *Cistaceae*
○ ⊜ ⊘ ⊕ ⊗ ⊛ ⊗
June–July. Red. H 15–25 cm (6–10 in). A 20 cm
(8 in). S dry, chalky. P cuttings. The flowers
close or drop off after a sunny day.

***Helianthemum* hybrid 'Golden Queen'**
Rock Rose / fam. *Cistaceae*
○ ⊜ ⊘ ⊕ ⊗ ⊛ ⊗
June–July. Yellow. H 15–25 cm (6–10 in).
A 20 cm (8 in). S dry, chalky. P cuttings. Grey-
green elliptical leaves. It bears a profusion of
flowers which re-open in sunny weather.

Helianthus annuus
Sunflower / fam. *Compositae*
○ ⊙ ⊗ ⊛ ⊕ ⊗
Sow in March–April and thin out to A 60–
80 cm (24–32 in). H 4 m (13 ft). Yellow / brown.
S fertile. Important agricultural crop yielding
oil and edible seeds. Large flowers.

***Helianthus annuus* 'Evening Sun'**
Sunflower / fam. *Compositae*
○ ⊙ ⊗ ⊛ ⊕ ⊗
Sow in April–May and thin out to A 30–45 cm
(12–18 in). H 2 m (6 ft). Yellow / brown-red.
S fertile. Unbranched stems with nodding
flowers which turn towards the sun.

***Helianthus annuus* 'Tubulosus'**
Sunflower / fam. *Compositae*
○ ⊙ ⊗ ⊛ ⊕ ⊗
Sow in April–May and thin out to A 30–45 cm
(12–18 in). H 2 m (6 ft). Yellow. S fertile.
Double-flowered variety with tubular ray
florets. All florets are the same colour.

***Helianthus decapetalus* 'Soleil d'Or'**
Sunflower / fam. *Compositae*
○ ⊘ ⊙ ⊗ ⊗
August–October. Yellow. H 150 cm (5 ft).
A 80 cm (32 in). S fertile. P division. Border
plant with medium-sized double flowers.
Thin out repeatedly.

Helianthus

Helianthus × laetiflorus 'Miss Mellish'
Sunflower / fam. *Compositae*
○ ◇ ⊙ ♀ ⊗
July–September. Yellow. H 140 cm (4½ ft).
A 80 cm (32 in). S fertile. P division. Cross
between *H. rigidus* and *H. tuberosus*. Needs a
great deal of moisture. Thin out well.

Helianthus salicifolius (H. orgyalis)
Sunflower / fam. *Compositae*
○ ⊛ ⊙ ⊘
October. Yellow. H 100–150 cm (3–5 ft). A 1 m
(3 ft). S fertile. P division. Inconspicuous
flowers. Grown for its gracefully arching
leaves.

Helichrysum bracteatum 'Compositum'
Straw Flower / fam. *Compositae*
○ ⊙ ♀ ⊗
Sow in March under glass or in April outside.
Thin / plant out at A 20–30 cm (8–12 in). H 40–
100 cm (16–36 in). Various colours. S normal
garden soil. Popular dried flower but difficult
to grow.

Helichrysum bracteatum 'Monstruosum'
Straw Flower / fam. *Compositae*
○ ⊙ ♀ ⊗
Sow in March under glass or in April outside.
Thin / plant out at A 20–30 cm (8–12 in). H 40–
100 cm (16–36 in). Various colours. S normal
garden soil. Cut just before flowers open, and
dry.

**Helictotrichon sempervirens (Avena
sempervirens)** / fam. *Gramineae*
○ ⊜ ⊙ ♀ ⊛ ⊕ ⊗
May–June. White. H 150 cm (5 ft). A 1 m (3 ft).
S normal garden soil. P division, seed.
Decorative blue-green grass with a profusion
of flowers in the summer. Very hardy.

Heliopsis helianthoides 'Goldgrünherz'
fam. *Compositae*
○ ⊙ ♀ ⊗
July–September. Yellow. H 90 cm (3 ft).
A 50 cm (20 in). S normal garden soil.
P division, cuttings. Plant in an easily
accessible position in the border. Good for
cutting.

Heliopsis helianthoides var. helianthoides
fam. *Compositae*
○ ⊙ ♀ ⊗
July–September. Yellow. H 100–125 cm (3–
4 ft). A 60 cm (2 ft). S normal garden soil.
P division, cuttings. Outstanding border
plant. Needs much water during flowering
period.

**Heliopsis helianthoides var. scabra
'Sommersonne'** / fam. *Compositae*
○ ⊙ ♀ ⊗
July–September. Yellow. H 100–125 cm (3–
4 ft). A 60 cm (2 ft). S normal. P division,
cuttings. Long-flowering plant with attractive
single blooms. Water generously in dry
weather.

Heliotropium arborescens (H. peruvianum)
Heliotrope / fam. *Boraginaceae*
○ ⊛ ⊙ ♀
Sow in March in a heated greenhouse. Plant
out at A 50 cm (20 in) after hardening off.
H 70 cm (28 in). Violet-blue. S fertile soil.
Variable, more or less shrub-like species.
Very sensitive to frosts.

Helipterum manglesii 'Rosea'
Everlasting Flower / fam. *Compositae*
○ ⊝ ⊙ ⓨ ⊗ ⊗
Sow in April under glass or in May outside.
Thin / plant out at A 15–20 cm (6–8 in). H 30–
50 cm (12–20 in). Red / yellow. S humus-rich.
Particularly attractive straw-textured flowers.

Helipterum roseum (Acroclinium roseum)
Everlasting Flower / fam. *Compositae*
○ ⊝ ⊙ ⓨ ⓧ
Sow in April under glass or in May in the
open. Thin / plant out at A 15–20 cm (6–8 in).
H 20–60 (8–24 in). Red / yellow. S humus-
rich. The most popular species. Leaves green,
not hairy.

Helleborus foetidus
Stinking Hellebore / fam. *Ranunculaceae*
◐ ⓜ ⊗ ⊙ ⓨ ⊛ ⓒ
March–May. Green. H 50 cm (20 in). A 30 cm
(1 ft). S fertile soil. P seed, division.
Evergreen, very early-flowering plant. Bell-
shaped red flowers with a red edge.

Helleborus × hybridus (H. orientalis)
Lenten Rose / fam. *Ranunculaceae*
◐ ⓞ ⓨ ⊛ ⓐ ⓒ
March–May. Green. H 30–50 cm (12–20 in).
A 30 cm (1 ft). S fertile soil. P seed, division.
The colour of these hybrids ranges from white
through green and pink to purple.

Helleborus niger
Christmas Rose / fam. *Ranunculaceae*
◐ ⓜ ⊝ ⊙ ⓨ ⓒ
December–March. White. H 30–45 cm (12–
18 in). A 45 cm (18 in). S fertile. P seed,
division. Valued for its early blooms. Flowers
change colour. Black roots.

Hemerocallis citrina
Day Lily / fam. *Liliaceae*
◐ ⊗ ⊙ ⓨ
July–August. Yellow. H 70–100 cm (28–36 in).
A 80 cm (32 in). S fertile soil. P division, seed.
The lily-like flowers do not open until the
evening, when they give off a delightful
fragrance.

Hemerocallis hybrid 'Atlas'
Day Lily / fam. *Liliaceae*
◐ ⊗ ⊙ ⓨ
July–August. Yellow H 110 cm (3½ ft). A 60–
80 cm (24–32 in). S fertile soil. P division.
Large-flowered cultivar with sturdy stems.
Leaves keep their bright green colour in
autumn.

Hemerocallis hybrid 'Crimson Pirate'
Day Lily / fam. *Liliaceae*
◐ ⊗ ⊙ ⓨ
July–August. Red. H 60 cm (2 ft). A 30–40 cm
(12–16 in). S fertile. P division. Small-
flowered cultivar with star-shaped crimson
blooms which go well with the leaves.

Hemerocallis hybrid 'Frans Hals'
Day Lily / fam. *Liliaceae*
◐ ⊗ ⊙ ⓨ
July–August. Yellow / red. H 1 m (3 ft).
A 50 cm (20 in). S fertile soil. P division.
Vigorous plant with striking flowers in an
unusual shade. Long flowering.

Hemerocallis

Hemerocallis hybrid 'Nol Hill'
Day Lily / fam. *Liliaceae*
Ⓘ ⊗ Ⓞ Ⓨ
July–August. Pink. H 60–80 cm (24–32 in).
A 40 cm (16 in). S fertile. P division. Unusual,
soft shade of pink. Not very strong but very
attractive in combinations. Rarely seen.

Hemerocallis hybrid 'Orange Man'
Day Lily / fam. *Liliaceae*
Ⓘ ⊗ Ⓞ Ⓨ
July–August. Orange-red. H 60–80 cm (24–
32 in). A 40 cm (16 in). S fertile soil. P division.
Masses of large flowers into September.
Suitable for growing under shrubs.

Hemerocallis hybrid 'Patricia Fay'
Day Lily / fam. *Liliaceae*
Ⓘ ⊗ Ⓞ Ⓨ
July–August. Pink. H 60–80 cm (24–32 in).
A 40 cm (16 in). S fertile. P seed, division.
New cultivar in what has become a favourite
colour.

Hemerocallis hybrid 'Sammy Russell'
Day Lily / fam. *Liliaceae*
Ⓘ ⊗ Ⓞ Ⓨ
July–August. Red. H 80 cm (32 in). A 40 cm
(16 in). S fertile. P division. An obvious
partner for purple-violet hostas.

Hemerocallis hybrid 'Tejas'
Day Lily / fam. *Liliaceae*
Ⓘ ⊗ Ⓞ Ⓨ
July–August. Yellow. H 120 cm (4 ft). A 60 cm
(2 ft). S fertile. P division, seed. Masses of
large, soft yellow flowers. A strong and
popular hybrid.

Hemerocallis lilio-asphodelus (H. flava)
Day Lily / fam. *Liliaceae*
Ⓘ ⊗ Ⓞ Ⓨ ⊗
May–June. Yellow. H 80 cm (32 in). A 40 cm
(16 in). S fertile. P division, seed. Strong,
decorative plant with lanceolate leaves and
beautifully scented flowers. Suitable for
naturalising.

Hepatica nobilis (H. triloba)
fam. *Ranunculaceae*
Ⓘ ⊗ ⊗ Ⓨ
March–April. Violet. H 10 cm (4 in). A 10 cm
(4 in). S fertile soil. P division, seed. Rare
plant with liver-coloured leaves. Suitable for
planting in a woody spot.

Heracleum mantegazzianum
Giant Hogweed / fam. *Umbelliferae*
Ⓘ Ⓘ ⊗ ☉ Ⓨ Ⓞ ⊕ ⊗
Sow in seed bed in July. Plant out in late
September at A 2 m (6 ft). H 3 m (10 ft). White.
S fertile soil. Splendid specimen plant: very
large lobate, deeply divided leaves and hairy
stems.

Hesperis dinarica
fam. *Cruciferae*
Ⓘ ☉ Ⓞ Ⓨ ⊗
May–June. Violet. H 50–80 cm (20–32 in).
A 40 cm (16 in). S fertile, light. P division,
seed. Night-scented flowers. Perennial often
grown as a biennial.

Hesperis matronalis
Damask Violet / fam. *Cruciferae*
◑ ☉ ⓨ ⊗
Sow in June in a seed bed. Plant out in late
September at A 45 cm (18 in). H 1 m (3 ft).
White, mauve. S fertile. Only species of
horticultural importance. Night scented.

Heuchera hybrid 'Huntsman'
fam. *Saxifragaceae*
◑ ◓ ⓨ ⊗
May–July. Red. H 60 cm (2 ft). A 30 cm (1 ft).
S normal garden soil. P division. Rewarding
plant with clusters of round leaves and
flowers in panicles.

Heuchera sanguinea 'Splendens'
fam. *Saxifragaceae*
◑ ◓ ◔ ◓ ⊗
May–July. Red. H 50 cm (20 in). A 30 cm (1 ft).
S normal. P division. Excellent for the border,
blending well with blue and grey plants.
Stays in bloom for a considerable time.

**× *Heucherella* × *tiarelloides* (*Heuchera* ×
Tiarella)** / fam. *Saxifragaceae*
◑ ◒ ◔ ⓨ ⊗
May–June. Pink. H 20–30 cm (8–12 in).
A 30 cm (1 ft). S normal garden soil.
P division. Masses of flowers and round,
heart-shaped leaves. Long lived.

Hibiscus moscheutos
fam. *Malvaceae*
○ ◒ ◔ ◔ ⓨ
August–October. Rose-purple. H 1–2 m (3–
6 ft). A 80 cm (32 in). S chalky loam. P cuttings
(summer). Hardy perennial usually grown as
an annual. Does well in mild regions.

Hibiscus syriacus 'Coelestis'
fam. *Malvaceae*
○ ◔ ◍ ⓨ ⊕
August–September. Blue. H 3 m (10 ft). W 2 m
(6 ft). Zone 5. S fertile garden soil. P cuttings.
Multi-branched shrub with erect stems.
Flowers borne singly in leaf axils.

Hibiscus syriacus 'Hamabo'
fam. *Malvaceae*
○ ◔ ◍ ⓨ ⊕
August–September. Pink. H 3 m (10 ft). W 2 m
(6 ft). Zone 5. S fertile soil. P cuttings. Multi-
branched shrub with ascending stems. Large
flowers borne singly in the leaf axils.

Hibiscus syriacus 'Rubis'
fam. *Malvaceae*
○ ◔ ◍ ⓨ ⊕
August–September. Pale ruby. H 3 m (10 ft).
W 2 m (6 ft). Zone 5. S fertile soil. P cuttings.
Multi-branched, low-growing shrub with
ascending stems. Comes into leaf fairly late
in the year.

Hibiscus trionum
Flower-of-an-Hour / fam. *Malvaceae*
○ ☉ ⓨ
July–September. Sow in April in a cold frame.
Plant out at A 30 cm (1 ft). H 40–60 cm (16–
24 in). Yellow / black. S normal garden soil.
Easily cultivated in good summers.

Hieracium aurantiacum
Hawkweed / fam. *Compositae*
○ ◑ ⊖ ⊘ ⊗ ⊛
June–August. Orange. H 40 cm (16 in).
A 20 cm (8 in). S any garden soil. P division,
seed. Long leafless stems and rosette-like
basal leaves. Invasive creeper.

Hieracium × rubrum
fam. *Compositae*
○ ◑ ⊖ ⊘ ⊗ ⊛
June–August. Orange-red. H 20 cm (8 in).
A 20 cm (8 in). S not critical. P division.
Hybrid with hairy leaves and very bright
flowers. Robust and easily kept in check.

Hippophaë rhamnoides
Sea Buckthorn / fam. *Elaeagnaceae*
○ ◑ ⊕ ⊘ ⊛ ⊛ ⊗
March–April. Greeny yellow. H 3 m (10 ft).
W 3 m (10 ft). Zone 3. S not critical. P seed.
Dense, dioecious shrub with sharp spines.
The flowers come out before the leaves.

Hippuris vulgaris
Mare's Tail / fam. *Hippuridaceae*
○ ≋ ◉ ⊘
July–August. Green. H 30 cm (1 ft). A 30 cm
(1 ft). S clay, or standard potting compost.
P seed, division. Leaves in whorls. Fast-
growing water and marsh plant.

Holcus lanatus 'Albovariegatus'
Yorkshire Fog / fam. *Gramineae*
○ ◑ ⊛ ⊛ ⊗
June–August. White / violet. H 30–90 cm (1–
3 ft). A 25 cm (10 in). S not critical. P division.
A very strong mat-forming grass with flowers
in attractive, loose spikelets. Hairy leaves.

Holodiscus discolor (Spiraea discolor)
fam. *Rosaceae*
○ ◑ ⊛ ⊛ ⊛ ⊛ ⊕
July–August. Creamy white. H 4 m (13 ft).
W 2.5 m (8 ft). Zone 5. S not critical. P cuttings,
layering. Stout shrub with arching branches
and flowers in large panicles.

Holodiscus discolor var. *discolor*
fam. *Rosaceae*
○ ◑ ⊛ ⊛ ⊛ ⊛ ⊕
July–August. White. H 4 m (13 ft). W 3 m
(10 ft). Zone 5. S humus-rich. P cuttings. Stout
shrub with overhanging branches, ovate and
lobed leaves and flowers in large panicles.

Holodiscus dumosus (Spiraea dumosa)
fam. *Rosaceae*
○ ◑ ⊛ ⊛ ⊛ ⊛ ⊕
July–August. White. H 1 m (3 ft). W 2 m (6 ft).
Zone 5. S humus-rich. P cuttings. Fairly rare
species with slightly more upright panicles
than most others. Stems almost prostrate.

Hordeum jubatum
Squirrel-tail Grass / fam. *Gramineae*
○ ○ ⊙ ⊛ ⊗
Sow in April and thin out to A 20 cm (8 in).
H 40–70 cm (16–28 in). Green. S normal
garden soil. Attractive grass grown for its
inflorescences. Also suitable for dried
arrangements.

Hosta albo-marginata (H. sieboldii)
Plantain Lily / fam. *Liliaceae*
① ⑩ ⊛ ○ ⊗ ⊘ ⊖
July–September. Purple. H 40 cm (16 in).
A 20 cm (8 in). S fertile garden soil. P division,
seed. From Japan. Cultivars grown from seed
do not come true.

Hosta capitata 'Nakaiamo'
Plantain Lily / fam. *Liliaceae*
① ⑩ ⊛ ○ ⊗ ⊘ ⊖
June–August. Violet. H 50–75 cm (20–30 in). A
30–40 cm (12–16 in). S fertile. P division.
Fairly unusual cultivar from Japan with
attractively grooved leaves.

Hosta decorata 'Betsy King'
Plantain Lily / fam. *Liliaceae*
① ⑩ ⊛ ○ ⊗ ⊘ ⊖
July–August. Purple-violet. H 50–75 cm (20–
30 in). A 30–40 cm (12–16 in). S fertile.
P division. Probably the garden variety with
the most profuse show of flowers.

Hosta × fortunei 'Obscura'
Plantain Lily / fam. *Liliaceae*
① ⑩ ⊛ ○ ⊗ ⊘ ⊖
July–August. Violet. H 60–80 cm (24–32 in).
A 50 cm (20 in). S fertile garden soil.
P division. Very large leaves. Grows
vigorously and makes a massive impression.
Very strong.

Hosta lancifolia 'Albo-Marginata'
Plantain Lily / fam. *Liliaceae*
① ⑩ ⊛ ◌ ○ ⊗ ⊘ ⊖
July–August. Purple-violet. H 50 cm (20 in).
A 30–40 cm (12–16 in). S fertile. P division.
Oblong, glossy leaves with a white edge.
Produces 15 to 20 racemes a year.

Hosta sieboldiana 'Glauca' (H. glauca)
Plantain Lily / fam. *Liliaceae*
① ⑩ ⊛ ○ ⊗ ⊘ ⊖
June–July. Off-white. H 60–80 cm (24–32 in).
A 40–60 cm (16–24 in). S fertile. P division.
Hostas with the most attractive grey-green
leaves but with less appealing flowers.
Sturdy.

Hosta × undulata 'Univittata'
Plantain Lily / fam. *Liliaceae*
① ⑩ ⊛ ○ ⊗ ⊘ ⊖
July–September. Violet. H 30–50 cm (12–
20 in). A 20–30 cm (8–12 in). S fertile garden
soil. P division. Long flower stems. Leaves
have wavy margins and are glossy
underneath. Slow growing.

Hosta ventricosa 'Aureomaculata'
Plantain Lily / fam. *Liliaceae*
① ⑩ ⊛ ○ ⊗ ⊘ ⊖
July–August. Violet. H 60–100 cm (2–3 ft).
A 50 cm (20 in). S normal. P division. Glossy,
wide, heart-shaped leaves, finely variegated
with yellow. Bell-shaped flowers.

Houstonia caerulea (Hedyotis caerulea)
Bluets / fam. *Rubiaceae*
① ⊛ ○ ⊗ ⊖
May–June. Violet-blue. H 20 cm (8 in). A 10–
20 cm (4–8 in). S moist. P division, seed.
Forms bright green carpets of leaves
completely covered in blooms during the
flowering season.

223

Humulus lupulus
Hop / fam. ***Moraceae***
◯ ◑ ◐ ⊛
July–August. Yellow-green. H 5 m (16 ft).
A 2 m (6 ft). S not critical. Attractive, vigorous,
native dioecious climber. Cone-shaped fruits.

Hutchinsia alpina ssp. ***alpina***
fam. ***Cruciferae***
◯ ◑ ◐ ◇ ⊛ ⊝
May–June. White. H 5–10 cm (2–4 in). A 10–
20 cm (4–8 in). S chalky. P division, seed.
From the Alps and Pyrenees. Spreads
vigorously. Protected plant. Moist soil.

Hyacinthus orientalis 'Amethyst'
Common Hyacinth / fam. ***Liliaceae***
◯ ◑ ◐ ◇ ⊛ ⊗ ⊚
April–May. Lilac-mauve. H 20–30 cm (8–
12 in). A 10–15 cm (4–6 in). D 5–10 cm (2–4 in).
S normal garden soil. P offsets. Remove dead
stalks and foliage after flowering season.

Hyacinthus orientalis 'Blue Giant'
Common Hyacinth / fam. ***Liliaceae***
◯ ◑ ◐ ◇ ◈ ⊛ ⊗ ⊚
April–May. Violet. H 20–30 cm (8–12 in).
A 10–15 cm (4–6 in). D 5–10 cm (2–4 in).
S normal garden soil. P offsets. Best planted
in October–November. Do not use fresh
manure.

Hydrangea anomala ssp. ***petiolaris***
fam. ***Saxifragaceae***
◑ ◐ ◎ ◈ ⊛ ⊚
July. White. H 7 m (23 ft). W 5 m (16 ft). Zone
4. S humus-rich. P cuttings. Vigorous
climbing shrub which clings to moist walls.
Browny-red branches.

Hydrangea aspera ssp. ***sargentiana***
fam. ***Saxifragaceae***
◯ ◑ ◐ ◎ ◈ ⊛ ⊚ ⊕ ⊖ ⊗
July–August. Violet. H 2 m (6 ft). W 2 m (6 ft).
Zone 5–6. S humus-rich. P cuttings. Fast-
growing, erect plant with downy ovate leaves
and white, sterile outer florets.

Hydrangea heteromalla (*H. bretschneideri*)
fam. ***Saxifragaceae***
◯ ◑ ◐ ◎ ◈ ⊛ ⊚ ⊕
June–July. Reddish purple. H 3 m (10 ft).
W 3 m (10 ft). Zone 5. S humus-rich, acid.
P cuttings. Less well known but attractive
hydrangea with a fine show of colour.

Hydrangea macrophylla
fam. ***Saxifragaceae***
◯ ◑ ◐ ◎ ◇ ◈ ⊛ ⊚ ⊗
June–September. Pink to blue. H 2 m (6 ft).
W 2 m (6 ft). Zone 5–6. S humus-rich, acid.
P cuttings. Colour of flowers varies with iron
content of soil. Can also be grown indoors.

Hydrangea macrophylla 'Bouquet Rose'
fam. ***Saxifragaceae***
◯ ◑ ◐ ◎ ◇ ◈ ◉ ⊛ ⊚
June–September. Pink. H 1.25 m (4 ft). W 1 m
(3 ft). Zone 5–6. S humus-rich. P cuttings.
Rounded shrub with broadly ovate, toothed
leaves and flowers in characteristic round
corymbs ('mopheads').

Hydrangea macrophylla **'Lilacina'**
fam. ***Saxifragaceae***
June–September. Lilac. H 1.5 m (5 ft). W 2 m (6 ft). Zone 5–6. S humus-rich. P cuttings. Good example of the Lacecap group of hydrangeas. Outer florets are pink.

Hydrangea macrophylla **ssp.** ***serrata***
fam. ***Saxifragaceae***
July–August. Mauve. H 1 m (3 ft). W 1 m (3 ft). Zone 5–6. S humus-rich. P cuttings. Erect shrub with thin stems and flat corymbs. Large outer florets.

Hydrangea paniculata
fam. ***Saxifragaceae***
July–August. White. H 4.5 m (15 ft). W 4.5 m (15 ft). Zone 4. S humus-rich. P cuttings. Upright shrub with flowers in large pyramidal panicles turning pale pink.

Hydrangea paniculata **'Grandiflora'**
fam. ***Saxifragaceae***
July–August. White. H 4.5 m (15 ft). W 4.5 m (15 ft). Zone 4. S humus-rich. P cuttings. Erect shrub with flowers in massive panicles. The outer florets change colour after flowering.

Hydrangea paniculata **'Praecox'**
fam. ***Saxifragaceae***
June–July. White. H 4.5 m (15 ft). W 4.5 m (15 ft). Zone 4. S humus-rich. P cuttings. Upright shrub with flowers in shorter and looser panicles. Large outer florets.

Hydrocharis morsus-ranae
Frog-bit / fam. ***Hydrocharitaceae***
July–August. White. H 5 cm (2 in). A 20 cm (8 in). Floating aquatic plant. Buds overwinter at the bottom. It is important to provide enough soil in the pool.

Hypericum calycinum
Rose of Sharon / fam. ***Guttiferae***
July–September. Yellow. H 45 cm (18 in). W 120 cm (4 ft). Zone 5. S humus-rich. P division, cuttings. Prostrate shrub which forms a dense carpet. Dark green leaves. Flowers borne singly.

Hypericum hookeranum **'Hidcote'**
St John's Wort / fam. ***Guttiferae***
July–September. Yellow. H 2 m (6 ft). W 2 m (6 ft). Zone 5. S humus-rich. P cuttings. A particularly useful, frost-resistant hybrid with blue-green leaves and large flowers.

Hypericum **×** ***inodorum*** **'Elstead'**
St John's Wort / fam. ***Guttiferae***
July–August. Yellow. H 1 m (3 ft). W 1 m (3 ft). Zone 5. S fertile, humus-rich. P cuttings. Dense, upright semi-hardy shrub with angular shoots. Attractive red fruits follow the flowers.

Hypericum

Hypericum × inodorum 'Goudelsje'
St John's Wort / fam. *Guttiferae*
○ ◑ ⊘ ⌃ ⌂ ⊛
July–August. Yellow. H 1 m (3 ft). W 2 m (6 ft).
Zone 5. S fertile and humus-rich. P cuttings.
Dense shrub of erect habit. Calyx turns black.

Hypericum × moseranum
St John's Wort / fam. *Guttiferae*
○ ◑ ⊘ ⌃ ⌂ ⊛
July–August. Yellow. H 60 cm (2 ft). W 120 cm
(4 ft). Zone 6. S humus-rich. P cuttings. Wide-
spreading shrub, semi-hardy. Large flowers
in clusters. Angular shoots.

Hyssopus officinalis
Hyssop / fam. *Labiatae*
○ ◑ ⌂ ⊗ ⌀
June–September. Purple-blue. H 45 cm (18 in).
W 50 cm (20 in). S normal garden soil. P seed.
Partly evergreen shrub with aromatic leaves.
Grown as a low hedge or as a culinary herb.

Hypericum olympicum
St John's Wort / fam. *Guttiferae*
○ ⊖ ⊜ ⌃ ⌂ ⊗ ⊟
June–July. Yellow. H 10–20 cm (4–8 in). A 10–
20 cm (4–8 in). S normal garden soil.
P division, seed. Erect stems and small bright
green leaves. Flowers in profusion. Rock
plant.

Iberis amara (I. coronaria)
Candytuft / fam. *Cruciferae*
○ ⊙ ⌂
Sow in February in a heated greenhouse or
March–April outside. Thin / plant out at A
15 cm (6 in). H 30 cm (1 ft). Red-purple.
S normal garden soil. Fragrant flowers.
Suitable for the border.

Iberis amara 'Iceberg'
Candytuft / fam. *Cruciferae*
○ ⊙ ⌂
Sow in February in a heated greenhouse or
March–April outside. Thin / plant out at
A 15 cm (6 in). H 30 cm (1 ft). White. S normal
garden soil. Flowers look askew because two
petals are large.

Iberis sempervirens 'Snowflake'
Candytuft / fam. *Cruciferae*
○ ⊖ ⊜ ⌃ ⌂ ⌂ ⊗ ⊗ ⊟
May–June. White. H 30 cm (1 ft). A 20 cm
(8 in). S chalky. P division. Free-flowering
semi-shrub. Cut back slightly immediately
after flowering period. Evergreen.

Iberis umbellata 'Pumila'
Candytuft / fam. *Cruciferae*
○ ⊙ ⌂
Sow in February in a heated greenhouse or
in March–April outside. Thin / plant out at
A 20 cm (8 in). H 40 cm (16 in). Red-purple,
violet, white. S normal garden soil. Flowers
in umbels.

Ilex × altaclarensis 'Camelliaefolia'
Holly / fam. *Aquifoliaceae*
○ ◑ ⊕ ⌃ ◉ ⌂ ⊛ ⌂ ⊛ ⊘ ⊖ ⊞ ⊗
April–May. White. H 7 m (23 ft). W 4 m (13 ft).
Zone 6. S humus-rich. P cuttings, layering.
Broadly erect, more or less pyramidal shrub
or small tree with glossy dark green leaves.

226

Ilex × altaclarensis 'Golden King'
Holly / fam. *Aquifoliaceae*
○ ◐ ➤ ⟐ ❋ ⊛ ❀ ⊛ ☺ ⊕ ▥ ⊗
April–May. White. H 8 m (26 ft). W 4 m (13 ft).
Zone 6. S humus-rich. P cuttings, layering.
Broad, slightly pyramidal shrub with fairly
large and broad golden-edged leaves.

Ilex aquifolium 'Argentea Longifolia'
Common Holly / fam. *Aquifoliaceae*
○ ◐ ➤ ⟐ ❋ ⊛ ❀ ⊛ ☺ ⊕ ▥ ⊗
May–June. White. H 8 m (26 ft). W 5 m (16 ft).
Zone 6. S humus-rich. P cuttings, layering,
grafting. Small trees or robust shrub with
toothed, white-edged leaves and red berries.
Monoecious.

Ilex aquifolium 'J. C. van Tol'
Common Holly / fam. *Aquifoliaceae*
○ ◐ ▥ ➤ ⟐ ❋ ⊛ ❀ ⊛ ☺ ⊕ ▥ ⊗
May–June. Green. H 5 m (16 ft). W 3 m (10 ft).
Zone 5. S humus-rich. P cuttings, layering,
grafting. Small tree or stout shrub with glossy
green, not very serrate leaves and masses of
red berries.

Ilex crenata 'Golden Gem'
Japanese Holly / fam. *Aquifoliaceae*
○ ◐ ▥ ➤ ⟐ ❀ ⊛ ☺ ⊗
May–June. Green. H 80 cm (32 in). W 150 cm
(5 ft). Zone 6. S humus-rich. P cuttings,
grafting, layering. Densely branched,
handsome shrub with golden leaves and
black berries.

Ilex verticillata
Black Alder / fam. *Aquifoliaceae*
○ ◐ ▥ ➤ ⟐ ⊛ ☺ ⊕ ⊗
June–July. Greeny white. H 3 m (10 ft). W 3 m
(10 ft). Zone 3. S humus-rich. P seed, cuttings,
layering. Attractive dioecious and deciduous
densely branched shrub with bright red
berries.

Impatiens balsamina 'Cinnabar'
Balsam / fam. *Balsaminaceae*
◐ ☺ ⊗
Sow in March in heated greenhouse or in
April outside. Thin / plant out at A 25 cm
(10 in). H 50 cm (20 in). S fertile. 'Bushflower'
type in which flowers are borne on the upper
leaves.

Impatiens balsamina 'Harlequin'
Busy Lizzie / fam. *Balsaminaceae*
◐ ☺ ⊗
Sow in March in a heated greenhouse or in
April outside. Thin / plant out at A 30 cm
(1 ft). H 30 cm (1 ft). Red / white. S fertile. One
of many two-coloured hybrids suitable for
bedding.

Impatiens balsamina 'Super Elfin Orchid'
Balsam / fam. *Balsaminaceae*
◐ ☺ ⊗
Sow in March in a heated greenhouse or in
April outside. Thin / plant out at A 30 cm
(1 ft). H 30 cm (1 ft). Purple-violet. S fertile.
Hybrid with large flowers which come out
very early.

Impatiens balsamina 'Tom Thumb Purple'
Balsam / fam. *Balsaminaceae*
◐ ☺ ⊗
Sow in March in a heated greenhouse or in
April outside. Thin / plant out at A 40 cm
(16 in). H 25 cm (10 in). Purple. S fertile.
Cultivar with masses of large double flowers.
Compact habit.

Impatiens

Impatiens glandulifera /Himalayan
Touch-me-not/fam. ***Balsaminaceae***
○ ◐ ○ ⦸
Sow in March in a heated greenhouse or in
April outside. Thin/plant out at A 25 cm
(10 in). H 75 cm (30 in). Various colours.
S fertile. Fleshy, erect plant with succulent
stems and a mass of flowers.

Incarvillea delavayi
Chinese Trumpet Flower/fam. ***Bignoniaceae***
○ ⌃ ○ ⓨ ⦸
June–July. Rich rose-pink. H 60 cm (2 ft).
A 35 cm (14 in). S fertile, well drained.
P division, seed. Thick, fleshy roots. Difficult
to cultivate. Cover well in winter.

Incarvillea mairei var. ***grandiflora***
Chinese Trumpet Flower/fam. ***Bignoniaceae***
○ ◐ ⌃ ○ ⓨ ⦸
May–June. Red. H 15–30 cm (6–12 in). A 20–
30 cm (8–12 in). S fertile and well drained.
P division, seed. Flowers set off well by the
pleated leaves. From West China and Tibet.

Indigofera amblyantha
fam. ***Leguminosae***
○ ◐ ⌃ ⧈ ⓨ
July–October. Pink. H 1.5 m (5 ft). W 1.25 m
(4 ft). Zone 5. S normal garden soil. P seed,
cuttings. Shrub with angular young stems
covered in white hairs. Flowers in dense
clusters.

Indigofera gerardiana (I. dosua)
fam. ***Leguminosae***
○ ◐ ⌃ ⧈ ⓨ
July–August. Pink. H 2 m (6 ft). W 1.5 m (5 ft).
Zone 5. S normal garden soil. P seed, cuttings.
Attractive flowering shrub with unevenly
pinnate leaves and flowers in long, dense
racemes.

Indigofera kirilowii
fam. ***Leguminosae***
○ ◐ ⧈ ⓨ
June. Rose-purple. H 1 m (3 ft). W 2 m (6 ft).
Zone 4. S normal garden soil. P seed, cuttings.
Shrub, densely covered in downy leaves.
Flowers in fairly dense clusters.

***Inula ensifolia* 'Compacta'**
fam. ***Compositae***
○ ⊜ ○ ⓨ ⊗
July–August. Yellow. H 20 cm (8 in). A 20 cm
(8 in). S chalky. P division. Attractive bushy
plant for the front of the border or the rock
garden. Attractive flower heads.

Inula magnifica
fam. ***Compositae***
○ ○ ⓨ ⊗
July–August. Yellow. H 150–180 cm (5–6 ft).
A 80 cm (32 in). S normal. P division, seed.
Robust plant for the border. The wide flowers
open in a characteristic manner. Stout stems.

Inula orientalis (I. glandulosa)
fam. ***Compositae***
○ ○ ⓨ ⊗
July–August. Yellow H 50–70 cm (20–28 in).
A 60 cm (2 ft). S normal garden soil.
P division, seed. Large flower heads, 10–
12 cm (4–5 in) across. Short flowering period.

Ipheion uniflorum
fam. *Liliaceae*
○ ⊕ ⊘ ⊗
February–April. Violet. H 10 cm (4 in). A 6–
8 cm (2¼–3 in). D 3–5 cm (1–2 in). S normal
garden soil. P offsets. Flowers open in sunny
weather and close up when it rains.

Ipomoea tricolor (I. rubrocaerulea)
Morning Glory / fam. *Convolvulaceae*
○ ⊙ ⊘
Sow in March in a heated greenhouse or in
May outside. Thin / plant out at A 30 cm (1 ft).
H 3 m (10 ft). Violet-blue. S fertile. Not
particularly strong climber with a profusion
of fast-fading flowers.

Ipomopsis rubra (I. elegans, Gilia rubra)
fam. *Polemoniaceae*
○ ⊙ ⊘ ⊗
Sow in February in a heated greenhouse or
in June in a cold greenhouse. Plant out at
A 25 cm (10 in). H 90 cm (3 ft). Red. S humus-
rich. Comes into full bloom in July. Elegant
stems; flowers trumpet shaped.

Iris aphylla (I. nudicaulis)
fam. *Iridaceae*
○ ⊘ ⊛ ⊘ ⊗
May. Purple. H 30–40 cm (12–16 in). A 20 cm
(8 in). S chalky, dry. P division. Richly
flowering, attractive form. The sword-shaped
leaves die off after the flowering period.

Iris bucharica
fam. *Iridaceae*
○ ⊜ ⊛ ⊘ ⊗
March–April. Creamy white. H 45 cm (18 in).
A 15 cm (6 in). D 5 cm (2 in). S humus-rich,
chalky. P division. Bulbous iris with leafy
stems and flowers in the leaf axils. Hardy.

Iris chamaeiris
fam. *Iridaceae*
○ ⊙ ⊛ ⊘ ⊗
April–May. Purple. H 15–25 cm (6–10 in).
A 15 cm (6 in). S chalky, dry. P division.
Dwarf bearded iris resembling *I. pumila* but
more robust. From South-east France and
Italy.

Iris danfordiae
fam. *Iridaceae*
○ ⊜ ⊛ ⊘ ⊗
March. Yellow. H 15 cm (6 in). A 5–7 cm (2–
2¾ in). D 5–10 cm (2–4 in). S chalky.
P division. Very early iris with a magnificent
fragrance. Particularly suitable for the rock
garden.

Iris foetidissima
fam. *Iridaceae*
○ ⊕ ⊛ ⊛ ⊗
June. Yellowish-green / lilac. H 80–100 cm
(32–36 in). A 40 cm (16 in). S moist. P division
of rhizomes. Most attractive orange-red seeds.
Leaves give off a rank smell when bruised.

Iris germanica hybrid 'Radiant Apogee'
fam. *Iridaceae*
○ ⊜ ⊛ ⊘ ⊗
May–June. Yellow / white. H 70 cm (28 in).
A 30 cm (1 ft). S dry, chalky. P division. This
cultivar is one of the intermediate bearded
irises which come in hundreds of varieties.

Iris

Iris germanica hybrid 'Rippling Waters'
fam. *Iridaceae*

○ ⊖ ⊛ ⊛ ⊛

May–June. Violet. H 80 cm (32 in). A 30 cm
(1 ft). S dry, chalky. P division. The leaves of
bearded irises must be kept as dry as
possible, especially winter, or plants will rot.

Iris germanica 'Stepping Out'
fam. *Iridaceae*

○ ⊖ ⊛ ⊛ ⊛

May–June. Purple / white. H 80 cm (32 in).
A 30 cm (1 ft). S dry, chalky. P division. A
particularly robust hybrid from the USA in a
striking colour combination. Dress the soil
well.

Iris germanica 'White Lightning'
fam. *Iridaceae*

○ ⊖ ⊛ ⊛ ⊛

May–June. White. H 80 cm (32 in). A 30 cm
(1 ft). S dry, chalky. P division. Lift every
three years in August and replant outermost
parts of the rhizome.

Iris hollandica hybrid 'Exotic Beauty'
fam. *Iridaceae*

○ ◧ ⊛ ⊛ ⊛ ⊛

May. Various colours. H 70–80 cm (28–32 in).
A 10–12 cm (4–5 in). D 10–15 cm (4–6 in).
S fertile. P offsets. Bulbous irises will last
longer if lifted and kept for a time after
flowering.

Iris hollandica hybrid 'Telstar'
fam. *Iridaceae*

○ ◧ ⊛ ⊛ ⊛ ⊛

May. Various colours. H 70–80 cm (28–32 in).
A 10–12 cm (4–5 in). D 10–15 cm (4–6 in).
S fertile soil. P offsets. Plant in autumn. Cover
thickly to protect from frost. Excellent for
cutting.

Iris kaempferi hybrid
fam. *Iridaceae*

○ ◧ ⊛ ⊛ ⊛ ⊛

July–August. Various colours. H 60–100 cm
(2–3 ft). A 30 cm (1 ft). D 20 cm (8 in). S acid
and fertile. P division. In containers, keep in
5 cm (2 in) water in spring, dry after flowering
and heel in for winter.

Iris pseudacorus
fam. *Iridaceae*

○ ◧ ⊛ ⊛ ⊛ ⊛

May–June. Yellow. H 80–100 cm (32–36 in).
A 40 cm (16 in). S not critical. P division, seed.
Outstanding for shallow pools. Plant at water
depth of about 20 cm (8 in). Very vigorous.

Iris pseudacorus 'Variegata'
fam. *Iridaceae*

○ ◧ ⊛ ⊛ ⊛ ⊛

May–June. Yellow. H 60 cm (2 ft). A 30 cm
(1 ft). S not critical. Leaves lightly striped. For
banks or shallow ponds – 20 cm (8 in). Good
contrast effect.

Iris pumila 'Tonya'
fam. *Iridaceae*

○ ⊛ ⊛ ⊛

April–May. Purple / violet. H 10–15 cm (4–
6 in). A 10 cm (4 in). S chalky, well drained.
P division. Good rock and edging plant.
Grows wild in South-east Europe (protected
plant).

Iris regeliocyclus hybrids
fam. *Iridaceae*
○ ◑ ⊖ ⌢ ◉ ⑲ ⊗
May–June. Various colours. H 80 cm (32 in).
A 40 cm (16 in). D 10 cm (4 in). S fertile.
P division. Attractive crosses between *Regelia*
and *Onocyclus* groups. Lift in July and store
in a dry place.

Iris reticulata
fam. *Iridaceae*
○ ◑ ⊖ ⌢ ◉ ⑲ ⊗
March–April. Various colours. H 15 cm (6 in).
A 5–7 cm (2–2¾ in). D 7 cm (2¾ in). S normal
garden soil. P cuttings. Also suitable for
balconies, tubs, naturalisation and as a border
plant.

Iris sanguinea (I. orientalis)
fam. *Iridaceae*
○ ◑ ⊖ ◉ ⑲ ⊗
May–June. Purple. H 60 cm (2 ft). A 30 cm
(1 ft). S moist, acid. P division. Resembles *I.
sibirica* but has larger flowers in groups of two
or three and is shorter.

Iris sibirica
fam. *Iridaceae*
○ ◑ ⊗ ⌢ ◉ ⑲ ⊗
June. Blue. H 70–100 cm (28–36 in). A 40 cm
(16 in). S moist, acid. P division. Tall plant
with hollow stems and slender leaves which
turn brown in autumn.

Iris sibirica 'Blue King'
fam. *Iridaceae*
○ ◑ ⊖ ⌢ ◉ ⑲ ⊗
June. Royal blue. H 70–100 cm (28–36 in).
A 40 cm (16 in). S moist, acid. P division.
Thrives along the edge of ponds but also does
well in drier soil. Hardy.

Iris xiphioides 'King of the Blues'
fam. *Iridaceae*
○ ◑ ⌢ ◉ ⑲ ⊗
June–July. Purple. H 50 cm (20 in). A 10 cm
(4 in). D 10–12 cm (4–6 in). S fertile. P offsets.
English iris, not very robust. Plant early (in
August) and cover well in the winter.

Ixia hybrid
fam. *Iridaceae*
○ ⌢ ⊗ ◉ ⑲ ⊗
June. Various colours. H 45 cm (18 in). A 2–
5 cm (¾–2 in). D 5–10 cm (2–4 in). S normal
garden soil. P offsets. Plant the corms in
November–December. Cover with a thick
layer of straw.

Ixiolirion tataricum
fam. *Amaryllidaceae*
○ ⌢ ◉ ⑲ ⊗
June. Lavender. H 30–45 cm (12–18 in). A 7–
10 cm (2¾–4 in). D 5–7 cm (2–2¾ in). S normal
garden soil. Bulbous plant suitable for a
border. The flowers measure 5 cm (2 in).

Jasione laevis (J. perennis)
fam. *Campanulaceae*
○ ◑ ⊖ ◉ ◉ ⊗
July–August. Blue. H 30 cm (1 ft). A 20 cm
(8 in). S chalky. P division, seed. Attractive
rock plant from Central Europe and the
Balkans. Easily cultivated: thrives on poor
soil.

231

Jasminum

Jasminum mesnyi (J. primulinum)
Jasmine / fam. *Oleaceae*
○◐◖△◍☾◉❋
March–April. Yellow. H 3 m (10 ft). W 3 m
(10 ft). Zone 8. S normal garden soil. P seed,
cuttings, layering. Broad and dense shrub
with glossy dark green leaves and singly
borne flowers.

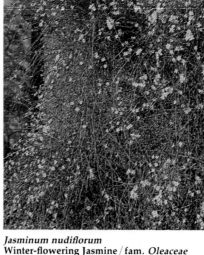

Jasminum nudiflorum
Winter-flowering Jasmine / fam. *Oleaceae*
○◐❋◍☾◉⊗
December–February. Yellow. H 3 m (10 ft).
W 2 m (6 ft). Zone 5. S normal garden soil.
P seed, cuttings, layering. Climbing shrub
needing support. Limp green twigs. For
training on walls.

Jovibarba heuffelii (Sempervivum heuffelii)
Houseleek / fam. *Crassulaceae*
○⊜◉☾◉⊗
July–August. Yellow. H 15 cm (6 in). A 10 cm
(4 in). S chalky. P seed, division. The rosettes
are 5–7 cm (2–2¾ in) wide and divide. From
South-east Europe.

Juglans cinerea
Butternut / fam. *Juglandaceae*
○◐✿❀⊛❀⊕
May. Green H 25 m (80 ft). W 20 m (65 ft). Zone
3. S fertile. P seed. Fairly slow-growing tree
with a wide-spreading crown and oblong
nuts on hairy stalks.

Juniperus chinensis 'Blaauw'
Chinese Juniper / fam. *Cupressaceae*
○◐◍◉❀◉◉⊕
Compact dwarf juniper of bushy habit.
Feathery twigs and green needles with two
white stripes. Dioecious. H 1.5 m (5 ft). W 1 m
(3 ft). S not critical. P cuttings. Zone 5.

Juniperus chinensis 'Blue and Gold'
Chinese Juniper / fam. *Cupressaceae*
○◐◍◉❀◉◉⊕
Very attractive shrub of open and loose habit.
Golden and blue-green scales and needle-
shaped leaves. H 2 m (6 ft). W 2 m (6 ft). S not
critical. P cuttings. Zone 4.

Juniperus chinensis 'Hetzii' (J. × media
'Hetzii' / Chinese Juniper / Cupressaceae
○◐◍◉❀◉◉⊕
Vigorous shrub of spreading habit. Prune
regularly to retain shape and fullness. Needs
space. H 2 m (6 ft). W 5 m (16 ft). S not critical.
P cuttings. Zone 4.

Juniperus chinensis 'Parsonii'
Chinese Juniper / fam. *Cupressaceae*
○◐◍◉❀◉◉⊕
Dwarf shrub with stiff, almost horizontal
branches covered in scales. Green leaves.
H 1 m (3 ft). W 3 m (10 ft). S not critical.
P cuttings. Zone 5–6.

Juniperus chinensis 'Pfitzeriana'
Chinese Juniper / fam. *Cupressaceae*
○◐◍◉❀◉◉⊖
Stout, spreading shrub with green leaves and
pendulous growing tips. Needs pruning.
H 2 m (6 ft). W 5 m (16 ft). S not critical.
P cuttings. Zone 4.

***Juniperus chinensis* 'Pfitzeriana Aurea'**
Chinese Juniper / fam. *Cupressaceae*
○ ◑ ⓜ ⊛ ✿ ❀ ❀ ◎ ⊖
Wide-spreading shrub with branches in flat
arrays. Yellowish needles and scales turning
bronze in the winter. H 2 m (6 ft). W 5 m (16 ft).
S not critical. P cuttings. Zone 5.

***Juniperus chinensis* 'Plumosa Aurea'**
Chinese Juniper / fam. *Cupressaceae*
○ ◑ ⓜ ⓐ ⊛ ❀ ❀ ◎
Dwarf juniper of irregular, spreading habit.
Feathery twigs and yellow-green foliage.
H 80 cm (32 in). W 2 m (6 ft). S not critical.
P cuttings. Zone 5.

***Juniperus chinensis* 'Wilson's Weeping'**
Chinese Juniper / fam. *Cupressaceae*
○ ◑ ⊛ ⓐ ⊛ ❀ ❀ ◎ ⊕
Tall, open tree with ascending branches and
pendent scaly and needle-shaped leaves
densely packed round the shoots. H 20 m
(65 ft). W 8 m (26 ft). S not critical. P cuttings.
Zone 4.

***Juniperus communis* 'Compressa'**
Common Juniper / fam. *Cupressaceae*
○ ◑ ⓜ ⊛ ⓜ ⓐ ⊛ ❀ ◎ ⊕ ⊗
Slow-growing dwarf juniper. The foliage is
entirely juvenile; awl-shaped needles with a
white stripe. H 1 m (3 ft). W 30 cm (1 ft). S not
critical. P cuttings. Zone 4.

***Juniperus communis* 'Depressa Aurea'**
Common Juniper / fam. *Cupressaceae*
○ ◑ ⓜ ⓐ ⊛ ❀ ◎
Ornamental conifer, bronze coloured in the
winter and with golden tips in the summer.
Cones have a blue bloom. Needs pruning.
H 1 m (3 ft). W 4 m (13 ft). S not critical.
P cuttings. Zone 4.

***Juniperus communis* 'Echinoformis'**
Common Juniper / fam. *Cupressaceae*
○ ◑ ⓜ ⓐ ⊛ ❀ ◎
Slow-growing, irregularly rounded dwarf
shrub with fairly thick, opposite needles.
H 30 cm (1 ft). W 60 cm (2 ft). S not critical.
P cuttings. Zone 4.

***Juniperus communis* 'Hibernica'**
Irish Juniper / fam. *Cupressaceae*
○ ◑ ⊜ ⓜ ⊛ ❀ ⊕ ⊗ ⓜ
Erect, narrowly columnar juniper with blue-
green leaves. Very popular. Needs pruning.
H 6 m (20 ft). W 2 m (6 ft). Zone 4. S not critical.
P cuttings.

Juniperus communis* var. *depressa
Common Juniper / fam. *Cupressaceae*
○ ◑ ⓜ ⓐ ⊛ ❀ ◎
Usually spreading but very variable shrub.
Upper needles are a light tan in the winter.
H 50 cm (20 in). W 10 m (4 in). S not critical.
P cuttings. Zone 4.

***Juniperus conferta* (*J. litoralis*)**
Juniper / fam. *Cupressaceae*
○ ◑ ⓜ ⓐ ⊛ ❀ ◎ ⊗ ⊖
Very strong conifer which looks most
attractive hanging over a wall. Very sharp and
prickly. Fresh green leaves. H 60 cm (2 ft).
W 4 m (13 ft). S not critical. P seed, cuttings.
Zone 5.

233

Juniperus horizontalis 'Douglasii'
Creeping Juniper / fam. *Cupressaceae*
Prostrate, strong-growing shrub with slender leaves, blue-green in the summer and violet-blue in the winter. H 50 cm (20 in). W 4–5 m (13–16 ft). S not critical. P cuttings. Zone 4.

Juniperus procumbens 'Nana'
Creeping Juniper / fam. *Cupressaceae*
Attractive flat-growing form which makes a dense mat of short, closely overlapping needles. Also suitable for bonsai. H 30 cm (1 ft). W 3 m (10 ft). S not critical. P cuttings. Zone 4.

Juniperus recurva var. *coxii*
Drooping Juniper / fam. *Cupressaceae*
Tall, pyramidal tree with gracefully arching branches. Dark greyish-purple cones. H 30 m (100 ft). W 10 m (33 ft). S not critical. P cuttings. Zone 7.

Juniperus sabina 'Musgrave'
Savin / fam. *Cupressaceae*
Conifer of low, spreading habit. Juvenile and adult foliage. Cones with a bluish bloom. H 60 cm (2 ft). W 2.5 m (8 ft). S not critical. P cuttings. Zone 4.

Juniperus sabina 'Tamariscifolia'
Savin / fam. *Cupressaceae*
Low-growing, spreading shrub with attractively overlapping branches and predominantly juvenile, pointed foliage. H 50 cm (20 in). W 4 m (13 ft). S not critical. P cuttings. Zone 5.

Juniperus squamata 'Blue Star' / Scaly-leaved
Nepal Juniper / fam. *Cupressaceae*
Attractive, spreading shrub of very graceful, rounded habit. Deep blue-grey needles. Dwarf form. H 1 m (3 ft). W 1.5 m (5 ft). S not critical. P cuttings. Zone 4.

Juniperus squamata 'Boulevard' / Scaly-leaved Nepal Juniper / fam. *Cupressaceae*
Fairly compact conifer with blue-green foliage bearing two bluish-white stripes underneath. Oval cones. H 2 m (6 ft). W 1 m (3 ft). S not critical. P cuttings. Zone 4.

Juniperus squamata 'Loderi' / Scaly-leaved Nepal Juniper / fam. *Cupressaceae*
Dense, cone-shaped shrub with juvenile foliage on all shoot tips and adult foliage everywhere else. H 3 m (10 ft). W 2 m (6 ft). S not critical. P cuttings. Zone 4.

Juniperus squamata 'Meyeri' / Scaly-leaved Nepal Juniper / fam. *Cupressaceae*
Broad, erect, bushy shrub. Older specimens must be cut back hard or they will go bald. Dense blue foliage. H 3–5 m (10–16 ft). W 2 m (6 ft). S not critical. P cuttings. Zone 4.

Juniperus squamata 'Wilsonii' / Scaly-leaved
Nepal Juniper / fam. *Cupressaceae*
Compact conical conifer which must be
pruned into shape. Awl-shaped leaves and
curving shoot tips. H 2 m (6 ft). W 1 m (3 ft).
S not critical. P cuttings. Zone 4.

Juniperus virginiana 'Glauca'
Pencil Cedar / fam. *Cupressaceae*
Columnar conifer of open habit. Young
shoots have pink-purple bark. Pale blue
scales. H 3–5 m (10–16 ft). W 1.5 m (5 ft). S not
critical. P cuttings. Zone 4.

Juniperus virginiana 'Reptans'
Pencil Cedar / fam. *Cupressaceae*
Low-growing shrub with stiff, fairly erect
branches. The scaly and awl-shaped, light
green leaves are rough to the touch. H 60 cm
(2 ft). W 2 m (6 ft). S not critical. P cuttings.
Zone 5.

Juniperus virginiana 'Skyrocket'
Pencil Cedar / fam. *Cupressaceae*
Very slender conifer with fine adult foliage.
Interesting variety, very suitable for heather
gardens. H 4 m (13 ft). W 60 cm (2 ft). S not
critical. P cuttings. Zone 5.

*Kalimeris incisa (Aster incisus, Calimeris
integrifolia)* / fam. *Compositae*
August–September. White. H 70 cm (28 in).
A 30–40 cm (12–16 in). S humus-rich, moist.
P division, seed. Wide-spreading plant which
tolerates a good deal of shade.

Kalmia angustifolia
Sheep Laurel / fam. *Ericaceae*
June–July. Rose-red. H 1 m (3 ft). W 1 m (3 ft).
Zone 2. S humus-rich. P layering, seed,
cuttings. Small shrub with erect branches and
grey-green, lanceolate leaves. Flowers in
clusters.

Kalmia latifolia
Calico Bush / fam. *Ericaceae*
May–June. Pink. H 3 m (10 ft). W 2.5 m (8 ft).
Zone 4. S humus-rich. P layering, seed,
cuttings. Shrub densely covered in glossy,
dark green leaves. Bare branches. Flowers in
large clusters.

Kerria japonica
Jew's Mallow / fam. *Rosaceae*
April–May. Yellow. H 2 m (6 ft). W 2 m (6 ft).
Zone 4. S normal garden soil. P cuttings,
division. Wide-spreading shrub with bare
green branches. Solitary double flowers.

Kerria japonica var. *simplex*
Jew's Mallow / fam. *Rosaceae*
April–May. Yellow. H 2 m (6 ft). W 2 m (6 ft).
Zone 4. S normal garden soil. P cuttings,
division. Wide-spreading shrub with arching
green shoots and single flowers.

235

Kirengeshoma

Kirengeshoma palmata
Waxbells / fam. *Saxifragaceae*
◐ ◑ ▣ ⌃ ◉ ⊕ ⊛
August–September. Yellow. H 60–100 cm (2–3 ft). A 30 cm (1 ft). S humus-rich. P seed, cuttings, division. Interesting and attractive plant with drooping flowers of waxy appearance.

Knautia dipsacifolia (K. sylvatica)
fam. *Dipsacaceae*
○ ○ ⓨ ⊗
June–August. Purple-violet. H 50–75 cm (20–30 in). A 30 cm (1 ft). S normal garden soil. P division, seed. Suitable for wild gardens, particularly with other 'wild' species from North America.

Kniphofia galpinii
Red Hot Poker / fam. *Liliaceae*
○ ⌃ ◉ ⓨ ⊗
September–October. Orange. H 50–60 cm (20–30 in). A 30 cm (1 ft). S humus-rich. P division, seed. A fairly unknown, very late-flowering species. Goes well with *Miscanthus*.

Kniphofia hybrid 'Alcazar'
Red Hot Poker / fam. *Liliaceae*
○ ⌃ ◉ ⓨ ⊗
June–August. Orange. H 90 cm (3 ft). A 40 cm (16 in). S humus-rich. P division. These plants make a good deal of growth the first year after planting. They prefer to be dry in the winter.

Kniphofia hybrid 'Shining Sceptre'
Red Hot Poker / fam. *Liliaceae*
○ ⌃ ◉ ⓨ ⊗
June–October. Yellow. H 125 cm (4 ft). A 40 cm (16 in). S humus-rich. P division. Very decorative plant with graceful grass-like leaves and a profusion of flowers.

Kniphofia hybrid 'The Rocket' ('Saturnus')
Red Hot Poker / fam. *Liliaceae*
○ ⌃ ◉ ⓨ ⊗
June–September. Red / yellow. H 1 m (3 ft). A 60 cm (2 ft). S humus-rich. P division. Profuse flowers in very large spikes; they will keep very well in water.

Kochia scoparia var. trichopylla
Burning Bush / fam. *Chenopodiaceae*
○ ☉ ⊕
Sow in March under glass or in April–May outside. Thin / plant out at 60 cm (2 ft). H 1 m (3 ft). Green. S fertile. Erect habit with bright green leaves which turn red in the autumn.

Kochia scoparia var. trichophylla 'Acapulco Silver' / Burning Bush / fam. *Chenopodiaceae*
○ ☉ ⊕
Sow in March under glass at 16°C (60°F). H 1 m (3 ft). Green. S fertile. The flowers, small, green and insignificant, are followed by a resting period.

Koeleria glauca
fam. *Gramineae*
○ ◐ ◑
June–July. Grey-blue. H 20–30 cm (8–12 in). A 20 cm (8 in). S normal. P division, seed. Does not flower every year. Modest ornamental grass, attractive only because of its blue tint.

236

Koelreuteria paniculata (fruit)
fam. *Sapindaceae*
○ ⬤ ✦ ⓨ ⓒ ⊞ ⊥
July–August. Yellow. H 5 m (16 ft). W 3 m
(10 ft). Zone 5. S fertile. P seed. Flowers in
large terminal panicles. Large bladder-shaped
green fruits.

Koelreuteria paniculata (foliage)
fam. *Sapindaceae*
○ ⬤ ✦ ⓨ ⓒ ⊞ ⊥
July–August. Yellow. H 5 m (16 ft). W 3 m
(10 ft). Zone 5. S fertile. P seed. Attractive
specimen or park tree with long pinnate mid-
green leaves which turn yellow in the
autumn.

Kolkwitzia amabilis
Beauty Bush / fam. *Caprifoliaceae*
○ ⓑ ⬤ ⓨ ⊥
May–June. Pink. H 2.5 m (8 ft). W 2 m (6 ft).
Zone 4. S normal garden soil. P seed, cuttings.
Erect shrub with arching branches and
peeling brown bark.

Laburnum anagyroides (L. vulgare)
Common Laburnum / fam. *Leguminosae*
○ ⓘ ⬤ ✦ ⓨ ⓒ ⊗
May–June. Yellow. H 8 m (26 ft). W 4 m (13 ft).
Zone 5. S normal garden soil. P seed. Erect
shrub or small tree with dark green trifoliate
leaves and fragrant flowers in long racemes.

Laburnum anagyroides 'Pendulum'
Common Laburnum / fam. *Leguminosae*
○ ⓘ ⬤ ✦ ⓨ ⓒ ⊗
May–June. Yellow. H 4 m (13 ft). W 3.5 m
(11 ft). Zone 5. S normal garden soil.
P grafting. Small tree with arching branches.
Suitable for the smaller garden.

Laburnum × watereri 'Vossii'
Laburnum / fam. *Leguminosae*
○ ⓘ ⬤ ✦ ⓨ ⓒ ⊗
May–June. Yellow. H 8 m (26 ft). W 4 m (13 ft).
Zone 5. S not critical. P cuttings, grafting,
budding. Most attractive of all varieties.
Destroy seed pods. All parts are poisonous.

Lagurus ovatus
Hare's Tail Grass / fam. *Gramineae*
○ ○ ⓨ ⊗
Sow in March in a heated greenhouse or in
April outside. Thin / plant out at A 20 cm (8
in). H 20–40 cm (8–16 in). White. S fertile.
Elegant grass with fluffy, ovoid
inflorescences. Can be dried.

Lamium garganicum ssp. laevigatum
Dead Nettle / fam. *Labiatae*
○ ⓘ ⓜ ⓜ ⓒ ⊘ ⊝
June–August. Rose-purple. H 25 cm (10 in).
A 30 cm (1 ft). S normal garden soil.
P division. Unusual species in an appealing
colour.

Lamium maculatum
Spotted Dead Nettle / fam. *Labiatae*
○ ⓘ ⓜ ⓜ ⓒ ⓨ ⓒ ⊘ ⊝
June–August. Pink-purple. H 30 cm (1 ft).
A 30 cm (1 ft). S normal. P division. Hardy
plant for wild parts of the garden. Good
ground cover, spreading quickly.

237

Lantana

Lantana camara hybrid
fam. *Verbenaceae*
○ ☼ ⊗
Sow in January–February in a heated
greenhouse. Plant out at A 60 cm (2 ft). H 1 m
(3 ft). Various colours. S fertile soil. Grown as
an annual or a perennial. Older blooms are
darker. Free flowering.

Larix decidua (L. europaea)
Common Larch / fam. *Pinaceae*
○ ❋ ☻ ☸ ⊕
Tall, conical tree with arching branches which
gives particularly durable timber. Fine
autumn foliage. H 25 m (80 ft). W 7 m (23 ft).
S humus-rich. P seed. Zone 2.

Larix gmelinii (L. dahurica)
Larch / fam. *Pinaceae*
○ ❋ ☻ ☸ ⊕
In poor conditions this larch will form a low
or spreading tree. Yellowish juvenile foliage;
ovid to cylindrical cones. H 20 m (65 ft). W 4 m
(13 ft). S humus-rich. P seed. Zone 4.

Larix laricina (L. americana)
Larch / fam. *Pinaceae*
○ ❋ ☻ ☸ ⊕
Fairly tall tree with a reddish trunk, needle-
shaped leaves that turn yellow just before
they are shed and small ovoid cones. H 30 m
(100 ft). W 8 m (26 ft). S humus-rich. P seed.
Zone 1.

Lathrea clandestina
fam. *Scrophulariaceae*
◑ ◐ ○
April–May. Purple. H 10 cm (4 in). A 10 cm
(4 in). P division. Parasitic plant that grows
on the roots of *Salix, Alnus* and other trees.

Lathyrus latifolius
Everlasting Pea / fam. *Leguminosae*
◑ ○ ◐ ☻ ☺ ⊗
June–August. Purple or white. H 3 m (10 ft).
A 1 m (3 ft). S normal. P division, seed. Strong
plant. Less attractive flowers than those of the
sweet pea. Suitable for training to supports.

Lathyrus odoratus
Sweet Pea / fam. *Leguminosae*
○ ○ ☻ ☺ ☻ ⊗
Sow in February–March in a heated
greenhouse or in April outside. Thin / plant
out at A 15–25 cm (6–10 in). H 3 m (10 ft).
Various colours. S humus-rich. Climbing
annual with fragrant flowers on long stems.

**Lathyrus vernus 'Lusus Variegatus' (*Orobus
variegatus*)** / Sweet Pea / fam. *Leguminosae*
◑ ◐ ◑ ☻ ☺ ⊗
April–June. White / red. H 20–40 cm (8–16 in).
A 20 cm (8 in). S fertile soil. P division. Non-
climbing sweet pea. Woody stems. Highly
suitable for naturalisation. Bushy habit.

Lavandula angustifolia (L. officinalis)
Lavender / fam. *Labiatae*
○ ⊜ ◐ ◑ ☻ ☺ ⊗
June–July. Dark mauve. H 30–60 cm (1–2 ft).
A 30–40 cm (12–16 in). S chalky. P cuttings of
ripe, non-flowering shoots in August.
Fragrant dwarf shrub. Cut back after
flowering.

Lavandula stoechas ssp. *stoechas*
Lavender / fam. *Labiatae*
○ ⊖ ⌾ ⓦ ⓨ ⊗ ⊗
July–October. Purple. H 30–60 cm (1–2 ft).
A 30 cm (1 ft). S chalky. P cuttings of half-ripe
shoots in summer. Mediterranean coast,
Portugal. Very fragrant dwarf shrub. Prune
after flowering.

Lavatera olbia 'Rosea'
Tree Mallow / fam. *Malvaceae*
○ ⌾ ⓦ ⓨ ⊕ ⊗
July–October. Rosy pink. H 2 m (6 ft). W 1 m
(3 ft). Zone 5. S fertile soil. P cuttings. Tender
semi-shrub with large flowers. For the border.

Lavatera thuringiaca
Tree Mallow / fam. *Malvaceae*
○ ◑ ⊖ ○ ⓨ ⊗
July–September. Rose-purple. H 150 cm (5 ft).
A 60–80 cm (24–32 in). S fertile. P division,
seed. Wide-spreading plant for the border.
Excellent for cutting.

Lavatera trimestris 'Sunset'
Tree Mallow / fam. *Malvaceae*
○ ⊖ ⊙ ⓦ ⊗
Sow in April and thin out to A 40–50 cm (16–
20 in). H 1 m (3 ft). Reddish purple. S normal
garden soil. Popular variety. Erect, bushy
habit with hibiscus-like flowers.

Layia elegans
Tidy Tips / fam. *Compositae*
○ ○ ⓨ
Sow in April–May and thin out to A 20 cm
(8 in). H 40 cm (16 in). Yellow-orange. S not
critical. Low, hairy and undemanding plant,
bushy and well branched.

Ledum palustre ssp. *groenlandicum*
'Compactum' / fam. *Ericaceae*
◑ ⓦ ⊗ ⓨ ⓜ ⓨ
May–June. White. H 50 cm (20 in). W 75 cm
(30 in). Zone 2. S not critical. P seed, cuttings,
layering. Dense and very broad little shrub
with masses of small flowers in umbels.

Leontopodium alpinum
Edelweiss / fam. *Compositae*
○ ⊖ ⊖ ⓨ ⓦ ⓨ ⊗ ⊗
June–August. White. H 20 cm (8 in). A 20 cm
(8 in). S chalky. P division, seed. Well-loved
plant from the European Alps. Colours best
in full sun. Well-drained sandy soil.

Leonurus cardiaca
Motherwort / fam. *Labiatae*
○ ◑ ○ ⓨ
June–October. White / red. H 1 m (3 ft).
A 50 cm (20 in). S fertile soil. P division, seed.
Decorative native plant with erect stems.
Rarely seen in garden centres.

Lespedeza thunbergii (L. formosa)
fam. *Leguminosae*
○ ◑ ⊖ ⌾ ⓦ ⓨ
September–October. Red-purple. H 2 m (6 ft).
W 2 m (6 ft). Zone 5. S humus-rich. P cuttings,
division. Graceful shrub with arching
branches and flowers in very long panicles.

239

Leucojum aestivum
Summer Snowflake / fam. ***Amaryllidaceae***
○ ◐ ≈ ⊘ ◎ ⊛ ☙
May–June. White. H 30–50 cm (12–20 in).
A 20–25 cm (8–10 in). D 10–15 cm (4–6 in).
S heavy, fertile soil. P offsets. Plant fresh
bulbs in October – deeper if soil is dry.
Replant every three years.

Leucothoe axillaris (Andromeda axillaris)
fam. ***Ericaceae***
○ ◐ ≈ ⊛ ⊛ ☙
May–June. White. H 1.5 m (5 ft). W 2 m (6 ft).
Zone 6. S humus-rich. P seed, division. Shrub
with long, arching stems, glossy leaves and
bell-shaped flowers.

Levisticum officinale
Lovage / fam. ***Umbelliferae***
○ ◐ ◎ ⊛ ⊗
July–August. Yellow. H 190 cm (6 ft). A 80 cm
(32 in). S fertile. P division, seed. Culinary
herb with strongly aromatic seeds, stems and
roots.

Lewisia heckneri hybrid
fam. ***Portulacaceae***
○ ◐ ≈ ⊘ ⊛ ⊗
June. Violet. H 25 cm (10 in). A 20 cm (8 in).
S fertile, lime free. P division, seed. Cool
position. Protect from winter sun. Water in
spring and growing period, then keep barely
moist.

Leycesteria formosa
Himalayan Honeysuckle / ***Caprifoliaceae***
○ ◐ ≈ ◎ ⊛
August–September. White. H 2 m (6 ft). W 1 m
(3 ft). Zone 7. S fertile. P seed. Tall, erect shrub
with ovate leaves. Flowers with claret bracts
in pendent, long racemes.

***Liatris spicata* 'Kobold'**
Blazing Star / fam. ***Compositae***
○ ◐ ⊜ ◎ ⊛ ⊗
July–September. Reddish purple. H 50 cm
(20 in). A 30 cm (1 ft). S normal garden soil.
P division. Compact variety which makes a
fine, strong border plant.

Ligularia dentata (L. clivorum)
fam. ***Compositae***
◐ ≈ ⊘ ⊛ ⊜ ⊕ ⊗
July–September. Yellow-orange. H 100–
150 cm (3–5 ft). A 60–80 cm (24–32 in). S moist,
peaty. P division, seed. Fine plant with large
leaves. Plant near water where there is plenty
of space.

Ligularia przewalskii (Senecio przewalskii)
fam. ***Compositae***
○ ◐ ≈ ⊘ ⊛ ⊕ ⊗
August–September. Yellow. H 150 cm (5 ft).
A 60–80 cm (24–32 in). S moist, peaty.
P division, seed. Impressive in a border. Must
be watered during dry spells.

Ligularia veitchiana (Senecio veitchianus)
fam. ***Compositae***
○ ◐ ≈ ⊘ ⊛ ⊕ ⊗
August–October. Yellow. H 2 m (6 ft). A 80 cm
(32 in). S moist, peaty. P division, seed. Tall
plant with very large heart-shaped leaves.
Plant near water.

Ligularia wilsoniana (Senecio wilsonianus)
fam. *Compositae*
○ ◑ ▣ ⊛ ◯ ⊕ ⊕ ⊗
August–September. Yellow. H 160 cm (5 ft).
A 80 cm (32 in). S moist, peaty. P division,
seed. Circular leaves. Tall and strong flower
stems. Strikingly beautiful in late autumn.

Ligustrum ovalifolium
Common Privet / fam. *Oleaceae*
○ ◑ ▣ ▥ ◔ ⊛ ◯
July. White. H 4.5 m (15 ft). W 4.5 m (15 ft).
Zone 5. S not critical. P cuttings. Semi-
deciduous shrub with hairless shoots and
leaves and flowers in panicles.

Ligustrum sinense var. stauntonii
Chinese Privet / fam. *Oleaceae*
○ ◑ ▣ ▥ ⊕ ◯
July–August. White. H 2 m (6 ft). W 3 m (10 ft).
Zone 7. S not critical. P cuttings. Low, very
wide-spreading shrub. Leaves densely
covered in hair. Flowers in large, loose
panicles.

Ligustrum vulgare 'Aureum'
Golden Privet / fam. *Oleaceae*
○ ◑ ▣ ▥ ⊕ ◯
June–July. White. H 4.5 m (15 ft). W 4 m (13 ft).
Zone 4. S not critical. P cuttings. Tall, wide-
spreading shrub with yellow-green leaves
and fragrant flowers in panicles.

Lilium bulbiferum var. croceum
Lily / fam. *Liliaceae*
○ ◑ ▣ ◔ ⊕ ◯ ⊗
July. Orange. H 60–120 cm (2–4 ft). A 20–30 cm
(8–12 in). D 10–15 cm (4–6 in). S fertile.
P offsets, seed. Larvae of the lily beetle may
cause severe damage.

Lilium candidum
Madonna Lily / fam. *Liliaceae*
▣ ◔ ⊕ ◯ ⊗
June–July. White. H 60–150 cm (2–5 ft).
A 25 cm (10 in). D 3 cm (1 in). S humus-rich.
P seed, division, axillary bulbils. Needs
spraying against botrytis. Plant in August for
best display.

Lilium concolor
Lily / fam. *Liliaceae*
○ ◑ ▣ ◔ ⊕ ◯ ⊗
July. Orange. H 30–90 cm (1–3 ft). A 20–30 cm
(8–12 in). D 10 cm (4 in). S fertile. P offsets,
seed. A small lily with one to ten star-shaped
flowers. The small bulbs are short lived.

Lilium davidii
Lily / fam. *Liliaceae*
○ ◑ ▣ ◔ ⊕ ◯ ⊕ ⊗
July. Orange. H 125 cm (4 ft). A 20–30 cm (8–
12 in). D 10–15 cm (4–6 in). S fertile. P offsets,
seed. Strong and straight stem with up to 40
flowers. From China.

Lilium hansonii
Lily / fam. *Liliaceae*
▣ ◔ ⊕ ◯ ⊕ ⊗
June. Orange. H 60–150 cm (2–5 ft). A 20–
30 cm (8–12 in). D 10–15 cm (4–6 in). S fertile.
P offsets, seed. Fragrant lily from Korea which
will survive in the garden for many years.

241

Lilium

Lilium henryi
Lily / fam. *Liliaceae*
◯ ◖ ⓐ ⓨ ⊙ ⊕ ⊗
July–August. Yellow-orange. H 150–200 cm
(5–6 ft). A 40–50 (16–20 in). D 15 cm (6 in).
S fertile. P offsets, seed. Indestructible lily
that will even grow on chalky soil.

Lilium hybrid (American) 'Bellingham'
Lily / fam. *Liliaceae*
◯ ◖ ⓐ ⓨ ⊙ ⊕ ⊗
July. Orange. H 150 cm (5 ft). A 40 cm (16 in).
D 10–15 cm (4–6 in). S fertile. P offsets. Petals
deeply reflexed. Flowers in large
inflorescences. Attractive border plant.

Lilium hybrid (Asiatic) 'Enchantment'
Lily / fam. *Liliaceae*
◯ ◖ ⓐ ⓨ ⊙ ⊕ ⊗
July. Orange. H 60–100 cm (2–3 ft). A 20–30 cm
(8–12 in). D 10–15 cm (4–6 in). S fertile.
P offsets. Popular and vigorous lily grown
chiefly for cut flowers. A 'Mid-Century'
hybrid.

Lilium hybrid (Asiatic) 'Fire King'
Lily / fam. *Liliaceae*
◯ ◖ ⓐ ⓨ ⓥ ⊙ ⊕ ⊗
May–June. Orange. H 125 cm (5 ft). A 20–
30 cm (8–12 in). D 10–15 cm (4–6 in). S normal
garden soil. P offsets. Well-known lily with
horizontal flower stems.

Lilium hybrid (Asiatic) 'Golden Chalice'
Lily / fam. *Liliaceae*
◯ ◖ ⓐ ⓨ ⓥ ⊙ ⊕ ⊗
July. Yellow-orange. H 120 cm (4 ft). A 30 cm
(1 ft). D 10–15 cm (4–6 in). S fertile. P offsets.
'Mid-Century' cross developed by Jan de
Graaff, Oregon, USA.

Lilium hybrid (Asiatic) 'Harmony'
Lily / fam. *Liliaceae*
◯ ◖ ⓐ ⓨ ⓥ ⊙ ⊕ ⊗
July. Orange. H 50–80 cm (20–32 in). A 20–
30 cm (8–12 in). D 10–15 cm (4–6 in). S fertile.
P offsets. 'Mid-Century' hybrid. Popular cut
flower, but also good in the garden.

Lilium hybrid (Asiatic) 'Helona'
Lily / fam. *Liliaceae*
◯ ◖ ⓐ ⓨ ⓥ ⊙ ⊕ ⊗
July. Creamy orange. H 60–80 cm (24–32 in).
A 20–30 cm (8–12 in). D 15 cm (6 in). S fertile.
P offsets. Dutch cross produced in 1975.
Wide-open flowers in an unusual pastel
shade.

Lilium hybrid (Asiatic) 'Pink Tiger'
Lily / fam. *Liliaceae*
◯ ◖ ⓐ ⓨ ⓥ ⊙ ⊕ ⊗
July. Pink. H 150 cm (5 ft). A 40 cm (16 in).
D 15 cm (6 in). S fertile. P offsets. Produced in
1975 by crossing a *L. tigrinum* hybrid with
'Discovery'. Very attractive garden lily.

Lilium hybrid (Asiatic) 'Uncle Sam'
Lily / fam. *Liliaceae*
◯ ◖ ⓐ ⓨ ⓥ ⊙ ⊕ ⊗
July. Yellow. H 90 cm (3 ft). A 40 cm (16 in).
D 10–15 cm (4–6 in). S fertile. P offsets.
Handsome lily though very susceptible to
virus disease. Created in 1964 by Jan de
Graaff.

Lilium hybrid (oriental) 'Chinook'
Lily / fam. *Liliaceae*
○ ◐ ⓐ ⓨ ⓦ ⊕ ⊗
July. Apricot-orange. H 120 cm (4 ft). A 40 cm
(16 in). D 10–15 cm (4–6 in). S fertile. P offsets.
Cross between 'Mid-Century' and
'Harlequin' hybrids.

Lilium hybrid (trumpet) 'African Queen'
Lily / fam. *Liliaceae*
○ ◐ ⓐ ⓨ ⓦ ⊕ ⊗
July. Yellow-orange. H 150–180 cm (5–6 ft).
A 20–30 cm (8–12 in). D 10–15 cm (4–6 in).
S fertile. P offsets. Lilies do not mind the sun
but their base must be shaded.

Lilium hybrid (trumpet) 'Bright Star'
Lily / fam. *Liliaceae*
○ ◐ ⓐ ⓨ ⓦ ⊕ ⊗
July. White / yellow. H 150–180 cm (5–6 ft).
A 20–30 cm (8–12 in). D 10–15 cm (4–6 in).
S fertile. P offsets. Most lilies are planted in
the spring because they are not completely
hardy.

Lilium hybrid (trumpet) 'Golden Splendour'
Lily / fam. *Liliaceae*
○ ◐ ⓐ ⓨ ⓦ ⊕ ⊗
July. Yellow. H 150–180 cm (5–6 ft). A 20–
30 cm (8–12 in). D 10–15 cm (4–6 in). S fertile.
P offsets. Lilies are not suitable for planting
in permanently moist ground.

Lilium hybrid (trumpet) 'Green Dawn'
Lily / fam. *Liliaceae*
○ ◐ ⓐ ⓨ ⓦ ⊕ ⊖
July. White. H 150–180 cm (5–6 ft). A 20–30 cm
(8–12 in). D 10–20 cm (4–8 in). S fertile.
P offsets. Lilies prefer rich, well-drained soil.

Lilium hybrid (trumpet) 'Pink Perfection'
Lily / fam. *Liliaceae*
○ ◐ ⓐ ⓨ ⓦ ⊕ ⊗
July. Rose-purple. H 150–180 cm (5–6 ft).
A 20–30 cm (8–12 in). D 10–15 cm (4–6 in).
S fertile. P offsets. Most lilies form roots
above the bulb and hence need fertile soil.

Lilium martagon var. ***album***
Turk's Cap Lily / fam. *Liliaceae*
○ ◐ ⓐ ⓨ ⓦ ⊕ ⊗
May–June. White. H 120–180 cm (4–6 ft).
A 50 cm (20 in). D 10–15 cm (4–6 in). S normal
garden soil. P offsets, seed. White variety of
the rose-coloured species. Attractive against
a dark background.

Lilium hybrid (oriental) 'Imperial Gold'
Lily / fam. *Liliaceae*
◐ ⓐ ⓨ ⓦ ⊕ ⊗
June–August. White / yellow / red. H 2 m
(6 ft). A 30 cm (1 ft). D 15 cm (6 in). S humus-
rich. P division, axillary bulbils. Hybrid from
the USA. Remarkable for its large bowl-
shaped flowers.

Lilium pardalinum
Panther Lily / fam. *Liliaceae*
○ ⓐ ⓨ ⓦ ⊕
July. Red / orange-red / brown. H 90–180 cm
(3–6 ft). A 30 cm (1 ft). D 20 cm (8 in). S good
garden soil. P division. Easily cultivated. Lift
every three years, divide and replant.
Fragrant.

Lilium

Lilium pumilum (L. tenuifolium)
fam. *Liliaceae*
○ ◑ ⚬ ⚭ ⚮ ⊗
June. Red. H 40–50 cm (16–20 in). A 20 cm
(8 in). D 10 cm (4 in). S fertile. P offsets, seed.
A graceful lily with grass-like leaves and one
to twenty fragrant flowers.

Lilium pyrenaicum
Yellow Turk's Cap Lily / fam. *Liliaceae*
○ ◑ ⚬ ⚭ ⚮ ⊗
May–June. Yellow. H 20–120 cm (8–48 in).
A 20–30 cm (8–12 in). D 10 cm (4 in). S fertile,
may be chalky. P offsets, seed. A lily with one
to twelve flowers up to 3.5 cm (1¼ in) across
and with a rank smell.

Lilium regale
Royal Lily / fam. *Liliaceae*
○ ◑ ⚬ ⚭ ⚮ ⊕ ⊗
July–August. White. H 80–150 cm (32–60 in).
A 40 cm (16 in). D 10–15 cm (4–6 in). S fertile.
P seed. The flowers of this vigorous lily are
trumpet shaped and very fragrant.

Lilium speciosum var. album 'White
Champion' / Lily / fam. *Liliaceae*
○ ⚬ ⚭ ⚮ ⊕
September. White / green. H 50–150 cm (20–
60 in). A 30 cm (1 ft). D 15 cm (6 in). S humus-
rich. P division, axillary bulbils. Very
attractive. Plant in spring; bury bulbs in sand
for winter.

Lilium × testaceum
Nankeen Lily / fam. *Liliaceae*
○ ◑ ⚬ ⚭ ⚮ ⊕ ⊗
July–August. Yellow. H 100–150 cm (3–5 ft).
A 40 cm (16 in). D 10–15 cm (4–6 in). S fertile.
P offsets. Resembles the Madonna Lily from
which it is derived. Not very easily grown.
Plant in autumn.

Limnanthes douglasii
Poached Egg Flower / fam. *Limnanthaceae*
○ ○ ⚭ ⊗
Sow in March–April under glass or in May in
the open. Thin / plant out at A 20 cm (8 in).
H 15 cm (6 in). White / yellow. S humus-rich.
The fragrant flowers attract bees. Good at the
front of a border.

Limonium bonduellei 'Superba'
Sea Lavender / fam. *Plumbaginaceae*
○ ⊙ ⚭ ⊗
Sow in April in a heated greenhouse. Plant
out at A 25–30 cm (10–12 in). H 30–60 cm (1–
2 ft). Yellow. S fertile soil. Popular and eye-
catching plant used for drying or cutting.

Limonium latifolium 'Violetta' (Statice
latifolia) / Sea Lavender / *Plumbaginaceae*
○ ○ ⚬ ⚭ ⊗
July–August. Purple-violet. H 20–50 cm (8–
20 in). A 30–40 cm (12–16 in). S fertile soil.
P division, seed. Will also grow on very dry
soil. Suitable for a border and for drying.

Limonium sinuataum (Statice sinuata)
Sea Lavender / fam. *Plumbaginaceae*
○ ⊙ ⚭ ⊗
Sow in April in heated greenhouse. Plant out
at A 25–30 cm (10–12 in). H 40–60 cm (16–
24 in). White, yellow, red, blue. S fertile. Very
popular. Cut when in full bloom, and then
dry.

Limonium suworowii (Statice suworowii)
Sea Lavender / fam. *Plumbaginaceae*
〇 ⦶ ⊗ ⊗
Sow in April in a heated greenhouse. Plant
out at A 25–30 cm (10–12 in). H 40–60 cm (16–
24 in). Rose pink. S fertile soil. The plume-
shaped panicles make excellent cut or dried
flowers.

Linanthus androsaceus (Gilia androsaceus)
fam. *Polemoniaceae*
〇 ⊙ ⊗
Sow in April–May. Thin out to A 15 cm (6 in).
H 15–30 cm (6–12 in). Various colours.
S normal. Erect plant, well branched from the
ground upwards. Striking flowers and
attractive leaves.

Linaria bipartita hybrid *(L. maroccana*
hybrid) / Toadflax / fam. *Scrophulariaceae*
〇 ⦶ ⊙ ⊗
Sow in March under glass or in April outside.
Thin / plant out at A 15 cm (6 in). H 20–30 cm
(8–12 in). Purple-violet with a yellow blotch.
S not critical. Brief flowering period.

Linaria vulgaris
Common Toadflax / fam. *Scrophulariaceae*
〇 ⦶ ⊜ ⊗ ⊗ ⊗
May–October. Yellow. H 80 cm (32 in).
A 40 cm (16 in). S poor, chalky. P division,
seed. Wild flower. For stone walls and rock
gardens. Liked for its pastel shade.

Lindheimera texana
fam. *Compositae*
〇 ⊙ ⊗
Sow in March in a heated greenhouse or in
April outside. Thin / plant out at A 20–25 cm
(8–10 in). H 30–60 cm (1–2 ft). Yellow.
S normal. Rarely seen, long-flowering plant
with a slight vanilla scent.

Linum flavum
Flax / fam. *Linaceae*
⦶ ⊜ ⊗ ⊙ ⊗
June–August. Yellow. H 40 cm (16 in). A 20 cm
(8 in). S dry garden soil. P division, seed.
Demands a warm and sheltered position.
Free-flowering herbaceous perennial or sub-
shrub.

Linum grandiflorum 'Bright Eyes'
Flax / fam. *Linaceae*
〇 ⦶ ⊙ ⊗ ⊗
Sow in April and thin out to A 15 cm (6 in).
H 20–40 cm (8–16 in). White / red. S normal
garden soil. Numerous shallow, funnel-
shaped flowers throughout the summer.

Linum grandiflorum 'Rubrum'
Scarlet Flax / fam. *Linaceae*
〇 ⦶ ⊙ ⊗ ⊗
Sow in April and thin out to A 15 cm (6 in).
H 20–40 cm (8–16 in). Crimson. S normal
garden soil. Well-loved summer flower, easily
grown but hard to transplant.

Linum narbonense
Flax / fam. *Linaceae*
〇 ⊜ ⊙ ⊗ ⊗
June–July. Violet. H 40 cm (16 in). A 20 cm
(8 in). S dry garden soil. P division, seed.
Perennial from the Mediterranean coast.
Fragrant. Demands a warm and sheltered
position.

Linum perenne
Blue Fax / fam. *Linaceae*
○ ⊖ ⊝ ⊘ ○ ⊗ ⊗
June–August. Blue. H 40–60 cm (16–24 in).
A 20–30 cm (8–12 in). S dry garden soil.
P division, seed. Strong plant with erect
stems and dense foliage. Fragrant. Grows
wild on chalk and limestone.

Liquidambar styraciflua
Sweet Gum / fam. *Hamamelidaceae*
○ ⊕ ⊗ ⊗ ⊗ ⊛ ⊛ ⊕
May. Greeny yellow. H 15 m (50 ft). W 15 m
(50 ft). Zone 5. S fertile. P seed, layering.
Slender, pyramidal tree with corky branches
and leaves colouring in autumn.

Liriodendron tulipifera
Tulip Tree / fam. *Magnoliaceae*
○ ⊛ ⊛ ⊗ ⊘ ⊕
June–July. Yellow-green / orange. H 20 m
(65 ft). W 8–10 m (26–33 ft). Zone 4. S humus-
rich. P seed, layering. Imposing tree with
leaves turning butter-yellow in autumn and
slender fruits.

***Liriodendron tulipifera* 'Fastigiatum'**
Tulip Tree / fam. *Magnoliaceae*
○ ⊛ ⊛ ⊘ ⊕
June–July. Yellow-green. H 15 m (50 ft). W 5 m
(16 ft). Zone 4. S humus-rich. P cuttings,
layering. Conical tree with light green leaves
which change colour in the autumn. Tulip-
shaped flowers.

Liriope platyphylla
fam. *Liliaceae*
⊕ ⊕ ⊗ ⊗ ○ ⊛ ⊗ ⊖
August–September. Purple-violet. H 20–
40 cm (8–16 in). A 20 cm (8 in). S fertile.
P division, seed. Decorative autumn-
flowering plant for a warm spot. Goes well
with rhododendrons.

Lithodora diffusa (Lithospermum diffusum)
fam. *Boraginaceae*
○ ⊗ ⊛ ⊛ ⊛ ⊗ ⊖
May–July. Blue. H 15 cm (6 in). W 80 cm
(32 in). Zone 6–7. S not critical. P seed,
cuttings, layering. Sub-shrub of creeping
habit. Has hairy branches with sessile leaves.

Lobelia erinus
fam. *Campanulaceae*
○ ⊕ ⊙ ⊛
Sow in February–March in a heated
greenhouse or frame. Thin / plant out at
A 20 cm (8 in). H 8–25 cm (3–10 in). Various
colours. S humus-rich. Wide-spreading dwarf
flowering from May until first frosts.

***Lobelia erinus compacta* 'Cambridge Blue'**
fam. *Campanulaceae*
○ ⊕ ⊙ ⊛
Sow in February–March in a heated
greenhouse or frame. Thin / plant out at
A 20 cm (8 in). H 10–12 cm (4–4¾ in). Violet-
blue. S humus-rich. Popular summer bedding
plant for small gardens; also window-boxes.

***Lobelia erinus compacta* 'Rosamond'**
fam. *Campanulaceae*
○ ⊕ ⊙ ⊛
Sow in February–March in a heated
greenhouse or frame. Thin / plant out at 20 cm
(8 in). H 10–12 cm (4–4¾ in). Carmine red /
white. S humus-rich. Attractive cultivar
which remains compact. Suitable for edging.

Lobelia erinus compacta 'Snowball'
fam. Campanulaceae
Sow in February–March in a heated
greenhouse. Thin/plant out at A 20 cm (8 in).
H 10–12 cm (4–4¾ in). White. S humus-rich. If
cut back after flowering, it will bloom again
later.

Lobelia erinus pendula 'Sapphire'
fam. Campanulaceae
Sow in February–March in a heated
greenhouse. Thin/plant out at A 20 cm (8 in).
H 15–30 cm (6–12 in). Purple-violet/white.
S humus-rich. One of the best pendulous
lobelias.

Lobelia fulgens 'Queen Victoria'
fam. Campanulaceae
August–October. Red. H 60–90 cm (2–3 ft).
A 30–40 cm (12–16 in). S fertile. P division,
cuttings. Exceptionally attractive, but
sensitive to frost and must be well covered.

Lobularia maritima 'Schneeteppich'
(Alyssum maritimum)/fam. Cruciferae
Sow in April–May. Thin out to A 20 cm (8 in).
H 10 cm (4 in). White. Normal garden soil,
chalky. Will make enormous hummocks in a
very short time.

Lobularia maritima 'Wonderland' (Alyssum
maritimum)/fam. Cruciferae
Sow in April–May and thin out to A 20 cm
(8 in). H 10–45 cm (4–18 in). Purple. S normal
garden soil, chalky. Rewarding plant in full
flower all summer. Dead-head for a second
show of flowers.

Lonas annua (L. inodora)
fam. Compositae
Sow in April and thin out to A 25 cm (10 in).
H 30–60 cm (1–2 ft). Yellow. S chalky.
Undemanding, free-flowering plant with
hoary stems bearing leaflets. Good for drying.

Lonicera × brownii 'Punicea'/Scarlet
Trumpet Honeysuckle/fam. Caprifoliaceae
May–August. Orange-red. H 4.5 m (15 ft).
W 2 m (6 ft). Zone 5. Humus-rich. P cuttings.
Moderately vigorous climbing shrub with
mid-green leaves, blue tinged and downy
underneath.

Lonicera × heckrottii
Honeysuckle/fam. Caprifoliaceae
June–September. Red-purple/yellow. H 6 m
(20 ft). W 3 m (10 ft). Zone 5. S not critical.
P cuttings. A less vigorous climbing species
with bare stems and a profusion of fragrant
flowers.

Lonicera involucrata f. serotina
Honeysuckle/fam. Caprifoliaceae
July–August. Yellow-orange. H 2 m (6 ft).
W 2 m (6 ft). Zone 5. S not critical. P seed,
cuttings. Erect shrub with fairly large, ovate
to oblong leaves and bare branches.

Lonicera

Lonicera japonica var. repens
'Aureoreticulata'/Japanese Honeysuckle
fam. *Caprifoliaceae*
June–July. White. H 6 m (20 ft). W 3 m (10 ft).
Zone 6–7. S humus-rich. P cuttings. Vigorous
twining plant with red branches. Ovate
greeny-yellow leaves.

Lonicera korolkowii 'Aurora'
Honeysuckle/fam. *Caprifoliaceae*
June. Pink. H 2.5 m (8 ft). W 3 m (10 ft). Zone
5. S not critical. P cuttings. Elegant shrub with
ascending and arching branches and grey-
green ovate to oblong leaves.

Lonicera maackii
Honeysuckle/fam. *Caprifoliaceae*
June. White. H 3 m (10 ft). W 3 m (10 ft). S not
critical. P cuttings. Dense, bushy shrub with
elliptical to ovate, pointed leaves and fragrant
flowers. Zone 2.

Lonicera microphylla
Honeysuckle/fam. *Caprifoliaceae*
May. Creamy white. H 1 m (3 ft). W 1 m (3 ft).
Zone 5. S not critical. P cuttings. Well-
branched, upright shrub with bare or downy
stems and short-stalked leaves.

Lonicera nitida 'Hohenheimer Findling'
Honeysuckle/fam. *Caprifoliaceae*
May. Yellow-green. H 1.5 m (5 ft). W 1.5 m
(5 ft). Zone 5. S not critical. P cuttings. Broad,
erect shrub with long arching branches. The
hardiest variety of all.

Lonicera orientalis
Honeysuckle/fam. *Caprifoliaceae*
June. Pink. H 3 m (10 ft). W 2 m (6 ft). Zone 5.
S not critical. P cuttings. Erect shrub with
bare branches and ovate to lanceolate, dark
green leaves.

Lonicera periclymenum 'Belgica'
Woodbine/fam. *Caprifoliaceae*
June–July. Purple-red/white. H 4 m (13 ft).
W 3 m (10 ft). Zone 4. S humus-rich. P seed,
cuttings. Tall climbing plant, more compact
than the species and strong growing. Fragrant
flowers.

Lonicera sempervirens 'Sulphurea'
Honeysuckle/fam. *Caprifoliaceae*
May–August. Yellow. H 6 m (20 ft). W 3 m
(10 ft). S not critical. P cuttings. Tall climber,
not reliable hardy. Elliptical to ovate leaves.
Flowers in whorls. Zone 3.

Lonicera syringantha
Honeysuckle/fam. *Caprifoliaceae*
May–June. Pink. H 2 m (6 ft). W 2 m (6 ft).
Zone 4. S not critical. P cuttings. Upright,
densely branched shrub with bare stems and
short-stalked oblong leaves.

Lonicera tatarica
Honeysuckle / fam. *Caprifoliaceae*
Ⓘ Ⓘ Ⓘ Ⓘ Ⓘ Ⓘ
June. Pink. H 3 m (10 ft). W 3 m (10 ft). S not
critical. P cuttings. Upright shrub with ovate
leaves, blue-green underneath. Flowers in
small clusters of pairs. Zone 3.

Lonicera tatarica 'Alba'
Honeysuckle / fam. *Caprifoliaceae*
Ⓘ Ⓘ Ⓘ Ⓘ Ⓘ Ⓘ
June. White. H 3 m (10 ft). W 2 m (6 ft). S not
critical. P cuttings. Robust, erect shrub with
ovate leaves and fairly large flowers in small
clusters. Zone 3.

Lonicera × tellmanniana
Honeysuckle / fam. *Caprifoliaceae*
Ⓘ Ⓘ Ⓘ Ⓘ Ⓘ
June. Orange-red. H 5 m (16 ft). W 3 m (10 ft).
Zone 5. S not critical. P cuttings. Strong-
growing climber, very suitable for training
against a south-west wall.

Lunaria annua (L. biennis)
Honesty / fam. *Cruciferae*
Ⓘ Ⓘ Ⓘ Ⓘ Ⓘ Ⓘ
Sow in June in a nursery bed. Plant out in
late September at A 50 cm (20 in). H 30–100 cm
(1–3 ft). Purple. S normal garden soil. Fragrant
flowers followed by silvery seed pods.

Lunaria annua 'Variegata'
Honesty / fam. *Cruciferae*
Ⓘ Ⓘ Ⓘ Ⓘ Ⓘ Ⓘ Ⓘ
Sow in June in a nursery bed. Plant out in
late September at A 50 cm (20 in). H 30–100 cm
(1–3 ft). Purple. S normal garden soil. Fast-
growing. Fragrant; heart-shaped, white-
edged leaves.

Lunaria rediviva
Honesty / fam. *Cruciferae*
Ⓘ Ⓘ Ⓘ Ⓘ Ⓘ
May–June. Mauve. H 1 m (3 ft). A 40 cm
(16 in). S normal. P division, seed. A very
unusual, hardy species with masses of flowers
in the early summer.

Lupinus hartwegii
Lupin / fam. *Leguminosae*
Ⓘ Ⓘ Ⓘ Ⓘ Ⓘ
Sow in March in a heated greenhouse. Plant
out at A 20–30 cm (8–12 in). H 50–70 cm (20–
28 in). Blue / white / red. S good garden soil.
Hairy, very attractive but late-flowering
lupin.

Lupinus hybrid 'Pixie Delight'
Lupin / fam. *Leguminosae*
Ⓘ Ⓘ Ⓘ Ⓘ Ⓘ
Sow in April and thin out to A 20–30 cm (8–
12 in). H 70 cm (28 in). Various colours. S good
garden soil. Suitable for planting in large
groups. Uniform growth and attractive
colours.

Lupinus polyphyllus 'Abendglut'
Lupin / fam. *Leguminosae*
Ⓘ Ⓘ Ⓘ Ⓘ Ⓘ Ⓘ Ⓘ Ⓘ
June–August. Red. H 1 m (3 ft). A 40 cm
(16 in). S acid, moist. P division, cuttings.
Particularly attractive shade of red. Soil must
not be too heavy.

Lupinus

Lupinus polyphyllus 'Noble Maiden'
Lupin/fam. *Leguminosae*
Ⓞ ◑ ⊗ ⌃ ⌖ Ⓞ Ⓨ ⊗
June–August. White. H 1 m (3 ft). A 40 cm
(16 in). S acid, moist. P division, cuttings.
Older specimens are difficult to transplant.
Suitable for a white border.

Lupinus polyphyllus 'The Chatelaine'
Lupin/fam. *Leguminosae*
Ⓞ ◑ ⊗ ⌃ ⌖ Ⓞ Ⓨ ⊗
June–August. Pink. H 1 m (3 ft). A 40 cm
(16 in). S acid, moist. P division, cuttings.
Two-tone cultivar with a white standard.
Attractive and strong garden strain.

Luzula nivea
Woodrush/fam. *Juncaceae*
Ⓞ ◑ Ⓞ ⊛ ⌖ ⊖ ⊗
July–August. White. H 30–50 cm (12–20 in).
A 30 cm (1 ft). S humus-rich. P seed, division.
Wild plant with narrow, bright green, ciliate
leaves.

Luzula sylvatica
Great Woodrush/fam. *Juncaceae*
◑ ◐ Ⓞ ⊛ ⌖ ⊖
April–June. White. H 25–40 cm (10–16 in).
A 30 cm (1 ft). S normal. P division. Glossy
evergreen leaves. Suitable for large areas.
Very hardy.

Lychnis arkwrightii 'Vesuvius'
Campion/fam. *Caryophyllaceae*
Ⓞ ◑ ⌃ Ⓞ Ⓨ ⊗
June–August. Scarlet. H 25–50 cm (10–20 in).
A 30–40 cm (12–16 in). S normal. P division,
seed. Not very long lived and best treated as
a biennial. Striking colour.

Lychnis chalcedonica
Maltese Cross/fam. *Caryophyllaceae*
Ⓞ ◑ Ⓞ Ⓨ ⊗
June–August. Red. H 75–100 cm (30–36 in).
A 50–60 cm (20–24 in). S normal garden soil.
P division, seed. Erect habit. Cut back after
flowering. May be attacked by root aphids if
soil is too dry.

Lychnis coronaria (C. tomentosa)
Rose Campion/fam. *Caryophyllaceae*
Ⓞ ◑ ◑ ⊖ Ⓨ ⊗
June–August. Red. H 30–60 cm (1–2 ft). A 40–
50 cm (16–20 in). S normal garden soil.
P division, seed. Biennial to hardy perennial.
Very rewarding because of its grey foliage
and sturdy stems.

Lychnis coronaria 'Alba'
White Campion/fam. *Caryophyllaceae*
Ⓞ ◑ ⊖ ⊙ Ⓞ Ⓨ ⊗
June–August. White. H 60 cm (2 ft). A 40–
50 cm (16–20 in). S normal. P division, seed.
Very long flowering. Recommended for white
borders.

Lychnis viscaria (Viscaria vulgaris)
Catchfly/fam. *Caryophyllaceae*
Ⓞ ◑ ⊖ Ⓞ Ⓨ ⊗
May–June. Violet-rose. H 30–50 cm (12–20 in).
A 40 cm (16 in). Herbaceous perennial from
the Mediterranean. Sticky stems. Also comes
in a white variety.

Lysichitum americanum
Skunk Cabbage / **fam. *Araceae***
○ ◐ ⊛ ○ ♈ ⊘
April–May. Yellow. H 50–70 cm (20–28 in).
A 30–40 cm (12–16 in). S fertile, moist soil.
P division, seed. Hardy perennial from North
America. Spectacular when planted alongside
pools or streams.

Lysichitum camtschatcense
fam. *Araceae*
○ ◐ ⊛ ○ ♈ ⊘
May–June. White. H 1 m (3 ft). A 40–50 cm
(16–20 in). S fertile, moist soil. P division,
seed. Water and marsh plant. The large leaves
do not develop until after the flowering
period.

Lysimachia clethroides
Loosestrife / **fam. *Primulaceae***
○ ◐ ⊛ ○ ♈
June–August. White. H 60–80 cm (24–32 in).
A 30–40 cm (12–16 in). S fertile, moist.
P division, seed. Long-flowering, attractive
plant for the border. Plant at the back, as
stems become bare.

Lysimachia nummularia
Creeping Jenny / **fam. *Primulaceae***
○ ◐ ● ⊛ ○ ♠ ⊛ ⊖
June–July. Yellow. H 5 cm (2 in). A 20 cm
(8 in). S moist, fertile. P division. Creeping,
fast-growing plant suitable for the edge of
ponds or for moist positions.

Lysimachia punctata
Loosestrife / **fam. *Primulaceae***
○ ◐ ○ ♈
June–August. Yellow. H 80–100 cm (32–36 in).
A 40–50 cm (16–20 in). S normal garden soil.
P division. Suckering perennial of erect habit.
Very invasive.

Lysimachia verticillaris
Loosestrife / **fam. *Primulaceae***
○ ◐ ○ ♈
June–August. Yellow. H 80–100 cm (32–36 in).
A 50 cm (20 in). S normal. P division, seed.
Less well-known species with flowers massed
in attractive spikes. Suitable for a border.

***Lythrum* hybrid**
fam. *Lythraceae*
◐ ◑ ⊛ ○ ♈ ⊗
June–September. Violet. H 125 cm (4 ft).
A 50 cm (20 in). S moist, humus-rich.
P division, cuttings. Will bear most attractive
flowers if planted out of full sun. Many
colours.

***Lythrum* hybrid 'The Rocket'**
fam. *Lythraceae*
○ ◑ ⊛ ○ ♈ ⊕
July–September. Deep rose pink. H 150 cm
(5 ft). A 60 cm (2 ft). S moist, humus-rich.
P division, cuttings. Goes well with spring
flowers that have to be dead-headed.

Lythrum salicaria
Purple Loosestrife / **fam. *Lythraceae***
○ ◐ ● ⊛ ○ ♈ ⊕
July–September. Red-purple. H 150–200 cm
(5–6 ft). A 80 cm (32 in). S normal garden soil.
P division, cuttings, seed. Long flowering
period. The spire-like racemes are 30 cm (1 ft)
long.

Macleaya

Macleaya cordata (Bocconia cordata)
Plume Poppy / fam. *Papaveraceae*
◐ ▣ ⊛ ⊗ ⊛ ⊕ ⊕
July–August. White. H 2–3 m (6–10 ft). A 1 m
(3 ft). S normal garden soil. P division, root
cuttings, seed. Tall, with plumes of small
pearly-white flowers. Invasive.

Magnolia grandiflora
fam. *Magnoliaceae*
⊛ ⊗ ⊕ ⊛ ⊛ ⊕ ⊕
June–August. White. H 20 m (65 ft). W 8 m
(26 ft). Zone 7. S humus-rich. P seed, cuttings,
layering. Handsome cone-shaped tree. Shoots
and buds reddish brown and woolly. Fragrant
flowers.

Magnolia kobus (M. tomentosa)
fam. *Magnoliaceae*
○ ⊗ ⊛ ⊛ ⊛ ⊕ ⊕
April–May. White. H 10 m (33 ft). W 5 m
(16 ft). Zone 5. S not critical. P layering,
grafting, seed. Tall shrub or small tree with
long red fruits. Bark fragrant when rubbed.

Magnolia liliiflora 'Nigra'
fam. *Magnoliaceae*
○ ⊕ ⊛ ⊛ ⊛ ⊕ ⊕
May. Red-purple. H 3 m (10 ft). W 3 m (10 ft).
Zone 5. S humus-rich. P cuttings, layering.
Broad, erect shrub with glossy, dark green
leaves. The large flowers open in late spring.

Magnolia × soulangiana
fam. *Magnoliaceae*
○ ⊕ ⊛ ⊛ ⊛ ⊕ ⊕ ⊗
April–May. White / red. H 7 m (23 ft). W 4 m
(13 ft). Zone 5. S humus-rich. P seed, cuttings,
layering. Shrub or small tree with lanceolate
leaves and masses of chalice-shaped flowers.

Magnolia × soulangiana 'Lennei'
fam. *Magnoliaceae*
○ ⊕ ⊛ ⊛ ⊛ ⊕ ⊕ ⊗
April–May. Purple / white. H 7 m (23 ft).
W 4 m (13 ft). Zone 5. S humus-rich.
P cuttings, layering. Shrub or small tree with
broadly ovate leaves and broad, bell-shaped
flowers.

Magnolia stellata (M. kobus var. stellata)
fam. *Magnoliaceae*
○ ⊕ ⊛ ⊕ ⊕
March–April. White. H 2 m (6 ft). W 2 m (6 ft).
Zone 5. S humus-rich. P seed, cuttings,
layering. Dense and wide-spreading shrub.
The star-shaped flowers are 7–10 cm (2¾–4 in)
across.

Magnolia stellata 'Rosea'
fam. *Magnoliaceae*
○ ⊛ ⊕ ⊕
March–April. Pink / white. H 2 m (6 ft). W 2 m
(6 ft). Zone 5. S humus-rich. P cuttings,
layering. Dense, wide-spreading, erect shrub
with lanceolate leaves and star-shaped,
fragrant flowers.

Mahonia aquifolium (Berberis aquifolium)
Oregon Grape / fam. *Berberidaceae*
○ ◐ ▣ ⊗ ⊛ ⊕ ⊛ ⊗ ⊕ ⊛ ⊕ ⊖
April–May. Yellow. H 2 m (6 ft). W 2.5 m (8 ft).
Zone 5. S good garden soil. P cuttings, seed.
Wide-spreading erect shrub with glossy
green, ovate, sharp-toothed leaves and
fragrant flowers.

Mahonia bealei (Berberis japonica var. *bealei)*/fam. *Berberidaceae*

〇◐◓❀⬗⬙🌳🏵🏵
February–May. Yellow. H 1 m (3 ft). W 1 m (3 ft). Zone 6. S good garden soil. P seed, cuttings. Upright shrub with blue-green leaves and flowers in stiffly erect racemes.

Mahonia japonica 'Hiemalis' fam. *Berberidaceae*

〇◐◓❀⬗⬙🌳🏵🏵
February–May. Yellow. H 1 m (3 ft). W 1 m (3 ft). Zone 7. S good garden soil. P cuttings. Shrub with glossy, dark green, composite, sharply toothed leaves which retain their colour.

Maianthemum bifolium (Convallaria bifolia) May Lily/fam. *Liliaceae*

◐◑❀⬗〇〇🏵
May–June. White. H 10–15 cm (4–6 in). A 10–20 cm (4–8 in). S poor, moist soil. P division, seed. Occurs locally in woods but is very rare. Berries green, turning red.

Malcolmia bicolor fam. *Cruciferae*

〇◐🌣⬗🌫⊗
Sow in March–June and thin out to A 10 cm (4 in). H 15 cm (6 in) Purple/creamy yellow. S good garden soil. Compact plant. Cut back after flowering to encourage a second show.

Malope trifida 'Purpurea' fam. *Malvaceae*

〇◐🌣⬗
Sow in February in a heated greenhouse or in April outside. Thin/plant at A 40–50 cm (16–20 in). H 1 m (3 ft). Red-purple, white. S fertile soil. Bushy plant with erect, branching stems.

Malus 'Adams' Flowering Crab/fam. *Rosaceae*

〇❀⬗🌳🏵🕘
May. Red. H 10 m (33 ft). W 8 m (26 ft). Zone 4. S normal garden soil. P grafting. Tree of dense habit. Single flowers, pink buds and small red fruits.

Malus baccata 'Gracilis' Flowering Crab/fam. *Rosaceae*

〇◐❀⬗🌳🏵🕘
April–May. White. H 8 m (26 ft). W 5 m (16 ft). S normal garden soil. P grafting. Small tree of dense, bushy habit. Has slender branches and small red fruits. Zone 2.

Malus 'Butterball' (fruit) Flowering Crab/fam. *Rosaceae*

〇❀⬗🌳🏵🕘
May. Pink. H 6 m (20 ft). W 6 m (20 ft). Zone 4. S normal garden soil. P grafting. Attractive new cultivar with numerous round, golden-yellow fruits which gradually turn orange.

Malus 'Echtermeyer' Flowering Crab/fam. *Rosaceae*

〇❀⬗🌳🏵🕘
May. Red-purple. H 3 m (10 ft). W 5 m (16 ft). Zone 4. S normal garden soil. P grafting. Weeping tree with slender, supple branches, single flowers and brown-red leaves with good autumn colour.

253

Malus

Malus floribunda
Flowering Crab / fam. *Rosaceae*
○ ❋ ⊛ ❀ ⊕
May. Pink. H 8 m (26 ft). W 8 m (26 ft). Zone 4.
S normal garden soil. P seed, grafting. Very
attractive tree with arching branches and
small yellow fruits.

Malus 'Golden Hornet' (fruits)
Flowering Crab / fam. *Rosaceae*
○ ❋ ⊛ ❀ ⊕
May. White. H 8 m (26 ft). W 6 m (20 ft). Zone
4. S normal garden soil. P grafting. Broad tree
with green leaves, pink buds, small flowers
and fruits which last until December.

Malus 'Gorgeous' (fruits)
Flowering Crab / fam. *Rosaceae*
○ ❋ ⊛ ❀ ⊕
May. Pink-white. H 5 m (16 ft). W 5 m (16 ft).
Zone 4. S normal garden soil. P grafting.
Moderately tall tree with decorative fruits that
persist on the tree for a long time.

Malus × hartwegii
Flowering Crab / fam. *Rosaceae*
○ ❋ ⊛ ❀ ⊕
May. White. H 8 m (26 ft). W 8 m (26 ft). Zone
4. S normal garden soil. P grafting, budding.
Broad, erect tree with yellow-green fruits,
dark brown branches and semi-double
flowers.

Malus 'Hopa'
Flowering Crab / fam. *Rosaceae*
○ ❋ ⊛ ❀ ⊕
April–May. Red. H 8 m (26 ft). W 8 m (26 ft).
Zone 4. S normal garden soil. P grafting.
Robust tree, later with spreading branches,
fairly large fruits and single flowers.

Malus 'Liset'
Flowering Crab / fam. *Rosaceae*
○ ❋ ⊛ ❀ ⊕
April–May. Red. H 5 m (16 ft). W 4 m (13 ft).
Zone 4. S normal garden soil. P grafting.
Medium-sized crab tree with a mass of
flowers and of small red-purple fruits.

Malus 'Mary Potter'
Flowering Crab / fam. *Rosaceae*
○ ❋ ⊛ ⊕
May. White. H 3 m (10 ft). W 5 m (16 ft). Zone
4. S normal garden soil. P grafting. Very
broad shrub with arching branches and
masses of ruby-red fruits into November.

Malus × micromalus
Flowering Crab / fam. *Rosaceae*
○ ❋ ⊛ ❀ ⊕
May. Pink. H 4 m (13 ft). W 3 m (10 ft). Zone 4.
S normal garden soil. P grafting. Erect,
densely branched tree with large leaves and
yellow fruits which do not persist long on the
tree.

Malus 'Montreal Beauty' (fruits)
Flowering Crab / fam. *Rosaceae*
○ ❋ ⊛ ❀ ⊕
May. White. H 6 m (20 ft). W 5 m (16 ft). Zone
4. S normal garden soil. P grafting. Small tree
or large shrub with single flowers 5 cm (2 in)
across and fruits 4 cm (1½ in) across.

Malus 'Professor Sprenger' (fruits)
Flowering Crab / fam. *Rosaceae*
○❀☿❀⊕⊕
May. Pink / white. H 6 m (20 ft). W 5 m (16 ft).
Zone 4. S normal garden soil. P grafting.
Apple-scab resistant small tree with golden-
yellow autumn foliage and small fruits that
last well.

Malus 'Rosseau'
Flowering Crab / fam. *Rosaceae*
○❀☿❀⊕⊕
May. Red-purple. H 6 m (20 ft). W 6 m (20 ft).
Zone 4. S normal garden soil. P grafting.
Small tree with bronze-red leaves turning red,
and red fruits from August to mid-October.

Malus 'Wintergold'
Flowering Crab / fam. *Rosaceae*
○❀☿❀⊕⊕
May. White. H 10 (33 ft). W 8 m (26 ft). Zone 4.
S normal garden soil. P grafting. Robust tree
with a round crown, glossy green leaves and
yellow fruits into December. For a large
garden.

Malus 'Wisley Crab'
Flowering Crab / fam. *Rosaceae*
○❀☿❀⊕⊕
May. Red-purple. H 6 m (20 ft). W 5 m (16 ft).
Zone 4. S normal garden soil. P grafting.
Strong-growing, erect tree with large leaves
and flowers measuring 5 cm (2 in) across.

Malus 'Zita' (fruits)
Flowering Crab / fam. *Rosaceae*
○❀☿❀⊕⊕
May. Pink. H 3 m (10 ft). W 5 m (16 ft). Zone 4.
S normal garden soil. P grafting to a 2–3-m
(6–10-ft) tall rootstock. Attractive weeping
form.

Malva alcea
Mallow / fam. *Malvaceae*
○○☿☿⊗
June–September. Mauve-pink. H 80–100 cm
(32–36 in). A 40 cm (16 in). S chalky.
P division, seed. A mass of 5-cm (2-in) wide
flowers. Seeds itself. Demands a warm
position.

Marrubium incanum
Horehound / fam. *Labiatae*
○⊖☿☿☿☿
June–July. White. H 25–40 cm (10–16 in).
A 20 cm (8 in). S normal garden soil.
P division, seed, cuttings. Suitable for a white
border. Silver-grey, woolly leaves.

Matteuccia struthiopteris (Struthiopteris germanica) / Ostrich Feather Fern / fam.
Onocleaceae
◑◖○⊗☿☿⊖
No flowers. H 80–130 cm (32–51 in). A 40–
50 cm (16–20 in). S fertile, moist. P offsets.
Attractive garden fern. If kept too dry, the
leaves turn yellow early.

Matthiola incana
Stock / fam. *Cruciferae*
○◑○☿☿
Sow in February–March in a heated
greenhouse or in April outside. Thin / plant
out at A 20 cm (8 in). H 20–75 cm (8–30 in).
Pale purple. S fertile. Upright plant with
fragrant flowers.

255

Meconopsis

Meconopsis betonicifolia
Himalayan Blue Poppy / fam. *Papaveraceae*
◑ ◐ ⊕ ◯ ◉ ◉
June–July. Blue. H 100–120 cm (3–4 ft).
A 50 cm (20 in). S acid, humus-rich.
P division, seed. Hard to cultivate; often
grown as a biennial. For true garden lovers
only.

Meconopsis cambrica 'Aurantiaca'
Welsh Poppy / fam. *Papaveraceae*
◯ ◑ ◯ ◯ ◉
June–October. Orange. H 25–50 cm (10–20 in).
A 30 cm (1 ft). S sandy. P division, seed. Often
seeds itself. Needs much moisture while
flowering, but should be kept fairly dry in the
winter.

Meconopsis regia
fam. *Papaveraceae*
◑ ⊗ ⊕ ◯ ◉ ◉
July–August. Yellow. H 180 cm (6 ft). A 50 cm
(20 in). S acid, humus-rich. P division, seed.
Usually flowers during the second year and
then dies.

Melissa officianalis 'Aurea'
Balm / fam. *Labiatae*
◯ ◑ ◯ ◉
June–August. Rose-purple. H 50–75 cm (20–
30 in). A 30 cm (1 ft). S normal garden soil.
P division. This plant with a strong smell of
lemon belongs in the herb garden or a border.

Mentha aquatica
Water Mint / fam. *Labiatae*
◯ ◑ ⊗ ◯ ⊛ ◉ ⊛ ⊗
July–August. Purple-violet. H 30–90 cm (1–
3 ft). A 60 cm (2 ft). S normal garden soil.
P seed, cuttings, division. Very fragrant
native mint found in wet places. Makes
runners and suckers.

Mentha longifolia var. **longifolia**
Horse Mint / fam. *Labiatae*
◯ ◑ ⊗ ◯ ⊛ ⊗
July–September. Purple-violet. H 50–80 cm
(20–32 in). A 30–40 cm (12–16 in). S normal
garden soil. P division, seed, cuttings.
Aromatic plant for the edge of pools. Sends
out suckers.

Mentha rotundifolia 'Variegata'
Apple Mint / fam. *Labiatae*
◯ ◑ ⊗ ◯ ◉ ⊗
July–October. White. H 30–60 cm (1–2 ft).
A 30 cm (1 ft). S normal garden soil.
P division, cuttings. Gives off an unpleasant
smell. Has runners and suckers. For the rock
garden.

Mentha spicata (M. virides)
Spear Mint / fam. *Labiatae*
◯ ◑ ⊗ ◯ ⊛
July–September. Purple-violet. H 60 cm (2 ft).
A 30 cm (1 ft). S humus-rich. P cuttings,
division. A herb with flowers in an appealing
colour.

Mentzelia lindleyi (Bartonia aurea)
Blazing Star / fam. *Loasaceae*
◯ ⊖ ⊜ ◯ ⊛ ⊗
Sow in March in a heated greenhouse or in
May outside. Thin / plant out at A 30–50 cm
(12–20 in). H 25–60 cm (10–24 in). Yellow.
S normal garden soil. A beautiful species with
fragrant flowers.

Menyanthes trifoliata
Bogbean / fam. *Menyanthaceae*
○ ◖ ⊗ ⊙ ⊚
May–June. White. H 15–40 cm (6–16 in).
A 20 cm (8 in). S clay. P runners (spring,
autumn). Marsh plant that tolerates water to
a depth of 30 cm (1 ft). Common in watery
bogs.

*Mertensia virginica (Pulmonaria virginica,
M. pulmonarioides)* / Virginian Cowslip
fam. **Boraginaceae**
◖ ⊗ ⊙ ○ ⊚ ⊗
April–May. Purplish blue. H 50 cm (20 in).
A 20–30 cm (8–12 in). S fertile soil. P division,
seed. Tuberous black roots. Blue-green
foliage, dark red when young.

Mesembryanthemum crystallinum
fam. *Aizoaceae*
○ ⊜ ⊙ ⊙ ⊚
Sow in January in a heated greenhouse. Plant
out at A 30 cm (1 ft). H 15 cm (6 in). Various
colours. S not critical. Bedding plant; covered
with pearly papillae. Colourful flowers.

Mespilus germanica 'Macrocarpa'
Medlar / fam. *Rosaceae*
○ ◖ ✳ ⊙ ⊚ ⊚ ⊕
May–June. White. H 5 m (16 ft). W 4 m (13 ft).
Zone 5. S not critical. P seed, grafting. Small
tree with spiny branches and shoots, edible
(over-ripe) fruits and oblong leaves.

*Metasequoia glyptostroboides (Sequoia
glyptostroboides)* / Dawn Redwood / fam.
Taxodiaceae
○ ✳ ⊚ ⊚ ⊕
Fast-growing conifer of open habit. The light
green leaves colour in autumn and fall mid-
November. H 35 m (115 ft). W 12 m (40 ft).
S fertile. P seed, cuttings. Zone 5.

Mimulus × *burnettii* 'A. T. Johnson'
Musk / fam. *Scrophulariaceae*
○ ◖ ⊗ ⊙ ○ ⊙
June–August. Yellow / red. H 25 cm (10 in).
A 20 cm (8 in). S normal. P division. A hybrid
with flowers in profusion. Not very hardy so
may have to be replaced in the spring.

Mimulus hybrid 'Orange King'
(M. × *tigrinus)* / Musk / fam.
Scrophulariaceae
○ ◖ ⊗ ⊙ ○ ⊙
June–August. Orange-red. H 25 cm (10 in).
A 20 cm (8 in). S normal garden soil.
P division. Plentiful flowers over a long
period. Will survive normal winters.

Mimulus luteus
Monkey Flower / fam. *Scrophulariaceae*
○ ◖ ⊗ ⊙ ○ ⊙
May–August. Yellow. H 40 cm (16 in). A 20 cm
(8 in). S normal. P division, seed. Plants
grown from seed flower later. Mid-green
leaves. The most popular variety is 'Trigrimus
Grandiflorus'.

Mirabilis jalapa
Marvel of Peru / fam. *Nyctaginaceae*
○ ⊗ ⊙ ○ ⊙
June–October. Red-crimson. H 1 m (3 ft).
A 40–50 cm (16–20 in). S fertile. P seed,
division, root cuttings. Perennial, usually
grown as an annual. Fragrant flowers open
mid to late afternoon.

Miscanthus

Miscanthus floridulus 'Variegata'
fam. Graminea
◐ ⊛ ⊘ ◯ ⊘
No flowers. H 2 m (6 ft). A 60 cm (2 ft). S fertile soil. P division. Ornamental grass. Can do with protection in severe winters.

Miscanthus sacchariflorus (Imperata sacchariflora) / **fam. Graminea**
◯ ◐ ⊛ ⊙ ◯ ⊗ ⊘ ⊗
August–October. Silvery brown. H 2 m (6 ft). A 1 m (3 ft). S not critical. P seed, division. Attractive ornamental grass which only blooms in warm summers. Splendid panicles.

Miscanthus sinensis 'Giganteus'
fam. Graminea
◯ ◐ ◯ ⊘ ⊕
Does not flower. H 200–250 cm (6–8 ft). A 80 cm (32 in). S normal. P division. Hardiest of ornamental grasses. Attractively arching foliage.

Miscanthus sinensis 'Gracillimus'
fam. Graminea
◯ ◐ ◯ ⊘ ⊗
Flowers rarely. H 150 cm (5 ft). A 45–60 cm (18–24 in). S fertile garden soil. P division. Graceful reed-like grass with very narrow blades and a whitish midrib.

Miscanthus sinensis 'Silberfeder'
fam. Graminea
◐ ⊛ ◯ ⊙ ⊘ ⊗
September–October. Silvery brown. H 180 cm (6 ft). A 1 m (3 ft). S fertile garden soil. P division. Most attractive flowers and arching, reed-like blades with a white midrib.

Miscanthus sinensis 'Strictus'
fam. Graminea
◯ ◐ ⊛ ◯ ⊘
Does not flower. H 120 cm (4 ft). A 1 m (3 ft). S fertile garden soil. P division. Stiff ornamental grass with ascending leaves and characteristic yellow cross-stripes.

Miscanthus sinensis 'Zebrinus' (Eulalia japonica) / **fam. Graminea**
◯ ◐ ⊛ ◯ ⊘
September–October. White. H 150 cm (5 ft). A 60 cm (2 ft). S fertile. Leaves marked alternately green and white by crossbands. Flowers rarely.

Molinia arundinaceae (M. litoralis)
fam. Graminea
◯ ◯ ⊘
June–August. White. H 50–120 cm (20–48 in). A 60 cm (2 ft). S fertile. P division. Thrives in dry as well as in moist positions. Leaves turn golden-yellow in the autumn.

Molinia caerulea 'Variegata'
Purple Moor Grass / **fam. Graminea**
◯ ◯ ⊘
July–September. White. H 50–100 cm. A 60 cm (2 ft). S fertile soil. P division. The white-green leaves turn browny red in the autumn. Must not be planted too close to water.

Moluccella laevis
Bells of Ireland / fam. *Labiatae*
○ ⊙ ⊗
Sow in March in a heated greenhouse or in April outside. Thin / plant out to A 30–40 cm (12–16 in). H 60–100 cm (2–3 ft). White. S fertile. Dried for the sake of its attractive calyces. Fragrant.

Monarda hybrid 'Croftway Pink'
Bergamot / fam. *Labiatae*
○ ◑ ⊙ ⊛ ⊗
July–September. Rose pink, violet. H 1 m (3 ft). A 45 cm (18 in). S fertile. P division. Attractive, sturdy and erect plant for the border. Unusual aroma. Free-flowering.

Monarda hybrid 'Prairienacht'
Bergamot / fam. *Labiatae*
○ ◑ ⊛ ⊙ ⊛ ⊗
July–September. Purple-violet. H 80 cm (32 in). A 40 cm (16 in). S normal. P division. Attractive free-flowering plant for a large border.

Morus alba 'Pendula'
White Mulberry / fam. *Moraceae*
○ ◑ ⊛ ⊛ ⊛
May. Greeny yellow. H 6 m (20 ft). W 4.5 m (15 ft). Zone 4. S not critical. P cuttings, grafting. Monoecious tree with slender arching branches and edible berries.

Muehlenbeckia axillaris
fam. *Polygonaceae*
◑ ⌃ ⊛ ⊖
May–June. Yellow-green. H 10 cm (4 in). W 50 cm (20 in). Zone 6. S fertile. P cuttings. Dense mat-forming little trailing plant with very fine, soft, hairy stems with rising tips.

Muscari armeniacum
Grape Hyacinth / fam. *Liliaceae*
○ ⊛ ⊛ ⊗
April–May. Deep blue. H 10–20 cm (4–8 in). A 7 cm (2¾ in). D 5–7 cm (2–2¾ in). S normal garden soil. P offsets. Suitable for naturalisation. Also attractive between short ground-cover plants.

Muscari armeniacum 'Blue Spike'
Grape Hyacinth / fam. *Liliaceae*
○ ⊛ ⊛ ⊗
April–May. Blue. H 20–25 cm (8–10 in). A 7 cm (2¾ in). D 5–7 cm (2–2¾ in). S normal garden soil. P offsets. Unusual double-flowered cultivar. Plant in September–October.

Muscari azurea (Hyacinthella azurea)
Grape Hyacinth / fam. *Liliaceae*
○ ⊛ ⊗
April–May. Blue. H 20–25 cm (8–10 in). A 6 cm (2¼ in). D 5–7 cm (2–2¾ in). S normal garden soil. P offsets. Grape hyacinths may be planted on the lawn provided mowing is left until late spring.

Muscari botryoides 'Album'
Grape Hyacinth / fam. *Liliaceae*
○ ⌃ ⊛ ⊗
March–April. White. H 15–20 cm (6–8 in). A 7 cm (2¾ in). D 5–7 cm (2–2¾ in). S normal garden soil. P offsets. A less well-known, white variety. Must be covered in winter.

259

Muscari

Muscari latifolium
Grape Hyacinth / fam. *Liliaceae*
○ ◐ ◈ ◉ ⊗
May. Blue. H 30–40 cm (12–16 in). A 7–10 cm
(2¾–4 in). D 5–7 cm (2–2¾ in). S normal garden
soil. P offsets in August / early September at
D 3–4 cm (1–1½ in).

Myosotis palustris.
Water Forget-me-not / fam. *Boraginaceae*
○ ◐ ◈ ◉ ◉ ⊛
May–August. Violet. H 25–50 cm (10–20 in).
A 30 cm (1 ft). S wet banks. P division, seed.
Richly flowering wild plant. Dislikes too
much sun. Attractive near water.

Myosotis sylvatica (M. alpestris)
Forget-me-not / fam. *Boraginaceae*
○ ◐ ◉ ⊙ ◉ ⊛
Sow in June. Plant out at A 15–20 cm (6–8 in).
H 15–50 cm (6–20 in). Various colours.
S humus-rich garden soil. Outstanding
bedding plant because of its low height, long
and early flowering period.

Narcissus cyclamineus 'February Gold'
fam. *Amaryllidaceae*
○ ◐ ◈ ◉ ◉ ⊗
February–March. Yellow. H 15–25 cm (6–
10 in). A 10 cm (4 in). D 10 cm (4 in). S normal
garden soil. P offsets. Cyclamineus varieties
are derived from hybrids. Their petals sweep
up and back.

Narcissus cyclamineus 'Jack Snipe'
fam. *Amaryllidaceae*
○ ◐ ◈ ◉ ◉ ⊗
March–April. Various colours. H 20 cm (8 in).
A 10 cm (4 in). D 10 cm (4 in). S normal garden
soil. P offsets. All narcissi like well-worked,
moist soil.

Narcissus cyclamineus 'Jenny'
fam. *Amaryllidaceae*
○ ◐ ◈ ◉ ◉ ⊗
March–April. Various colours. H 20–25 cm (8–
10 in). A 10 cm (4 in). D 10 cm (4 in). S normal
garden soil. P offsets. Once established for a
while, these plants need not be covered in
winter.

Narcissus cyclamineus 'Little Witch'
fam. *Amaryllidaceae*
○ ◐ ◈ ◉ ◉ ⊗
March–April. Yellow. H 25 cm (10 in). A 10 cm
(4 in). D 10 cm (4 in). S normal garden soil.
P offsets. This daffodil is especially suitable
for pot cultivation and for naturalisation.

Narcissus cyclamineus 'Tête à Tête'
fam. *Amaryllidaceae*
○ ◐ ◈ ◉ ◉ ⊗
February–March. Yellow. H 15–20 cm (6–8 in).
A 10 cm (4 in). D 10 cm (4 in). S normal garden
soil. P offsets. Do not mow the lawn until the
leaves of narcissi have partly died down.

Narcissus (double) 'Flower Dream'
fam. *Amaryllidaceae*
○ ◐ ◈ ⊕ ◉ ◉ ⊗
April–May. White / yellow. H 30–40 cm (12–
16 in). A 15–20 cm (6–8 in). D 10–15 cm (4–
6 in). S normal garden soil. P offsets. Large-
flowered cultivar with a larger than usual
number of petals.

260

Narcissus (double) 'Texas'
fam. *Amaryllidaceae*
○ ◑ ⌂ ⊛ ⊛ ⊛ ⊗

April–May. Yellow. H 35 cm (14 in). A 15 cm
(6 in). D 10–15 cm (4–6 in). S normal garden
soil. P offsets. Double-flowered daffodils are
not as strong as single-flowered. Shelter from
wind.

Narcissus (large-cupped) 'Ice Follies'
fam. *Amaryllidaceae*
○ ◑ ⌂ ⌂ ⊛ ⊗

April–May. White / yellow. H 40–50 cm (16–
20 in). A 15–20 in (6–8 in). D 10–15 cm (4–6 in).
S normal. P offsets. Large-cupped narcissi fall
between trumpet daffodils and small-cupped
narcissi.

Narcissus (large-cupped) 'Mercato'
fam. *Amaryllidaceae*
○ ◑ ⌂ ⌂ ⊛ ⊗

April–May. White / orange. H 40–50 cm (16–
20 in). A 15–20 cm (6–8 in). D 10–15 cm (4–
6 in). S normal garden soil. P offsets. All
large-cupped narcissi are suitable for
naturalisation.

Narcissus jonquilla
Wild Jonquil / fam. *Amaryllidaceae*
○ ◑ ⌂ ⌂ ⊛ ⊗

April. Deep yellow. H 30 cm (1 ft). A 12 cm
(4½ in). D 10 cm (4 in). S humus-rich. P seed,
offsets. Species with cylindrical leaves and
strongly scented flowers in clusters. Small
trumpets.

**Narcissus (small-cupped) 'Barrett
Browning' / fam. *Amaryllidaceae***
○ ◑ ⌂ ⌂ ⊛ ⊗

April. White / orange. H 45 cm (18 in). A 15 cm
(6 in). D 10–15 cm (4–6 in). S normal garden
soil. P offsets. Small-cupped narcissus with a
relatively large, flat cup. Robust variety.

Narcissus (small-cupped) 'Quirinus'
fam. *Amaryllidaceae*
○ ◑ ⌂ ⌂ ⊛ ⊗

April. Deep yellow. H 40–50 cm (16–20 in).
A 15 cm (6 in). D 10–15 cm (4–6 in). S normal
garden soil. P offsets. Flowers profusely. Very
suitable for naturalisation and cutting.

Narcissus poeticus
Poet's Narcissus / fam. *Amaryllidaceae*
○ ◑ ⌂ ⌂ ⊛ ⊗

May. Yellow. H 40–45 cm (16–18 in). A 10–
15 cm (4–6 in). D 10–15 cm (4–6 in). S normal
garden soil. P offsets. Particularly suitable for
naturalisation. Delightful fragrance.

Narcissus poeticus 'Actaea'
Poet's Narcissus / fam. *Amaryllidaceae*
○ ◑ ⌂ ⌂ ⊛ ⊗

April–May. White. H 45 cm (18 in). A 10–
15 cm (4–6 in). D 10–15 cm (4–6 in). S normal
garden soil. P offsets. Very attractive cultivar
with extra large, highly fragrant flowers.

Narcissus (split corona) 'Orangerie'
Narcissus / fam. *Amaryllidaceae*
○ ◑ ⌂ ⌂ ⊛ ⊗

April. Various colours. H 40–50 cm (16–20 in).
A 15 cm (6 in). D 10–15 cm (4–6 in). S normal
garden soil. P offsets. Very striking plant with
an irregular, curling and divided corona.

261

Narcissus

Narcissus tazetta 'Cheerfulness' / Polyanthus
Narcissus / fam. *Amaryllidaceae*
○ ◐ ◖ ⊘ ⊗ ⊗ ⊗
April–May. White. H 50 cm (20 in). A 10–
15 cm (4–6 in). D 10–15 cm (4–6 in). S normal
garden soil. P offsets. Fragrant narcissus with
several flowers per stem. Also for pot
cultivation.

Narcissus tazetta 'Cragford' / Polyanthus
Narcissus / fam. *Amaryllidaceae*
○ ◐ ◖ ⊘ ⊗ ⊗ ⊗
April–May. Various colours. H 50 cm (20 in).
A 10–15 cm (4–6 in). D 10–15 cm (4–6 in).
S normal garden soil. P offests. Fairly large
flowers, five or six on a stem. Also suitable
for pots.

Narcissus triandrus 'Albus'
Angel's Tears / fam. *Amaryllidaceae*
○ ◐ ◖ ⊘ ⊗ ⊗ ⊗
April. White. H 15 cm (6 in). A 10 cm (4 in).
D 10 cm (4 in). S normal garden soil. P offsets.
Late-flowering rock-garden plant with
pendent flowers, two or three to the stem.

Narcissus triandrus 'April Tears'
fam. *Amaryllidaceae*
○ ◐ ◖ ⊘ ⊗ ⊗ ⊗
May. Yellow. H 15–30 cm (6–12 in). A 10 cm
(4 in). D 10 cm (4 in). S normal garden soil.
P offsets. The best-known cultivar in its
species. Do not plant in groups that are too
small.

Narcissus triandrus 'Thalia'
fam. *Amaryllidaceae*
○ ◐ ◖ ⊘ ⊗ ⊗ ⊗
April–May. White. H 40 cm (16 in). A 10 cm
(4 in). D 10 cm (4 in). S normal garden soil.
P offsets. Less well known but very attractive
cultivar. Plant close to paths or terraces.

Narcissus (trumpet) 'Golden Harvest'
Daffodil / fam. *Amaryllidaceae*
○ ◐ ◖ ⊘ ⊗ ⊗ ⊗
March–April. Yellow. H 55 cm (22 in). A 15–
20 cm (6–8 in). D 10–15 cm (4–6 in). S normal
garden soil. P offsets. Trumpet daffodils have
the longest coronas of all. Easily forced.

Narcissus (trumpet) 'Satin Pink'
Daffodil / fam. *Amaryllidaceae*
○ ◐ ◖ ⊘ ⊗ ⊗ ⊗
May. White / deep yellow. H 40 cm (16 in).
A 15–20 cm (6–8 in). D 10–15 cm (4–6 in).
S normal garden soil. P offsets. Trumpet
daffodils with a pink corona are a recent
addition.

Nemesia strumosa
fam. *Scrophulariaceae*
○ ⊙ ⊗ ⊗
Sow in March in a heated greenhouse or in
April in a cold frame. Plant out at A 15–20 cm
(6–8 in). H 30–60 cm (1–2 ft). Various colours.
S humus-rich. One of the loveliest of all
summer flowers.

Nemophila maculata
fam. *Hydrophyllaceae*
○ ⊙ ⊗
Sow in April–June and thin out to A 10–15 cm
(4–6 in). H 35 cm (14 in). White / violet.
S normal garden soil. Suitable as edging for
borders or paths. Attractive saucer-shaped
flowers.

Nemophila menziesii (N. insignis)
Baby Blue Eyes / fam. *Hydrophyllaceae*
◐ ⊙ ⊛
Sow in April–June. Thin out to A 10–15 cm
(4–6 in). H 20 cm (8 in). Blue / white. S normal
garden soil. Wide-spreading plant covered in
rough hair. Feathery leaves and striking
flowers.

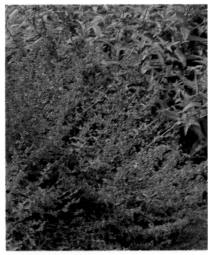

Nepeta × *faassenii*
Catmint / fam. *Labiatae*
◯ ◐ ◬ ◯ ⊛
June–August (October). Lavender blue. H 35–
45 cm (14–18 in). A 20 cm (8 in). S normal
garden soil. P division, cuttings. Aromatic; it
attracts cats. Good edging and border plant.

Nepeta grandiflora
fam. *Labiatae*
◯ ◐ ◯ ⊛
June–July. Violet-blue. H 60–80 cm (24–32 in).
A 30 cm (1 ft). S normal garden soil.
P division, cuttings. Stout stems. Leaves very
aromatic when rubbed. Attractive border
plant.

Nepeta sibirica (Dracocephalum sibiricum,
N. macrantha) / fam. *Labiatae*
◯ ◯ ⊛ ⊗
July–September. Blue. H 75 cm (30 in). A 30 cm
(1 ft). S normal garden soil. P division,
cuttings. Must be cut back after flowering.
Replant in spring. Do not remove foliage in
the winter.

Nerine bowdenii
fam. *Amaryllidaceae*
◐ ◬ ◬ ⊛ ⊛ ⊗
September–October. Pink. H 60 cm (2 ft).
A 15 cm (6 in). D 5–10 cm (2–4 in). S fertile,
well drained. P offsets. Bulbs must be covered
or grown under glass in winter. Striking
flowers.

Nerine sarniensis var. *corusca* 'Major'
Guernsey Lily / fam. *Amaryllidaceae*
◐ ◬ ◬ ⊛ ⊛ ⊗
September–October. Orange-red. H 60 cm
(2 ft). A 15 cm (6 in). D 5–10 cm (2–4 in).
S fertile. P offsets. Magnificent large flowers,
few leaves. Cover well or grow under glass in
winter.

Nicotiana alata hybrids *(N. affinis)*
Tobacco Plant / fam. *Solanaceae*
◯ ◐ ◐ ⊛ ⊙ ⊛ ⊛ ⊗
Sow in March in a heated greenhouse or in
April outside. Thin / plant out at A 25–30 cm
(10–12 in). H 1 m (3 ft). Various colours. Heavy
fragrance in the evening.

Nicotania hybrid 'White Bedder'
Tobacco Plant / fam. *Solanaceae*
◯ ⊛ ⊙ ⊛ ⊛ ⊗
Sow in March in a heated greenhouse or in
April outside. Thin / plant out at A 25–30 cm
(10–12 in). H 70 cm (28 in). White. S fertile
garden soil. There is also a green-flowered
variety.

Nierembergia repens (N. rivularis)
fam. *Solanaceae*
◯ ⊛ ◬ ◯ ⊛ ⊗
July–September. White. H 5 cm (2 in). A 20 cm
(8 in). S well drained. P division, seed. Bowl-
shaped flowers. Creeping plant suitable for
damp areas near rocks.

Nigella damascena
Love-in-a-Mist / fam. *Ranunculaceae*
Sow in April–May and thin out to A 20 cm
(8 in). H 40–60 cm (16–24 in). Red-purple, blue
or white. S good garden soil. Ornamental
plant with many possibilities; sensitive to
rain.

Nothofagus antarctica
Antarctic Beech / fam. *Fagaceae*
May. Green. H 10 m (33 ft). W 10 m (33 ft).
Zone 5. S humus-rich. P seed, cuttings.
Ornamental tree with fern-like, downy young
shoots and ovate leaves.

Nuphar lutea
Yellow Water Lily / fam. *Nymphaeaceae*
June–August. Yellow. D 60–250 cm (2–8 ft).
A 6 m (20 ft). Still water. P division of
rootstock. Invasive aquatic plant, not suitable
for small ponds. Triangular leaf stems.

Nymphaea caerulea
Water Lily / fam. *Nymphaeaceae*
May–August. Violet. H 15 cm (6 in). A 1 m
(3 ft). D 50–80 cm (20–32 in). S fertile.
P division of rootstock. Not hardy, so is
suitable only for heated pools, such as in
botanical gardens.

Nymphaea hybrid 'Aurora'
Water Lily / fam. *Nymphaeaceae*
June–August. Orange. H 15 cm (6 in). A 1 m
(3 ft). S fertile. P division of rootstock. Flowers
10 cm (4 in) across. Water depth 20–40 cm (8–
16 in). Flowers red-orange, turning copper-
coloured.

Nymphaea hybrid 'Gloriosa'
Water Lily / fam. *Nymphaeaceae*
June–August. Rose red. H 15 cm (6 in).
A 150 cm (5 ft). S fertile. P division of
rootstock. Flowers 16–18 cm (6½–7 in) across.
Water depth 40–90 cm (16–36 in). Robust
cultivar.

Nymphaea hybrid 'Hollandia'
Water Lily / fam. *Nymphaeaceae*
June–August. Pink. H 15 cm (6 in). A 2 m (6 ft).
D 50–100 cm (20–36 in). S fertile. P division of
rootstock. Most water lilies were developed
by French grower M. Latour-Marliac, but not
this.

Nymphaea hybrid 'James Brydon'
Water Lily / fam. *Nymphaeaceae*
June–August. Red. H 15 cm (6 in). A 150 cm
(5 ft). S fertile. P division of rootstock. Flowers
14 cm (5½ in) across on average. Water depth
30–70 cm (12–28 in). Valuable, typical water
lily.

Nymphaea hybrid 'Laydekeri Purpurata'
Water Lily / fam. *Nymphaeaceae*
June–August. Red. H 15 cm (6 in). A 1 m (3 ft).
S fertile. P division of rootstock. Flowers
10 cm (4 in) across. Water depth 30–50 cm (12–
20 in). Remains half-open for a long time.

Nymphaea hybrid 'Marliacea chromatella'
Water Lily / fam. *Nymphaeaceae*
○ ⊗ Ⓐ Ⓨ ⍢
Ⓢ
June–August. Yellow. H 15 cm (6 in). A 2 m
(6 ft). S fertile. P division of rootstock. Flowers
16–18 cm (6½–7 in) across. Water depth 60–
90 cm (2–3 ft). Grows vigorously in hot
weather.

Nymphaea hybrid 'Sioux'
Water Lily / fam. *Nymphaeaceae*
○ ⊗ Ⓐ Ⓨ ⍢
June–August. Orange-red. H 15 cm (6 in).
A 2 m (6 ft). S fertile. P division of rootstock.
Flowers 10–15 cm (4–6 in) across. Water depth
30–50 cm (12–20 in). Hardy at this depth.

Nymphaea hybrid 'Virginalis'
Water Lily / fam. *Nymphaeaceae*
○ ⊗ Ⓐ Ⓨ ⍢
June–August. Yellow. H 15 cm (6 in). A 4 m
(13 ft). D 60–120 cm (2–4 ft). S fertile.
P division of rootstock. In artificial ponds,
best grown in baskets filled with turf, soil,
farmyard manure.

Nymphaea pygmaea (N. tetragona)
Water Lily / fam. *Nymphaeaceae*
○ ⊗ Ⓐ Ⓨ ⍢
June–August. White. H 15 cm (6 in). A 40 cm
(16 in). S fertile. P division of rootstock.
Flowers 2.5–4 cm (1–1½ in) across. Water
depth 10–20 cm (4–8 in). The smallest of all
water lilies, suitable for containers.

*Nymphoides peltata (Limnanthemum
peltatum)* / fam. *Menyanthaceae*
○ ◐ ⊗ Ⓐ Ⓨ ⍢
July–August. Yellow. H 10 cm (4 in). A 3 m
(10 ft). D 50–150 cm (20–60 in). S fertile.
P division of rootstock. Slender, long and
creeping rootstock. Plant in pots or tubs.

Nyssa sylvatica
Tupelo / fam. *Nyssaceae*
○ ◐ ✳ ⊛ ⊛ ☺
June. Green. H 20 m (65 ft). W 12 m (40 ft).
Zone 6. S humus-rich. P seed. Tall tree with
branches that hang down to the ground. Bitter
fruits; striking autumn colouring.

*Oenanthe aquatica (Phellandrium
aquaticum)* / Fine-leaved Water Dropwort
fam. *Umbelliferae*
○ ◐ ⊗ ○ ⍢ ⍢
Sow in April. Thin out to A 30 cm (1 ft). H 20–
30 cm (8–12 in). White. S not critical. Found
in ponds, dykes and ditches. Flowers in July–
August.

Oenothera caespitosa
Evening Primrose / fam. *Onagraceae*
○ ◐ ⊗ ○ Ⓨ ⊗
June–August. Yellow. H 40–80 cm (16–32 in).
A 30 cm (1 ft). S sandy. P division, seed.
Biennial to perennial, not entirely hardy.
Suitable for paved areas and rock gardens.

Oenothera fruticosa 'Youngii'
Evening Primrose / fam. *Onagraceae*
○ ◐ ○ Ⓨ
June–August. Yellow. H 25–50 cm (10–20 in).
A 30 cm (1 ft). S normal. P division. Lightly
scented, profusely flowering border plant.
Erect stems, woody below.

Oenothera

Oenothera missouriensis
Evening Primrose / fam. *Onagraceae*
○ ◑ Ⓜ Ⓞ Ⓨ ⊛
July–October. Yellow. H 20–30 cm (8–12 in).
A 20 cm (8 in). S normal garden soil.
P division, seed. Particularly suited to rock
gardens and the front of a border. Prostrate
stems.

Omphalodes cappadocica
fam. *Boraginaceae*
○ ◑ ⌒ Ⓞ Ⓨ ⊖
April–June. Blue. H 15 cm (6 in). A 15 cm
(6 in). S normal. P division, seed. Suitable for
planting under shrubs or for northern edge
of a garden.

Omphalodes verna (O. repens)
fam. *Boraginaceae*
◑ Ⓜ Ⓞ Ⓢ ⊖
March–May. Blue. H 5–20 cm (2–8 in). A 15 cm
(6 in). S normal. P division, seed. The most
popular of the omphalodes. Not very
appealing, but makes good ground cover.

Onoclea sensibilis
Sensitive Fern / fam. *Onocleaceae*
◑ Ⓜ Ⓞ ⊗ Ⓢ ⊕
Does not flower. H 90 cm (3 ft). A 40 cm (16 in).
S fertile. P runners. Leaves open early in the
year. Vigorous grower spreading rapidly in
wet soil.

Onopordum bracteatum
fam. *Compositae*
○ ⊜ ☺ ⊛ ⊕
Sow in June and thin out to about 75 cm
(30 in). H 3 m (10 ft). Red-purple. S normal
garden soil, chalky. Imposing grey plant.
Dead-head before seed ripens.

Orchis mascula
Early Purple Orchid / fam. *Orchidaceae*
○ ◑ Ⓞ Ⓨ
May–June. Purple. H 40 cm (16 in). A 30 cm
(1 ft). S chalky. P division, seed. Very variable
species, common in shady places. Protected
plant.

Origanum vulgare
Marjoram / fam. *Labiatae*
○ ⊜ Ⓞ Ⓨ ⊛
July–September. Pale purple. H 30–60 cm (1–
2 ft). A 30 cm (1 ft). S normal garden soil.
P division, seed, cuttings. For border and rock
gardens. Does not like moisture in winter.
Wild flower.

Ornithogalum nutans
fam. *Liliaceae*
◑ ◔ ⊛ ◕ Ⓞ ⊗
April–May. White. H 20–40 cm (8–16 in).
A 10 cm (4 in). D 8–10 cm (3–4 in). S normal
garden soil. P offsets. Wild flower for the
natural garden or for cutting. Hardy.

Ornithogalum thyrsoides
Chincherinchee / fam. *Liliaceae*
○ ⊛ ◕ Ⓨ Ⓞ ⊗
August. White. H 40 cm (16 in). A 12–15 cm
(4½–6 in). D 8–10 cm (3–4 in). S normal garden
soil. P offsets. Not hardy. Plant out in late
April and lift in October. Excellent for cutting.

Ornithogalum umbellatum
Star of Bethlehem / fam. *Liliaceae*
○ ◑ ⬓ ⚛ ⚘ ⚘
April–May. White. H 15–30 cm (6–12 in).
A 20 cm (8 in). D 7 cm (2¾ in). S normal. P seed,
offsets. Suitable for naturalisation under
shrubs and woods. Flowers open at about
11 a.m.

Osmanthus yunnanensis (O. forrestii)
fam. *Oleaceae*
○ ◑ ⬓ ⚛ ⚘ ⚛ ⚘
May. Creamy white. H 8 m (26 ft). W 9 m
(30 ft). Zone 7. S humus-rich. P seed, cuttings,
layering. Tall shrub with bare branches, very
fragrant flowers and ovate, dark blue fruits.

Osmarea burkwoodii
fam. *Oleaceae*
○ ◑ ⬓ ⚛ ⚘ ⚛ ⚘
April–May. White. H 1 m (3 ft). W 1 m (3 ft).
Zone 6. S normal garden soil. P cuttings.
Dense shrub with ovate, glossy and pointed
leaves. Fragrant flowers in clusters.

Osmunda regalis
Royal Fern / fam. *Osmundaceae*
○ ◑ ⬓ ⚘ ⚘ ⬓
Does not flower. H 70–100 cm (30–36 in).
A 40 cm (16 in). S humus-rich, moist. P seed,
division of rootstock. Brown, woolly fronds
which later grow very large and turn bright
green.

Ostrya virginiana / American Hop Hornbeam
fam. *Betulaceae*
○ ◑ ⬓ ⚛ ⚘ ⬓
May. Green. H 20 m (65 ft). W 15 m (50 ft).
Zone 4. S fertile. P seed. Attractive tree of
round or pyramidal habit and bearing
spindle-shaped nuts.

Pachysandra procumbens
fam. *Buxaceae*
◑ ⬓ ⬓ ⚛ ⚛ ⬓
March–April. White / red-purple. H 25 cm
(10 in). W 30 cm (1 ft). Zone 4. S fertile soil.
P division, cuttings. Evergreen spreading
shrub with fragrant flowers.

Pachysandra terminalis
fam. *Buxaceae*
◑ ⬓ ⬓ ⚛ ⚛ ⬓
April. White. H 30 cm (1 ft). W 30 cm (1 ft).
Zone 5. S fertile soil. P division, cuttings.
Creeping semi-shrub with glossy, coarsely
toothed leaves and tiny flowers in spikes.

Paeonia lactiflora (P. albiflora, P. sinensis)
Paeony / fam. *Paeoniaceae*
○ ○ ⚛ ⚛
June–July. Pink. H 70–100 cm (28–36 in).
A 50 cm (20 in). S very fertile (clay).
P division. Often sold as a paeony hybrid:
there are at least 3000 cultivars. From China.

Paeonia lactiflora 'Duchesse de Nemours'
Paeony / fam. *Paeoniaceae*
○ ○ ⚛ ⚛
June–July. White. H 70–100 cm (28–36 in).
A 50 cm (20 in). S very fertile (clay).
P division. Fine hardy perennial. Very
suitable for a mixed border.

Paeonia

Paeonia lactiflora hybrid 'Bunker Hill'
Paeony / fam. *Paeoniaceae*
○○⓰ⓨ⊗
June–July. Red. H 70–100 cm (28–36 in).
A 50 cm (20 in). S very fertile (clay).
P division. Complaints that hybrids do not
flower must be blamed on the soil.

**Paeonia lactifloria hybrid 'Dr Alexander
Fleming'** / Paeony / fam. *Paeoniaceae*
○○⓰ⓨ⊗
June–July. Pink. H 70–100 cm (28–36 in).
A 50 cm (20 in). S very fertile (clay).
P division. Replant hybrids in August–
September, but not in the first five to ten
years of life. Thin out.

Paeonia lactiflora 'Reine Hortense'
Paeony / fam. *Paeoniaceae*
○○⓰ⓨ⊗
June–July. White / red. H 70–100 cm (28–
36 in). A 50 cm (20 in). S very fertile (clay).
P division. Hybrids develop rather slowly,
over several years. Support with twiggy
sticks.

Paeonia mascula ssp. arietina
Paeony / fam. *Paeoniaceae*
○◑⓰ⓨ⊗
May. Red. H 120 cm (4 ft). A 50–60 cm (20–
24 in). S fertile. P division. Magnificent silky
petals. Wild flower, resistant to drought.

Paeonia mlokosewitschii
Paeony / fam. *Paeoniaceae*
○◑⓰ⓨ⊗
April–May. White. H 50–60 cm (20–24 in).
A 30 cm (1 ft). S fertile. P division, seed. Not
suitable for heavy soil. Does badly in wet
summers.

Paeonia officinalis 'Rubra Plena'
Paeony / fam. *Paeoniaceae*
○◑⓰ⓨ⊗
May–June. Crimson-red. H 35–75 cm (14–
30 in). A 1 m (3 ft). S fertile. P division.
Attractive strong-growing plant with dense
double, globular flowers. The most popular
paeony.

Paeonia suffruticosa hybrid
Paeony / fam. *Paeoniaceae*
○⌃⓰ⓨ
May–June. White / pink. H 1.5 m (5 ft).
W 1.5 m (5 ft). Zone 6. S fertile soil. P division,
cuttings. Shrub with thick branches, large
trifoliate leaves and large double flowers.

Paeonia tenuifolia 'Plena'
Paeony / fam. *Paeoniaceae*
○⌃⓰ⓨ⊗
May–June. Rose-red. H 60 cm (2 ft). A 30 cm
(1 ft). S fertile. P division, seed. Graceful plant
with fine foliage from South-east Europe. For
a warm position.

Paeonia wittmanniana hybrid 'Maimorgen'
Paeony / fam. *Paeoniaceae*
○○ⓨ⊗
May. Red. H 1 m (3 ft). A 80 cm (32 in).
S fertile, fairly dry. P division. Large, single
flowers. Demands well-drained loamy soil.

Panicum virgatum 'Rehbraun'
fam. *Gramineae*
○ ⊝ ⊙ ⓨ ⊛ ⊗
July–September. Reddish brown. H 60–
150 cm (2–5 ft). A 50 cm (20 in). S fertile garden
soil. P seed, division. Ornamental grass
forming dense bushy clumps. Erect, smooth
stems. Vigorous.

Papaver nudicaule
Iceland Poppy/**fam. *Papaveraceae***
○ ◐ ⊙ ⊝ ⓨ ⊛ ⊗
June–September. Various colours. H 30–45 cm
(12–18 in). A 20 cm (8 in). S normal garden
soil. P division, seed. Flowers profusely for a
long time. Often grown as a biennial.

Papaver orientale 'Perry's White'
Poppy/**fam. *Papaveraceae***
○ ◐ ⊙ ⓨ ⊛ ⊗
June. White. H 60–90 cm (2–3 ft). A 40 cm
(16 in). S normal garden soil. P division, root
cuttings. Suitable for a border. Most leaves
die after the flowering period.

Papaver rhoeas
Field Poppy/**fam. *Papaveraceae***
○ ◐ ◐ ⊝ ⊙ ⓨ ⊛ ⊗
Sow in April and thin out to A 25–30 cm (10–
12 in). H 30–90 cm (1–3 ft). Red. S not critical.
Very variable species. Recommended for
annual borders.

Papaver somniferum
Poppy/**fam. *Papaveraceae***
○ ◐ ◐ ⊝ ⊙ ⓨ ⊗
Sow in April and thin out to A 25–30 cm (10–
12 in). H 1 m (3 ft). Various colours. S not
critical. Also grown for its edible seeds.

Parrotia persica
fam. *Hamamelidaceae*
○ ◐ ◐ ◐ ⊛ ⊛ ⓨ ⊘ ⊕
March–April. Yellow. H 10 m (33 ft). W 8 m
(26 ft). Zone 5. S normal. P seed, cuttings,
layering. Tree with a broad, rounded crown,
often grown as a shrub. Flowers in clusters;
no petals.

Parthenocissus henryana (Vitis henryana)
Chinese Virginia Creeper/**fam. *Vitaceae***
○ ◐ ◐ ⊘ ⊛ ⊛ ⊛
June–July. Green. H 9 m (30 ft). W 6 m (20 ft).
Zone 6. S humus-rich. P seed, cuttings,
layering. Self-attaching climber with leaves
that turn brilliant red in the autumn.

Parthenocissus inserta (P. vitacea var. typica)
Common Virginia Creeper/**fam. *Vitaceae***
○ ◐ ◐ ⊘ ⊛ ⊛ ⊛
June–July. Green. H 10 m (33 ft). W 4 m (13 ft).
Zone 5. S humus-rich. P seed, cuttings,
layering. Low climbing shrub, not self-
clinging. Blue-black fruits.

*Parthenocissus quinquefolia (Ampelopsis
quinquefolia)*/Virginia Creeper/**fam.
*Vitaceae***
○ ◐ ◐ ⊘ ⊛ ⊛ ⊛
June–July. Green. H 20 m (65 ft). W 6 m (20 ft).
Zone 5. S humus-rich. P seed, cuttings,
layering. Spreading climber, not self-clinging.
Autumn colour.

Parthenocissus tricuspidata (autumn)
Boston Ivy / fam. *Vitaceae*
○ ◐ ⊛ ⊛ ⊛
For description and P see last entry.
Attractive, deciduous climber with
inconspicuous flowers and fruits and simple
or trifoliate leaves.

Passiflora caerulea
Passion Flower / fam. *Passifloraceae*
○ ⊘ ⊛ ⊛ ⊛
June–September. White-green / blue. H 3 m
(10 ft). W 1 m (3 ft). Zone 7. S fertile. P seed,
cuttings. Will grow outdoors in sheltered sites
in the south and west. Cover during the
winter.

Paulownia tomentosa (P. imperialis)
fam. *Scrophulariaceae*
○ ◐ ⊛ ⊛ ⊛ ⊛ ⊛
April–May. Violet, yellow. H 10 m (33 ft).
W 4.5 m (15 ft). Zone 5. S fertile. P seed,
cuttings. Sturdy tree with a broad crown and
spreading branches. Flowers appear before
leaves.

***Pelargonium zonale* 'Mustang'**
fam. *Geraniaceae*
○ ⊜ ⊙ ⊛ ⊛
Sow in February in a heated greenhouse.
Plant out at A 25 cm (10 in). H 30 cm (1 ft). Red.
S humus-rich. Early-flowering and rain-
resistant hybrid.

***Pelargonium zonale* 'Ringo Dolly'**
fam. *Geraniaceae*
○ ⊜ ⊙ ⊛ ⊛
For propagation and description see last
entry. Growing pelargoniums from seed
rather than from cuttings saves time.

Peltiphyllum peltatum (leaves)
Umbrella Plant / fam. *Saxifragaceae*
◐ ◑ ⊛ ○ ⊛ ⊛ ⊕
April–May. Pink. H 50–100 cm (20–36 in).
A 40–50 cm (16–20 in). S fertile. P division,
seed. The large, glossy, shield-shaped leaves
come out after the flowers. Plant in a cool site.

Peltiphyllum peltatum (flowers)
Umbrella Plant / fam. *Saxifragaceae*
◐ ◑ ⊛ ○ ⊛ ⊛ ⊕
April–May. Pink. H 50–100 cm (20–36 in).
A 40–50 cm (16–20 in). S fertile. P division,
seed. The flowers, 40 cm (16 in) tall, appear
before the leaves unfold. Attractive near
ponds.

Pennisetum alopecuroides (P. compressum)
fam. *Gramineae*
○ ⊛ ⊛ ⊛ ⊛ ⊗
August–September. Grey-brown. H 1 m (3 ft).
A 50 cm (20 in). S good garden soil. P seed,
division. Attractive ornamental grass for
warm sites. Forms dense clumps with many
flower spikes.

Pennisetum villosum (P. longistylum)
fam. *Gramineae*
○ ⊙ ⊛ ⊛ ⊗
Sow in April in the open. Thin to A 40 cm
(16 in). H 50–75 cm (20–30 in). Greeny yellow.
S not critical. Not hardy in cold areas; usually
grown as an annual.

Penstemon campanulatus
fam. *Scrophulariaceae*
○ ⊙ ◎ ⊛ ⊗
July–September. Rose-purple. H 30–50 cm
(12–20 in). A 20 cm (8 in). S good garden soil.
P division, seed, cuttings. Free flowering and
drought resistant. Needs some cover in severe
winters.

Penstemon hartwegii 'Blue Gem'
fam. *Scrophulariaceae*
○ ⊙ ◎ ⊛ ⊗
July–October. Violet. H 40–60 cm (16–24 in).
A 20–30 cm (8–12 in). S humus-rich, sandy.
P division, cuttings, seed. Attractive border
plant but not very hardy. Long flowering
period.

Penstemon hybrid 'Sensation'
fam. *Scrophulariaceae*
○ ⊙ ⊛ ⊗
Sow in February–March in a heated
greenhouse. Plant out at A 30 cm (1 ft). H 30–
80 cm (12–32 in). Various colours. S humus-
rich. Graceful stems and large flowers.
Dislikes damp.

Penstemon scouleri
fam. *Scrophulariaceae*
○ ⊙ ◎ ⊛ ⊗
May–June. Purple-violet. H 15 cm (6 in).
A 20 cm (8 in). S good garden soil. P division,
seed, cuttings. Needs a warm and dry
position; lime free. Very free flowering.

Perilla frutescens 'Atropurpurea'
fam. *Labiatae*
○ ⊙ ⊚
Sow in March in a heated greenhouse. Plant
out at A 30 cm (1 ft). H 1 m (3 ft). White. S good
garden soil. Magnificent foliage plant for beds
and containers. Spicy smell when bruised.

Pernettya mucronata
fam. *Ericaceae*
○ ⊙ ⊛ ⊛ ⊛ ⊛ ⊗
May–June. White. H 1 m (3 ft). W 1 m (3 ft).
Zone 5. S lime free. P seed, cuttings.
Dioecious shrub with small, glossy, dark
green leaves coming to a prickly point.

Perovskia atriplicifolia 'Blue Spire'
fam. *Labiatae*
○ ⊖ ◎ ⊛ ⊛ ⊗
August–September. Violet-blue. H 150 cm
(5 ft). A 45 cm (18 in). S chalky, well drained.
P seed, cuttings. Sub-shrub of very erect
habit, covered in white wool. Leaves smell of
sage.

Petteria ramentacea
fam. *Leguminosae*
○ ⊛ ⊙ ⊛
June. Yellow. H 2 m (6 ft). W 3 m (10 ft). Zone
5. S normal garden soil. P seed. Stiffly erect
shrub with bare branches, trifoliate leaves
and fragrant flowers.

Petunia grandiflora 'Duo Karmijn'
fam. *Solanaceae*
○ ⊛ ⊙
For P see *Petunia* hybrid 'Circus'. H 30 cm
(1 ft). White / red. S humus-rich. Large-
flowered cultivar. Flowers ruffled and frilled.

271

Petunia

Petunia hybrid 'Circus'
fam. Solanaceae
○ ⊛ ⊙ ⊗
Sow in January–March in a heated greenhouse. Plant out at A 30 cm (1 ft). H 40 cm (16 in). Red. S humus-rich. Large double flowers. Petunias are slightly sticky to the touch. They flower profusely.

Petunia hybrid 'Orchid Cloud'
fam. Solanaceae
○ ⊛ ⊙ ⊗
For P see *Petunia* hybrid 'Circus'. H 40 cm (16 in). Red-purple. S humus-rich. Large single flowers. Petunias flower most prolifically in sheltered sites.

Petunia hybrid 'Star Joy' (front)
fam. Solanaceae
○ ⊛ ⊙ ⊗
Sow in January–March in a heated greenhouse. Plant out at A 30 cm (1 ft). H 40 cm (16 in). Red-purple / white. S humus-rich. Member of the *Nana Compacta Multiflora* group. Weather resistant.

Phacelia campanularia
fam. Hydrophyllaceae
○ ⊙ ⊗
Sow in April and thin out to A 15 cm (6 in). H 25 cm (10 in). Gentian blue. S not critical. Bushy plant with densely branched stems and very fragrant leaves. For the front of the border.

Phacelia tanacetifolia
fam. Hydrophyllaceae
○ ⊙ ⊗
Sow in April outside. Thin out to A 15 cm (6 in). H 30–70 cm (12–28 in). Lavender. S not critical. Entire plant is hairy. Makes good green manure. Attractive to bees.

Phalaris arundinacea 'Picta'
Reed Canary Grass / fam. Gramineae
○ ⊗ ○ ⊗
June–July. White. H 1 m (3 ft). A 50 cm (20 in). S normal garden soil. P division. Variegated ornamental grass that spreads very rapidly. Can even grow in water.

Phalaris canariensis
Canary Grass / fam. Gramineae
○ ⊙ ⊗ ⊗
Sow in April and thin out to A 25 cm (10 in). H 15–60 cm (6–24 in). White. S fertile. Grown commercially for bird seed but can also be dried for winter decoration. Attractive spikelets.

Phellodendron amurense
fam. Rutaceae
○ ◑ ⊛ ⊗ ⊗
June. Green-yellow. H 15 m (50 ft). W 10 m (33 ft). S not critical. P seed, cuttings. Tree with cork-like bark. Leaves smell of turpentine when bruised. Zone 3.

Phellodendron japonicum
fam. Rutaceae
○ ◑ ⊛ ⊗ ⊗ ⊗
June. Yellow-green. H 15 m (50 ft). W 12 m (40 ft). Zone 4. S not critical. P seed, division. Stout tree of broad habit. Thin, dark brown bark. Leaves downy underneath.

***Philadelphus* hybrid 'Belle Etoile'**
Mock Orange / fam. *Saxifragaceae*
○ ◑ ⊕ ⊗ ⊕ ⊥ ⊗
June–July. White. H 3 m (10 ft). W 2 m (6 ft).
Zone 5. S normal garden soil. P cuttings.
Robust shrub with peeling stems. The single
flowers are saucer shaped and slightly frilled.
Fragrant.

Philadelphus* × *lemoinei
Mock Orange / fam. *Saxifragaceae*
○ ◑ ⊕ ⊗ ⊥ ⊗
June–July. White. H 2 m (6 ft). W 1.5 (5 ft).
Zone 5. S normal garden soil. P cuttings.
Upright shrub with slender branches, small
leaves and single, highly fragrant flowers.

Philadelphus lewisii* var. *gordonianus
Mock Orange / fam. *Saxifragaceae*
○ ◑ ⊕ ⊗ ⊥ ⊗
June–July. White. H 4 m (13 ft). W 3 m (10 ft).
Zone 5. S normal garden soil. P cuttings.
Upright shrub of broad habit. Hairy stems
and lightly scented flowers.

Phlomis samia
fam. *Labiatae*
○ ⊼ ◐ ⊗ ⊗
June–July. Yellow. H 60–100 cm (2–3 ft).
A 30 cm (1 ft). S humus-rich. P seed, division.
Hairy plant, suitable for a border, for planting
alongside a light hedge or for dry walls.

Phlomis tuberosa
fam. *Labiatae*
○ ⊛ ⊗
July–August. Purple-violet. H 60–100 cm (2–
3 ft). A 40 cm (16 in). S normal garden soil.
P division, seed, cuttings. This strong-
growing plant demands a sheltered position.

Phlox amoena
fam. *Polemoniaceae*
○ ◑ ⊜ ⊼ ◐ ⊗ ⊗
April–May. Purple. H 15–30 cm (6–12 in).
A 30 cm (1 ft). S humus-rich, fertile. P root
cuttings, seed. Variable species with short,
erect stalks, lanceolate leaves and flowers in
clusters.

Phlox douglasii
fam. *Polemoniaceae*
○ ◑ ⊜ ⊼ ◐ ⊗ ⊛ ⊗
May–June. Purple. H 10 cm (4 in). A 10 cm
(4 in). S chalky. P division, seed. Evergreen.
Flowers in profusion. Mat-forming plant
suitable for rock gardens and dry walls.

Phlox douglasii* var. *diffusa
fam. *Polemoniaceae*
○ ◑ ◑ ⊼ ◐ ⊗ ⊛ ⊗ ⊜
May–June. Violet. H 10 cm (4 in). A 10 cm
(4 in). S chalky. P division, seed. Evergreen,
richly flowering, fast-growing rock and
splendid ground-cover plant.

***Phlox drummondii* 'Cuspidata'**
fam. *Polemoniaceae*
○ ⊙ ⊗ ⊗
Sow in March–April in a heated greenhouse
or in May outside. Thin / plant out at A 20 cm
(8 in). H 30 cm (1 ft). Red. S fertile. Popular
garden plant with erect stems and prettily
shaped flowers.

Phlox

Phlox drummondii 'Globe'
fam. *Polemoniaceae*
○ ⊙ ⊗ ⊗
For P see *Phlox drummondii* 'Cuspidata'.
H 15 cm (6 in). White / red. S fertile soil.
Rewarding flowers in summer and autumn.
Attractive compact habit. Lanceolate leaves.

Phlox drummondii 'Stellata'
fam. *Polemoniaceae*
○ ⊙ ⊗ ⊗
For P see *Phlox drummondii* 'Cuspidata'.
H 30 cm (1 ft). Red / white. S fertile soil.
Sensitive to cold at the juvenile stage. Flowers
in dense clusters from July to September.

Phlox paniculata 'Bright Eyes'
fam. *Polemoniaceae*
○ ⊕ ○ ⊗ ⊗
August–September. Rose-purple. H 100 cm
(3 ft). A 40 cm (16 in). S fertile. P division, root
cuttings. Reliable border plant. A variety with
a spectacular 'eye'.

Phlox paniculata hybrid 'Mies Copijn'
fam. *Polemoniaceae*
○ ⊕ ○ ⊗ ⊗
August–September. Pink. H 100 cm (3 ft).
A 40 cm (16 in). S fertile. P division, root
cuttings. Attractive border plant. Dress
regularly and water liberally during the
growing season.

Phlox paniculata hybrid 'White Admiral'
fam. *Polemoniaceae*
○ ⊕ ○ ⊗ ⊗
August–September. White. H 100 cm (3 ft).
A 40 cm (16 in). S fertile. P division, root
cuttings. Difficult to cultivate. Flowers
profusely. Lends itself to many combinations.

Phlox paniculata 'Mrs Ethel Prichard'
fam. *Polemoniaceae*
○ ⊕ ○ ⊗ ⊗
August–September. Red. H 90 cm (3 ft).
A 40 cm (16 in). S fertile. P division, root
cuttings. Phlox is often attacked by stem and
bulb eelworms. Prevent by treating the soil.

Phlox paniculata 'Spitfire'
fam. *Polemoniaceae*
○ ⊕ ○ ⊗ ⊗
August–September. Red. H 90 cm (3 ft).
A 40 cm (16 in). S fertile. P division, root
cuttings. Very bright colour, difficult to
combine with other flowers. Blooms in
profusion over a long period.

Phlox subulata 'Apple Blossom'
fam. *Polemoniaceae*
○ ⊕ ○ ⊗ ⊗
April–June Violet. H 10 cm (4 in). A 10 cm
(4 in). S fertile. P division, cuttings. Mat-
forming plant. Requires a well-drained and
warm site.

Phormium tenax 'Atropurpureum'
New Zealand Flax / fam. *Liliaceae*
○ ⊗ ○ ⊛ ⊛ ⊕
July–August. Violet. H 2 m (6 ft). A 1 m (3 ft).
S potting compost. P division, seed. Half-
hardy. Plant in deep, moist soil in a sunny
position and protect with straw or bracken in
winter.

Photinia villosa
fam. *Rosaceae*
○ ⊛ ✽ ⊚ ⊛ ⊕
June. White. H 5 m (16 ft). W 3 m (10 ft). Zone 4. S light, sandy. P seed, layering, grafting. Large shrub with thin stems, ovate red fruits and foliage colouring in autumn.

Phuopsis stylosa (Crucianella stylosa)
fam. *Rubiaceae*
○ ⊕ ⊙ ⊚
June–August. Purple. H 20 cm (8 in). A 20 cm (8 in). S fertile. P division. Mat-forming plant with a profusion of flowers over an exceptionally long period. Excellent in a border.

Phygelius capensis
Cape Figwort / fam. *Scrophulariaceae*
○ ○ ⊘ ⊚ ⊛
July–October. Red, yellow. H 90 cm (3 ft). A 50 cm (20 in). S humus-rich. P seed, cuttings. Small sub-shrub that can flower long and freely. Protect against frost.

Phyllitis scolopendrium (S. vulgare)
Hart's Tongue Fern / fam. *Aspleniaceae*
⊕ ⊕ ⊞ ○ ○ ⊚ ⊛
Does not flower. H 40 cm (16 in). A 20 cm (8 in). P division. Evergreen. Found on cool mountain slopes (protected). A fern with glossy fronds.

Physalis alkekengi var. *franchetii*
Chinese Lantern / fam. *Solanaceae*
○ ⊕ ⊕ ⊛ ⊗
July. White. H 1 m (3 ft). A 50 cm (20 in). S fertile. P division, seed. Its orange-red berries are the chief attraction of this plant. Very invasive.

Physocarpus capitatus
fam. *Rosaceae*
○ ⊕ ⊛ ⊚ ⊛
June. Pink. H 3 m (10 ft). W 3 m (10 ft). Zone 5. S not critical. P seed, cuttings. Upright, broadly arching shrub with leafy flower stems and bladder-like fruits.

Physostegia virginiana 'Bouquet Rose'
Obedient Plant / fam. *Labiatae*
○ ○ ⊚ ⊚ ⊛ ⊗
July–September. Rose-pink. H 90 cm (3 ft). A 30 cm (1 ft). S good garden soil. P division. Free-flowering plant with rather weak stems. Better for cutting than for a border.

Physostegia virginiana 'Rosy Spire'
Obedient Plant / fam. *Labiatae*
○ ○ ⊚ ⊚ ⊛ ⊗
July–September. Rose-purple. H 90 cm (3 ft). A 30 cm (1 ft). S good garden soil. P division. Erect plant. The flowers can be pushed to any side and will remain in that position.

Physostegia virginiana 'Summer Snow'
Obedient Plant / fam. *Labiatae*
○ ○ ⊚ ⊛ ⊗
July–September. White. H 90 cm (3 ft). A 40 cm (16 in). S fertile. P division. Also comes in purple varieties. Sturdy and hardy.

275

Phyteuma orbiculare
fam. _Campanulaceae_
May–September. Violet-blue. H 20–40 cm (8–16 in). A 15 cm (6 in). S humus-rich. P seed. Mat-forming plant with bare and erect flower stems and flowers closely set on spikes.

Phytolacca acinosa (P. esculenta)
fam. _Phytolaccaceae_
June–July. White. H 2 m (6 ft). A 90 cm (3 ft). S good garden soil. P seed, division. Hardy, wide-spreading plant from Asia with long erect spikes of flowers.

Picea abies 'Acrocona'
Norway Spruce / fam. _Pinaceae_
Large conifer which will spread out considerably if not pruned in youth. Fine cones. H 6–8 m (20–26 ft). W 8 m (26 ft). S normal garden soil. P cuttings. Zone 4.

Picea abies 'Clanbrassiliana'
Norway Spruce / fam. _Pinaceae_
Compact, conical conifer. Grows so slowly it may be considered a shrub. Round crown, reddish-brown buds, hard needles. H 2 m (6 ft). W 3 m (10 ft). S normal garden soil. P cuttings. Zone 4.

Picea abies 'Nidiformis'
Norway Spruce / fam. _Pinaceae_
Very slow-growing conifer. Young plants have a nest-shaped depression in the middle. Hard needles. H 1–2 m (3–6 ft). W 2–3 m (6–10 ft). S normal garden soil. P cuttings. Zone 4.

Picea abies 'Repens'
Norway Spruce / fam. _Pinaceae_
Broad conifer with branches flat on the ground and short, radially arranged needles. Ideal for slopes. H 50 cm (20 in). W 1.5 m (5 ft). S normal. P cuttings. Zone 4.

Picea abies 'Wartburg'
Norway Spruce / fam. _Pinaceae_
Attractive, densely branched weeping stem, its branches hanging straight down. H 4 m (13 ft). W 2 m (6 ft). S normal garden soil. P cuttings. Zone 4.

Picea brewerana
Brewer's Spruce / fam. _Pinaceae_
Graceful spruce with long curtains of shoots. Large cones. H 30 m (100 ft). W 6 m (20 ft). S not critical. P cuttings. Zone 2.

Picea glauca 'Albertiana'
Canadian Spruce / fam. _Pinaceae_
Slow-growing dwarf conifer of regular, conical and compact habit. Thin needles. H 3 m (10 ft). W 1 m (3 ft). S humus-rich. P cuttings. Zone 4.

Picea glauca 'Conica'
Canadian Spruce / fam. *Pinaceae*
○ ◐ ⊛ ◉ ⊛
Slow-growing conifer of regular, narrowly conical habit. Covered densely with soft, light green needles. H 2–3 m (6–10 ft). W 1 m (3 ft). S normal garden soil. P cuttings. Zone 4.

Picea glauca 'Echiniformis'
Canadian Spruce / fam. *Pinaceae*
○ ◐ ⊛ ◉ ⊛
Slow-growing dwarf shrub of dense rounded habit. Forms a little mound with a flat crown. H 80 cm (32 in). W 1.5 m (5 ft). S normal garden soil. P cuttings. Zone 4.

Picea likiangensis var. *balfouriana*
Spruce / fam. *Pinaceae*
○ ⊛ ◉ ⊕
Tree with dark green needles set closely against hairy shoots. Crimson cones. Erect shoot tips. H 40 m (135 ft). W 6 m (20 ft). S normal garden soil. P cuttings. Zone 4.

Picea mariana (P. nigra)
Black Spruce / fam. *Pinaceae*
○ ◐ ⊛ ◉ ⊛ ⊛ ⊕
Pyramidal tree. Branches densely packed with shoots. Red-brown ovate cones. An important source of newsprint. H 15 m (50 ft). W 7 m (23 ft). S normal garden soil. P cuttings. Zone 2.

Picea omorika (Pinus omorika)
Serbian Spruce / fam. *Pinaceae*
○ ◐ ⊛ ◉ ⊛ ⊛ ⊕
Fast-growing, narrowly pyramidal, almost columnar conifer with blunt needles and violet-blue cones that appear at a young stage. H 20 m (65 ft). W 3–5 m (10–16 ft). S not critical. P seed. Zone 4.

Picea omorika 'Nana'
Serbian Spruce / fam. *Pinaceae*
○ ◐ ⊛ ◉ ⊛ ⊛ ⊕
Dwarf form, broadly conical habit. The radially spreading needles have two white and blue stripes underneath. H 1.5 m (5 ft). W 1 m (3 ft). S not critical. P cuttings. Zone 4.

Picea pungens 'Argentea'
Colorado Spruce / fam. *Pinaceae*
○ ◐ ⊛ ◉ ⊛ ⊕
Conical tree with bright silvery-blue foliage that looks attractive even in winter. Short needles. H 10 m (33 ft). W 6 m (20 ft). S not critical. P grafting. Zone 2.

Picea pungens 'Glauca'
Colorado Spruce / fam. *Pinaceae*
○ ◐ ⊛ ◉ ⊛ ⊕ ⊗
Conical tree, fairly quick growing and with sharp, radially set grey-blue and blue-green needles. H 25 m (80 ft). W 5 m (16 ft). S not critical. P cuttings. Zone 2.

Picea pungens 'Glauca Globosa' ('Globosa')
Colorado Spruce / fam. *Pinaceae*
○ ◐ ⊛ ◉ ⊛ ⊛
Slow-growing dense, blue-green conifer of irregular shape. Retains its colour throughout the year. Large cones. H 1 m (3 ft). W 1 m (3 ft). S not critical. P cuttings. Zone 2.

Picea

Picea pungens 'Koster'
Colorado Spruce / fam. *Pinaceae*
○ ◖ ❊ ⊛ 🐾 ⊕ ⊛
One of the finest cultivars with magnificent blue needles and glossy 10-cm (4-in) cones ripening to a shiny pale brown. H 10 m (33 ft). W 4 m (13 ft). S not critical. P grafting. Zone 2.

Picea wilsonii
Spruce / fam. *Pinaceae*
○ ◖ ❊ ⊛ 🐾 ⊕ ⊛
Pyramidal tree with short horizontal branches, sharp, broad needles and oval cones. H 7 m (23 ft). W 7 m (23 ft). S normal garden soil. P cuttings. Zone 5.

Pieris floribunda (Andromeda floribunda)
fam. *Ericaceae*
○ ◖ ◍ 🌱 ⊛
April–May. White. H 2 m (6 ft). W 2 m (6 ft). Zone 4. S humus-rich, lime free. P seed, cuttings. Dense shrub with leathery leaves and bell-shaped flowers in erect panicles.

Pieris forrestii (P. formosa var. forrestii)
fam. *Ericaceae*
○ ◖ ◍ 🌱 🐾 ⊛
April–May. White. H 3 m (10 ft). W 4 m (13 ft). Zone 6–7. S humus-rich, lime free. P seed, cuttings. Shrub with red juvenile foliage. Fragrant flowers in pendent panicles.

Pieris japonica (Andromeda japonica)
fam. *Ericaceae*
○ ◖ ◍ 🌱 🐾 ⊕
March–May. White. H 3 m (10 ft). W 3 m (10 ft). Zone 5. S humus-rich, lime free. P seed, cuttings. Broad, erect shrub with flowers in drooping panicles and red juvenile foliage.

Pinus cembra 'Compacta Glauca'
Stone Pine / fam. *Pinaceae*
○ ◍ 🐾 ⊛ ⊕
Slender conifer, densely branched all the way down. Needles blue-green on top and blue-white underneath. H 2 m (6 ft). W 1 m (3 ft). S humus-rich. P cuttings. Zone 4.

Pinus contorta (P. inops)
Beach Pine / fam. *Pinaceae*
○ ◖ ❊ 🐾 ⊛ ⊕
Good garden tree with needles in pairs, often strangely contorted when young. Yellow-brown cones. H 5–6 m (16–20 ft). W 4 m (13 ft). S not critical. P seed. Zone 7.

Pinus densiflora 'Umbraculifera'
Japanese Red Pine / fam. *Pinaceae*
○ ◍ 🐾 ⊛ ⊕ ⊛
Attractive conifer, slow growing, with an umbrella-shaped crown and dark green limp needles in pairs. H 3 m (10 ft). W 3 m (10 ft). S humus-rich. P cuttings. Zone 4.

Pinus heldreichii
Pine / fam. *Pinaceae*
○ ❊ 🐾 ⊛ ⊕
Vigorous conifer of attractive conical habit. Dark green needles and blue cones. H 20 m (65 ft). W 8 m (26 ft). S humus-rich. P seed, cuttings. Zone 5.

278

Pinus leucodermis 'Satellit'
Bosnian Pine / fam. *Pinaceae*
◯ ⊖ ⊛ ⊘ ⊛ ⊕
Slender, fairly loosely branched, conical tree
with light green, long needles bent towards
the branches. H 20 m (65 ft). W 8 m (26 ft).
S humus-rich. P cuttings. Zone 5.

Pinus mugo 'Gnom'
Mountain Pine / fam. *Pinaceae*
◯ ⊕ ⊘ ⊛ ⊛ ⊗
Shrubby pine with needles in pairs and white
juvenile shoots in the spring. H 1.5–2 m (5–
6 ft). W 1.5–2 m (5–6 ft). S not critical.
P grafting. Zone 2.

Pinus mugo 'Mops'
Mountain Pine / fam. *Pinaceae*
◯ ⊕ ⊘ ⊛ ⊛ ⊗
Attractive low-growing pine of compact
rounded habit. Reddish-brown resinous
buds. H 1 m (3 ft). W 1.5 m (5 ft). S not critical.
P grafting, cuttings. Zone 2.

Pinus nigra ssp. *nigra*
Austrian Pine / fam. *Pinaceae*
◯ ⊖ ⊚ ⊛ ⊘ ⊛ ⊕
Robust tree, later with an umbrella-shaped
crown, dark green, long and stiff needles, in
pairs. Broad cones. H 20 m (65 ft). W 6 m (20 ft).
S not critical. P cuttings. Zone 4.

Pinus parviflora 'Glauca'
Japanese White Pine / fam. *Pinaceae*
◯ ⊖ ⊛ ⊛ ⊛ ⊕
Attractive specimen tree with striking blue
needles in bunches of five. Cones compact,
erect, ovate. H 15 m (50 ft). W 4–6 m (13–20 ft).
Zone 5. S slightly acid. P cuttings, grafting.

Pinus pinea
Italian Stone Pine / fam. *Pinaceae*
◯ ⊛ ⊘ ⊛ ⊛ ⊕
Picturesque tree with a thick, rough, reddish-
brown trunk, long, bright green, slightly
twisted needles and large reddish cones.
H 30 m (100 ft). W 20 m (65 ft). S humus-rich.
P seed. Zone 8.

Pinus ponderosa
Western Yellow Pine / fam. *Pinaceae*
◯ ⊛ ⊘ ⊛ ⊛ ⊕
Fast-growing tree with a small number of
short branches set regularly round the stem.
Very long needles, large cones. H 40 m (135 ft).
W 20 m (65 ft). S humus-rich. P seed, cuttings.
Zone 5.

Pinus pumila
Dwarf Pine / fam. *Pinaceae*
◯ ⊖ ⊕ ⊛ ⊘ ⊛ ⊗
Shrub with blue-green needles in groups of
five, 4–7 cm (1½–2¾ in) in length. The purple-
violet cones turn reddish brown. H 3 m (10 ft).
W 5 m (16 ft). S not critical. P seed. Zone 3.

Pinus pumila 'Glauca'
Dwarf Pine / fam. *Pinaceae*
◯ ⊕ ⊚ ⊛ ⊘ ⊛ ⊗
Very slow-growing shrub with fairly short,
blue-grey needles. Compact habit. Arresting
cones set close together. H 3 m (10 ft). W 3 m
(10 ft). S not critical. P cuttings. Zone 5.

Pinus

Pinus radiata (P. insignis)
Monterey Pine / fam. *Pinaceae*
○ ➔ ✿ 🌿 🌲 🌼 ⏚
Fast-growing tree with a rough trunk. The bright green needles in groups of three are shed in the third year. Elongated cones. H 35 m (115 ft). W 20 m (65 ft). S humus-rich. P seed. Zone 6–7.

Pinus strobus
Weymouth Pine / fam. *Pinaceae*
○ ✿ 🌿 🌲 🌼 ⏚
Pyramidal tree with slender branches, blue-green, often pendent needles and elongated cones in small bunches. H 40 m (135 ft). W 20 m (65 ft). S humus-rich. P seed, cuttings. Zone 3.

Pinus strobus 'Radiata'
Weymouth Pine / fam. *Pinaceae*
○ 🌰 🌿 🌲 ⏚
Dense dwarf conifer of compact, globular habit. Needles green on top, bluish underneath and pressed close to the shoots. H 2 m (6 ft). W 2 m (6 ft). S humus-rich. P cuttings. Zone 3.

Pinus sylvestris
Scots Pine / fam. *Pinaceae*
○ ⊜ ✿ 🌿 🌲
Tree with an umbrella-shaped crown, bare yellow-grey branches, pointed, non-resinous buds and blue-green needles. H 35 m (115 ft). W 10 m (33 ft). S not critical. P seed. Zone 3.

Pinus sylvestris 'Beuvronensis'
Scots Pine / fam. *Pinaceae*
○ ⊜ 🌰 🌿 🌲 ⏚
Broad, rounded, slow-growing dwarf pine, first compact but later somewhat looser in habit. Striking brown winter buds. H 1 m (3 ft). W 2 m (6 ft). S humus-rich. P cuttings. Zone 3.

Pinus sylvestris 'Watereri'
Scots Pine / fam. *Pinaceae*
○ ⊜ ✿ 🌿 🌲
Slow-growing, rounded conifer with blue-grey needles in pairs. Older bark is reddish brown with dark scales. H 5–7 m (16–23 ft). W 5 m (16 ft). S humus-rich. P cuttings. Zone 2.

Pinus wallachiana (P. griffithii)
Bhutan Pine / fam. *Pinaceae*
○ ➔ ✿ 🌿 🌲 ⏚
Particularly graceful tree with very long, drooping blue-grey needles and long, pendent cones encrusted with white resin. H 30 m (100 ft). W 20 m (65 ft). S humus-rich. P seed. Zone 5.

Platycodon grandiflorus 'Mariesii'
Balloon Flower / fam. *Campanulaceae*
○ ◑ 🌕 🌿 ⊗
July–September. Violet. H 40 cm (16 in). A 20 cm (8 in). S fertile, sandy. P division. Resembles campanula. Excellent border plant that needs a great deal of moisture.

Pleione bulbocodioides (P. limprichtii)
fam. *Orchidaceae*
◑ ◇ 🌿 ⊗
April–May. Purple-white. H 15 cm (6 in). A 15 cm (6 in). S very fertile. P division, seed. Needs a lot of moisture in spring and summer. Keep dry in autumn and winter: cover with glass.

Podocarpus nivalis
fam. ***Podocarpaceae***
○ ◐ ❀ ⊕ ⊗ ⊖
Ground-covering, slow-growing shrub with
narrow dark green leaves. Very tough and
tolerant of lime. H 1 m (3 ft). W 3 m (10 ft).
P seed. Zone 6.

Podophyllum hexandrum (P. emodi)
Himalayan Mayflower / fam. ***Berberidaceae***
◐ ◐ ○ ⊕ ⊕ ⊕ ⊗ ⊘
May. White. H 30–45 cm (12–18 in). A 20 cm
(8 in). S humus-rich. P division of rootstock,
seed. Ornamental plant with large, edible red
fruits. Stems, leaves and roots are poisonous.

Polemonium reptans
fam. ***Polemoniaceae***
○ ◐ ○ ⊕
April–June. Violet. H 30 cm (1 ft). A 20 cm
(8 in). S fertile. P division, seed. Creeping
plant. Seeds itself. Cut back after flowering.
Needs moisture.

Polygonatum multiflorum
Solomon's Seal / fam. ***Liliaceae***
◐ ◐ ⊕ ⊕ ⊕
May–June. White. H 60 cm (2 ft). A 30 cm (1 ft).
S humus-rich, moist. P division. Ornamental
native plant that needs little attention and
thrives in most positions.

Polygonum affine 'Superbum'
Knotweed / fam. ***Polygonaceae***
○ ◐ ○ ⊕ ⊛ ⊗ ⊖
August–September. Red-purple. H 25 cm
(10 in). A 20 cm (8 in). S fertile. P division.
Creeping plant with evergreen leaves. Well-
known ground coverer on dry walls and
stones.

Polygonum amplexicaule
Knotweed / fam. ***Polygonaceae***
○ ◐ ⊗ ○ ⊕ ⊗
July–October. Red-purple. H 90 cm (3 ft).
A 40 cm (16 in). S fertile. P division, seed.
Good border plant of dense habit. Robust: it
can withstand dry spells.

Polygonum bistorta
Snakeweed / fam. ***Polygonaceae***
◐ ⊗ ○ ⊕
May–August. Pink. H 1 m (3 ft). A 50 cm
(20 in). S fertile. P division, seed. Suitable for
planting near water and in herbaceous
borders. Invasive.

Polygonum campanulatum
Knotweed / fam. ***Polygonaceae***
○ ◐ ⊗ ⊗ ○ ⊕
August–October. Pink. H 60–100 cm (2–3 ft).
A 40 cm (16 in). S fertile. P division, seed.
Masses of flowers. Slightly sensitive to frost.
Somewhat woody at the base.

Polygonum capitatum
Knotweed / fam. ***Polygonaceae***
○ ◐ ◐ ⊙ ⊗ ⊗
Sow in April outside and thin out to A 15 cm
(6 in). H 15 cm (6 in). Red. S fertile. Creeping
plant with reddish stems. Flowers profusely.
Makes an attractive hanging plant.

281

Polygonum

Polygonum macrophyllum (P. sphaerosta-chyum) / Knotweed / fam. *Polygonaceae*
○ ◑ ○ ⓨ ⊗
July–September. Purple. H 50 cm (20 in).
A 30 cm (1 ft). S fertile. P division, seed. Less
well known but attractive knotweed with
large flower spikes in an attractive colour.

Polygonum orientale (Persicaria orientalis)
Knotweed / fam. *Polygonaceae*
○ ◑ ○ ⓨ ⊗
Sow in April outside and thin out to A 15 cm
(6 in). H 1–3 m (3–10 ft). Red-purple. S fertile
soil. Not very well known but easily
cultivated and appreciated for its colour.

Polygonum sericeum
Knotweed / fam. *Polygonaceae*
○ ◑ ⊗ ⊝ ⓨ
May–June. White. H 60 cm (2 ft). A 30 cm (1 ft).
S fertile. P division, seed. Bushy habit. Non-
invasive knotweed with masses of flowers.
Cut back after flowering period.

Polygonum vacciniifolium
Knotweed / fam. *Polygonaceae*
○ ⌃ ◑ ⓨ ⊗
August–September. Purple. H 25 cm (10 in).
A 20 cm (8 in). S normal. P division, seed.
Creeping plant from the Himalayas. Suitable
for trailing over walls. Demands a warm
position.

Polypodium vulgare
Polypody / fam. *Polypodiaceae*
◑ ◑ ○ ✿ ⚘ ⊗
Does not flower. H 15–40 cm (6–16 in). A 30–
40 cm (12–16 in). S humus-rich. P division of
rhizomes. Fairly slow-growing fern with
quadripinnate and gracefully arching fronds.

Polystichum setiferum (P. angulare)
Soft Shield Fern / fam. *Aspidiaceae*
◑ ◑ ⊗ ⌃ ○ ✿ ⊗
Does not flower. H 60–100 cm (2–3 ft).
A 150 cm (5 ft). S humus-rich. P spores,
division. Very graceful, strong fern with
bipinnate fronds and rounded spore clusters.

Polystichum tripteron
Kidney Fern / fam. *Aspidiaceae*
◑ ◑ ⊗ ⌃ ○ ✿ ⚘ ⊗
Does not flower. H 40 cm (16 in). A 30 cm (1 ft).
S humus-rich. P spores, division. Attractive
and robust fern seen to best advantage among
light shrubs.

Poncirus trifoliatus (flowers)
fam. *Rutaceae*
○ ◑ ⋇ ⚘ ✳ ⓨ ⊗ ⊗
April–May. White. H 3 m (10 ft). W 3 m (10 ft).
Zone 5. S fertile soil. P seed, cuttings. Small
tree or shrub with dark green branches,
spines and large, fragrant flowers.

Poncirus trifoliatus (fruits)
fam. *Rutaceae*
○ ◑ ⋇ ⚘ ✳ ⓨ ⊗ ⊗
For description and P see last entry. Shrub of
globular habit. The bare winter stems have a
most decorative shape and are often cut and
used for decoration. Inedible aromatic fruits.

Pontederia cordata
Pickerel Weed / fam. *Pontederiaceae*
◯ ⊛ ⌒ ◯ ⊛
June–August. Violet. H 60–70 cm (24–28 in).
A 30 cm (1 ft). S clay. P division, seed.
Profusely flowering plant with glossy leaves.
For marshy ground or water with a depth of
up to 40 cm (16 in).

Populus alba
White Poplar / fam. *Salicaceae*
◯ ◑ ⊜ ⊝ ⊛ ◐
March–April. Greeny yellow. H 30 m (100 ft).
W 10–15 m (33–50 ft). S not critical.
P hardwood cuttings in winter. Sometimes
grown as a shrub. White felt under leaves.
Zone 3.

***Populus alba* 'Rocket'**
White Poplar / fam. *Salicaceae*
◯ ◑ ⊜ ⊝ ⊛ ⊕
March–April. Yellow-green. H 30 m (100 ft).
W 10 m (33 ft). Exceptionally slender tree with
a straight trunk. Good for windbreaks.
Zone 3.

Populus balsamifera (P. tacamahacca)
Balsam Poplar / fam. *Salicaceae*
◯ ◑ ⊜ ⊝ ⊛
March–April. Yellow-green. H 25–40 m (80–
135 ft). W 10 m (33 ft). S not critical.
P hardwood cuttings in winter. Buds large
and sticky. Leaves smell of balsam. Zone 2.

***Populus balsamifera* 'Aurora'**
Balsam Poplar / fam. *Salicaceae*
◯ ◑ ⊜ ⊝ ⊛ ⊛ ⊛
March–April. Yellow-green. H 10 m (33 ft).
W 3 m (10 ft). Zone 4. S not critical.
P hardwood cuttings in winter. More valuable
as a shrub. Prune hard in winter to bring out
the variegated effect.

***Populus canadensis* hybrid**
Canadian Poplar / fam. *Salicaceae*
◯ ◑ ⊝ ⊛ ⊛ ⊛ ⊕
April–May. Yellow-green. H 25 m (80 ft).
W 8 m (26 ft). Zone 4. S not critical. P cuttings.
Robust, fast-growing tree with sticky winter
buds, shown here in pollarded form.

***Populus nigra* 'Italica'**
Lombardy Poplar / fam. *Salicaceae*
◯ ◑ ⊛ ⊝ ⊛ ⊕ ▥
March–April. Yellow-green. H 30 m (100 ft).
W 10 m (33 ft). S not critical. P hardwood
cuttings in winter. Fast-growing, columnar
tree with angular branches. Good for
windbreaks. Zone 2.

***Portulaca* hybrid 'Sunglo Orchid'**
Purslane / fam. *Portulacaceae*
◯ ⊜ ⊛ ◐ ⊛ ⊛ ⊛
Sow in April in a heated greenhouse or in
May outside. Thin / plant out at A 15–20 cm
(6–8 in). H 10–25 cm (4–10 in). Purple. S not
critical. Low-growing plant; fleshy leaves.
Flowers open in sun.

Potentilla fruticosa
Cinquefoil / fam. *Rosaceae*
◯ ◑ ⊛ ⊛ ⊛
May–August. Yellow. H 1 m (3 ft). W 1 m (3 ft).
S not critical. P seed, cuttings. Compact shrub
with erect, peeling stems and composite
leaves.

283

Potentilla

Potentilla hybrid 'Gibson's Scarlet'
Cinquefoil / fam. *Rosaceae*
○ ◐ ◐ ⊛ ⊛
June–August. Scarlet. H 25–50 cm (10–20 in).
A 30 cm (1 ft). S normal garden soil.
P division, cuttings. Flowers in profusion.
Deep rooting and drought resistant.

Potentilla hybrid 'William Rollison'
Cinquefoil / fam. *Rosaceae*
○ ◐ ◐ ⊛ ⊛
June–August. Flame-orange. H 25–50 cm (10–
20 in). A 30 cm (1 ft). S normal garden soil.
P division, cuttings. These hybrids have
straighter stems than *P. nepalensis*. Free
flowering.

Potentilla hybrid 'Yellow Queen'
Cinquefoil / fam. *Rosaceae*
○ ◐ ◐ ⊛ ⊛
June–August. Yellow. H 25–50 cm (10–20 in).
A 30 cm (1 ft). S normal garden soil.
P division, cuttings. Attractive plant for
borders and rock gardens. Cut back hard to
extend flowering.

Potentilla nepalensis 'Miss Willmot'
Cinquefoil / fam. *Rosaceae*
○ ○ ⊛ ⊛ ⊛
June–August. Cherry pink. H 40–60 cm (16–
24 in). A 30 cm (1 ft). S normal. P division,
cuttings. Richly flowering plant for the
border. Needs a sunny, warm site.

Potentilla recta 'Warreniii'
Cinquefoil / fam. *Rosaceae*
○ ◐ ◐ ⊛ ⊛
June–July. Yellow. H 30–70 cm (12–28 in).
A 30 cm (1 ft). S normal garden soil.
P division, cuttings. Excellent border plant.
Upright stems. The best cultivar. Flowers
profusely.

Potentilla × tonguei
Cinquefoil / fam. *Rosaceae*
○ ◐ ◐ ⊛ ⊛
June–August. Yellow / orange. H 10–25 cm
(4–10 in). A 20 cm (8 in). S normal garden soil.
P division, cuttings. Creeping and invasive
plant, suitable for rock gardens. Flowers
profusely.

Primula bullesiana hybrid
fam. *Primulaceae*
◐ ⊛ ○ ⊛
June–July. Various colours. H 50 cm (20 in).
A 30 cm (1 ft). S normal, moist. P division,
seed. Florists usually offer mixed colours.
Fast-growing plant for moist and cool sites.

Primula capitata hybrid
fam. *Primulaceae*
○ ◐ ◐ ⊛ ⊛
July–August. Violet-blue. H 30 cm (1 ft).
A 20 cm (8 in). S good garden soil. P division.
A particularly attractive species; nearly
globular flower heads and small funnel-
shaped flowers.

Primula denticulata
Drumstick Primrose / fam. *Primulaceae*
◐ ⊛ ○ ⊛ ⊛
March–April. Purple. H 10–25 cm (4–10 in).
A 20 cm (8 in). S normal, moist. P division,
seed. Leaves come out after flowers.
Attractive varieties in many colours.

Primula elatior 'Aurea'
fam. Primulaceae
○ ◐ ⊗ ⊙ ⊗ ⊗
March–May. Yellow. H 20 cm (8 in). A 20 cm
(8 in). S loamy, moist. P division. Will
sometimes flower again in the autumn.
Prefers light shade, such as a cool position at
the edge of woods.

Primula elatior hybrids
fam. Primulaceae
○ ◐ ⊗ ⊙ ⊗ ⊗
March–May. Red. H 10–25 cm (4–10 in).
A 20 cm (8 in). S loamy, moist. P division.
Very popular old-fashioned garden primula.
Can be bought in a host of named varieties
and colours.

Primula elatior ssp. pallassi
fam. Primulaceae
○ ◐ ⊗ ⊙ ⊗ ⊗
March–May. Yellow. H 20 cm (8 in). A 20 cm
(8 in). S loamy, moist. P division, seed. Will
sometimes flower again in the autumn. No
scent. Plant in groups in a cool position.

Primula farinosa
Bird's Eye Primula / **fam. Primulaceae**
○ ◐ ⊗ ⊗ ∧ ⊙ ⊗ ⊘
April–May. Lilac-pink. H 20 cm (8 in). A 20 cm
(8 in). S moist meadowland. P division, seed.
The leaves seem to be covered with flour.
Must not be allowed to get too wet in winter.

Primula florindae
Himalayan Cowslip / **fam. Primulaceae**
○ ◐ ⊗ ⊙ ⊙
July–August. Yellow. H 50–75 cm (20–30 in).
A 30 cm (1 ft). S normal, moist. P division,
seed. If the site is moist enough, this plant
will tolerate full sun.

Primula japonica
fam. Primulaceae
◐ ⊗ ∧ ⊙ ⊙
June–July. Purplish-red. H 50 cm (20 in).
A 30 cm (1 ft). S loamy, moist. P division,
seed. Very attractive and strong primula.
Sensitive to frost: cover with bracken in
winter.

Primula juliae hybrid 'Wanda'
fam. Primulaceae
◐ ⊗ ⊙ ⊙ ⊗
March–May. Purple. H 5–10 cm (2–4 in).
A 10 cm (4 in). S normal, moist. P division.
Mat-forming plant with creeping stems.
Attractive in the rock garden. Masses of
flowers. Cool site.

Primula pulverulenta
fam. Primulaceae
○ ◐ ⊗ ⊙ ⊙
June–July. Claret red. H 80 cm (32 in). A 30 cm
(1 ft). S normal, moist. Flowers in tiers.
Powdery leaves. Will tolerate full sun if the
soil is moist.

Primula rosea
fam. Primulaceae
◐ ⊗ ∧ ⊙ ⊙
April–May. Rose pink. H 15 cm (6 in). A 15 cm
(6 in). S normal, moist. P division, seed.
Attractive spring-flowering primula from the
North-west Himalayas. Cover with bracken
in winter.

285

Primula

Primula secundiflora (P. vittata)
fam. Primulaceae
May–June. Purple. H 70 cm (28 in). A 30 cm
(1 ft). S normal, moist. P division, seed.
Attractive small, bell-shaped flowers. Needs
a great deal of moisture. Keep out of full sun.

Primula sieboldii 'Shinkiro'
fam. Primulaceae
May–June. Purple-violet. H 20 cm (8 in).
A 20 cm (8 in). S very moist, humus-rich, lime
free. P division. Not easy to cultivate. Flowers
in profusion. Best in small groups.

Primula sikkimensis
fam. Primulaceae
June–July. Yellow. H 25–50 cm (10–20 in).
A 30 cm (1 ft). S humus-rich, moist.
P division, seed. Sturdy flower stems, often
powdery. No midday sun. Goes well with
ferns.

Primula vialii (P. littoniana)
fam. Primulaceae
June–July. Bluish-violet. H 60 cm (2 ft).
A 30 cm (1 ft). S humus-rich, moist.
P division, seed. Keep very moist before
flowering period; afterwards fairly dry. Good
companion for ferns.

Primula vulgaris (P. acaulis)
Primrose / fam. Primulaceae
March–April. Various colours. H 10 cm (4 in).
A 15 cm (6 in). S humus-rich. P division, seed.
Common in woods and on shady banks. Cool
position. Looks attractive in the shadow of
shrubs.

Prunella grandiflora
fam. Labiatae
June–September. Purple-violet. H 10–20 cm
(4–8 in). A 20 cm (8 in). S fertile, well drained.
P division, seed. For the border or for
naturalising. Attractive in combinations.
Long flowering period.

Prunella hastifolia 'Rosea'
fam. Labiatae
June–September. Reddish-purple. H 20 cm
(8 in). A 20 cm (8 in). S fertile, well drained.
Not common despite its appealing colour and
profusion of flowers. First-class border plant.

Prunella × webbiana 'Loveliness'
fam. Labiatae
June–September. Purple. H 20 cm (8 in).
A 20 cm (8 in). S fertile, well drained.
P division. Suitable for borders and rock
gardens. Cross between *P. grandiflora* and *P. hastifolia*.

Prunus × amygdalopersica
Pollardii Almond / fam. Rosaceae
March–April. Rich pink. H 6 m (20 ft). W 4 m
(13 ft). Zone 5. S fertile, humus-rich.
P cuttings. Attractive and vigorous cross
between peach and almond. Grooved nuts.

Prunus avium 'Decumana'
Wild Cherry / fam. *Rosaceae*
○ ✳ ❀ ⊙ ⊙ ⊕
April–May. White. H 15 m (50 ft). W 9 m
(30 ft). S fertile. P grafting, budding. Vigorous
tree with large leaves colouring in autumn
and very dark, sweet fruits. Zone 3.

Prunus avium 'Plena'
Wild Cherry / fam. *Rosaceae*
○ ✳ ❀ ⊙ ⊛ ⊙ ⊕
April–May. White. H 18 m (60 ft). W 10 m
(33 ft). S fertile. P grafting, budding.
Magnificent ornamental cherry with a broad
pyramidal crown and nodding double
flowers. Zone 3.

Prunus cerasifera 'Atropurpurea'
Cherry Plum / fam. *Rosaceae*
○ ⊛ ✳ ❀ ⊙ ⊕
March–April. White. H 6 m (20 ft). W 6 m
(20 ft). S fertile, humus-rich. P grafting. Erect
shrub or small tree with a rounded crown and
reddish-brown leaves. Sweet red fruits.
Zone 3.

**Prunus × cistena (P. cerasifera
'Atropurpurea' × P. pumila) / fam. Rosaceae**
○ ⊛ ❀ ✳ ⊛ ⊙ ⊕
May. White. H 1.5 m (5 ft). W 1.5 m (5 ft).
S fertile, humus-rich. P cuttings. Small shrub
with narrow, dark reddish-brown leaves and
deep purple fruits. Zone 2.

Prunus fontanesiana (P. avium × P. mahaleb)
fam. *Rosaceae*
○ ✳ ❀ ⊛ ⊙
April–May. White. H 9 m (30 ft). W 6 m (20 ft).
Zone 4. S fertile, humus-rich. P cuttings. Tree
resembling *P. avium* but with downy young
shoots and small red fruits.

Prunus 'Kursar' (P. kurilensis × P. sargentii)
Ornamental Cherry / fam. *Rosaceae*
○ ⊛ ✳ ❀ ⊙
April. Pink. H 5 m (16 ft). W 4 m (13 ft). Zone
4. S fertile, humus-rich. P grafting, cuttings.
Shrub or small tree with a profusion of large
single flowers in clusters.

Prunus laurocerasus 'Rotundifolia'
Common Laurel / fam. *Rosaceae*
○ ⊛ ❀ ✳ ⊛ ⊙ ⊕ ⊕
April–May. White. H 4 m (13 ft). W 5.5 m
(18 ft). Zone 5–6. S fertile, humus-rich.
Vigorous, wide-spreading shrub with
elongated leathery leaves and small black
fruits.

Prunus lusitanica 'Angustifolia'
Portugal Laurel / fam. *Rosaceae*
○ ⊛ ❀ ✳ ⊛ ⊙
June. White. H 3 m (10 ft). W 3 m (10 ft). Zone
5–6. S fertile, humus-rich. Dense, wide-
spreading shrub with small, narrow dark
green leaves and flowers in long clusters.

Prunus maackii
Ornamental Cherry / fam. *Rosaceae*
○ ⊛ ❀ ✳ ⊙ ⊕
April. White. H 10 m (33 ft). W 8 m (26 ft).
S fertile, humus-rich. P seed, cuttings.
Vigorous tree with ovate leaves and black
fruits. Flowers come out before leaves.
Zone 2.

Prunus

Prunus mahaleb (Cerasus mahaleb)
Mahaleb Cherry / fam. *Rosaceae*
○ ⊕ ✳ ⊛ ⊕ ⊚
April–May. White. H 10 m (33 ft). W 10 m
(33 ft). Zone 5. S fertile, humus-rich. P seed,
cuttings. Small tree to broad shrub. Almost
circular leaves, black fruits. Rootstock for
morellos.

Prunus padus (Cerasus padus)
Bird Cherry / fam. *Rosaceae*
○ ⓪ ✳ ⊛ ⊕ ⊚
May. White. H 9 m (30 ft). W 6 m (20 ft).
S fertile, humus-rich. P seed. Tall shrub with
strongly scented flowers in drooping racemes.
Black fruits. Zone 3.

Prunus persica 'Klara Mayer'
Ornamental Peach / fam. *Rosaceae*
○ ⊕ ✳ ⊛ ⊕ ⊚
April. Pink. H 7 m (23 ft). W 5 m (16 ft). Zone
5. S fertile, humus-rich. P grafting, budding.
Tall shrub or small tree with lanceolate leaves,
double flowers and green fruits.

Prunus sargentii (P. serrulata var.
sachalinensis) (summer) / fam. *Rosaceae*
○ ✳ ⊛ ⊕ ⊕ ⊚
May. Pink. H 10 m (33 ft). W 8 m (26 ft). Zone
4. S fertile, humus-rich. P seed. One of the
finest flowering cherries. Flowers in sessile
clusters. Reddish bark. Not for small gardens.

Prunus sargentii (P. serrulata var.
sachalinensis) (autumn) / fam. *Rosaceae*
○ ⓪ ✳ ⊕ ⊕ ⊚
May. Pink. H 10 m (33 ft). W 8 m (26 ft). Zone
4. S fertile, humus-rich. P seed. Vigorous tree
with brilliant red or orange autumn
colouring. Dark red fruits.

Prunus sargentii 'Rancho' (autumn)
fam. *Rosaceae*
○ ✳ ⊛ ⊕ ⊚
May. Pink. H 8 m (26 ft). W 2 m (6 ft). Zone 4.
S fertile, humus-rich. P grafting. Columnar
tree with splendid autumn colour and fairly
large flowers in sessile clusters.

Prunus serotina (Padus serotina)
Wild Black Cherry / fam. *Rosaceae*
○ ⓪ ⓿ ⊕ ✳ ⊛ ⊕ ⊚
May–June. White. H 10 m (33 ft). W 8 m (26 ft).
S fertile, humus-rich. P seed. Often a
troublesome tree or shrub with glossy green
leaves and bitter or sweet black fruits. Zone 3.

Prunus serrula
Ornamental Cherry / fam. *Rosaceae*
○ ✳ ⊕ ⊕ ⊚
April–May. White. H 8 m (26 ft). W 5 m (16 ft).
Zone 5. S fertile, humus-rich. P seed, cuttings.
Small tree with leaves colouring in autumn,
small fruits and a glossy reddish-brown
trunk.

Prunus serrulata 'Amanogawa'
Japanese Flowering Cherry / fam. *Rosaceae*
○ ⊕ ⊛ ✳ ⊕ ⊚ ⊕
April–May. Pink. H 9 m (30 ft). W 2 m (6 ft).
Zone 5. S fertile, humus-rich. P grafting.
Small tree or shrub of narrowly columnar
habit and fragrant, sometimes double,
flowers.

Prunus serrulata 'Kiku-shidare-sakura'
Japanese Ornamental Cherry / fam. *Rosaceae*
○ ❀ ⓨ ⊚ ⊕
April. Pink. H 3 m (10 ft). W 4 m (13 ft). Zone 5. S fertile, humus-rich. P grafting. Weeping form with double flowers.

Prunus serrulata 'Kwanzan' / Japanese Ornamental Cherry / fam. *Rosaceae*
○ ❀ ❁ ⓨ ⊚ ⊘
May. Pink. H 12 m (40 ft). W 10 m (33 ft). Zone 5. S fertile, humus-rich. P grafting. Tree with a flattened crown, wide-spreading branches and numerous fringed double flowers.

Prunus serrulata 'Shimidsu-Zakura' / Japanese Ornamental Cherry / fam. *Rosaceae*
○ ❀ ⓨ ⊚ ⊘
April–May. White. H 5 m (16 ft). W 8 m (26 ft). Zone 5. S fertile, humus-rich. P grafting. Tree with a flat crown, wide-spreading branches and double, fringed flowers in great profusion.

Prunus serrulata 'Shirotae' / Japanese Ornamental Cherry / fam. *Rosaceae*
○ ⓦ ⓨ ⊚
April–May. White. H 3 m (10 ft). W 6 m (20 ft). Zone 5. S fertile, humus-rich. P grafting. Moderately fast-growing shrub with wide-spreading branches and large, semi-double flowers.

Prunus serrulata 'Ukon' / Japanese Ornamental Cherry / fam. *Rosaceae*
○ ⓦ ⓨ ⊚ ⊘
May. Creamy white. H 6 m (20 ft). W 8 m (26 ft). Zone 5. S fertile, humus-rich. P grafting. Robust shrub or tree with leaves that are bronze-brown when unfolding. Small double flowers.

Prunus serrulata var. hupehensis / Japanese Ornamental Cherry / fam. *Rosaceae*
○ ❀ ⓨ ⊚ ⊘
April. White. H 10 m (33 ft). W 8 m (26 ft). Zone 5. S fertile, humus-rich. P grafting. Robust tree with a broad crown, leaves that are light bronze on opening and small double flowers.

Prunus subhirtella 'Pendula'
Spring Cherry / fam. *Rosaceae*
○ ❀ ❁ ⓨ ⊚ ⊚ ⊕
April. Pink. H 3 m (10 ft). W 5 m (16 ft). Zone 5. S fertile, humus-rich. P grafting. Weeping form with drooping branches, small flowers and black fruits.

Prunus triloba
Ornamental Almond / fam. *Rosaceae*
○ ⓦ ❀ ⓨ ⊚ ⊕ ⊗
March–April. Pink. H 2 m (6 ft). W 2 m (6 ft). Zone 5. S fertile, humus-rich. P seed, cuttings. Small shrub with crowded, ascending branches and semi-double flowers. May be grown as a low standard.

Prunus × yedoensis
Yoshino Cherry / fam. *Rosaceae*
○ ❀ ⓨ ❁ ⊚
April. White. H 15 m (50 ft). W 12 m (40 ft). Zone 5. S fertile, humus-rich. P cuttings. Tree with a broad, flattened crown, smooth bark, single, fragrant flowers and black fruits.

Pseudolarix kaempferi (P. amabilis)
Golden Larch / fam. *Pinaceae*
○ ❀ 🌀 🐌 🕷
Tree with a broad pyramidal crown,
horizontally extending branches, light green
needles turning gold in autumn and cones.
H 45 m (150 ft). W 20 m (65 ft). S fertile. P seed.
Zone 5.

Pseudosasa japonica (Bambusa japonica)
fam. *Gramineae*
🌀 ◑ ❀ 🌀 ❀ 🐌 🕷
Flowers very rarely. H 4 m (13 ft). A 50 cm
(20 in). Zone 8. S humus-rich. P division.
Very tall bamboo with bristly brown stems
and creeping rhizomes.

Pseudotsuga menziesii (P. taxifolia)
Douglas Fir / fam. *Pinaceae*
○ ❀ 🌀 🐌 🕷
Tree of conical habit. Straight trunk with
smooth, resinous bark. Thickening, narrow,
pendent cones. H 30 m (100 ft). W 10 m (33 ft).
S not critical. P seed. Zone 5.

***Pseudotsuga menziesii* 'Brevifolia'**
Douglas Fir / fam. *Pinaceae*
○ ❀ 🌀 🐌 🕷 🕷 ⊕
Bushy, narrow tree with almost radial needles
and red buds. Used for timber and paper
making. H 30 m (100 ft). W 20 m (65 ft). S not
critical. P grafting. Zone 5.

***Pseudotsuga menziesii* 'Tempelhof**
Compacta' / Douglas Fir / fam. *Pinaceae*
○ ❀ 🌀 🐌 🕷 ⊕ 🕷
Spreading dwarf form with a flattened top.
The greyish-green foliage can be used for
decoration. H 2 m (6 ft). W 2 m (6 ft). S fertile.
P cuttings. Zone 6.

Pterocarya rhoifolia
fam. *Juglandaceae*
○ ◑ ❀ 🕷
June. Green. H 25 m (80 ft). W 15 m (50 ft).
Zone 5. S fertile soil. P seed, layering. Tree
with two or three large scales round its leaf
buds. Flowers borne in catkins.

Pulmonaria angustifolia
Narrow-leaved Lungwort / fam. *Boraginaceae*
◑ ◐ ◔ ⊙ ❀
March–April. Violet. H 20–30 cm (8–12 in).
A 20 cm (8 in). S humus-rich. P division, seed.
Hairy herbaceous perennial from moist
woods. Spreads quickly after flowering
period.

Pulmonaria rubra
Lungwort / fam. *Boraginaceae*
◑ ◐ ◔ ⊙ ❀
March–April. Red. H 30–40 cm (12–16 in).
A 20 cm (8 in). S humus-rich. P division, seed.
Covered with soft hairs. Very inconspicuous
ground-cover plant. Vigorous and fast
growing.

***Pulmonaria saccharata* 'Mrs Moon'**
Lungwort / fam. *Boraginaceae*
◑ ◐ ◔ ⊙ ❀
April–May. Purple. H 30–40 cm (12–16 in).
A 20 cm (8 in). S humus-rich. P division.
Flowers red at first, turning purple. Vigorous
ground-cover plant with spotted leaves.

Pulsatilla vulgaris (Anemone pulsatilla)
Pasque Flower / fam. *Ranunculaceae*
○ ◑ ⊘ ⊗ ⊘ ⓨ ⊘ ⊗
April–May. Violet-purple. H 10–25 cm (4–
10 in). A 20 cm (8 in). S humus-rich.
P division, seed. The finely divided leaves are
seen to best advantage after the flowering
period.

Puschkinia scilloides 'Alba'
fam. *Liliaceae*
○ ◑ ⓵ ⓺ ⓨ ⊗
April–May. Blue. H 15 cm (6 in). A 5–10 cm (2–
4 in). D 5 cm (2 in). S normal garden soil.
P offsets. White form lacks the blue central
stripe found on the petals of the (blue)
species.

Puschkinia scilloides var. *libanotica*
fam. *Liliaceae*
○ ◑ ⓵ ⓺ ⓨ ⊗
April. Blue. H 10 cm (4 in). A 5–10 cm (2–4 in).
D 7 cm (2¾ in). S normal garden soil. P offsets.
Suitable for rock gardens and naturalisation.
May be left undisturbed for years.

Pyracantha coccinea (Cotoneaster pyracantha)
Firethorn / fam. *Rosaceae*
○ ◑ ⓦ ⓨ ⊛ ⊛ ⊚ ⓰ ⊗
May. White. H 2 m (6 ft). W 4 m (13 ft). Zone 5.
S fertile. P cuttings, seed. Attractive
ornamental shrub with hawthorn-like flowers
and leathery leaves. Often trained on walls.

Pyrus communis (P. domestica)
Pear / fam. *Rosaceae*
○ ⊛ ⓨ ⊛
April–May. White. H 15 m (50 ft). W 10 m
(33 ft). Zone 4. S fertile garden soil. P grafting.
Tree of broadly conical habit. Yellow-green
fruits. Comes in many varieties.

Pyrus elaeagnifolia
Ornamental Pear / fam. *Rosaceae*
○ ⊛ ⓨ ⊛
April–May. White. H 6 m (20 ft). W 5 m (16 ft).
Zone 4. S fertile garden soil. P seed. Small tree
with thorns, woolly young shoots, flowers in
clusters and round, green fruits.

Quercus coccinea 'Splendens'
Scarlet Oak / fam. *Fagaceae*
○ ◑ ⊛ ⓰ ⊛
May. Green. H 25 m (80 ft). W 7 m (23 ft). Zone
4. S not critical. P grafting. Fast-growing tree.
Seven to nine-lobed ovate to obovate leaves,
brilliant scarlet in the autumn.

Quercus dentata (Q. obovata)
Japanese Emperor Oak / fam. *Fagaceae*
○ ◑ ⊛ ⓰ ⊛
May. Green. H 20 m (65 ft). W 15 m (50 ft).
Zone 5. S not critical. P seed. Very imposing
tree with a thick, cracked bark. The sessile
acorns are half surrounded by cups.

Quercus ilex
Holm Oak / fam. *Fagaceae*
◑ ◐ ⊛ ⓰ ⓨ
April. Yellow-green. H 30 m (100 ft). W 20 m
(65 ft). Zone 7–8. S not critical. P seed. Very
strong tree with leathery leaves. Although
hardy, it is not suitable for very cold districts.

Quercus

Quercus macranthera
Persian Oak / fam. *Fagaceae*
○ ◐ ✳ ∅ ⊛
May. Green. H 20 m (65 ft). W 8 m (26 ft). Zone 5. S not critical. P seed. Tree with thick, woolly, juvenile branches. Leaves with ovate lobes. Sessile acorns.

Quercus pontica
Armenian Oak / fam. *Fagaceae*
○ ◐ ✳ ∅ ⊛
May. Yellow-green. H 6 m (20 ft). W 5 m (16 ft). Zone 4. S not critical. P seed. Small tree or tall shrub with ovate acorns, 2 cm (¾ in) in length and half surrounded by cups.

Quercus robur (Q. pedunculata)
Common Oak / fam. *Fagaceae*
○ ◐ ✳ ∅ ⊛
May. Yellow-green. H 25–30 m (80–100 ft). W 20 m (65 ft). Zone 5. S not critical. P seed. The common oak has a broad, irregular crown, deeply lobed leaves and acorns on short stalks.

Quercus robur 'Fastigiata'
Common Oak / fam. *Fagaceae*
○ ◐ ✳ ∅ ⊛
May. Yellow-green. H 15 m (50 ft). W 7 m (23 ft). Zone 5. S not critical. P grafting. Erect oak of narrow conical habit. Retains its brown foliage far into the autumn.

Quercus robur 'Pectinata'
Common Oak / fam. *Fagaceae*
○ ◐ ✳ ∅ ⊛
May. Yellow-green. H 20 m (65 ft). W 12 m (40 ft). Zone 5. S not critical. P grafting. Elegant, slow-growing tree with inconspicuous flowers and finely shaped leaves.

Quercus rubra (Q. borealis)
Red Oak / fam. *Fagaceae*
○ ◐ ✳ ∅ ⊛ ⊗
May. Yellow-green. H 25 m (80 ft). W 12 m (40 ft). S not critical. P seed. Tree with a broad, open crown and long, cylindrical acorns set in cups for one fifth of their length.

Quercus × schochiana (Q. palustris × Q. phellos) / Oak / fam. *Fagaceae*
○ ◐ ✳ ∅ ⊛
May. Yellow-green. H 15 m (50 ft). W 15 m (50 ft). Zone 5. S not critical. P grafting. Tree with elongated to lanceolate entire, wavy or lobed leaves.

Quercus suber
Cork Oak / fam. *Fagaceae*
◐ ◑ ✳ ⊛ ∅ ⊡
April. Yellow-green. H 6–20 m (20–65 ft). W 20 m (65 ft). Zone 7. S not critical. P seed. Trunk covered in furrowed cork. Old trees tend to lean dangerously.

Ramonda myconii (R. pyrenaica)
fam. *Gesneriaceae*
◐ ◑ ◐ ∞ ○ ⊙ ⊗
May–June. Pale mauve. H 5–10 cm (2–4 in). A 10–20 cm (4–8 in). S normal. P division, seed, cuttings. Hardy herbaceous perennial from the Pyrenees, where it grows in damp rock crevices.

Ranunculus aconitifolius
Fair Maids of France / fam. *Ranunculaceae*
Ⓘ Ⓘ ○ ⓨ ☺ ⊗
May–July. White. H 40–60 cm (16–24 in).
A 30 cm (1 ft). S normal garden soil.
P division. Attractive foliage. Bushes out and
thrives in shade.

Ranunculus asiaticus (R. hortensis)
Turban Ranunculus / fam. *Ranunculaceae*
Ⓘ Ⓘ ⊛ ⊛ ⓨ ⓨ ⊗
May–June. Mixed colours. H 15–30 cm (6–
12 in). A 15 cm (6 in). D 4–8 cm (1½–3 in).
S humus-rich. P seed, division. Large double,
paeony-like flowers. Tubers with claw-like
ends.

Ranunculus lingua
Great Spearwort / fam. *Ranunculaceae*
○ Ⓘ ⊛ ⊛ ⓨ ⊗
June–August. Yellow. H 60–80 cm (24–32 in).
A 30 cm (1 ft). S normal. P division, seed. For
shallow garden pools, ponds and marshy
ground.

Reseda odorata 'Manchet'
Mignonette / fam. *Resedaceae*
○ Ⓘ ⊙ ⊙ ⓨ ⊗
Sow in April outside and thin out to A 15 cm
(6 in). H 15–75 cm (6–30 in). Greeny-yellow.
S fertile garden soil. Densely branched plant
with fragrant flowers in packed, cylindrical
spikes.

*Reynoutria japonica (Polygonum
cuspidatum)* / fam. *Polygonaceae*
Ⓘ Ⓘ ○ ⓨ ⊗
August–October. White. H 1–3 m (3–10 ft).
A 90 cm (3 ft). S not critical. P seed, cuttings.
Strong-growing plant with invasive
rhizomes. For large-scale planting projects.

Rhamnus frangula (F. alnus)
Berry-bearing Alder / fam. *Rhamnaceae*
Ⓘ Ⓘ ⊛ ⓦ ⊛ Ⓘ
May–June. Greeny white. H 4 m (13 ft). W 3 m
(10 ft). S not critical. P seed. Robust shrub.
Brown branches with corky tubercles, woolly
brown buds and black berries. Zone 2.

Rheum alexandrae
Ornamental Rhubarb / fam. *Polygonaceae*
○ ⊛ ○ ⓰ ⊕
June–July. Greeny yellow. H 70–90 cm (28–
36 in). A 50 cm (20 in). S fertile. P seed,
division. Basal leaves on long stalks; elegantly
shaped foliage, insignificant flowers.

Rheum palmatum
Ornamental Rhubarb / fam. *Polygonaceae*
○ ⊛ ○ ⓰ ⊕
June. Creamy white. H 2.5 m (8 ft). A 1 m (3 ft).
S fertile. P seed, division. Tall plant that
needs space. Leaves nearly circular, very large
and deeply divided.

Rheum palmatum 'Bowles'
Ornamental Rhubarb / fam. *Polygonaceae*
○ ⊛ ○ ⓰ ⊕
May–June. Red. H 2.5 m (8 ft). A 1 m (3 ft).
S fertile. P division. Attractive foliage plant
with purple-red, deeply divided leaves that
turn green after flowering.

Rhododendron

Rhododendron 'Aida' (Azalea rustica hybrid)
fam. Ericaceae

May. Purple-pink. H 2 m (6 ft). W 2.5 m (8 ft). Zone 5. S humus-rich, acid. P cuttings. Hardy shrub with fragrant double flowers, each measuring 6 cm (2¼ in) across. Good value.

Rhododendron 'Blue Tit'
Augustinii hybrid / fam. Ericaceae

April–May. Violet-blue. H 1 m (3 ft). W 1 m (3 ft). Zone 5. S humus-rich, acid. P grafting, cuttings. Compact, round shrub with a profusion of small flowers. Very good value.

Rhododendron 'Blue Tit Major'
Augustinii hybrid / fam. Ericaceae

April–May. Violet-blue. H 1 m (3 ft). W 1 m (3 ft). Zone 5. S humus-rich, acid. P cuttings, grafting. Low, compact shrub with unusually large flowers.

Rhododendron cinnabarinum var. roylei
fam. Ericaceae

May–June. Red. H 3 m (10 ft). W 2 m (6 ft). Zone 6. S humus-rich, acid. P layering, cuttings. Shrub with ovate leaves and waxy, tubular flowers. High value.

Rhododendron ferrugineum
Alpenrose / fam. Ericaceae

May–June. Rosy crimson. H 1 m (3 ft). W 1 m (3 ft). Zone 4. S humus-rich. P cuttings, grafting, layering. Small, compact shrub with masses of flowers. Reddish scales under the leaves.

Rhododendron 'Hardijzer Beauty'
Japanese Azalea / fam. Ericaceae

May. Rose red. H 1 m (3 ft). W 1 m (3 ft). Zone 5. S humus-rich, acid. P grafting. Shrub with 3-cm (1-in) wide flowers in groups of two to four and with five or six stamens each.

Rhododendron 'Irene Koster' (Azalea occidentale hybrid) / fam. Ericaceae

May. Pink. H 2.5 m (8 ft). W 3 m (10 ft). Zone 5. S humus-rich, acid. P cuttings. Low shrub with fragrant, funnel-shaped, yellow-spotted flowers, 5–8 cm (2–3 in) across.

Rhododendron 'Klondyke' / Knap Hill-Exbury Azalea / fam. Ericaceae

May–June. Yellow. H 2 m (6 ft). W 2 m (6 ft). Zone 5. S humus-rich, acid. P cuttings. Large-flowered shrub of broad, erect habit. Leaves dark brown when unfolding.

Rhododendron 'Koster's Brilliant Red' (Azalea mollis hybrid) / fam. Ericaceae

May. Orange-red. H 1.5 m (5 ft). W 3 m (10 ft). Zone 5. S humus-rich, acid. P cuttings. Shrub with non-fragrant, funnel-shaped flowers. Excellent value.

Rhododendron 'Narcissiflora' *(Azalea pontica* hybrid)/fam. *Ericaceae*
May. Yellow. H 2 m (6 ft). W 2 m (6 ft). Zone 4.
S humus-rich. P grafting, cuttings. Hardy
shrub with fragrant double, not very large
flowers. Good value.

Rhododendron 'Persil'/Knap Hill-Exbury Azalea/fam. *Ericaceae*
May. White. H 2 m (6 ft). W 2 m (6 ft). Zone 5.
S humus-rich, acid. P cuttings. Shrub bearing
pure white flowers with a yellow spot. Very
good value.

Rhododendron × *praecox (R. ciliatum* × *R. dauricum)*/fam. *Ericaceae*
March–April. Pink. H 2 m (6 ft). W 2 m (6 ft).
Zone 5. S humus-rich, acid. P cuttings.
Attractive and popular garden shrub. Flowers
sensitive to night frost.

Rhododendron repens hybrid 'Elisabeth Hobbie'/fam. *Ericaceae*
May. Red. H 1.5 m (5 ft). W 2 m (6 ft). Zone 5.
S humus-rich, acid. P cuttings, layering.
Hybrid with dull green leaves, flowers in
groups of three to five. Hardy in normal
winters.

Rhododendron 'Samuel T. Coleridge' *(Azalea mollis* hybrid)/fam. *Ericaceae*
May. Pink. H 1.5 m (5 ft). W 3 m (10 ft). Zone
5. S humus-rich, acid. P cuttings. Non-
fragrant, funnel-shaped flowers and rough,
hairy leaves which change colour in autumn.

Rhododendron sinogrande fam. *Ericaceae*
April. Creamy white. H 6 m (20 ft). W 6 m
(20 ft). Zone 6. S humus-rich, acid. P seed,
layering, cutting. Shrub with elliptic to
oblong leaves, silvery grey underneath.

Rhododendron 'Tottenham' fam. *Ericaceae*
May–June. Pink. H 60 cm (2 ft). W 60 cm (2 ft).
Zone 5–6. S humus-rich, acid. P cuttings.
Dense shrub. Fairly fleshy leaves with
reddish-brown scales underneath.

Rhododendron (garden hybrid) 'Blue Ensign'/fam. *Ericaceae*
May. Violet. H 3 m (10 ft). W 4 m (13 ft). Zone
5. S humus-rich, acid. P cuttings, layering.
Hybrid with fringed flowers in tall and
compact clusters. Very good value.

Rhododendron (garden hybrid) 'Catawbiense Album'/fam. *Ericaceae*
May–June. White. H 3 m (10 ft). W 3 m (10 ft).
Zone 4. S humus-rich, acid. P cuttings,
layering. Tolerates very severe winters. Buds
light purple at first. Good value.

295

Rhododendron

Rhododendron (garden hybrid) 'Furnivall's Daughter' / fam. *Ericaceae*
ⓘ ⊜ ⌂ ⊕ ⌞ ⓨ ⊘ ⊛ ⊗
May. Pink. H 4 m (13 ft). W 4 m (13 ft). Zone 5. S humus-rich, acid. P cuttings, layering. Large-flowered hybrid. Flowers with a prominent dark red spot. Very good value.

Rhododendron (garden hybrid) 'Hollandia' fam. *Ericaceae*
ⓘ ⊜ ⌂ ⊕ ⌞ ⓨ ⊘ ⊛ ⊗
May. Rose-purple. H 4 m (13 ft). W 6 m (20 ft). Zone 5. S humus-rich. P cuttings, layering. Large-flowered hybrid with attractive foliage and flowers in compact clusters. Excellent value.

Rhododendron (garden hybrid) 'Koster's Cream' / fam. *Ericaceae*
ⓘ ⊜ ⌂ ⊕ ⌞ ⓨ ⊘ ⊛ ⊗
May. Yellow. H 2 m (6 ft). W 3 m (10 ft). Zone 5. S humus-rich, acid. P cuttings, layering. Hardier than most yellow rhododendrons.

Rhododendron (garden hybrid) 'Louis Pasteur' / fam. *Ericaceae*
ⓘ ⊜ ⌂ ⊕ ⌞ ⓨ ⊘ ⊛ ⊗
May–June. Red. H 4 m (13 ft). W 5 m (16 ft). Zone 5. S humus-rich, acid. P cuttings, layering. Soft shoots and flowers with a bicolor effect. Good value.

Rhododendron (garden hybrid) 'Mermaid' fam. *Ericaceae*
ⓘ ⊜ ⌂ ⊕ ⌞ ⓨ ⊘ ⊛ ⊗
May. Pink. H 3 m (10 ft). W 4 m (13 ft). Zone 5–6. S humus-rich, acid. P cuttings. Attractive, large garden hybrid, recommended for its big salmon-pink flowers.

Rhododendron (garden hybrid) 'Mme Ida Rubinstein' / fam. *Ericaceae*
ⓘ ⊜ ⌂ ⊕ ⌞ ⓨ ⊘ ⊛ ⊗
May. Red. H 3 m (10 ft). W 3 m (10 ft). Zone 5. S humus-rich, acid. P cuttings, layering. Garden hybrid with large flowers in closed clusters. Very good value.

Rhododendron (garden hybrid) 'Mrs Betty Robertson' / fam. *Ericaceae*
ⓘ ⊜ ⌂ ⊕ ⌞ ⓨ ⊘ ⊛ ⊗
May. Yellow. H 2 m (6 ft). W 3 m (10 ft). Zone 6. S humus-rich, acid. P cuttings, layering. Flowers turn creamy. Very good value.

Rhododendron (garden hybrid) 'Mount Everest' / fam. *Ericaceae*
ⓘ ⊜ ⌂ ⊕ ⌞ ⓨ ⊘ ⊛ ⊗
May. White. H 4 m (13 ft). W 4 m (13 ft). Zone 6. S humus-rich, acid. P cuttings, layering. One of the most attractive white rhododendrons with slightly fragrant flowers.

Rhododendron williamsianum fam. Ericaceae
ⓘ ⊜ ⌂ ⊕ ⌞ ⓨ ⊛ ⊗
April. Pink. H 1 m (3 ft). W 2 m (6 ft). Zone 5. S humus-rich, acid. P layering, cuttings. Small spreading shrub with ovate leaves, bronze when unfolding. Bell-shaped flowers.

Rhododendron yunnanense
fam. *Ericaceae*
Ⓐ ⊛ ⊛ ⊛ ⊛
May. White. H 4 m (13 ft). W 4 m (13 ft). Zone
7. S humus-rich, acid. P seed, layering.
Spreading shrub with dark green leaves and
funnel-shaped flowers in clusters of three to
six.

Rhus trichocarpa
Sumach / fam. *Anacardiaceae*
○ ⊛ ⊛ ⊛ ⊛ ○ ⊕
June. Green. H 5 m (16 ft). W 4 m (13 ft). Zone
4. S not critical. P suckers. Small tree with a
flattened crown, pinnate leaves colouring well
in autumn and yellowish, hairy fruits.

Rhus typhina
Stag's Horn Sumach / fam. *Anacardiaceae*
○ ⊛ ⊛ ⊛ ⊛ ○ ⊕
June–July. Red. H 5 m (16 ft). W 5 m (16 ft).
S not critical. P suckers. Shrub or small tree
with green, later red and finally brown, hairy
branches. Dioecious.

Rhus typhina 'Laciniata' / Stag's Horn
Sumach / fam. *Anacardiaceae*
○ ⊛ ⊛ ⊛ ⊛ ⊛ ○ ⊕
June–July. Green. H 5 m (16 ft). W 5 m (16 ft).
S not critical. P suckers. Attractive tree with
deeply divided to pinnate leaves that change
colour in the autumn.

Ribes sanguineum
Flowering Currant / fam. *Saxifragaceae*
○ ◐ ◍ ⊛ ⊛ ⊛ ⊗
April–May. Red. H 3 m (10 ft). W 2 m (6 ft).
Zone 4. S normal garden soil. P cuttings.
Shrub with rough leaves, a profusion of
flowers in dense pendent clusters and blue-
black berries.

Ribes sanguineum 'Carneum'
Flowering Currant / fam. *Saxifragaceae*
○ ◐ ◍ ⊛ ⊛ ⊛ ⊗
April–May. Pink. H 3 m (10 ft). W 2 m (6 ft).
Zone 5. S normal garden soil. P cuttings.
Shrub with rough leaves, strikingly coloured
flowers in pendent clusters and blue-black
berries.

Ricinus communis
Castor Oil Plant / fam. *Euphorbiaceae*
○ ⊕ ◐ ○ ⊛ ⊕
Sow in March in a heated greenhouse,
separating the seeds. Plant out at A 1 m (3 ft).
H 3 m (10 ft). Green. S fertile soil. Fast
growing. Inconspicuous flowers; round seed
pods.

Robinia hispida
Rose Acacia / fam. *Leguminosae*
○ ⊜ ⊕ ◍ ⊛ ⊕
June. Pink. H 3 m (10 ft). W 1.5 m (5 ft). Zone
5. S normal garden soil. P seed, layering.
Shrub with spineless branches, red and
covered with stiff hairs, later green with red
tips.

Robinia pseudoacacia 'Frisia' / Common or
False Acacia / fam. *Leguminosae*
○ ⊜ ⊕ ⊛ ⊛ ⊛ ○ ⊕
June. White. H 9 m (30 ft). W 4.5 m (15 ft).
S normal garden soil. P grafting. Tree with
red-spined young twigs and ovate, bright
yellow-green leaflets. Zone 3.

297

Robinia

***Robinia pseudoacacia* 'Myrtifolia'**
Common or False Acacia / fam. *Leguminosae*
June. White. H 10 m (33 ft). W 8 m (26 ft).
S good garden soil. P grafting. Tree with
pinnate leaves; 11 to 19 leaflets, ovate, 10–
15 mm (½ in) long. Zone 3.

***Robinia pseudoacacia* 'Tortuosa' / Common**
or False Acacia / fam. *Leguminosae*
June. White. H 15 m (50 ft). W 12 m (40 ft).
S normal garden soil. P grafting. Tree with
twisted trunk and branches. Leaves often
pendent. It rarely bears flowers. Zone 3.

Rodgersia aesculifolia
fam. *Saxifragaceae*
July–August. Pale yellow. H 1 m (3 ft). A 50 cm
(20 in). S fertile. P division, root cuttings,
seed. Attractive plant with chestnut-like
leaves. Protect against strong wind and sun.

***Rodgersia pinnata* 'Superba'**
Feathered Bronze Leaf / fam. *Saxifragaceae*
June–July. Red. H 120 cm (4 ft). A 50 cm (20 in).
S fertile. P division, root cuttings, seed. Dark
green glossy leaves made up of six to nine
leaflets. Goes well with ferns.

Rodgersia podophylla
fam. *Saxifragaceae*
June–July. Light yellow. H 100–160 cm (3–
5 ft). A 50 cm (20 in). S fertile. P division, root
cuttings, seed. Flowers profusely. Glossy
leaves, bronze coloured when young. Japan,
Korea.

Rodgersia purdomii
fam. *Saxifragaceae*
June–July. White. H 1 m (3 ft). A 50 cm (20 in).
S fertile. P division, root cuttings, seed.
Reddish-brown juvenile foliage. Ornamental
plant that does best in a cool position.

Romneya coulteri
Tree Poppy / fam. *Papaveraceae*
July–September. White. H 150 cm (5 ft).
A 60 cm (2 ft). S fertile. P division, root
cuttings, seed. Dry, warm position. Water
sparingly even during dry spells (susceptible
to root rot).

***Rosa banksiae* 'Lutescens'**
Banksia Rose / fam. *Rosaceae*
April–July. Yellow. H 20 m (65 ft). W 5 m
(16 ft). Zone 7. S humus-rich, fertile. P seed,
cuttings. Strong-growing climber, sweetly
scented flowers, fresh green leaves. Needs
sheltered position.

***Rosa blanda* (*R. fraxinifolia*)**
fam. *Rosaceae*
May–June. Pink. H 2 m (6 ft). W 3 m (10 ft).
S humus-rich, fertile. P seed, cuttings.
Species rose with (usually) a mass of single
flowers. Smooth flower stems and round hips.
Zone 2.

298

Rosa centifolia
Provence Rose / **fam.** *Rosaceae*
○ ◐ ⊗ ⊛ ⊗
June–July. Pink. H 2 m (6 ft). W 2 m (6 ft). Zone
5. S humus-rich, fertile. P seed, cuttings. Very
thorny plant of open habit. Flowers scented
and nodding. Leaves have a reddish edge.

***Rosa centifolia* 'Fantin Latour'**
Provence Rose / **fam.** *Rosaceae*
○ ◐ ⊗ ⊛ ⊗
June–July. Pink. H 1.5 m (5 ft). W 1.5 m (5 ft).
Zone 5. S humus-rich, fertile. P cuttings.
Exceptionally beautiful, bushy shrub with
fragrant, flat-topped flowers and large, dark
leaves.

***Rosa centifolia* 'Red Moss'**
Provence Rose / **fam.** *Rosaceae*
○ ◐ ⊗ ⊛ ⊗
June–July. Red. H 2 m (6 ft). W 2 m (6 ft). Zone
5. S humus-rich, fertile. P cuttings. Moss rose
with large, semi-double, fragrant flowers with
mossy sepals.

***Rosa chinensis* var. *minima* (*R. roulettii*)**
China Rose / **fam.** *Rosaceae*
○ ◐ ⊗ ⊗ ⊗
June–July. Pink. H 20 cm (8 in). W 20 cm (8 in).
Zone 5. S humus-rich, fertile. P cuttings. The
original Swiss parent of miniature roses,
lightly scented and suitable for balconies.

***Rosa* 'Constance Spry'**
Shrub Rose / **fam.** *Rosaceae*
○ ◐ ⊗ ⊗
June–July. Pink. H 2.5 m (8 ft). W 2 m (6 ft).
Zone 5. S humus-rich, fertile. P cuttings.
Fragrant rose of old-fashioned appearance.
Rough leaves. Bowl-shaped flowers in long
arching sprays.

***Rosa* 'Wife of Bath'**
Shrub Rose / **fam.** *Rosaceae*
○ ⊙ ◐ ⊗ ⊗
June–July. Pink. H 90 cm (3 ft). W 80 cm (32 in).
Zone 5. S humus-rich, fertile. P budding.
Small, densely branched long-flowering
shrub. Double bowl-shaped flowers with a
fine fragrance.

***Rosa* 'Yellow Doll'**
Miniature Rose / **fam.** *Rosaceae*
○ ⊙ ◐ ⊗ ⊗ ⊗
June–July. Yellow. H 30 cm (1 ft). W 20 cm
(8 in). Zone 5. S humus-rich, fertile.
P cuttings. Dwarf suitable for pots on
balconies. Flowers turn ivory white.

***Rosa gallica* 'Officinalis'**
French Rose / **fam.** *Rosaceae*
○ ◐ ⊗ ⊛ ⊗
June. Red. H 2.5 m (8 ft). W 3 m (10 ft). Zone 5.
S humus-rich, fertile. P cuttings. Very old
garden rose of fairly stiff habit. Fragrant
double flowers. Hips on occasion.

***Rosa gallica* 'Versicolor' (*Rosa* 'Mundi')**
French Rose / **fam.** *Rosaceae*
○ ◐ ⊗ ⊛ ⊜ ⊗
June. Red / white. H 1.5 m (5 ft). W 2 m (6 ft).
Zone 5. S humus-rich, fertile. P cuttings. Eye-
catching rose with striped petals. Fairly stiff
habit and matt green leaves.

Rosa

Rosa glutinosa
fam. *Rosaceae*
◯ ⚘ ⚙ ⚘ ⊗
June. Pink. H 30–70 cm (12–28 in). W 1 m (3 ft).
Zone 5. S humus-rich. P seed, cuttings. Very
dense, thorny shrub with small single flowers
and small circular leaves.

Rosa 'American Pillar'
Climbing Rose / fam. *Rosaceae*
June–July. Dark pink. H 4–6 m (13–20 ft).
W 2 m (6 ft). Zone 5. S humus-rich, fertile.
P budding. Very strong, not a perpetual-
flowering climber. No fragrance. Single
flowers in clusters.

Rosa 'Bantry Bay'
Climbing Rose / fam. *Rosaceae*
◯ ⚘ ⚙ ⊗
June–July. Bright pink. H 3 m (10 ft). W 2 m
(6 ft). Zone 5. S humus-rich, fertile.
P budding. Fairly soft branches. Semi-double,
lightly scented climber for walls and pillars.

Rosa 'Clair Matin'
Climbing Rose / fam. *Rosaceae*
◯ ⚘ ⚙ ⊗
June–July. Pink. H 2–3 m (6–10 ft). W 2 m
(6 ft). Zone 5. S humus-rich, fertile.
P budding. Perpetual-flowering rose; also
suitable as a shrub. Semi-double, fragrant
flowers.

Rosa 'Climbing Sarabande'
Climbing Rose / fam. *Rosaceae*
◯ ⚘ ⚙ ⊗
June–July. Red. H 4 m (13 ft). W 2 m (6 ft).
Zone 5. S humus-rich, fertile. P budding.
Free-flowering rose with slightly fragrant,
semi-double flowers. Award of merit.

Rosa 'Danse du Feu'
Climbing Rose / fam. *Rosaceae*
◯ ⚘ ⚙ ⊗
June–July. Orange-scarlet. H 3.5 m (11 ft).
W 2 m (6 ft). Zone 5. S humus-rich, fertile.
P budding. Fairly vigorous plant. repeat
flowering. Double flowers. Train against walls
or fences.

Rosa 'Fritz Nobis'
Climbing Rose / fam. *Rosaceae*
◯ ⚘ ⚙ ⚘ ⊗
June–July. Pink. H 2 m (6 ft). W 2 m (6 ft). Zone
5. S humus-rich, fertile. P budding. Bushy
rose with arching branches. Fragrant flowers
in profusion. Reddish-brown hips.

Rosa 'Handel'
Climbing Rose / fam. *Rosaceae*
◯ ⚘ ⚙ ⊗
June–July. Carmine-rose / white. H 3.5 m
(11 ft). W 2 m (6 ft). Zone 5. S humus-rich,
fertile. P budding. Highly recommended.
Very healthy, densely branched, perpetual-
flowering rose.

Rosa 'Parkdirektor Riggers'
Climbing Rose / fam. *Rosaceae*
◯ ⚘ ⚙ ⊗
June–July. Blood red. H 4.5 m (15 ft). W 2 m
(6 ft). Zone 5. S humus-rich, fertile.
P budding. Perpetual-flowering climber with
lightly scented, velvety, semi-double flowers
in clusters.

Rosa 'Pink Cloud'
Climbing Rose / fam. *Rosaceae*
○ 🌰 ⊛ ⊗
June–July. Rose red. H 3 m (10 ft). W 2 m (6 ft).
Zone 5. S humus-rich, fertile. P budding. A
rather old-fashioned rose with pliant
branches, easily trained against walls.
Fragrant.

Rosa 'Réveil Dijonnais'
Climbing Rose / fam. *Rosaceae*
○ ⊘ ⊛ ⊗
June–July. Red / yellow. H 4 m (13 ft). W 2 m
(6 ft). Zone 5. S humus-rich, fertile.
P budding. Robust, bushy shrub, not
recommended for walls or pillars. Lightly
scented flowers.

Rosa 'Zéphirine Drouhin'
Climbing Rose / fam. *Rosaceae*
○ ⊘ ⊛ ⊗
June–July. Carmine pink. H 1.5–4.5 m (5–
15 ft). W 2 m (6 ft). Zone 5. S humus-rich,
fertile. P budding. Old, valuable variety,
continuously blooming, no thorns. Fragrant
semi-double flowers.

Rosa laevigata
Cherokee Rose / fam. *Rosaceae*
○ 🌰 ⊛ ⊛ ⊕
June. White. H 6 m (20 ft). W 2 m (6 ft). Zone 7.
S humus-rich, fertile. P seed, cuttings.
Fragrant rose with single flowers and large,
oval and bristly hips.

Rosa macrantha 'Raubritter'
Sweet Briar / fam. *Rosaceae*
○ 🌰 ⊛ ⊖ ⊗
July–August. Pink. H 1 m (3 ft). W 2 m (6 ft).
Zone 5. S humus-rich, fertile. P cuttings.
Shrub with crooked branches covered with
clusters of globular, semi-double flowers.

Rosa moyesii 'Geranium' (autumn)
fam. *Rosaceae*
○ 🌰 ⊛ ⊛ ⊕ ⊗
June. Blood red. H 2 m (6 ft). W 2 m (6 ft). Zone
5. S humus-rich, fertile. P cuttings. Fine shrub
of compact habit with large flowers followed
by urn-shaped hips.

Rosa moyesii 'Nevada'
fam. *Rosaceae*
○ 🌰 ⊛ ⊛ ⊕ ⊗
June–July. Creamy white. H 2 m (6 ft). W 3 m
(10 ft). Zone 5. S humus-rich, fertile.
P cuttings. Exceptionally attractive, recurrent-
flowering shrub with large single flowers.
Arching habit.

Rosa 'Fred Loads'
Modern Shrub Rose / fam. *Rosaceae*
○ 🌰 ⊛ ⊕ ⊗
May–June. Bright orange or vermilion.
H 1.5 m (5 ft). W 1 m (3 ft). Zone 5. S humus-
rich, fertile. P cuttings. Outstanding,
especially suitable for parks. Fragrant semi-
double flowers.

Rosa pimpinellifolia 'Frühlingsmorgen'
Scots Briar / fam. *Rosaceae*
○ 🌰 ⊛ ⊛ ⊗
May–June. Pink / creamy yellow. H 2 m (6 ft).
W 3 m (10 ft). Zone 5. S humus-rich, fertile.
P cuttings. Strikingly beautiful rose with large
single flowers. Often recurs in autumn.

301

Rosa

Rosa × richardii (R. gallica × R. phoenicia)
St John's Rose / **fam.** *Rosaceae*
◯ ⊘ ⍟ ⍟ ⍟ ⍟ ⍟ ⍟
June. Pink. H 3 m (10 ft). W 3 m (10 ft). Zone 6.
S humus-rich, fertile. P cuttings. Cross
between French Rose and the tender
Phoenician Rose first introduced in 1902.

Rosa rubiginosa (R. eglanteria)
Sweetbriar or Eglantine / **fam.** *Rosaceae*
◯ ⊖ ⍟ ⍟ ⍟ ⍟ ⍟
June. Pink. H 2.5 m (8 ft). W 2.5 m (8 ft). Zone
4. S humus-rich, fertile. P seed, cuttings.
Robust shrub with very thorny branches.
Leaves and flowers emit an apple-like
fragrance.

Rosa rubiginosa (R. eglanteria)
Sweetbriar or Eglantine / **fam.** *Rosaceae*
◯ ⊖ ⍟ ⍟ ⍟ ⍟ ⍟
For description and P see previous entry.
Makes an almost impenetrable hedge. Single
flowers, attractive hips and hook-shaped
thorns.

***Rosa sempervirens* 'Felicité et Perpetué'**
Rambling Rose / **fam.** *Rosaceae*
◯ ⍟ ⍟ ⍟ ⍟ ⍟
June. White. H 2–3 m (6–10 ft). W 3 m (10 ft).
Zone 5. S humus-rich, fertile. P cuttings.
Lightly scented, subtly beautiful rose with
small, dark leaves. Flowers in large clusters.

***Rosa setipoda* (autumn)**
Chinese Rose / **fam.** *Rosaceae*
◯ ⍟ ⍟ ⍟ ⍟
July. Pink. H 3 m (10 ft). W 2 m (6 ft). Zone 5.
S humus-rich, fertile. P seed, cuttings.
Impressive rose with fragrant flowers in small
clusters and apple-scented leaves.

Rosa × stylosa (R. canina × R. arvensis)
fam. *Rosaceae*
◯ ⍟ ⍟ ⍟
June–July. White. H 2 m (6 ft). W 3 m (10 ft).
Zone 5. S humus-rich, fertile. P cuttings.
Cross between the Dog Rose and Trailing
Rose first cultivated in 1838. Possibly an even
older hybrid.

***Rosa* 'Arianna'**
Hybrid Tea Rose / **fam.** *Rosaceae*
◯ ⊘ ⍟ ⍟ ⍟
June–July. Red. H 80 cm (32 in). W 60 cm (2 ft).
Zone 5. S humus-rich, fertile. P budding.
Lightly scented, erect shrub with a profusion
of flowers. Winner of five European gold
medals.

***Rosa* 'Chicago Peace'**
Hybrid Tea Rose / **fam.** *Rosaceae*
◯ ⊘ ⍟ ⍟ ⍟
June–July. Phlox pink / yellow. H 1 m (3 ft).
W 70 cm (28 in). Zone 5. S humus-rich, fertile.
P budding. Free-flowering, compact shrub
with graceful, lightly scented double flowers.

***Rosa* 'Dainty Bess'**
Hybrid Tea Rose / **fam.** *Rosaceae*
◯ ⊘ ⍟ ⍟ ⍟
June–July. Pink. H 80 cm (32 in). W 60 cm (2 ft).
Zone 5. S humus-rich, fertile. P budding. A
very leafy rose with single, fragrant flowers.
The petals have wavy edges.

Rosa 'Fragrant Cloud'
Hybrid Tea Rose / fam. *Rosaceae*
○ ⊙ ⊛ ⊕ ⊗
June–July. Coral-salmon. H 125 cm (4 ft).
W 80 cm (32 in). Zone 5. S humus-rich, fertile.
P budding. Free-flowering, very healthy rose
with a delightful fragrance. Red in bud.

Rosa 'Grandpa Dickson'
Hybrid Tea Rose / fam. *Rosaceae*
○ ⊙ ⊛ ⊕ ⊗
June–July. Yellow. H 90 cm (3 ft). W 60 cm
(2 ft). Zone 5. S humus-rich, fertile.
P budding. Erect shrub with very thorny
stems. Fragrant. Suitable for rose beds.

Rosa 'Interflora'
Hybrid Tea Rose / fam. *Rosaceae*
○ ⊙ ⊛ ⊕ ⊗
June–July. Orange-red. H 80 cm (32 in).
W 60 cm (2 ft). Zone 7. S humus-rich, fertile.
P budding. Erect greenhouse rose with lightly
scented double flowers and dark green leaves.

Rosa 'Mullard Jubilee'
Hybrid Tea Rose / fam. *Rosaceae*
○ ⊙ ⊛ ⊕ ⊗
June–July. Deep rose pink. H 80 cm (32 in).
W 60 cm (2 ft). Zone 5. S humus-rich, fertile.
P budding. Compact shrub with large,
shapely and fragrant flowers. Award winner.

Rosa 'Super Star'
Hybrid Tea Rose / fam. *Rosaceae*
○ ⊙ ⊛ ⊕ ⊗
June–July. Light vermilion. H 125 cm (4 ft).
W 70 cm (28 in). Zone 6. S humus-rich, fertile.
P budding. Sturdy plant; thorny stems.
Masses of flowers with a rich fruity fragrance.

Rosa 'Virgo'
Hybrid Tea Rose / fam. *Rosaceae*
○ ⊙ ⊛ ⊕ ⊗
June–July. White. H 70 cm (28 in). W 60 cm
(2 ft). Zone 5. S humus-rich, fertile.
P budding. Elegant rose with shapely and
lightly scented flowers. Also suitable for the
greenhouse.

Rosa 'Wendy Cussons'
Hybrid Tea Rose / fam. *Rosaceae*
○ ⊙ ⊛ ⊕ ⊗
June–July. Cerise. H 1 m (3 ft). W 70 cm (28 in).
Zone 5. S humus-rich, fertile. P budding.
Prize-winning, leafy rose with a profusion of
delightfully fragrant flowers.

Rosa 'White Wings'
Hybrid Tea Rose / fam. *Rosaceae*
○ ⊙ ⊛ ⊕ ⊗
June–July. White. H 1 m (3 ft). W 60 cm (2 ft).
Zone 5. S humus-rich, fertile. P budding. Not
very strong but outstandingly beautiful with
large single flowers and a light fragrance.

Rosa 'Betty Prior'
Floribunda Rose / fam. *Rosaceae*
○ ⊙ ⊛ ⊕ ⊗
June–July. Purple-red. H 100–150 cm (3–5 ft).
W 80 cm (32 in). Zone 4. S humus-rich, fertile.
P budding. Exceptionally hardy, disease-
resistant rose with a light fragrance. Single
flowers.

Rosa

Rosa 'Chinatown'
Floribunda Rose / fam. *Rosaceae*
June–July. Yellow. H 170 cm (5½ ft). W 1 m
(3 ft). Zone 5. S humus-rich, fertile.
P budding. Vigorous shrub of symmetrical
habit. Fragrant double flowers. Prune lightly.

Rosa 'Pernille Poulsen'
Floribunda Rose / fam. *Rosaceae*
June–July. Pink. H 70 cm (28 in). W 60 cm (2 ft).
Zone 5. S humus-rich, fertile. P budding.
Long-flowering and disease-resistant rose
with attractive, fragrant double flowers.

Rosa 'Queen Elizabeth' / Floribunda
(Grandiflora) Rose / fam. *Rosaceae*
June–July. Clear pink. H 1.5 m (5 ft). W 1 m
(3 ft). Zone 5. S humus-rich, fertile.
P budding. Strong-growing rose with long
stems almost completely devoid of thorns.
Gold medal winner.

Rosa 'Red Gold'
Floribunda Rose / fam. *Rosaceae*
June–July. Golden yellow / cherry red.
H 80 cm (32 in). W 60 cm (2 ft). Zone 5.
S humus-rich, fertile. P budding. Bears a host
of lightly scented double flowers. Weather
resistant.

Rosa 'Sarabande'
Floribunda Rose / fam. *Rosaceae*
June–July. Bright orange-red. H 65 cm (26 in).
W 50 cm (20 in). Zone 5. S humus-rich, fertile.
Good for beds or front of a border. Light
scent; very hardy and weather resistant.

Rosa 'Schneewittchen'
Polyantha Rose / fam. *Rosaceae*
June–July. White. H 1 m (3 ft). W 70 cm (28 in).
Zone 5. S humus-rich, fertile. P budding.
Bushy shrub with a mass of fragrant semi-
double flowers. Disease resistant.

Rosa 'Schweizer Gruss'
Floribunda Rose / fam. *Rosaceae*
June–July. Blood red. H 50 cm (20 in). W 50 cm
(20 in). Zone 5. S humus-rich, fertile.
P cuttings. Erect, bushy and free-flowering
shrub. Lightly scented, semi-double flowers.

Rosa villosa (R. pomifera)
Apple Rose / fam. *Rosaceae*
June–July. Pink. H 2 m (6 ft). W 2 m (6 ft). Zone
5. S humus-rich, fertile. P seed, cuttings.
Shrub with grey-green, resin-scented leaves
and fairly large solitary flowers.

Rosmarinus officinalis
Rosemary / fam. *Labiatae*
May–June. Mauve. H 1 m (3 ft). W 1 m (3 ft).
Zone 6–7. S not critical. P cuttings. Woody
shrub with elongated, aromatic leaves.
Flowers in axillary clusters.

Rubus calycinoides (R. fockeanus)
Bramble / fam. ***Rosaceae***
◐ ⊗ ⊘ ⚬ 🌲 ⊖
May–June. White. H 10 cm (4 in). W 2 m (6 ft).
Zone 5. S normal garden soil. P cuttings,
division. Creeping shrub with relatively few
thorns and red fruits.

Rubus thibetanus
Bramble / fam. ***Rosaceae***
◯ ◐ ⊗ 🌲 ⊖
June. Violet-purple. H 2 m (6 ft). W 3 m (10 ft).
Zone 5. S normal garden soil. P cuttings. Erect
shrub with bluish white glaucous branches
and black or red glaucous fruits.

Rudbeckia fulgida var. ***speciosa***
Coneflower / fam. ***Compositae***
◯ ◐ ◯ ☿ ⊗
August–October. Yellow. H 60 cm (2 ft).
A 30 cm (1 ft). S fertile. P division. Herbaceous
perennial with sturdy stems and a mass of
flowers over a long period. Water in dry
spells.

Rudbeckia fulgida var. ***sullivantii***
'Goldsturm' / fam. ***Compositae***
◯ ◐ ◯ ☿ ⊗
August–October. Yellow. H 60 cm (2 ft).
A 30 cm (1 ft). S fertile. P division. Free-
flowering. Good border plant. Soil must not
be allowed to get too dry. Good for cutting.

Rudbeckia hirta
Black-Eyed Susan / fam. ***Compositae***
◯ ⊖ ⊛ ⚬ ☿ ⊗
Sow in late March under glass. Plant out at
A 25–30 cm (10–12 in). H 60–100 cm (2–3 ft).
Yellow-orange. S fertile. Profusely flowering
and spreading. For large borders.

Rudbeckia hirta var. ***pulcherrima***
Black-Eyed Susan / fam. ***Compositae***
◯ ⊖ ⊗ ⊛ ⚬ ☿ ⊗
Sow in late March under glass and plant out
at A 30–40 cm (12–16 in). H 30–60 cm (1–2 ft).
Orange. S fertile. Differs little from *R. hirta*
but its ray florets may be longer, up to 5 cm
(2 in).

Rudbeckia laciniata
Coneflower / fam. ***Compositae***
◯ ◐ ◯ ☿ ⊗
July–September. Yellow. H 80–250 cm (32–
100 in). A 60–80 cm (24–32 in). S fertile.
P division. 'Golden Glow' 2 m (6 ft);
'Goldkugel' 1.5 m (5 ft); 'Goldquelle' 80 cm
(32 in).

Rudbeckia nitida **'Herbstsonne'**
Coneflower / fam. ***Compositae***
◯ ◐ ◯ ☿ ⊗
August–September. Yellow. H 2 m (6 ft). A 60–
80 cm (24–32 in). S fertile. P division. Flowers
have reflexed petals. Fairly tolerant of shade.

Ruscus hypophyllum
fam. ***Liliaceae***
◯ ◐ ⊖ ⚬ 🌲 ⊛
May–June. White. H 30 cm (1 ft). W 80 cm
(32 in). Zone 6. S not critical. P division. Sub-
shrub with leaf-like stems and red fruits.

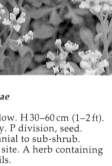

Ruta graveolens
Rue / fam. *Rutaceae*
○ ⊜ ◎ ⍟ ⊛
June–August. Yellow. H 30–60 cm (1–2 ft).
A 30 cm (1 ft). S dry. P division, seed.
Herbaceous perennial to sub-shrub.
Demands a warm site. A herb containing
highly aromatic oils.

Sagina subulata (S. pilifera)
Heath Pearlwort / fam. *Caryophyllaceae*
○ ◐ ◓ ◎ ⍟ ⊛
July–August. White. H 2–7 cm (¾–2¾ in).
A 15 cm (6 in). S normal. P division, seed.
Forms very low, mossy cushions covered with
small white flowers. Must not be trodden on.

Sagittaria sagittifolia
Arrowhead / fam. *Alismataceae*
○ ◓ ◎ ⊛ ◎ ⍟ ⊛
June–July (August). White. H 30–70 cm (12–
28 in). A 40 cm (16 in). S muddy. P division,
seed. Water depth 10–40 cm (4–16 in).
Decorative, arrow-shaped leaves. Tubers are
liked by ducks.

Salix alba 'Tristis'
White Weeping Willow / fam. *Salicaceae*
○ ◐ ◓ ⊛ ⊛ ◎ ⊕
April–May. Greeny yellow. H 15 m (50 ft).
W 12 m (40 ft). Zone 2. S not critical.
P cuttings. Vigorous tree with a very broad
crown and yellow shoots that droop to the
ground.

Salix hastata 'Wehrhahnii'
Willow / fam. *Salicaceae*
○ ◐ ◓ ⊛ ⍟ ⊛ ⊛
April–May. Silvery white. H 1.5 m (5 ft).
W 2 m (6 ft). Zone 4. S not critical. P cuttings.
Exceptionally beautiful catkins. Ovate leaves.
Best in groups or in heather and rock gardens.

Salix irrorata (autumn)
Willow / fam. *Salicaceae*
○ ◐ ◓ ⍟ ⊛
April. White. H 3 m (10 ft). W 5 m (16 ft). Zone
4. S not critical. P cuttings. Vigorous shrub
with very glaucous purple branches and
short, dense catkins.

Salix matsudana 'Tortuosa'
Willow / fam. *Salicaceae*
○ ◐ ◓ ⊛ ⍟ ⊛ ⊛
April–May. Greeny yellow. H 9 m (30 ft).
W 6 m (20 ft). Zone 4. S not critical. P cuttings.
Fairly tall, attractive shrub with twisted
branches and leaves.

Salix moupinensis
Willow / fam. *Salicaceae*
○ ◐ ◓ ⊛ ⍟ ⊛ ⊛
May–June. Yellow-green. H 6 m (20 ft). W 2 m
(6 ft). Zone 5. S not critical. P cuttings.
Exceptionally lovely, unusual shrub with long
catkins and reddish-brown sturdy branches.

Salix sachalinensis 'Sekka'
Willow / fam. *Salicaceae*
○ ◐ ◓ ⊛ ⍟ ⊛ ⊛
March–April. Yellow-green. H 4.5 m (15 ft).
W 3 m (10 ft). Zone 4. S not critical. P cuttings.
Vigorous, broad, open shrub with corrugated
branches. Long catkins.

Salpiglossis sinuata (S. variabilis)
fam. *Solanaceae*
◯ ◖ ☉ ⊗ ⊗
Sow in March in a heated greenhouse or in
May outside. Thin / plant out at A 15 cm (6 in).
H 50–100 cm (20–36 in). Mixed colours.
S fertile. Outstanding border plant; unusual
colour pattern.

Salpiglossis sinuata 'Emperor'
fam. *Solanaceae*
◯ ☉ ☉ ⊗ ⊗
For P see *S. sinuata*. H 50–100 cm (20–36 in).
Red / yellow. S fertile. Large-flowered
cultivar with slender, multi-branched stems
and sticky flowers. Good for cutting.

Salvia farinacea
Sage / fam. *Labiatae*
◯ ◖ ◖ ☉ ⊗ ⊗
Sow in February–March in a heated
greenhouse. Harden off. Plant out at A 25 cm
(10 in). H 60–80 cm (24–32 in). Violet-blue.
S fertile. Bushy, rewarding border plant with
a long flowering period.

Salvia fulgens
fam. *Labiatae*
◯ ◖ ⊘ ⊕ ⊗
August–October. Red. H 1 m (3 ft). W 1 m
(3 ft). Zone 5–6. S fertile garden soil. P seed,
division. Densely branched, tender shrub.
Leaves hairy underneath. Flowers in long
clusters.

Salvia patens
Sage / fam. *Labiatae*
◯ ◖ ◖ ⊗ ⊗
July–September. Blue. H 60–80 cm (24–32 in).
A 30–40 cm (12–16 in). S humus-rich, fertile.
P division, seed. Graceful plant with large
flowers. Cover in winter.

Salvia pratensis
Meadow Clary / fam. *Labiatae*
◯ ◖ ⊗ ⊗
June–August. Violet. H 50–60 cm (20–24 in).
A 30 cm (1 ft). S sandy loam. P division, seed.
Very suitable for grassy areas. Vigorously
self-seeding. Wrinkled leaves.

Salvia przewalskii
Sage / fam. *Labiatae*
◯ ◖ ⊗
July–August. Purple. H 50–75 cm (20–30 in).
A 40 cm (16 in). S normal. P division, seed.
Attractive but not widely grown plant with
sturdy stems. Suitable for a border.

Salvia sclarea
Clary / fam. *Labiatae*
◯ ◖ ☉ ⊗
Sow in June, outside. Thin out to A 35 cm
(14 in). H 150 cm (5 ft). Bluish-white. S good
garden soil. Ornamental plant with pungently
aromatic leaves. A medicinal and culinary
herb.

Salvia splendens
Scarlet Sage / fam. *Labiatae*
◯ ◖ ☉ ⊗
For P see *S. farinacea*. H 50 cm (20 in). Red,
pink, white. S fertile soil. Popular border and
bedding plant. Flowers surrounded by bracts.
Long flowering period.

307

Salvia

***Salvia × superba* 'Ostfriesland'**
Sage / fam. *Labiatae*
○ ○ ◉ ⊗
June–September. Violet-purple. H 50 cm
(20 in). A 30 cm (1 ft). S normal. P division.
Rewarding, sturdy, densely branched border
plant. Also suitable for poorer soil.

Salvia verticillata
fam. *Labiatae*
○ ○ ◉
July–September. Violet. H 50 cm (20 in).
A 30 cm (1 ft). S normal. P seed, division.
Native plant with grey-green, hairy leaves.
Suitable for borders.

Salvia viridis (S. horminum)
fam. *Labiatae*
○ ◉ ◉ ⊙ ⊗
Sow in April under glass. Plant out at A 20 cm
(8 in). H 50 cm (20 in). Mauve-violet. S normal
garden soil. Slightly hairy plant. Small
flowers, large, coloured bracts. Long
flowering period.

***Sambucus canadensis* 'Maxima'**
American Elder / fam. *Caprifoliaceae*
○ ◉ ◐ ◑ ◓ ⊗ ◈ ◉
June–July. White. H 3–4 m (10–13 ft). W 4 m
(13 ft). Zone 3. S not critical. P cuttings. Very
attractive elder with large leaves, black and
purple fruits. Autumn colouring.

Sambucus ebulus
Dwarf Elder / fam. *Caprifoliaceae*
○ ◉ ◐ ◓ ⊗ ◈ ◉
July–August. White. H 2 m (6 ft). A 2 m (6 ft).
S not critical. P cuttings, seed. *S. ebulus* is not
a shrub like the other elders but a herbaceous
perennial.

Sambucus nigra
Common Elder / fam. *Caprifoliaceae*
◉ ◐ ⊕ ❋ ⊗ ◈ ◉
June–July. White. H 6 m (20 ft). W 5 m (16 ft).
Zone 5. S not critical. P cuttings. Shrub or
small tree with pinnate leaves, flowers in
flattened umbels, and black berries.

***Sambucus nigra* 'Aurea'**
Golden Elder / fam. *Caprifoliaceae*
◉ ◐ ◓ ⊗ ❋ ◈ ◉
June–July. White. H 6 m (20 ft). W 4 m (13 ft).
Zone 5. S not critical. P cuttings. Cut back to
the ground each spring for best effect.

***Sambucus racemosa* 'Plumosa Aurea'**
Scarlet-Berried Elder / fam. *Caprifoliaceae*
◉ ◐ ◑ ◓ ⊗ ◈ ◉
April–May. Yellow-green. H 4 m (13 ft). W 4 m
(13 ft). Zone 4. S not critical. P cuttings. Shrub
with flowers in globular panicles, red berries,
and deeply cut, golden leaves.

Sanguinaria canadensis
Bloodroot / fam. *Papaveraceae*
◉ ◐ ◑ ⊗
April–May. White. H 20 cm (8 in). A 10–20 cm
(4–8 in). S sandy, acid. P division, seed.
Anemone-like flowers. The kidney-shaped
leaves come out after the flowers.

Sanguinaria canadensis 'Multiplex'
Bloodroot / fam. *Papaveraceae*
April–May. White. H 20 cm (8 in). A 10–20 cm (4–8 in). S sandy, acid, P division, seed. Preferred to the species because of its very full double flowers. Replant in the autumn.

Sanguisorba obtusa
Burnet / fam. *Rosaceae*
July–September. Purple. H 60–100 cm (2–3 ft). A 40 cm (16 in). S fertile. P division, seed. Found in moist meadows, but suitable for borders. Flowers quickly change colour to white.

Sanguinaria obtusa 'Albiflora'
Burnet / fam. *Rosaceae*
July–September. White. H 60–100 cm (2–3 ft). A 40 cm (16 in). S fertile. P division. Colour does not change, so it is more suitable for the border than the species.

Santolina chamaecyparissus
Lavender Cotton / fam. *Compositae*
July–August. Yellow. H 45–60 cm (18–24 in). W 60 cm (2 ft). Zone 6–7. S not critical. P cuttings. Bushy, aromatic sub-shrub with finely cut grey leaves and woolly stems.

Sanvitalia procumbens
Creeping Zinnia / fam. *Compositae*
Sow in April under glass or in May outside. Thin / plant out at A 20 cm (8 in). H 15 cm (6 in). Yellow-orange. S humus-rich. Free-flowering; hairy, prostrate and densely branched stems.

Saponaria ocymoides
Rock Soapwort / fam. *Caryophyllaceae*
May–June. Rose pink. H 30 cm (1 ft). A 20 cm (8 in). S fertile. P division, seed. Unassuming creeping plant from the Alps suitable for rock gardens, dry walls and edging.

Saponaria officinalis
Soapwort / fam. *Caryophyllaceae*
July–September. Purplish pink. H 50–80 cm (20–32 in). A 40 cm (16 in). S fertile. P division, seed. Invasive plant. Cut roots were once used to wash sheep's wool.

Saponaria officinalis 'Plena'
Soapwort / fam. *Caryophyllaceae*
July–September. Pink. H 50–80 cm (20–32 in). A 40 cm (16 in). S fertile. P division, seed. Double flowers. Suitable for a border. Produces underground runners which need curbing.

Sarcococca humilis (S. hookerana var. humilis) / fam. *Buxaceae*
January–March. White. H 50 cm (20 in). W 50 cm (20 in). Zone 5. S humus-rich. P seed, division. Dwarf shrub with splendid, fragrant flowers, black berries and lanceolate leaves.

Sasa veitchii (Bambusa veitchii)
fam. *Gramineae*

Usually without flowers. H 60–100 cm (2–3 ft).
W 70 cm (28 in). Zone 8. S humus-rich.
P division, root cuttings. Elegant bamboo
with yellow, desiccated leaf margins in the
autumn.

Saxifraga arendsii hybrid 'Ware's Crimson'
Saxifrage / fam. *Saxifragaceae*

May–June. Crimson. H 15–25 cm (6–10 in).
A 20 cm (8 in). S normal. P division. Carpet-
forming plant with fresh green leaves.
Spreads quickly. Divide after flowering.

Saxifraga × haagii
Saxifrage / fam. *Saxifragaceae*

April–May. Yellow. H 10 cm (4 in). A 10–20 cm
(4–8 in). S normal (chalky). P division. Mat-
forming plant with plentiful flowers. Grows
in crevices and holes in rock gardens and on
dry walls.

Saxifraga umbrosa
London Pride / fam. *Saxifragaceae*

May–June. White. H 20–40 cm (8–16 in). A 30–
45 cm (12–18 in). S normal. P seed, division.
Very sturdy plant with masses of flowers in
sprays. Rather fleshy rosettes. Suitable for
edging.

Saxifraga umbrosa 'Variegata'
London Pride / fam. *Saxifragaceae*

May–June. White / red. H 30–40 cm (12–
16 in). A 20 cm (8 in). S normal. P division.
Strong plant, native to Europe. Variegated
form. Makes excellent ground cover.

Scabiosa atropurpurea
Sweet Scabious / fam. *Dipsacaceae*

Sow in March under glass or in April outside.
Thin / plant out at A 25 cm (10 in). H 1 m (3 ft).
Mixed colours. S good garden soil. Easily
cultivated plant with musk-scented double
flowers.

Scabiosa caucasica 'Clive Greaves'
Scabious / fam. *Dipsacaceae*

June–September. Rich mauve. H 80 cm (32 in).
A 40 cm (16 in). S normal. P division (spring,
summer). Few flowers but a beautiful colour.
Strong stems, good for cutting.

Scabiosa ochroleuca
Scabious / fam. *Dipsacaceae*

June–October. Yellow. H 60 cm (2 ft). A 30 cm
(1 ft). S fertile. P division (spring, summer).
Good for cutting – keeps well in water.
Sowing not recommended.

Schizanthus pinnatus 'Star Parade'
Butterfly Flower / fam. *Solanaceae*

Sow in March under glass or in April outside.
Thin out to A 20 cm (8 in). H 45 cm (18 in).
Reddish-purple / yellow. S fertile. Bushy,
with orchid-like flowers. Long flowering
period.

Schizanthus wisetonensis hybrid
fam. *Solanaceae*
For P see *S. pinnatus*. H 30–40 cm (12–16 in).
Various colours. S fertile. Densely branched
plant with pinnate to bipinnate leaves and
flowers in panicles.

Schizostylis coccinea 'Sunrise'
Kaffir Lily / fam. *Iridaceae*
October–November. Pink. H 40–50 cm (16–
20 in). A 5–10 cm (2–4 in). D 8–10 cm (3–4 in).
S humus-rich. P division. Flowers in
profusion for three to four weeks. Protect with
bracken in winter.

Sciadopitys verticillata
Japanese Umbrella Pine / fam. *Taxodiaceae*
Attractive conifer of narrowly pyramidal
habit. Long needles arranged in whorls as
well as scaly needles. Oval cones. H 20 m
(65 ft). W 12 m (40 ft). S fertile. P seed. Zone 5.

Scilla hispanica
Spanish Bluebell / fam. *Liliaceae*
May–June. Blue. H 20–30 cm (8–12 in).
A 10 cm (4 in). D 8–10 cm (3–4 in). S normal
garden soil. P offsets, seed. Cover during the
first winter. Useful for naturalisation under
shrubs.

Scilla mischtschenkoana (S. tubergeniana)
fam. *Liliaceae*
March. Blue. H 10 cm (4 in). A 10 cm (4 in).
D 8–10 cm (3–4 in). S normal garden soil.
P offsets, seed. Flowers at the same time as
Galanthus nivalis and *Eranthis hyemalis*.

Scilla peruviana
Cuban Lily / fam. *Liliaceae*
May–June. Blue. H 20–30 cm (8–12 in).
A 25 cm (10 in). D 15–20 cm (6–8 in). S well
drained. P offsets, seed. Attractive, tender
species from the Mediterranean coast.

Scilla pratensis
fam. *Liliaceae*
May–June. Blue. H 20 cm (8 in). A 10 cm (4 in).
D 8–10 cm (3–4 in). S normal. P offsets, seed.
Late-flowering species from the Balkans. Not
very common.

Scilla sibirica 'Spring Beauty'
Squill / fam. *Liliaceae*
March–April. Violet-blue. H 10–20 cm (4–
8 in). A 10 cm (4 in). D 8–10 cm (3–4 in).
S normal garden soil. P offsets. Most popular
of all varieties, especially suitable for
naturalisation.

Scirpus tabernaemontani 'Zebrinus'
Zebra Rush / fam. *Cyperaceae*
June–July. Reddish brown. H 150 cm (5 ft).
A 60 cm (2 ft). S not critical. P division. Very
decorative marsh plant with round stems and
no real leaves.

311

Scutellaria

Scutellaria incana (S. canescens)
Skullcap / fam. *Labiatae*
◯ ◐ ⊝ ⊘ ◉ ✿ ⊗
August–September. Purple. H 60–100 cm (2–3 ft). A 30 cm (1 ft). S not critical. P seed, division. Attractive border plant with strong and erect stems. Flowers in dense clusters.

Sedum acre
Wall Pepper / fam. *Crassulaceae*
◯ ◐ ⊝ ◉ ⑲ ✿ ◎ ⊗ ⊖
June–July. Yellow. H 15 cm (6 in). A 10–20 cm (4–8 in). S normal. P division, seed, cuttings. Drought resistant. Grows on sites where nothing else seems to thrive.

Sedum aizoon (S. maximowiczii)
fam. *Crassulaceae*
◯ ◐ ⊝ ◉ ◎ ⊗
June–July. Yellow. H 40 cm (16 in). A 20 cm (8 in). S normal. P division, seed, stem cuttings (in summer). Suitable for rock gardens and borders. Loses its looks on moist sites.

Sedum album 'Coral Carpet'
White Stonecrop / fam. *Crassulaceae*
◯ ◐ ⊝ ◉ ⑲ ✿ ◎ ⊗ ⊖
June–July. White. H 10 cm (4 in). A 10–20 cm (4–8 in). S normal. P division. Very fleshy leaves. Creeping leaf stalks; erect flower stems. Suitable for dry walls.

Sedum cauticolum 'Robustum'
fam. *Crassulaceae*
◯ ⊝ ◉ ⑲ ⊗
July. Crimson. H 20–25 cm (8–10 in). A 20 cm (8 in). S normal garden soil. P division, cuttings. Creeping plant. Prostrate to erect stems, bluish-grey leaves and flowers in dense heads.

Sedum cyaneum 'Rosenteppich'
fam. *Crassulaceae*
◯ ◐ ⊝ ◉ ◎ ⊗ ⊖
June–August. Red. H 10 cm (4 in). A 10–20 cm (4–8 in). S normal. P division, seed, cuttings. Mat-forming plant with blue-green leaves. Drought resistant. Suitable for a rock garden.

Sedum floriferum 'Weihenstephaner Gold'
fam. *Crassulaceae*
◯ ◐ ⊝ ◉ ⑲ ◎ ⊗ ⊖
June–August. Yellow. H 15 cm (6 in). A 10–20 cm (4–8 in). S normal. P division, seed, cuttings. Mat-forming, attractive plant even after flowering. Bronze foliage in autumn.

Sedum middendorffianum
fam. *Crassulaceae*
◯ ◐ ⊝ ◉ ⑲ ✿ ◎ ⊗ ⊖
July–August. Yellow. H 10–20 cm (4–8 in). A 10–20 cm (4–8 in). S normal. P division, seed, cuttings. Strong, fast-growing, mat-forming plant. Bronze autumn foliage. For rock gardens.

Sedum spectabile 'Brilliant'
fam. *Crassulaceae*
◯ ◐ ◉ ⑲ ◎ ⊗
August–September. Rose-purple. H 30–45 cm (12–18 in). A 45 cm (18 in). S normal garden soil. P division, cuttings. Outstanding plant. Leaves in whorls, flowers in flattened heads.

Sedum telephium
fam. Crassulaceae
◯ ◑ ◯ ◯ ⊗
July–August. Red. H 20–40 cm (8–16 in).
A 20 cm (8 in). S normal. P division, seed.
Common in woods. May flower into October.
Very sturdy plant.

Sempervivum arachnoideum ssp. tomento-
sum / Cobweb Houseleek / **Crassulaceae**
◯ ◑ ⊖ ◯ ⊘ ⊛ ⊗ ⊖
July–August. Rose red. H 10 cm (4 in). A 30 cm
(1 ft). S not critical. P division. One of the
most attractive varieties; the globular rosettes
are covered with filmy hairs.

Sempervivum ciliosum (S. borisii)
Houseleek / fam. **Crassulaceae**
◯ ◑ ⊖ ◯ ⊘ ⊛ ⊗ ⊖
June–July. Yellow. H 5 cm (2 in). A 30 cm (1 ft).
S not critical. P division. Attractive small
plant from Greece. Rosettes densely covered
with hair.

Sempervivum tectorum
Common Houseleek / fam. **Crassulaceae**
◯ ◑ ⊖ ◯ ◯ ⊘ ⊛ ⊗ ⊖
June–August. Rose-purple. H 5 cm (2 in).
A 30 cm (1 ft). S not critical. P division. The
oldest of cultivated houseleeks. Forms large
rosettes with green, maroon-tipped leaves.

Sempervivum zelebori 'Alpha'
Houseleek / fam. **Crassulaceae**
◯ ◑ ◑ ⊖ ◯ ◯ ⊘ ⊛ ⊗ ⊖
June–July. Pink. H 10 cm (4 in). A 30 cm (1 ft).
S not critical. P division. Grows in dry places.
Greyish-green rosettes measuring 3 cm (1 in)
across.

Senecio bicolor 'Silverdust' (Cineraria
bicolor, C. maritima) / fam. **Compositae**
◯ ◑ ◑ ⊙ ⊘ ◯
Sow in February in a heated greenhouse.
Plant out at A 25 cm (10 in). H 60 cm (2 ft).
Yellow. S not too moist. Ornamental leaves
covered in white wool. Popular bedding
plant.

Senecio doria
fam. Compositae
◯ ◑ ◑ ⊗ ◯ ◯ ⊘
July–August. Yellow. H 180 cm (6 ft). A 60–
80 cm (24–32 in). S fertile. P division, seed.
Free-flowering plant and fast growing.
Suitable for naturalisation on moist sites.

Sequoiadendron giganteum (Wellingtonia
gigantea) / Giant Sequoia / fam. **Taxodiaceae**
◯ ◯ ⊗ ⊛ ⊛ ◯
Slender, very tall tree with a thick trunk,
brownish-red, soft bark, small cones. H 70 m
(230 ft). W 20 m (65 ft). S fertile. P seed,
cuttings. Zone 6.

Setaria italica
Italian Bristle Grass / fam. **Gramineae**
◯ ◑ ◑ ⊙ ◯ ⊗
Sow in April and thin out to A 30 cm (1 ft).
H 1 m (3 ft). Green. S not critical. Ornamental
grass with slender spikes, bristles than turn
yellow to black and coarse leaves.

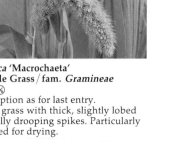

Setaria italica 'Macrochaeta'
Italian Bristle Grass / fam. *Gramineae*
○ ◐ ⊙ ✿ ⊗
P and description as for last entry.
Ornamental grass with thick, slightly lobed
and eventually drooping spikes. Particularly
recommended for drying.

Sidalcea hybrid 'Elsie Heugh'
fam. *Malvaceae*
○ ◐ ○ ✿ ⊗
June–August. Rose-purple. H 60–80 cm (24–
32 in). A 20–30 cm (8–12 in). S normal.
P division, cuttings. Fragrant flowers in
profusion. S lime free, very moist. Cut back
after flowering.

Sidalcea hybrid 'Sussex Beauty'
fam. *Malvaceae*
○ ◐ ○ ✿ ⊗
June–August. Pink. H 60–80 cm (24–32 in).
A 20–30 cm (8–12 in). S normal. P division,
cuttings. All varieties make excellent border
plants. Good for colour combinations.

Sidalcea hybrid 'William Smith'
fam. *Malvaceae*
○ ◐ ○ ⊗
June–August. Salmon pink. H 60–80 cm (24–
32 in). A 20–30 cm (8–12 in). S normal.
P division, cuttings. Must be watered
regularly during dry spells. No other
problems.

Silene acaulis
Moss Campion / fam. *Caryophyllaceae*
○ ⊘ ○ ✿ ⊗
May–August. Vivid pink. H 5 cm (2 in).
A 10 cm (4 in). S normal garden soil. P seed,
division. Dense mat-forming plant with small
rosettes. Awl-shaped leaves.

Silene armeria
fam. *Caryophyllaceae*
○ ○ ⊙ ✿
Sow in April and thin out to A 10–20 cm (4–
8 in). H 30–60 cm (1–2 ft). Rose-purple.
S normal garden soil. Can be found all over
the world. Stems sticky on top.

Silene coeli-rosa (Viscaria oculata)
Rose of Heaven / fam. *Caryophyllaceae*
○ ⊙ ✿
Sow in April and thin out to A 20–30 cm (8–
12 in). H 30–80 cm (12–32 in). Rose-purple.
S normal garden soil. Very easily cultivated
plant. Flowers in profusion. Pointed,
lanceolate leaves.

Silene coeli-rosa 'Formule'
Rose of Heaven / fam. *Caryophyllaceae*
○ ⊙ ✿
For P see last entry. H 80 cm (32 in). Mixed
colours. S normal garden soil. Long-flowering
small plant. Several flowers combined in loose
clusters.

Silene maritima 'Weisskelchen'
Sea Campion / fam. *Caryophyllaceae*
○ ○ ✿ ⊗
May–August. White. H 20 cm (8 in). A 20 cm
(8 in). S normal. P division, cuttings. Mat-
forming plant. Must not become too wet in
the winter. Long flowering season.

Silene schafta 'Splendens'
Campion / fam. *Caryophyllaceae*
○ ◑ ⦷ ⓨ ⊗
August–September. Rose-purple. H 10–15 cm
(4–6 in). A 30 cm (1 ft). S normal garden soil.
P division, seed. Free-flowering, mat-forming
little plant. Flowers have reddish, hairy
sepals.

Silphium perfoliatum
fam. *Compositae*
○ ○ ⓨ
July–September. Yellow. H 150–250 cm (5–
8 ft). A 60 cm (2 ft). S good garden soil. P seed,
division. Unpretentious plant with angular
stems. Upper leaves fused into cups.

Silybum marianum
Holy Thistle / fam. *Compositae*
○ ◑ ⊙ ⦿ ⊕
Sow in April and thin out to A 60 cm (2 ft).
H 150 cm (5 ft). Rosy-purple. S humus-rich.
Naturalised plant from the Mediterranean.
Very attractive, spiny leaves. Edible and
medicinal.

**Sinarundinaria murielae (Arundinaria
murielae)** / fam. *Gramineae*
○ ◑ ⊘ ⦿ ⦿ ⊛
Does not flower in cultivation. H 2.5 m (8 ft).
W 1 m (3 ft). Zone 5. S normal garden soil.
P division. Spreading ornamental grass with
very strong, greeny-yellow stems arching out.

**Skimmia × foremannii (S. japonica × S.
reevesiana)** / fam. *Rutaceae*
○ ◑ ⊘ ⦿ ⦿ ⊛
May. White. H 1.25 m (4 ft). W 1.25 m (4 ft).
Zone 5. S humus-rich, acid. P seed, cuttings.
Modest little shrub with large obovate leaves,
flowers in panicles and red berries.

Skimmia japonica (S. fragrans) male flowers
fam. *Rutaceae*
○ ◑ ⊘ ⦿ ⓨ ⦿ ⊛
May. White. H 1.5 m (5 ft). W 2 m (6 ft). Zone
5. S humus-rich, acid. Slow-growing shrub
with leathery leaves and masses of flowers in
large panicles.

Skimmia japonica (S. oblata) female plant
fam. *Rutaceae*
○ ◑ ⊘ ⦿ ⓨ ⦿ ⊛ ⊛
May. White. H 1.5 m (5 ft). W 2 m (6 ft). Zone
5. S humus-rich, acid. P seed, cuttings.
Variable, often densely globular, dioecious
shrub. Fruits remain long on the tree.

Solanum crispum
Chilean Potato Tree / fam. *Solanaceae*
○ ⦿ ⓨ ⊛
June–September. Purple-blue. H 6 m (20 ft).
W 2 m (6 ft). Zone 8. S not critical. P cuttings.
Bushy, climbing, sometimes evergreen shrub
with ovate leaves and fragrant flowers.

Solidago caesia
Golden Rod / fam. *Compositae*
○ ○ ⓨ ⊗
August–September. Yellow. H 60 cm (2 ft).
A 30–40 cm (12–16 in). S normal. P division,
seed, cuttings. Sturdy perennial for borders,
also for naturalised groups. Slightly arching
stems.

315

Solidago hybrid 'Goldenmosa'
Golden Rod / fam. *Compositae*
○ ⓞ ⓨ ⓧ
August–October. Yellow. H 80 cm (32 in).
A 40 cm (16 in). S normal garden soil.
P division, cuttings. Resembles mimosa.
Sprays of fluffy flowers. Very good for
cutting.

Solidago hybrid 'Goldstrahl'
Golden Rod / fam. *Compositae*
○ ⓞ ⓨ ⓧ
August–September. Yellow. H 80 cm (32 in).
A 40 cm (16 in). S normal. P division, seed.
Erect stems. Strong plant. Attacked by mildew
in bad weather.

× *Solidaster luteus*
fam. *Compositae*
○ ⓞ ⓨ ⓧ
July–September. Yellow. H 60–100 cm (2–3 ft).
A 40 cm (16 in). S normal garden soil.
P division, cuttings. Cross between *Solidago*
and *Aster*. Not very sturdy stems. Flowers in
profusion.

Sophora japonica
Japanese Pagoda Tree / fam. *Leguminosae*
○ ✳ ⓨ ⓦ ⓦ
August. White. H 25 m (80 ft). W 15 m (50 ft).
Zone 4. S fertile garden soil. P seed. Tree with
pinnate leaves, pea-like flowers in pendent
racemes followed by seed pods.

Sorbaria aitchisonii
fam. *Rosaceae*
○ ⓘ ⓦ ⓨ
July–August. White. H 3 m (10 ft). W 3.5 m
(11 ft). Zone 5. S normal garden soil. P rooted
suckers, cuttings. Tall shrub with dark red
stems, composite leaves and flowers in
plumes of long panicles.

Sorbaria arborea var. *subtomentosa*
fam. *Rosaceae*
○ ⓘ ⓦ ⓨ
July–August. White. H 4 m (13 ft). W 4 m
(13 ft). Zone 5. S not critical. P cuttings, rooted
suckers. Flowering shrub with reddish, hairy
young shoots and leaves hairy underneath.

Sorbaria sorbifolia (Spiraea sorbifolia)
fam. *Rosaceae*
○ ⓘ ⓦ ⓨ
June–July. White. H 2 m (6 ft). W 2.5 m (8 ft).
Zone 2. S normal garden soil. P rooted
suckers, cuttings. Low shrub with erect
branches covered with fine hairs. Flowers in
erect panicles.

Sorbus alnifolia (Micromeles alnifolia)
fam. *Rosaceae*
○ ⓘ ✳ ⓦ ⓦ
May–June. White. H 12 m (40 ft). W 5 m (16 ft).
Zone 5. S not critical. P seed. Erect tree with
reddish-brown, glossy branches, foliage
colouring in autumn and red fruits.

Sorbus americana 'Belmonte'
fam. *Rosaceae*
○ ⓘ ✳ ⓨ ⓦ ⓦ
May–June. White. H 8 m (26 ft). W 7 m (23 ft).
S not critical. P grafting. Tree with a dense
oval crown, erect branches and attractive
orange-red autumn foliage.

***Sorbus aria* 'Majestica'**
Whitebeam / fam. *Rosaceae*
○ ◐ ➲ ❀ ❀
May. White. H 10 m (33 ft). W 8 m (26 ft). Zone
5. S not critical. P grafting. Vigorous tree
bearing large, dull green leaves, whitish
underneath, and changing colour in autumn.
Red fruits.

***Sorbus aucuparia* 'Beissneri'**
Rowan / fam. *Rosaceae*
○ ◐ ❀ ❀
May. White. H 15 m (50 ft). W 7.5 m (24 ft).
S not critical. P grafting. Vigorous tree with
reddish stems and shoots. Fruits are not
bitter. Zone 2.

Sorbus austriaca
fam. *Rosaceae*
○ ◐ ❀ ❀ ❀ ❀
May. White. H 7 m (23 ft). W 4 m (13 ft). Zone
4. S not critical. P seed. Small tree of a
pyramidal habit. Serrate leaves and more or
less spherical fruits.

***Sorbus* 'Copper Glow'**
fam. *Rosaceae*
○ ◐ ❀ ❀ ❀ ❀
May. White. H 8 m (26 ft). W 6 m (20 ft). Zone
4. S not critical. P grafting. Handsome
ornamental tree, very attractive when in
flower or bearing fruit.

Sorbus decora
fam. *Rosaceae*
○ ◐ ❀ ❀
May. White. H 6 m (20 ft). W 5 m (16 ft). S not
critical. P seed. Small tree with a compact,
broad crown and large red fruits in
spectacular clusters. Zone 2.

Sorbus discolor
fam. *Rosaceae*
○ ◐ ❀ ❀ ❀ ❀ ❀
May. White. H 10 m (33 ft). W 8 m (26 ft). Zone
5. S not critical. P seed. Loosely branched
ornamental tree without a main stem. Very
spectacular fruits.

***Sorbus hupehensis* 'November Pink'**
fam. *Rosaceae*
○ ◐ ❀ ❀
May. White. H 7 m (23 ft). W 4 m (13 ft). Zone
4. S not critical. P grafting. Moderately tall
tree with a loose crown. Pink fruits covered
with red dots stay on the tree until December.

***Sorbus* 'Joseph Rock'**
fam. *Rosaceae*
○ ◐ ❀ ❀ ❀
May. White. H 9 m (30 ft). W 3 m (10 ft). Zone
4. S not critical. P grafting. Sturdy and
compact pyramidal tree. A particularly
attractive and recommended form of rowan.

***Sorbus* 'Mitchellii' ('John Mitchell')**
fam. *Rosaceae*
○ ◐ ❀ ❀
May. White. H 8 m (26 ft). W 6 m (20 ft). Zone
5–6. S not critical. P seed. Moderately tall tree.
Large green and brown fruits in loose
clusters. Attractive, large, woolly leaves.

317

Sparaxis tricolor hybrid
Harlequin Flower / fam. *Iridaceae*
○ ⊙ ⊙ ⊛ ⊗
June. Various colours. H 35 cm (14 in). A 8–
10 cm (3–4 in). D 8 cm (3 in). S normal garden
soil. P offsets. Plant the corms in autumn and
cover well. Lift in July and store.

Spartium junceum
Spanish Broom / fam. *Leguminosae*
○ ⊙ ⊙ ⊛ ⊗
September. Yellow. H 3 m (10 ft). W 2.5 m
(8 ft). Zone 7. S normal garden soil. P seed.
Flowering shrub with tough, rush-like green
stems and small deciduous leaves. Fragrant.

Spiraea × arguta
Bridal Wreath / fam. *Rosaceae*
○ ⊙ ⊙ ⊛ ⊗
April–May. White. H 2.5 m (8 ft). W 2.5 m
(8 ft). Zone 4. S fertile soil. P cuttings,
layering. Flowering shrub with arching,
slender branches and flowers in dense
umbels.

Spiraea × billardii
fam. *Rosaceae*
○ ⊙ ⊜ ⊙ ⊙ ⊗
June–August. Pink. H 2 m (6 ft). W 2 m (6 ft).
Zone 4. S fertile. P cuttings, layering.
Vigorous flowering shrub. Leaves woolly
underneath. Flowers in dense plume-shaped
heads.

Spiraea × bumalda 'Anthony Waterer'
fam. *Rosaceae*
○ ⊙ ⊜ ⊙ ⊙ ⊗
July–September. Rose-purple. H 80 cm (32 in).
W 1 m (3 ft). Zone 5. S fertile. P cuttings,
layering. Small shrub with narrow leaves,
often variegated cream and pink. Prune in
spring.

Spiraea chamaedryfolia (S. flexuosa)
fam. *Rosaceae*
⊙ ⊜ ⊙ ⊙ ⊙
May–June. White. H 2 m (6 ft). W 2 m (6 ft).
Zone 5. S fertile soil. P cuttings, layering.
Broad shrub with arching branches. Suitable
for large areas and the edge of woods.

Spiraea nipponica
fam. *Rosaceae*
○ ⊙ ⊜ ⊙ ⊙ ⊗
June. White. H 2.5 m (8 ft). W 2.5 m (8 ft). Zone
4. S fertile soil. P cuttings, layering. Stiffly
erect shrub with arching branches and small
ovate, dark green leaves.

Spiraea thunbergii
fam. *Rosaceae*
○ ⊙ ⊙ ⊜ ⊙ ⊙
April–May. White. H 2 m (6 ft). W 2.5 m (8 ft).
Zone 4. S fertile soil. P cuttings, layering.
Finely branched little shrub with light green,
narrow leaves and reddish-brown branches.

**Spiraea × vanhouttei (S. cantoniensis × S.
trilobata)** / fam. *Rosaceae*
○ ⊙ ⊜ ⊙ ⊙ ⊙ ⊜
May–June. White. H 2 m (6 ft). W 2 m (6 ft).
Zone 4. S fertile soil. P cuttings, layering.
Shrub with arching branches, reddish-brown,
smooth branchlets and a mass of flowers.

Spiraea veitchii
fam. *Rosaceae*
○ⓘⓛ◯ⓨⓥⓥ
July. White. H3m (10ft). W3m (10ft). Zone
5. S fertile soil. P cuttings, layering.
Handsome bushy shrub with arching
branches. Leaves downy underneath.

Stachys byzantina (S. lanata, S. olympica)
fam. *Labiatae*
○ⓘⓛ◯ⓨⓥⓥ
June–August. Purple. H25–50cm (10–20in).
A20cm (8in). S normal. P division, seed,
cuttings. Grown chiefly for its attractive
woolly leaves. Looks well with blue plants.

Stachys grandiflora (Betonica macrantha)
fam. *Labiatae*
○ⓘⓛ◯ⓨ
June–August. Purple. H40–70cm (20–28in).
A30cm (1ft). S normal. P division, seed,
cuttings. Decorative and strong-growing
plant for the border. Woolly leaves and stems.

Stachys officinalis
Wood Betony / fam. *Labiatae*
○ⓘⓛ◯ⓨ
July–August. Purple. H30–60cm (1–3ft).
A30cm (1ft). S normal garden soil.
P division, seed, cuttings. Stems bear few
leaves. Good for naturalising and is very
undemanding.

Stachyurus praecox
fam. *Stachyuraceae*
○ⓘⓛ◯ⓨⓥⓥ
March–April. Yellow-green. H2m (6ft).
W2m (6ft). Zone 5. S humus-rich. P cuttings.
Shrub with arching, very dark branches.
Flowers come out before the leaves. Yellow-
green berries.

Staphylea colchica
fam. *Staphyleaceae*
ⓘⓛ◯⊗ⓥⓥ⊕
May. White. H3m (10ft). W2m (6ft). Zone 5.
S normal garden soil. P seed, layering. Erect
shrub with irregularly pinnate leaves and
flowers in erect or arching plume-like sprays.

Staphylea pinnata
Bladder-nut / fam. *Staphyleaceae*
○ⓘⓛ◯ⓥⓥ⊗⊕
May–June. White. H5m (16ft). W3m (10ft).
Zone 5. S humus-rich. P seed, cuttings,
layering. Erect shrub with sharply toothed
leaves, globular fruits and yellow-brown
seeds.

Stellaria holostea
Greater Stichwort / fam. *Caryophyllaceae*
ⓘⓛ◯ⓨ
April–June. White. H20–40cm (8–16in).
A20cm (8in). S normal garden soil.
P division, seed. Herbaceous perennial
suitable for naturalising among shrubs.

Stephanandra incisa 'Crispa' (autumn)
fam. *Rosaceae*
○ⓘⓛ◯ⓥⓥ
June. White. H60cm (2ft). W150cm (5ft).
Zone 5. S humus-rich. P cuttings, division.
Small shrub with stems that arch down to the
ground and a more or less creeping habit.

Stewartia sinensis
fam. *Theaceae*
○ ✱ ⊛ Ⓨ
June–July. White. H 20 m (65 ft). W 15 m (50 ft).
Zone 6. S humus-rich. P seed, cuttings. Tree
with peeling brown bark and fragrant cup-
shaped flowers.

Stipa barbata
Feather Grass / fam. *Gramineae*
○ ⊖ ⊘ ⌃ Ⓥ Ⓨ ⊛ ⊗ ⊗
July–August. White. H 75–100 cm (30–36 in).
A 30–40 cm (12–16 in). S dry. P division, seed.
Graceful blades suitable for drying. One of
the most decorative of ornamental grasses.

Stipa gigantea
Feather Grass / fam. *Gramineae*
○ ⊖ ⊘ ⌃ Ⓥ Ⓨ ⊛ ⊕ ⊗
June–July. White. H 75–100 cm (30–36 in).
A 30–40 cm (12–16 in). S dry garden soil.
P division, seed. Graceful grass seen to best
advantage in exposed sites where the wind
blows freely.

Stokesia laevis
Stoke's Aster / fam. *Compositae*
○ ⌃ ⊙ Ⓥ Ⓨ
July–September. Purple. H 25 cm (10 in).
A 20 cm (8 in). S normal garden soil.
P division, seed, cuttings. Flower resembles
China Aster. Sensitive to wet and cold
winters.

Stranvaesia davidiana
fam. *Rosaceae*
○ ◑ ⊕ Ⓨ ⊛
June. White. H 2.5 m (8 ft). W 2.5 m (8 ft). Zone
5–6. S fertile soil. P seed, cuttings. Broad
shrub with dark green lanceolate leaves,
crimson from September on. Flowers in wide,
flat heads.

Streptosolen jamesonii
fam. *Solanaceae*
○ ◑ ⊕ Ⓥ ⊛
April–June. Orange. H 1.5 m (5 ft). W 1.5 m
(5 ft). Zone 10. S fertile. P cuttings. Climbing
shrub of irregular habit. Needs sub-tropical
conditions. Spectacular flowers.

Styrax obassia
fam. *Styracaceae*
○ ◑ ✱ Ⓨ ⊛
May–June. White. H 9 m (30 ft). W 7 m (23 ft).
Zone 6. S light, sandy. P seed, layering,
cuttings. Shrub or tree with erect branches
and fragrant flowers in arching clusters.

Symphoricarpos albus var. *laevigatus*
Snowberry / fam. *Caprifoliaceae*
○ ◑ ◐ ⊕ ⊘ ⊛ ⊜ ⊗
July–August. Pink. H 1.5 m (5 ft). W 2 m (6 ft).
S normal garden soil. P rooted suckers. Broad,
erect shrub with many suckers, flowers in
small clusters, berries until November or
December. Zone 3.

Symphoricarpos × doorenbosii 'Magic Berry'
fam. *Caprifoliaceae*
○ ◑ ◐ ⊕ ⊘ ⊛ ⊜ ⊗
June–July. Pink. H 80 cm (32 in). W 100 cm
(3 ft). Zone 4. S normal garden soil. P cuttings.
Low, bushy shrub with fairly large, reddish-
purple berries in dense clusters.

Symphoricarpos × doorenbosii 'Mother of Pearl' / fam. Caprifoliaceae
○ ◐ ⊕ ⊛ ⊛ ⊛
June–July. Pink. H 1.25 m (4 ft). W 1.50 m (5 ft). Zone 4. S normal garden soil. P cuttings. Vigorous shrub with mother-of-pearl coloured large berries. Very attractive variety.

Symphytum grandiflorum
Comfrey / fam. Boraginaceae
April–June. Creamy white. H 10–25 cm (4–10 in). A 20 cm (8 in). S normal. P division, seed, cuttings. Spreading. Good ground-cover plant which comes in a number of garden varieties.

Symphytum × uplandicum 'Variegatum'
fam. Boraginaceae
○ ◐ ○ ⊘
June–July. Rose-purple. H 1 m (3 ft). A 60–80 cm (24–32 in). S normal garden soil. P division, cuttings. Vigorous plant suitable for naturalising between conifers. Tubular flowers.

Syringa josikaea
Hungarian Lilac / fam. Oleaceae
○ ⊕ ⊕ ⊙ ⊗
May–June. Deep violet. H 3 m (10 ft). W 2 m (6 ft). S fertile garden soil. P seed. Vigorous shrub with flowers in pyramidal panicles. Reddish-brown buds. Zone 2.

Syringa komarowii
Lilac / fam. Oleaceae
○ ⊕ ⊕ ⊙ ⊗
June. Pink. H 4 m (13 ft). W 5 m (16 ft). Zone 4. S fertile garden soil. P seed. Shrub with light brown warty branches and flowers in dense, ovate panicles.

Syringa × persica (S. afghanica × S. laciniata)
Persian Lilac / fam. Oleaceae
○ ⊕ ⊕ ⊙ ⊗
May. Violet. H 5 m (16 ft). W 4 m (13 ft). Zone 5. S fertile garden soil. Dense, rounded shrub with fairly soft branches and fragrant flowers in loose panicles.

Syringa × swegiflexa (S. reflexa × S. sweginzowii) / Lilac / fam. Oleaceae
○ ⊕ ⊕ ⊙ ⊗
June. Pink. H 3 m (10 ft). W 2.5 m (8 ft). Zone 5. S fertile garden soil. P cuttings, seed. Erect shrub with flowers in gracefully arching panicles and dark red buds.

Syringa tigerstedtii
Lilac / fam. Oleaceae
○ ⊕ ⊕ ⊙ ⊗
June. Pale violet. H 3 m (10 ft). W 5 m (16 ft). Zone 4. S fertile garden soil. P cuttings, seed. Shrub with slender branches, ovate and pointed leaves. Fragrant flowers in erect panicles.

Syringa vulgaris 'Cavour'
Common Lilac / fam. Oleaceae
○ ⊕ ⊕ ⊙ ⊗
May. Lilac. H 5 m (16 ft). W 4 m (13 ft). S fertile garden soil. P grafting, layering. Erect shrub with single flowers in long, dense, conical panicles. Zone 3.

321

Syringa

Syringa vulgaris 'General Sherman'
Common Lilac / fam. *Oleaceae*
○ ✿ ⊛ ⦿ ⊗
May. Lilac-pink. H 5 m (16 ft). W 4 m (13 ft).
S fertile garden soil. P grafting. Cut lilacs back
hard after flowering to preserve their compact
shape. Zone 3.

Syringa vulgaris 'Maréchal Lannes'
Common Lilac / fam. *Oleaceae*
○ ✿ ⊛ ⦿ ⊗
May. Mauve-pink. H 5 m (16 ft). W 4 m (13 ft).
S fertile garden soil. P grafting, layering. Tall,
erect shrub with semi-double flowers in
broad, dense panicles. Zone 3.

Syringa wolfii (S. formosissima)
Lilac / fam. *Oleaceae*
○ ✿ ⊛ ⦿ ⊗
June. Purple-rose. H 5 m (16 ft). W 4 m (13 ft).
Zone 5. S fertile garden soil. P seed. Shrub
with smooth branches and fragrant flowers in
downy panicles.

Tagetes erecta hybrid 'First Lady'
African Marigold / fam. *Compositae*
○ ◑ ⊙ ⦿
Sow in April under glass and plant out at
A 20–25 cm (8–10 in). H 30 cm (1 ft). Yellow.
S not critical. Attractive and compact plant
with double flowers. Leaves smell pungent if
bruised.

Tagetes erecta hybrid 'First Whites'
African Marigold / fam. *Compositae*
○ ◑ ⊙ ⦿
Sow in April under glass and plant out at
A 25–35 cm (10–14 in). H 45 cm (18 in). White.
S not critical. Fairly low-growing cultivar
suitable for bedding. Flowers over a long
period.

Tagetes erecta hybrid 'Golden Jubilee'
African Marigold / fam. *Compositae*
○ ◑ ⊙ ⦿
Sow in April under glass. Plant out at A 25–
35 cm (10–14 in). H 50 cm (20 in). Yellow-
orange. S not critical. Semi-tall variety with
large double flowers. Weather resistant.

Tagetes erecta hybrid 'Orange Jubilee'
African Marigold / fam. *Compositae*
○ ◑ ⊙ ⦿
For P and description see last entry. Densely
branched, fast-growing plant. Good for
cutting, though it has a pungent smell.

Tagetes patula 'Honeycomb'
French Marigold / fam. *Compositae*
○ ◑ ⊙ ⦿
Sow in April under glass and plant out at
A 15–20 cm (6–8 in). H 25 cm (10 in). Orange /
red. S not critical. Hybrid with large, double,
bicoloured flowers. Good bedding plant.

Tagetes patula hybrid 'Dainty Marietta'
French Marigold / fam. *Compositae*
○ ◑ ⊙ ⦿
Sow in April under glass and plant out at
A 15–20 cm (6–8 in). H 30 cm (1 ft). Yellow /
red. S not critical. Single-flowered, compact
variety highly recommended for bedding.

***Tagetes patula* hybrid 'Florence'**
French Marigold / fam. *Compositae*
◯ ◗ ⊙ ⊛
Sow in April under glass and plant out at
A 15–20 cm (6–14 in). H 20 cm (8 in). Orange-
yellow. S not critical. Fleuroselect winner in
1982. Single to semi-double flowers; fine
foliage.

***Tagetes patula* hybrid 'Queen Bee'**
French Marigold / fam. *Compositae*
◯ ◗ ⊙ ⊛
For P and description see *T. patula*
'Honeycomb'. Fleuroselect winner in 1980.
From Mexico. Densely branched and long-
flowering.

***Tagetes patula* 'Silvia'**
French Marigold / fam. *Compositae*
◯ ◗ ⊙ ⊛
Sow in April under glass and plant out at
A 15–20 cm (6–8 in). H 15 cm (6 in). Yellow.
S not critical. Fleuroselect winner in 1982. For
balconies. Flowers early. Uniform growth.

***Tagetes patula* 'Yellow Jacket'**
French Marigold / fam. *Compositae*
◯ ◗ ⊙ ⊛
Sow in April under glass and plant out at
A 20–25 cm (8–10 in). H 25 cm (10 in). Yellow.
S not critical. Fleuroselect winner in 1982.
Attractive hybrid with fully double flowers.

***Tagetes tenuifolia* 'Golden Gem'**
fam. *Compositae*
◯ ◗ ⊙ ⊛
Sow in April under glass and plant out at
A 20–25 cm (8–10 in). H 30 cm (1 ft). Yellow-
orange. S not critical. Compact plant with
star-shaped single flowers.

***Tagetes tenuifolia* 'Lemon Queen'**
fam. *Compositae*
◯ ◗ ⊙ ⊛
Sow in April under glass and plant out at
A 20–25 cm (8–10 in). H 30 cm (1 ft). Yellow.
S not critical. A cross developed from *T. t.*
'Pumila'. All tagetes plants come from Mexico.

***Tagetes tenuifolia* 'Pumila'**
fam. *Compositae*
◯ ◗ ⊙ ⊛
Sow in April under glass and plant out at
A 20–25 cm (8–10 in). H 20–30 cm (8–12 in).
S not critical. Attractive plant, usually free-
flowering, with aromatic, finely divided
leaves.

Tamarix ramosissima (T. odessana)
Tamarisk / fam. *Tamaricaceae*
◯ ◗ ⊕ ⊛ ⊗
June–August. Pink. H 2–4 m (6–13 ft). W 3 m
(10 ft). Zone 4. S fertile, well drained.
P cuttings. Vigorous, tall shrub with arching
branches. Suitable for informal hedges.

Tamarix tetrandra
Tamarisk / fam. *Tamaricaceae*
◯ ◗ ◖ ⊕ ⊛ ⊗
April–May. Pink. H 3 m (10 ft). W 2 m (6 ft).
Zone 5. S fertile. P cuttings. Robust shrub
with arching, reddish-brown branches.
Flowers on last year's wood.

Taxodium distichum
Swamp Cypress/fam. *Taxodiaceae*
○ ≋ ✳ ⊛ ⦾ ⊕
Pyramidal tree for wet ground. Yellow-green
needles change colour in autumn. Develops
breathing roots called 'knees'. H 30 m (100 ft).
W 10 m (33 ft). S humus-rich. P seed, cuttings.
Zone 4.

Taxus baccata
Common Yew/fam. *Taxaceae*
○ ◑ ⦾ ⦾ ⊛ ⦿ ⊛ ⦾ ⊙ ⦿
Broad, well-branched tree easily clipped into
all sorts of shapes. Fleshy, oval, red or yellow
fruits. H 10 m (33 ft). W 10 m (33 ft). S plenty of
humus. P seed. Zone 5.

***Taxus baccata* 'Aurea'**
Common Yew/fam. *Taxaceae*
○ ◑ ⦾ ⦾ ⊛ ⦿ ⊛ ⦾ ⊙ ⦿
Small compact shrub. The golden leaves turn
green during the second year. Will stand
clipping into any shapes. H 6 m (20 ft). W 4 m
(13 ft). S humus-rich. P cuttings. Zone 5.

***Taxus baccata* 'Cavendishii'**
Common Yew/fam. *Taxaceae*
○ ◑ ⦾ ⦾ ⊛ ⦿ ⊛ ⦾
Low, spreading shrub of irregular habit. Blue-
green needles. H 2 m (6 ft). W 4 m (13 ft).
S humus-rich. P cuttings. Zone 5.

***Taxus baccata* 'Dovastonii Aurea'**
Common Yew/fam. *Taxaceae*
○ ◑ ⦾ ⦾ ⊛ ⦿ ⊛ ⦾ ⊕
Broadly pyramidal, upright conifer with
spreading yellow branches and curtains of
branchlets. Golden needles. H 3 m (10 ft). W 3–
4 m (10–13 ft). S humus-rich. P cuttings.
Zone 5.

***Taxus baccata* 'Fastigiata'**
Irish Yew/fam. *Taxaceae*
○ ◑ ✳ ⦾ ⊛ ⦿ ⊛ ⦾ ⊙ ⊕
Erect, columnar, eventually broadly elliptical
tree with a multi-pointed top. Prune regularly
to prevent top-heaviness. H 4 m (13 ft). W 1 m
(3 ft). S humus-rich. P cuttings. Zone 5.

***Taxus baccata* 'Fastigiata Aurea'**
Irish Yew/fam. *Taxaceae*
○ ◑ ✳ ⦾ ⦾ ⊛ ⦾ ⊙ ⊕
Erect, columnar, and broadly elliptical conifer
with a dense crown and multi-pointed top.
Golden yellow needles all the year. H 4 m
(13 ft). W 1 m (3 ft). S humus-rich. P cuttings.
Zone 5.

***Taxus baccata* (hedge)**
Common Yew/fam. *Taxaceae*
○ ⦾ ⦾ ⊛ ⦿ ⊛ ⦾ ⊙ ⦿
Very suitable for hedging, but in that case
less tolerant of shade. Excellent for topiary
work. Do not plant near cattle or horses – the
plant is extremely poisonous.

***Taxus baccata* 'Lutea'**
Common Yew/fam. *Taxaceae*
○ ◑ ⦾ ⦾ ✳ ⊛ ⦿ ⊛ ⦾ ⊙ ⦿
Small tree or tall bushy shrub with pointed,
glossy needles in two tiers on horizontal
branches. Yellow-orange fruits. H 10 m (33 ft).
W 6 m (20 ft). S humus-rich. P seed. Zone 5.

Taxus baccata 'Pyramidalis Variegata'
Common Yew / fam. *Taxaceae*
○ ◐ ◍ ❋ ⊛ ⊕ ⊛ ☺ ⊖
Very broad, fairly tall, densely branched tree
of upright habit. The short needles are yellow
with a central green stripe. H 6 m (20 ft). W 2 m
(6 ft). S humus-rich. P cuttings. Zone 5.

Taxus baccata 'Repandens'
Common Yew / fam. *Taxaceae*
○ ◐ ◍ ⊕ ⊛ ☺ ⊖
Low, broad flat-topped shrub with long, dark,
blue-green needles bent upwards. Suitable
for slopes and as background. H 50 cm (20 in).
W 3 m (10 ft). S humus-rich. P cuttings.
Zone 5.

Taxus baccata 'Semperaurea'
Common Yew / fam. *Taxaceae*
○ ◐ ◍ ⊕ ⊛ ☺ ⊖
Broad, spreading, densely branched shrub
with small, beautifully coloured golden-
yellow needles throughout the year. H 1.5–
3 m (5–10 ft). W 2–3 m (6–10 ft). S humus-rich.
P cuttings. Zone 5.

Taxus canadensis 'Variegata'
Yew / fam. *Taxaceae*
○ ◐ ◍ ⊕ ⊛ ❋ ☺ ⊕
Shrub of spreading, often low and irregular,
habit. Yellow and green needles. Red fruits.
H 3 m (10 ft). W 3 m (10 ft). S humus-rich.
P cuttings. Zone 3.

Taxus cuspidata 'Aurescens'
Japanese Yew / fam. *Taxaceae*
○ ◐ ◍ ⊕ ⊛ ☺ ⊕
Slow-growing dwarf conifer with a yellow
colour most of the year. H 1 m (3 ft). W 3 m
(10 ft). S humus-rich. P cuttings. Zone 4.

Taxus cuspidata 'Nana Aurea'
Japanese Yew / fam. *Taxaceae*
○ ◐ ◍ ⊕ ⊛ ❋
Slow-growing conifer of compact habit when
young. Must be clipped later to prevent loss
of shape. Needles arranged radially. H 1 m
(3 ft). W 2–3 m (6–10 ft). S humus-rich.
P cuttings. Zone 4.

Taxus × *media* 'Hatfieldii'
Yew / fam. *Taxaceae*
○ ◐ ◍ ⊕ ⊛ ❋
Broad, bushy conifer with dark green needles
on stiffly erect branches. Tends to assume a
pyramidal shape. H 4 m (13 ft). W 4 m (13 ft).
S humus-rich. P cuttings. Zone 4.

Telekia speciosa
fam. *Compositae*
○ ◐ ⊛ ○ ☺ ⊕
June–August. Yellow. H 150 cm (5 ft). A 60 cm
(2 ft). S normal. P division, seed. Attractive
large leaves. Does best when grown in the
shade of a group of trees.

Thalictrum aquilegifolium
Meadow Rue / fam. *Ranunculaceae*
○ ◐ ⌂ ○ ☺ ☺ ⊗
May–July. Reddish purple. H 40–150 cm (16–
60 in). A 30–45 cm (12–18 in). S fertile. P seed,
division. Fine plant with flowers (petal-like
sepals with numerous stamens) in spreading
panicles.

325

Thalictrum

Thalictrum dipterocarpum
Chinese Meadow Rue / fam. *Ranunculaceae*
◯ ◑ ⬙ ⌃ ⌄ ⑨ ⊗ ⊗
June–August. Mauve. H 160–200 cm (5–6 ft).
A 80 cm (32 in). S fertile. P division, seed.
Ornamental plant with flowers in graceful,
pyramidal sprays. Needs tying.

Thalictrum flavum ssp. *glaucum*
Meadow Rue / fam. *Ranunculaceae*
◯ ◑ ⬙ ⌃ ⌄ ⑨ ⊗ ⊗
June–July. Yellow. H 2 m (6 ft). A 80 cm (32 in).
S fertile. P division, seed. Attractive but
rather inconspicuous plant, tolerant of a great
deal of shade.

Thalictrum speciosissimum 'Majus'
Meadow Rue / fam. *Ranunculaceae*
◯ ◑ ⬙ ⌄ ⑨ ⊗ ⊗
June–July. Yellow. H 2 m (6 ft). A 80 cm (32 in).
S fertile. P division, seed. Very striking,
recently introduced cultivar. Still rather
difficult to obtain.

Thermopsis lanceolata (T. lupinoides)
fam. *Leguminosae*
◯ ◯ ⑨
June–August. Yellow. H 50–75 cm (20–30 in).
A 30–40 cm (12–16 in). S fertile. P division,
seed. Similar to a lupin in habit and
inflorescence. Dislikes being transplanted.

Thladiantha dubia
fam. *Cucurbitaceae*
◯ ⊛ ⑨ ⊘ ⊛
June–July. Yellow. H 2–3 m (6–10 ft). A 60 cm
(2 ft). S normal. P division, seed. Fast-
growing climber with ovate red fruits, 4–5 cm
(1½–2 in) long.

Thuja occidentalis (hedge)
White Cedar / fam. *Cupressaceae*
◯ ◑ ✳ ⊛ ⊛ ⑨ ⊙ ▣
Pyramidal tree tolerant of clipping. Strongly
branched. Flat, scale-like leaves with an
apple-like scent when bruised. H 20 m (65 ft).
W 6 m (20 ft). S good garden soil. P seed.
Zone 4.

Thuja occidentalis 'Aurea'
White Cedar / fam. *Cupressaceae*
◯ ◑ ✳ ⊛ ⊛ ⑨ ⊙ ▣
Tall, broadly conical tree with golden leaves
turning golden bronze in winter. Cones up to
12 mm (½ in) in length. H 15 m (50 ft). W 6 m
(20 ft). S good garden soil. P cuttings. Zone 4.

Thuja occidentalis 'Danica'
White Cedar / fam. *Cupressaceae*
◯ ◑ ⬙ ⊛ ⊛ ⊛
Globular dwarf form with green foliage
turning slightly brown in the winter. Straight
shoots at the top. H 1 m (3 ft). W 1 m (3 ft).
S good garden soil. P cuttings. Zone 4.

Thuja occidentalis 'Pygmaea'
White Cedar / fam. *Cupressaceae*
◯ ◑ ⬙ ⊛ ⊛ ⊛
Densely branched dwarf shrub of irregular
habit. Slightly glossy, flat scales. H 1.5 m (5 ft).
W 1 m (3 ft). S good garden soil. P cuttings.
Zone 4.

Thuja occidentalis 'Rheingold'
White Cedar / fam. *Cupressaceae*
○ ◖ ✿ ✿ ✿ ✿
Globular to broadly conical shrub with
multiple tops. Golden-yellow scales. H 2 m
(6 ft). W 2 m (6 ft). S good garden soil.
P cuttings. Zone 4.

Thuja occidentalis 'Woodwardii'
White Cedar / fam. *Cupressaceae*
○ ◖ ✿ ✿ ✿ ✿
Vigorous, dense, globular shrub of open
habit. Does not need pruning. Foliage turns
brown in the winter. H 2 m (6 ft). W 2–3 m (6–
10 ft). S good garden soil. P cuttings. Zone 4.

Thuja orientalis 'Aurea Nana'
Chinese Arbor-Vitae / fam. *Cupressaceae*
○ ◖ ✿ ✿ ✿ ✿
Dense, egg-shaped dwarf conifer with a
round to flattened top and bright green
foliage, yellow-bronze in winter. H 2 m (6 ft).
W 2 m (6 ft). S good garden soil. P cuttings.
Zone 5.

Thuja orientalis 'Elegantissima'
Chinese Arbor-Vitae / fam. *Cupressaceae*
○ ◖ ✿ ✿ ✿ ✿
Conifer of conical habit. Yellow foliage
turning golden bronze in winter. Young
plants are sensitive to frost. H 5 m (16 ft).
W 2 m (6 ft). S good garden soil. P cuttings.
Zone 5.

Thuja plicata (T. gigantea)
Western Red Cedar / fam. *Cupressaceae*
○ ◖ ✿ ✿ ✿ ✿ ✿
Fast-growing, conical tree with light brown
peeling bark and yellow-brown cones with
few scales. H 30–60 m (100–200 ft). W 25 m
(80 ft). S good garden soil. P cuttings. Zone 5.

Thuja plicata 'Cuprea'
Western Red Cedar / fam. *Cupressaceae*
○ ◖ ✿ ✿ ✿ ✿ ✿
Slow-growing dwarf conifer of broadly
pyramidal habit. Bronze-green foliage.
Branches pendent at the tips. H 1 m (3 ft).
W 1 m (3 ft). S good garden soil. P cuttings.
Zone 5.

Thuja plicata 'Gracilis Aurea'
Western Red Cedar / fam. *Cupressaceae*
○ ◖ ✿ ✿ ✿ ✿ ✿
Vigorous shrub of conical habit. Very fine
loose branchlets and delicate golden-yellow
summer foliage. H 6 m (20 ft). W 4 m (13 ft).
S good garden soil. P cuttings. Zone 5.

Thuja plicata 'Rogersii'
Western Red Cedar / fam. *Cupressaceae*
○ ◖ ✿ ✿ ✿ ✿ ✿
Rounded dwarf conifer with a pointed top.
Dark green, very fine and compact foliage
with golden-yellow tips. Easily pruned. H 1 m
(3 ft). W 1 m (3 ft). S good garden soil.
P cuttings. Zone 5.

Thuja plicata 'Stoneham Gold'
Western Red Cedar / fam. *Cupressaceae*
○ ◖ ✿ ✿ ✿ ✿ ✿
Slow-growing, bushy shrub. Foliage dark
green with deep golden tips. Very attractive
in winter. H 2 m (6 ft). W 2 m (6 ft). S good
garden soil. P cuttings. Zone 5.

327

Thujopsis dolobrata 'Nana'
fam. Cupressaceae
◯ ⓘ ⊕ ⊛ ⊕ ⊛ ⊛ ⊕
Dense, shrubby dwarf conifer with fine
shoots, glossy flat needles and globular light
brown cones. H 1 m (3 ft). W 3 m (10 ft). S good
garden soil. P cuttings. Zone 5–6.

Thymus × citriodorus 'Aureus'
Lemon Thyme / fam. Labiatae
◯ ⊖ ⌃ ⓜ ⓨ ⓦ ⊛ ⊠ ⊖
July–August. Mauve. H 10–25 cm (4–10 in).
A 20 cm (8 in). S well drained. P division,
cuttings. Aromatic (lemon scented). Valuable
ground-cover plant for rock gardens.

Thymus serpyllum 'Albus'
Wild Thyme / fam. Labiatae
◯ ⊖ ⌃ ⓜ ⓨ ⊛ ⊠ ⊖
June–August. White. H 10 cm (4 in). A 20 cm
(8 in). S well drained. Small, creeping shrub.
Makes good ground cover in rock gardens.

Thymus serpyllum 'Pygmaeus'
Wild Thyme / fam. Labiatae
◯ ⊖ ⌃ ⓜ ⓨ ⊛ ⊠ ⊖
June–August. Purple. H 10 cm (4 in). A 20 cm
(8 in). S well drained. P division, cuttings.
Creeping plant, very attractive to bees and
other insects.

Tiarella cordifolia
Foam Flower / fam. Saxifragaceae
ⓘ ⓘ ⓞ ⓨ ⓦ ⊖
May–June. White. H 10–20 cm (4–8 in).
A 20 cm (8 in). S fertile. P division, seed.
Attractive ground-cover plant with graceful
leaves. Foliage turns bronze in the autumn.

Tigridia pavonia
Tiger Flower / fam. Iridaceae
◯ ⓐ ⓨ ⊗
July–October. Yellow / crimson-brown. H 25–
45 cm (10–18 in). A 10 cm (4 in). D 7 cm (2¾ in).
S fertile. P seed, offsets. Brown, ovate bulbs.
Spectacular flowers which last for just one
day.

Tilia × euchlora (T. cordata × T. dasystyla)
Lime / fam. Tiliaceae
◯ ⓘ ⊛ ⊛ ⓦ ⊕
July. Yellow-white. H 20 m (65 ft). W 7 m
(23 ft). Zone 4. S normal garden soil. P seed.
Vigorous tree with glossy, green, serrated
leaves. Excellent source of honey.

Tilia europaea (T. cordata × T. vulgaris)
Common Lime / fam. Tiliaceae
◯ ⓘ ⊛ ⊛ ⊕
July. Yellow-white. H 40 m (135 ft). W 10 m
(33 ft). Zone 3. S normal garden soil. P seed.
Vigorous hybrid with woolly, spherical fruits
Prone to severe aphid infestation.

Tilia moltkei (T. americana × T. petiolaris)
Lime / fam. Tiliaceae
◯ ⓘ ⊛ ⊛ ⊕
July. Yellow-white. H 20 m (65 ft). W 6 m
(20 ft). Zone 4. S normal garden soil. P seed.
Fine tree with a loose crown, slightly arching
branches and flowers in dense clusters.

Tilia platyphyllos (T. grandifolia) fruits
Broad-leaved Lime / fam. *Tiliaceae*
○ ◖ ✿ ❀ ⊕
June. Yellow-white. H 30 m (100 ft). W 12 m
(40 ft). S normal. P seed, grafting, layering.
Large tree with a dense, almost spherical
crown and flowers in long pendent cymes.
Suitable for parks.

Tilia platyphyllos (T. grandifolia)
Broad-leaved Lime / fam. *Tiliaceae*
○ ❀ ❀ ❀ ⊕
For description and P see last entry. Broad-
leaved lime with near-circular leaves, and
spherical nuts. Does not 'drip', makes few
seeds and yields a great deal of honey.

Tithonia rotundifolia (T. speciosa)
Mexican Sunflower / fam. *Compositae*
○ ○ ❀ ⊗
Sow in March in a heated greenhouse and
plant out at A 10–75 cm (4–30 in). H 3 m (10 ft).
Orange-scarlet. S fertile. Densely branched,
fast-growing plant with hairy leaves.

Trachelium caeruleum 'Balaton'
fam. *Campanulaceae*
○ ☉ ☉ ❀
Sow in January–April in a heated greenhouse
or in June–July in a cold frame. Plant out at
A 20 cm (8 in). H 60–100 cm (2–3 ft). Purple.
S humus-rich. Masses of flowers on erect
stems.

Tradescantia andersoniana hybrid 'Osprey'
Spiderwort / fam. *Commelinaceae*
◖ ○ ❀
June–September. White, blue. H 50–60 cm
(20–24 in). A 30 cm (1 ft). S fertile. P division.
Long flowering period. Demands a great deal
of moisture, or it will turn yellow.

Tradescantia andersoniana 'Zwanenburg
Blue' / **Spiderwort** / fam. *Commelinaceae*
◖ ○ ❀
June–September. Purple-blue. H 50–60 cm
(20–24 in). A 30 cm (1 ft). S fertile. P division.
Masses of flowers over a long period,
especially in moist positions.

Tradescantia virginiana 'Innocence'
Spiderwort / fam. *Commelinaceae*
◖ ○ ❀
June–September. White. H 50–75 cm (20–
30 in). A 30 cm (12 in). S fertile. P division.
Attractive white garden form. Also in shades
ranging from violet to purple. Very long
flowering period.

Tricyrtis formosana (T. stolonifera)
Toad Lily / fam. *Liliaceae*
◖ ◖ ⌒ ○ ❀
August–September. White / mauve. H 50–
100 cm (20–36 in). A 40 cm (16 in). S humus-
rich. P seed, cuttings, division. Unusual plant
with short creeping rhizomes and stem-
enveloping leaves.

Trifolium pannonicum
Clover / fam. *Leguminosae*
○ ○ ❀
June–July. Yellow. H 30 cm (1 ft). A 20 cm
(8 in). S normal. P division, seed. Well-known
cattle-fodder plant from Central Europe.
Grown in gardens for its attractive colour.

329

Trillium

Trillium grandiflorum
Wake Robin / fam. *Liliaceae*
Ⓞ Ⓘ Ⓞ Ⓞ Ⓞ
May–June. Rose pink. H 30 cm (1 ft). A 20 cm (8 in). S fertile, moisture retaining. P division, seed. Attractive herbaceous perennial from the forests of N. America. Dies down in summer.

Triteleia laxa (Brodiaea laxa)
fam. *Liliaceae*
Ⓞ Ⓘ Ⓐ Ⓨ Ⓧ
July. Various shades. H 30–60 cm (1–2 ft). A 10–15 cm (4–6 in). D 7 cm (2¾ in). S normal garden soil. P offsets. Plant in October and cover during the first winter.

***Trollius europaeus* 'Orange Globe'**
Globe Flower / fam. *Ranunculaceae*
Ⓞ Ⓘ Ⓞ Ⓟ Ⓞ Ⓧ
May–June. Yellow-orange. H 50–75 cm (20–30 in). A 30 cm (1 ft). S normal, moisture retaining. P division. Cut back after flowering for a second show in the autumn. Good for cutting.

***Trollius europaeus* 'Superbus'**
Globe Flower / fam. *Ranunculaceae*
Ⓞ Ⓘ Ⓞ Ⓟ Ⓞ Ⓧ
May–June. Yellow (sepals). H 50–75 cm (20–30 in). A 30 cm (1 ft). S normal, moisture retaining. P division.

***Trollius* hybrid 'First Lancers'**
Globe Flower / fam. *Ranunculaceae*
Ⓞ Ⓘ Ⓞ Ⓟ Ⓞ Ⓧ
May–June. Orange. H 50–75 cm (20–30 in). A 30 cm (1 ft). S normal, moisture retaining. P division. Cut back after flowering for a second show in the autumn. Suitable for borders.

Tropaeolum majus
Nasturtium / fam. *Tropaeolaceae*
Ⓞ Ⓘ Ⓞ Ⓨ Ⓧ
Sow in April under glass or in May outside. Thin / plant out at A 30 cm (1 ft). H 30–300 cm (1–10 ft). Mixed colours. S normal garden soil. Popular plant with lightly scented flowers.

***Tropaeolum majus* 'Empress of India'**
Nasturtium / fam. *Tropaeolaceae*
Ⓞ Ⓘ Ⓞ Ⓨ Ⓧ
Sow in April under glass or in May outside. Thin out to A 20–25 cm (8–10 in). H 30 cm (1 ft). Red. S normal garden soil. Low, non-trailing plant for flower beds or containers.

***Tropaeolum majus* 'Jewel'**
Nasturtium / fam. *Tropaeolaceae*
Ⓞ Ⓘ Ⓞ Ⓨ Ⓧ
For P see last entry. H 30 cm (1 ft). Mixed colours. S normal garden soil. Very low-growing, non-trailing nasturtium with semi-double, fragrant and richly varied flowers.

***Tropaeolum majus* 'Whirleybird Cherry Rose'** / **Nasturtium** / fam. *Tropaeolaceae*
Ⓞ Ⓘ Ⓞ Ⓨ Ⓧ
Sow in April under glass or in May outside. Thin / plant out at A 25 cm (10 in). H 30 cm (1 ft). Red. S normal. Attractive semi-double dwarf form, very suitable for flower beds or balconies.

Tropaeolum majus 'Whirleybird Orange'
Nasturtium / fam. *Tropaeolaceae*
○ ◑ ☉ ⑨ ⊗
Sow in April under glass or in May outside.
Thin / plant out at A 25 cm (10 in). H 30 cm
(1 ft). Yellow-orange. S normal garden soil.
Very strong and permanently compact plant.

Tropaeolum peltophorum (T. lobbianum)
Nasturtium / fam. *Tropaeolaceae*
○ ◑ ☉ ⑨ ⊗
Sow in April under glass or in May outside.
Thin / plant out at A 40 cm (16 in). H 4 m
(13 ft). S normal garden soil. Vigorous
climbing plant, ideal for sunny slopes.

Tropaeolum pentaphyllum
Nasturtium / fam. *Tropaeolaceae*
○ ⌂ ⑨ ⑳ ⑨
July–November. Red. H 2–3 m (6–10 ft).
A 60 cm (2 ft). S humus-rich. P division, seed.
Climbing plant, not very hardy. Plant the
tubers at a depth of 20 cm (8 in) and cover
well.

Tropaeolum peregrinum (T. aduncum,
T. canariense) / Canary Creeper / fam.
Tropaeolaceae
○ ◑ ☉ ⑨
Sow in April under glass or in May outside.
Thin / plant out at A 25–30 cm (10–12 in).
H 3 m (10 ft). Yellow. S normal garden soil.
Graceful climbing plant.

Tropaeolum speciosum
Flame Creeper / fam. *Tropaeolaceae*
○ ◑ ⌂ ◑ ⑨
August–October. Red. H 2–3 m (6–10 ft).
A 60 cm (2 ft). S humus-rich. P division, seed.
Protect roots from fierce sunlight. Cover well
in winter. Climbing plant.

Tsuga canadensis 'Bennett'
Eastern Hemlock / fam. *Pinaceae*
○ ◑ ⚊ ⚉ ⚇ ⚈ ⚌
Handsome compact shrub with a flattened
top and slightly pendulous shoot tips. H 1 m
(3 ft). W 2–3 m (6–10 ft). S humus-rich.
P cuttings. Zone 4. Unusual shape.

Tsuga canadensis 'Pendula'
Eastern Hemlock / fam. *Pinaceae*
○ ◑ ⚊ ⚉ ⚇ ⚌
Shrubby weeping tree. Fairly low and dense
form with pendulous branches. Very
decorative on slopes. H 2–3 m (6–10 ft). W 3–
5 m (10–16 ft). S humus-rich. P cuttings.
Zone 5.

Tsuga heterophylla 'Conica'
Western Hemlock / fam. *Pinaceae*
○ ◑ ⚊ ⚉ ⚇ ⚈ ⚌
Shapely, conical shrub with hairy brown
branches, blunt, grey-green buds, and tear-
shaped cones. H 4 m (13 ft). W 3 m (10 ft).
S humus-rich. P cuttings. Zone 6.

Tsuga mertensiana (T. pattoniana)
Mountain Hemlock / fam. *Pinaceae*
○ ◑ ⚉ ⚉ ⚇ ⚈ ⚌
Slow-growing tree. Branches densely covered
with curved needles. Rough, scaly dark
reddish-brown bark. H 30 m (100 ft). W 12 m
(40 ft). S humus-rich. P seed. Zone 5.

Tulipa

Tulipa 'Acuminata'
Horned Tulip / fam. *Liliaceae*
○ ⓐ ⓨ ⓦ ⊗
April. Red / yellow. H 30–40 cm (12–16 in).
A 10 cm (4 in). D 8–10 cm (3–4 in). S light,
sandy. P offsets. Cultivar with curiously
shaped flowers: narrow, twisted petals.

Tulipa clusiana
Lady Tulip / fam. *Liliaceae*
○ ⓐ ⓨ ⓦ ⊗
April. White / red. H 20–30 cm (8–12 in).
A 10 cm (4 in). D 8–10 cm (3–4 in). S light,
sandy. P offsets. Long, slender flowers.
Outermost petals have cherry-red stripes.

Tulipa 'Maureen'
Cottage Tulip / fam. *Liliaceae*
○ ⊕ ⓐ ⓨ ⊗
April–May. White. H 90 cm (3 ft). A 10 cm
(4 in). D 8–10 cm (3–4 in). S light, sandy.
P cuttings. Cottage tulips are a very old group
and are nowadays rarely cultivated.

Tulipa 'Black Swan'
Darwin Hybrid Tulip / fam. *Liliaceae*
○ ⊕ ⓐ ⓨ ⊗
May. Dark purple. H 60–80 cm (24–32 in).
A 15 cm (6 in). D 8–10 cm (3–4 in). S light,
sandy. P offsets. One of the so-called 'black'
tulips.

Tulipa 'Eric Hofsjö'
Darwin Hybrid Tulip / fam. *Liliaceae*
○ ⊕ ⓐ ⓨ ⊗
May. Orange-red. H 60–80 cm (24–32 in).
A 15 cm (6 in). D 8–10 cm (3–4 in). S light,
sandy. P offsets. Darwin hybrids are crosses
between Darwin tulips and *Tulipa fosterana*.

Tulipa 'Olympic Flame'
Darwin Hybrid Tulip / fam. *Liliaceae*
○ ⊕ ⓐ ⓨ ⊗
May. Yellow / orange-red. H 60–80 cm (24–
32 in). A 15 cm (6 in). D 8–10 cm (3–4 in).
S light, sandy. P offsets. Darwin hybrids have
unusually large flowers.

Tulipa 'Paradise'
Darwin Tulip / fam. *Liliaceae*
○ ⊕ ⓐ ⓨ ⊗
May. White / scarlet. H 60–80 cm (24–32 in).
A 15 cm (6 in). D 8–10 cm (3–4 in). S light,
sandy. P offsets. Darwin tulips are of Belgian
origin. The flowers have squared-off
receptacles.

Tulipa 'Angelique'
Double Late Tulip / fam. *Liliaceae*
○ ⊕ ⓐ ⓨ ⊗
May. Rose pink. H 40–60 cm (16–24 in).
A 10 cm (4 in). D 8–10 cm (3–4 in). S light,
sandy. P offset bulbs. A late-flowering tulip.
Sensitive to rain and wind.

Tulipa 'Fringed Beauty'
Double Early Tulip / fam. *Liliaceae*
○ ⊕ ⓐ ⓨ
April. Various colours. H 30–40 cm (12–16 in).
A 10 cm (4 in). D 8–10 cm (3–4 in). S light,
sandy. P offsets. A double variety with
fringed petals.

Tulipa 'Keizerskroon'
Single Early Tulip / fam. *Liliaceae*
○ ⑥ ⑨ ⊗
April. Yellow / red. H 35–40 cm (14–16 in).
A 10–15 cm (4–6 in). D 8–10 cm (3–4 in).
S light, sandy. P offsets. Single early tulips
have sturdy stems and are often forced
indoors.

Tulipa 'Prinses Irene'
Single Early Tulip / fam. *Liliaceae*
○ ⑥ ⑨ ⊗
April. Orange. H 35 cm (14 in). A 10 cm (4 in).
D 8–10 cm (3–4 in). S light, sandy. P offset
bulbs. Single early tulips are excellent for
cutting, and especially this fine variety.

Tulipa fosterana 'Spring Pearl'
Tulip / fam. *Liliaceae*
○ ⑥ ⑨ ⊗
April. Red. H 25–40 cm (10–16 in). A 10 cm
(4 in). D 8–10 cm (3–4 in). S light, sandy.
P offset bulbs. Strong, short-stemmed tulip.
Flowers early and stands up to the wind.

Tulipa fosterana 'Sylvia van Lennep'
Tulip / fam. *Liliaceae*
○ ⑥ ⑨ ⊗
April. Scarlet. H 30–40 cm (12–16 in). A 10 cm
(4 in). 8–10 cm (3–4 in). S light, sandy. P offset
bulbs. *T. fosterana* is one of the parents of
Darwin hybrids.

Tulipa greigii 'Charmeuse'
Tulip / fam. *Liliaceae*
○ ⑥ ⑨ ⊗
April–May. Yellow / scarlet. H 20–30 cm (8–
12 in). A 10 cm (4 in). D 8–10 cm (3–4 in).
S light, sandy. Greigii strains are easily
identified by their broad, striped leaves.

Tulipa greigii 'Dreamboat'
Tulip / fam. *Liliaceae*
○ ⑥ ⑨ ⊗
April–May. Orange-scarlet. H 20 cm (8 in).
A 10 cm (4 in). D 8–10 cm (3–4 in). S light,
sandy. P offset bulbs. Particularly beautiful,
soft-coloured flowers. One of the finest
strains.

Tulipa greigii 'Plaisir'
Tulip / fam. *Liliaceae*
○ ⑥ ⑨ ⊗
April–May. White / red. H 20 cm (8 in).
A 10 cm (4 in). D 8–10 cm (3–4 in). S light,
sandy. P offset bulbs. Brightly coloured,
short-stemmed tulip, effective in borders.

Tulipa kaufmanniana 'Ancilla'
Water-Lily Tulip / fam. *Liliaceae*
○ ⑥ ⑨ ⊗
March–April. White / yellow. H 15–20 cm (6–
8 in). A 10 cm (4 in). D 8–10 cm (3–4 in).
S light, sandy. P offset bulbs. Water-lily tulips
flower very early and do not grow too tall.

Tulipa kaufmanniana 'Stresa'
Water-Lily Tulip / fam. *Liliaceae*
○ ⑥ ⑨ ⊗
March–April. Mixed colours. H 20 cm (8 in).
A 10 cm (4 in). D 8–10 cm (3–4 in). S light,
sandy. P offset bulbs. One of the best-known
cultivars. Sturdy plant with broad, striped
leaves.

333

Tulipa

Tulipa kolpakowskiana
Tulip / fam. *Liliaceae*
○ ⌀ ⌀ ⌀ ⌀
April. Various colours. H 15–20 cm (6–8 in).
A 10 cm (4 in). D 8–10 cm (3–4 in). S light,
sandy. P offset bulbs, seed. Attractive
botanical tulip from West Tien Shan with a
very natural look.

Tulipa 'Queen of Sheba'
Lily-Flowered Tulip / fam. *Liliaceae*
○ ⌀ ⌀ ⌀ ⌀
May. Various colours. H 60 cm (2 ft). A 10 cm
(4 in). D 8–10 cm (3–4 in). S light, sandy.
P offset bulbs. Lily-flowered tulips have
graceful petals curving outwards.

Tulipa maximowiczii
Tulip / fam. *Liliaceae*
○ ⌀ ⌀ ⌀ ⌀
May. Crimson. H 20–25 cm (8–10 in). A 10 cm
(4 in). D 10 cm (4 in). S light, sandy. P offset
bulbs, seed. Rare botanical tulip in a beautiful
shade of red. Flowers are bluish at the base.

Tulipa 'Apricot Beauty'
Mendel Tulip / fam. *Liliaceae*
○ ⌀ ⌀ ⌀ ⌀
April. Orange-red. H 40 cm (16 in). A 10 cm
(4 in). D 8–10 cm (3–4 in). S light, sandy.
P offset bulbs. Hybrid between 'Duc van Tol'
and Darwin tulips. Stems not very sturdy.

Tulipa 'Estella Rijnveld'
Parrot Tulip / fam. *Liliaceae*
○ ⌀ ⌀ ⌀ ⌀
May. Various colours. H 45 cm (18 in). A 10 cm
(4 in). D 8–10 cm (3–4 in). S light, sandy.
P offset bulbs. The usually two-coloured
petals are twisted and fringed.

Tulipa praestans 'Fusilier'
Tulip / fam. *Liliaceae*
○ ⌀ ⌀ ⌀
April. Red. H 25 cm (10 in). A 10 cm (4 in). D 8–
10 cm (3–4 in). S light, sandy. P offset bulbs.
Free-flowering, with three to five flowers to
the stem. Very effective in a border.

Tulipa saxatilis
Tulip / fam. *Liliaceae*
○ ⌀ ⌀ ⌀
April. Violet-purple / yellow. H 15–20 cm (6–
8 in). A 10 cm (4 in). D 8–10 cm (3–4 in).
S light, sandy. P offset bulbs, seed. Tulip of
Cretan origin for warm spots. Up to three
flowers per stem.

Tulipa tarda (T. dasystemon)
Tulip / fam. *Liliaceae*
○ ⌀ ⌀ ⌀
March–April. White / yellow. H 20 cm (8 in).
A 10 cm (4 in). D 8–10 cm (3–4 in). S light,
sandy. P offset bulbs, seed. Striking star-
shaped flowers, three to five to each stem.

Tulipa 'Aleppo'
Triumph Tulip / fam. *Liliaceae*
○ ⌀ ⌀ ⌀
April. Yellow / orange-red. H 30–45 cm (12–
18 in). A 10 cm (4 in). D 8–10 cm (3–4 in).
S light, sandy. P offset bulbs. A fairly recently
introduced fringed cultivar.

Tulipa 'Capri'
Triumph Tulip / **fam.** *Liliaceae*
○ ⊚ ⓨ ⊛ ⊗
April. Red. H 45 cm (18 in). A 10 cm (4 in). D 8–
10 cm (3–4 in). S light, sandy. P offset bulbs.
Cross between single early and Darwin tulips.

Tulipa 'Don Quixote'
Triumph Tulip / **fam.** *Liliaceae*
○ ⊚ ⓨ ⊗
April. Reddish-purple. H 30–45 cm (12–18 in).
A 10 cm (4 in). D 8–10 cm (3–4 in). S light,
sandy. P offset bulbs. Flowers later than
single early and earlier than Darwin tulips.

Tulipa 'Dreaming Maid'
Triumph Tulip / **fam.** *Liliaceae*
○ ⊚ ⓨ ⊗
April. Apricot-pink. H 30–45 cm (12–18 in).
A 10 cm (4 in). D 8–10 cm (3–4 in). S light,
sandy. P offset bulbs. Particularly sturdy
stems. Petals not glossy.

Tulipa 'Golden Arguno'
Triumph Tulip / **fam.** *Liliaceae*
○ ⊚ ⓨ ⊗
April. Orange-red. H 30–45 cm (12–18 in).
A 10 cm (4 in). D 8–10 cm (3–4 in). S light,
sandy. P offset bulbs. The petals of Triumph
tulips often have a lighter edge. Excellent for
cutting.

Tulipa turkestanica
Tulip / **fam.** *Liliaceae*
○ ⊚ ⓨ ⊛
April. Yellow. H 10–15 cm (4–6 in). A 10 cm
(4 in). D 8–10 cm (3–4 in). S light, sandy.
P offset bulbs, seed. One of the best-known
botanical species. Five to nine flowers per
stem. Good for naturalising.

Tulipa urumiensis
Tulip / **fam.** *Liliaceae*
○ ⊚ ⓨ ⊛
April. Yellow. H 10–15 cm (4–6 in). A 10 cm
(4 in). D 8–10 cm (3–4 in). S light, sandy.
P offset bulbs, seed. Four to five flowers per
stem. Suitable for naturalising.

Tulipa violacea (T. pulchella var. violacea)
Tulip / **fam.** *Liliaceae*
○ ⊚ ⓨ ⊛
March. Violet-red. H 10–15 cm (4–6 in).
A 10 cm (4 in). D 8–10 cm (3–4 in). S light,
sandy. P offset bulbs, seed. Flowers measure
3–5 cm (1–2 in) and are blue-black at the base.
Flowers early.

Tulipa viridiflora 'Eye Catcher'
Tulip / **fam.** *Liliaceae*
○ ⊚ ⓨ
May. Green / red. H 60 cm (2 ft). A 20 cm (8 in).
D 10 cm (4 in). S light, sandy. P offset bulbs.
Green tulip that has become red as a result of
numerous crossings.

Tulipa viridiflora 'Spring Queen'
Tulip / **fam.** *Liliaceae*
○ ⊚ ⓨ
May. Greeny-yellow. H 60 cm (2 ft). A 20 cm
(8 in). D 10 cm (4 in). S light, sandy. P offset
bulbs. Green tulips are becoming increasingly
popular and there are now many cultivars.

Typha latifolia
Great Reedmace / fam. *Typhaceae*
○ ◑ ⊗ ○ ○ ⊙ ⊗
July–August. Brown. H 1–2.5 m (3–8 ft). A 60–
80 cm (24–32 in). D 1 m (3 ft). S normal.
P division, seed. Common beside streams
and ponds. Mistakenly referred to as a
bulrush.

Ulmus glabra 'Camperdownii'
Camperdown Elm / fam. *Ulmaceae*
○ ❀ ⊛ ⊕
March–April. Green. H 5 m (16 ft). W 5 m
(16 ft). Zone 4. S normal garden soil.
P grafting. Leaves are pressed tight against
the stiffly pendulous branches, forming a
kind of.bower.

Ulmus glabra 'Horizontalis'
Wych or Scots Elm / fam. *Ulmaceae*
○ ❀ ⊛ ⊛ ⊕
March–April. Green. H 10 m (33 ft). W 15 m
(50 ft). Zone 4. S normal garden soil.
P grafting. Branches horizontal at first, then
gently arching.

Ulmus minor 'Sarniensis' *(U. carpinifolia)*
Wheatley Elm / fam. *Ulmaceae*
○ ◑ ❀ ⊛ ⊕
March–April. Green. H 9 m (30 ft). W 6 m
(20 ft). Zone 4. S normal garden soil.
P grafting. Tree with closely set, ascending
branches. Susceptible to Dutch elm disease.

Ulmus minor 'Wredrei'
Golden Elm / fam. *Ulmaceae*
○ ❀ ⊛ ⊕
March–April. Green. H 9 m (30 ft). W 2.5 m
(8 ft). Zone 4. S normal. P cuttings, layering.
Small tree (here shown clipped into columnar
shape) with close-growing golden-yellow
leaves.

Ursinia anethoides
fam. *Compositae*
○ ○ ⊙ ⊗
Sow in March in a heated greenhouse or in
April outside. Thin / plant out at A 30 cm
(1 ft). H 30–60 cm (1–2 ft). Yellow-orange.
S fertile. Bushy, half-hardy annual. For sunny
positions.

Uvularia grandiflora
fam. *Liliaceae*
◑ ◐ ○ ⊙
April–June. Yellow. H 30 cm (1 ft). A 15 cm
(6 in). S humus-rich. P division of rhizomes.
Rewarding plant with stem-enveloping leaves
and small groups of up to three pendulous
flowers.

Vaccinium corymbosum
Swamp Blueberry / fam. *Ericaceae*
○ ◑ ⊗ ⊛ ⊛ ⊛
May. Pink. H 2 m (6 ft). W 2.5 m (8 ft).
S humus-rich. P seed, layering, cuttings.
Hardy shrub with flowers in racemes.
Delicious blue berries with a white bloom.
Zone 3.

Vaccinium vitis-idaea 'Koralle'
Cowberry / fam. *Ericaceae*
◑ ◐ ◑ ⊗ ❀ ⊛ ⊛ ⊖
May–June. White. H 30 cm (1 ft). W 50 cm
(20 in). S humus-rich. P cuttings, layering.
Good ground coverer with leathery leaves and
masses of large berries in pendulous clusters.
Zone 2.

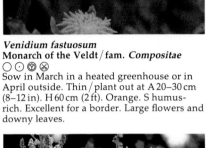

Venidium fastuosum
Monarch of the Veldt / fam. *Compositae*
○ ☉ ⊛ ⊗
Sow in March in a heated greenhouse or in
April outside. Thin / plant out at A 20–30 cm
(8–12 in). H 60 cm (2 ft). Orange. S humus-
rich. Excellent for a border. Large flowers and
downy leaves.

Veratrum nigrum
fam. *Liliaceae*
○ ◑ ⊛ ○ ⊛
July–August. Red. H 50–100 cm (20–36 in).
A 50 cm (20 in). S normal garden soil.
P division, seed. Most unusual, hairy plant
with succulent leaves. Goes well with shrubs.

Verbascum bombyciferum (V. lagurus)
Mullein / fam. *Scrophulariaceae*
○ ◑ ☉ ⊛ ⊛ ⊕
Sow in June–July under glass. Plant out at a
60 cm (2 ft). H 2 m (6 ft). Yellow. S normal
garden soil. Impressive plant with grey,
woolly leaves in rosettes. Suitable for the back
of a border.

Verbascum chaixii
Mullein / fam. *Scrophulariaceae*
○ ◑ ◐ ⊛ ⊕
July–August. Yellow. H 100–130 cm (3–4 ft).
A 50 cm (20 in). S normal garden soil. P seed,
cuttings. Eye-catching large pyramidal
inflorescences. Good specimen plant.

Verbascum densiflorum (V. thapsiforme)
Mullein / fam. *Scrophulariaceae*
○ ◑ ☉ ⊛ ⊕
For P and description see *V. phlomoides*
(below). Found on sandy river banks in
Europe. Attractive yellow-grey, woolly plant
with leaves decurrent on the stems.

Verbascum hybrid 'Gainsborough'
Mullein / fam. *Scrophulariaceae*
○ ⊘ ○ ⊛ ⊗
June–August. Yellow. H 75–100 cm (32–36 in).
A 50 cm (20 in). S normal garden soil.
P division, cuttings. Ornamental plant seen to
best advantage in a mixed border.

Verbascum hybrid 'Pink Domino'
Mullein / fam. *Scrophulariaceae*
○ ◑ ⊘ ⊘ ⊛ ⊗
June–August. Deep rose pink. H 75–100 cm
(32–36 in). A 50 cm (20 in). S normal garden
soil. P division, cuttings. Ornamental plant
for large border and the edge of woods. Best
in big groups.

Verbascum nigrum
Dark Mullein / fam. *Scrophulariaceae*
○ ◑ ○ ⊛ ⊕
June–October. Yellow. H 125–160 cm (4–5 ft).
A 60–80 cm (24–32 in). S normal. P seed,
cuttings. Mulleins are often treated as
biennials. For a warm and sunny position.

Verbascum phlomoides
Mullein / fam. *Scrophulariaceae*
○ ◑ ☉ ⊛
Sow in June–July under glass. Plant out at
A 60 cm (2 ft). H 2 m (6 ft). Yellow. S normal
garden soil. Yellowish, woolly plant with
fairly broad leaves and round stems.

337

Verbascum

Verbascum 'Polarsonne'
Mullein / fam. *Scrophulariaceae*

◯ ◑ ☺ ⊕

Sow in June–July under glass and plant out
at A 60 cm (2 ft). H 30 cm (1 ft). Grey leaves.
S normal garden soil. Fairly new cultivar
developed for its large, grey rosettes of leaves.

Verbena hybrid 'Blaze'
fam. *Verbenaceae*

◯ ☺ ⓨ

Sow in March in a heated greenhouse. Plant
out at A 20 cm (8 in). H 20 cm (8 in). Scarlet.
S normal garden soil. Bushy dwarf strain with
bright flowers over a long period.

Verbena rigida (V. venosa)
fam. *Verbenaceae*

◯ ⊘ ◯ ◯ ⓨ ⊗

Sow in March in a heated greenhouse. Plant
out at A 40 cm (16 in). H 30–50 cm (12–20 in).
Purple. S normal garden soil. Attractive plant,
densely branched and woolly. Erect stems.

Verbena bonariensis
fam. *Verbenaceae*

◯ ⊘ ◯ ◯ ⓨ ⊗

Sow in January–March in a heated
greenhouse or in April under glass. Plant out
at A 60 cm (2 ft). H 150 cm (5 ft). Rose-lavender.
S normal garden soil. Long flowering period.
Densely branched.

Verbena hybrid 'Olympia'
fam. *Verbenaceae*

◯ ☺ ⓨ

Sow in March in a heated greenhouse. Plant
out at A 20 cm (8 in). H 30 cm (1 ft). Mixed
colours. S normal garden soil. Member of the
'Compacta' group. For flower beds and
containers.

Vernonia fassiculata
fam. *Compositae*

◯ ⊛ ◯ ◯ ⓨ ⊗

August–September. Purple. H 1.5 m (5 ft).
A 60–80 cm (24–32 in). S normal garden soil.
P division, seed, cuttings. Rarely seen.
Strong, erect stems. Useful in a large border.

Verbena bonariensis 'Tenuisecta'
fam. *Verbenaceae*

◯ ⊘ ◯ ◯ ⓨ ⊗

Sow in January–February in a heated
greenhouse or in April under glass. Plant out
at A 30 cm (1 ft). H 50 cm (20 in). Violet-purple.
S normal garden soil. Compact cultivar;
masses of flowers.

Verbena hybrids (V. × hybrida)
fam. *Verbenaceae*

◯ ☺ ⓨ

Sow in March in a heated greenhouse. Plant
out at A 30 cm (1 ft). H 40 cm (16 in). Various
colours. S normal garden soil. Good plant for
containers and among shrubs. Free-
flowering.

**Veronica austriaca ssp. teucrium 'Royal
Blue' / Speedwell / fam. *Scrophulariaceae***

◯ ◑ ⓨ ◯ ⊛ ◯ ⊗

June–July. Violet. H 30 cm (1 ft). A 20 cm (8 in).
S normal. P division, cuttings. Well-known
perennial which flowers profusely. Good for
cutting. Not too sunny a position.

Veronica chamaedrys / Germander Speedwell / fam. *Scrophulariaceae*
◯ ◍ ◍ ◬ ◯ ⊛ ⊗
May–July. Blue. H 15–45 cm (6–18 in). A 20 cm (8 in). S normal garden soil. P division, cuttings. Prostrate to erect stems. Very attractive plant with flowers in profusion.

Veronica filiformis Speedwell / fam. *Scrophulariaceae*
◯ ◍ ◬ ◯ ⊛ ⊗
April–May. Violet-blue. H 10 cm (4 in). A 10–20 cm (4–8 in). S normal. P division, cuttings. Mat-forming, very invasive plant. Protect in severe winters.

Veronica longifolia Speedwell / fam. *Scrophulariaceae*
◯ ◍ ◍ ◯ ⊗
June–August. Purple. H 50–75 cm (20–30 in). A 30 cm (1 ft). S normal garden soil. P division, cuttings. Free-flowering border plant with erect stems. Also a white variety.

Veronica spicata 'Erica' Spiked Speedwell / fam. *Scrophulariaceae*
◯ ⊖ ◬ ◯ ⊛ ⊗
July–August. Purple. H 25–50 cm (10–20 in). A 20–30 cm (8–12 in). S normal garden soil. P division, cuttings. Attractive plant with erect stems. Needs a fairly dry position.

Veronica spicata ssp. *spicata* Spiked Speedwell / fam. *Scrophulariaceae*
◯ ⊖ ◬ ◯ ⊛ ⊗
July–September. Violet. H 25–50 cm (10–20 in). A 30 cm (1 ft). S normal garden soil. P division, cuttings. Free-flowering plant for fairly dry sites. Erect stems. Good for cutting.

Viburnum × burkwoodii fam. *Caprifoliaceae*
◯ ◍ ◍ ◍ ⊛ ◉
March–April. White. H 2.5 m (8 ft). W 3.75 m (12 ft). Zone 5. S good garden soil. P cuttings, layering. Broad, semi-hardy shrub with arching branches and fragrant flowers.

Viburnum × carlcephalum fam. *Caprifoliaceae*
◯ ◍ ◍ ⊛ ◉
April–May. White. H 2.5 m (8 ft). W 2.5 m (8 ft). Zone 5. S good garden soil. P cuttings, layering. Vigorous shrub with fragrant flowers in semi-spherical heads.

Viburnum carlesii fam. *Caprifoliaceae*
◯ ◍ ◍ ⊛ ◉
April–May. White. H 1.5 m (5 ft). W 1.5 m (5 ft). Zone 4. S humus-rich, moist. P seed, cuttings. More or less compact, round and hardy shrub. The fragrant flowers are pink at first.

Viburnum davidii fam. *Caprifoliaceae*
◯ ◍ ◬ ◍ ⊛ ◉ ⊗ ⊖
June. White. H 40 cm (16 in). W 80 cm (32 in). Zone 7. S humus-rich, acid. P seed, cuttings. Good for the rock garden. Plant male and female specimens side by side. Blue berries.

Viburnum

Viburnum farreri (V. fragrans)
fam. Caprifoliaceae
◯ ◑ ⊘ ⊗ ⊙
November–December. H 2.5 m (8 ft). W 2.5 m
(8 ft). Zone 6. S good garden soil. P cuttings,
division. Erect, fairly slender shrub with very
fragrant flowers in small clusters.

Viburnum henryi
fam. Caprifoliaceae
◯ ◑ ⊘ ⊗ ⊙
August. White. H 3 m (10 ft). W 3 m (10 ft).
Zone 7. S good garden soil. P cuttings,
layering. Fairly tall, more or less open shrub
with flowers in pendent clusters. Reddish-
black fruits.

Viburnum × juddii (V. bitchiuense × V.
carlesii) / fam. Caprifoliaceae
◯ ◑ ⊘ ⊗ ⊙
April–May. White. H 1.5 m (5 ft). W 2 m (6 ft).
Zone 5. S good garden soil. P cuttings,
layering. Resembles *V. carlesii* but has looser
and larger flower clusters.

Viburnum lantana
Wayfaring Tree / fam. Caprifoliaceae
◯ ◑ ◍ ◍ ⊗ ⊗ ⊙
May–June. White. H 3 m (10 ft). W 2.5 m (8 ft).
S good garden soil. P cuttings, layering.
Broad, erect shrub with downy leaves. Fruit
red at first, turning black. Zone 3.

Viburnum opulus
Guelder Rose / fam. Caprifoliaceae
◯ ◑ ◍ ⊛ ◍ ⊗ ⊗ ⊙
May–June. White. H 4.5 m (15 ft). W 4.5 m
(15 ft). S good garden soil. P cuttings,
layering. Bushy shrub with very fragrant
fertile flowers surrounded by sterile bracts.
Zone 3.

Viburnum opulus 'Notcutt'
Guelder Rose / fam. Caprifoliaceae
◯ ◑ ◍ ⊛ ◍ ⊗ ⊗
May–June. H 4.5 m (15 ft). W 4.5 m (15 ft).
S good garden soil. P cuttings, layering.
Vigorous shrub. Flowers in large heads
surrounded by conspicuous sterile bracts.
Zone 3.

Viburnum opulus 'Xanthocarpum'
Guelder Rose / fam. Caprifoliaceae
◯ ◑ ◍ ◍ ⊗ ⊗ ⊙
May–June. White. H 4 m (13 ft). W 4 m (13 ft).
S good garden soil. P cuttings, layering.
Stout, erect shrub with flowers in flat heads.
Fruits remain yellow. Zone 3.

Viburnum plicatum 'Rotundifolium'
fam. Caprifoliaceae
◯ ◑ ◍ ◍ ◍ ⊗ ⊗ ◍ ⊕
May–June. White. H 2 m (6 ft). W 2 m (6 ft).
Zone 4. S good garden soil. P cuttings,
layering. Broad shrub with foliage colour in
autumn and sterile flowers in globular
clusters.

Viburnum plicatum var. tomentosum
fam. Caprifoliaceae
◯ ◑ ◍ ◍ ◍ ⊛ ⊗ ◯ ⊕
May–June. White. H 2.5 m (8 ft). W 2.5 m (8 ft).
Zone 4. S good garden soil. P cuttings,
layering. Broad shrub of an erect habit. Flat
flower heads. Blue-black fruits. Wild-growing
form.

Viburnum × rhytidophylloides 'Alleghany'
fam. Caprifoliaceae
◯ ◑ 🌱 🌸 ❀ ✿
May–June. White. H 3 m (10 ft). W 3 m (10 ft).
Zone 5. S good garden soil. P cuttings,
layering. Strong-growing, broad shrub.
Flowers in great profusion. Red fruits turning
black.

Viburnum rhytidophyllum
fam. Caprifoliaceae
◯ ◑ 🌱 🌸 ❀ ✿ ❀
May–June. White. H 4 m (13 ft). W 3 m (10 ft).
Zone 5. S humus-rich, well drained.
P cuttings, grafting. Vigorous shrub with
deeply furrowed leaves. Ovate red berries
later turning black.

Viburnum tinus
Laurustinus / fam. Caprifoliaceae
◯ ◑ 🌱 🌸 ❀ ✿ ❀
November–April. White. H 2.5 m (8 ft).
W 2.5 m (8 ft). Zone 7–8. S good garden soil.
P cuttings, layering. Dense shrub, evergreen.
Lightly fragrant flowers. Blue berries.

Vinca major 'Variegata'
Greater Periwinkle / fam. Apocynaceae
◑ 🌱 △ ◯ ❀ △ ◯ ⊖
April–May. Violet-blue. H 30 cm (1 ft).
A 30 cm (1 ft). S humus-rich. P division,
cuttings. Very vigorous and invasive semi-
shrub with yellow-spotted and yellow-edged
leaves.

Vinca minor
Lesser Periwinkle / fam. Apocynaceae
◑ 🌱 △ ❀ △ ◯ ⊖
April–June. Violet. H 10 cm (4 in). A 20 cm
(8 in). S normal garden soil. P division,
cuttings. Invasive, very vigorous semi-shrub
suitable for northern slopes under deciduous
trees.

Vinca minor 'Atropurpurea Compacta'
Lesser Periwinkle / fam. Apocynaceae
◑ 🌱 △ ❀ △ ◯ ⊖
April–June. Purple. H 10 cm (4 in). A 20 cm
(8 in). S normal. Unusual colour but few
flowers, like all Lesser Periwinkles.

Viola cornuta 'Hansa'
Horned Violet / fam. Violaceae
◯ ◑ △ ◯ 🌸 ✿ ⊗
May–July. Deep lavender. H 25 cm (10 in).
A 20 cm (8 in). S normal garden soil.
P division, cuttings. Flowers profusely. May
be kept for many years in a cool site. Dead-
head as soon as the flowers fade.

Viola cornuta hybrid 'Amethyst'
Horned Violet / fam. Violaceae
◯ ◑ △ ◯ 🌸 ✿ ⊗
May–July. Purple. H 10 cm (4 in). A 20 cm
(8 in). S normal garden soil. P division,
cuttings. Flowers profusely, often into the
autumn. Erect stems. Very leafy plant.

Viola odorata
Sweet Violet / fam. Violaceae
◑ 🌱 ❀ △ ◯ 🌸 ⊖
March–April. Purple-violet. H 10–20 cm (4–
8 in). A 20 cm (8 in). S normal. P division,
seed, cuttings. Very old garden plant with a
delightful fragrance. Also suitable for
containers.

341

Viola

Viola tricolor
Heartsease / fam. *Violaceae*
○ ◖◗ ☉ ⊕ ⊗ ⊗
Sow in June–July and thin out to A 15–30 cm
(6–12 in). H 15–30 cm (6–12 in). Purple /
yellow / white. S humus-rich. Bedding plant
with a profusion of early blooms. Leaves
ovate to lanceolate.

Viola wittrockiana hybrid
Garden Pansy / fam. *Violaceae*
○ ◖◗ ☉ ⊕ ⊗ ⊗
For P see *V. tricolor*. H 15–30 cm (6–12 in).
Various colours. S humus-rich. Long
flowering period. Comes in an enormous
number of varieties. Outstandingly good
bedding plant.

Viscum album
Mistletoe / fam. *Loranthaceae*
◖◗ ◖◗ ⊕ ⊛ ⊕ ⊕ ⊙
March–April. Yellow-green. H 1 m (3 ft).
W 1 m (3 ft). Zone 7. Parasitic on a number of
trees. P sqeeeze ripe berries into bark
crevices. Globular plant. Dioecious. White
fruits and sticky seeds.

Vitis amurensis (autumn)
Amurland Grape / fam. *Vitaceae*
○ ◖◗ ⊕ ⊕ ⊕
June. Green. H 15 m (50 ft). W 6 m (20 ft). Zone
4. S fertile soil. P seed, layering. Vigorous
climbing shrub with broadly ovate to round
leaves. Splendid autumn colouring.

Vitis coignetiae (V. labrusca) / **Japanese**
Crimson Glory Vine / fam. *Vitaceae*
○ ◖◗ ⊕ ⊕ ⊕
June–July. Green. H 25 m (80 ft). W 6 m (20 ft).
Zone 5. S fertile soil. P cuttings, layering.
Vigorous climbing shrub with flowers in long
panicles. Inedible black grapes.

Vitis palmata
fam. *Vitaceae*
○ ◖◗ ⊕ ⊕ ⊕
July–August. Green. H 15 m (50 ft). W 6 m
(20 ft). S fertile. P seed, layering. Vigorous
climber with slender branches, red leafstalks
and black grapes with no bloom.

Vitis vinifera
Grape Vine / fam. *Vitaceae*
○ ◖◗ ⊕ ⊕ ⊕
June–July. Green. H 15 m (50 ft). W 6 m (20 ft).
Zone 5. S fertile garden soil. P cuttings,
layering. Climber with very long tendrils. The
grapes, blue, green or yellow, have a waxy
bloom.

Vitis vinifera 'Brant' ('Brandt')
Grape Vine / fam. *Vitaceae*
○ ⊖ ⊘ ⊕ ◖◗ ⊕ ⊕
June–July. Yellow-green. H 7 m (23 ft). W 2 m
(6 ft). Zone 6. S fertile. P layering, eye
cuttings. Vigorous, mostly hardy with
attractive autumn colouring. Edible grapes.

Waldsteinia ternata (W. sibirica)
fam. *Rosaceae*
◖◗ ◖◗ ◖◗ ⊕ ⊕ ⊕ ⊕ ⊖
April–May. Yellow. H 15–25 cm (6–10 in).
A 20 cm (8 in). S fertile. P division. Evergreen,
glossy foliage. Hairy runners (invasive).
Excellent ground-cover plant.

Weigela floribunda 'Grandiflora'
fam. *Caprifoliaceae*
○ ◑ ◍ ⊗
May–June. White / pink. H 3 m (10 ft). W 3 m
(10 ft). Zone 4. S fertile garden soil. P cuttings.
Shrub with slender branches, larger flowers
than the species and sessile, downy leaves.

Weigela florida 'Purpurea'
fam. *Caprifoliaceae*
○ ◑ ◍ ⊗ ⊗
May–June. Pink. H 2 m (6 ft). W 2 m (6 ft).
Zone 5. S fertile soil. P cuttings. Slow-
growing, compact shrub with reddish-brown
leaves and arching branches.

Weigela middendorffiana (Macrodiervilla
middendorffiana) / fam. *Caprifoliaceae*
○ ⊗ ⊖ ◍ ⊗
May–June. Yellow. H 1.5 m (5 ft). W 1.5 m
(5 ft). Zone 4. S fertile. P cuttings. Shrub with
ovate-lanceolate leaves. The greyish-brown
branches carry two rows of hair.

Weigela praecox 'Bailey'
fam. *Caprifoliaceae*
○ ◑ ◍ ⊗
May. Reddish purple. H 2 m (6 ft). W 2 m (6 ft).
Zone 5. S fertile soil. P cuttings. Broad,
densely branched shrub with downy leaves
and flowers in small clusters.

Wisteria sinensis
Chinese Wisteria / fam. *Leguminosae*
○ ◑ ⊖ ◍ ⊗ ⊗ ⊕
April–May. Violet-blue. H 10 m (33 ft). W 4 m
(13 ft). Zone 5. S fertile. P grafting, cuttings,
layering. Tall, twining climber with a mass of
fragrant flowers coming out before the leaves.

Wisteria sinensis 'Alba'
fam. *Leguminosae*
○ ◑ ⊖ ◍ ⊗ ⊗ ⊕
April–May. White. H 10 m (33 ft). W 4 m
(13 ft). Zone 5. S fertile soil. P grafting,
cuttings, layering. Resembles the species.
Flowers in long racemes. Pinnate leaves
composed of 11–13 leaflets.

Wulfenia baldaccii
fam. *Scrophulariaceae*
◑ ⊗ ○ ⊗ ⊗
May–June. Purple. H 10–15 cm (4–6 in).
A 20 cm (8 in). S fertile. P division, seed.
Suitable for moist, cool positions in a rock
garden. Likes semi-shade.

Xanthoceras sorbifolium
fam. *Sapindaceae*
○ ◍ ⊛ ⊛ ⊗
May–June. White. H 8 m (26 ft). W 6 m (20 ft).
Zone 5–6. S good garden soil. P seed,
cuttings. Upright shrub with bare, brown
branches and apple-shaped fruits with many
black seeds.

Xeranthemum annuum
Immortelle / fam. *Compositae*
○ ⊙ ⊗ ⊗
Sow in April under glass or in May outside.
Thin / plant out at A 25 cm (10 in). H 30–60 cm
(1–2 ft). Mixed colours. S normal soil. Woolly
grey stems. Oblong, entire leaves. Good for
cutting.

343

Yucca

Yucca flaccida (Y. puberula)
fam. *Agavaceae*
○ ⊘ ○ ⊙ ⊛ ⊛ ⊙ ⊕
July–September. White. H 1–2 m (3–6 ft).
A 80 cm (32 in). S fertile, well drained.
P division, seed. Cut back after flowering.
Cover well in severe winters.

Yucca gloriosa
fam. *Agavaceae*
○ ⊘ ○ ⊙ ⊛ ⊙ ⊕
July–September. White. H 1–1.5 m (3–5 ft).
A 80 cm (32 in). S fertile, well drained.
P division, seed. Decorative species from
North Carolina and Florida. Slow-growing;
not very hardy.

Zelkova abelicea (Z. cretica)
fam. *Ulmaceae*
○ ⊛ ⊕
July. Green. H 10 m (33 ft). W 6 m (20 ft). Zone
5–6. S fertile. P seed, layering. Fairly tall
branching tree with a smooth trunk, ovate
crown and inconspicuous flowers.

Zigadenus glaucus
fam. *Liliaceae*
○ ◈ ⊛ ⊙
June–August. Pale yellow. H 80 cm (32 in).
A 40 cm (16 in). S normal. P division, seed.
Star-shaped flowers. Upright stems. Long,
narrow leaves. Of American origin.

Zinnia angustifolia (Z. haageana)
fam. *Compositae*
○ ⊛ ⊙ ⊙ ⊗
Sow in April under glass. Plant out at A 20–
50 cm (8–20 in). H 30–50 cm (12–20 in).
Yellow / red. S fertile. Spreading sub-shrub
with a long flowering period. Suitable for
border or bedding.

Zinnia elegans
fam. *Compositae*
○ ⊛ ⊙ ⊙ ⊗
Sow in April under glass. Plant out at A 20–
50 cm (8–20 in). H 90 cm (3 ft). Yellow-orange.
S fertile soil. Dahlia-flowered variety with
flowers measuring 10–15 cm (4–6 in). Good
for cutting.

Zinnia elegans 'Dasher Scarlet'
fam. *Compositae*
○ ⊙ ⊙ ⊗
For P see Z. *elegans*. H 30 cm (1 ft). Scarlet.
S fertile soil. Very compact bedding plant in
a spectacular colour. Likes a slightly sheltered
position.

Zinnia elegans 'Pink Button'
fam. *Compositae*
○ ⊙ ⊙ ⊗
For P see Z. *elegans*. H 35 cm (14 in). Red.
S fertile soil. Hybrid with a profusion of
rather small flowers.

Zinnia elegans 'Sprite'
fam. *Compositae*
○ ⊙ ⊙ ⊗
Sow in April under glass. Plant out at 20–
50 cm (8–20 in). H 50 cm (20 in). Mixed
colours. S fertile. Attractive cultivar with
weather-resistant flowers.

Plants for Special Conditions

In the last section, all plants have been given symbols reflecting their special needs and uses. In what follows, plants will be listed in accordance with these symbols, so that those with the same needs may be found together. The first list is for house plants and the second for garden plants.

Indoor Plants

All house plants having the same set of symbols will be listed together so that you will be able to choose the right plants for particular situations. Suppose you have an east-facing window in a normally heated room and you want to select a suitable plant? All you have to do is to look for the following symbols in the list:

◐ semi-shade
⊕ keep warm
⊚, ⊗ or ⊙ water liberally, moderately or sparingly
◔ low humidity (no need to spray every day)
▣ standard potting compost (no need to make up a special mix)

The main classifying criterion used is the amount of light needed:

Full sun
Full sun or semi-shade
Semi-shade
Semi-shade or shade
Shade

Our subsidiary classifications are temperature and water needs, from high to low.

FULL SUN

Keep warm; water sparingly

○ ⊕ ⊙ ◔ ▣
1. Moderately humid; special potting mix.

Rebutia gracilis
Rebutia minuscula var. *grandiflora*
Rebutia senilis

○ ⊕ ⊙ ◔ ▣
2. Tolerates a dry atmosphere; standard potting mix.

Sansevieria trifasciata
Sansevieria trifasciata 'Golden Hahnii'
Sansevieria trifasciata 'Laurentii'

○ ⊕ ⊙ ◔ ▣
3. Tolerates a dry atmosphere; special potting mix.

Hamatocactus setispinus
Jatropha podagrica
Parodia aureispina
Parodia chlorocarpa
Parodia commutans
Parodia gracilis
Parodia minima
Pyrrhocactus reconditus
Pyrrhocactus scoparius
Senecio citriformis
Senecio herreanus
Senecio rowleyanus
Senecio serpens

High or moderate temperature; water freely

○ ⊕ ⊕ ⊚ ▣ ◔ ▣
4. Humid or fairly humid atmosphere; special potting mix.

Musa × *paradisiaca*

High or moderate temperature; water moderately

○ ⊕ ⊕ ⊗ ◔ ▣
5. Moderately humid atmosphere; standard potting mix.

Canna indica hybrid 'Lucifer'
Hippeastrum hybrid
Hippeastrum hybrid 'Belinda'
Hippeastrum hybrid 'Fire Dance'
Hippeastrum hybrid 'Picotee'

○ ⊕ ⊕ ⊗ ◔ ▣
6. Moderately humid atmosphere; special potting mix.

Malvaviscus arboreus

○ ⊕ ⊕ ⊗ ◔ ▣
7. Tolerates a dry atmosphere; special potting mix.

Euphorbia heteracantha

High or moderate temperature; water sparingly

○ ⊕ ⊕ ⊙ ◔ ▣ ▣
8. Moderately humid atmosphere; special or standard potting mix.

Opuntia ficus-indica
Opuntia microdasys var. *undulata*
Opuntia scheeri
Opuntia vulgaris

○ ⊕ ⊙ ⊙ ⊙ ⊙
9. Tolerates dry atmosphere; special potting mix.

Astrophytum capricorne senile
Astrophytum myriostigma
Astrophytum ornatum
Lithops ruschiorum
× *Pachyveria clavifolium*
× *Pachyveria* 'Glauca'

○ ⊕ ⊕ ⊙ ⊙ ⊙ ⊙
10. Moderately humid atmosphere; tolerates a dry atmosphere; special potting mix.

Ferocactus acanthodes
Ferocactus latispinus
Ferocactus recurvus

Moderate temperature; water freely

○ ⊕ ⊗ ⊙ ⊙
11. Moderately humid atmosphere; special potting mix.

Nerium oleander

Moderate temperature; water freely or moderately

○ ⊕ ⊗ ⊗ ⊙ ⊙
12. Moderately humid atmosphere; standard potting mix.

Cyanotis kewensis

○ ⊕ ⊗ ⊗ ⊙ ⊙
13. Moderately humid atmosphere; special potting mix.

Datura candida 'Plena'
Datura hybrid
Datura suaveolens

Moderate temperature; water moderately

○ ⊕ ⊗ ⊙ ⊙
14. Humid atmosphere; special potting mix.

Sandersonia aurantiaca

○ ⊕ ⊗ ⊙ ⊙
15. Moderately humid atmosphere; standard potting mix.

Amaryllis belladonna
Capsicum annuum
Carissa spectabilis
Catharanthus roseus 'Ocellatus'
Lapeirousia laxa
Malvastrum capense
Oreopanax capitatus
Thunbergia alata
Vallota speciosa

○ ⊕ ⊗ ⊙ ⊙
16. Moderately humid atmosphere; special potting mix.

Myrtus communis
Callistemon citrinus
Cleistocactus strausii
Dasylirion serratifolium
Elisena longipetala
Erythrina crista-galli
Gerbera jamesonii
Haemanthus multiflorus
Hymenocallis narcissiflora
Hymenocallis speciosa
Jasminum officinale 'Grandiflorum'
Leptospermum scoparium
Littonia modesta
Pachycereus pringlei
Strelitzia reginae
Yucca aloifolia 'Marginata'
Yucca elephantipes

○ ⊕ ⊗ ⊙ ⊙ ⊙
17. Moderately humid atmosphere; special or standard potting mix.

Hibiscus rosa-sinensis
Hibiscus rosa-sinensis 'Cooperi'
Hibiscus rosa-sinensis 'Holiday'
Homalocladium platycladum
Oxalis purpurea
Oxalis vulcanicola
Punica granatum 'Nana'
Trichocereus pasacana
Trichocereus spachianus

○ ⊕ ⊗ ⊙ ⊙
18. Tolerates a dry atmosphere; standard potting mix.

Kalanchoe daigremontiana
Kalanchoe laxiflora 'Fedschenko'
Kalanchoe tubiflora

○ ⊕ ⊗ ⊙ ⊙
19. Tolerates a dry atmosphere; special potting mix.

Aporocactus flagelliformis
Eriocactus leninghausii
Eriocactus magnificus var. *nigrispinus*
Euphorbia meloformis

Moderate temperature; water moderately or sparingly

○ ⊕ ⊗ ⊙ ⊙ ⊙
20. Humid atmosphere; standard potting mix.

Austrocephalocereus dybowskii

○ ⊕ ⊗ ⊙ ⊙ ⊙
21. Moderately humid atmosphere; standard potting mix.

Echinofossulocactus zacatecasensis

○ ⊕ ⊗ ⊙ ⊙ ⊙
22. Tolerates a dry atmosphere; special potting mix.

Borzicactus samaipatanus
Echeveria agavoides
Echeveria agavoides 'Cristata'
Echeveria elegans
Echeveria gibbiflora var. *carnunculata*
Echeveria gigantea
Echeveria harmsii
Echeveria leucotricha
Echeveria pulvinata 'Ruby'
Echeveria secunda 'Pumila'
Echeveria setosa
Euphorbia milii
Euphorbia pseudocactus
Glottiphyllum nelii
Haageocereus chosicensis
Kalanchoe tomentosa
Leptocladodia elongata
Mammillaria elongata var. *echinaria*
Mammillaria pennispinosa
Mammillaria prolifera var. *texana*
Mammillaria spinosissima
Mammillaria zeilmanniana

○ ⊕ ⊗ ⊙ ⊙ ⊙ ⊙
23. Moderately humid atmosphere; tolerates a dry atmosphere; special potting mix.

Faucaria tigrina

Moderate temperature; water sparingly

○ ⊕ ⊙ ⊙ ⊙
24. Moderately humid atmosphere; standard potting mix.

Arachis hypogaea

○ ⊕ ◉ ◔ ▣

25. Moderately humid atmosphere; special potting mix.

Conophytum corculum
Conophytum wettsteinii
Cotyledon orbiculata
Cotyledon undulata
Melocactus bahiensis
Melocactus maxonii
Opuntia clavarioides
Tillandsia ionantha

○ ⊕ ◉ ◔ ▣

26. Tolerates a dry atmosphere; special potting mix.

Adromischus trigynus
Cereus peruvianus
Cereus peruvianus 'Monstrosus'
Crassula arborescens
Crassula conjuncta
Crassula falcata
Crassula lycopodioides
Crassula portulacea
Crassula rupestris
Crassula tetragona
Euphorbia cap st. mariensis
Euphorbia grandicornis
Euphorbia horrida
Euphorbia pugniformis
Euphorbia tirucalli
Euphorbia trigona
Lampranthus blandus
Leuchtenbergia principis
Mammillaria albicans
Mammillaria bellacantha
Mammillaria parkinsonii
Mammillaria sheldonii
Mammillaria vaupelii 'Cristata'
Mammillaria winteriae
Neoporteria paucicostata
Neoporteria senilis
Neoporteria wagenknechtii
Obregonia denegrii
Pachyphytum funifera
Pachyphytum marneriana
Pelargonium tetragonum
Sedum griseum
Sedum morganianum
Sedum pachyphyllum
Sedum rubrotinctum
Sedum stahlii
Sedum suaveolens

○ ⊕ ◉ ◔ ◔ ▣

27. Moderately humid atmosphere; tolerates a dry atmosphere; special potting mix.

Conophytum cornatum
Graptopetalum amethystinum

Moderate or low temperature; water liberally

○ ⊕ ◡ ◎ ◔ ▣

28. Moderately humid atmosphere; standard potting mix.

Zephyranthes candida

Moderate or low temperature; water liberally or moderately

○ ⊕ ◡ ◎ ◉ ◔ ▣

29. Humid atmosphere; standard potting mix.

Habranthus robustus

Moderate or low temperature; water moderately

○ ⊕ ◡ ◎ ◔ ▣

30. Moderately humid atmosphere; standard potting mix.

Cyrtanthus parviflorus

○ ⊕ ◡ ◎ ◔ ▣

31. Moderately humid atmosphere; special potting mix.

Narcissus 'Carlton'

○ ⊕ ◡ ◎ ◔ ▣ ▣

32. Moderately humid atmosphere; special or standard potting mix.

Jacobinia pauciflora
Lachenalia aloides hybrid
Lachenalia bulbifera

Moderate or low temperature; water moderately or sparingly

○ ⊕ ◡ ◎ ◉ ◔ ▣

33. Moderately humid atmosphere; special potting mix.

Opuntia microdasys 'Albispina'

Moderate or low temperature; water sparingly

○ ⊕ ◡ ◉ ◔ ▣

34. Moderately humid atmosphere; special potting mix.

Opuntia clavarioides var. *cristata*
Opuntia tunicata

○ ⊕ ◡ ◉ ◔ ▣

35. Tolerates a dry atmosphere; special potting mix.

Agave albicans 'Albopicta'
Colletia cruciata

Low temperature; water freely

○ ◡ ◎ ◔ ▣

36. Moderately humid atmosphere; standard potting mix.

Acacia armata
Passiflora caerulea
Solanum pseudocapsicum

Low temperature; water moderately

○ ◡ ◎ ◔ ▣

37. Moderately humid atmosphere; standard potting mix.

Campanula fragilis 'Carol Foster'
Eucomis bicolor
Olea europeana
Pelargonium peltatum 'l'Elegante'

○ ◡ ◎ ◔ ▣

38. Moderately humid atmosphere; special potting mix.

Eugenia paniculata
Hebe andersonii hybrid
Hebe andersonii 'Variegata'
Hebe speciosa
Laurus nobilis
Oreocereus celsianus
Phoenix canariensis

○ ◡ ◎ ◔ ▣ ▣

39. Moderately humid atmosphere; special or standard potting mix.

Lagerstroemia indica
Oxalis deppei
Tritonia crocata hybrid

40. Tolerates a dry atmosphere; special potting mix.

Beaucarnea recurvata
Coryphantha cornifera
Coryphantha hesterii

41. Moderately humid atmosphere; tolerates a dry atmosphere; special potting mix.

Eucalyptus cinerea

Low temperature, water moderately or sparingly

42. Moderately humid atmosphere; standard potting mix.

Opuntia rufida

43. Moderately humid atmosphere; special potting mix.

Cephalocereus senilis

Low temperature; water sparingly

44. Moderately humid atmosphere; standard potting mix.

Saxifraga cotyledon

45. Tolerates a dry atmosphere; special potting mix.

Aeonium arboreum
Aeonium tabuliforme
Agave americana
Agave americana 'Marginata'
Agave americana 'Stricta'
Agave ferdinandi-regis
Agave parrasana
Agave schidigera
Agave stricta
Aloe arborescens
Aloe barbadensis
Aloe ferox
Aloe mitriformis
Aloe plicatilis
Aloe spinosissima
Aloe striata
Aloe variegata
Arequipa paucicostata
Lobivia famatimensis
Lobivia hertrichiana
Lobivia nealeana
Mammillaria bachmannii
Mammillaria plumosa
Mammillaria vagaspina

FULL SUN OR SEMI-SHADE

High temperature; water liberally

46. Humid atmosphere; special potting mix.

Cyperus haspan

High temperature; water moderately

47. Moderately humid atmosphere; standard potting mix.

Ficus benjamina 'Variegata'
Kalanchoe hybrid 'Wendy'

48. Moderately humid atmosphere; special potting mix.

Kalanchoe blossfeldiana hybrid 'Solferino Purper'
Kalanchoe blossfeldiana 'Kuiper's Orange'
Kalanchoe manginii
Notocactus horstii
Notocactus leninghausii
Notocactus mammulosus 'Masollerensis'
Notocactus ottonis
Notocactus purpureus

49. Tolerates a dry atmosphere; special potting mix.

Kalanchoë farinacea

High temperature; water sparingly.

50. Tolerates a dry atmosphere; special potting mix.

Senecio macroglossus 'Variegatum'

High or moderate temperature; water freely

51. Humid atmosphere; standard potting mix

Coleus blumei hybrid
Coleus blumei hybrid 'Pagoda'
Coleus blumei hybrid 'Sabre Pastel'

52. Moderately humid atmosphere; standard potting mix.

Plectranthus fruticosus

High or moderate temperature; water liberally or moderately

53. Moderately humid atmosphere; special potting mix.

Chlorophytum comosum 'Variegatum'

High or moderate temperature; water moderately

54. Humid atmosphere; special potting mix.

Catasetum trulla

High or moderate temperature; water sparingly

55. Moderately humid atmosphere; special potting mix.

Huernia brevirostris
Peperomia obtusifolia
Stapelia variegata

56. Water sparingly; tolerates a dry atmosphere; special potting mix.

Ceropegia barkleyi
Ceropegia sandersonii
Ceropegia woodii ssp. *woodii*

Moderate temperature; water freely

○ ◑ ☺ ∞ ☺ ▣
57. Moderately humid atmosphere; standard potting mix.

Beloperone guttata
Impatiens walleriana
Impatiens hybrid 'Confetti'

Moderate temperature; water moderately

○ ◑ ☺ ∞ ☺ ▣
58. Humid atmosphere; special potting mix.

Gloriosa rothschildiana
Heliconia illustris 'Aureostriata'
Persea americana

○ ◑ ☺ ∞ ☺ ▣
59. Humid atmosphere; standard potting mix.

Passiflora violacea

○ ◑ ☺ ∞ ☺ ▣ ▣
60. Humid atmosphere; special or standard potting mix.

Dionaea muscipula
Mikania ternata
Rhodochiton atrosanguineus

○ ◑ ☺ ∞ ☺ ▣
61. Moderately humid atmosphere; standard potting mix.

Cocculus laurifolius
Cuphea ignea
Ophiopogon jaburan 'Vittatus'
Pelargonium grandiflorum hybrid 'Marechal Foch'
Pelargonium graveolens 'Variegatum'
Pelargonium × citrosmum 'Variegatum'
Pelargonium zonale hybrid 'Dawn'
Pelargonium zonale hybrid 'Friesdorf'
Pelargonium zonale hybrid 'Lady Cullum'

○ ◑ ☺ ∞ ☺ ▣
62. Moderately humid atmosphere; special potting mix.

Citrus limon
Citrus microcarpa
Corynocarpus laevigatus
Haemanthus albiflos
Hypocyrta glabra

○ ◑ ☺ ∞ ☺ ▣ ▣
63. Moderately humid atmosphere; special or standard potting mix.

Hoya carnosa
Piper nigrum

○ ◑ ☺ ∞ ☺ ▣
64. Tolerates a dry atmosphere; special potting mix.

Mammillaria rhodantha

○ ◑ ☺ ∞ ☺ ☺ ▣
65. Humid or moderately humid atmosphere; standard potting mix.

Passiflora alata

○ ◑ ☺ ∞ ☺ ☺ ▣
66. Humid or moderately humid atmosphere; special potting mix.

Washingtonia filifera

○ ◑ ☺ ∞ ☺ ☺ ▣
67. Moderately humid atmosphere but will tolerate a dry atmosphere; special potting mix.

Gasteria caespitosa
Gasteria maculata

Moderate temperature; water sparingly

○ ◑ ☺ ○ ☺ ▣
68. Tolerates a dry atmosphere; special potting mix.

Echinopsis intricatissima
Lithops bromfieldii
Myrtillocactus geometrizans
Pseudomammillaria camptotricha

○ ◑ ☺ ○ ☺ ☺ ▣
69. Moderately humid atmosphere but will tolerate a dry atmosphere; special potting mix.

Gasteria verrucosa

Moderate or low temperature; water moderately

○ ◑ ☺ ☺ ∞ ☺ ▣
70. Moderately humid atmosphere; standard potting mix.

Abutilon hybrid 'Feuerglocke'
Abutilon hybrid 'Golden Fleece'
Abutilon megapotamicum 'Variegatum'
Abutilon striatum 'Thompsonii'
Cordyline indivisa
Setcreasea purpurea

○ ◑ ☺ ☺ ∞ ☺ ▣ ▣
71. Moderately humid atmosphere; special or standard potting mix.

Parthenocissus henryana

Low temperature; water moderately

○ ◑ ☺ ∞ ☺ ▣
72. Humid atmosphere; standard potting mix.

Euonymus japonicus 'Albomarginatus'

○ ◑ ☺ ∞ ☺ ▣
73. Humid atmosphere; special potting mix.

Lycaste virginalis

○ ◑ ☺ ∞ ☺ ▣
74. Moderately humid atmosphere; standard potting mix

Campanula isophylla 'Alba'
Campanula isophylla 'Mayi'

○ ◑ ☺ ∞ ☺ ▣
75. Moderately humid atmosphere; special potting mix.

Illicium verum
Pinus 'Silver Crest'
Pittosporum eugenioides
Pittosporum tobira
Pittosporum tobira 'Variegatum'
Pittosporum undulatum
Podocarpus macrophyllus
Veltheimia capensis

○ ◑ ☺ ∞ ☺ ▣ ▣
76. Moderately humid atmosphere; special or standard potting mix.

Harpephyllum caffrum

SEMI-SHADE

High temperature; water freely

◑ ⊕ ∞ ☺ ⬓
77. Humid atmosphere; acid potting mix.

Calathea crocata
Sinningia speciosa

◑ ⊕ ∞ ☺ ⬓
78. Humid atmosphere; special potting mix.

Anthurium andreanum
Anthurium crystallinum
Anthurium magnificum
Anthurium scherzeranum
Brassavola nodosa
Brassavola perrinii
Coelia bella
Cyperus papyrus
Eulophia porphyroglossa
Nepenthes hybrid

◑ ⊕ ∞ ☺ ⬓
79. Moderately humid atmosphere; standard potting mix.

Billbergia nutans

◑ ⊕ ∞ ☺ ⬓
80. Moderately humid atmosphere; special potting mix.

Areca lutescens
Caryota mitis

◑ ⊕ ∞ ∞ ☺ ⬓
81. Humid or moderately humid atmosphere; special potting mix.

Caladium bicolor 'Candidum'
Caladium bicolor 'Crimson Glow'
Microcoelum weddellianum

High temperature; water liberally or moderately

◑ ⊕ ∞ ∞ ☺ ⬓
82. Humid atmosphere; standard potting mix.

Cocos nucifera

◑ ⊕ ∞ ∞ ☺ ⬓
83. Humid atmosphere; special potting mix.

Coffea arabica
Fittonia verschaffeltii
Fittonia verschaffeltii 'Argyroneura'
Fittonia verschaffeltii 'Pearcei'

◑ ⊕ ∞ ∞ ∞ ☺ ⬓
84. Humid or moderately humid atmosphere; special potting mix.

Codiaeum variegatum var. *pictum*

High temperature; water moderately

◑ ⊕ ∞ ☺ ⬓
85. Humid atmosphere; standard potting mix.

Alloplectus capitatus
Cissus discolor
Hypoestes phyllostachya
Pseuderanthemum sinuatum

◑ ⊕ ∞ ☺ ⬓
86. Humid atmosphere; acid potting mix.

Achimenes erecta
Achimenes hybrid 'India'
Achimenes hybrid 'J. Michelsen'
Achimenes hybrid 'Little Beauty'

Achimenes hybrid 'Paul Arnold'
Kohleria amabilis
Kohleria bogotensis
Kohleria eriantha

◑ ⊕ ∞ ∞ ☺ ⬓
87. Humid atmosphere; special potting mix.

Aeschynanthus lobbianus
Aeschynanthus marmoratus
Aeschynanthus radicans
Aeschynanthus speciosus
Allamanda cathartica
Alocasia lowii
Alpinia sanderae
Aphelandra maculata
Bulbophyllum becquartii
Calanthe vestita 'William Murray'
Clerodendrum speciosissimum
Clerodendrum thomsoniae
Columnea gloriosa
Columnea gloriosa 'Purpurea'
Columnea hirta
Columnea microphylla
Cordyline terminalis
Cordyline terminalis 'Mme André'
Ctenanthe lubbersiana
Ctenanthe oppenheimiana 'Variegata'
Ctenanthe rubra
Dendrobium phalaenopsis hybrid
Dichorisandra reginae
Dipladenia atropurpurea
Dipladenia boliviensis
Dipladenia sanderi 'Rosea'
Dipteracanthus devosianus
Dipteracanthus makoyanus
Doritaenopsis 'Jason Beard' × *manni*
Doritis pulcherrima
Encyclia vitellina
Eucharis grandiflora
Guzmania dissitiflora
Guzmania lindenii
Guzmania lingulata
Guzmania minor 'Orange'
Guzamina zahnii
Hemigraphis alternata
Hoya bella
Hoya multiflora
Ixora hybrid
Maranta bicolor
Maranta leuconeura
Maranta leuconeura 'Erythroneura'
Maranta leuconeura 'Fascinator'
Maranta leuconeura 'Kerchoveana'
Medinilla magnifica
Nautilocalyx lynchii
Pavonia multiflora
Pellionia pulchra
Pellionia repens
Phoenix roebelenii
Pseuderanthemum atropurpureum 'Tricolor'
Rechsteineria cardinalis
Rechsteineria leuchotricha
Scindapsus pictus 'Argyreus'
Seemania latifolia
Smithiantha cinnabarina
Smithiantha hybrid
Sonerila margaritacea
Stromanthe amabilis
Tillandsia flabellata
Tillandsia leiboldiana
Tillandsia lindenii
Vriesea carinata
Vriesea hieroglyphica
Vriesea psittacina
Vriesea rodigasiana
Vriesea splendens 'Major'
Vriesea viminalis 'Rex'
Vriesea × *poelmannii*
× *Vuylstekeara* 'Cambria Plush'

◐ ⊕ ∞ ◔ ▣ ▤
88. Humid atmosphere; acid or standard potting mix.

Crossandra infundibuliformis 'Mona Wallhed'
Perilepta dyerana

◐ ⊕ ∞ ◔ ▣ ▤
89. Humid atmosphere; special or standard potting mix.

Costus igneus
Jacobinia carnea
Pandanus veitchii
Piper crocatum
Pisonia umbellifera 'Variegata'
Plumbago indica
Xanthosoma nigrum

◐ ⊕ ∞ ◔ ▣
90. Moderately humid atmosphere; standard potting mix.

Elettaria cardamomum
Ficus altissima
Ficus aspera 'Parcellii'
Ficus benghalensis
Ficus benjamina
Ficus benjamina 'Rijssenhout'
Ficus cyathistipula
Ficus deltoidea
Ficus elastica 'Decora'
Ficus elastica 'Schryveriana'
Ficus schlechteri
Ficus triangularis
Pedilanthus tithymaloides 'Variegata'
Steriphoma paradoxum

◐ ⊕ ∞ ◔ ▤
91. Moderately humid atmosphere; acid potting mix.

Begonia boweri
Begonia conchifolia
Begonia corallina
Begonia decora
Begonia foliosa
Begonia heracleifolia
Begonia hispida var. *cucullifera*
Begonia hydrocotylifolia
Begonia imperialis
Begonia limmingheana
Begonia maculata
Begonia manicata 'Aureomaculata'
Begonia masoniana 'Iron Cross'
Begonia metallica
Begonia rex hybrid
Begonia serratipetala
Begonia socotrana
Begonia × *erythrophylla*
Calathea lancifolia
Calathea leitzei
Calathea makoyana
Calathea ornata 'Sanderiana'
Calathea zebrina

◐ ⊕ ∞ ◔ ▤
92. Moderately humid atmosphere; special potting mix.

Aechmea fasciata
Aechmea fulgens
Aechmea recurvata var. *benrathii*
Aechmea weilbachii
Aglaonema commutatum 'Pseudobracteatum'
Aglaonema costatum
Aglaonema modestum 'Variegatum'
Aglaonema nitidum f. *curtsii*
Aglaonema treubii 'Silver King'
Aglaonema treubii 'Silver Queen'
Columnea × *banksii*
Dieffenbachia amoena 'Tropic Snow'
Dieffenbachia bowmannii 'Arvida'
Dieffenbachia × *bausei*
Dracaena fragrans 'Massangeana'
Dracaena fragrans 'Victoria'
Dracaena marginata
Dracaena reflexa 'Song of India'
Dracaena sanderana
Euterpe edulis
Syngonium podophyllum 'Greengold'

◐ ⊕ ∞ ◔ ▣ ▤
93. Moderately humid atmosphere; acid or standard potting mix.

Calliandra tweedyi

◐ ⊕ ∞ ◔ ▣ ▤
94. Moderately humid atmosphere; special or standard potting mix.

Dracaena deremensis 'Warneckii'
Epipremnum aureum 'Marble Queen'
Ficus elastica 'Belgaplant'
Ficus sagittata 'Variegata'
Stephanotis floribunda

◐ ⊕ ∞ ◔ ◔ ▣
95. Humid or moderately humid atmosphere; standard potting mix.

Aphelandra aurantiaca var. *roezlii*
Breynia disticha 'Rosea Pictum'
Ficus lyrata
Monstera deliciosa 'Variegata'

◐ ⊕ ∞ ◔ ◔ ▤
96. Humid or moderately humid atmosphere; acid potting mix.

Aphelandra squarrosa
Aphelandra squarrosa hybrid

◐ ⊕ ∞ ◔ ◔ ▤
97. Humid or moderately humid atmosphere; special potting mix.

Cycas revoluta
Cycnoches chlorochilum
Dendrobium ciliatum
Dendrobium phalaenopsis var. *schroederianum*
Neoregelia carolinae
Neoregelia carolinae 'Stricata'
Neoregelia carolinae 'Tricolor'
Neoregelia concentrica
Philodendron sagittifolium 'Ilsemannii'
Rhipsalidopsis gaertneri
Rhipsalidopsis rosea
Testundinaria elephantipes

◐ ⊕ ∞ ◔ ◔ ▣ ▤
98. Humid or moderately humid atmosphere; standard or special potting mix.

Cryptanthus beuckeri
Cryptanthus bivittatus
Cryptanthus fosteranus
Cryptanthus zonatus 'Zebrinus'
Polystichum tsus-simense

◐ ⊕ ∞ ◔ ◔ ▤
99. Moderately humid atmosphere but will tolerate a dry atmosphere; special potting mix.

Coccoloba uvifera
Codonanthe crassifolia
Dracaena surculosa

High temperature; water moderately or sparingly

◐ ⊕ ∞ ◉ ◔ ▤
100. Humid atmosphere; special potting mix.

Phyllanthus angustifolius

High temperature; water sparingly

◐ ⊕ ◉ ◔ ▣
101. Moderately humid atmosphere; standard potting mix.

Siderasis fuscata

◐ ⊕ ☺ ◔ ◠ 🗁

102. Tolerates a dry atmosphere; special potting mix.

Haworthia attenuata
Haworthia fasciata
Haworthia reinwardtii

High or moderate temperature; water liberally

◐ ⊕ ☺ ∞ ◠ 🖳

103. Humid atmosphere; standard potting mix.

Scirpus cernuus

◐ ⊕ ☺ ∞ ◠ 🗁

104. Humid atmosphere; special potting mix.

Catasetum callosum

High or moderate temperature; water liberally or moderately

◐ ⊕ ☺ ∞ ∞ ◠ 🗁

105. Humid atmosphere; special potting mix.

Aerangis rhodosticta
Polyscias balfouriana 'Pennockii'
Polyscias fruticosa
Polyscias guilfoylei

◐ ⊕ ☺ ∞ ∞ ◠ 🖳

106. Moderately humid atmosphere; standard potting mix.

Plectranthus coleoides 'Marginatus'

◐ ⊕ ☺ ∞ ∞ ◠ ◠ 🗁

107. Humid or moderately humid atmosphere; special potting mix.

Acalypha hispida
Acalypha wilkesiana 'Musaica'

High or moderate temperature; water moderately

◐ ⊕ ☺ ∞ ◠ 🖳

108. Humid atmosphere; standard potting mix.

Zebrina pendula
Zebrina pendula 'Quadricolor'
Zebrina purpusii

◐ ⊕ ☺ ∞ ◠ 🗁

109. Humid atmosphere; special potting mix.

Cordyline terminalis 'Tricolor'
Habenaria rhodocheila
Murraya paniculata
Oncidium flexuosum
Oncidium krameranum
Oncidium sphacelatum
Rodriguezia secunda

◐ ⊕ ☺ ∞ ◠ 🖳

110. Moderately humid atmosphere; acid potting mix.

Euphorbia pulcherrima
Ficus rubiginosa 'Variegata'
Hedera helix ssp. *canariensis* 'Variegata'

◐ ⊕ ☺ ∞ ◠ 🗁

111. Moderately humid atmosphere; special potting mix.

Davallia mariesii
Dracaena draco
Gynura aurantiaca

◐ ⊕ ☺ ∞ ∞ ◠ 🖳

112. Humid or moderately humid atmosphere; standard potting mix.

Rivinia humilis

◐ ⊕ ☺ ∞ ∞ ◠ 🖳 🗁

113. Humid or moderately humid atmosphere; standard or special potting mix.

Zamia pumila

High or moderate temperature; water sparingly

◐ ⊕ ☺ ∞ ◔ ◠ 🗁

114. Moderately humid atmosphere; special potting mix.

Peperomia argyreia
Peperomia blanda
Peperomia caperata
Peperomia clusiifolia
Peperomia fraseri
Peperomia glabella 'Variegata'
Peperomia griseo-argentea
Peperomia metallica
Peperomia puteolata
Peperomia rotundifolia
Peperomia serpens

High, moderate or low temperature; water moderately

◐ ⊕ ☺ ☺ ∞ ◠ 🖳

115. Moderately humid atmosphere; special or standard potting mix.

Tolmiea menziesii

◐ ⊕ ☺ ☺ ∞ ◠ ◠ 🖳 🗁

116. Humid or moderately humid atmosphere; special or standard potting mix.

Ficus pumila

Moderate temperature; water liberally

◐ ☺ ∞ ◠ 🖳

117. Moderately humid atmosphere; standard potting mix.

Cyperus alternifolius
Cyperus argentiostriatus
Oplismenus hirtellus

◐ ☺ ∞ ◠ 🗁

118. Moderately humid atmosphere; special potting mix.

Chysis aurea
Coelogyne flaccida
× *Brassolaeliacattleya* 'Heron Gyll'
Zantedeschia aethiopica
Zantedeschia aethiopica 'Green Goddess'

Moderate temperature; water liberally or moderately

◐ ☺ ∞ ∞ ◠ 🖳

119. Moderately humid atmosphere; standard potting mix.

Asparagus asparagoides
Asparagus densiflorus 'Meyeri'
Asparagus densiflorus 'Myriocladus'
Asparagus falcatus

◐ ☺ ∞ ∞ ◠ 🗁

120. Moderately humid atmosphere; special potting mix.

Chamaerops humilis
Manettia inflata

◐ 😊 ⊗ ⊗ ◔ ◔ 🔟
121. Humid or moderately humid atmosphere; special potting mix.

Asparagus setaceus

Moderate temperature; water moderately

◐ 😊 ⊗ ◔ 🔟
122. Humid atmosphere; acid potting mix.

Jacaranda mimosifolia

◐ 😊 ⊗ ◔ 🔟
123. Humid atmosphere; special potting mix.

Arpophyllum giganteum
Cattleya bowringiana
Cattleya forbesii
Cattleya labiata
Cattleya mossiae
Cattleya skinneri
Lycaste lasioglossa
Mimosa pudica
Oncidium incurvum
Pentas lanceolata
Selaginella apoda
Selaginella kraussiana
Selaginella lepidophylla
Selaginella martensii
Tetraclinis articulata
Vanda coerulea
Vanda roeblingiana
× *Laeliocattleya* 'Hugo de Groot'
× *Odontioda* 'Lilly Menuet'
× *Odontocidium* 'Anneliese Rothenberger'
× *Odontocidium* 'Tiger Hambuhren'
× *Wilsonara* hybrid

◐ 😊 ⊗ ◔ 🔳 🔟
124. Humid atmosphere; standard or special potting mix.

Dizygotheca elegantissima
Dizygotheca veitchii
Dizygotheca veitchii 'Castor'
Dizygotheca veitchii 'Gracillima'
Heterocentron elegans
Pteris cretica 'Albolineata'
Pteris cretica 'Alexandria'
Pteris ensiformis 'Victoriae'

◐ 😊 ⊗ ◔ 🔳
125. Moderately humid atmosphere; standard potting mix.

Ardisia crenata
Begonia elatior hybrid 'Rieger'
Begonia semperflorens hybrid
Bowiea volubilis
Brunfelsia pauciflora var. *calycina*
Callisia elegans
Carex brunnea 'Variegata'
Chrysanthemum indicum hybrid
Cissus striata
Coprosma baueri 'Marginata'
Cyperus diffusus
Liriope muscari 'Variegatus'
Rhoeo spathacea 'Vittata'
Saxifraga stolonifera
Saxifraga stolonifera 'Tricolor'
Schefflera actinophylla
Schefflera digitata
Schefflera octophyllum
Schefflera venulosa
Schizanthus pinnatus 'Dwarf Bouquet'
Serissa foetida 'Variegata'
Sprekelia formosissima
Streptocarpus caulescens
Streptocarpus hybrid
Streptocarpus hybrid 'Laura Nimf'
Streptocarpus polyanthus
Torenia fournieri
Tradescantia albiflora 'Albovittata'
Tradescantia blossfeldiana 'Variegata'
Trevesia burckii

◐ 😊 ⊗ ◔ 🔟
126. Moderately humid atmosphere; acid potting mix.

Begonia acutifolia
Begonia chlorosticta
Begonia lorraine hybrid

◐ 😊 ⊗ ◔ 🔟
127. Moderately humid atmosphere; special potting mix.

Chamaedorea elegans
Clivia miniata 'Citrina'
Cymbidium hybrid 'Norma Talmadge'
Cymbidium 'Zuma Beach'
Epiphyllum hybrid 'Anton Gunther'
Euphorbia lophogona
Exacum affine
Gardenia jasminoides
Gerbera hybrid 'Orange Queen'
Hatiora cylindrica
Hechtia stenopetala
Hibbertia scandens
Howeia belmoreana
Howeia fosteriana
Narcissus 'Grand Soleil d'Or'
Nematanthus strigillosus
Nematanthus strigillosus 'Variegatus'
Schlumbergera hybrid

◐ 😊 ⊗ ◔ 🔳 🔟
128. Moderately humid atmosphere; standard or special potting mix.

Bouvardia hybrid 'Mary'
Browallia speciosa
Fuchsia hybrid 'Alice Hoffman'
Fuschia hybrid 'Bernadette'
Fuschia hybrid 'Cover Girl'
Fuchsia hybrid 'Dollarprinzessin'
Fuchsia hybrid 'El Camino'
Fuchsia hybrid 'Gartenmeister B'
Fuchsia hybrid 'La Campanella'
Fuchsia hybrid 'Mme Cornelissen'
Fuchsia hybrid 'Pink Galore'
Fuchsia hybrid 'Pink Temptation'
Fuchsia hybrid 'White Prixii'
Hoya carnosa 'Exotica'
Plumbago auriculata

◐ 😊 ⊗ ◔ ◔ 🔳
129. Humid or moderately humid atmosphere; standard potting mix.

Soleirolia soleirolii
Tetrastigma voinierianum
Trevesia palmata

◐ 😊 ⊗ ◔ ◔ 🔳
130. Humid or moderately humid atmosphere; acid potting mix.

Saintpaulia ionantha

◐ 😊 ⊗ ◔ ◔ 🔟
131. Humid or moderately humid atmosphere; special potting mix.

Nephrolepis cordifolia 'Plumosa'
Nephrolepis exaltata 'Maassii'
Nephrolepis exaltata 'Rooseveltii'
Nephrolepis exaltata 'Teddy Junior'
Pilea cadierei
Pilea involucrata
Pilea microphylla
Pilea spruceana 'Norfolk'
Pilea spruceana 'Silver Tree'
× *Odontonia* 'Boussole Blanche'

◐ 😊 ⊗ ◔ ◔ 🔳
132. Moderately humid atmosphere but will tolerate a dry atmosphere; standard potting mix.

Aspidistra elatior 'Variegata'

⬤ 😊 ∞ ☽ 🔲

133. Moderately humid atmosphere but will tolerate a dry atmosphere; special potting mix.

Brassia maculata

Moderate temperature; water moderately or sparingly

⬤ 😊 ∞ ⊙ ☽ 🔲

134. Tolerates a dry atmosphere; special potting mix.

Gymnocalycium bicolor
Nopalxochia phyllanthoides 'Grandiflorum'

⬤ 😊 ∞ ⊙ ☽ 🔲

135. Moderately humid atmosphere but will tolerate a dry atmosphere; special potting mix.

Gymnocalycium mihanovichii
Gymnocalycium pileomayensis
Gymnocalycium quehlianum

Moderate temperature; water sparingly

⬤ 😊 ⊙ ☽ 🔲

136. Humid atmosphere; special potting mix.

Epidendrum ciliare
Epidendrum cochleatum
Epidendrum fragrans
Epidendrum radiatum

⬤ 😊 ⊙ ☽ 🔲

137. Moderately humid atmosphere; special potting mix.

Tillandsia recurvata
Tillandsia tricholepis
Tillandsia usneoides
Tillandsia xerographica

⬤ 😊 ⊙ ☽ 🔲

138. Tolerates a dry atmosphere; special potting mix.

Chaemaecereus silvestrii

Moderate or low temperature; water moderately

⬤ 😊 😊 ∞ ☽ 🔲

139. Water moderately; humid atmosphere; special potting mix.

Calanthe masuca

⬤ 😊 😊 ∞ ☽ ▣

140. Water moderately; moderately humid atmosphere; standard potting mix.

Cleyera japonica 'Tricolor'
Ficus australis
Glecoma hederacea 'Variegata'
Primula malacoides 'Pink Panther'
Primula obconica
Primula praenitens

⬤ 😊 😊 ∞ ☽ 🔲

141. Water moderately; moderately humid atmosphere; acid potting mix.

Rhododendron obtusum
Rhododendron simsii
× *Fatshedera lizei*
× *Fatshedera lizei* 'Variegata'

⬤ 😊 😊 ∞ ☽ 🔲

142. Water moderately; moderately humid atmosphere; special potting mix.

Arisaema candidissimum
Grevillea robusta
Hyacinthus orientalis hybrid 'Blue Jacket'

Odontoglossum bictoniense
Odontoglossum grande
Odontoglossum pulchellum
Tulipa 'Brilliant Star'
Tulipa 'Prince Carnaval'

⬤ 😊 😊 ∞ ☽ ▣ 🔲

143. Water moderately; moderately humid atmosphere; special or standard potting mix.

Hedera helix 'Harald'

Moderate or low temperature; water sparingly

⬤ 😊 😊 ⊙ ☽ 🔲

144. Moderately humid atmosphere; special potting mix.

Rochea coccinea

⬤ 😊 😊 ⊙ ☽ 🔲

145. Tolerates a dry atmosphere; acid potting mix.

Tulipa 'Rose Copland'

Low temperature; water freely

⬤ 😊 ∞ ☽ ▣

146. Humid atmosphere; standard potting mix.

Primula vulgaris

⬤ 😊 ∞ ☽ ▣

147. Moderately humid atmosphere; standard potting mix.

Acorus gramineus 'Aureovariegatus'
Duchesnea indica
Senecio cruentus

Low temperature; water moderately

⬤ 😊 ∞ ☽ 🔲

148. Humid atmosphere; special potting mix.

Araucaria heterophylla 'Gracilis'
Lycaste cruenta

⬤ 😊 ∞ ☽ ▣

149. Moderately humid atmosphere; standard potting mix.

Ampelopsis brevipedunculata maximow 'Elegans'
Cytisus × *racemosus*
Fatsia japonica
Fatsia japonica 'Albomarginata'
Rehmannia elata
Sauromatum venosum
Sparmannia africana
Stenocarpus sinuatus

⬤ 😊 ∞ ☽ 🔲

150. Moderately humid atmosphere; acid potting mix.

Calceolaria hybrid
Camellia japonica
Camellia sinensis
Erica gracilis

⬤ 😊 ∞ ☽ 🔲

151. Moderately humid atmosphere; special potting mix.

Cyclamen persicum hybrid
Cyclamen persicum 'Vuurbaak'
Cyclamen persicum 'Wellensiek'
Erica × *willmorei*
Nertera granadensis

SEMI-SHADE OR SHADE

High temperature; water liberally

152. Humid atmosphere; standard potting mix.

Spathiphyllum wallisii

153. Humid atmosphere; special potting mix.

Microlepia platyphylla
Microlepia speluncae

154. Moderately humid atmosphere; special potting mix.

Comparettia speciosa
Episcia cupreata
Episcia cupreata 'Silver Queen'
Episcia dianthiflora
Episcia lilacina
Macroplectrum sesquipedale

155. Moderately humid atmosphere; standard potting mix.

Brosimum alicastrum

High temperature; water moderately

156. Moderately humid atmosphere; special potting mix.

Aglaonema commutatum
Dieffenbachia maculata
Syngonium podophyllum
Syngonium podophyllum 'Albolineatum'
Syngonium vellozianum 'Albolineatum'

157. Humid or moderately humid atmosphere; standard potting mix.

Monstera deliciosa
Monstera obliqua var. *expilata*

158. Humid or moderately humid atmosphere; special potting mix.

Philodendron domesticum
Philodendron elegans
Philodendron erubescens hybrid
Philodendron laciniatum
Philodendron longilaminatum
Philodendron melanochrysum 'Andreanum'
Philodendron micans
Philodendron panduriforme
Philodendron radiatum
Philodendron scandens
Philodendron selloum
Philodendron sodiroi
Philodendron squamiferum

159. Moderately humid atmosphere but will tolerate a dry atmosphere; special or standard potting mix.

Epipremnum aureum

High or moderate temperature; water moderately

160. Moderately humid atmosphere; special potting mix.

Platycerium bifurcatum
Platycerium grande

161. Moderately humid atmosphere but will tolerate a dry atmosphere; special potting mix.

Phlebodium aureum
Phlebodium aureum 'Mandaianum'

Moderate temperature; water liberally or moderately

162. Moderately humid atmosphere; special potting mix.

Asparagus densiflorus 'Sprengeri'

Moderate temperature; water moderately

163. Humid atmosphere; special potting mix.

Asplenium nidus
Miltonia hybrid
Miltonia paterson × 'Limelight'
Miltonia spectabilis var. *bicolor*

164. Humid atmosphere; special or standard potting mix.

Pteris cretica 'Major'
Pteris cretica 'Parkeri'
Pteris quadriaurita

165. Moderately humid atmosphere; standard potting mix.

Cissus antarctica
Cissus rhombifolia
Cissus rhombifolia 'Ellen Danica'
Liriope spicata
Rhoicissus capensis

166. Moderately humid atmosphere; special potting mix.

Clivia miniata

Moderate or low temperature; water moderately

167. Humid atmosphere; special potting mix.

Miltoniopsis vexillaria

168. Moderately humid atmosphere; standard potting mix.

Hedera helix 'Erecta'
Hedera helix 'Garland'
Hedera helix 'Goldheart'

169. Moderately humid atmosphere but will tolerate a dry atmosphere; standard potting mix.

Aspidistra elatior

Low temperature; water liberally

170. Humid atmosphere; special potting mix.

Hydrangea macrophylla ssp. *m.* f. *otaksa*

Low temperature; water moderately

◐ ◑ ⊙ ⊗ ⊖ ⊡

171. Moderately humid atmosphere; special potting mix.

Helleborus niger

Low temperature; water sparingly

◐ ◑ ⊙ ⊙ ⊖ ⊡

172. Humid atmosphere; special potting mix.

Masdevallia 'Doris'

SHADE

High temperature; water liberally

◐ ⊕ ⊗ ⊖ ⊡

173. Humid atmosphere; special potting mix.

Adiantum fulvum
Adiantum raddianum
Adiantum raddianum 'Goldelse'
Adiantum tenerum 'Scutum'
Didymochlaena truncatula

High temperature; water moderately

◐ ⊕ ⊗ ⊖ ⊡

174. Humid atmosphere; special potting mix.

Barkeria lindleyanum
Bertolonia maculata
Bertolonia marmorata
Paphiopedilum sukhakulii
Phalaenopsis amabilis var.
Phalaenopsis amboinensis
Phalaenopsis fasciata
Phalaenopsis hybrid
Phalaenopsis hybrid (rose)

◐ ⊕ ⊗ ⊖ ⊟

175. Moderately humid atmosphere; acid potting mix.

Blechnum occidentale

Moderate temperature; water liberally

◐ ⊕ ⊗ ⊖ ⊡

176. Humid atmosphere; special potting mix.

Asplenium bulbiferum
Asplenium daucifolium

Moderate temperature; water liberally or moderately

◐ ⊕ ⊗ ⊗ ⊙ ⊖ ⊡

177. Humid or moderately humid atmosphere; special potting mix.

Cyrtomium falcatum

Moderate temperature; water moderately

◐ ⊕ ⊗ ⊖ ⊡

178. Humid atmosphere; special potting mix.

Doryopteris palmata
Paphiopedilum fairieanum
Pahpiopedilum hybrid 'F. M. Ogilvie'

◐ ⊕ ⊗ ⊖ ⊡

179. Moderately humid atmosphere; acid potting mix.

Blechnum gibbum

◐ ⊕ ⊗ ⊖ ⊖ ⊡

180. Moderately humid atmosphere; will tolerate a dry atmosphere; special potting mix.

Pellaea falcata
Pellaea rotundifolia

Moderate or low temperature; water moderately

◐ ⊕ ⊙ ⊗ ⊖ ⊡

181. Humid atmosphere; special potting mix.

Paphiopedilum venustum

Low temperature; water liberally

◐ ⊙ ⊗ ⊖ ⊡

182. Humid atmosphere; special potting mix.

Darlingtonia californica

Low temperature; water moderately

◐ ⊙ ⊗ ⊖ ⊡

183. Humid atmosphere; special potting mix.

Paphiopedilum insigne

◐ ⊙ ⊗ ⊖ ⊟

184. Humid or moderately humid atmosphere; standard potting mix.

Phyllitis scolopendrium
Phyllitis scolopendrium 'Undulatum'

Garden Plants

As with house plants, we have listed plants with the same demands or properties together, so that the best choice can easily be made for, say, a sunny spot, for hedges, ground cover and so on.

The Latin names of the plants are followed by a reference to their colour and height.

Colour usually refers to the flowers, but in lists of fruiting shrubs, colour usually refers to the berries or fruits.

Colours have been abbreviated as follows:

B = blue
G = green
O = orange
P = purple
R = red
V = violet
W = white
Y = yellow

R/P means that both red and purple are present; R–P means that the colour lies between red and purple, that is, reddish-purple.

If a plant comes in mixed colours, the list will state 'var. col.'.

Heights are given in metres (m) and centimetres (cm) as well as the approximate equivalents in feet (ft) and inches (in). 'To 1.5 m (5 ft),' or '–1.5 m (5 ft)' means that the plant in question is usually smaller than the given figure. In general, however, the given heights are maximum measurements – heights that some shrubs may take many years to attain.

The main classifying criterion used in this list of garden plants is the amount of light and soil moisture needed:

Full sun
Full sun and a dry or moist site
Full sun and a dry site
Full sun and semi-shade
Full sun, semi-shade, moist site
Full sun, semi-shade, dry site
Full sun, semi-shade and shade
Semi-shade and a moist site
Semi-shade and a dry site
Semi-shade and shade
Shade

Our secondary classifications are:

Annuals
Biennials
Herbaceous perennials
Bulbs
Tubers
Shrubs
Trees

FULL SUN

Annuals

○ ⊙
1. No special features.

Alonsoa warscewiczii, O–R, –90 cm (3 ft)
Argemone mexicana, Y–O, –80 cm (32 in)
Brachycome iberidifolia, var. col., 45 cm (18 in)
Celosia argentea var. *cristata*, R, 30 cm (12 in)
Chrysanthemum frutescens, W/Y, 45 cm (18 in)
Chrysanthemum paludosum, W–Y, 25 cm (10 in)
Chrysanthemum parthenium 'Ball's White', W/Y, –80 cm (32 in)
Chrysanthemum parthenium 'Snowball', W–Y, 70 cm (28 in)
Cobaea scandens, V–B, 3 m (10 ft)
Coreopsis basalis 'Goldkrone', Y/R–P, 50 cm (20 in)
Coreopsis tinctoria 'Tetra Mistigry', Y/R–P, 1 m (3 ft)
Dianthus chinensis 'Heddewigii', R/W, 25 cm (10 in)
Dimorphotheca pluvialis, W/V/O, 40 cm (16 in)
Eccremocarpus scaber, O–R, R/Y, 5 m (16 ft)
Echium plantagineum, B, 90 cm (3 ft)
Echium plantagineum hybrid, V–B, 70 cm (28 in)
Erysimum perovskianum, O, 50 cm (20 in)
Felicia bergerana, B/Y, 15 cm (6 in)
Heliotropium arborescens, V–B, 70 cm (28 in)
Hibiscus trionum, Y/Black, –60 cm (24 in)
Iberis amara, R–P, 30 cm (12 in)
Iberis amara 'Iceberg', W, 30 cm (12 in)
Ipomoea tricolor, V–B, 3 m (10 ft)
Kochia scoparaia var. *trichophylla*, G, 1 m (3 ft)
Kochia scoparia var. *trichophylla* 'Acapulco Silver', 1 m (3 ft)
Lantana camara hybrid, var. col., 1 m (3 ft)
Layia elegans, Y–O, 40 cm (16 in)
Lindheimera texana, Y, –60 cm (24 in)
Malope trifida 'Purpurea', R–P, 1 m (3 ft)
Mirabilis jalapa, R–P, 1 m (3 ft)
Nemophila maculata, W/V, 35 cm (14 in)
Nemophila menziesii, B/W, 20 cm (8 in)
Perilla frutescens 'Atropurpurea', W, 1 m (3 ft)
Petunia grandiflora 'Duo Karmijn', W/R, 30 cm (12 in)
Petunia hybrid 'Circus', R, 40 cm (16 in)
Petunia hybrid 'Star Joy', R–P, W, 40 cm (16 in)
Phacelia campanularia, B, 25 cm (10 in)
Phacelia tanacetifolia, P–V, –70 cm (28 in)
Silene armeria, R–P, –60 cm (24 in)
Silene coeli-rosa, P, –80 cm (32 in)
Silene coeli-rosa 'Formule', var. col., 80 cm (32 in)
Trachelium caeruleum 'Balaton', P, –1 m (3 ft)
Verbena hybrid, var. col., 40 cm (16 in)
Verbena hybrid 'Blaze', R, 20 cm (8 in)
Verbena hybrid 'Olympia', var. col., 30 cm (12 in)

○ ⊙ ✽
2. With attractive berries or fruits.

Basella alba, R–P, –20 cm (8 in)
Eschscholzia caespitosa 'Sundew', Y, 40 cm (16 in)
Eschscholzia californica 'Mission Bells', var. col., 60 cm (24 in)
Helianthus annuus, Y/Brown, 4 m (13 ft)
Nicotiana hybrid 'White Bedder', W, 70 cm (28 in)
Nigella damascena, R–P, B/W, –60 cm (24 in)

○ ⊙ ◎
3. Partly or wholly poisonous.

Agrostemma githago, R–P, 80 cm (32 in)
Delphinium ajacis 'Blue Bells', V–B, –25 cm (10 in)
Delphinium ajacis 'Brilliant Rose', R–P, –25 cm (10 in)
Delphinium ajacis 1.2 m (4 ft), 'Giant Imperial', var. col., 1.2 m (4 ft)
Eschscholzia caespitosa 'Sundew', Y, 40 cm (16 in)
Eschscholzia californica 'Mission Bells', var. col., 60 cm (24 in)
Euphorbia marginata, W, 90 cm (3 ft)
Lathyrus odoratus, var. col., –25 cm (10 in)
Ricinus communis, G, 3 m (10 ft)

○ ⊙ ⊕
4. Suitable as a speciment plant.

Alcea rosea 'Silver Puffs', R–P, 1.5 m (5 ft)
Cleome spinosa 'Kirschköningin', R–P, –40 cm (16 in)
Helianthus annuus, Y/Brown, 4 m (13 ft)
Helianthus annuus 'Evening Sun', Y, Brown/R, 2 m (6 ft)
Helianthus annuus 'Tubulosus', Y, 2 m (6 ft)
Ricinus communis, G, 3 m (10 ft)

⊙⊙ ⊗

5. Suitable for rock gardens and crevices in paving.

Anagallis arvensis, R/B, 5 cm (2 in)
Anagallis arvensis ssp *coerulea*, 5 cm (2 in)
Limnanthes douglasii, W/Y, 15 cm (6 in)
Linanthus androsceaus, var. col., –30 cm (12 in)
Lobularia maritima 'Schneeteppich', W, 10 cm (4 in)
Lobularia maritima 'Wonderland', P, –45 cm (18 in)
Malcolmia bicolor P/Y, 15 cm (6 in)
Sanvitalia procumbens, Y–O, 20 cm (8 in)

○ ⊙ ⊖

6. Suitable for ground cover.

Alternanthera bettzickiana, 20 cm (8 in)
Basella alba, R–P, –20 cm (8 in)
Iberis umbellata 'Pumila', R/P, V/W, 40 cm (16 in)

○ ⊙ ⊗

7. Suitable for cutting.

Agrostemma githago, R–P, 80 cm (32 in)
Alcea rosea 'Silver Puffs', R–P, 1.5 m (5 ft)
Amaranthus caudatus, R, 1 m (3 ft)
Amaranthus tricolor 'Splendens', R, –45 cm (18 in)
Amberboa moschata 'Imperialis', R–V, 80 cm (32 in)
Anchusa capensis 'Blue Bird', B, 45 cm (18 in)
Anethum graveolens var. *hortorum*, Y, 1 m (3 ft)
Arctotis hybrid, var. col. 60 cm (24 in)
Callistephus chinensis, 'Azure Blue', var. col., 60 cm (24 in)
Callistephus chinensis 'Deep Blue', var. col., 30 cm (12 in)
Callistephus chinensis 'Hellblaue Prinzessin', var. col., 75 cm (30 in)
Callistephus chinensis 'Pinocchio's Mittelblau', var. col., 45 cm (18 in)
Centaurea cyanus, var. col., –40 cm (16 in)
Centaurea cynaus, 'Blue Diadem', B, 1 m (3 ft)
Chrysanthemum carinatum, var. col., 60 cm (24 in)
Chrysanthemum carinatum 'Merry', var. col., 60 cm (24 in)
Chrysanthemum segetum 'Eastern Star', Y–Brown, 60 cm (24 in)
Chrysanthemum segetum 'Eldorado', Y–Brown, –60 cm (24 in)
Clarkia unguiculata 'Ruby King', var. col., 60 cm (24 in)
Convolvulus tricolor, var. col., –40 cm (16 in)
Cosmos bipinnatus 'Gloria', R–P, –60 cm (24 in)
Cosmos bipinnatus 'Purity', R, 1.2 m (4 ft)
Delphinium ajacis 'Blue Bell' V–B, –25 cm (10 in)
Delphinium ajacis 'Brilliant Rose', R–P, –25 cm (10 in)
Delphinium ajacis 1.2 m (4 ft), 'Giant Imperial', var. col., 1.2 m (4 ft)
Dianthus 'Brilliancy', R–P, 25 cm (10 in)
Dianthus 'Queen of Hearts', R, 25 cm (10 in)
Dianthus 'Telstar', W, R–P, 25 cm (10 in)
Dianthus caryophyllus 'Juliet', R, 15 cm (6 in)
Dimorphotheca sinuata, O–Brown, 30 cm (12 in)
Euphorbia marginata, W, 90 cm (3 ft)
Gaillardia pulchella var. *picta*, var. col., 45 cm (18 in)
Gaillardia pulchella var. *picta* 'Lollipop', var. col., 45 cm (18 in)
Gailliarda pulchella var. *picta* 'Lorenziana', 50 cm (20 in)
Godetia hybrid, var. col., 75 cm (30 in)
Gomphrena globosa, var. col., 30 cm (12 in)
Helianthus annuus, Y/Brown, 4 m (13 ft)
Helianthus annuus, 'Evening Sun', Y, Brown–R, 2 m (6 ft)
Helianthus annuus, 'Tubulosus', Y, 2 m (6 ft)
Helichrysum bracteatum 'Compositum', var. col., –1 m (3 ft)
Helichrysum bracteatum 'Monstruosum', var. col., –1 m (3 ft)
Hordeum jubatum, G, –70 cm (28 in)
Ipomopsis rubra, R, 90 cm (3 ft)
Lagurus ovatus, W, –40 cm (16 in)
Lathyrus odoratus, var. col., –25 cm (10 in)
Limonium bonduellei 'Superba', Y, –60 cm (24 in)
Limonium sinuatum, W,Y,R,B, –60 cm (24 in)
Limonium suworowii, R–P, –60 cm (24 in)
Lonas annua, Y, –60 cm (24 in)
Malcolmia bicolor, P/Y, 15 cm (6 in)
Moluccella laevis, W, –1 m (3 ft)
Nicotiana hybrid 'White Bedder', W, 70 cm (28 in)
Nigella damascena, R–P, B/W, –60 cm (24 in)
Pennisetum villosum, G–Y, –75 cm (30 in)
Penstemon hybrid 'Sensation', var. col., –80 cm (32 in)
Phalaris canariensis, W, –60 cm (24 in)
Phlox drummondii 'Cuspidata', R, 30 cm (12 in)
Phlox drummondii 'Globe', W/R, 15 cm (6 in)
Phlox drummondii 'Stellata', R, 30 cm (12 in)
Salpiglossis sinuata, var. col., –1 m (3 ft)
Salpiglossis sinuata 'Emperor', R/Y, –1 m (3 ft)
Sanvitalia procumbens, Y–O, 20 cm (8 in)
Schizanthus pinnatus 'Star Parade', R–P, Y, 45 cm (18 in)
Tithonia rotundifolia, O–R, 3 m (10 ft)
Ursinia anethoides, Y–O, –60 cm (24 in)

Venidium fastuosum, O, 60 cm (24 in)
Verbena bonariensis, V–B, 1.5 m (5 ft)
Verbena bonariensis 'Tenuisecta', P/V, 50 cm (20 in)
Verbena rigida, P, –50 cm (20 in)
Xeranthemum annuum, var. col., –60 cm (24 in)
Zinnia elegans, Y–O, –50 cm (20 in)
Zinnia elegans, 'Dasher Scarlet', R, 30 cm (12 in)
Zinnia elegans 'Pink Button', 35 cm (14 in)
Zinnia elegans 'Sprite', var. col., –50 cm (20 in)

Biennials

○ ⊙ ⊕

8. Suitable as a specimen plant.

Alcea rosea, R, 3 m (10 ft)
Alcea rosea, W, 3 m (10 ft)
Alcea rosea 'Chater's Double Choice', R, 3 m (10 ft)

○ ⊙ ⊗

9. Suitable for cutting.

Alcea rosea, R, 3 m (10 ft)
Alcea rosea, W, 3 m (10 ft)
Alcea rosea 'Chater's Double Choice', R, 3 m (10 ft)
Dianthus barbatus, 'Wee Willie', R/W, –15 cm (6 in)
Dipsacus sativus, P, 2 m (6 ft)
Ipomopsis rubra, R, 90 cm (3 ft)

Herbaceous perennials

○ ◎

10. No special features.

Anchusa azurea 'Loddon Royalist', B, 90 cm (3 ft)
Arundo donax, –3 m (10 ft)
Aster ericoides 'Delight', W, –1 m (3 ft)
Cajophora laterita, Y–O, 3 m (10 ft)
Chrysanthemum arcticum, Y, –40 cm (16 in)
Epilobium angustifolium, P, 1.5 m (5 ft)
Mirabilis jalapa, R–P, 1 m (3 ft)
Molinia arundinacea, W, –1.2 m (4 ft)
Molinia caerulea 'Variegata', W, –1 m (3 ft)
Salvia przewalskii, P, –75 cm (30 in)
Salvia verticillata, P, 50 cm (20 in)
Silphium perfoliatum, Y, –2.5 m (8 ft)
Stokesia laevis, P, 25 cm (10 in)
Thermopsis lanceolata, Y, –75 cm (30 in)
Trifolium pannonicum, Y, 30 cm (12 in)

○ ◎ ✸

11. Evergreen.

Armeria maritima, P, 15 cm (6 in)
Armeria maritima 'Rosea', R, 15 cm (6 in)
Yucca flaccida, W, –2 m (6 ft)
Yucca gloriosa, W, –1.5 m (5 ft)

○ ◎ ◎

12. Wholly or partly poisonous.

Aquilegia vulgaris, P, –80 cm (32 in)
Delphinium Pacific hybrid 'Galahad', W, –1.8 m (6 ft)
Delphinium Pacific hybrid 'Oberon', B, –1.8 m (6 ft)
Delphinium Pacific hybrid 'Summer Skies', V, –1.8 m (6 ft)
Delphinium hybrid 'Finsteraahorn', P–V, 1.7 m (5½ ft)
Delphinium hybrid 'Gletscherwasser', B, 1.8 m (6 ft)
Delphinium hybrid 'Ouverture', P–V, 1.6 m (5 ft)
Delphinium hybrid 'Sommerwind', V–B, 1.6 m (5 ft)
Delphinium hybrid 'Völkerfrieden', B, 1 m (3 ft)
Delphinium × *ruysii* 'Pink Sensation', R, 80 cm (32 in)
Euphorbia characias ssp. *wulfenii*, Y, 90 cm (3 ft)
Euphorbia griffithii 'Fireglow', O, 50 cm (20 in)
Yucca flaccida, W, –2 m (6 ft)
Yucca gloriosa, W, –1.5 m (5 ft)

○ ◎ ⊕

13. Suitable as a specimen plant.

Cortaderia selloana, W, –3 m (10 ft)
Cynara cardunculus, P, 1.5 m (5 ft)
Eremurus elwesii, R, 2 m (6 ft)
Pennisetum alopecuroides, G/Brown, 1 m (3 ft)

Yucca flaccida, W, –2 m (6 ft)
Yucca gloriosa, W, –1.5 m (5 ft)

○ ◎ ⊗

14. Suitable for rock gardens and crevices in paving.

Antennaria dioica 'Rubra', R, –20 cm (8 in)
Anthericum liliago, W, –80 cm (32 in)
Arabis ferdinandi-coburgi 'Variegata', W, –25 cm (10 in)
Armeria maritima, P, 15 cm (6 in)
Armeria maritima 'Rosea', R, 15 cm (6 in)
Aster alpinus, P, –25 cm (10 in)
Eriophyllum lanatum, Y, 25 cm (10 in)
Incarvillea delavayi, R–P, 60 cm (24 in)
Phlomis samia, Y, –1 m (3 ft)
Phygelius capensis, R/Y, 90 cm (3 ft)
Polygonum vacciniifolium, P, 25 cm (10 in)
Potentilla nepalensis 'Miss Wilmott', R–P, –60 cm (24 in)
Romneya coulteri, W, 1.5 m (5 ft)
Silene acaulis, R–P, 5 cm (2 in)
Silene maritima 'Weisskehlchen', W, 20 cm (8 in)

○ ◎ ⊖

15. Suitable for ground cover.

Arabis ferdinandi-coburgi 'Variegata', W, –25 cm (10 in)
Armeria maritima, P, 15 cm (6 in)
Armeria maritima 'Rosea', R, 15 cm (6 in)

○ ◎ ⊗

16. Suitable for cutting.

Agapanthus praecox ssp. *orientalis,* V, –70 cm (28 in)
Alstroemeria aurantiaca 'Lutea', Y–O, –1.2 m (4 ft)
Alstroemeria aurantiaca 'Orange Kingp, O, –1.2 m (4 ft)
Antennaria dioica 'Rubra', R, –20 cm (8 in)
Anthericum liliago, W, –80 cm (32 in)
Aquilegia vulgaris, P, –80 cm (32 in)
Aster amellus 'Rudolf Goethe', P, –70 cm (28 in)
Aster dumosus 'Alice Haslam', R–P, 25 cm (10 in)
Aster dumosus 'Little Boy Blue', V, 40 cm (16 in)
Aster farreri 'Berggarten', P, 50 cm (20 in)
Aster linosyris, Y, –60 cm (24 in)
Aster novae-angliae 'Dr Eckener', P, –1.6 m (5 ft)
Aster novae-angliae 'Roter Stern', P, 1.35 m (4½ ft)
Aster novae-angliae 'Rudelsberg', P, 1.2 m (4 ft)
Aster novi-belgii 'Dauerblau', V, 1.25 m (4 ft)
Aster novi-belgii 'Eventide', V, 1 m (3 ft)
Aster sedifolius, P–V, –1 m (3 ft)
Aster shortii, P, –1 m (3 ft)
Aster tongolensis 'Wartburgstern', P, –40 cm (16 in)
Aster × frikartii, P–V, –70 cm (28 in), P, 50 cm (20 in)
Buphthalmum salicifolium, Y, –60 cm (24 in)
Centranthus ruber, R, 80 cm (32 in)
Centranthus ruber 'Roseus', R, 80 cm (32 in)
Chrysanthemum 'Blanche Poiteviene', W, 1.2 m (4 ft)
Chrysanthemum 'Fairweather', R–P, 1.2 m (4 ft)
Chrysanthemum 'Golden Chance', Y, 60 cm (24 in)
Chrysanthemum 'Jimmy Mottram', O–R, 60 cm (24 in)
Chrysanthemum 'Maiko', R–P, 1 m (3 ft)
Chrysanthemum 'Perfection', R–P, 80 cm (32 in)
Chrysanthemum 'Red Breast', R, 60 cm (24 in)
Chrysanthemum 'Ringdove', R–P, 60 cm (24 in)
Chrysanthemum 'Rytop', R–P, 80 cm (32 in)
Chrysanthemum 'Ugetsu', W, 1.2 m (4 ft)
Chrysanthemum 'Balcombe Perfection', O, 1.2 m (4 ft)
Chrysanthemum coccineum 'Brenda', R, 1 m (3 ft)
Chrysanthemum corymbosum, W, 1.2 m (4 ft)
Chrysanthemum leucanthemum, W–Y, –60 cm (24 in)
Chrysanthemum maximum hybrid 'Marvellous', W, –70 cm (28 in)
Chrysanthemum rubellum 'Clara Curtis', P, –1 m (3 ft)
Chrysanthemum serotinum, W, 1 m (3 ft)
Coreopsis grandiflora 'Sunburst', Y, –1 m (3 ft)
Coreopsis lancelolata 'Babygold', Y, –60 cm (24 in)
Coreopsis tripteris, Y, –75 cm (30 in)
Coreopsis verticillata, Y, –75 cm (30 in)
Coreopsis verticillata 'Grandiflora', Y, –75 cm (30 in)
Cortaderia selloana, W, –3 m (10 ft)
Cynara cardunculus, P, 1.5 m (5 ft)
Delphinium hybrid 'Finsteraarhorn', P–V, 1.7 m (5½ ft)
Delphinium hybrid 'Gletscherwasser', B, 1.8 m (6 ft)
Delphinium hybrid 'Ouverture', P–V, 1.7 m (5½ ft)
Delphinium hybrid 'Sommerwind', V–B, 1.6 m (5 ft)
Delphinium hybrid 'Völkerfrieden', B, 1 m (3 ft)
Delphinium Pacific hybrid 'Galahad', W, –1.8 m (6 ft)
Delphinium Pacific hybrid 'Oberon', B, –1.8 m (6 ft)
Delphinium Pacific hybrid 'Summer Skies', V, –1.8 m (6 ft)

Delphinium × ruysii 'Pink Sensation', R, 80 cm (32 in)
Didiscus caeruleus, V–B, 45 cm (18 in)
Dierama pendulum, V, 60 cm (24 in)
Echinea purpurea, R–P, –1 m (3 ft)
Eremurus elwesii, R, 2 m (6 ft)
Erigeron speciosus var. *macranthus,* V, 40 cm (18 in)
Erigeron hybrid 'Dunkelste Aller', P, 60 cm (24 in)
Erigeron hybrid 'Foerster's Liebling', V, 60 cm (24 in)
Erigeron hybrid 'Quakeress', V, 70 cm (28 in)
Erigeron hybrid 'Sommerabend', W, 30 cm (12 in)
Erigeron hybrid 'Strahlenmeer', V, 70 cm (28 in)
Eriophyllum lanatum, Y, 25 cm (10 in)
Eupatorium purpureum 'Glutball', P, 2 m (6 ft)
Euphorbia characias ssp. *wulfenii,* Y, 90 cm (3 ft)
Euphorbia griffithii 'Fireglow', O, 50 cm (20 in)
Foeniculum vulgare, Y, 1.5 m (5 ft)
Galega × hartlandii 'Duchess of Bedford', W/V, 1.5 m (5 ft)
Geranium tuberosum, P, –30 cm (12 in)
Helenium hybrid 'Altgoldriese', R, 2 m (6 ft)
Helenium hybrid 'Chipperfield Orange', Y–O, 2 m (6 ft)
Helenium hybrid 'Julisonne', Y, 1 m (3 ft)
Helenium hybrid 'Superbum Rubrum', O, 2 m (6 ft)
Helenium hybrid 'Symbol', Y, 1.5 m (5 ft)
Helianthus decapetalus 'Soleil d'Or', Y, 1.5 m (5 ft)
Helianthus × laetiflorus 'Miss Mellish', Y, 1.4 m (4½ ft)
Heliopsis helianthoides 'Goldgrünherz', Y, 90 cm (3 ft)
Heliopsis helianthoides var. *helianthoides,* Y, 1.25 cm (4 ft)
Heliopsis helianthoides var. *scabra,* Y, 1.25 cm (4 ft)
Holcus lanatus 'Albovariegatus', W/V, 90 cm (3 ft)
Inula magnifica, Y, –1.8 m (6 ft)
Inula orientalis, Y, –70 cm (28 in)
Knautia dipsacifolia, P–V, –75 cm (30 in)
Kniphofia galpinii, O, –60 cm (24 in)
Kniphofia hybrid 'Alcazar', O, 90 cm (3 ft)
Kniphofia hybrid 'Shining Sceptre', Y, 1.25 m (4 ft)
Kniphofia hybrid 'The Rocket', R/Y, 1 m (3 ft)
Levisticum officinale, Y, 1.9 m (6 ft)
Limonium latifolium 'Violetta', P–V, –40 cm (16 in)
Malva alcea, R–P, –1 m (3 ft)
Nepeta sibirica, B, 75 cm (30 in)
Paeonia lactiflora, R, 1 m (3 ft)
Paeonia lactiflora 'Bunker Hill', R, –1 m (3 ft)
Paeonia lactiflora 'Dr Alex Fleming', R, 1 m (3 ft)
Paeonia lactiflora 'Duchesse de Nemours', W, 1 m (3 ft)
Paeonia lactiflora 'Reine Hortense', W–R, 1 m (3 ft)
Paeonia tenuifolia 'Plena', R, 60 cm (24 in)
Paeonia wittmanniana hybrid 'Maimorgen', R, 1 m (3 ft)
Panicum virgatum 'Rehbraun', R–Brown, –1.5 m (5 ft)
Pennisetum alopecuroides, G–Brown, 1 m (3 ft)
Penstemon campanulatus, R–P, 50 cm (20 in)
Penstemon hartwegii 'Blue Gem', V, –60 cm (24 in)
Penstemon scouleri, P–V, 15 cm (6 in)
Physocarpus virginiana 'Bouquet Rose', R–P, 90 cm (3 ft)
Physocarpus virginiana 'Rosy Spire', R–P, 90 cm (3 ft)
Physocarpus virginiana 'Summer Snow', W, 90 cm (3 ft)
Potentilla nepalensis 'Miss Wilmott', R–P, –60 cm (24 in)
Salvia pratensis, V, –60 cm (24 in)
Salvia × superba 'Ostfriesland', P, 50 cm (20 in)
Solidago caesia, Y, 60 cm (24 in)
Solidago hybrid 'Goldenmosa', Y, 80 cm (32 in)
Solidago hybrid 'Goldstrahl', Y, 80 cm (32 in)
Solidaster × luteus, Y, 1 m (3 ft)
Verbascum hybrid 'Gainsborough', Y, 1 m (3 ft)
Verbena bonariensis, V–B, 1.5 m (5 ft)

Bulbs

○

17. No special features

Cardiocrinum giganteum, W, –4 m (13 ft)
Cypella herberti, var. col., –90 cm (13 ft)
Tulipa (double early) 'Fringed Beauty', var. col., 40 cm (16 in)
Tulipa viridiflora 'Eye Catcher', G/R, 60 cm (24 in)
Tulipa viridiflora 'Spring Queen', G–Y, 60 cm (24 in)

○

18. Wholly or partly poisonous.

Fritillaria imperialis, O, 1 m (3 ft)
Fritillaria imperialis 'Lutea', O, 1 m (3 ft)
Fritillaria persica 'Adiyaman', P, 75 cm (30 in)
Lilium speciosum var. *album* 'White Champion', W, –1.5 m (5 ft)
Ornithogalum thyrsoides, W, 40 cm (16 in)

○ ⊛ ⊕
19. Suitable as a specimen plant.

Fritillaria imperialis, O, 1 m (3 ft)
Fritillaria imperialis 'Lutea', O, 1 m (3 ft)
Lilium pardalinum, R, O–R, Brown, –1.8 m (6 ft)
Lilium speciosum var. *album* 'White Champion', W, –1.5 m (5 ft)

○ ⊛ ⊗
20. Suitable for rock gardens and crevices in paving.

Ipheion uniflorum, V, 10 cm (4 in)
Muscaria azurea, B, –25 cm (10 in)
Muscaria armeniacum, B, –20 cm (8 in)
Muscaria armeniacum 'Blue Spike', B, –25 cm (10 in)
Muscaria botryoides 'Album', W, –20 cm (8 in)
Muscaria latifolium, B, –40 cm (16 in)
Scilla peruviana, B, –30 cm (12 in)
Tulipa acuminata, R–Y, –40 cm (16 in)
Tulipa clusiana, W–R, –30 cm (12 in)
Tulipa (cottage) 'Maureen', W, 90 cm (3 ft)
Tulipa fosterana 'Spring Pearl', R, –40 cm (16 in)
Tulipa fosterana 'Sylvia van Lennep', R, –40 cm (16 in)
Tulipa greigii 'Charmeuse', Y–R, –30 cm (12 in)
Tulipa greigii 'Dreamboat', O–R, 20 cm (8 in)
Tulipa greigii 'Plaisir', W, R, 20 cm (8 in)
Tulipa kaufmanniana 'Ancilla', W/Y, –20 cm (8 in)
Tulipa kaufmanniana 'Stresa', var. col., 20 cm (8 in)
Tulipa kopakowskiana, var. col., –20 cm (8 in)
Tulipa maximowiczii, R, –25 cm (10 in)
Tulipa praestans 'Fusilier', R, 25 cm (10 in)
Tulipa saxatilis, P–V, Y, –20 cm (8 in)
Tulipa tarda, W/Y, 20 cm (8 in)
Tulipa (triumph) 'Aleppo', Y, O–R, –45 cm (18 in)
Tulipa (triumph) 'Capri', R, –45 cm (18 in)
Tulipa turkestanica, W/O, 25 cm (10 in)
Tulipa urumiensis, Y, –15 cm (6 in)
Tulipa violacea, R–P, –15 cm (6 in)

○ ⊛ ⊗
21. Suitable for cutting.

Crinum × *powellii*, R/W, 1.2 m (4 ft)
Ixiolirion tataricum, B, –45 cm (18 in)
Ornithogalum thyrsoides, W, 40 cm (16 in)
Sparaxis tricolor hybrid, var. col., 35 cm (14 in)
Tigridia pavonia, Y–R, –45 cm (18 in)
Tulipa (Darwin) 'Paradise', W–R, –80 cm (32 in)
Tulipa (Darwin hybrid) 'Black Swan', P, –80 cm (32 in)
Tulipa (Darwin hybrid) 'Eric Hofsjo', O–R, –80 cm (32 in)
Tulipa (Darwin hybrid) 'Olympic Flame', Y, O–R, 80 cm (32 in)
Tulipa (double late) 'Angelique', R, –60 cm (24 in)
Tulipa (single early) 'Keizerskroon', Y–R, –40 cm (16 in)
Tulipa (single early) 'Prinses Irene', O, 35 cm (14 in)
Tulipa (lily-flowered) 'Queen of Sheba', var. col., 60 cm (24 in)
Tulipa (Mendel) 'Apricot Beauty', O/R, 40 cm (16 in)
Tulipa (parrot) 'Estella Rijnveld', var. col., 45 cm (18 in)
Tulipa (triumph) 'Capri', R, 45 cm (18 in)
Tulipa (triumph) 'Don Quichotte', R–P, 45 cm (18 in)
Tulipa (triumph) 'Dreaming Maid', R, –45 cm (18 in)
Tulipa (triumph) 'Golden Arguno', O–R, –45 cm (18 in)

Tubers

○ ⊛
22. No special features.

Phlomis tuberosa, P–V, –1 m (3 ft)
Tropaeolum pentaphyllum, R, –3 m (10 ft)

○ ⊛ ⊛
23. With attractive fruits or berries.

Thladiantha dubia, Y, –3 m (10 ft)

○ ⊛ ☻
24. Wholly or partly poisonous.

Anemone coronaria 'Sylphide', P, –35 cm (14 in)
Bulbocodium vernum, P, 20 cm (8 in)

○ ⊛ ⊕
25. Suitable as a specimen plant.

Canna indica hybrid, var. col., –1.5 m (5 ft)
Eremurus 'Shelford Hybrids', R, 2.25 m (7½ ft)
Eremurus himalaicus, W, –1.2 m (4 ft)
Eremurus robustus, R, –3 m (10 ft)

○ ⊛ ⊗
26. Suitable for rock gardens and crevices in paving.

Bulbocodium vernum, P, 20 cm (8 in)
Dahlia 'Top Mix Rose', R, 25 cm (10 in)
Iris aphylla, P, –40 cm (16 in)
Iris pumila 'Tonya', P/V, –15 cm (6 in)

○ ⊛ ⊗
27. Suitable for cutting.

Anemone coronaria 'Sylphide', P, 35 cm (14 in)
Dahlia (anemone-flowered), var. col. –60 cm (24 in)
Dahlia (cactus) 'Madeleine St Germain', R–P, 1.5 m (5 ft)
Dahlia (cactus) 'Television', O–R, Y, 1.5 m (5 ft)
Dahlia (decorative) 'Emile Zola', O–R, 1.5 m (5 ft)
Dahlia (decorative) 'Frendy', Y/R, 1.5 m (5 ft)
Dahlia (collarette) O–R, Y, 1.25 m (4 ft)
Dahlia (dwarf single) 'Excellent Dwarf', O–R, 50 cm (20 in)
Dahlia (orchid-flowered), 'Rote Giraffe', R, 80 cm (32 in)
Dahlia (paeony-flowered) 'Dandy', R, 80 cm (32 in)
Dahlia (pompon) 'Charles Dickens', R–P, 90 cm (3 ft)
Dahlia (pompon) 'Kinky', R–P, 80 cm (32 in)
Dahlia (pompon) 'Kitty Hawk', P, 80 cm (32 in)
Dahlia (pompon) 'Liane', R, 80 cm (32 in)
Dahlia (semi-cactus) 'Hatsekatourian', Y, 1.5 m (5 ft)
Dahlia (semi-cactus) 'Show', Y–R, 1.5 m (5 ft)
Dahlia (simplex) 'Emilio Dahlio', P, 50 cm (20 in)
Dahlia (simplex) 'Schneekönigin', W, 50 cm (20 in)
Dahlia (top mix) 'Top Mix Rose', R, 25 cm (10 in)
Eremurus 'Shelford Hybrids', R, 2.25 m (7½ ft)
Eremurus himalaicus, W, –1.2 m (4 ft)
Eremurus robustus, R, –3 m (10 ft)
Freesia hybrid 'Rijnvelds Golden Yellow', Y, 30 cm (12 in)
Ixia hybrid, var. col., 45 cm (18 in)
Triteleia laxa, var. col., –60 cm (24 in)

Shrubs

○ ⊛
28. No special features.

Campsis radicans, O/Y, 10 m (33 ft)
Caryopteris × *clandonesis*, B, 1.25 m (4 ft)
Ceanothus hybrid 'Gloire de Versailles', V–B, 1 m (3 ft)
Escallonia virgata, W, 2 m (6 ft)
Escallonia × *langleyensis*, W, 2.5 m (8 ft)
Hyssopus officinalis, V–B, 45 cm (18 in)
Paeonia suffruticosa hybrid, W/R, 1.5 m (5 ft)

○ ⊛ ⊛
29. Evergreen.

Abies balsamea f. *hudsonia*, 1 m (3 ft)
Chamaecyparis lawsoniana 'Gimbornii', 80 cm (32 in)
Chamaecyparis lawsoniana 'Minima Aurea', 1.5 m (5 ft)
Chamaecyparis obtusa 'Nana Gracilis', 2.5 m (8 ft)
Chamaecyparis pisifera 'Nana', 60 cm (24 in)
Chamaecyparis pisifera 'Plumosa Aurea Nana', 1.5 m (5 ft)
Chamaecyparis thyoides 'Ericoides', 2 mg (6 ft)
Empetrum nigrum, R–P, 25 cm (10 in)
Hebe 'Autumn Blue', V–B, 40 cm (16 in)
Hebe armstrongii, W, 60 cm (24 in)
Hebe salificolia, W/V, 3 m (10 ft)
Hebe traversii, W/V, 3 m (10 ft)
Hebe × *andersonii*, V, 1 m (3 ft)
Juniperus procumbens 'Nana', 30 cm (12 in)
Lithodora diffusa, B, 15 cm (6 in)
Pernettya mucronata, W, 1 m (3 ft)
Pinus cembra 'Compacta Glauca', 2 m (6 ft)
Pinus densiflora 'Umbraculifera', 3 m (10 ft)
Pinus mugo 'Gnom', –2 m (6 ft)
Pinus mugo 'Mops', 1 m (3 ft)
Pinus strobus 'Radiata', 2 m (6 ft)
Prunus laurocerasus 'Rotundifolia', W, 4 m (13 ft)
Prunus lusitanica 'Angustifolia', W, 3 m (10 ft)
Pseudotsuga menziesii 'Tempelhof Compacta', 2 m (6 ft)

Rosa sempervirens 'Felicité et Perpetue', W, 3 m (10 ft)
Santolina chamaecyparissus, Y, –60 cm (24 in)
Solanum crispum, V–B, 6 m (20 ft)
Taxus baccata (hedge), 10 m (33 ft)

30. With attractive berries or fruits.

Berberis 'Barbarossa', Y, –1.5 m (5 ft)
Berberis 'Bunch o' Grapes', Y, –1.5 m (5 ft)
Berberis carminea (×) 'Buccaneer', R, 1 m (3 ft)
Berberis thunbergii, Y, 1.5 m (5 ft)
Berberis wilsoniae, R, 1 m (3 ft)
Berberis wilsoniae 'Orangeade', Y, 1 m (3 ft)
Chamaecyparis lawsoniana 'Gimbornii', 80 cm (32 in)
Chamaecyparis lawsoniana 'Minima Aurea', 1.5 m (5 ft)
Chamaecyparis obtusa 'Nana Gracilis', 2.5 m (8 ft)
Chamaecyparis pisifera 'Nana', 60 cm (24 in)
Chamaecyparis pisifera 'Plumosa Aurea Nana' 1.5 m (5 ft)
Chamaecyparis thyoides 'Ericoides', 2 m (6 ft)
Clerodendrum trichotomum, W, 8 m (26 ft)
Coriaria japonica, G, 1 m (3 ft)
Cotinus coggygria, G, 3 m (10 ft)
Cotinus coggygria 'Royal Purple', G, 2 m (6 ft)
Cotinus obovatus, G, 6 m (20 ft)
Cytisus dallimorei (×) 'Adreanus Splendens', Y/R, 2.5 m (8 ft)
Empetrum nigrum, R–P, 25 cm (10 in)
Euonymus sachalinensis, R, 3 m (10 ft)
Exochorda giraldii var. *wilsonii*, W, 3 m (10 ft)
Exochorda racemosa, W, 3 m (10 ft)
Juniperus procumbens 'Nana', 30 cm (12 in)
Malus 'Mary Potter', W, 3 m (10 ft)
Passiflora caerulea, W/G/B, 3 m (10 ft)
Pernettya mucronata, W, 1 m (3 ft)
Prunus cistena (×), W, 1 m (3 ft)
Prunus laurocerasus 'Rotundifolia', W, 4 m (13 ft)
Rosa (climber) 'Fritz Nobis', R, 2 m (6 ft)
Rosa blanda, R, 2 m (6 ft)
Rosa centifolia, R, 2 m (6 ft)
Rosa centifolia 'Fantin Latour', R, 1.5 m (5 ft)
Rosa centifolia 'Red Moss', R, 2 m (6 ft)
Rosa gallica 'Officinalis', R, 2.5 m (8 ft)
Rosa gallica 'Versicolor' R–W, 1.5 m (5 ft)
Rosa glutinosa, R, –70 cm (28 in)
Rosa laevigata, W, 6 m (20 ft)
Rosa moyesii 'Geranium' R, 2 m (6 ft)
Rosa moyesii 'Nevada', W, 2 m (6 ft)
Rosa pimpinellifolia 'Frühlingsmorgen', R–Y, 2 m (6 ft)
Rosa richardii (×), R, 3 m (10 ft)
Rosa setipoda, R, 3 m (10 ft)
Rosa villosa, R, 2 m (6 ft)
Taxus baccata (hedge), 10 m (33 ft)
Vitis amurensis, G, 15 m (50 ft)

31. Wholly or partly poisonous.

Berberis thunbergii, Y, 1.5 m (5 ft)
Chamaecyparis lawsoniana 'Gimbornii', 80 cm (32 in)
Chamaecyparis lawsoniana 'Minima Aurea', 1.5 m (5 ft)
Chamaecyparis obtusa 'Nana Gracilis', 2.5 m (8 ft)
Chamaecyparis pisifera 'Nana', 60 cm (24 in)
Chamaecyparis pisifera 'Plumosa Aurea Nana', 1.5 m (5 ft)
Chamaecyparis thyoides 'Ericoides', 2 m (6 ft)
Coriaria japonica, G, 1 m (3 ft)
Cotinus coggygria, G, 3 m (10 ft)
Cotinus coggygria 'Royal Purple', G, 2 m (6 ft)
Cotinus obovatus, G, 6 m (20 ft)
Cytisus kewensis (×), Y, 60 cm (24 in)
Cytisus nigricans, Y, 1.5 m (5 ft)
Cytisus praecox (×), Y, 2 m (6 ft)
Cytisus praecox (×) 'Zeelandia', R–P, 1.8 m (6 ft)
Cytisus purpureus, R, 60 cm (24 in)
Cytisus scoparius 'Luna', Y, 2 m (6 ft)
Genista aetnensis, Y, 4 m (13 ft)
Genista lydia, Y, 60 cm (24 in)
Juniperus procumbens 'Nana', 30 cm (12 in)
Prunus cistena (×), W, 1.5 m (5 ft)
Prunus laurocerasus 'Rotundifolia', W, 4 m (13 ft)
Prunus lusitanica 'Angustifolia', W, 3 m (10 ft)
Prunus serrulata 'Shirotae', W, 3 m (10 ft)
Prunus serrulata 'Ukon', Y–W, 6 m (20 ft)
Taxus baccata (hedge), 10 m (33 ft)
Wisteria sinensis 'Alba', W, 10 m (33 ft)

32. Suitable as a specimen plant.

Chamaecyparis obtusa 'Nana Gracilis', 2.5 m (8 ft)
Chamaecyparis pisifera 'Nana', 60 cm (24 in)
Chamaecyparis pisifera 'Plumosa Aurea Nana', 1.5 m (5 ft)
Chamaecyparis thyoides 'Ericoides', 2 m (6 ft)
Cotinus coggygria, G, 3 m (10 ft)
Cotinus coggygria 'Royal Purple', G, 2 m (6 ft)
Cotinus obovatus, G, 6 m (20 ft)
Exochorda giraldii var. *wilsonii*, W, 3 m (10 ft)
Exochorda racemosa, W, 3 m (10 ft)
Hibiscus syriacus 'Coelestis', B, 3 m (10 ft)
Hibiscus syriacus 'Hamabo', R, 3 m (10 ft)
Hibiscus syriacus 'Rubis', R, 3 m (10 ft)
Kolkwitzia amabilis, R, 2.5 m (8 ft)
Lavatera olbia 'Rosea', R/W, 2 m (6 ft)
Magnolia liliiflora, R–P, 3 m (10 ft)
Magnolia soulangiana (×), W–R, 7 m (23 ft)
Magnolia soulangiana (×) 'Lennei', P/W, 7 m (23 ft)
Magnolia stellata, W, 2 m (6 ft)
Magnolia stellata 'Rosea', R/W, 2 m (6 ft)
Malus 'Mary Potter', W, 3 m (10 ft)
Pinus cembra 'Compacta Glauca', 2 m (6 ft)
Pinus densiflora 'Umbraculifera', 3 m (10 ft)
Pinus strobus 'Radiata', 2 m (6 ft)
Prunus cistena (×), W, 1.5 m (5 ft)
Pseudotsuga menziesii 'Tempelhof Compacta', 2 m (6 ft)
Rosa (shrub) 'Fred Loads', R, 1.5 m (5 ft)
Rosa moyesii 'Geranium', R, 2 m (6 ft)
Rosa moyesii 'Nevada', W, 2 m (6 ft)
Wisteria sinensis 'Alba', W, 10 m (33 ft)

33. Suitable for rock gardens and crevices in paving.

Abies balsamea f. *hudsonia*, 1 m (3 ft)
Cytisus kewensis (×), Y, 60 cm (24 in)
Empetrum nigrum, R–P, 25 cm (10 in)
Genista lydia, Y, 60 cm (24 in)
Hebe armstrongii, W, 60 cm (24 in)
Lithodora diffusa, B, 15 cm (6 in)
Pinus densiflora 'Umbraculifera', 3 m (10 ft)
Pinus mugo 'Gnom', –2 m (6 ft)
Pinus mugo 'Mops', 1 m (3 ft)
Pseudotsuga menziesii 'Tempelhof Compacta', 2 m (6 ft)
Rosa (dwarf) 'Yellow Doll', Y, –30 cm (12 in)
Rosa chinensis var. *minima*, R, 20 cm (8 in)
Thymus serpyllum 'Albus', W, 10 cm (4 in)

34. Suitable for hedging.

Berberis thunbergii, Y, 1.5 m (5 ft)
Cytisus praecox (×), Y, 2 m (6 ft)
Cytisus praecox (×) 'Zeelandia', R–P, 1.8 m (6 ft)
Escallonia hybrid 'Donard Seedling', R, 2 m (6 ft)
Prunus laurocerasus 'Rotundifolia', W, 4 m (13 ft)
Rosa (floribunda) 'Queen Elizabeth', R, 1.5 m (5 ft)
Rosa gallica 'Versicolor', R–W, 1.5 m (5 ft)
Taxus baccata (hedge), 10 m (33 ft)

35. Suitable for ground cover.

Empetrum nigrum, R–P, 25 cm (10 in)
Juniperus procumbens 'Nana', 30 cm (12 in)
Lithodora diffusa, B, 15 cm (6 in)
Rosa macrantha 'Raubritter', R, 1 m (3 ft)

36. Suitable for cutting.

Berberis 'Barbarossa', Y, –1.5 m (5 ft)
Berberis 'Bunch o' Grapes', Y, –1.5 m (5 ft)
Buddleia davidii, W, 3 m (10 ft)
Buddleia davidii 'Fascination', P–V, 3 m (10 ft)
Buddleia davidii 'Nanho Purple', R–P, 1 m (3 ft)
Buddleia davidii var. *nanhoensis*, P, 1.5 m (5 ft)
Euonymus sachalinensis, R, 3 m (10 ft)
Lavatera olbia 'Rosea', R, 2 m (6 ft)
Magnolia soulangiana (×), W–R, 7 m (23 ft)
Magnolia soulangiana hybrid 'Lennei', P–W, 7 m (23 ft)
Pernettya mucronata, W, 1 m (3 ft)
Rosa banksiae 'Lutescens', Y, 20 m (65 ft)
Rosa blands, R, 2 m (6 ft)
Rosa centifolia, R, 2 m (6 ft)
Rosa centifolia 'Fantin Latour', R, 1.5 m (5 ft)
Rosa centifolia 'Red Moss', R, 2 m (6 ft)
Rosa chinensis var. *minima*, R, 2 m (6 ft)
Rosa (David Austin) 'Constance Spry', R, 2.5 m (8 ft)
Rosa (David Austin) 'Wife of Bath', R, 90 cm (3 ft)
Rosa (dwarf) 'Yellow Doll', Y, –30 cm (12 in)
Rosa gallica 'Officinalis', R, 2.5 m (8 ft)
Rosa gallica 'Veriscolor', R–W, 1.5 m (5 ft)
Rosa glutinosa, R, –70 cm (28 in)
Rosa (climber) 'American Pillar', R–P, 6 m (20 ft)
Rosa (climber) 'Bantry Bay', R, 3 m (10 ft)
Rosa (climber) 'Clair Martin', R, –3 m (10 ft)
Rosa (climber) 'Climbing Sarabande', R, 4 m (13 ft)
Rosa (climber) 'Danse du Feu', R, 3.5 m (11 ft)
Rosa (climber) 'Fritz Nobis', R, 2 m (6 ft)
Rosa (climber) 'Handel', R–P, 3.5 m (11 ft)
Rosa (climber) 'Parkdirektor Riggers', R, 4.5 m (15 ft)
Rosa (climber) 'Pink Cloud', R, 3 m (10 ft)
Rosa (climber) 'Revell Dijonnais', R/Y, 4 m (13 ft)
Rosa (climber) 'Zepherine Drouhin', R, 4.5 m (15 ft)
Rosa laevigata, W, 6 m (20 ft)
Rosa macrantha 'Raubritter', R, 1 m (3 ft)
Rosa moyesii 'Geranium', R, 2 m (6 ft)
Rosa moyesii 'Nevada', W, 2 m (6 ft)
Rosa (shrub) 'Fred Loads', R, 1.5 (5 ft)
Rosa pimpinellifolia 'Fruhlingsmorgen', R–Y, 2 m (6 ft)
Rosa richardii (×), R, 3 m (10 ft)
Rosa sempervirens 'Felicité et Perpetue', W, 3 m (10 ft)
Rosa setipoda, R, 3 m (10 ft)
Rosa stylosa (×), W, 2 m (6 ft)
Rosa (hybrid tea) 'Arianne', R, 80 cm (32 in)
Rosa (hybrid tea) 'Chicago Peace', R–Y, 1 m (3 ft)
Rosa (hybrid tea) 'Dainty Bess', R, 80 cm (32 in)
Rosa (hybrid tea) 'Duftwolke', R–P, 1.25 m (4 ft)
Rosa (hybrid tea) 'Grandpa Dickson', Y, 90 cm (3 ft)
Rosa (hybrid tea) 'Interflora', O–R, 80 cm (32 in)
Rosa (hybrid tea) 'Mullard Jubilee', R, 80 cm (32 in)
Rosa (hybrid tea) 'Super Star', R, 1.25 m (4 ft)
Rosa (hybrid tea) 'Virgo', W, 70 cm (28 in)
Rosa (hybrid tea) 'Wendy Cussons', R–P, 1 m (3 ft)
Rosa (hybrid tea) 'White Wings', W, 1 m (3 ft)
Rosa (floribunda) 'Betty Prior', R–P, –1.5 m (5 ft)
Rosa (floribunda) 'Chinatown', , 1.7 m (5½ ft)
Rosa (floribunda) 'Pernille Poulsen', R, 70 cm (28 in)
Rosa (floribunda) 'Queen Elizabeth', R, 1.5 m (5 ft)
Rosa (floribunda) 'Redgold', Y/R, 80 cm (32 in)
Rosa (floribunda) 'Sarabande', R, 65 cm (26 in)
Rosa (floribunda) 'Schneewittchen', W, 1 m (3 ft)
Rosa (floribunda) 'Schweizer Gruss', R, 50 cm (20 in)
Rosa villosa, R, 2 m (6 ft)
Syringa josikaea, P, 3 m (10 ft)
Syringa komarowii, R, 4 m (13 ft)
Syringa × *persica*, V, 5 m (16 ft)
Syringa × *swegiflexa*, R, 3 m (10 ft)
Syringa tigerstedtii, W–V, 3 m (10 ft)
Syringa vulgaris 'Cavour', V–B, 5 m (16 ft)
Syringa vulgaris 'General Sherman', V, 5 m (16 ft)
Syringa vulgaris 'Marechal Lannes', V, 5 m (16 ft)
Syringa wolfii, R–P, 5 m (16 ft)

Trees

37. Evergreen.

Abies grandis, 30 m (100 ft)
Abies pinsapo 'Glauca', 20 m (65 ft)
Araucaria araucana, 20 m (65 ft)
Cedrus atlantica 'Glauca', 30 m (100 ft)
Cedrus deodara, 20 m (65 ft)
Cedrus deodara 'Aurea', 10 m (33 ft)
Cedrus libani, –40 m (135 ft)
Chamaecyparis lawsoniana 'Lana', 6 m (20 ft)
Chamaecyparis lawsoniana 'Lutea', 10 m (33 ft)
Chamaecyparis lawsoniana 'Pendula', 20 m (65 ft)
Chamaecyparis lawsoniana 'Winston Churchill', 8 m (26 ft)
Chamaecyparis nootkatensis 'Pendula', 10 m (33 ft)
Cunninghamia lanceolata, –15 m (50 ft)
Cupressus arizonica, 20 m (65 ft)
Juniperus recurva var. *coxil*, 30 m (100 ft)
Magnolia grandiflora, W, 20 m (65 ft)
Picea likiangensis var. *balfouriana*, 40 m (135 ft)
Pinus heldreichii, 20 m (65 ft)
Pinus leucodermis 'Satellit', 20 m (65 ft)
Pinus pinea, 20 m (65 ft)
Pinus ponderosa, 40 m (135 ft)
Pinus radiata, 35 m (115 ft)
Pinus strobus, 40 m (135 ft)
Pinus wallichiana, 30 m (100 ft)
Pseudotsuga menziesii 'Brevifolia', 30 m (100 ft)
Sciadopitys verticillata, 20 m (65 ft)
Sequoiadendron giganteum, 70 m (230 ft)

38. Attractive fruits or berries.

Abies grandis, 30 m (100 ft)
Abies koreana, 15 m (50 ft)
Abies lasiocarpa var. *arizonica*, 20 m (65 ft)
Abies pinsapo 'Glauca', 20 m (65 ft)
Ammobium alatum 'Grandiflorum', W–Y, 50 cm (20 in)
Betula pendula 'Dalecarlica', Y–G, 20 m (65 ft)
Betula pubescens, Y–G, 20 m (65 ft)
Catalpa erubescens (×), W, 10 m (33 ft)
Catalpa ovata, W, 10 m (33 ft)
Cedrus atlantica 'Glauca', 30 m (100 ft)
Cedrus deodara, 20 m (65 ft)
Cedrus deodara 'Aurea', 10 m (33 ft)
Cedrus libani, –40 m (135 ft)
Cercis siliquastrum, P, 7 m (23 ft)
Chamaecyparis lawsoniana 'Lana', 6 m (20 ft)
Chamaecyparis lawsoniana 'Lutea', 10 m (33 ft)
Chamaecyparis lawsoniana 'Pendula', 20 m (65 ft)
Chamaecyparis lawsoniana 'Winston Churchill', 8 m (26 ft)
Chamaecyparis nootkatensis 'Pendula', 10 m (33 ft)
Cladrastis lutea, W/R, 10 m (33 ft)
Cunninghamia lanceolata, R, –5 m (16 ft)
Fraxinus excelsior, Y–G, 40 m (135 ft)
Fraxinus excelsior 'Aurea', Y–G, 15 m (50 ft)
Fraxinus excelsior 'Jaspidea', Y–G, 20 m (65 ft)
Ginkgo biloba, 20 m (65 ft)
Gymnocladus dioicus, G/W, 20 m (65 ft)
Juniperus recurva var. *coxil*, 30 m (100 ft)
Larix decidua, 25 m (80 ft)
Larix gmelinii, 20 m (65 ft)
Larix laricina, 30 m (100 ft)
Malus 'Adams', R, 10 m (33 ft)
Malus 'Butterball', R, 6 m (20 ft)
Malus 'Echtermeyer', R–P, 3 m (10 ft)
Malus 'Golden Hornet', W, 8 m (26 ft)
Malus 'Gorgeous', R/W, 5 m (16 ft)
Malus 'Hopa', R, 8 m (26 ft)
Malus 'Liset', R, 5 m (16 ft)
Malus 'Montreal Beauty', W, 6 m (20 ft)
Malus 'Professor Sprenger', R/W, 6 m (20 ft)
Malus 'Rosseau', R–P, 6 m (20 ft)
Malus 'Wintergold', W, 10 m (33 ft)
Malus 'Wisley Crab', R–P, 6 m (20 ft)
Malus 'Zita', R, 3 m (10 ft)
Malus floribunda, R, 8 m (26 ft)
Malus hartwegii (×), W, 8 m (26 ft)
Malus micromalus (×), R, 4 m (13 ft)
Metasequoia glyptostroboides, 35 m (115 ft)
Picea likiangensis var. *balfouriana*, 40 m (135 ft)
Pinus leucodermis 'Satellit', 20 m (65 ft)
Pinus pinea, 20 m (65 ft)
Pinus ponderosa, 40 m (135 ft)
Pinus radiata, 35 m (115 ft)
Pinus strobus, 40 m (135 ft)
Pinus wallichiana, 30 m (100 ft)
Prunus avium 'Decumana', W, 15 m (50 ft)
Prunus fontanesiana (×), W, 9 m (30 ft)
Prunus maackii, W, 10 m (33 ft)
Prunus sargentii, R, 8 m (26 ft)
Prunus serrula, W, 8 m (26 ft)
Prunus subhirtella 'Pendula', R, 3 m (10 ft)

Prunus yedoensis (×), W, 15 m (50 ft)
Pseudolarix kaempferi, 20 m (65 ft)
Pseudotsuga menziesii 'Brevifolia', 30 m (100 ft)
Pyrus communis, W, 15 m (50 ft)
Pyrus elaeagnifolia, W, 6 m (20 ft)
Rhus trichocarpa, G, 5 m (16 ft)
Sciadopitys verticillata, 20 m (65 ft)
Sophora japonica, W, 25 m (80 ft)
Ulmus glabra 'Horizontalis', G, 10 m (33 ft)

○ ❀ ◎
39. Wholly or partly poisonous.

Chamaecyparis lawsoniana 'Lana', 6 m (20 ft)
Chamaecyparis lawsoniana 'Lutea', 10 m (33 ft)
Chamaecyparis lawsoniana 'Pendula', 20 m (65 ft)
Chamaecyparis lawsoniana 'Winston Churchill', 8 m (26 ft)
Chamaecyparis nootkatensis 'Pendula', 10 m (33 ft)
Juniperus recurva var. *coxil*, 30 m (100 ft)
Prunus avium 'Decumana', W, 15 m (50 ft)
Prunus avium 'Plena', W, 18 m (60 ft)
Prunus fontanesiana (×), W, 9 m (30 ft)
Prunus maackii, W, 10 m (33 ft)
Prunus sargentii, R, 8 m (26 ft)
Prunus sargentii 'Rancho', R, 8 m (26 ft)
Prunus serrula, W, 8 m (26 ft)
Prunus serrulata 'Kiku-shidare-sakura', R, 3 m (10 ft)
Prunus serrulata 'Shimidsu-Zakura', W, 5 m (16 ft)
Prunus serrulata var. *hupehensis*, W, 10 m (33 ft)
Prunus subhirtella 'Pendula', R, 3 m (10 ft)
Prunus yedoensis (×), W, 15 m (50 ft)
Rhus trichocarpa, G, 5 m (16 ft)

○ ❀ ⊕
40. Suitable as a specimen plant.

Araucaria araucana, 20 m (65 ft)
Betula papyrifera, Y–G, 25 m (80 ft)
Betula pendula 'Dalecarlica', Y–G, 20 m (65 ft)
Betula pubescens, Y–G, 20 m (65 ft)
Catalpa erubescens (×), W, 10 m (33 ft)
Catalpa ovata, W, 10 m (33 ft)
Cedrus atlantica 'Glauca', 30 m (100 ft)
Cedrus deodara, 20 m (65 ft)
Cedrus deodara 'Aurea', 10 m (33 ft)
Cedrus libani, –40 m (135 ft)
Cercis siliquastrum, P, 7 m (23 ft)
Chamaecyparis lawsoniana 'Lana', 6 m (20 ft)
Chamaecyparis lawsoniana 'Lutea', 10 m (33 ft)
Chamaecyparis lawsoniana 'Pendula', 20 m (65 ft)
Chamaecyparis lawsoniana 'Winston Churchill', 8 m (26 ft)
Chamaecyparis nootkatensis 'Pendula', 10 m (33 ft)
Cladrastis lutea, W/R, 10 m (33 ft)
Cupressus arizonica, 20 m (65 ft)
Eucalyptus niphophila, G, 7 m (23 ft)
Fraxinus excelsior, Y–G, 40 m (135 ft)
Fraxinus excelsior 'Aurea', Y–G, 15 m (50 ft)
Fraxinus excelsior 'Jaspidea', Y–G, 20 m (65 ft)
Ginkgo biloba, 20 m (65 ft)
Gymnocladus dioicus, G/W, 20 m (65 ft)
Juniperus recurva var. *coxil*, 30 m (100 ft)
Larix decidua, 25 m (80 ft)
Larix gmelinii, 20 m (65 ft)
Larix laricina, 30 m (100 ft)
Liriodendron tulipifera, Y–G, O, 20 m (65 ft)
Liriodendron tulipifera 'Fastigiatum', Y–G, 15 m (50 ft)
Magnolia grandiflora, W, 20 m (65 ft)
Malus 'Adams', R, 10 m (33 ft)
Malus 'Butterball', R, 6 m (20 ft)
Malus 'Echtermeyer', R–P, 3 m (10 ft)
Malus 'Golden Hornet', W, 8 m (26 ft)
Malus 'Gorgeous', R/W, 5 m (16 ft)
Malus 'Hopa', R, 8 m (26 ft)
Malus 'Liset', R, 5 m (16 ft)
Malus 'Montreal Beauty', W, 6 m (20 ft)
Malus 'Professor Sprenger', R/W, 6 m (20 ft)
Malus 'Rosseau', R–P, 6 m (20 ft)
Malus 'Wintergold', W, 10 m (33 ft)
Malus 'Wisley Crab', R–P, 6 m (20 ft)
Malus floribunda, R, 8 m (26 ft)
Malus hartwegii (×), W, 8 m (26 ft)
Malus micromalus (×), R, 4 m (13 ft)
Metasequoia glyptostroboides, 35 m (115 ft)
Picea likiangensis var. *balfouriana*, 40 m (135 ft)
Pinus heldreichii, 20 m (65 ft)
Pinus leucodermis 'Satellit', 20 m (65 ft)
Pinus pinea, 20 m (65 ft)

Pinus ponderosa, 40 m (135 ft)
Pinus radiata, 35 m (115 ft)
Pinus strobus, 40 m (135 ft)
Pinus wallichiana, 30 m (100 ft)
Prunus avium 'Decumana', W, 15 m (50 ft)
Prunus avium 'Plena', W, 18 m (60 ft)
Prunus maackii, W, 10 m (33 ft)
Prunus serrulata 'Kiku-shidare-sakura', R, 3 m (10 ft)
Prunus subhirtella 'Pendula', R, 3 m (10 ft)
Pseudotsuga menziesii 'Brevifolia', 30 m (100 ft)
Rhus trichocarpa, G, 5 m (16 ft)
Sciadopitys verticillata, 20 m (65 ft)
Sequoiadendron giganteum, 70 m (230 ft)
Ulmus glabra 'Camperdownii', G, 5 m (16 ft)
Ulmus glabra 'Horizontalis', G, 10 m (33 ft)
Ulmus minor 'Sarniensis', G, 9 m (30 ft)
Ulmus minor 'Wredei', G, 9 m (30 ft)
Zelkova abelicea, G, 10 m (33 ft)

Shrubs and trees

○ ⦿ ❀ ❀ ⊛
41. With attractive berries and fruits.

Catalpa bignonioides, W, 10 m (33 ft)
Chamaecyparis pisifera 'Filifera Aurea', 5 m (16 ft)
Koelreuteria paniculata, Y, 5 m (16 ft)
Photinia villosa, W, 5 m (16 ft)
Prunus amygdalopersica (×), R, 6 m (20 ft)
Prunus cerasifera 'Atropurpurea', W, 6 m (20 ft)
Prunus mahaleb, W, 10 m (33 ft)
Rhus typhina, R, 5 m (16 ft)
Rhus typhina 'Laciniata', G, 5 m (16 ft)
Xanthoceras sorbifolium, W, 8 m (26 ft)

○ ⦿ ❀ ◎
42. Wholly or partly poisonous.

Chamaecyparis pisifera 'Filifera Aurea', 5 m (16 ft)
Prunus 'Kursar', R, 5 m (16 ft)
Prunus manaleb, W, 10 m (33 ft)
Prunus persica 'Klara Mayer', R, 7 m (23 ft)
Prunus serrula 'Amanogawa', R, 9 m (30 ft)
Prunus serrulata 'Kwanzan', R, 12 m (40 ft)
Prunus triloba, R, 2 m (6 ft)
Rhus typhina, R, 5 m (16 ft)
Rhus typhina 'Laciniata', G, 5 m (16 ft)

○ ⦿ ❀ ⊕
43. Suitable as a specimen plant.

Catalpa bignonioides, W, 10 m (33 ft)
Chamaecyparis pisifera 'Filifera Aurea', 5 m (16 ft)
Koelreuteria paniculata, Y, 5 m (16 ft)
Photinia villosa, W, 5 m (16 ft)
Prunus serrula 'Amanogawa', R, 9 m (30 ft)
Prunus triloba, R, 2 m (6 ft)
Rhus typhina, R, 5 m (16 ft)
Rhus typhina 'Laciniata', G, 5 m (16 ft)

FULL SUN; MOIST SITES

Herbaceous perennials

○ ⊗ ◎
44. No special features.

Butomus umbellatus, R, –1.2 m (4 ft)
Eichhornia crassipes, V, –10 cm (4 in)
Helianthus salicifolius, Y, –2.5 m (8 ft)
Hippuris vulgaris, Y, 30 cm (12 in)
Phalaris arundinacea 'Picta', W, 1 m (3 ft)
Pontederia cordata, V, –70 cm (28 in)

○ ⊗ ◎ ❀
45. Evergreen.

Phormium tenax 'Atropurpureum', V, 2 m (6 ft)

○ ⊗ ◎ ⊕
46. Suitable as a specimen plant.

Phormium tenax 'Atropurpureum', V, 2 m (6 ft)
Rheum alexandrae, G–Y, –90 cm (3 ft)
Rheum palmatum, W–Y, 2.5 m (8 ft)
Rheum palmatum 'Bowles', R, 2.5 m (8 ft)

○ ⊗ ◐ ⊗
47. Suitable for rock gardens and crevices in paving.

Gentiana septemfida, V–B, –30 cm (12 in)
Nierembergia repens, W, 5 cm (2 in)

○ ⊗ ◐ ⊖
48. Suitable for ground cover.

Gentiana septemfida, V–B, –30 cm (12 in)

○ ⊗ ◐ ⊗
49. Suitable for cutting.

Dactylorhiza maculata, P, –50 cm (20 in)
Hibiscus moscheutos, R–P, –2 m (6 ft)
Vernonia fassiculata, P, 1.5 m (5 ft)

○ ⊗ ⊕
50. Water lilies.

Nymphaea caerulea, V, 15 cm (6 in)
Nymphaea pygmaea, W, 15 cm (6 in)
Nymphaea hybrid 'Aurora', O, 15 cm (6 in)
Nymphaea hybrid 'Gloriosa', R, 15 cm (6 in)
Nymphaea hybrid 'Hollandia', R, 15 cm (6 in)
Nymphaea hybrid 'James Brydon', R, 15 cm (6 in)
Nymphaea hybrid 'Laydekeri Purpurata', R, 15 cm (6 in)
Nymphaea hybrid 'Marliacea chromatella', Y, 15 cm (6 in)
Nymphaea hybrid 'Sioux', O/R, 15 cm (6 in)
Nymphaea hybrid 'Virginalis', Y, 15 cm (6 in)

Bulbs

○ ⊗ ⊚
51. No special features.

Zigadenus glaucus, Y, 80 cm (32 in)

Shrubs

○ ⊗ ⊛
52. No peculiarities.

Amorpha fruticosa, P, 5 m (16 ft)

○ ⊗ ⊛ ⊛
53. Evergreen

Chamaedaphne calyculata, var. nana, W, 30 cm (12 in)
Erica cinerea 'Cevennes', P, 25 cm (10 in)
Erica cinerea 'Golden Drop', R–P, 25 cm (10 in)
Erica cinerea 'Pallas', P, 35 cm (14 in)
Erica cinerea 'Pink Ice', R–P, 20 cm (8 in)

○ ⊗ ⊛ ⊛
54. With attractive berries or fruits.

Cornus amomum, Y–W, 4 m (13 ft)

○ ⊗ ⊛ ◎
55. Wholly or partly poisonous.

Erica cinerea 'Cevennes', P, 25 cm (10 in)
Erica cinerea 'Golden Drop', R–P, 25 cm (10 in)
Erica cinerea 'Pallas', P, 35 cm (14 in)
Erica cinerea 'Pink Ice', R–P, 20 cm (8 in)

○ ⊗ ⊛ ⊕
56. Suitable as a specimen plant.

Magnolia kobus, W, 10 m (33 ft)

○ ⊗ ⊛ ⊕⊛
57. Suitable for ground cover.

Erica cinerea 'Cevennes', P, 25 cm (10 in)
Erica cinerea 'Golden Drop', R–P, 25 cm (10 in)
Erica cinerea 'Pallas', P. 35 cm (14 in)
Erica cinerea 'Pink Ice', R–P, 20 cm (8 in)

○ ⊗ ⊛ ⊗
58. Suitable for cutting.

Eriophorum latifolium, W, 50 cm (20 in)

Trees

○ ⊗ ✳ ⊛
59. Evergreen.

Pseudotsuga menziesii, 30 m (100 ft)

○ ⊗ ✳ ⊛
60. With attractive fruits or berries.

Pseudotsuga menziesii, 30 m (100 ft)
Taxodium distichum, 30 m (100 ft)

○ ⊗ ✳ ⊕
61. Suitable as a speciman plant.

Betula nigra, Y–G, 20 m (65 ft)
Pseudotsuga menziesii, 30 m (100 ft)
Taxodium distichum, 30 m (100 ft)

FULL SUN; DRY OR MOIST SITES

Trees

○ ⊖ ⊗ ✳ ⊛
62. With attractive fruits or berries.

Betula jaquemontii, Y–G, 12 m (40 ft)

○ ⊖ ⊗ ✳ ⊕
63. Suitable as a specimen plant.

Betula jaquemontii, Y–G, 12 m (40 ft)

FULL SUN; DRY SITES

Annuals

○ ⊖ ☉ ⊗
64. Suitable for rock gardens and crevices in paving.

Adonis aestivalis, R, –50 cm (20 in)
Cladanthus arabicus, Y, –30 cm (12 in)
Delosperma pruinosum, R–P, 50 cm (20 in)
Gazania hybrid 'Ministar', var. col., 25 cm (10 in)
Gazania hybrid 'Ministar Yellow', Y, 25 cm (10 in)
Helipterum manglesii 'Rosea', R/Y, –50 cm (20 in)
Mentzelia lindleyi, Y, –60 cm (24 in)
Mesembryanthemum crystallinum, var. col., 15 cm (6 in)
Pelargonium zonale 'Mustang', R, 30 cm (12 in)
Pelargonium zonale 'Ringo Dolly', R, 30 cm (12 in)
Portulaca hybrid 'Sunglo Orchid', P, 25 cm (10 in)

○ ⊖ ⊙ ⊗

65. Suitable for cutting.

Adonis aestivalis, R, –50 cm (20 in)
Gypsophila elegans 'Alba', W, 60 cm (24 in)
Helipterum manglesii 'Rosea', R/Y, –50 cm (20 in)
Helipterum roseum, R/Y, –60 cm (24 in)
Lavatera trimestris 'Sunset', R–P, 1 m (3 ft)
Rudbeckia hirta, Y–O, –1 m (3 ft)
Rudbeckia hirta var. *pulcherrima*, O, –60 cm (24 in)

Herbaceous perennials

○ ⊖ ◐

66. No special features.

Alyssum saxatile 'Dudley Neville', Y, –30 cm (12 in)
Marrubium incanum, W, –40 cm (16 in)
Ruta graveolens, Y, –60 cm (24 in)

○ ⊖ ◐ ✿

67. Evergreen.

Acantholimon olivieri, R, 20 cm (8 in)
Dryas octopetala, W, 15 cm (6 in)

○ ⊖ ◐ ✾

68. With attractive fruits or berries.

Acaena anserinifolia, R–P, 15 cm (6 in)
Acaena buchananii, Brown, 5 cm (2 in)
Acaena novae-zelandiae, R, 10 cm (4 in)

○ ⊖ ◐ ◉

69. Wholly or partly poisonous.

Adonis vernalis, Y, –30 cm (12 in)
Eryngium alpinum, V, –80 cm (32 in)
Eryngium amethystinum, V, 80 cm (32 in)
Eryngium planum, V, 1 m (3 ft)
Euphorbia myrsinites, Y, –20 cm (8 in)

○ ⊖ ◐ ⊕

70. Suitable as a specimen plant.

Echinops bannaticus, V, –1.1 m (3½ ft)
Echinops bannaticus 'Blue Globe', P–V, 1.1 m (3½ ft)
Helictotrichon sempervirens, W, 1.5 m (5 ft)
Stipa gigantea, W, –1 m (3 ft)

○ ⊖ ◐ ⊗

71. Suitable for rock gardens and crevices in paving.

Acaena anserinifolia, R–P, 15 cm (6 in)
Acaena buchananii, Brown, 5 cm (2 in)
Acantholimon olivieri, R, 20 cm (8 in)
Adonis vernalis, Y, –30 cm (12 in)
Aethionema hybrid 'Warley Ruber', P, –25 cm (10 in)
Alyssum montanum ssp. *montanum*, Y, –20 cm (8 in)
Alyssum saxatile, Y, –30 cm (12 in)
Anthemis cupaniana, W, 60 cm (24 in)
Anthemis tinctoria, Y, –80 cm (32 in)
Arabis aubrietioides, P–V, –25 cm (10 in)
Arabis caucasica, W, –30 in (12 in)
Asphodeline lutea, Y, –80 cm (32 in)
Aubrieta libanotica, P–V, –10 cm (4 in)
Aubrieta hybrid, var. col., –10 cm (4 in)
Campanula poscharskyana, V, –20 cm (8 in)
Carlina acaulis, W, –15 cm (6 in)
Cerastium biebersteinii, W, 30 cm (12 in)
Chrysanthemum millefoliatum, Y, –50 cm (20 in)
Chrysogonum virginianum, Y, –40 cm (16 in)
Dianthus allwoodii (×), R, –35 cm (14 in)
Dianthus deltoides hybrid, R, –30 cm (12 in)
Dianthus gratianopolitanus, R, –15 cm (6 in)
Dianthus petraeus, W, –25 cm (10 in)
Drosanthemum pulchellum, R–P, –10 cm (4 in)
Dryas octopetala, W, 15 cm (6 in)
Eryngium alpinum, V, –80 cm (32 in)
Eryngium amethystinum, V, 80 cm (32 in)
Erysimum decumbens, Y, 25 cm (10 in)
Euphorbia myrsinites, Y, –20 cm (8 in)
Euphorbia polychorma, Y, –40 cm (16 in)
Gypsophila repens 'Rosea', R–P, 10 cm (4 in)
Gypsophila hybrid 'Rosenschleier', W/P, 30 cm (12 in)

Helictotrichon sempervirens, W, 1.5 m (5 ft)
Hypericum olympicum, Y, –30 cm (12 in)
Inula ensifolia 'Compacta', Y, 20 cm (8 in)
Jovibarba heuffelii, Y, 15 cm (6 in)
Leontopodium alpinum, W, 20 cm (8 in)
Linum perenne, B, –60 cm (24 in)
Origanum vulgare, P, –60 cm (24 in)
Perovskia atriplicifolia 'Blue Spire', V–B, 1.5 m (5 ft)
Saponaria ocymoides, P, 30 cm (12 in)
Sedum cauticolum 'Robustum', R, –25 cm (10 in)
Stipa barbata, W, –1 m (3 ft)

○ ⊖ ◐ ◐

72. Suitable for ground cover.

Acaena anserinifolia, R–P, 15 cm (6 in)
Acaena buchananii, Brown, 5 cm (2 in)
Acaena novae-zelandiae, R, 10 cm (4 in)
Acantholimon olivieri, R, 20 cm (8 in)
Arabis aubrietioides, P–V, –25 cm (10 in)
Arabis caucasica, W, –30 cm (12 in)
Cerastium biebersteinii, W, 30 cm (12 in)
Dianthus deltoides hybrid, R, –30 cm (12 in)
Dianthus petraeus, W, –25 cm (10 in)
Dianthus plumarius, R, –25 cm (10 in)
Dryas octopetala, W, 15 cm (6 in)
Hypericum olympicum, Y, –30 cm (12 in)
Saponaria ocymoides, P, 30 cm (12 in)

○ ⊖ ◐ ⊗

73. Suitable for cutting.

Achnatherum calamagrostis, Y–W, –1 m (3 ft)
Anthemis cupaniana, W, 60 cm (24 in)
Anthemis tinctoria, Y, –80 cm (32 in)
Arabis caucasica, W, –30 cm (12 in)
Catananche caerulea, P–V, –80 cm (32 in)
Centaurea macrocephala, Y, –90 cm (3 ft)
Chamaemelum nobile, W, 30 cm (12 in)
Chrysanthemum millefoliatum, Y, –50 cm (20 in)
Dianthus allwoodii (×), R, –35 cm (14 in)
Dianthus gratianopolitanus, R, –15 cm (6 in)
Dictamnus albus, R–P, –1 m (3 ft)
Echinops bannaticus, V, –1.1 m (3½ ft)
Echinops bannaticus 'Blue Globe', P–V, 1.1 m (3½ ft)
Eryngium alpinum, V, –80 cm (32 in)
Eryngium amethystinum, V, 80 cm (32 in)
Eryngium planum, V, 1 m (3 ft)
Erysimum decumbens, Y, 25 cm (10 in)
Gypsophila paniculata, W/V, 1 m (3 ft)
Leontopodium alpinum, W, 20 cm (8 in)
Linum perenne, B, –60 cm (24 in)
Stipa barbata, W, –1 m (3 ft)
Stipa gigantea, W, –1 m (3 ft)
Veronica spicata 'Erica', P, –50 cm (20 in)
Veronica spicata ssp. *spicata*, V, –50 cm (20 in)

Bulbs

○ ⊖ ◈

74. No special features.

Allium cernuum, P, 60 cm (24 in)
Allium flavum, Y, 30 cm (12 in)

○ ⊖ ◈ ⊕

75. Chalky soil; suitable as a specimen plant.

Allium giganteum, P, 1.75 m (5¾ ft)

○ ⊖ ◈ ⊗

76. Suitable for rock gardens and crevices in paving.

Allium karataviense, R, 30 cm (12 in)
Allium oreophilum, P–R, 15 cm (6 in)
Allium ursinum, W, –40 cm (16 in)
Iris bucharica, W/Y, 45 cm (18 in)
Iris danfordiae, Y, 15 cm (16 in)

○ ⊜ ⚙ ⊗

77. Suitable for cutting.

Acidanthera bicolor var. *murielae*, W, –40 cm (16 in)
Allium christophii, P–V, 60 cm (24 in)
Allium giganteum, P, 1.75 m (5¾ ft)
Allium sphaerocephalon, P, –60 cm (24 in)

Tubers

○ ⊜ ⚛ ⊗

78. Suitable for rock gardens and crevices in paving.

Iris chamaeiris, P, –25 cm (10 in)
Iris germanica 'Radiant Apogee', Y/W, 70 cm (28 in)
Iris germanica 'Rippling Waters', V, 80 cm (32 in)
Iris germanica 'Stepping Out', P/W, 80 cm (32 in)
Iris germanica 'White Lightning', W, 80 cm (32 in)

Shrubs

79. Evergreen.

Helianthemum hybrid 'Cerise Queen', R, 25 cm (10 in)
Helianthemum hybrid 'Fire Dragon', R, –25 cm (10 in)
Helianthemum hybrid 'Golden Queen', Y, –25 cm (10 in)
Iberis sempervirens 'Snowflake', W, 30 cm (12 in)
Pinus pumila, 3 m (10 ft)
Pinus pumila 'Glauca', 3 m (10 ft)
Pinus sylvestris 'Beuvronensis', 1 m (3 ft)
Rosmarinus officinalis, B, 1 m (3 ft)
Thymus citriodorus (×) 'Aureus', V, –25 cm (10 in)
Thymus serpyllum 'Albus', W, 10 cm (4 in)
Thymus serpyllum 'Pygmaeus', P, 10 cm (4 in)

○ ⊜ ⚙ ⊛

80. With attractive fruits or berries.

Pinus pumila, 3 m (10 ft)
Pinus pumila 'Glauca', 3 m (10 ft)
Rosa rubiginosa, R, 2.5 m (8 ft)
Vitis vinifera 'Brandt', Y–G, 7 m (23 ft)

○ ⊜ ⚙ ◎

81. Wholly or partly poisonous.

Cytisus ardoini, Y, 20 cm (8 in)
Cytisus decumbens, Y, 1 m (3 ft)

○ ⊜ ⚙ ⊕

82. Chalky soil; suitable as a specimen plant.

Buddleia alternifolia, V, 4 m (13 ft)
Pinus sylvestris 'Beuvronensis', 1 m (3 ft)
Robinia hispida, R, 3 m (10 ft)

○ ⊜ ⚙ ⊗

83. Suitable for rock gardens and crevices in paving.

Cytisus ardoini, Y, 20 cm (8 in)
Cytisus decumbens, Y, 1 m (3 ft)
Eriogonum umbellatum, Y, 30 cm (12 in)
Helianthemum hybrid 'Cerise Queen', R, 25 cm (10 in)
Helianthemum hybrid 'Fire Dragon', R, –25 cm (10 in)
Helianthemum hybrid 'Golden Queen', Y, –25 cm (10 in)
Iberis sempervirens 'Snowflake', W, 30 cm (12 in)
Lavandula angustifolia, P–V, –60 cm (24 in)
Lavandula stoechas ssp. *stoechas*, P, –60 cm (24 in)
Perovskia atriplicifolia 'Blue Spire', V–B, 1.5 m (5 ft)
Pinus pumila, 3 m (10 ft)
Pinus pumila 'Glauca', 3 m (10 ft)
Thymus citriodorus (×) 'Aureus', V, –25 cm (10 in)
Thymus serpyllum 'Albus', W, 10 cm (4 in)
Thymus serpyllum 'Pygmaeus', P, 10 cm (4 in)

○ ⊜ ⚙ ⬛

84. Suitable for hedging.

Rosa rubiginosa, R, 2.5 m (8 ft)
Rosmarinus officinalis, B, 1 m (3 ft)

○ ⊜ ⚙ ◔

85. Suitable for ground cover.

Cytisus decumbens, Y, 1 m (3 ft)
Iberis sempervirens 'Snowflake', W, 30 cm (12 in)
Thymus serpyllum 'Albus', W, 10 cm (4 in)
Thymus serpyllum 'Pygmaeus', P, 10 cm (4 in)

○ ⊜ ⚙ ⊗

86. Suitable for cutting.

Buddleia alternifolia, V, 4 m (13 ft)
Lavandula angustifolia, P–V, –60 cm (24 in)
Lavandula stoechas ssp. *stoechas*, P, –60 cm (24 in)
Rosa rubiginosa, R, 2.5 m (8 ft)

Trees

○ ⊜ ❋ ❀

87. Evergreen.

Pinus nigra ssp. *nigra*, 20 m (65 ft)
Pinus parviflora 'Glauca', 15 m (50 ft)
Pinus sylvestris, 35 m (115 ft)
Pinus sylvestris 'Watereri', –7 m (23 ft)

○ ⊜ ❋ ⊛

88. With attractive fruits or berries.

Betula albosinensis septentrionalis, Y–G, 25 m (80 ft)
Betula costata, Y–G, 15 m (50 ft)
Betula pendula, Y–G, 20 m (65 ft)
Betula pendula 'Youngii', Y–G, 4 m (13 ft)
Gleditsia aquatica, G, 15 m (50 ft)
Gleditsia japonica, G, 20 m (65 ft)
Gleditsia macrantha, G, 15 m (50 ft)
Gleditsia triacanthos 'Sunburst', Y, 8 m (26 ft)
Pinus nigra ssp. *nigra*, 20 m (65 ft)
Pinus sylvestris, 35 m (115 ft)

○ ⊜ ❋ ◎

89. Wholly or partly poisonous.

Robinia pseudoacacia 'Frisia', W, 9 m (30 ft)
Robinia psuedoacacia 'Myrtifolia', W, 10 m (33 ft)
Robinia pseudoacacia 'Tortuosa', W, 15 m (50 ft)

○ ⊜ ❋ ⊕

90. Suitable as a specimen plant.

Betula albosinensis septentrionalis, Y–G, 25 m (80 ft)
Betula costata, Y–G, 15 m (50 ft)
Betula pendula, Y–G, 20 m (65 ft)
Betula pendula 'Youngii', Y–G, 4 m (13 ft)
Fraxinus ornus, W, 10 m (33 ft)
Gleditsia aquatica, G, 15 m (50 ft)
Gleditsia japonica, G, 20 m (65 ft)
Gleditsia macrantha, G, 15 m (50 ft)
Gleditsia triacanthos 'Sunburst', Y, 8 m (26 ft)
Pinus nigra ssp. *nigra*, 20 m (65 ft)
Pinus parviflora 'Glauca', 15 m (50 ft)
Robinia pseudoacacia 'Frisia', W, 9 m (30 ft)
Robinia pseudoacacia 'Myrtifolia', W, 10 m (33 ft)
Robinia pseudoacacia 'Tortuosa', W, 15 m (50 ft)

○ ⊜ ❋ ⚙

91. Also suitable for hedging.

Carpinus betulus, Y–G, 20 m (65 ft)

FULL SUN AND SEMI-SHADE

Annuals

○ ◐ ☉
92. No special features.

Ageratum 'Dondo', V–B, 15 cm (6 in)
Ageratum houstonianum, V–B, –60 cm (24 in)
Asperula orientalis, B, 25 cm (10 in)
Brassica oleracea 'Plumosa', Y–W, 25 cm (10 in)
Calceolaria integrifolia, Y, 60 cm (24 in)
Calceolaria tripartita, Y, –70 cm (28 in)
Chamomilla recutita, W–Y, 40 cm (16 in)
Collinsia heterophylla, V–W, 30 cm (12 in)
Cuphea ignea, R, 30 cm (12 in)
Cynoglossum amabile, B/W/R, –60 cm (24 in)
Impatiens glandulifera, var. col., 75 cm (30 in)
Linaria bipartita hybrid, P–V, –30 cm (12 in)
Lobelia erinus, var. col., –25 cm (10 in)
Lobelia erinus compacta 'Cambridge Blue', V–B, 12 cm (4¾ in)
Lobelia erinus compacta 'Rosamond', R–P, –12 cm (4¾ in)
Lobelia erinus compacta 'Snowball', W, –12 cm (4¾ in)
Lobelia erinus pendula 'Sapphire', P–V, W, –30 cm (12 in)
Salvia splendens, R/W, 50 cm (20 in)
Salvia viridis, R–P, V, 50 cm (20 in)
Tagetes erecta hybrid 'First Lady', Y, 30 cm (12 in)
Tagetes erecta hybrid 'First Whites', W, –35 cm (14 in)
Tagetes erecta hybrid 'Golden Jubilee', Y–O, –35 cm (14 in)
Tagetes erecta hybrid 'Orange Jubilee', Y–O, –35 cm (14 in)
Tagetes patula hybrid 'Dainty Marietta', Y/R, 20 cm (8 in)
Tagetes patula hybrid 'Florence', O–Y, 20 cm (8 in)
Tagetes patula hybrid 'Honeycomb', O–R, –20 cm (8 in)
Tagetes patula hybrid 'Queen Bee', O–Y, 20 cm (8 in)
Tagetes patula hybrid 'Silvia', Y, 20 cm (8 in)
Tagetes patula hybrid 'Yellow Jacket', Y, –25 cm (10 in)
Tagetes tenuifolia hybrid 'Golden Gem', Y–O, –25 cm (10 in)
Tagetes tenuifolia hybrid 'Lemon Queen', Y, –25 cm (10 in)
Tagetes tenuifolia hybrid 'Pumila', Y–O, –25 cm (10 in)
Tropaeolum peregrinum, Y, 3 m (10 ft)

○ ◐ ☉ ❀
93. With attractive fruits or berries.

Cucurbita pepo var. *ovifera*, O–Y, 60 cm (24 in)
Lunaria annua 'Variegata', P, –1 m (3 ft)

○ ◐ ☉ ◉
94. Wholly or partly poisonous.

Lupinus hartwegii, B/W/R, –70 cm (28 in)
Lupinus hybrid 'Pixie Delight', var. col., –30 cm (12 in)
Nicotiana alata hybrid, var. col., –30 cm (12 in)
Senecio bicolor 'Silverdust', Y, 60 cm (24 in)

○ ◐ ☉ ⊕
95. Suitable as a specimen plant.

Silybum marianum, R–P, 1.5 m (5 ft)

○ ◐ ☉ ⊗
96. Suitable for rock gardens and crevices in paving.

Borago officinalis, B, 60 cm (24 in)
Linum grandiflorum 'Bright Eyes', W/R, –40 cm (16 in)
Linum grandiflorum 'Rubrum', R, –40 cm (16 in)
Polygonum capitatum, R, 15 cm (16 in)

○ ◐ ☉ ⊗
97. Suitable for cutting.

Antirrhinum majus 'Butterfly Little Darling', var. col., 75 cm (30 in)
Antirrhinum majus 'Madame Butterfly', O, 35 cm (14 in)
Antirrhinum majus 'Panorama', R–Y, 80 cm (32 in)
Borago officinalis, B, 60 cm (24 in)
Briza maxima, 50 cm (20 in)
Bromus macrostachys, 60 cm (24 in)
Calendula officinalis, Y–O, 60 cm (24 in)
Calendula officinalis 'Golden King', Y–O, 60 cm (24 in)
Calendula officinalis 'Plena', Y–O, 60 cm (24 in)
Calendula officinalis 'Radio', O, 60 cm (24 in)
Lunaria annua 'Variegata', P, –1 m (3 ft)

Lupinus hartwegii, B/W/R, –70 cm (28 in)
Lupinus hybrid 'Pixie Delight', var. col., –30 cm (12 in)
Matthiola incana, R–P, –75 cm (30 in)
Nemesia strumosa, var. col., –60 cm (24 in)
Nicotiana alata hybrid, var. col., –30 cm (12 in)
Polygonum orientale, R–P, –3 m (10 ft)
Salvia farinacea, V–B, 80 cm (32 in)
Scabiosa atropurpurea, var. col., 1 m (3 ft)
Schizanthus wisetonensis hybrid, var. col., –40 cm (16 in)
Setaria italica, 1 m (3 ft)
Setaria italica 'Macrochaeta', 1 m (3 ft)
Tagetes erecta hybrid 'Orange Jubilee', Y–O, –35 cm (14 in)
Tropaeolum majus, var. col., 3 m (10 ft)
Tropaeolum majus 'Empress of India', R, 30 cm (12 in)
Tropaeolum majus 'Jewel', var. col., 30 cm (12 in)
Tropaeolum majus 'Whirleybird Cherry Rose', R, 30 cm (12 in)
Tropaeolum majus 'Whirleybird Orange', Y–O, 30 cm (12 in)
Tropaeolum peltophorum, O, 4 m (13 ft)

Biennials

○ ◐ ☉
98. No special features.

Bellis perennis 'Hortensis', W/R, 15 cm (6 in)
Salvia sclarea, B–W, 1.5 m (5 ft)
Verbascum phlomoides, Y, 60 cm (24 in)
Verbascum 'Polarsonne', Grey–B, 30 cm (12 in)

○ ◐ ☉ ❀
99. With attractive fruits or berries.

Lunaria annua, P, –1 m (3 ft)

○ ◐ ☉ ⊕
100. Suitable as a specimen plant.

Verbascum bombyciferum, Y, 2 m (6 ft)
Verbascum densiflorum, Y, 2 m (6 ft)

○ ◐ ☉ ⊗
101. Suitable for rock gardens and crevices in paving.

Myosotis sylvatica, var. col., –20 cm (8 in)
Oenothera caespitosa, Y, –80 cm (32 in)
Viola tricolor, P/Y/W, –30 cm (12 in)
Viola wittrockiana hybrid, var. col., –30 cm (12 in)

○ ◐ ☉ ⊗
102. Suitable for cutting.

Lunaria annua, P, –1 m (3 ft)
Viola tricolor, P/Y/W, –30 cm (12 in)
Viola wittrockiana hybrid, var. col., –30 cm (12 in)

Herbaceous perennials

○ ◐ ◑
103. No special features.

Agastache foeniculum, P, 70 cm (28 in)
Aponogeton distachyus, W, 10 cm (4 in)
Asperula tinctoria, W, 50 cm (20 in)
Campanula lactiflora 'Pouffe', V, 30 cm (12 in)
Geranium sanguineum var. *prostratum*, R, –25 cm (10 in)
Geranium sanguineum var. *sanguineum*, R–P, –25 cm (10 in)
Gillenia trifoliata, W/R, –70 cm (28 in)
Koeleria glauca, G–B, –30 cm (12 in)
Leonurus cardiaca, W/R, 1 m (3 ft)
Lysimachia punctata, Y, –1 m (3 ft)
Lysimachia verticillaris, Y, –1 m (3 ft)
Melissa officinalis 'Aurea', P, –75 cm (30 in)
Miscanthus sinensis 'Strictus', 1.2 m (4 ft)
Nepeta faassenii, (×), P–V, –45 cm (18 in)
Nepeta grandiflora, V–B, –80 cm (32 in)
Oenothera fruticosa 'Youngii', Y, –50 cm (20 in)
Orchis mascula, P, 40 cm (16 in)
Polemonium reptans, V, 30 cm (12 in)
Sanguinaria obtusa, P, –1 m (3 ft)
Stachys grandiflora, P, 70 cm (28 in)
Stachys officinalis, P, –60 cm (24 in)
Symphytum × *uplandicum* 'Variegatum', P, 1 m (3 ft)
Tropaeolum speciosum, R, –3 m (10 ft)

○ ◐ ○ ❀
104. Evergreen.

Geranium palmatum, R–P, –80 cm (32 in)
Polygonum affine 'Superbum', R–P, 25 cm (10 in)
Sagina subulata, W, 7 cm (2¾ in)

○ ◐ ○ ❀
105. With attractive fruits or berries.

Humulus lupulus, Y/G 5 m (16 ft)
Lunaria rediviva, P, 1 m (3 ft)
Physalis alkekengi var. *franchetii*, W, 1 m (3 ft)
Phytolacca acinosa, W, 2 m (6 ft)
Sambucus ebulus, W, 2 m (6 ft)

○ ◐ ○ ◎
106. Wholly or partly poisonous.

Anemone hupehensis var. *japonica*, R, 75 cm (30 in)
Anemone japonica 'Elegans', W, –1 m (3 ft)
Anemone sylvestris 'Macrantha', W, –40 cm (16 in)
Anemone tomentosa 'Albadura', R, 50 cm (20 in)
Anemone tomentosa 'Robustissima', P–R, –50 cm (20 in)
Clematis integrifolia, V, 1.5 m (5 ft)
Clematis integrifolia 'Hendersoni', V, –50 cm (20 in)
Digitalis nervosa, Y, –1.8 m (6 ft)
Meconopsis cambrica 'Aurantiaca', O, –50 cm (20 in)
Phytolacca acinosa, W, 2 m (6 ft)
Thalictrum aquilegifolium, R–P, 1.5 m (5 ft)
Thalictrum dipterocarpum, V, –2 m (6 ft)
Thalictrum flavum ssp. *glaucum*, Y, 2 m (6 ft)
Thalictrum speciosissimum 'Majus', Y, 2 m (6 ft)
Trollius europaeus 'Orange Globe', Y–O, –75 cm (30 in)
Trollius europaeus 'Superbus', Y, –75 cm (30 in)
Trollius hybrid 'First Lancers', O, –75 cm (30 in)

○ ◐ ○ ☯
107. Suitable as a specimen plant.

Acanthus mollis, W–P, 1 m (3 ft)
Aruncus aerthusifolius, W, –2 m (6 ft)
Crambe cordifolia, W, –1.6 m (5¼ ft)
Miscanthus sinensis 'Giganteus', –2.5 m (8 ft)
Phuopsis stylosa, P, 20 cm (8 in)
Phytolacca acinosa, W, 2 m (6 ft)
Verbascum chaixii, Y, 1.3 m (4¼ ft)
Verbascum nigrum, Y, –1.6 m (5¼ ft)

○ ◐ ○ ⊗
108. Suitable for rock gardens and crevices in paving.

Campanula carpatica, V, 45 cm (18 in)
Campanula portenschlagiana 'Birch Hybrid', P–V, 10 cm (4 in)
Chiastophyllum oppositifolium, Y, –25 cm (10 in)
Crepis pyrenaica, Y, –60 cm (24 in)
Festuca scoparia, Y–W, –15 cm (6 in)
Gentiana sino-ornata, B, –20 cm (8 in)
Gentiana verna, B, 10 cm (4 in)
Geranium cinereum 'Ballerina', P–V, 15 cm (6 in)
Geranium dalmaticum, P–V, 10 cm (4 in)
Geranium palmatum, R–P, –80 cm (32 in)
Hutchinsia alpina ssp. *alpina*, W, –10 cm (4 in)
Incarvillea mairei var. *grandiflora*, R, –30 cm (12 in)
Oenothera caespitosa, Y, –80 cm (32 in)
Oenothera missouriensis, Y, –30 cm (12 in)
Polygonum affine 'Superbum', R–P, 25 cm (10 in)
Potentilla recta 'Warrenii', Y, –70 cm (28 in)
Potentilla tonguei (×), Y–O, –25 cm (10 in)
Potentilla hybrid 'Gibson's Scarlet', R, 50 cm (20 in)
Potentilla hybrid 'William Rollison', R, 50 cm (20 in)
Potentilla hybrid 'Yellow Queen', Y, –50 cm (20 in)
Primula capitata hybrid, V–B, 30 cm (12 in)
Prunella grandiflora, P, –20 cm (8 in)
Prunella hastifolia 'Rosea', R–P, 20 cm (8 in)
Prunella (×) *webbiana* 'Loveliness'
Sagina subulata, W, 7 cm (2¾ in)
Silene schafta 'Splendens', R–P, –15 cm (6 in)
Veronica austriaca ssp. *teucrium* 'Royal Blue', V, 30 cm (12 in)
Veronica chamaedrys, B, –45 cm (18 in)
Veronica filiformis, V–B, 10 cm (4 in)
Viola cornuta 'Hansa', P, 25 cm (10 in)
Viola cornuta hybrid 'Amethyst', P, 10 cm (4 in)

○ ◐ ○ ⊖
109. Suitable for ground cover.

Astilbe chinensis var. *pumila*, R–P, 30 cm (12 in)
Campanula portenschlagiana 'Birch Hybrid', P–V, 10 cm (4 in)
Festuca scoparia, Y/W, –15 cm (6 in)
Gentiana sino-ornata, B, –20 cm (8 in)
Geranium dalmaticum, P–V, 10 cm (4 in)
Hutchinsia alpina ssp. *alpina*, W, 10 cm (4 in)
Luzula sylvatica, W, –40 cm (16 in)
Omphalodes cappadocica, B, 15 cm (6 in)
Polygonum affine 'Superbum', R–P, 25 cm (10 in)

○ ◐ ○ ⊗
110. Suitable for cutting.

Acanthus mollis, W–P, 1 m (3 ft)
Achillea 'Coronation Gold', Y, –1 m (3 ft)
Achillea filipendulina, Y, 1.2 m (4 ft)
Achillea millefolium, R, –75 cm (30 in)
Achillea taygetea, Y, –40 cm (16 in)
Alchemilla mollis, Y, –40 cm (16 in)
Anemone hupehensis var. *japonica*, R, –75 cm (30 in)
Anemone japonica 'Elegans', W, –1 m (3 ft)
Anemone tomentosa 'Albadura', R, 50 cm (20 in)
Anemone tomentosa 'Robustissima', P–R, 50 cm (20 in)
Aster divaricatus, W, 60 cm (24 in)
Calamagrostis × *acutiflora* 'Karl Foerster', Y–O, 1.5 m (5 ft)
Campanula glomerata, P–V, –60 cm (24 in)
Campanula lactiflora, V–B, –1.5 m (5 ft)
Campanula lactiflora 'Alba', W, –1.5 m (5 ft)
Campanula lactiflora 'Loddon Anna', P, 1 m (3 ft)
Campanula lactiflora 'Pritchard', V, 60 cm (24 in)
Campanula latifolia 'Alba', W, –1.5 m (5 ft)
Campanula latifolia 'Macrantha', P–V, 1 m (3 ft)
Campanula persicifolia, V, –1 m (3 ft)
Centaurea montana 'Alba', W, 50 cm (20 in)
Cephalaria gigantea, Y, –1.6 m (5¼ ft)
Clematis integrifolia, V, 1.5 m (5 ft)
Crambe cordifolia, W, –1.6 m (5¼ ft)
Crepis pyrenaica, Y, –60 cm (24 in)
Dianthus seguieri ssp. *seguieri*, R–P, 30 cm (12 in)
Geranium × *magnificum*, P–V, –70 cm (28 in)
Geranium meeboldii 'Johnson's Blue', V–B, 50 cm (20 in)
Geranium palmatum, R–P, –80 cm (32 in)
Geranium phaeum, P, 50 cm (20 in)
Geranium psilostemon, R, 90 cm (3 ft)
Geum chiloense 'Mrs Bradshaw', R, –60 cm (24 in)
Geum hybrid 'Prinses Juliana', O, –60 cm (24 in)
Lavatera thuringiaca, R–P, 1.5 m (5 ft)
Lewisia heckneri hybrid, V, 25 cm (10 in)
Lobelia fulgens 'Queen Victoria', R, –90 cm (3 ft)
Lunaria rediviva, P, 1 m (3 ft)
Lychnis arkwrightii 'Vesuvius', R, –50 cm (20 in)
Lychnis chalcedonica, R, –1 m (3 ft)
Miscanthus sinensis 'Gracillimus', 1.5 m (5 ft)
Monarda hybrid 'Croftway Pink', P/V, 1 m (3 ft)
Paeonia mascula ssp. *arietina*, R, 1.2 m (4 ft)
Paeonia mlokosewitschii, W, –60 cm (24 in)
Paeonia officinalis 'Rubra Plena', R–P, –75 cm (30 in)
Papaver orientale 'Perry's White', W, –90 cm (3 ft)
Phlox paniculata 'Bright Eyes', R–P, –1 m (3 ft)
Phlox paniculata 'Mrs E. Prichard', R, 90 cm (3 ft)
Phlox paniculata hybrid 'Mies Copijn', R, –1 m (3 ft)
Phlox paniculata hybrid 'White Admiral', W, –1 m (3 ft)
Physalis alkekangi var. *franchetii*, W, 1 m (3 ft)
Platycodon grandiflorus 'Mariesii', V, 40 cm (16 in)
Polygonum macrophyllum, P, 50 cm (20 in)
Rudbeckia fulgida var. *speciosa*, Y, 60 cm (24 in)
Rudbeckia fulgida var. *sullivantii*, Y, 60 cm (24 in)
Rudbeckia laciniata, Y, 2.5 m (8 ft)
Rudbeckia nitida 'Herbstsonne', Y, 2 m (6 ft)
Salvia patens, B, –80 cm (32 in)
Sanguinaria obtusa, P, –1 m (3 ft)
Sanguisorba obtusa 'Albiflora', W, –1 m (3 ft)
Scabiosa caucasica 'Clive Greaves', P–V, 80 cm (32 in)
Scabiosa ochroleuca, Y, 60 cm (24 in)
Sedum spectabile 'Brilliant', R–P, –45 cm (18 in)
Sedum telephium, R, 40 cm (16 in)
Sidalcea hybrid 'Elsie Heugh', P, –80 cm (32 in)
Sidalcea hybrid 'Sussex Beauty', R, –80 cm (32 in)
Sidalcea hybrid 'William Smith', P, –80 cm (32 in)
Thalictrum aquilegifolium, R–P, 1.5 m (5 ft)
Thalictrum dipterocarpum, V, –2 m (6 ft)
Thalictrum flavum ssp. *glaucum*, Y, 2 m (6 ft)
Thalictrum speciosissimum 'Majus', Y, 2 m (6 ft)
Trollius europaeus 'Orange Globe', Y–O, –75 cm (30 in)

Trollius europaeus 'Superbus', Y, –75 cm (30 in)
Trollius hybrid 'First Lancers', O, –75 cm (30 in)
Verbascum hybrid 'Pink Domino', P, –1 m (3 ft)
Veronica austriaca ssp. *teucrium* 'Royal Blue', V, 30 cm (12 in)
Veronica chamaedrys, B, –45 cm (18 in)
Veronica longifolia, P, –75 cm (30 in)
Viola cornuta 'Hansa', P, 25 cm (10 in)
Viola cornuta hybrid 'Amethyst', P, 10 cm (4 in)

Bulbs

○ ◐ ◉

111. No special features.

Chionodoxa gigantea, B, 20 cm (8 in)
Chionodoxa luciliae, B, –15 cm (6 in)
Chionodoxa luciliae 'Pink Giant', R–P, –15 cm (6 in)
Galtonia candicans, W, –1.25 m (4 ft)
Scilla pratensis, B, 20 cm (8 in)

○ ◐ ◉ ⊗

112. Wholly or partly poisonous.

Colchicum autumnale, R–P, W, 20 cm (8 in)
Colchicum bowlesianum, R–P, –20 cm (8 in)
Colchicum byzantinum, P–V, –20 cm (8 in)
Colchicum speciosum, P–V, –20 cm (8 in)
Hyacinthus orientalis 'Amethyst', P, –30 cm (12 in)
Hyacinthus orientalis 'Blue Giant', V, –30 cm (12 in)
Lilium (American hybrid) 'Bellingham', O, 1.5 m (5 ft)
Lilium (Asiatic hybrid) 'Enchantment', O, –1 m (3 ft)
Lilium (Asiatic hybrid) 'Fire King', O, 1.2 m (4 ft)
Lilium (Asiatic hybrid) 'Golden Chalice', Y–O, 1.2 m (4 ft)
Lilium (Asiatic hybrid) 'Harmony', O, 80 cm (32 in)
Lilium (Asiatic hybrid) 'Helona', Y–O, –80 cm (32 in)
Lilium (Asiatic hybrid) 'Pink Tiger', R, 1.5 m (5 ft)
Lilium (Asiatic hybrid) 'Uncle Sam', Y, 1.9 m (6 ft)
Lilium bulbiferum var. *croceum*, O, –1.2 m (4 ft)
Lilium concolor, O, 90 cm (3 ft)
Lilium davidii, O, 1.2 m (4 ft)
Lilium martagon var. *album*, W, –1.8 m (6 ft)
Lilium (oriental hybrid) 'Chinook', Y–O, 1.2 m (4 ft)
Lilium pumilum, R, –50 cm (20 in)
Lilium pyrenaicum, Y, –1.2 m (4 ft)
Lilium regale, W, –1.5 m (5 ft)
Lilium testaceum (×), Y, –1.5 m (5 ft)
Lilium (trumpet) 'African Queen', Y–O, 1.8 m (6 ft)
Lilium (trumpet) 'Bright Star', Y, –1.8 m (6 ft)
Lilium (trumpet) 'Golden Splendour', Y, –1.8 m (6 ft)
Lilium (trumpet) 'Green Dawn', W, –1.8 m (6 ft)
Lilium (trumpet) 'Pink Perfection', R–P, 1.8 m (6 ft)
Ornithogalum umbellatum, W, –30 cm (12 in)

○ ◐ ◉ ⊕

113. Suitable as a specimen plant.

Lilium (American hybrid) 'Bellingham', O, 1.5 m (5 ft)
Lilium (Asiatic hybrid) 'Enchantment', O, –1 m (3 ft)
Lilium (Asiatic hybrid) 'Fire King', O, 1.2 m (4 ft)
Lilium (Asiatic hybrid) 'Golden Chalice', Y–O, 1.2 m (4 ft)
Lilium (Asiatic hybrid) 'Harmony', O, 80 cm (32 in)
Lilium (Asiatic hybrid), 'Helona', Y–O, –80 cm (32 in)
Lilium (Asiatic hybrid) 'Pink Tiger', R, 1.5 m (5 ft)
Lilium (Asiatic hybrid) 'Uncle Sam', Y, 1.9 m (6 ft)
Lilium davidii, O, 1.2 m (4 ft)
Lilium martagon var. *album*, W, –1.8 m (6 ft)
Lilium (oriental hybrid) 'Chinook', Y–O, 1.2 m (4 ft)
Lilium regale, W, –1.5 m (5 ft)
Lilium testaceum (×), Y, –1.5 m (5 ft)
Lilium (trumpet) 'African Queen', Y–O, 1.8 m (6 ft)
Lilium (trumpet) 'Bright Star', Y, –1.8 m (6 ft)
Lilium (trumpet) 'Golden Splendour', Y, –1.8 m (6 ft)
Lilium (trumpet) 'Green Dawn', W, –1.8 m (6 ft)
Lilium (trumpet) 'Pink Perfection', R–P, 1.8 m (6 ft)

○ ◐ ◉ ⊗

114. Suitable for rock gardens and crevices in paving.

Narcissus cyclamineus 'February Gold', Y, –25 cm (10 in)
Narcissus cyclamineus 'Jack Snipe', var. col., 20 cm (8 in)
Narcissus cyclamineus 'Jenny', var. col., –25 cm (10 in)
Narcissus cyclamineus 'Little Witch', Y, 25 cm (10 in)
Narcissus cyclamineus 'Tête à Tête', Y, –20 cm (10 in)
Narcissus jonquilla, Y–O, 30 cm (12 in)
Narcissus triandrus 'Albus', W, 15 cm (6 in)

Narcissus triandrus 'April Tears', Y, –30 cm (12 in)
Narcissus triandrus 'Thalia', W, 40 cm (16 in)
Puschkinia scilloides 'Alba', B, 15 cm (6 in)
Puschkinia scilloides var. *libanotica*, B, 10 cm (4 in)
Scilla sibirica 'Spring Beauty', V–B, –20 cm (8 in)

○ ◐ ◉ ⊗

115. Suitable for cutting.

Iris hollandica hybrid 'Exotic Beauty', var. col., 80 cm (32 in)
Iris hollandica hybrid 'Telstar', var. col., –80 cm (32 in)
Iris xiphioides 'King of the Blues', P, 50 cm (20 in)
Lilium (American hybrid) 'Bellingham', O, 1.5 m (5 ft)
Lilium (Asiatic hybrid) 'Enchantment', O, –1 m (3 ft)
Lilium (Asiatic hybrid) 'Fire King', O, 1.2 m (4 ft)
Lilium (Asiatic hybrid) 'Golden Chalice', Y–O, 1.2 m (4 ft)
Lilium (Asiatic hybrid) 'Harmony', O, 80 cm (32 in)
Lilium (Asiatic hybrid) 'Helona', Y–O, –80 cm (32 in)
Lilium (Asiatic hybrid) 'Pink Tiger', R, 1.5 m (5 ft)
Lilium (Asiatic hybrid) 'Uncle Sam', Y, 1.9 m (6 ft)
Lilium bulbiferum var. *croceum*, O, –1.2 m (4 ft)
Lilium concolor, O, –90 cm (3 ft)
Lilium davidii, O, 1.2 m (4 ft)
Lilium martagon var. *album*, W, –1.8 m (6 ft)
Lilium (oriental hybrid) 'Chinook', Y–O, 1.2 m (4 ft)
Lilium pumilum, R, –50 cm (20 in)
Lilium pyrenaicum, Y, –1.2 m (4 ft)
Lilium regale, W, –1.5 m (5 ft)
Lilium testaceum (×), Y, –1.5 m (5 ft)
Lilium (trumpet) 'African Queen', Y–O, 1.8 m (6 ft)
Lilium (trumpet) 'Bright Star', Y, –1.8 m (6 ft)
Lilium (trumpet) 'Golden Splendour', Y, –1.8 m (6 ft)
Lilium (trumpet) 'Green Dawn', W, –1.8 m (6 ft)
Lilium (trumpet) 'Pink Perfection', R–P, 1.8 m (6 ft)
Narcissus (double) 'Flowerdream', W/Y, 40 cm (16 in)
Narcissus (double) 'Texas', Y, 35 cm (14 in)
Narcissus (large-cupped), 'Ice Follies', W/Y, –50 cm (20 in)
Narcissus (large-cupped) 'Mercato', W/O, –50 cm (20 in)
Narcissus jonquilla, Y–O, 30 cm (12 in)
Narcissus (small-cupped) 'Barrett Browning', W/O, 45 cm (18 in)
Narcissus (small-cupped) 'Quirinus', Y/O, 45 cm (18 in)
Narcissus poeticus, Y, –45 cm (18 in)
Narcissus poeticus 'Actaea', W, 45 cm (18 in)
Narcissus (split corona) 'Orangerie', var. col., 50 cm (20 in)
Narcissus tazetta 'Cheerfulness', W, 50 cm (20 in)
Narcissus tazetta 'Cragford', var. col., 50 cm (20 in)
Narcissus triandrus 'Thalia', W, 40 cm (16 in)
Narcissus (trumpet) 'Golden Harvest', Y, 55 cm (22 in)
Narcissus (trumpet) 'Satin Pink', W, H–O, 40 cm (16 in)
Scilla hispanica, B, –30 cm (12 in)
Scilla mischtschenkoana, B, 10 cm (4 in)

Tubers

○ ◐ ⓐ ⊛

116. With attractive fruits or berries.

Iris foetidissima Y–P, –1 m (3 ft)

○ ◐ ⓐ ◉

117. Wholly or partly poisonous.

Anemone appenina, var. col., –20 cm (8 in)
Anemone blanda, var. col., –15 cm (6 in)
Anemone × *fulgens* 'Annulata Grandiflora', R, 30 cm (12 in)

○ ◐ ⓐ ⊗

118. Suitable for rock gardens and crevices in paving.

Anemone appenina, var. col., –20 cm (8 in)
Anemone blanda, var. col., –15 cm (6 in)
Anemone × *fulgens* 'Annulata Grandiflora', R, 30 cm (12 in)
Crocus biflorus, P, 10 cm (4 in)
Crocus chrysanthus 'Blue Bird', W–B, –10 cm (4 in)
Crocus chrysanthus 'Cream Beauty', Y, –10 cm (4 in)
Crocus flavus, Y, –10 cm (4 in)
Crocus kotschyanus, P–V, –10 cm (4 in)
Crocus longiflorus, P, 10 cm (4 in)
Crocus speciosus, P, 15 cm (6 in)
Crocus tommasinianus, B, –10 cm (4 in)
Crocus versicolor, W, 10 cm (4 in)
Crocus hybrid, var. col., –10 cm (4 in)
Eranthis hyemalis, Y, 15 cm (6 in)

○ ◐ ㉑ ⊗

119. Suitable for cutting.

Anemone × fulgens 'Annulata Grandiflora', R, 30 cm (12 in)
Gladiolus (butterfly) 'A. Capella', Y/R, –1.2 m (4 ft)
Gladiolus (butterfly) 'Bambino', R–P, 1.2 m (4 ft)
Gladiolus (butterfly) 'Norma', O/Y, –1.2 m (4 ft)
Gladiolus (buttefly) 'Prelude', W/R, –1.2 m (4 ft)
Gladiolus (butterfly) 'Turandot', Y, –1.2 m (4 ft)
Gladiolus byzantinus, R–P, 1 m (3 ft)
Gladiolus hybrid, R/W, –1.5 m (5 ft)
Gladiolus hybrid 'Clio', R–P, W, 1 m (3 ft)
Gladiolus hybrid 'Franz Liszt', R/Y, 1 m (3 ft)
Gladiolus hybrid 'Herman van der Mark', R, 1.5 m (5 ft)
Gladiolus hybrid 'Melodie', var. col., –1.5 m (5 ft)
Gladiolus hybrid 'Oscar', R, –1.5 m (5 ft)
Gladiolus hybrid 'Papillo', V/W/Y, 1.5 m (5 ft)
Gladiolus hybrid 'Sweepstake', O–R, Y, 1.5 m (5 ft)
Iris foetidissima, Y–P, –1 m (3 ft)
Schizostylis coccinea 'Sunrise', R, –50 cm (20 in)

Shrubs

120. No special features.

Ceratostigma willmottianum, B, 1 m (3 ft)
Clethra alnifolia, W, 2 m (6 ft)
Clethra barbinervis, W, 4 m (13 ft)
Coronilla emerus ssp. *emeroides*, Y, 1 m (3 ft)
Fallopia aubertii, W, 12 m (40 ft)
Hydrangea anomala ssp. *petiolaris*, W, 7 m (23 ft)
Hypericum hookeranum 'Hidcote', Y, 2 m (6 ft)
Indigofera amblyantha, R, 1.5 m (5 ft)
Indigofera gerardiana, R, 2 m (6 ft)
Indigofera kirilowii, R–P, 1 m (3 ft)
Salvia fulgens, R, 1 m (3 ft)
Sorbaria aitchisonii, W, 3 m (10 ft)
Sorbaria arborea var. *subtomentosa*, W, 4 m (13 ft)
Sorbaria sorbifolia, W, 2 m (6 ft)
Stachys byzantina, P, –50 cm (20 in)
Weigela floribunda 'Grandiflora', W/R, 3 m (10 ft)
Weigela floribunda 'Purpurea', R, 2 m (6 ft)

121. Evergreen.

Andromeda polifolia, R, –30 m (100 ft)
Berberis candidula, Y, 50 cm (20 in)
Berberis gagnepainii var. *lanceifolia*, Y, 2 m (6 ft)
Berberis hybridogagnepainii (×), Y, 1.5 m (5 ft)
Berberis stenophylla (×), Y–O, 2 m (6 ft)
Bruckenthalia spiculifolia, R–P, 15 cm (6 in)
Buxus sempervirens 'Argenteovariegata', Y, 2 m (6 ft)
Buxus sempervirens 'Suffruticosa', Y, 1 m (3 ft)
Calluna vulgaris 'Darkness', R–P, 35 cm (14 in)
Calluna vulgaris 'Elsie Purnell', R, 60 cm (24 in)
Calluna vulgaris 'Gold Haze', W, 25 cm (10 in)
Calluna vulgaris 'Golden Rivulet', P, 20 cm (8 in)
Calluna vulgaris 'H. E. Beale', R–P, 30 cm (12 in)
Calluna vulgaris 'Marleen', R–P, 30 cm (12 in)
Calluna vulgaris 'Multicolor', P, 20 cm (8 in)
Calluna vulgaris 'Peter Sparkes', R, 60 cm (24 in)
Calluna vulgaris 'Radnor', R, 30 cm (12 in)
Camellia japonica, var. col., 4 m (13 ft)
Camellia japonica 'Beatrice Burns', R, 4 m (13 ft)
Cephalotaxus harringtonia 'Fastigiata', 5 m (16 ft)
Cestrum 'Newellii', R, 3 m (10 ft)
Cestrum purpureum, R–P, 3 m (10 ft)
Chamaecyparis lawsoniana 'Albovariegata', 7 m (23 ft)
Chamaecyparis lawsoniana 'Dow's Gem', 3 m (10 ft)
Chamaecyparis lawsoniana 'Erecta Aurea', 4 m (13 ft)
Chamaecyparis lawsoniana 'Filiformis Comp.', 2 m (6 ft)
Chamaecyparis lawsoniana 'Minima Glauca', 1.5 m (5 ft)
Chamaecyparis lawsoniana 'Nana', 1.2 m (4 ft)
Chamaecyparis lawsoniana 'Nidiformis', 1.5 m (5 ft)
Chamaecyparis obtusa 'Pygmaea', 75 cm (30 in)
Chamaecyparis obtusa 'Tetragona Aurea', 4 m (13 ft)
Chamaecyparis pisifera 'Boulevard', 4 m (13 ft)
Chamaecyparis pisifera 'Compacta', 50 cm (20 in)
Chamaecyparis pisifera 'Filifera Nana', 50 cm (20 in)
Chamaecyparis pisifera 'Plumosa Minima', 1 m (3 ft)
Chamaecyparis pisifera 'Pygmaea', 2 m (6 ft)
Choisya ternata, W, 1 m (3 ft)
Cotoneaster simonsii, W, 3 m (10 ft)
Cryptomeria japonica 'Elegans Nana', 2 m (6 ft)

Cryptomeria japonica 'Globosa Nana', 3 m (10 ft)
Cryptomeria japonica 'Pygmaea', 2 m (6 ft)
Cupressocyparis (×) *leylandii*, 20 m (65 ft)
Daboecia cantabrica 'Atropurpurea', P, 40 cm (16 in)
Elaeagnus pungens 'Maculata', W, 4 m (13 ft)
Elaeagnus × ebbingei, W, 3 m (10 ft)
Erica ciliaris 'Globosa', R–P, 35 cm (14 in)
Erica erigena, R. 1.5 m (5 ft)
Erica herbacea, R–P, 25 cm (10 in)
Erica herbacea 'Myretoun Ruby', R–P, 30 cm (12 in)
Erica tetralix 'Helma', R–P, 40 cm (16 in)
Erica tetralix 'Ken Underwood', R–P, 30 cm (12 in)
Erica vagans 'George Underwood', R–P, 25 cm (10 in)
Erica vagans 'Mrs D. F. Maxwell', R, 35 cm (14 in)
Erica vagans 'St Keverne', R–P, 35 cm (14 in)
Erica watsonii (×) 'Truro', R–P, 15 cm (6 in)
Euonymus japonicus 'Aureomarginatus', Y–W, 3 m (10 ft)
Hedera colchica (9 m) 'Dentatovariegata', G/Y, 9 m (3 ft)
Hypericum calycinum, Y, 45 cm (18 in)
Hypericum inodorum (×) 'Elstead', Y, 1 m (3 ft)
Hypericum inodorum (×) 'Goudelsje', Y, 1 m (3 ft)
Hypericum moseranum (×), Y, 60 cm (24 in)
Jasminum mesnyi, Y, 3 m (10 ft)
Juniperus chinensis 'Blaauw', 1.5 m (5 ft)
Juniperus chinensis 'Blue and Gold', 2 m (6 ft)
Juniperus chinensis 'Hetzii', 2 m (6 ft)
Juniperus chinensis 'Parsonii', 1 m (3 ft)
Juniperus chinensis 'Pfitzeriana', 2 m (6 ft)
Juniperus chinensis 'Pfitzeriana Aurea', 2 m (6 ft)
Juniperus chinensis 'Plumosa Aurea', 80 cm (32 in)
Juniperus communis 'Compressa', 1 m (3 ft)
Juniperus communis 'Depressa Aurea', 1 m (3 ft)
Juniperus communis 'Echiniformis', 30 cm (12 in)
Juniperus communis var. *depressa*, 50 cm (20 in)
Juniperus conferta, 60 cm (24 in)
Juniperus horizontalis 'Douglasii', 50 cm (20 in)
Juniperus sabina 'Tamariscifolia', 50 cm (20 in)
Juniperus squamata 'Blue Star', 1 m (3 ft)
Juniperus squamata 'Boulevard', 2 m (6 ft)
Juniperus squamata 'Loderi', 3 m (10 ft)
Juniperus squamata 'Meyeri', –5 m (16 ft)
Juniperus squamata 'Wilsonii', 2 m (6 ft)
Juniperus virginiana 'Reptans', 60 cm (24 in)
Lonicera japonica repens 'Aureoreticulata', W, 6 m (20 ft)
Lonicera sempervirens 'Sulphurea', Y, 6 m (20 ft)
Osmarea burkwoodii, W, 1 m (3 ft)
Picea abies 'Acrocona', –8 m (26 ft)
Picea abies 'Clanbrassiliana', 2 m (6 ft)
Picea abies 'Nidiformis', –2 m (6 ft)
Picea abies 'Repens', 50 cm (20 in)
Picea abies 'Wartburg', 4 m (13 ft)
Picea glauca 'Albertiana', 3 m (10 ft)
Picea glauca 'Conica', –3 m (10 ft)
Picea glauca 'Echiniformis', 80 cm (32 in)
Picea omorika 'Nana', 1.5 m (5 ft)
Picea pungens 'Glauca Globosa', 1 m (3 ft)
Pieris floribunda, W, 2 m (6 ft)
Pieris forrestii, W, 3 m (10 ft)
Pieris japonica, W, 3 m (10 ft)
Podocarpus nivalis, 1 m (3 ft)
Pyracantha coccinea, W, 4 m (13 ft)
Skimmia foremanii (×), W, 1.2 m (4 ft)
Skimmia japonica, W, 1.5 m (5 ft)
Streptosolen jamesonii, O, 1.5 m (5 ft)
Taxus baccata 'Aurea', 6 m (20 ft)
Taxus baccata 'Cavendishii', 2 m (6 ft)
Taxus baccata 'Dovastonii Aurea', 3 m (10 ft)
Taxus baccata 'Repandens', 50 cm (20 in)
Taxus baccata 'Semperaurea', –3 m (10 ft)
Taxus canadensis 'Variegata', 3 m (10 ft)
Taxus cuspidata 'Aurescens', 1 m (3 ft)
Taxus media (×) 'Hatfieldii', 4 m (13 ft)
Thuja occidentalis 'Danica', 1 m (3 ft)
Thuja occidentalis 'Pygmaea', 1.5 m (5 ft)
Thuja occidentalis 'Rheingold', 2 m (6 ft)
Thuja occidentalis 'Woodwardii', 2 m (6 ft)
Thuja orientalis 'Aurea Nana', 2 m (6 ft)
Thuja plicata 'Cuprea', 1 m (3 ft)
Thuja plicata 'Gracilis Aurea', 6 m (20 ft)
Thuja plicata 'Rogersii', 1 m (3 ft)
Thuja plicata 'Stoneham Gold', 2 m (6 ft)
Thujopsis dolobrata 'Nana', 1 m (3 ft)
Tsuga canadensis 'Bennett', 1 m (3 ft)
Tsuga canadensis 'Pendula', –3 m (10 ft)
Tsuga heterophylla 'Conica', 4 m (13 ft)
Viburnum davidii, W, (16 in)
Viburnum rhytidophyllum, W, 4 m (13 ft)
Viburnum tinus, W, 2.5 m (8 ft)

○ ◐ ◑ ❀
122. With attractive fruits or berries.

Actinidia chinensis, Y–W, 8 m (26 ft)
Actinidia kolomikta, W, 2 m (6 ft)
Akebia quinata, P, 10 m (33 ft)
Amelanchier canadensis, W, 8 m (26 ft)
Ampelopsis brevipedunculata, G, 12 m (40 ft)
Ampelopsis megalophylla, G, 12 m (40 ft)
Andromeda polifolia, R. –30 m (100 ft)
Berberis candidula, Black, 50 cm (20 in)
Berberis gagnepainii var. *lanceifolia*, Black, 2 m (6 ft)
Berberis giraldii, Y, 2 m (6 ft)
Berberis hybridogagnepainii (×), Y, 1.5 m (5 ft)
Berberis siedboldii, R, 1 m (3 ft)
Berberis stenophylla (×), Black, 2 m (6 ft)
Broussonetia papyrifera, O–R, 4 m (13 ft)
Calycanthus floridus, R–Brown, 3 m (10 ft)
Calycanthus occidentalis, R–Brown, 3 m (10 ft)
Celastrus orbiculatus, Y–G, 10 m (33 ft)
Celastrus scandens, G–Y, 7 m (23 ft)
Cephalotaxus harringtonia 'Fastigiata', 5 m (16 ft)
Cestrum 'Newelli', R, 3 m (10 ft)
Cestrum purpureum, R–P, 3 m (10 ft)
Chaenomeles superba (×), R, 2 m (6 ft)
Chamaecyparis lawsoniana 'Albovariegata', 7 m (23 ft)
Chamaecyparis lawsoniana 'Dow's Gem', 3 m (10 ft)
Chamaecyparis lawsoniana 'Erecta Aurea', 4 m (13 ft)
Chamaecyparis lawsoniana 'Filiformis Comp.', 2 m (6 ft)
Chamaecyparis lawsoniana 'Minima Glauca', 1.5 m (5 ft)
Chamaecyparis lawsoniana 'Nana', 1.2 m (4 ft)
Chamaecyparis lawsoniana 'Nidiformis', 1.5 m (5 ft)
Chamaecyparis obtusa 'Pygmaea', 75 cm (30 in)
Chamaecyparis obtusa 'Tetragona Aurea', 4 m (13 ft)
Chamaecyparis pisifera 'Boulevard', 4 m (13 ft)
Chamaecyparis pisifera 'Compacta', 50 cm (20 in)
Chamaecyparis pisifera 'Filifera Nana', 50 cm (20 in)
Chamaecyparis pisifera 'Plumosa Minima', 1 m (3 ft)
Chamaecyparis pisifera 'Pygmaea', 2 m (6 ft)
Chionanthus virginicus, B, –3 m (10 ft)
Clematis tangutica, Y, 6 m (20 ft)
Clerodendrum bungei, R, 2.5 m (8 ft)
Colutea arborescens, Y, 3 m (10 ft)
Cornus controversa 'Variegata', W, 5 m (16 ft)
Cornus florida 'Rubra', R–P, 6 m (20 ft)
Cornus kousa, W, 6 m (20 ft)
Cornus mas, Y, 7 m (23 ft)
Cornus nuttallii 'Ascona', W, 6 m (20 ft)
Cotoneaster simonsii, R, 3 m (10 ft)
Cotoneaster watereri (×) 'Brandkjaer', R, 4.5 m (15 ft)
Cotoneaster watereri (×) 'Pendula', R, 4.5 m (15 ft)
Crataegus nitida, W, 7 m (23 ft)
Crataegus × prunifolia, W, 4 m (13 ft)
Crataegus pubescens f. *stipulaceae*, W, 4 m (13 ft)
Cryptomeria japonica 'Pygmaea', 2 m (6 ft)
Cydonia oblonga, W, 8 m (26 ft)
Daphne mezereum, P–V, 1 m (3 ft)
Decaisnea fargesii, Y–G, 2.5 m (8 ft)
Elaeagnus multiflora, Y, 2 m (6 ft)
Euonymus alatus, G–Y, 2 m (6 ft)
Euonymus europaeus 'Red Cascade', W, 3 m (10 ft)
Euonymus hamiltonianus var. *hians*, Y/W, 3 m (10 ft)
Fortunella margarita, W, 1.5 m (5 ft)
Hippophae rhamnoides, G–Y, 3 m (10 ft)
Holodiscus discolor, Y/W, 4 m (13 ft)
Holodiscus discolor var. *discolor*, W, 4 m (13 ft)
Holodiscus dumosus, W, 1 m (3 ft)
Hypericum inodurum (×) 'Elstead', Y, 1 m (3 ft)
Hypericum inodorum (×) 'Goudelsje', Y, 1 m (3 ft)
Juniperus chinensis 'Blaauw', 1.5 m (5 ft)
Juniperus chinensis 'Blue and Gold', 2 m (6 ft)
Juniperus chinensis 'Hetzii', 2 m (6 ft)
Juniperus chinensis 'Parsonii', 1 m (3 ft)
Juniperus chinensis 'Pfitzeriana', 2 m (6 ft)
Juniperus chinensis 'Pfitzeriana Aurea', 2 m (6 ft)
Juniperus chinensis 'Plumosa Aurea', 80 cm (32 in)
Juniperus communis 'Compressa', 1 m (3 ft)
Juniperus communis 'Depressa Aurea', 1 m (3 ft)
Juniperus communis 'Echiniformis', 30 cm (12 in)
Juniperus communis var. *depressa*, 50 cm (20 in)
Juniperus conferta, 60 cm (24 in)
Juniperus sabina 'Tamariscifolia', 50 cm (20 in)
Juniperus squamata 'Blue Star', 1 m (3 ft)
Juniperus squamata 'Boulevard', 2 m (6 ft)
Juniperus squamata 'Loderi', 3 m (10 ft)
Juniperus squamata 'Meyeri', –5 m (16 ft)
Juniperus squamata 'Wilsonii', 2 m (6 ft)

Juniperus virginiana 'Reptans', 60 cm (24 in)
Leycestreria formosa, R, 2 m (6 ft)
Loncera japonica repens 'Aureoreticulata', W, 6 m (20 ft)
Lonicera periculmenum 'Belgica', R–P, W, 4 m (13 ft)
Lonicera sempervirens 'Sulphurea', Y, 6 m (20 ft)
Parthenocissus henryana, G, 9 m (30 ft)
Parthenocissus inserta, G, 10 m (33 ft)
Parthenocissus quinquefolia, G, 20 m (65 ft)
Parthenocissus tricuspidata, G, 20 m (65 ft)
Physocarpus capitatus, R, 3 m (10 ft)
Picea abies 'Acrocona', –8 m (26 ft)
Picea omorika 'Nana', 1.5 m (5 ft)
Picea pungens 'Glauca Globosa', 1 m (3 ft)
Prunus padus, W, 9 m (30 ft)
Pyracantha coccinea, W, 4 m (13 ft)
Ribes sanguineum, R, 3 m (10 ft)
Ribes sanguineum 'Carneum', R, 3 m (10 ft)
Skimmia foremanii (×), W, 1.2 m (4 ft)
Skimmia japonica, R, 1.5 m (5 ft)
Stachyurus praecox, Y–G, 2 m (6 ft)
Staphylea pinnata, W, 5 m (16 ft)
Stranvaesia davidiana, W, 2.5 m (8 ft)
Taxus baccata 'Aurea', 6 m (20 ft)
Taxus baccata 'Cavendishii', 2 m (6 ft)
Taxus canadensis 'Variegata', 3 m (10 ft)
Thuja orientalis 'Aurea Nana', 2 m (6 ft)
Thujopsis dolobrata 'Nana', 1 m (3 ft)
Tsuga heterophylla 'Conica', 4 m (13 ft)
Viburnum davidii, B, 40 cm (16 in)
Viburnum henryi, W, 3 m (10 ft)
Viburnum opulus 'Xanthocarpum', W, 4 m (13 ft)
Viburnum plicatum f. *tomentosum*, B–Black, 2.5 m (8 ft)
Viburnum plicatum f. *tomentosum*, W, 2 m (6 ft)
Viburnum rhytidophylloides (×) 'Alleghany', R, 3 m (10 ft)
Viburnum rhytidophyllum, R, 4 m (13 ft)
Viburnum tinus, B, 2.5 m (8 ft)
Vitis coignetiae, G, 25 m (80 ft)
Vitis palmata, G, 15 m (50 ft)
Vitis vinifera, G, 15 m (50 ft)

○ ◐ ◑ ◎
123. Wholly or partly poisonous.

Buxus sempervirens 'Argenteovariegata', Y, 2 m (6 ft)
Buxus sempervirens 'Aureovariegata', Y, 2 m (6 ft)
Buxus sempervirens 'Suffruticosa', Y, 1 m (3 ft)
Calycanthus floridus, R–Brown, 3 m (10 ft)
Calycanthus occidentalis, R–Brown, 3 m (10 ft)
Cephalotaxus harringtonia 'Fastigiata', 5 m (16 ft)
Chaenomeles superba (×), R, 2 m (6 ft)
Chamaecyparis lawsoniana 'Albovariegata', 7 m (23 ft)
Chamaecyparis lawsoniana 'Dow's Gem', 3 m (10 ft)
Chamaecyparis lawsoniana 'Erecta Aurea', 4 m (13 ft)
Chamaecyparis lawsoniana 'Filiformis Comp.', 2 m (6 ft)
Chamaecyparis lawsoniana 'Minima Glauca', 1.5 m (5 ft)
Chamaecyparis lawsoniana 'Nana', 1.2 m (4 ft)
Chamaecyparis lawsoniana 'Nidiformis', 1.5 m (5 ft)
Chamaecyparis obtusa 'Pygmaea', 75 cm (30 in)
Chamaecyparis obtusa 'Tetragona Aurea', 4 m (13 ft)
Chamaecyparis pisifera 'Boulevard', 4 m (13 ft)
Chamaecyparis pisifera 'Compacta', 50 cm (20 in)
Chamaecyparis pisifera 'Filifera Nana', 50 cm (20 in)
Chamaecyparis pisifera 'Plumosa Minima', 1 m (3 ft)
Chamaecyparis pisifera 'Pygmaea', 2 m (6 ft)
Chamaecyparis pisifera 'Squarrosa Pygmaea', 80 cm (32 in)
Clematis macropetala, V–B, 3 m (10 ft)
Clematis macropetala 'Maidwell Hall', B, 3 m (10 ft)
Clematis macropetala 'Markhamii', R, 3 m (10 ft)
Clematis montana 'Rubens', R, 10 m (33 ft)
Clematis montana 'Tetrarose', R–P, 10 m (33 ft)
Clematis tangutica, Y, 6 m (20 ft)
Clematis hybrid 'Ernest Markham', R, 4 m (13 ft)
Clematis hybrid 'Fairy Queen', R, 3 m (10 ft)
Clematis hybrid 'Hagley Hybrid', R–P, 2 m (6 ft)
Clematis hybrid 'Jackmanii Superba', V–B, 10 m (33 ft)
Clematis hybrid 'Mrs Cholmondeley', B, 3 m (10 ft)
Clematis hybrid 'Nelly Moser', P, 4 m (13 ft)
Clematis hybrid 'The President', P–V, 4 m (13 ft)
Clematis hybrid 'Ville de Lyon', R, 4 m (13 ft)
Clematis hybrid 'Vyvyan Pennell', P–V, 4 m (13 ft)
Colutea arborescens, Y, 3 m (10 ft)
Cornus alba, W, 3 m (10 ft)
Cornus alba 'Elegantissima', W, 3 m (10 ft)
Cryptomeria japonica 'Pygmaea', 2 m (6 ft)
Daphne mezereum, P–V, 1 m (3 ft)
Erica ciliaris 'Globosa', R–P, 35 cm (14 in)
Erica erigena, R, 1.5 m (5 ft)

123. Wholly or partly poisonous (continued).

Erica herbacea, R–P, 25 cm (10 in)
Erica herbacea 'Myretoun Ruby', R–P, 30 cm (12 in)
Erica tetralix 'Helma', R–P, 40 cm (16 in)
Erica tetralix 'Ken Underwood', R–P, 30 cm (12 in)
Erica vagans 'George Underwood', R–P, 25 cm (10 in)
Erica vagans 'Mrs D. F. Maxwell', R, 35 cm (14 in)
Erica vagans 'St Keverne', R–P, 35 cm (14 in)
Euonymus europaeus 'Red Cascade', W, 3 m (10 ft)
Hedera colchica 'Dentatovariegata', G–Y, 9 m (30 ft)
Juniperus chinensis 'Blaauw', 1.5 m (5 ft)
Juniperus chinensis 'Blue and Gold', 2 m (6 ft)
Juniperus chinensis 'Hetzii', 2 m (6 ft)
Juniperus chinensis 'Parsonii', 1 m (3 ft)
Juniperus chinensis 'Pfitzeriana Aurea', 2 m (6 ft)
Juniperus chinensis 'Pfitzeriana', 2 m (6 ft)
Juniperus chinensis 'Plumosa Aurea', 80 cm (32 in)
Juniperus communis 'Compressa', 1 m (3 ft)
Juniperus communis 'Depressa Aurea', 1 m (3 ft)
Juniperus communis 'Echiniformis', 30 cm (12 in)
Juniperus communis var. *depressa*, 50 cm (20 in)
Juniperus conferta, 60 cm (24 in)
Juniperus sabina 'Tamariscifolia', 50 cm (20 in)
Juniperus squamata 'Blue Star', 1 m (3 ft)
Juniperus squamata 'Boulevard', 2 m (6 ft)
Juniperus squamata 'Loderi', 3 m (10 ft)
Juniperus squamata 'Meyeri', –5 m (16 ft)
Juniperus squamata 'Wilsonii', 2 m (6 ft)
Juniperus virginiana 'Reptans', 60 cm (24 in)
Kerria japonica, Y, 2 m (6 ft)
Kerria japonica var. *simplex*, Y, 2 m (6 ft)
Ligustrum sinense var. *stauntonii*, W, 2 m (6 ft)
Lonicera japonica repens 'Aureoreticulata', W, 6 m (20 ft)
Lonicera periclymenum 'Belgica', R–P, W, 4 m (13 ft)
Lonicera sempervirens 'Sulphurea', Y, 6 m (20 ft)
Petteria ramentacea, Y, 2 m (6 ft)
Prunus padus, W, 9 m (30 ft)
Pyracantha coccinea, W, 4 m (13 ft)
Spiraea arguta (×), W, 2.5 m (8 ft)
Spiraea billardii (×), R, 2 m (6 ft)
Spiraea bumalda (×) 'Anthony Waterer', R–P, 80 cm (32 in)
Spiraea nipponica, W, 2.5 m (8 ft)
Spiraea thunbergii, W, 2 m (6 ft)
Spiraea vanhouttei (×), W, 2 m (6 ft)
Spiraea veitchii, W, 3 m (10 ft)
Taxus baccata 'Aurea', 6 m (20 ft)
Taxus baccata 'Cavendishii', 2 m (6 ft)
Taxus baccata 'Dovastonii Aurea', 3 m (10 ft)
Taxus baccata 'Repandens', 50 cm (20 in)
Taxus baccata 'Semperaurea', –3 m (10 ft)
Taxus canadensis 'Variegata', 3 m (10 ft)
Taxus cuspidata 'Aurescens', 1 m (3 ft)
Taxus media (×) 'Hatfieldii', 4 m (13 ft)
Thuja occidentalis 'Danica', 1 m (3 ft)
Thuja occidentalis 'Pygmaea', 1.5 m (5 ft)
Thuja occidentalis 'Rheingold', 2 m (6 ft)
Thuja occidentalis 'Woodwardii', 2 m (6 ft)
Viburnum burkwoodii (×), W, 2.5 m (8 ft)
Viburnum carlcephalum (×), W, 2.5 m (8 ft)
Viburnum carlesii, W, 1.5 m (5 ft)
Viburnum davidii, B, 40 cm (16 in)
Viburnum farreri, W, 2.5 m (8 ft)
Viburnum henryi, W, 3 m (10 ft)
Viburnum juddii (×), W, 1.5 m (5 ft)
Viburnum opulus 'Xanthocarpum', W, 4 m (13 ft)
Viburnum plicatum 'Rotundifolium', W, 2 m (6 ft)
Viburnum plicatum f. *tomentosum*, W, 2.5 m (8 ft)
Viburnum rhytidophylloides (×), 'Alleghany', R, 3 m (10 ft)
Viburnum rhytidophyllum, R, 4 m (13 ft)
Viburnum tinus, B, 2.5 m (8 ft)
Wisteria sinensis, V–B, 10 m (33 ft)

○ ◑ ◍ ⊕

124. Suitable as a specimen plant.

Chamaecyparis lawsoniana 'Albovariegata', 7 m (23 ft)
Chamaecyparis lawsoniana 'Minima Glauca', 1.5 m (5 ft)
Chamaecyparis lawsoniana 'Nana', 1.2 m (4 ft)
Chamaecyparis lawsoniana 'Nidiformis', 1.5 m (5 ft)
Chamaecyparis obtusa 'Tetragona Aurea', 4 m (13 ft)
Chamaecyparis pisifera 'Compacta', 50 cm (20 ft)
Chamaecyparis pisifera 'Filifera Nana', 50 cm (20 ft)
Chamaecyparis pisifera 'Plumosa Minima', 1 m (3 ft)
Chamaecyparis pisifera 'Pygmaea', 2 m (6 ft)
Chamaecyparis pisifera 'Squarrosa Pygmaea', 80 cm (32 in)
Chionanthus virginicus, W, –3 m (10 ft)
Cornus controversa 'Variegata', W, 5 m (16 ft)

Cornus florida 'Rubra', R–P, 6 m (20 ft)
Cornus kousa, W, 6 m (20 ft)
Cornus mas, Y, 7 m (23 ft)
Cotoneaster watereri (×) 'Brandkjaer', R, 4.5 m (15 ft)
Cotoneaster watereri (×) 'Pendula', R, 4.5 m (15 ft)
Cryptomeria japonica 'Elegans Nana', 2 m (6 ft)
Cryptomeria japonica 'Globosa Nana', 3 m (10 ft)
Decaisnea fargesii, Y–G, 2.5 m (8 ft)
Enkianthus perulatus, W, 2 m (6 ft)
Hamamelis intermedia (×) 'Jelena', O, 3 m (10 ft)
Holodiscus discolor, Y/W, 4 m (13 ft)
Holodiscus discolor var. *discolor*, W, 4 m (13 ft)
Holodiscus dumosus, W, 1 m (3 ft)
Hydrangea paniculata, W, 4.5 m (15 ft)
Hydrangea paniculata 'Grandiflora', W, 4.5 m (15 ft)
Hydrangea paniculata 'Praecox', W, 4.5 m (15 ft)
Juniperus chinensis 'Blaauw', 1.5 m (5 ft)
Juniperus chinensis 'Blue and Gold', 2 m (6 ft)
Juniperus communis 'Compressa', 1 m (3 ft)
Juniperus sabina 'Tamariscifolia', 50 cm (20 in)
Juniperus squamata 'Blue Star', 1 m (3 ft)
Juniperus squamata 'Boulevard', 2 m (6 ft)
Juniperus squamata 'Loderi', 3 m (10 ft)
Juniperus squamata 'Meyeri', –5 m (16 ft)
Juniperus squamata 'Wilsonii', 2 m (6 ft)
Juniperus virginiana 'Reptans', 60 cm (24 in)
Philadelphus lemoinei (×), W, 2 m (6 ft)
Philadelphus lewisii var. *gordonianus*, W, 4 m (13 ft)
Philadelphus hybrid 'Belle Etoile', W, 3 m (10 ft)
Picea abies 'Acrocona', –8 m (26 ft)
Picea abies 'Clanbrassiliana', 2 m (6 ft)
Picea abies 'Nidiformis', –2 m (6 ft)
Picea abies 'Wartburg', 4 m (13 ft)
Picea omorika 'Nana', 1.5 m (5 ft)
Pieris japonica, W, 3 m (10 ft)
Spiraea vanhouttei (×), W, 2 m (6 ft)
Staphylea pinnata, W, 5 m (16 ft)
Taxus baccata 'Dovastonii Aurea', 3 m (10 ft)
Taxus canadensis 'Variegata', 3 m (10 ft)
Taxus cuspidata 'Aurescens', 1 m (3 ft)
Thuja plicata 'Cuprea', 1 m (3 ft)
Thuja plicata 'Rogersii', 1 m (3 ft)
Thuja plicata 'Stoneham Gold', 2 m (6 ft)
Thujopsis dolobrata 'Nana', 1 m (3 ft)
Tsuga canadensis 'Bennett', 1 m (3 ft)
Tsuga canadensis 'Pendula', –3 m (10 ft)
Tsuga heterophylla 'Conica', 4 m (13 ft)
Viburnum plicatum 'Rotundifolium', W, 2 m (6 ft)
Viburnum plicatum f. *tomentosum*, W, 2.5 m (8 ft)
Wisteria sinensis, V–B, 10 m (33 ft)

○ ◑ ◍ ⊗

125. Suitable for rock gardens and crevices in paving.

Andromeda polifolia, R, –30 cm (12 in)
Berberis candidula, Y, 50 cm (20 in)
Berberis hybridogagnepainii (×), Y, 1.5 m (5 ft)
Ceratostigma plumbaginoides, B, 30 cm (12 in)
Chamaecyparis pisifera 'Plumosa Minima', 1 m (3 ft)
Cryptomeria japonica 'Pygmaea', 2 m (6 ft)
Daphne burkwoodii (×) 'Somerset', W/R, 50 cm (20 in)
Erica herbacea, R–P, 25 cm (10 in)
Erica herbacea 'Myretoun Ruby', R–P, 30 cm (12 in)
Erica vagans 'Mrs D. F. Maxwell', R, 35 cm (14 in)
Juniperus communis 'Compressa', 1 m (3 ft)
Juniperus conferta, 60 cm (24 in)
Podocarpus nivalis, 1 m (3 ft)
Viburnum davidii, W, 40 cm (16 in)

○ ◑ ◍ ◓

126. Suitable for hedging.

Berberis stenophylla (×), Y–O, 2 m (6 ft)
Buxus sempervirens 'Argenteovariegata', Y, 2 m (6 ft)
Buxus sempervirens 'Aureovariegata', Y, 2 m (6 ft)
Buxus sempervirens 'Suffrutucosa', Y, 1 m (3 ft)
Cornus mas, Y, 7 m (23 ft)
Cotoneaster simonsii, W, 3 m (10 ft)
Cupressocyparis (×) *leylandii*, 20 m (65 ft)
Elaeagnus multiflora, Y, 2 m (6 ft)
Elaeagnus pungens 'Maculata', W, 4 m (13 ft)
Osmarea burkwoodii, W, 1 m (3 ft)
Potentilla fruticosa, Y, 1 m (3 ft)
Pyracantha coccinea, W, 4 m (13 ft)
Spiraea vanhoutei (×), W, 2 m (6 ft)
Taxus baccata 'Aurea', 6 m (20 ft)
Taxus baccata (hedge), 10 m (33 ft)

○ ◑ ◍ ⊖
127. Suitable for ground cover.

Berberis media (×) 'Parkjuweel', Y, 1 m (3 ft)
Calluna vulgaris 'Darkness', R–P, 35 cm (14 in)
Calluna vulgaris 'Elsie Purnell', R, 60 cm (24 in)
Calluna vulgaris 'Gold Haze', W, 25 cm (10 in)
Calluna vulgaris 'Golden Rivulet', P, 20 cm (8 in)
Calluna vulgaris 'H. E. Beale', R–P, 60 cm (24 in)
Calluna vulgaris 'Marleen', R–P, 30 cm (12 in)
Calluna vulgaris 'Multicolor', P, 20 cm (8 in)
Calluna vulgaris 'Peter Sparkes', R, 60 cm (24 in)
Calluna vulgaris 'Radnor', R, 30 cm (12 in)
Ceratostigma plumbaginoides, B, 30 cm (12 in)
Erica ciliaris 'Globosa', R–P, 35 cm (14 in)
Erica herbacea, R–P, 25 cm (10 in)
Erica herbacea 'Myretoun Ruby', R–P, 30 cm (12 in)
Erica tetralix 'Helma', R–P, 40 cm (16 in)
Erica tetralix 'Ken Underwood', R–P, 30 cm (12 in)
Erica vagans 'George Underwood', R–P, 25 cm (10 in)
Erica vagans 'Mrs D. F. Maxwell', R, 35 cm (14 in)
Erica vagans 'St Keverne', R–P, 35 cm (14 in)
Erica watsonii (×) 'Truro', R–P, 15 cm (6 in)
Euonymus japonicus 'Aureomarginatus', Y–W, 3 m (10 ft)
Hypericum calycinum, Y, 45 cm (18 in)
Juniperus chinensis 'Hetzii', 2 m (6 ft)
Juniperus chinensis 'Pfitzeriana', 2 m (6 ft)
Juniperus chinensis 'Pfitzeriana Aurea', 2 m (6 ft)
Juniperus conferta, 60 cm (24 in)
Juniperus horizontalis 'Douglasii', 50 cm (20 in)
Juniperus sabina 'Tamariscifolia', 50 cm (20 in)
Juniperus squamata 'Blue Star', 1 m (3 ft)
Juniperus squamata 'Meyeri', –5 m (16 ft)
Juniperus virginiana 'Reptans', 60 cm (24 in)
Picea abies 'Repens', 50 cm (20 in)
Podocarpus nivalis, 1 m (3 ft)
Stephanandra incisa 'Crispa', W, 60 cm (24 in)
Taxus baccata 'Repandens', 50 cm (20 in)
Viburnum davidii, W, 40 cm (16 in)

○ ◑ ◍ ⊗
128. Suitable for cutting.

Berberis sieboldii, Y, 1 m (3 ft)
Calluna vulgaris 'Darkness', R–P, 35 cm (14 in)
Calluna vulgaris 'Elsie Purnell', R, 60 cm (24 in)
Calluna vulgaris 'Golden Rivulet', P, 20 cm (8 in)
Calluna vulgaris 'H. E. Beale', R–P, 60 cm (24 in)
Calluna vulgaris 'Marleen', R–P, 30 cm (12 in)
Calluna vulgaris 'Multicolor', P, 20 cm (8 in)
Calluna vulgaris 'Peter Sparkes', R, 60 cm (24 in)
Calluna vulgaris 'Radnor', R, 30 cm (12 in)
Camellia japonica, var. col., 4 m (13 ft)
Camellia japonica 'Beatrice Burns', R, 4 m (13 ft)
Clematis jackmanii (×), V–B, 4 m (13 ft)
Clematis tangutica, Y, 6 m (20 ft)
Clematis hybrid 'Ernest Markham', R, 4 m (13 ft)
Clematis hybrid 'Fairy Queen', R, 3 m (10 ft)
Clematis hybrid 'Hagley Hybrid', R–P, 2 m (6 ft)
Clematis hybrid 'Jackmanii Superba', V–B, 10 m (33 ft)
Clematis hybrid 'Mrs Cholmondeley', B, 3 m (10 ft)
Clematis hybrid 'Nelly Moser', P, 4 m (13 ft)
Clematis hybrid 'The President', P–V, 4 m (13 ft)
Clematis hybrid 'Ville de Lyon', R, 4 m (13 ft)
Cornus mas, Y, 7 m (23 ft)
Deutzia hybrida (×) 'Mont Rosa', R, 2 m (6 ft)
Deutzia lemoinei (×), W, 1 m (3 ft)
Deutzia lemoinei (×), 'Boule de Neige', W, 1 m (3 ft)
Deutzia magnifica (×), W, 2.5 m (8 ft)
Deutzia maliflora (×), 'Boule Rose', W, 1 m (3 ft)
Deutzia rosea (×) 'Campanulata', W, 1 m (3 ft)
Deutzia scabra 'Campanulata', W, 1 m (3 ft)
Deutzia scabra 'Macropetala', W, 3 m (10 ft)
Deutzia sieboldiana, W, 1 m (3 ft)
Deutzia taiwanensis, W, 1.5 m (5 ft)
Deutzia vilmorinae, W, 1.5 m (5 ft)
Enkianthus campanulatus, R, 3 m (10 ft)
Erica herbacea, R–P, 25 cm (10 in)
Erica herbacea 'Myretoun Ruby', R–P, 30 cm (12 in)
Erica tetralix 'Helma', R–P, 40 cm (16 in)
Erica tetralix 'Ken Underwood', R–P, 30 cm (12 in)
Erica vagans 'George Underwood', R–P, 25 cm (10 in)
Erica vagans 'Mrs D. F. Maxwell', R, 35 cm (14 in)
Erica vagans 'St Keverne', R–P, 35 cm (14 in)
Euonymus alatus, G–Y, 2 m (6 ft)
Euonymus europaeus 'Red Cascade', W, 3 m (10 ft)
Euonymus hamiltonianus var. *hians*, Y/W, 3 m (10 ft)

Forsythia intermedia (×), Y, 2 m (6 ft)
Fuchsia magellanica 'Gracilis', R, 1 m (3 ft)
Fuchsia magellanica 'Riccartonii', R/V, 2 m (6 ft)
Hamamelis intermedia (×) 'Jelena', O, 3 m (10 ft)
Hippophae rhamnoides, G–Y, 3 m (10 ft)
Hydrangea paniculata, W, 4.5 m (15 ft)
Hydrangea paniculata 'Grandiflora', W, 4.5 m (15 ft)
Hydrangea paniculata 'Praecox', W, 4.5 m (15 ft)
Jasminum nudiflorum, Y, 3 m (10 ft)
Philadelphus hybrid 'Belle Etoile', W, 3 m (10 ft)
Philadelphus lemoinei (×) W, 2 m (6 ft)
Philadelphus lewisii var. *gordonianus*, W, 4 m (13 ft)
Pyracantha coccinea, W, 4 m (13 ft)
Ribes sanguineum, R, 3 m (10 ft)
Ribes sanguineum 'Carneum', R, 3 m (10 ft)
Salix irrorata, W, 3 m (10 ft)
Spiraea arguta (×), W, 2.5 m (8 ft)
Spiraea billardii (×), R, 2 m (6 ft)
Spiraea bumalda (×), 'Anthony Waterer', R–P, 80 cm (32 in)
Tamarix ramosissima, R, –4 m (13 ft)
Tamarix tetrandra, R, 3 m (10 ft)

Trees

○ ◑ ✳
129. No special features.

Acer platanoides, Y–G, 20 m (65 ft)
Acer platanoides, 'Goldsworth Purple', Y, 20 m (65 ft)
Acer pseudoplatanus, 'Costorphinense', Y–G, 30 m (100 ft)
Acer pseudoplatanus 'Luteo-virescens', Y–G, 30 m (100 ft)
Acer saccharinum, G, 30 m (100 ft)
Acer tegmentosum, Y, 9 m (30 ft)

○ ◑ ✳ ❀
130. Evergreen.

Acacia dealbata, Y, 20 m (65 ft)
Arbutus menziesii, W, 20 m (65 ft)
Calocedrus decurrens, 30 m (100 ft)
Camellia japonica 'Beatrice Burns', R, 4 m (13 ft)
Chamaecyparis lawsoniana, 35 m (115 ft)
Chamaecyparis lawsoniana 'Alumii', 20 m (65 ft)
Chamaecyparis lawsoniana 'Blue Nantais', 10 m (33 ft)
Chamaecyparis lawsoniana 'Ellwood's White', 8 m (26 ft)
Chamaecyparis lawsoniana 'Ellwoodii', 6 m (20 ft)
Chamaecyparis lawsoniana 'Fletcheri', 12 m (40 ft)
Chamaecyparis lawsoniana 'Intertexta', 20 m (65 ft)
Chamaecyparis lawsoniana 'Nyewoods', 10 m (33 ft)
Chamaecyparis lawsoniana 'Triomf van Boskoop', –18 m (60 ft)
Chamaecyparis obtusa, 8 m (26 ft)
Cryptomeria japonica, 25 m (80 ft)
Cryptomeria japonica 'Cristata', 3 m (10 ft)
Cupressocyparis (×) *leylandii* 'Castlewellan', 20 m (65 ft)
Cupressocyparis (×) *leylandii* 'Haggerston Grey', 20 m (65 ft)
Eucalpytus gunnii, W, 8 m (26 ft)
Eucalyptus urnigera var. *glauca*, W, 10 m (33 ft)
Juniperus chinensis 'Wilson's Weeping', 20 m (65 ft)
Juniperus virginiana 'Glauca', –5 m (16 ft)
Juniperus virginiana 'Skyrocket', 4 m (13 ft)
Picea mariana, 15 m (50 ft)
Picea omorika, 20 m (65 ft)
Picea pungens 'Argentea', 10 m (33 ft)
Picea pungens 'Glauca', 25 m (80 ft)
Picea pungens 'Koster', 10 m (33 ft)
Picea wilsonii, 7 m (23 ft)
Pinus contorta, 5 m (16 ft)
Taxus baccata 'Fastigiata', 4 m (13 ft)
Taxus baccata 'Pyramidalis Variegata', 6 m (20 ft)
Thuja occidentalis 'Aurea', 15 m (50 ft)
Thuja occidentalis, 20 m (65 ft)
Thuja orientalis 'Elegantissima', 5 m (16 ft)
Thuja plicata, –60 m (200 ft)
Tsuga mertensiana, 30 m (100 ft)

○ ◐ ❋ ❀

131. With attractive fruits or berries.

Acer cappadocicum, Y, 20 m (65 ft)
Acer griseum, Y, 12 m (40 ft)
Aesculus carnea (×), R, 15 m (50 ft)
Aesculus hippocastanum, W, 30 m (100 ft)
Aesculus hippocastanum 'Memmingeri', W, 30 m (100 ft)
Aesculus pavia, R, 15 m (50 ft)
Ailanthus altissima, O, 20 m (65 ft)
Arbutus menziesii, W, 20 m (65 ft)
Carpinus betulus, Y–G, 20 m (65 ft)
Castanea sativa 'Glabra', G–Y, 20 m (65 ft)
Chamaecyparis lawsoniana, 35 m (115 ft)
Chamaecyparis lawsoniana 'Alumii', 20 m (65 ft)
Chamaecyparis lawsoniana 'Blue Nantais', 10 m (33 ft)
Chamaecyparis lawsoniana 'Ellwood's White', 8 m (26 ft)
Chamaecyparis lawsoniana 'Ellwoodii', 6 m (20 ft)
Chamaecyparis lawsoniana 'Fletcheri', 12 m (40 ft)
Chamaecyparis lawsoniana 'Intertexta', 20 m (65 ft)
Chamaecyparis lawsoniana 'Nyewoods', 10 m (33 ft)
Chamaecyparis lawsoniana 'Triomf van Boskoop', –18 m (60 ft)
Chamaecyparis obtusa, 8 m (26 ft)
Crataegomespilus (×) *dardarii*, W, 6 m (20 ft)
Crataegus (×) *grignonensis*, W, 3.5 m (11 ft)
Crataegus laevigata 'Mutabilis', W, 4 m (13 ft)
Crataegus laevigata 'Paul's Scarlet', R, 7 m (23 ft)
Crataegus prunifolia (×), W, 4 m (13 ft)
Crataegus punctata, W, 6 m (20 ft)
Crataegus succulenta, R, 5 m (16 ft)
Fagus sylvatica, G, 40 m (135 ft)
Fagus sylvatica 'Asplenifolia', G, 25 m (80 ft)
Fagus sylvatica 'Atropunicea', G, 40 m (135 ft)
Fagus sylvatica 'Fastigiata', G, 20 m (65 ft)
Fagus sylvatica 'Zlatia', G, 40 m (135 ft)
Juglans cinerea, G, 25 m (80 ft)
Juniperus chinensis 'Wilson's Weeping', 20 m (65 ft)
Juniperus virginiana 'Glauca', –5 m (16 ft)
Juniperus virginiana 'Skyrocket', 4 m (13 ft)
Malus baccata 'Gracilis', W, 8 m (26 ft)
Mespilus germanica 'Macrocarpa', W, 5 m (16 ft)
Morus alba 'Pendula', G–Y, 6 m (20 ft)
Nyssa sylvatica, G, 20 m (65 ft)
Ostrya virginiana, G, 20 m (65 ft)
Phellodendron amurense, G–Y, 15 m (50 ft)
Phellodendron japonicum, Y–G, 15 m (50 ft)
Picea mariana, 15 m (50 ft)
Picea omorika, 20 m (65 ft)
Picea pungens 'Argentea', 10 m (33 ft)
Picea pungens 'Glauca', 25 m (80 ft)
Picea pungens 'Koster', 10 m (33 ft)
Picea wilsonii, 7 m (23 ft)
Pterocarya rhoifolia, G, 25 m (80 ft)
Quercus coccinea 'Splendens', G, 25 m (80 ft)
Quercus dentata, G, 20 m (65 ft)
Quercus macranthera, G, 20 m (65 ft)
Quercus robur, Y–G, –30 m (100 ft)
Quercus robur 'Fastigiata', Y–G, 15 m (50 ft)
Quercus robur 'Pectinata', Y–G, 20 m (65 ft)
Quercus rubra, Y–G, 25 m (80 ft)
Quercus schochiana (×), Y–G, 15 m (50 ft)
Sorbus alnifolia, W, 12 m (40 ft)
Sorbus americana 'Belmonte', W, 8 m (26 ft)
Sorbus aria 'Majestica', W, 10 m (33 ft)
Sorbus aucuparia 'Beissneri', W, 15 m (50 ft)
Sorbus austriaca, W, 7 m (23 ft)
Sorbus 'Copper Glow', W, 8 m (26 ft)
Sorbus decora, W, 6 m (20 ft)
Sorbus discolor, W, 10 m (33 ft)
Sorbus hupehensis 'November Pink', W, 7 m (23 ft)
Sorbus 'Joseph Rock', W, 9 m (30 ft)
Sorbus 'Mitchellii', W, 8 m (26 ft)
Styrax obassia, W, 9 m (30 ft)
Taxus baccata 'Fastigiata', 4 m (13 ft)
Taxus baccata 'Fastigiata Aurea', 4 m (13 ft)
Taxus baccata 'Pyramidalis Variegata', 6 m (20 ft)
Thuja occidentalis, 20 m (65 ft)
Thuja occidentalis 'Aurea', 15 m (50 ft)
Thuja orientalis 'Elegantissima', 5 m (16 ft)
Thuja plicata, 60 m (200 ft)
Tilia platyphyllos, Y–W, 30 m (100 ft)
Tsuga mertensiana, 30 m (100 ft)

○ ◐ ❋ ◎

132. Wholly or partly poisonous.

Aesculus carnea (×), R, 15 m (50 ft)
Aesculus hippocastanum, W, 30 m (100 ft)
Aesculus hippocastanum 'Memmingeri', W, 30 m (100 ft)
Chamaecyparis lawsoniana 35 m (115 ft)
Chamaecyparis lawsoniana 'Alumii', 20 m (65 ft)
Chamaecyparis lawsoniana 'Blue Nantais', 10 m (33 ft)
Chamaecyparis lawsoniana 'Ellwood's White', 8 m (26 ft)
Chamaecyparis lawsoniana 'Ellwoodii', 6 m (20 ft)
Chamaecyparis lawsoniana 'Fletcheri', 12 m (40 ft)
Chamaecyparis lawsoniana 'Intertexta', 20 m (65 ft)
Chamaecyparis lawsoniana 'Nyewoods', 10 m (33 ft)
Chamaecyparis lawsoniana 'Triomf van Boskoop', –18 m (60 ft)
Chamaecyparis obtusa, 8 m (26 ft)
Juniperus chinensis 'Wilson's Weeping', 20 m (65 ft)
Juniperus virginiana 'Glauca', –5 m (16 ft)
Juniperus virginiana 'Skyrocket', 4 m (13 ft)
Taxus baccata 'Fastigiata', 4 m (13 ft)
Taxus baccata 'Fastigiata Aurea', 4 m (13 ft)
Taxus baccata 'Pyramidalis Variegata', 6 m (20 ft)
Thuja occidentalis, 20 m (65 ft)
Thuja occidentalis 'Aurea', 15 m (50 ft)

○ ◐ ❋ ⊕

133. Suitable as a specimen tree.

Acacia dealbata, Y, 20 m (65 ft)
Acer cappadocicum, Y, 20 m (65 ft)
Acer griseum, Y, 12 m (40 ft)
Acer platanoides 'Drummondii', Y, 15 m (50 ft)
Acer platanoides 'Globosum', Y, 5 m (16 ft)
Acer pseudoplatanus 'Atropurpureum', Y–G, 15 m (50 ft)
Aesculus carnea (×), R, 15 m (50 ft)
Aesculus hippocastanum, W, 30 m (100 ft)
Aesculus hippocastanum 'Memmingeri', W, 30 m (100 ft)
Aesculus pavia, R, 15 m (50 ft)
Calocedrus decurrens, 30 m (100 ft)
Chamaecyparis lawsoniana, 35 m (115 ft)
Chamaecyparis lawsoniana 'Alumii', 20 m (65 ft)
Chamaecyparis lawsoniana 'Blue Nantais', 10 m (33 ft)
Chamaecyparis lawsoniana 'Ellwood's White', 8 m (26 ft)
Chamaecyparis lawsoniana 'Ellwoodii', 6 m (20 ft)
Chamaecyparis lawsoniana 'Fletcheri', 12 m (40 ft)
Chamaecyparis lawsoniana 'Intertexta', 20 m (65 ft)
Chamaecyparis lawsoniana 'Nyewoods', 10 m (33 ft)
Chamaecyparis lawsoniana 'Triomf van Boskoop', –18 m (60 ft)
Chamaecyparis obtusa, 8 m (26 ft)
Crataegus laevigata 'Paul's Scarlet', R, 7 m (23 ft)
Cryptomeria japonica, 25 m (80 ft)
Cryptomeria japonica 'Cristata', 3 m (10 ft)
Cupressocyparis (×) *leylandii* 'Castlewellan', 20 m (65 ft)
Cupressocyparis (×) *leylandii* 'Haggerston Grey', 20 m (65 ft)
Eucalyptus gunnii, W, 8 m (26 ft)
Eucalyptus urnigera var. *glauca*, W, 10 m (33 ft)
Fagus sylvatica, G, 40 m (135 ft)
Fagus sylvatica 'Asplenifolia', G, 25 m (80 ft)
Fagus sylvatica 'Atropunicea', 40 m (135 ft)
Fagus sylvatica 'Fastigiata', G, 20 m (65 ft)
Fagus sylvatica 'Zlatia', G, 40 m (135 ft)
Juglans cinerea, G, 25 m (80 ft)
Juniperus chinensis 'Wilson's Weeping', 20 m (65 ft)
Juniperus virginiana 'Glauca', –5 m (16 ft)
Juniperus virginiana 'Skyrocket', 4 m (13 ft)
Malus baccata 'Gracilis', W, 8 m (26 ft)
Mespilus germanica 'Macrocarpa', W, 5 m (16 ft)
Nothofagus antarctica, G, 10 m (33 ft)
Nyssa sylvatica, G, 20 m (65 ft)
Ostrya virginiana, 20 m (65 ft)
Paulownia tomentosa, V/Y, 10 m (33 ft)
Picea mariana, 15 m (50 ft)
Picea omorika, 20 m (65 ft)
Picea pungens 'Argentea', 10 m (33 ft)
Picea pungens 'Glauca', 25 m (80 ft)
Picea pungens 'Koster', 10 m (33 ft)
Picea wilsonii, 7 m (23 ft)
Pinus contorta, 5 m (16 ft)
Taxus baccata 'Fastigiata', 4 m (13 ft)
Taxus baccata 'Fastigiata Aurea', 4 m (13 ft)
Taxus baccata 'Pyramidalis Variegata', 6 m (20 ft)
Thuja occidentalis 'Aurea', 15 m (50 ft)
Thuja plicata, –60 m (200 ft)
Tilia euchlora (×), Y, 20 m (65 ft)
Tilia europaea, Y–W, 40 m (135 ft)
Tilia moltkei (×), Y–W, 20 m (65 ft)
Tilia platyphyllos, Y–W, 30 m (100 ft)
Tsuga mertensiana, 30 m (100 ft)

○ ◑ ❋ ⊗

134. Suitable for rock gardens.

Picea pungens 'Glauca', 25 m (80 ft)
Picea pungens 'Koster', 10 m (33 ft)

○ ◑ ❋ ▥

135. Also suitable for hedging.

Carpinus betulus, Y–G, 20 m (65 ft)
Chamaecyparis lawsoniana, 35 m (115 ft)
Chamaecyparis lawsoniana 'Alumii', 20 m (65 ft)
Chamaecyparis lawsoniana 'Triomf van Boskoop', –18 m (60 ft)
Cupressocyparis (×) *leylandii* 'Castlewellan', 20 m (65 ft)
Cupressocyparis (×) *leylandii* 'Haggerston Grey', 20 m (65 ft)
Fagus sylvatica, G, 40 m (135 ft)
Fagus sylvatica 'Atropunicea', G, 40 m (135 ft)
Populus canadensis hybrid, Y–G, 25 m (80 ft)
Thuja occidentalis, 20 m (65 ft)
Thuja occidentalis 'Aurea', 15 m (50 ft)

○ ◑ ❋ ⊗

136. Suitable for cutting.

Eucalyptus gunnii, W, 8 m (26 ft)
Quercus rubra, Y–G, 25 m (80 ft)

Trees and shrubs

○ ◑ ◍ ❋

137. No special features.

Acer pseudoplatanus 'Prinz Handjery', Y–G, 3 m (10 ft)
Acer rubrum 'Scanlon', R, 15 m (50 ft)

○ ◑ ◍ ❋ ❀

138. Evergreen.

Ilex altaclarensis (×) 'Camelliaefolia', W, 7 m (23 ft)
Ilex altaclarensis (×) 'Golden King', W, 8 m (26 ft)
Ilex aquifolium 'Argentea Longifolia', W, 8 m (26 ft)
Osmanthus yunnanensis, W–Y, 8 m (26 ft)
Taxus baccata, 10 m (33 ft)

○ ◑ ◍ ❋ ❀

139. With attractive fruits or berries.

Acer capilipes, Y–W, 6 m (20 ft)
Acer negundo ssp. *californicum,* Y–G, 15 m (50 ft)
Amelanchier lamarckii, W, 10 m (33 ft)
Aralia elata, W, 5 m (16 ft)
Aralia elata 'Variegata', W, 2 m (6 ft)
Crataegus lavallei (×), W, 5 m (16 ft)
Crataegus monogyna 'Pendula', W, 8 m (26 ft)
Dipteronia sinensis, G, 15 m (50 ft)
Elaeagnus angustifolia, Y, 7 m (23 ft)
Halesia carolina var. *monticola,* W, 6 m (20 ft)
Ilex altaclarensis (×), 'Camelliaefolia', W, 7 m (23 ft)
Ilex altaclarensis (×) 'Golden King', W, 8 m (26 ft)
Ilex aquifolium 'Argentea Longifolia', W, 8 m (26 ft)
Laburnum anagyroides, Y, 8 m (26 ft)
Laburnum anagyroides 'Pendulum', Y, 4 m (13 ft)
Laburnum watereri (×) 'Vossii', Y, 8 m (26 ft)
Osmanthus yunnanensis, W–Y, 8 m (26 ft)
Poncirus trifoliatus, W, 3 m (10 ft)
Quercus pontica, Y–G, 6 m (20 ft)
Taxus baccata, 10 m (33 ft)

○ ◑ ◍ ❋ ◎

140. Wholly or partly poisonous.

Ilex altaclarensis (×) 'Camelliaefolia', W, 7 m (23 ft)
Ilex altaclarensis (×) 'Golden King', W, 8 m (26 ft)
Ilex aquifolium 'Argentea Longifolia' W, 8 m (26 ft)
Laburnum anagyroides, Y, 8 m (26 ft)
Laburnum anagyroides 'Pendulum', Y, 4 m (13 ft)
Laburnum watereri (×) 'Vossii', Y, 8 m (26 ft)
Taxus baccata, 10 m (33 ft)

○ ◑ ◍ ❋ ⊕

141. Suitable as a specimen plant.

Acer japonicum 'Acontifolium', R, 5 m (16 ft)
Acer japonicum 'Aureum', R, 5 m (16 ft)
Aralia elata 'Variegata', W, 2 m (6 ft)

Crataegus lavallei (×), W, 5 m (16 ft)
Crataegus monogyna 'Pendula', W, 8 m (26 ft)
Davidia involucrata, W, 15 m (50 ft)
Eucryphia nymanensis, (×), W, 6 m (20 ft)
Ilex altaclarensis (×) 'Camelliaefolia', W, 7 m (23 ft)
Ilex altaclarensis (×) 'Golden King', W, 8 m (26 ft)
Ilex aquifolium 'Argentea Longifolia', W, 8 m (26 ft)

○ ◑ ◍ ❋ ▥

142. Suitable for hedging.

Ilex altaclarensis (×) 'Camelliaefolia', W, 7 m (23 ft)
Ilex altaclarensis (×) 'Golden King', W, 8 m (26 ft)
Ilex aquifolium 'Argentea Longifolia', W, 8 m (26 ft)
Taxus baccata, 10 m (33 ft)

○ ◑ ◍ ❋ ⊗

143. Suitable for cutting.

Ilex altaclarensis (×) 'Camelliaefolia', W, 7 m (23 ft)
Ilex altaclarensis (×) 'Golden King', W, 8 m (26 ft)
Ilex aquifolium 'Argentea Longifolia' W, 8 m (26 ft)
Laburnum anagyroides, Y, 8 m (26 ft)
Laburnum watereri (×) 'Vossii', Y, 8 m (26 ft)
Poncirus trifoliatus, W, 3 m (10 ft)

FULL SUN, SEMI-SHADE; MOIST GROUND

Herbaceous perennials

○ ◑ ⊗ ○

144. No special features.

Azolla filiculoides, R
Cardamine pratensis, P, –40 cm (16 in)
Cimicifuga dahurica, W, 2 m (6 ft)
Gentiana cruciata, B, 30 cm (12 in)
Glyceria maxima 'Variegata', 1.5 m (5 ft)
Hydrocharis morsus-ranae, W, 5 cm (2 in)
Iris kaempferi, var. col., –1 m (3 ft)
Lysichitum americanum, Y, –70 cm (28 in)
Lysichitum camtschatcence, W, 1 m (3 ft)
Lysimachia clethroides, W, –80 cm (32 in)
Mentha spicata, P–V, 60 cm (24 in)
Menyanthes trifoliata, W, –40 cm (16 in)
Mimulus burnettii (×) 'A. T. Johnson', Y–R, 25 cm (10 in)
Mimulus luteus, Y, 40 cm (16 in)
Mimulus hybrid 'Orange King', O/R, 25 cm (10 in)
Miscanthus sinensis 'Zebrinus', W, 1.5 m (5 ft)
Nuphar lutea, Y, –2.5 m (8 ft)
Polygonum campanulatum, R, –1 m (3 ft)
Primula florindae, Y, –75 cm (30 in)
Primula pulverulenta, P, 80 cm (32 in)
Scirpus tabernaemontani 'Zebrinus', R-Brown, 1.5 m (5 ft)
Telekia speciosa, Y, 1.5 m (5 ft)
Veratrum nigrum, R, –1 m (3 ft)

○ ◑ ⊗ ○ ❀

145. Evergreen.

Cotula squalida, G, 5 cm (2 in)
Myosotis palustris, V–B, –25 cm (10 in)

○ ◑ ⊗ ○ ◎

146. Wholly or partly poisonous.

Calla palustris, W, –40 cm (16 in)
Caltha palustris, Y, 50 cm (20 in)
Caltha palustris 'Plena', Y, 50 cm (20 in)
Iris pseudacorus, Y, –1 m (3 ft)
Lupinus polyphyllus 'Abendglut', R, 1 m (3 ft)
Lupinus polyphyllus 'Noble Maiden', W, 1 m (3 ft)
Lupinus polyphyllus 'The Chatelaine', R, 1 m (3 ft)
Pulsatilla vulgaris, P–V, –25 cm (10 in)
Ranunculus lingua, Y, –80 cm (32 in)

○ ◐ ⊗ ○ ⊕
147. Suitable as a specimen plant.

Carex pendula, G, –1.5 m (5 ft)
Gunnera manicata, Brown, –3 m (10 ft)
Gunnera tinctoria, Brown–R, –3 m (10 ft)
Ligularia przewalskii, Y, 1.5 m (5 ft)
Ligularia veitchiana, Y, 2 m (6 ft)
Ligularia wilsoniana, Y, 1.6 m (5½ ft)
Lythrum hybrid 'The Rocket', R–P, 1.5 m (5 ft)
Osmunda regalis, –1 m (3 ft)
Senecio doria, Y, 1.8 m (6 ft)

○ ◐ ⊗ ○ ⊗
148. Suitable for rock gardens and crevices in paving.

Cotula squalida, G, 5 cm (2 in)
Mentha rotundifolia 'Variegata', W, –60 cm (24 in)
Primula elatior 'Aurea', Y, 20 cm (8 in)
Primula elatior hybrid, R, 25 cm (10 in)
Primula elatior ssp. *pallassii*, Y, 20 cm (8 in)
Primula farinosa, P, 20 cm (8 in)
Pulsatilla vulgaris, P–V, –25 cm (10 in)
Scutellaria incana, P, –1 m (3 ft)

○ ◐ ⊗ ○ ⊖
149. Suitable for ground cover.

Astibe hybrid 'Mowe', R, –60 cm (24 in)
Calla palustris, W, –40 cm (16 in)
Cotula squalida, G, 5 cm (2 in)
Mentha aquatica, P/V, –90 cm (3 ft)
Viola odorata, P–V, –20 cm (8 in)

○ ◐ ⊗ ○ ⊗
150. Suitable for cutting.

Alisma plantago-aquatica, W, –80 cm (32 in)
Astilbe hybrid 'Fanal', R, –75 cm (30 in)
Astilbe hybrid 'Peach Blossom', R, –60 cm (24 in)
Astilbe hybrid 'Vesuvius', R, –75 cm (30 in)
Cimicifuga ramosa, W, –1.5 m (5 ft)
Cimicifuga simplex, W, –1.2 m (4 ft)
Dactylorhiza foliosa, R–P, –80 cm (32 in)
Ligularia przewalskii, Y, 1.5 m (5 ft)
Ligularia veitchiana, Y, 2 m (6 ft)
Ligularia wilsoniana, Y, 1.6 m (5½ ft)
Lupinus polyphyllus 'Abendglut', R, 1 m (3 ft)
Lupinus polyphyllus 'Noble Maiden', W, 1 m (3 ft)
Lupinus polyphyllus 'The Chatelaine', R, 1 m (3 ft)
Lythrum salicaria, R–P, –2 m (6 ft)
Mentha aquatica, P/V, –90 cm (3 ft)
Mentha longifolia var. *longifolia*, P–V, –80 cm (32 in)
Monarda hybrid 'Prairienacht', P–V, 80 cm (32 in)
Polygonum amplexicaule, R–P, (3 ft)
Scutellaria incana, P, –1 m (3 ft)
Typha latifolia, Brown, 2.5 m (8 ft)

Bulbs

○ ◐ ⊗ ◎
151. No special features.

Camassia cusickii, B, 1 m (3 ft)
Corbularia bulbocodium, Y, 10 cm (4 in)

○ ◐ ⊗ ◎ ◎
152. Wholly or partly poisonous.

Fritillaria meleagris, var. col., –40 cm (16 in)
Leucojum aestivum, W, –50 cm (20 in)

Tubers

○ ◐ ⊗ ◎
153. No special features.

Nymphoides peltata, Y, 10 cm (4 in)
Sagittaria sagittifolia, W, –70 cm (28 in)

○ ◐ ⊗ ◎ ⊗
154. Suitable for cutting.

Crocosmia crocosmiiflora, (×), O–R, –1 m (3 ft)
Iris sibirica, B, –1 m (3 ft)
Iris sibirica 'Blue King', P, 1 m (3 ft)

Shrubs

○ ◐ ⊗ ◎
155. No special features.

Acer palmatum 'Corallinum', R, 3 m (10 ft)
Acer palmatum 'Roseomarginatum', R, 6 m (20 ft)
Cornus sericea 'Flaviramea', W, 2.5 m (8 ft)
Hydrangea macrophylla 'Bouquet Rose', R, 1.2 m (4 ft)

○ ◐ ⊗ ◎ ❀
156. Evergreen.

Erica arborea var. *alpina*, W, 1.5 m (5 ft)
Erica darleyensis (×) 'Darley Dale', R–P, 40 cm (16 in)
Kalmia angustifolia, R–P, 1 m (3 ft)
Kalmia latifolia, R, 3 m (10 ft)
Leucothoe axillaris, W, 1.5 m (5 ft)
Sinarundinaria murielae, 2.5 m (8 ft)

○ ◐ ⊗ ◎ ❀
157. With attractive fruits or berries.

Chaenomeles japonica, Y–G, 2.5 m (8 ft)
Chaenomeles speciosa 'Simonii', Y, 50 cm (20 in)
Chaenomeles superba (×) 'Crimson and Gold', Y, 1 m (3 ft)
Dipelta ventricosa, P–O, 2 m (6 ft)
Rubus thibetanus, P–V, 2 m (6 ft)
Vaccinium corymbosum, R, 2 m (6 ft)
Viburnum opulus 'Notcutt', W, 4.5 m (15 ft)

○ ◐ ⊗ ◎ ◎
158. Wholly or partly poisonous.

Chaenomeles japonica, Y–G, 2.5 m (8 ft)
Chaenomeles speciosa 'Simonii', Y, 50 cm (20 in)
Chaenomeles superba (×) 'Crimson and Gold', Y, 1 m (3 ft)
Erica arborea var. *alpina*, W. 1.5 m (5 ft)
Erica darleyensis (×) 'Darley Dale', R–P, 40 cm (16 in)
Kalmia angustifolia, R–P, 1 m (3 ft)
Kalmia latifolia, R, 3 m (10 ft)

○ ◐ ⊗ ◎ ⊕
159. Suitable as a specimen plant.

Acer palmatum 'Atropurpureum', R, 6 m (20 ft)
Acer palmatum var. *heptalobum*, R, 4.5 m (15 ft)
Fothergilla major, W, 2 m (6 ft)
Hydrangea aspera ssp. *sargentiana*, V, 2 m (6 ft)
Hydrangea heteromalla, R–P, 3 m (10 ft)
Hydrangea macrophylla, 'Lilacina', B, 1.5 m (5 ft)
Hydrangea macrophylla ssp. *serrata*, B, 1 m (3 ft)
Salix moupinensis, Y–G, 6 m (20 ft)

○ ◐ ⊗ ◎ ⊗
160. Suitable for rock gardens and crevices in paving.

Salix hastata 'Wehrhahnii', 1.5 m (5 ft)

○ ◐ ⊗ ◎ ⊖
161. Suitable for ground cover.

Chaenomeles speciosa 'Simonii', Y, 50 cm (20 in)
Chaenomeles superba (×) 'Crimson and Gold', Y, 1 m (3 ft)
Erica darleyensis (×) 'Darley Dale', R–P, 40 cm (16 in)

○ ◐ ⊗ ◎ ⊗
162. Suitable for cutting.

Erica arborea var. *alpina*, W, 1.5 m (5 ft)
Hydrangea aspera ssp. *sargentiana*, V, 2 m (6 ft)
Hydrangea macrophylla 'Lilacina', B, 1.5 m (5 ft)
Hydrangea macrophylla, R/B, 2 m (6 ft)
Salix hastata 'Wehrhahnii', 1.5 m (5 ft)
Salix moupinensis, Y–G, 6 m (20 ft)
Salix sachalinensis 'Sekka', Y–G, 4.5 m (15 ft)

Trees

○ ◑ ⊗ ✽ ✿
163. Evergreen.

Picea brewerana, 30 m (100 ft)

○ ◑ ⊗ ✽ ✾
164. With attractive fruits or berries.

Alnus glutinosa, 25 m (80 ft)
Picea brewerana, 30 m (100 ft)

○ ◑ ⊗ ✽ ⊕
165. Suitable as a specimen tree.

Cercidiphyllum japonicum, R, 10 m (33 ft)
Liquidambar styraciflua, G–Y, 15 m (50 ft)
Picea brewerana, 30 m (100 ft)
Populus nigra 'Italica', Y–G, 30 m (100 ft)
Salix alba 'Tristis', Y–G, 15 m (50 ft)

○ ◑ ⊗ ✽ ▥
166. Also suitable for hedging.

Alnus glutinosa, 25 m (80 ft)
Populus nigra 'Italica', Y–G, 30 m (100 ft)

○ ◑ ⊗ ✽ ⊗
167. Suitable for cutting.

Alnus glutinosa, 25 m (80 ft)

Shrubs and trees

○ ◑ ⊗ ⊛ ✽ ✾
168. With attractive fruits or berries.

Amelanchier florida, B-Black, 4 m (13 ft)

FULL SUN, SEMI-SHADE; DRY SITE

Annuals

○ ◑ ⊖ ⊙ ⊚
169. Wholly or partly poisonous.

Papaver rhoeas, R, –90 cm (3 ft)

○ ◑ ⊖ ⊙ ⊗
170. Suitable for cutting.

Papaver rhoeas, R, –90 cm (3 ft)
Papaver somniferum, var. col., 1 m (3 ft)
Reseda odorata 'Manchet', G–Y, –75 cm (30 in)

Biennials

○ ◑ ⊖ ⊙ ⊗
171. Suitable for rock gardens and crevices in paving.

Cheiranthus cheiri, var. col., 40 cm (16 in)
Papaver nudicaule, var. col., –45 cm (18 in)

○ ◑ ⊖ ⊙ ⊗
172. Suitable for cutting.

Cheiranthus cheiri, var. col., 40 cm (16 in)
Lychnis coronaria 'Alba', W, 60 cm (24 in)
Papaver nudicaule, var. col., –45 cm (18 in)

Herbaceous perennials

○ ◑ ⊖ ○
173. No special features.

Polygonum sericeum, W, 60 cm (24 in)

○ ◑ ⊖ ○ ✾
174. Evergreen.

Phlox douglasii, P, 10 cm (4 in)
Phlox douglasii var. *diffusa*, V, 10 cm (4 in)
Sedum acre, Y, 15 cm (6 in)
Sedum album 'Coral Carpet', W, 10 cm (4 in)
Sedum floriferum 'Weihenstephaner Gold', Y, 15 cm (6 in)
Sedum middendorffianum, Y, –20 cm (8 in)
Sempervivum arachnoideum ssp. *tomentosum*, R–P, 10 cm (4 in)
Sempervivum ciliosum, Y, 5 cm (2 in)
Sempervivum tectorum, R, 5 cm (2 in)
Sempervivum zelebori 'Alpha', R, 10 cm (4 in)

○ ◑ ⊖ ○ ☠
175. Wholly or partly poisonous.

Sedum acre, Y, 15 cm (6 in)

○ ◑ ⊖ ○ ⊗
176. Suitable for rock gardens and crevices in paving.

Anaphalis margaritacea, W, –75 cm (30 in)
Anaphalis triplinervis 'Schwefellicht', Y, –50 cm (20 in)
Androsace sarmentosa, R–P, 12 cm (4½ in)
Aster himalaicus, P, –30 cm (12 in)
Festuca cinerea, W, –40 cm (16 in)
Festuca ovina 'Silberreiher', W, 25 cm (10 in)
Jasione laevis, B, 30 cm (12 in)
Linaria vulgaris, Y, 80 cm (32 in)
Papaver nudicaule, var. col., –45 cm (18 in)
Phlox amoena, P. –30 cm (12 in)
Phlox douglasii, P, 10 cm (4 in)
Phlox douglasii var. *diffusa*. V, 10 cm (4 in)
Saponaria officinalis, P, –80 cm (32 in)
Saponaria officinalis 'Plena', P, –80 cm (32 in)
Sedum acre, Y, 15 cm (6 in)
Sedum aizoon, Y, 40 cm (16 in)
Sedum album 'Coral Carpet', W, 10 cm (4 in)
Sedum cyaneum 'Rosenteppich', R, 10 cm (4 in)
Sedum floriferum 'Weihenstephaner Gold', Y, 15 cm (6 in)
Sedum middendorffianum, Y, –20 cm (8 in)
Sempervivum arachnoideum ssp. *tomentosum*, R–P, 10 cm (4 in)
Sempervivum ciliosum, Y, 5 cm (2 in)
Sempervivum tectorum, R, 5 cm (2 in)
Sempervivum zelebori, 'Alpha', R, 10 cm (4 in)

○ ◑ ⊖ ○ ⊝
177. Suitable for ground cover.

Festuca cinerea, W, –40 cm (16 in)
Festuca ovina 'Silberreiher', W, 25 cm (10 in)
Sedum acre, Y, 15 cm (6 in)
Sedum album 'Coral Carpet', W, 10 cm (4 in)
Sedum cyaneum 'Rosenteppich', R, 10 cm (4 in)
Sedum floriferum 'Weihenstephaner gold', Y, 15 cm (6 in)
Sedum middendorffianum, Y, –20 cm (8 in)
Sempervivum arachnoideum ssp. *tomentosum*, R–P, 10 cm (4 in)
Sempervivum ciliosum, Y, 5 cm (2 in)
Sempervivum tectorum, R, 5 cm (2 in)
Sempervivum zelebori 'Alpha', R, 10 cm (4 in)

○ ◑ ⊖ ○ ⊗
178. Suitable for cutting.

Anaphalis margaritacea, W, –75 cm (30 in)
Anaphalis triplinervis 'Schwefellicht', Y, –50 cm(20 in)
Elymus arenarius, –1.5 m (5 ft)
Hieracium aurantiacum, O, 40 cm (16 in)
Hieracium rubrum (×) O–R, 20 cm (8 in)
Liatris spicata 'Kobald', P, 50 cm (20 in)
Linaria vulgaris, Y, 80 cm (32 in)
Lychnis coronaria, R, –60 cm (24 in)
Lychnis coronaria 'Alba', W, 60 cm (24 in)
Lychnis viscaria V–R, –50 cm (20 in)
Papaver nudicaule, var. col., –45 km (18 in)

Shrubs

○ ◐ ⊖ ◍

179. No special features.

Hedysarum multijugum, R, 1 m (3 ft)
Lespedeza thunbergii, R–P, 2 m (6 ft)
Spartium junceum, Y, 3 m (10 ft)

○ ◐ ⊖ ◍ ✾

180. Evergreen.

Coronilla valentina ssp. *glauca*, Y, 1 m (3 ft)
Daphne cneorum, R, 30 cm (12 in)
Juniperus communis 'Hibernica', 6 m (20 ft)
Juniperus sabina 'Musgrave', 60 cm (24 in)
Ruscus hypophyllum, W, 30 cm (12 in)

○ ◐ ⊖ ◍ ❀

181. With attractive fruits or berries.

Clematis alpina 'Willy', R–P, 3 m (10 ft)
Elaeagnus umbellata, W, 4 m (13 ft)
Juniperus sabina 'Musgrave', 60 cm (24 in)
Ruscus hypophyllum, W, 30 cm (12 in)

○ ◐ ⊖ ◍ ◎

182. Wholly or partly poisonous.

Clematis alpina 'Willy', R–P, 3 m (10 ft)
Clematis viticella, 'Minuet', R–P, 3 m (10 ft)
Juniperus communis 'Hibernica', 6 m (20 ft)
Juniperus sabina 'Musgrave', 60 cm (24 in)

○ ◐ ⊖ ◍ ⊕

183. Suitable as a specimen plant.

Juniperus communis 'Hibernica', 6 m (20 ft)

FULL SUN, SEMI-SHADE AND SHADE

Shrubs

○ ◐ ◍ ◍ ✾

184. Evergreen.

Cotoneaster dammeri, W, 20 cm (8 in)
Hedera helix, G–Y, 20 m (65 ft)
Ilex crenata 'Golden Gem', G, 80 cm (32 in)
Ligularia ovalifolium, W, 4.5 m (15 ft)
Mahonia bealii, Y, 1 m (3 ft)
Mahonia japonica 'Hiemalis', Y, 1 m (3 ft)
Taxus cupidata 'Nana Aurea', 1 m (3 ft)

○ ◐ ◍ ◍ ❀

185. With attractive fruits or berries.

Clematis vitalba, W, 15 m (50 ft)
Cotoneaster dammeri, R, 20 cm (8 in)
Ilex crenata 'Golden Gem', G, 80 cm (32 in)
Ilex verticillata, Y–W, 3 m (10 ft)
Ligustrum vulgare 'Aureum', W, 4.5 m (15 ft)
Lonicera involucrata f. *serotina*, Y–O, 2 m (6 ft)
Mahonia bealii, Y, 1 m (3 ft)
Mahonia japonica 'Hiemalis', Y, 1 m (3 ft)
Sambucus canadensis 'Maxima', W, –4 m (13 ft)
Symphoricarpos albus var. *laevigatus*, R, 1.5 m (5 ft)
Symphoricarpos doorenbosii (×) 'Magic Berry', R, 80 cm (32 in)
Symphoricarpos doorenbosii (×) 'Mother of Pearl', R, 1.2 m (4 ft)
Viburnum lantana, W, 3 m (10 ft)

○ ◐ ◍ ◍ ◎

186. Wholly or partly poisonous.

Clematis vitalba, W, 15 m (50 ft)
Hedera helix, G–Y, 20 m (65 ft)
Ilex crenata 'Golden Gem', G, 80 cm (32 in)
Ilex verticillata, Y–W, 3 m (10 ft)
Ligularia ovalifolium, W, 4.5 m (15 ft)

Ligustrum vulgare 'Aureum', W, 4.5 m (15 ft)
Lonicera heckrottii (×), 6 m (20 ft)
Lonicera involucrata f. *serotina*, Y–O, 2 m (6 ft)
Symphoricarpos albus var. *laevigatus*, R, 1.5 m (5 ft)
Taxus cuspidata 'Nana Aurea', 1 m (3 ft)

○ ◐ ◍ ◍ ⊗

187. Suitable for rock gardens and crevices in paving.

Cotoneaster dammeri, W, 20 cm (8 in)

○ ◐ ◍ ◍ ◍

188. Suitable for hedging.

Ilex crenata 'Golden Gem', G, 80 cm (32 in)
Ligularia ovalifolium, W, 4.5 m (15 ft)
Ligustrum vulgare 'Aureum', W, 4.5 m (15 ft)
Symphoricarpos albus var. *laevigatus*, R, 1.5 m (5 ft)
Symphoricarpos doorenbosii (×) 'Magic Berry', R, 80 cm (32 in)
Symphoricarpos doorenbosii (×) 'Mother of Pearl', R, 1.2 m (4 ft)

○ ◐ ◍ ◍ ⊖

189. Suitable for ground cover.

Cotoneaster dammeri, W, 20 cm (8 in)
Hedera helix, G–Y, 20 cm (65 ft)

○ ◐ ◍ ◍ ⊗

190. Suitable for cutting.

Ilex verticillata, Y–W, 3 m (10 ft)
Symphoricarpos albus var. *laevigatus*, R. 1.5 m (5 ft)
Symphoricarpos doorenbosii (×) 'Magic Berry', R, 80 cm (32 in)
Symphoricarpos doorenbosii (×) 'Mother of Pearl', R, 1.2 m (4 ft)

Shrubs and trees

○ ◐ ◍ ◍ ✾ ❀ ◎

191. With attractive fruits or berries; wholly or partly poisonous.

Ilex aquifolium 'J.C. van Tol', G, 5 m (16 ft)
Prunus serotina, W, 8 m (26 ft)

SEMI-SHADE

Annuals

◐ ☉

192. No special features.

Begonia semperflorens hybrid, var. col., 20 cm (8 in)
Browallia americana, B, 60 cm (24 in)
Impatiens balsamina 'Cinnabar', var. col., 50 cm (20 in)
Impatiens balsamina 'Harlequin', R/W 30 cm (12 in)
Impatiens balsamina 'Super Elfin Orchid', P–V, 30 cm (12 in)
Impatiens balsamina 'Tom Thumb Purple', P, 25 cm (10 in)

Biennials

◐ ☉ ⊕

193. Suitable as a specimen plant.

Digitalis ciliata, R–P, Y, 1 m (3 ft)
Digitalis grandiflora, Y/Brown, 1 m (3 ft)
Digitalis purpurea, R–P, W, 1.5 m (5 ft)
Digitalis purpurea 'Gloxiniaeflora', var. col., 1.5 m (5 ft)
Lilium candidum, W, –1.5 m (5 ft)

◐ ☉ ⊗

194. Suitable for cutting.

Campanula medium, var. col., 1 m (3 ft)
Campanula pyramidalis, V–B, 1.5 m (5 ft)
Digitalis purpurea, R–P, W, 1.5 m (5 ft)
Hesperis dinarica, V, –80 cm (32 in)
Hesperis matronalis, W, R–P, 1 m (3 ft)
Lilium candidum, W, –1.5 m (5 ft)

Herbaceous perennials

◐ ○
195. No special features.

Aegopodium podagraria 'Variegatum', W, –40 cm (16 in)
Cypripedium calceolus, R–Brown, Y, –40 cm (16 in)
Cypripedium reginae, W/R –60 cm (24 in)
Lathrea clandestina P, 10 cm (4 in)
Stellaria holostea, W, 40 cm (16 in)
Tradescantia andersoniana 'Zwanenburg', P, –60 cm (24 in)
Tradescantia andersoniana hybrid 'Osprey', W–P, –60 cm (24 in)
Tradescantia virginiana 'Innocence', W, –75 cm (30 in)

◐ ○ ❀
196. Evergreen.

Cornus canadensis, W, –20 cm (8 in)
Helleborus foetidus, Y, 50 cm (20 in)
Helleborus × hybridus, G, –50 cm (20 in)

◐ ○ ❀
197. With attractive fruits or berries.

Cornus canadensis, W, –20 cm (8 in)

◐ ○ ☻
198. Wholly or partly poisonous.

Aconitum arendsii (×), B, –1.3 m (4¼ ft)
Aconitum carmichaelii, V, –1 m (3 ft)
Aconitum fischeri, P–V, –70 cm (28 in)
Aconitum henryi, V–B, –1.6 m (5½ ft)
Aconitum lamarckii, Y, 1 m (3 ft)
Aconitum napellus ssp. *pyramidale*, P–V, 1.5 m (5 ft)
Dicentra formosa, R, 40 cm (16 in)
Dicentra spectabilis, R/W, 1 m (3 ft)
Digitalis grandiflora, Y/Brown, 1 m (3 ft)
Helleborus × hybridus, G, –50 cm (20 in)
Lathyrus latifolius, P/W, 3 m (10 ft)
Lathyrus vernus 'Lusus Variegatus', W/R, 40 cm (16 in)

◐ ○ ⊕
199. Suitable as a specimen plant.

Aruncum dioicus, W, 2 m (6 ft)

◐ ○ ⊗
200. Suitable for rock gardens and crevices in paving.

Aquilegia flabellata, R/W, 20 cm (8 in)
Cyananthus microphyllus, B, –20 cm (8 in)
Dodecatheon jeffreyi, P–V, –60 cm (24 in)
Dodecatheon meadia, R, 50 cm (20 in)
Phyteuma orbiculare, V–B, –40 cm (16 in)
Saxifraga arendsii hybrid 'Ware's Crimson', P, –25 cm (10 in)
Saxifraga haagii (×), Y, 10 cm (4 in)

◐ ○ ⊖
201. Suitable for ground cover.

Ajuga reptans, B, 20 cm (8 in)
Ajuga reptans 'Rubra', B, 30 cm (12 in)
Cornus canadensis, W, –20 cm (8 in)
Epimedium cantabrigense (×), O–R, –40 cm (16 in)
Epimedium perralderanum 'Fronleiten', Y, 35 cm (14 in)
Epimedium pinnatum var. *elegans.*, Y, 35 cm (14 in)
Epimedium pinnatum var. *elegans*, W, 35 cm (14 in)
Epimedium rubrum (×), Y/P, 35 cm (14 in)
Epimedium versicolor (×), W/Y, 35 cm (14 in)
Epimedium warleyense (×), O–R, 30 cm (12 in)
Heuchera hybrid 'Huntsman', R, 60 cm (24 in)
Heuchera sanguinea 'Splendens', R, 50 cm (20 in)
Saxifraga arendsii hybrid 'Ware's Crimson', P, –25 cm (10 in)
Saxifraga haagii (×), Y, 10 cm (4 in)
Symphytum grandiflorum, Y, –25 cm (10 in)
Symphytum grandiflorum 'Pearl', R, 1.2 m (4 ft)

◐ ○ ⊗
202. Suitable for cutting.

Aconitum arendsii (×), B, –1.3 cm (4¼ ft)
Aconitum carmichaelii, V, –1 m (3 ft)
Aconitum fischeri, P–V, –70 cm (28 in)
Aconitum henryi, V–B, –1.6 m (5¼ ft)
Aconitum lamarckii, Y, 1 m (3 ft)

Aconitum napellus ssp. *pyramidale*, P–V, 1.5 m (5 ft)
Aquilegia hybrid, var. col., –1.2 m (4 ft)
Astrantia carniolica, W, –75 cm (30 in)
Astrantia carniolica 'Rubra', R, –75 cm (30 in)
Astrantia major, W, R–P, –60 cm (24 in)
Chelone obliqua, R–P, 60 cm (24 in)
Cimicifuga rivulare 'Atropurpureum', R–P, 1.4 m (4½ ft)
Dicentra formosa, R, 40 cm (16 in)
Dicentra spectabilis, R/W, 1 m (3 ft)
Dodecatheon jeffreyi, P–V, –60 cm (24 in)
Dodecatheon meadia, R, 50 cm (20 in)
Geranium sylvaticum 'Mayflower', P–V, 60 cm (24 in)
Hesperis dinarica, V, –80 cm (32 in)
Heuchera hybrid 'Huntsman', R, 60 cm (24 in)
Heuchera sanguinea 'Splendens', R, 50 cm (20 in)
Lathyrus latifolius, P/W, 3 m (10 ft)
Miscanthus sinensis 'Silberfeder', Silver–Brown, 1.8 m (6 ft)
Reynoutria japonica, W, –3 m G–Y, –75 cm (30 in)

Bulbs

◐ ◓ ○
203. Wholly or partly poisonous.

Galanthus nivalis, W, –20 cm (8 in)
Lilium hansonii, O, –1.5 m (5 ft)
Lilium henryi, Y–O, –2 m (6 ft)
Lilium (oriental hybrid) 'Imperial Gold', W/Y/R, 2 m (6 ft)
Nerine bowdenii, R, 60 cm (24 in).

◐ ◓ ⊕
204. Suitable as a specimen plant.

Lilium hansonii, O, –1.5 m (5 ft)
Lilium henryi, Y–O, –2 m (6 ft)
Lilium (oriental hybrid) 'Imperial Gold', W/Y/R, 2 m (6 ft)

◐ ◓ ⊗
205. Suitable for rock gardens and crevices in paving.

Galanthus nivalis, W, –20 cm (8 in)

◐ ◓ ⊗
206. Suitable for cutting.

Lilium hansonii, O, –1.5 m (5 ft)
Lilium henryi, Y–O, –2 m (6 ft)
Lilium (oriental hybrid) 'Imperial Gold', W/Y/R, 2 m (6 ft)
Nerine bowdenii, R, 60 cm (24 in)
Nerine samiensis var. *corusca* 'Major', O–R, 60 cm (24 in)
Ornithogalum nutans, W, 40 cm (16 in)

Tubers

◐ ⊛
207. No special features.

Begonia tuberhybrida (×) var. col., 20 cm (8 in)
Begonia tuberhybrida (×) 'Bertinii', var. col., –25 cm (10 in)
Pleione bulbocodioides, P/W, 15 cm (6 in)

208. Suitable for rock gardens and crevices in paving.

Cyclamen coum ssp. *hiemale*, R–P, 10 cm (4 in)

Shrubs

◐ ❀
209. No special features.

Weigela praecox 'Bailey', R–P, 2 m (6 ft)

◐ ❀ ❀
210. Evergreen.

Aucuba japonica 'Variegata', W, 3 m (10 ft)
Chamaecyparis lawsonia 'Pygmaea Argentea', 1 m (3 ft)
Chusquea culeou, 3 m (10 ft)
Euonymus fortunei 'Emerald Gaiety', W, 2 m (6 ft)
Euonymus fortunei 'Silver Queen', W, 2 m (6 ft)

◐ ⊛ ⊛
211. With attractive fruits or berries.

Aucuba japonica 'Variegata', R, 3 m (10 ft)
Berberis vulgaris, R, 2 m (6 ft)
Callicarpa bodinieri var. *giraldii*, V, 2 m (6 ft)
Callicarpa dichotoma, R, 1.5 m (5 ft)
Chamaecyparis lawsoniana 'Pygmaea Argentea', 1 m (3 ft)
Corylus avellana 'Pendula', Y, 5 m (16 ft)

◐ ⊛ ⊚
212. Wholly or partly poisonous.

Berberis vulgaris, R, 2 m (6 ft)
Callicarpa bodinieri var. *giraldii*, V, 2 m (6 ft)
Chamaecyparis lawsoniana 'Pygmaea Argentea', 1 m (3 ft)

◐ ⊛ ⊕
213. Suitable as a specimen plant.

Chamaecyparis lawsoniana 'Pygmaea Argentea', 1 m (3 ft)
Corylus avellana 'Contorta', Y, 3 m (10 ft)
Corylus avellana 'Pendula', Y, 5 m (16 ft)
Hamamelis mollis, Y, 4 m (13 ft)
Hamamelis virginiana, Y, 4 m (13 ft)

◐ ⊛ ⊗
214. Suitable for rock gardens and crevices in paving.

Muehlenbeckia axillaris, G–Y, 10 cm (4 in)

◐ ⊛ ⊜
215. Suitable for hedging.

Berberis vulgaris, Y, 2 m (6 ft)
Euonymus fortunei 'Emerald Gaiety', W, 2 m (6 ft)
Euonymus fortunei 'Silver Queen', W, 2 m (6 ft)

◐ ⊛ ⊖
216. Suitable for ground cover.

Euonymus fortunei 'Emerald Gaiety', W, 2 m (6 ft)
Euonymus fortunei 'Silver Queen', W, 2 m (6 ft)
Muehlenbeckia axillaris, G–Y, 10 cm (4 in)

◐ ⊛ ⊗
217. Suitable for cutting.

Callicarpa bodinieri var. *giraldii*, V, 2 m (6 ft)
Callicarpa dichotoma, R, 1.5 m (5 ft)
Corylus avellana 'Contorta', Y, 3 m (10 ft)
Corylus avellana 'Pendula', Y, 5 m (16 ft)
Hamamelis mollis, Y, 4 m (13 ft)

Trees

◐ ⊛ ⊕
218. Suitable as a specimen tree.

Acer pseudoplatanus 'Brillantissimum', Y–G, 7 m (23 ft)

SEMI-SHADE; MOIST SITE

Herbaceous perennials

◐ ⊛ ○
219. No special features.

Filipendula ulmaria 'Plena', W, –1.2 m (4 ft)
Hakonechloa macra 'Aureola', G–Y, –50 cm (20 in)
Hemerocallis citrina, Y, –1 m (3 ft)
Hemerocallis hybrid 'Atlas', Y, 1.1 m (3½ ft)
Hemerocallis hybrid 'Crimson Pirate', R, 60 cm (24 in)
Hemerocallis hybrid 'Frans Hals', Y/R, 1 m (3 ft)
Hemerocallis hybrid 'Nol Hill', R, –80 cm (32 in)
Hemerocallis hybrid 'Orange Man', O–R, –80 cm (32 in)
Hemerocallis hybrid 'Patricia Fay', R, –80 cm (32 in)
Hemerocallis hybrid 'Sammy Russell', R, –80 cm (32 in)
Hemerocallis hybrid 'Tejas', Y, 1.2 m (4 ft)
Miscanthus floridulus 'Variegata', –2 m (6 ft)

Polygonum bistorta, R, 1 m (3 ft)
Primula bullesiana hybrid, var. col., 50 cm (20 in)
Primula japonica, R–P, 50 cm (20 in)
Primula rosea, P, 15 cm (6 in)
Primula secundiflora, P, 70 cm (28 in)
Primula sieboldii 'Shinkiro', P–V, 20 cm (8 in)
Primula sikkimensis, Y, –50 cm (20 in)
Primula vialii, P, 60 cm (24 in)

◐ ⊛ ○ ⊛
220. Evergreen.

Bergenia hybrid 'Morgenröte', P, –50 cm (20 in)
Bergenia hybrid 'Orangeade', Y, 1 m (3 ft)
Bergenia hybrid 'Silberlicht', P, 50 cm (20 in)
Bergenia schmidtii (×), P, –50 cm (20 in)
Carex plantaginea, G–W, 30 cm (6 in)

◐ ⊛ ○ ⊚
221. Wholly or partly poisonous.

Helleborus niger, W, –45 cm (18 in)
Meconopsis betonicifolia, B, –1.2 m (4 ft)
Meconopsis regia, Y, 1.8 m (6 ft)

◐ ⊛ ○ ⊕
222. Suitable as a specimen plant.

Ligularia dentata, Y–O, –1.5 m (5 ft)

◐ ⊛ ○ ⊗
223. Suitable for rock gardens or crevices in paving.

Houstonia caerulea, V–B, 20 cm (8 in)
Mertensia virginica, V–B, 50 cm (20 in)
Primula denticulata, P, –25 cm (10 in)
Primula juliae hybrid 'Wanda', P, 10 cm (4 in)
Primula vulgaris, var. col., 10 cm (4 in)
Wulfenia baldacci, P. –15 cm (6 in)

◐ ⊛ ○ ⊖
224. Suitable for ground cover.

Bergenia hybrid 'Morgenröte', P, –50 cm (20 in)
Bergenia hybrid 'Silberlicht', P, –50 cm (20 in)
Bergenia schmidtii (×), P, 50 cm (20 in)
Brunnera macrophylla, B, –40 cm (16 in)
Galium odoratum, W, –25 cm (10 in)

◐ ⊛ ○ ⊗
225. Suitable for cutting.

Astilbe chinensis, var. pumila, R–P, 30 cm (12 in)
Astilbe hybrid 'Emden', R, –75 cm (30 in)
Filipendula rubra 'Venusta', R, –1.5 m (5 ft)
Galium odoratum, W, 25 cm (10 in)
Hemerocallis lilio-asphodelus, Y, 80 cm (32 in)
Hepatica nobilis, V, 10 cm (4 in)
Heucherella tiarelloides (×), W–R, –30 cm (6 in)
Ligularia dentata, Y–O, –1.5 m (5 ft)

Bulbs

◐ ⊛ ⊚
226. No special features.

Allium moly, Y, 25 cm (10 in)
Erythronium tuolumnense 'Pagoda', Y, 25 cm (10 in)

◐ ⊛ ⊚ ⊗
227. Suitable for rock gardens and crevices in paving.

Erythronium dens-canis, R, –20 cm (8 in)

Tubers

◐ ⊛ ⊚
228. No special features.

Cyclamen hederifolium, R, 15 cm (6 in)

◑ ⊗ ⊛ ⊛
229. Evergreen

Bergenia hybrid 'Silberlicht', P, –50 cm (20 in)
Bergenia (×) *schmidtii* P, –50 cm (20 in)

◑ ⊗ ⊛ ⊛
230. Wholly or partly poisonous.

Ranunculus asiaticus, var. col., –30 cm (12 in)

◑ ⊗ ⊛ ⊖
231. Suitable for ground cover.

Bergenia hybrid 'Silberlicht', P, –50 cm (20 in)
Bergenia (×) *schmidtii*, P, –50 cm (20 in)

◑ ⊗ ⊛ ⊗
232. Suitable for cutting.

Ranunculus asiaticus, var. col., –30 cm (12 in)

Shrubs

◑ ⊗ ⊛
233. No special features.

Acer palmatum 'Ornatum', R, 4 m (13 ft)
Rhododendron (Ghent azalea) 'Narcissiflora', Y, 2 m (6 ft)
Rhododendron (Knap Hill azalea) 'Klondyke', Y, 2 m (6 ft)
Rhododendron (Knap Hill azalea) 'Persil', W, 2 m (6 ft)
Rhododendron (Mollis azalea), 'Kosters Brilliant Red', O–R, 1.5 m (5 ft)
Rhododendron (Mollis azalea) 'Samuel T. Coleridge', R, 1.5 m (5 ft)
Rhododendron (*R. occidentalis* hybrid) 'Irene Koster', R, 2.5 m (8 ft)
Rhododendron (Rustica azalea) 'Aida', R–P, 2 m (6 ft)
Weigela middendorffiana, Y, 1.5 m (5 ft)

◑ ⊗ ⊛ ⊛
234. Evergreen.

Danae racemosa, Y–G, 1 m (3 ft)
Ledum palustre ssp. 'Compactum', W, 50 cm (20 in)
Pseudosasa japonica, 4 m (13 ft)
Rhododendron (*R. augustinii* hybrid) 'Blue Tit', V–B, 1 m (3 ft)
Rhododendron (*R. augustinii* hybrid) 'Blue Tit Major', V–B, 1 m (3 ft)
Rhododendron (Azaleodendron) 'Tottenham', R, 60 cm (24 in)
Rhododendron cinnabarinum var. *roylei*, R, 3 m (10 ft)
Rhododendron ferrugineum, R, 1 m (3 ft)
Rhododendron (Japanese azalea) 'Hardijzer Beauty', R, 1 m (3 ft)
Rhododendron praecox (×), R–P, 2 m (6 ft)
Rhododendron (Repens hybrid) 'Elisabeth', R, 1.5 m (5 ft)
Rhododendron sinogrande, Y–W, 6 m (20 ft)
Rhododendron (garden hybrid) 'Blue Ensign', V, 3 m (10 ft)
Rhododendron (garden hybrid) 'Catawbiense', W, 3 m (10 ft)
Rhododendron (garden hybrid) 'Furnivall's Daughter', R, 4 m (13 ft)
Rhododendron (garden hybrid) 'Hollandia', R–P, 4 m (13 ft)
Rhododendron (garden hybrid) 'Koster's Cream', Y, 2 m (6 ft)
Rhododendron (garden hybrid) 'Louis Pasteur', R, 4 m (13 ft)
Rhododendron (garden hybrid) 'Mermaid', R, 3 m (10 ft)
Rhododendron (garden hybrid) 'Mme Ida Rubinstein', R, 3 m (10 ft)
Rhododendron (garden hybrid) 'Mount Everest', W, 4 m (13 ft)
Rhododendron (garden hybrid) 'Mrs Betty Robertson', Y, 2 m (6 ft)
Rhododendron williamsianum, R, 1 m (3 ft)
Rhododendron yunnanense, W, 4 m (13 ft)
Rubus calycinoides, W, 10 cm (4 in)
Sasa veitchii, –1 m (3 ft)

◑ ⊗ ⊛ ⊛
235. With attractive fruits or berries.

Danae racemosa, Y–G, 1 m (3 ft)
Rhamnus frangula, G–W, 4 m (13 ft)
Rubus calycinoides, W, 10 cm (4 in)
Staphylea colchica, W, 3 m (10 ft)

◑ ⊗ ⊛ ◎
236. Wholly or partly poisonous.

Ledum palustre ssp. 'Compactum', W, 50 cm (20 in)
Rhododendron ferrugineum, R, 1 m (3 ft)

◑ ⊗ ⊛ ⊕
237. Suitable as a specimen plant.

Acer palmatum 'Dissectum', R, 3 m (10 ft)
Pseudosasa japonica, 4 m (13 ft)
Staphylea colchica, W, 3 m (10 ft)

◑ ⊗ ⊛ ⊗
238. Suitable for rock gardens and crevices in paving.

Arundinaria pumila, 60 cm (24 in)
Rhododendron ferrugineum, R, 1 m (3 ft)

◑ ⊗ ⊛ ⊛
239. Suitable for hedging.

Rhamnus frangula, G–W, 4 m (13 ft)

◑ ⊗ ⊛ ⊖
240. Suitable for ground cover.

Arundinaria pumila, 60 cm (24 in)
Rubus calycinoides, W, 10 cm (4 in)

◑ ⊗ ⊛ ⊗
241. Suitable for cutting.

Danae racemosa, Y–G, 1 m (3 ft)
Rhododendron (Azaleodendron) 'Tottenham', R, 60 cm (24 in)
Rhododendron (garden hybrid) 'Catawbiense', W, 3 m (10 ft)
Rhododendron (garden hybrid) 'Furnivall's Daughter', R, 4 m (13 ft)
Rhododendron (garden hybrid) 'Hollandia', R–P, 4 m (13 ft)
Rhododendron (garden hybrid) 'Koster's Cream', Y, 2 m (6 ft)
Rhododendron (garden hybrid) 'Louis Pasteur', R, 4 m (13 ft)
Rhododendron (garden hybrid) 'Mermaid', R, 3 m (10 ft)
Rhododendron (garden hybrid) 'Mme Ida Rubinstein', R, 3 m (10 ft)
Rhododendron (garden hybrid) 'Mount Everest', W, 4 m (13 ft)
Rhododendron (garden hybrid) 'Mrs Betty Robertson', Y, 2 m (6 ft)
Rhododendron williamsianum, R, 1 m (3 ft)

SEMI-SHADE; DRY GROUND

Herbaceous perennials

◑ ⊖ ○
242. No special features.

Linum flavum, Y, 40 cm (16 in)

◑ ⊖ ○ ⊗
243. Suitable for rock gardens and crevices in paving.

Apocynum androsaemifolium, R, 30 cm (12 in)
Campanula cochlearifolia, V–B, 15 cm (6 in)

SEMI-SHADE AND SHADE

Herbaceous perennials

◑ ◑ ○
244. No special features.

Kirengeshoma palmata, Y, –1 m (3 ft)
Rodgersia pinnata 'Superba', R, 1.2 m (4 ft)
Rodgersia podophylla, Y, 1.6 m (5½ ft)
Rodgersia purdomii, W, 1 m (3 ft)
Sanguinaria canadensis, W, 20 cm (8 in)
Sanguinaria canadensis 'Multiplex', W, 20 cm (8 in)
Tricyrtis formosana, W, R–P, –1 m (3 ft)
Trillium grandiflorum, R–P, 30 cm (12 in)
Uvularia grandiflora, Y, 30 cm (12 in)

◐◑◉⊛
245. Evergreen.

Galeobdolon luteum 'Herman's Pride', Y, 30 cm (12 in)
Galeobdolon luteum 'Variegatum', Y, –30 cm (12 in)
Helleborus foetidus, Y, 50 cm (12 in)
Luzula sylvatica, W, –40 cm (16 in)
Phyllitis scolopendrium, 40 cm (16 in)
Polypodium vulgare, –40 cm (16 in)
Waldsteinia ternata, Y, 25 cm (10 in)

◐◑◉⊛
246. With attractive berries.

Podophyllum hexandrum, W, –45 cm (18 in)

◐◑◉◎
247. Wholly or partly poisonous.

Corydalis lutea, Y, 30 cm (12 in)
Corydalis solida, P, –25 cm (10 in)
Doronicum orientale, Y, –50 cm (20 in)
Doronicum pardalianches, Y, –1 m (3 ft)
Doronicum plantagineum 'Excelsum', Y, 80 cm (32 in)
Helleborus foetidus, Y, 50 cm (20 in)
Podophyllum hexandrum, W, –45 cm (18 in)
Ranunculus aconitifolius, W, –60 cm (24 in)

◐◑◉⊕
248. Suitable as a specimen plant.

Rodgersia aesculifolia, Y, 1 m (3 ft)

◐◑◉⊗
249. Suitable for rock gardens and crevices in paving.

Adiantum pedatum, –50 cm (20 in)
Arenaria balearica, W, 5 cm (2 in)
Corydalis lutea, Y, 30 cm (12 in)
Doronicum orientale, Y, –50 cm (20 in)
Doronicum plantagineum 'Excelsum', Y, 80 cm (32 in)
Galeobdolon luteum 'Herman's Pride', Y, 30 cm (12 in)
Podophyllum hexandrum, W, –45 cm (18 in)
Polypodium vulgare, –40 cm (16 in)
Saxifraga umbrosa 'Variegata', W/R, –40 cm (16 in)

◐◑◉⊖
250. Suitable for ground cover.

Arenaria balearica, W, 5 cm (2 in)
Galeobdolon luteum 'Herman's Pride', Y, 30 cm (12 in)
Galeobdolon luteum 'Variegatum', Y, 30 cm (12 in)
Omphalodes verna, B, –20 cm (8 in)
Pulmonaria angustifolia, V, –30 cm (12 in)
Pulmonaria rubra, R, –40 cm (16 in)
Pulmonaria saccharata 'Mrs Moon', P, –40 cm (16 in)
Saxifraga umbrosa, W, –40 cm (16 in)
Saxifraga umbrosa 'Variegata', W/R, –40 cm (16 in)
Tiarella cordifolia, W, –20 cm (8 in)
Waldsteinia ternata, Y, –25 cm (10 in)

◐◑◉⊗
251. Suitable for cutting.

Doronicum orientale, Y, –50 cm (20 in)
Doronicum pardalianches, Y, –1 m (3 ft)
Doronicum plantagineum 'Excelsum', Y, 80 cm (32 in)
Ranunculus aconitifolius, W, –60 cm (24 in)

Tubers

◐◑⊛
252. No special features.

Anemone ranunculoides, 'Plena', Y, –25 cm (10 in)
Polygonatum multiflorum, W, 60 cm (24 in)

◐◑⊛◎
253. Wholly or partly poisonous.

Anemone nemorosa, W, –25 cm (10 in)
Convallaria majalis, W, –25 cm (10 in)

Shrubs

◐◑◍⊛
254. Evergreen.

Gaultheria procumbens, W, R–P, 15 cm (6 in)
Hedera helix 'Arborescens', G–Y, 30 m (100 ft)
Hedera helix 'Ovata', G–Y, 20 m (65 ft)
Hedera helix 'Sagittaefolia', G–Y, 5 m (16 ft)
Hedera helix 'Spectabilis Aurea', G, 10 m (33 ft)
Lonicera nitida, 1.5 m (5 ft), 'Hohenheimer Findling', Y–G, 1.5 m (5 ft)
Pachysandra procumbens, W, P–R, 25 cm (10 in)
Pachysandra terminalis, W, 30 cm (12 in)
Sarcococca humilis, W, 50 cm (20 in)
Vinca major 'Variegata', V–B, 30 cm (12 in)
Vinca minor, V, 10 cm (4 in)
Vinca minor 'Atropurpurea Compacta', P, 10 cm (4 in)
Viscum album, Y–G, 1 m (3 ft)

◐◑◍⊛
255. With attractive fruits or berries.

Gaultheria procumbens, W, R–P, 15 cm (6 in)
Hedera helix 'Arborescens', G–Y, 30 m (100 ft)
Lonicera korolkowii 'Aurora', R, 2.5 m (8 ft)
Lonicera maackii, W, 3 m (10 ft)
Lonicera microphylla, Y–W, 1 m (3 ft)
Lonicera orientalis, R, 3 m (10 ft)
Lonicera tatarica 'Alba', W, 3 m (10 ft)
Lonicera tatarica, R, 3 m (10 ft)
Sambucus nigra, W, 6 m (20 ft)
Sambucus racemosa 'Plumosa Aurea', Y–G, 4 m (13 ft)
Viscum album, Y–G, 1 m (3 ft)

◐◑◍◎
256. Wholly or partly poisonous.

Hedera helix 'Arborescens', G–Y, 30 m (100 ft)
Hedera helix 'Ovata', G–Y, 20 m (65 ft)
Hedera helix 'Sagittaefolia', G–Y, 5 m (16 ft)
Hedera helix 'Spectabilis Aurea', G, 10 m (33 ft)
Lonicera brownii (×) 'Punicea', O–R, 4.5 m (15 ft)
Lonicera korolkowii 'Aurora', R, 2.5 m (8 ft)
Lonicera maackii, W, 3 m (10 ft)
Lonicera microphylla, Y–W, 1 m (3 ft)
Lonicera orientalis, R, 3 m (10 ft)
Lonicera tatarica, R, 3 m (10 ft)
Lonicera tatarica 'Alba', W, 3 m (10 ft)
Sambucus nigra, W, 6 m (20 ft)
Sambucus racemosa 'Plumosa Aurea', Y–G, 4 m (13 ft)
Spiraea chamaedryfolia, W, 2 m (6 ft)
Vinca major 'Variegata', V–B, 30 cm (12 in)
Vinca minor, V, 10 cm (4 in)
Vinca minor 'Atropurpurea Compacta', P, 10 cm (4 in)
Viscum album, Y–G, 1 m (3 ft)

◐◑◍⊖
257. Suitable for ground cover.

Gaultheria procumbens, W, R–P, 15 cm (6 in)
Hedera helix 'Arborescens', G–Y, 30 m (100 ft)
Hedera helix 'Ovata', G–Y, 20 m (65 ft)
Pachysandra procumbens, W, P–R, 25 cm (10 in)
Pachysandra terminalis, W, 30 cm (12 in)
Sarcococca humilis, W, 50 cm (20 in)
Vinca major 'Variegata', V–B, 30 cm (12 in)
Vinca minor, V, 10 cm (4 in)
Vinca minor 'Atropurpurea Compacta', P, 10 cm (4 in)

SHADE

Annuals

◑
258. No special features.

Begonia semperflorens 'Organdy', R–P, 20 cm (8 in)

Herbaceous perennials

259. Suitable for cutting.

Arrhenatherum elatius ssp. *bulbosum* 'Variegatum', W, –50 cm (20 in)

Shrubs

260. No special features.

Aristolochia macrophylla, Brown/G, 10 m (33 ft)
Corylopsis pauciflora, Y, 1 m (3 ft)

261. With attractive fruits or berries.

Aronia melanocarpa, W, 1 m (3 ft)
Aronia prunifolia, W, 4 m (13 ft)
Cotoneaster dielsianus, W, 2 m (6 ft)
Cotoneaster divaricatus, R, 2 m (6 ft)
Cotoneaster horizontalis, W, 1 m (3 ft)
Cotoneaster racemiflorus, W, 2.5 m (8 ft)
Cotoneaster roseus, W, 3 m (10 ft)
Cotoneaster salicifolius, W, 4.5 m (15 ft)

262. Suitable for rock gardens and crevices in paving.

Artemisia 'Silver Queen', W, –1 m (3 ft)
Artemisia ludoviciana, W, –1 m (3 ft)

Botanical Index

Indoor Plants

Garden Plants

Botanical Index: Garden Plants

Botanical Index: Garden Plants

Botanical Index: Garden Plants

Index of common names

Indoor Plants

Index of Common Names: Garden Plants

Garden Plants

Index of Common Names: Garden Plants

Glossary of American common names of indoor plants

Glossary of American common names of garden plants